"The challenge of promoting values beyond Western-style individual auton-
omy — but avoiding top-down oppression — is both a puzzle for academics
and a broad social problem with real-world consequences. This most welcome
book leverages an ancient and helpfully foreign concept — the biblical idea
of covenant — to move beyond this paralyzing binary. The trajectory set by
Marcia Pally, tightly argued and socially oriented, is one that many different
kinds of people can and should support."

— CHARLES CAMOSY
Fordham University

"Marcia Pally's *Commonwealth and Covenant* asks one of the big questions of
our time: What worldview is now needed for us to develop productive public
policy? Pally grasps that what we need is not more economic theory but, rather,
a full worldview. In addressing this fundamental and daunting task, she moves
elegantly and authoritatively through modern intellectual history as well as
Christian and Jewish theology. Marked by clear and graceful prose, this book
is a must-read for those concerned about our economic and political future."

— TSVI BLANCHARD
National Jewish Center for
Learning and Leadership

"Brilliant! In addition to its insightful lessons in history, philosophy, culture,
government, psychology, and moral theology, this book contains a description
of the virtue derived from the proper relationship between self and society.
. . . This book is so helpful to me as a pastor because it affirms the basic theme
that each person is a valuable creation of God, yet made for relationships."

— JOEL C. HUNTER
Northland, a Church
Distributed

COMMONWEALTH AND COVENANT

Economics, Politics, and Theologies of Relationality

Marcia Pally

William B. Eerdmans Publishing Company
Grand Rapids, Michigan

Wm. B. Eerdmans Publishing Co.
2140 Oak Industrial Drive N.E., Grand Rapids, Michigan 49505
www.eerdmans.com

Published 2016
Printed in the United States of America

22 21 20 19 18 17 16   2 3 4 5 6 7 8

Library of Congress Cataloging-in-Publication Data

Pally, Marcia.
    Commonwealth and covenant : economics, politics, and
    theologies of relationality / Marcia Pally.
        pages   cm
    Includes bibliographical references.
    ISBN 978-0-8028-7104-6 (pbk. : alk. paper)
    1. Covenants — Religious aspects — Christianity.
    2. Covenants. 3. Covenant theology.   I. Title.
    BT155.P28   2016
    231.7′6 — dc23
                            2015034475

Contents

Acknowledgments

My first thanks go to the many thinkers cited in this book and those who worked with and supported them in developing theologies of relationality. Their work in many different schools and traditions has made a profound contribution to the way we think about our relations to world, others, and transcendent. It gives us a way to assess what we do well and poorly and points us to solutions because it offers one of the most valuable of life's gifts: an undergirding ontology or understanding from which specific programs and practices may emerge. Every political decision and economic policy is an expression of an articulated or tacit view of the world. Theologies of relationality offer us one that makes greater well-being a real possibility. We may say we know it, but looking at the world's present difficulties, we don't — not really. It is my hope that this book in some small way makes us take their ideas seriously.

I am deeply grateful to those who worked with me through the development of this book and gave me invaluable feedback and wisdom. I have learned a great deal from John Milbank, Adrian Pabst, Peter Candler, Russell Pearce, Mathias Greffrath, and Tsvi Blanchard. I am thankful to Rabbi Avinoam Paul Sharon for his generosity with source materials and for his time as a "sounding board" for so many of this book's ideas. I am deeply thankful also to Joel Hunter, Becky Hunter, David Gushee, Greg Boyd, Dan Lacich, Barbara Lacich, Robert Andrescik, Charles Haynes, Tri Robinson, Tim McFarlane, and all others at Vineyard for showing me relationality in community in practice.

I am indebted — always — to my publishers, Bill Eerdmans and Anita Eerdmans, and editors James Ernest and Jon Pott, for their continuing support and for their unique feel for ideas and books. Their contribution to scholarship, theology, ethics, and just plain decent thinking is inestimable. Indeed, I am grateful to all the people at Eerdmans Publishing for their help in bringing this manuscript to the public: editors Tom Raabe and Mary Hietbrink, Willem Mineur (cover design), Rachel Bomberger, Victoria Fanning, Ingrid Wolf, Laura Bardolph Hubers, Philip Zoutendam, Amy Kent, and Holly Hoover, among others.

I wish to thank my colleagues at New York University, Fordham University, and Humboldt University in Berlin for the conversations they have shared with me and the insights they have given. I want to thank also the German Research Foundation (DFG) and German Academic Exchange (DAAD) for grants that have directly and indirectly enabled me to pursue the research included here.

To my assistants, Mareike Hansen, Kris Watson, Juliane Stork, Maria Schulz, and especially Doerthe Guelzow, I am very grateful for the hard work, attention to detail, and generosity of spirit.

For her support throughout the many stages of research and writing, I thank Pamela Parker, who has vetted so many ideas and given me such friendship and good cheer over the years. Here, too, no thanks are enough. I would like to express my gratitude also to my teachers at the Solomon Schechter School, who were my first guides to relationality, to community, and to thinking. Sending me to this school was a great gift from my parents, Nettie Rose Pally and Sidney Pally.

PART I

Separability-amid-Situatedness: An Ontology

CHAPTER 1

An Introduction to Separability, Situatedness, and the Two Together

Respondeo, ergo sum.[1]

Separability, Situatedness, and Their Discontents

The West is in yet another moment of self-reflection. Perhaps this is to be expected in a culture born of scientific and intellectual revolutions as well as political and economic ones. Yet here we are, pushed by global challenges in economics, geopolitics, disease, and war. What do we believe is important; is it really? Do we have the stuff to adapt to new circumstances — or has the West lost its pizzazz and gravitas? Other places in the world, East Asia and elsewhere, have increasingly good prospects. Are we shortchanging ourselves?

In this book, I will suggest that the West isn't short of anything but rather is long on what might be a good thing were there less of it. That thing is separability or distinction, the ability to leave one's place and develop oneself differently from past and neighbors. Separability has much for us, but more is not necessarily better. Its opposite, situatedness or relation, may also in excess yield difficulties, to which I'll turn. But first a moment on separability. (I am using the terms "separability"/"distinction" and "situatedness"/"relation" rather than "individualism," "collectivism," "communitarianism," "liberal," or "conservative" because the first sets are the basics, pointing to the primary conditions on which political and sociological notions are built. They more plainly describe the physical, mental, and politico-legal circumstances under

---

1. E. Meir, *Interreligious Theology: Its Value and Mooring in Modern Jewish Philosophy* (Berlin: De Gruyter, 2015), p. 159.

discussion, are less prone to multiple meanings [see pt. I, ch. 2], and are less burdened by philosophical or political partisanship.)

Separability yields such indispensable things as innovation and the freedom to follow opportunity and change one's way of thinking and living. It is the basis for human and civil rights that are guaranteed to each person regardless of background or station. It undergirds, as Gillian Rose notes, both the person who may think and act unconventionally and the laws that guarantee her the right to do so.[2] Yet excesses of separability yield abandonment, anomie, and self-absorption, with results in greed, an adversarial stance in politics, resource grabbing, political chicanery, and business and stock market cheating. It is a recipe for talent wasted by anomie and poverty and hobbles our ability to act together for the life we live in common. Its economic effects were noted in the mid–eighteenth century in Adam Smith's complaint that the new industrialization made workers dull, destroyed communities, vitiated morality, fostered anonymous cities, and allowed the flamboyant rich to corrupt all others. It was found in the Sadler Committee Report on British labor conditions in 1832[3] and in this lambaste by David Frum, a Republican conservative and speechwriter for G. W. Bush, who in 2011 wrote, "In the face of evidence of dwindling upward mobility and long-stagnating middle-class wages, my party's economic ideas sometimes seem to have shrunk to just one: more tax cuts for the very highest earners."[4] And it has brought us the tragicomic reflection of ourselves in these films: *The Wolf of Wall Street* (1929), *Wall Street* (1987),

2. See especially, G. Rose, *The Broken Middle: Out of Our Ancient Society* (Oxford: Blackwell, 1992).

3. M. Williams, ed., *Child Labor and Sweatshops* (San Diego: Greenhaven Press, 1999); see also, T. Piketty, *Capital in the Twenty-First Century*, trans. A. Goldhammer (Cambridge: Harvard University Press, 2014); L. Bruni and S. Zamagni, *Civil Economy: Efficiency, Equity, Public Happiness* (Bern: Peter Lang, 2007); D. Foley, *Adam's Fallacy: A Guide to Economic Theology* (Cambridge: Harvard University Press, Belknap Press, 2006); W. Greider, *One World, Ready or Not: The Manic Logic of Global Capitalism* (New York: Simon and Schuster, Touchstone, 1997); D. Hausman and M. McPherson, *Economic Analysis and Moral Philosophy* (Cambridge: Cambridge University Press, 1996); M. Lind, *The Next American Nation: The New Nationalism and the Fourth American Revolution* (New York: Free Press, 1995); J. Madrick, *Why Economics Grow: The Forces That Shape Prosperity and How We Can Get Them Working Again* (New York: Basic Books, Century Foundation Book, 2002); J. Stiglitz, *The Price of Inequality: How Today's Divided Society Endangers Our Future* (New York: Norton, 2013); L. Thurow, *The Future of Capitalism: How Today's Economic Forces Shape Tomorrow's World* (New York: Morrow, 1996).

4. D. Frum, "When Did the GOP Lose Touch with Reality?" *New York Magazine*, November 20, 2011.

Wall Street Warriors (2006), *Wall Street: Money Never Sleeps* (2010), *Margin Call* (2011), and *The Wolf of Wall Street* (2013).

For with persistent focus on separating — on the *exit* from common concerns and projects — one might well come to think only of oneself (one's party or firm) and to assume others are doing the same. This is the Hobbesian diagnosis: fear of grabbing by others sets one to inconsolable competition. The results are what Charles Taylor and Glen Stassen call the buffered self; Larry Rasmussen calls it "detached individualism." Luke Bretherton refers to "isolated choosers," and Pope Francis to a "throwaway" society where large numbers of people are considered disposable products if they are thought of at all.[5]

Politically, the focus on "exit" yields suspicion of societal projects and government per se. In a culture of self-concern, government, the largest agent of common effort, is mistrusted. As the enforcer of common responsibilities (taxes, market regulations), it is seen as the foe of freedom. This has come to such a pitch that sectors of America vote like the Redcoats are coming still and the Manchurian Candidate lurks on every ballot. The roles left to government are national security and the making of laws that institutionalize our self-concern in the deregulation of markets and politics.

The undue separability most pertinent to this book began in early modernity, resulting in a crescendo of separability to which we are heir (see pt. I, ch. 3). With the scientific and technological revolutions came substantial gain in our control of nature, to benefits in greater health and prosperity. Yet an unintended consequence was a shift in worldview from our being in nature, in interaction with all else in the natural world, to our being on top of it, separated and in control. Our appreciation of interconnectedness (of persons, world, and undergirding setup) thinned, and was replaced by various sorts of nominalism, a fascination with the mind and its ability to change what things mean — to change unpredictable nature, for instance, into a controllable tool.

In short, control yielding an inflated sense of self-sufficiency yielded undue separability, a focus on the self and how one can further control one's surroundings for oneself. This early modern tendency was abetted by improved transportation and economic opportunities that made for much wealth and

---

5. G. Stassen, *A Thicker Jesus: Incarnational Discipleship in a Secular Age* (Louisville: Westminster John Knox, 2012), p. 101; C. Taylor, "Buffered and Porous Selves," *The Immanent Frame*, September 2, 2008; retrieved from http://blogs.ssrc.org/tif/2008/09/02/buffered-and-porous-selves/; L. Rasmussen, *Moral Fragments and Moral Community: A Proposal for Church in Society* (Minneapolis: Augsburg Fortress, 1993), p. 11; L. Bretherton, *Hospitality as Holiness: Christian Witness amid Moral Diversity* (Farnham, U.K., and Burlington, Vt.: Ashgate, 2006), p. 16; Francis, *Evangelii gaudium*, November 24, 2013, para. 5.

opportunity but also an increasingly mobile populace, further disembedding persons from place and relationships and leaving one to rely, again, on oneself.

That said, undue situatedness — tight group embeddedness with few individual options or freedoms — is equally unproductive. Situatedness, like separability, has much for us; it brings security, support, and affection, and enables cooperative projects that sustain our physical and socioeconomic infrastructures. Yet, untempered by separability, it yields oppressive control (situatedness top-down) and stultifying conformity riddled with snooping and prejudice (situatedness from the crowd). Hannah Arendt diagnosed the top-down problem in totalitarian systems: because totalitarian states make all persons one mass, both the individual and relationships are erased, as persons must be distinct (not en-massed) to bring to each other the assistance and gift of their singular capacities.[6] Undue situatedness arises, however, absent state control. Precisely because one is affected by the conduct of others, one keeps an eye on it. From that may come not only a helping hand but much busybody policing and nasty in-group-ness — the sort of community control described in Michel Foucault's *Madness and Civilization* and *Discipline and Punish* and in studies, both literary and scientific, of town-without-pity conformity and local witch hunts.

Taylor, who has written such trenchant critiques of modern "disembeddedness," nonetheless notes, "we shouldn't forget the spiritual costs of various kinds of forced conformity: hypocrisy, spiritual stultification, inner revolt against the Gospel, the confusion of faith and power, and even worse. . . . I'm not sure we wouldn't be wiser to stick with the present dispensation."[7] In short, situatedness should not be confused with situation in only one's ancestral group, with "old boy networks," with lobbying government to enforce prejudices, or with the self-congratulatory in-group-ness of "people like us" — what Luigino Bruni calls "a gigantic I."[8] Without opt-out and opt-in possibilities and contact with new persons and ideas, one cannot judge one's situation and is a servant to the status quo and whisper campaigns.

As if these negative effects were not enough, separability or situatedness gone too far yields the other. A too-cozy situatedness in one's group may yield suspicion of other groups and lead to the "gigantic I" — separability, suspicion, and intergroup aggression. In early modernity, the collusion of states and state-

6. See, for instance, H. Arendt, *The Origin of Totalitarianism* (New York: Harcourt, Brace, 1973), p. 478.

7. C. Taylor, *A Secular Age* (Cambridge: Harvard University Press, 2007), p. 513.

8. L. Bruni, *The Wound and the Blessing: Economics, Relationships, and Happiness*, trans. N. M. Brennen (Hyde Park, N.Y.: New City Press, 2012), p. 59.

sanctioned churches to control the populace (doubly oppressive situatedness) led to wariness of situatedness per se, to valuing separability and conflating freedom with mere flight. That is, oppressive situatedness provokes excessive separation. Conversely, separability gone so far as to make people separat*ed* leads to competition and to self-interested violence — the resource grabbing, war, political chicanery, and cheating mentioned above. Thus, a rigorous set of controls is needed to address the resulting crime (street and white-collar), political corruption, poverty, and social instability. In this Hobbes was again right: from undue separability comes the Leviathan. Not only does government become more bureaucratic and controlling, but so too does civil society, with increased micromanagement and workplace surveillance. Relationships and commitment to the long-term big picture — how most snags are solved and ideas hatched — are eroded.

The Alternative of Separability-amid-Situatedness, Distinction-amid-Relation

All this is not to say that our workplaces and communities are separability or situatedness run amok. But where we do get one untempered by the other, we fare less well than with practices based on their mutual constitution: separability-*amid*-situatedness, distinction-*amid*-relation. Indeed, our distinctiveness is inextricable from our relations in what Bernard Lonergan calls "the dialectics of community," of individual intersubjectivity *and* our socioeconomic, technological, political, and legal systems.[9]

If he and I are correct, and the ills outlined above are partly or substantially grounded in undue separability, a resituating ontology might go some way to addressing them. That is, an *ontology of relationality*, which holds together each person's singular concerns and the common infrastructure that supports each person — and preferably an ontology that doesn't swing the pendulum to undue situatedness and its problems. Such an ontology-to-ethics program

---

9. Bernard Lonergan distinguishes between "ordinary meaningfulness," the assumptions, perspectives, values, etc., that we come into as we grow up in any society of "sedimented values," and "original meaningfulness," which occurs "when the subject stands on his or her own two feet, raises his or her own questions in acts of understanding and in judgments of fact and value." R. Doran, *What Is Systematic Theology?* (Toronto: University of Toronto Press, 2005), p. 130; see also p. 175; B. Lonergan, *Method in Theology* (Toronto: University of Toronto Press, 2000), pp. 31-32; R. Doran, *Theology and the Dialectics of History* (Toronto: University of Toronto Press, 1990, 2001), chs. 11–14.

would set the aims and mores of markets, civil society, and government into the setup of interdependence that we're indeed in. It is a cultural shift of perhaps some significance. But cultures do shift. I am proposing theologies of relationality as one such ontology — theologies that see us as distinct creatures sustained by relation and that *see to* this relationality, our distinction-amid-relation. The relationality or covenantality of our bond with God constitutes humanity in such a way as to make us distinct yet covenantally interdependent, and this covenantal interdependence among persons (in part) constitutes our relationship with God.

These theologies have throughout history been understood as truth, metaphor or illustration, revelation, and more. I am not suggesting that there is no difference between belief and metaphor, only that in both cases these theologies have provided insight and paths forward. Readers come to this book from many perspectives, and it is addressed to all who are concerned about the public sphere. For, lacking insight into what has gone awry, we often have only (panicked) impulses to go on. We understandably press leaders for quick-fix relief; leaders risk next-election populism. Or we risk a relativistic guessing game: all policies and practices seem of equal merit because each seeks support only from the group that already believes it, and once such support is garnered, all policies are considered equally plausible and productive.

A few words on ontology, multiplicity, and relativism might be helpful here. Because each of us experiences the world differently, our understandings of it also differ. Our accounts of the world are multiple, and different ones tell us different, valuable things about our circumstances, as no single one is complete. There have been, for instance, numerous distinct nontheological considerations of separability-amid-situatedness. David Hume understood that individual reason does not account for values or behavior, which emerge in response to experience, mores, and cultural practices — situatedness in one's surroundings. Rousseau too saw that moral, societally responsible conduct would emerge not from individual reason alone but also from communal experience and the "social spirit."[10] He was wrong about an imposed "general will" yielding the best society,[11] but right that individual reason is not how people come to be or come together. His contemporaries Antonio Genovesi and others in the Neapolitan school rejected the bifurcation between the sep-

---

10. J.-J. Rousseau, *Theology and the Dialectics of History* (Toronto: University of Toronto Press, 1990, 2001), bk. 2, ch. 7.

11. He thought it was possible only in communities small enough for direct, not representative, democracy.

arable individual and "persons bound in society." They held instead to their mutual constitution, finding that even ostensibly competitive markets flourish only when mutual societal trust and reciprocity do.[12] In the nineteenth century, Tocqueville described a meld of individual initiative (separability) and the common good (situatedness) in his analysis of America. In the twentieth, Henri Bergson held that communal spirit provides social cohesion, standards of morality, and much of personal identity — the "solidity" of the ego, he writes, "lies in its solidarity."[13] Yet he also saw that a prime human feature is freedom, the capacity for separability, to change and invent.

Part I of this volume contains a short review of secular proposals that account for separability-amid-situatedness, especially by those often claimed to be advocates of one "side" or the other. On more careful reading, one finds that many were not polarizers but rather held to a mutually constitutive meld. The purpose of this review in chapters 4 and 5 is by no means to give a complete account of this secular discussion but to look at proposals for various separability/situatedness melds that have been reinterpreted through our present high separability, losing us the nuance of the original ideas. Since I believe that separability-amid-situatedness is one good way to talk about well-being, chapters 4 and 5 make a small effort at reviving them.

Indeed, the accumulation of our plural efforts — theological or otherwise — to discover how the world works is how we discover it. Yet the thing about which our understanding is multiple is the world. We cannot say just anything about it but must try to get at what our ontology is. While persons, groups, and cultures have many ways of working out our natural and societal circumstances, we are obliged to account for what we encounter. Saying just anything is not multiculturalism but pre-judice, judging before taking account of what is there; or it is relativism (all utterances are equally plausible). "Might we once and for all," Catherine Keller writes, "recognize the difference between a value-free relativism and value-loaded relationalism — in its strict analogy to that

12. Genovesi in particular considered market relations as emerging from reciprocal bonds of cooperation and assistance. He saw "public faith" as threefold: political, economic, and ethical (familial and civil). The first two, including modern markets, are grounded by the last, which he described as "the shared confidence of people, families, and the social orders, founded on the view of the virtue and religion of the contracting parties.... When the foundations of ethical trust tremble in a nation, neither can economic or political trust remain firm." A. Genovesi, *Lezioni di commercio o sia di economia civile*, ed. M. L. Perna (Naples: Instituti italiano per gli studi filosofici, 2005; original 1765-1767), II, ch. 10, para. VI.

13. H. Bergson, *The Two Sources of Morality and Religion* (Notre Dame: University of Notre Dame Press, 1932, 1977), p. 15.

between separation [from others] and differentiation [amid others]?"[14] Claims that do not account for world (water boils at 50 degrees Celsius; true success needs no help from others) do not yield productive outcomes, as failing to sterilize medical instruments or living in unconsideration of others attests.

In focusing on ontology, I am intentionally not enumerating a list of goods or practices deemed productive. Many have been proposed by economists, ethicists, and political writers to include basic goods (those that are universal and necessary) such as health, security, association, respect/dignity, and "personality"[15] (individual interest/passions/aspirations). Others have pointed to the means[16] and actual capacity[17] for achieving these goods — civil rights and education, for instance. A number of these are described in the conclusion to this volume. But much of the book concerns the primary step before we make lists about what's wanted, by whom, and how to provide it. As Lewis Mudge and others have noted,[18] pragmatic suggestions have been discussed at various high-level meetings at Davos, the U.N., and elsewhere, among the G-7 and G-20 and others, with disappointing results.

It's not that the political or economic ideas are lacking but that the ontology is in what Lonergan called the "flight from insight."[19] Thus, the ontology of separability-amid-situatedness or distinction-amid-relation. The ethics it yields is not a prescription for separability and situatedness or a codex but a *process* of reciprocal consideration-worthiness, taking the concerns of the (distinct) other to be as worthy of consideration as one's own, to be accounted for as one's own are to be counted. Though he is now touted as the guru of

14. C. Keller, "Theology's Multitude: Polydoxy Reviewed and Renewed," *Modern Theology* 30, no. 3 (2014): 138.

15. R. Skidelsky and E. Skidelsky, *How Much Is Enough? Money and the Good Life* (New York: Other Press, 2012), p. 160.

16. John Rawls's notion of "primary goods" would fall in this grouping; see J. Rawls, *A Theory of Justice* (Cambridge: Harvard University Press, 1971), p. 433.

17. Martha Nussbaum has described a list of ten such capacities, including health and bodily integrity, imagination, thought, practical reason, affiliation, and play; see M. Nussbaum, *Women and Human Development: The Capabilities Approach* (Cambridge: Cambridge University Press, 2000).

18. L. Mudge, *We Can Make the World Economy a Sustainable Global Home* (Grand Rapids: Eerdmans, 2014), Kindle locations 1423-1477, 1510-1516, 1571-1579.

19. Lonergan holds that unexamined thinking and what counts as common sense may lead to inaccuracies regarding "the long view," which need correction by more rigorous, continuous effort to better get at what is the case rather than what is merely familiar. He writes, "the general bias of common sense involves sins of refusal as well as of mere omission"; *The Lonergan Reader*, ed. E. Morelli and M. Morelli (Toronto: University of Toronto Press, 1997), p. 138.

greed, Adam Smith proposed just this: in markets, as in all of society, he wrote, each should "endeavor, as much as he can, to put himself in the situation of the other, and to bring home to himself every little circumstance of distress which can possibly occur to the sufferer."[20] Smith's idea may today appear simplistic — or paradoxically, quite difficult. Yet it is difficult only if one assumes current praxis. Under a different understanding of world, it might appear reciprocally productive for the long run.

Reciprocal consideration-worthiness brings out common needs, goals, and interests, and differences. These, if we are to engage one another from a position other than separat*ed-ness,* need be approached by, in Joel Hunter's words, asking "why the other side is for the other side"[21] (even or especially if that is difficult to articulate), so that the answers may be brokered into practices and policies. Karl Rahner calls this "unity-in-difference";[22] James Olthuis refers to it as "non-oppositional difference"; Keller and Laurel Schneider call it "entangled," "non-separable," or "connected" difference.[23]

This does not suggest ceding one's views or that all that's wanted is given; rather, it suggests a process of each reciprocally getting at the other's underlying concerns (fears, needs, hopes) and understanding how both we and others have come to present views. In Rose's words, it is a sacred practice of conversational openness not from an imagined objective perch but from within one's situation, taking responsibility for the good and evil that have been done in its name. This might begin with near-others, but given the present mobility of persons, goods, microbes, and ideas, arenas of interdependent impact reach across the globe, requiring that we work, as Pope Francis notes, "in our own neighbourhood, but with a larger perspective."[24] The "larger perspective" is in any case affecting the neighborhood.

20. A. Smith, *The Theory of Moral Sentiments,* ed. D. Raphael and A. Macfie (Oxford: Clarendon, 1976; original 1759/1790), p. 21.

21. Hunter is a pastor and member of President Barack Obama's President's Advisory Council on Faith-Based and Neighborhood Partnerships, 2009-2010; see J. Hunter, *A New Kind of Conservative* (Ventura, Calif.: Gospel Light, 2008), pp. 84-85.

22. K. Rahner, *Foundations of Christian Faith: An Introduction to the Idea of Christianity,* trans. W. V. Dych (New York: Seabury Press, 1978), pp. 15, 17, 62, 447, 456; see also, K. Rahner, *Spirit in the World* (London: Sheed and Ward, 1968), p. 239.

23. J. Olthuis, "Face-to-Face: Ethical Asymmetry of the Symmetry of Mutuality?" in *The Hermeneutics of Charity: Interpretation, Selfhood, and Postmodern Faith; Studies in Honor of James H. Olthuis,* ed. J. K. Smith and H. I. Venema (Grand Rapids: Brazos, 1996, 2004), p. 151. C. Keller and L. Schneider, eds., *Polydoxy: Theology of Multiplicity and Relation* (New York: Routledge, 2010), p. 7.

24. Francis, *Evangelii gaudium,* para. 235.

Distinction-amid-relation and the process of reciprocal consideration-worthiness would affect "habitual attitudes" and "the mass and momentum of feeling" as well as our reasoning and its symbolic orders (law, politics, policy). It would offer an undergirding *"normative* source of meaning"[25] by which present practices and policies can be assessed and new ones proposed. In a practical example, the question might not be whether a timber firm and its employees (who want to retain jobs) may legally continue to log trees against the protests of the local community and environmental protection groups. Rather, it might be to recognize that loggers, shareholders, and management too have interests in forests surviving to the next generation (of building materials, jobs, and profits).

Thus: What would the outcome look like if all involved (owners, management, shareholders, employees, town residents, environmental protection organizations) believed in the way we believe we breathe that discussion begins with taking "why the other side is for the other side" as consideration-worthy? No one leaves the discussion until all have contributed substantially to the solution and until a solution is developed where no one's concerns are sidelined. It wouldn't occur to anyone to do anything else.

This is not to say that this will be achieved absent law. Law both expresses societal values and is a procedure to be used when usual means of addressing problems fail. That is, legal protections follow from ontology. One has laws against discrimination, for instance, because of the underlying belief in the dignity of each person, and it is difficult to imagine a society writing anti-discrimination laws absent that belief. Law may reflect what Eli Wald and Russell Pearce call a culture of "autonomous self-interest," where lawyers are taken as "hired guns" who try to get away with as much as possible just inside the letter of the law.[26] Or it may reflect "relational self-interest,"[27] where the interests of client and lawyer are seen as woven into the interests of society and its future.[28]

---

25. Doran, *What Is Systematic Theology?* pp. 166, 178.

26. See, for instance, L. A. Cunningham, "A Prescription to Retire the Rhetoric of 'Principles-Based Systems' in Corporate Law, Securities Regulation, and Accounting," *Vanderbilt Law Review* 60 (2007): 1423.

27. E. Wald and R. Pearce, "The Obligation of Lawyers to Heal Civic Culture: Confronting the Ideal of Incivility in the Practice of Law" (University of Denver Sturm College of Law, legal research paper series, working paper 11-27), *University of Arkansas Law Review* 34 (2011): 17ff.

28. "[T]he view that all actors are inter-connected, whether [as] individuals [or in groups] . . . [and] cannot maximize [their] own good in isolation." R. Pearce and E. Wald, "Rethinking Lawyer Regulation: How a Relational Approach Would Improve Professional Rules and Roles," *Michigan State Law Review* (2012): 514.

In addition to relational uses of the law, I am suggesting that ontologies of distinction-amid-relation from the get-go yield *usual* practices of reciprocal consideration-worthiness — it's just what's done — thus preempting an agonistic framework.

An Introduction to the Ontology of Distinction-amid-Relation and the Theology That Grounds It

We can begin by picturing subatomic particles, each of which is distinct yet each of whose trajectory is formed by "responding to" other subatomic particles and their trajectories. While remaining distinct, each develops and moves through its milieu by "taking others into account." All particles together constitute the environment of which each is a part. Distinction-amid-relation is in this sense basic to existence.

In the human realm, persons too are distinct — even identical twins differ in character and conduct. Yet distinctiveness emerges from interaction, beginning with our earliest caretakers, as only each can have those exchanges. (Infants do not develop absent relationship, yet the conduct of even twins differs in each relationship.)[29] While distinct, we are, as Donald Pfaff holds, set up not only for relationship but "wired for goodwill"[30] as a matter of evolution. "Reciprocal altruism antedates formal institutions, and," Edwin Scott Fruehwald explains, "appears to be hard-wired into human brains. In other words, there is a universal grammar of reciprocity just like there is a universal grammar of language."[31] This reciprocity structures not only dyadic exchange and family relations but also complex societal networks and, importantly, given present patterns of relocation, relationships among highly mobile persons absent long-term bonds (see pt. 1, ch. 3).[32]

29. See, for instance, R. Bellah et al., *Habits of the Heart: Individualism and Commitment in American Life* (Berkeley: University of California Press, 1985).

30. D. Pfaff, *The Altruistic Brain: How We Are Naturally Good* (New York: Oxford University Press, 2014), p. 5; see also, R. Churchland, *Braintrust: What Neuroscience Tells Us about Morality* (Princeton: Princeton University Press, 2012).

31. E. S. Fruehwald, "Reciprocal Altruism as the Basis for Contract," *University of Louisville Law Review* 47, no. 3 (2009), Hofstra University Legal Studies Research Paper no. 08-09; available at SSRN: http://ssrn.com/abstract=1270117.

32. See D. Cheney, "Extent and Limits of Cooperation in Animals," *Proceedings of the National Academy of Sciences* 108, suppl. 2 (2011): 10902-9; R. Davidson, *The Emotional Life of Your Brain* (New York: Penguin Group, 2012); F. De Waal, *The Age of Empathy* (London: Souvenir Press, 2010); A. M. Hurtado and K. Hill, *Ache Life History: The Ecology and Demography of a*

It also raises questions about the "naturalness" of war. Douglas Fry finds that the mores of consensus building in hunter-gatherer societies — the human condition for 95 percent of our evolution — "argue strongly against the belief that war is a natural attribute of humanity."[33] David Barash concurs: war is historically recent and a "capacity," that is, "derivative traits that are unlikely to have been directly selected for." And, he continues, "capacities are neither universal nor mandatory."[34] Thus generosity and "hyper-cooperativeness"[35] appear to be the human default, with aggression occurring when the usual cooperation fails. "The vast majority of the people on the planet," Fry writes, "awake on a typical morning and live through a violence-free day — and this experience generally continues day after day after day."[36]

Said another way, reciprocal consideration-worthiness is part of the biological grain. This answers David Bentley Hart's insightful question, how do people of good will account for their virtue?[37] While cooperation is vulnerable to distortion by individual chemical imbalance, unfortunate confluences of events (including shortages of essential goods), or the unintended consequences of benign developments (as in the technological shifts of early modernity), cooperation may also be enhanced by one's surroundings even after they have been damaged by trauma. This argues for ontology, policies, and practices that allow for the cooperation-default to develop naturally and that right it when it has been distorted.

Additional support for evolutionary findings comes from Maurice Merleau-Ponty's work on perception. He notes that even something so set in the individual self as "seeing" is never an act of apprehending raw data

---

Foraging People (Livingston, N.J.: Aldine Transaction, 1996); C. Roca and D. Helbing, "Emergence of Social Cohesion in a Model Society of Greedy, Mobile Individuals," *Proceedings of the National Academy of Sciences* (2011); retrieved from http://www.pnas.org/content/108/28/11370 .full; R. Seyfarth and D. Cheney, "The Evolutionary Origins of Friendship," *Annual Review of Psychology* 63 (2012): 179-99; J. Silk and B. House, "Evolutionary Foundations of Human Pro-social Sentiments," *Proceedings of the National Academy of Sciences* 108, suppl. 2 (2011): 10910-17; R. Trivers, "The Evolution of Reciprocal Altruism," *Quarterly Review of Biology* 46, no. 1 (1971): 35-57; E. O. Wilson, *The Social Conquest of Earth* (New York: Norton, Liveright, 2013).

33. D. Fry, *Beyond War: The Human Potential for Peace* (Oxford: Oxford University Press, 2007), p. 32.

34. D. Barash, "Is There a War Instinct?" *Aeon*, September 19, 2013.

35. Paul Schmid-Hempel, Institute for Integrative Biology, Zurich, Switzerland: Swiss Federal Institute of Technology, personal communication, May 15, 2015.

36. Fry, *Beyond War*, p. 22.

37. D. B. Hart, *In the Aftermath: Provocations and Laments* (Grand Rapids: Eerdmans, 2009), p. 16.

(unprocessed dots and colors) but is an act of noticing what means some-thing — what counts as some *thing* — in the situation or culture one is in.[38] An item that doesn't count might come into the range of vision but remain unnoticed and unnoticeable. (Peoples, for instance, who have no blue flowers, foods, or artifacts also have no word for blue and cannot distinguish it from other colors on color charts, though they can see the sky, which we call blue.) Our "interiors" have come into being in engagement with our situation. "The world," Merleau-Ponty writes, "is not at the end of our touch but rather the world in which we are entwined."[39] Hart explains the idea this way: "A mere agitation of molecules, for instance, does not simply 'amount to' a game of chess, even though every physical structure and activity involved in that game may be in one sense reducible without remainder to molecules and electrical impulses and so on; it is not the total ensemble of those material forces that adds up to the chess game, but only that ensemble as organized to an end by higher forms of causality."[40]

There is thus no one whose separable interiority and conduct aren't in-formed by her surroundings — no one who forms herself *de novo.* Or, as Stanley Hauerwas quips, the *de novo* idea is "the story that you should have no story except the story that you chose when you had no story," which is itself a story of unrealistic separability.[41]

Thus far, we have looked at the ontology of separability-amid-situatedness/distinction-amid-relation. The theological premise that grounds it is analogous participation. This is expressed in various ways in the Abrahamic traditions, and here I will focus on three: the ideas of co-creatorship, *tselem Elohim/imago Dei* (made in God's image), and the *analogia entis* (analogy of being). In the *analogia entis,* as explained by ibn Sina, Maimonides, Thomas Aquinas, and

38. M. Merleau-Ponty, "The Primacy of Perception and Its Philosophical Consequences," trans. J. Edie, in *The Primacy of Perception and Other Essays* (Evanston, Ill.: Northwestern University Press, 1964), pp. 12, 15. See also, M. Merleau-Ponty, *The Phenomenology of Perception,* trans. C. Smith (London: Routledge, 2002); for a concise and insightful discussion of this point, see O. Edgar, "Seeing as Communion: Merleau-Ponty's Embodied Phenomenology of Vision and the Trinitarian Ontology of John Zizioulas" (paper presented at the Centre of Theology and Philosophy conference on the soul, St. Anne's College, Oxford, June 28–July 1, 2013).

39. M. Merleau-Ponty, "Eye and Mind," in *The Primacy of Perception and Other Essays,* p. 178.

40. D. B. Hart, *The Experience of God: Being, Consciousness, Bliss* (New Haven: Yale University Press, 2013), p. 78.

41. S. Hauerwas, *War and the American Difference* (Grand Rapids: Baker Academic, 2011), p. 18.

Nicholas of Cusa,[42] causes yield resembling results. Thus humanity, caused by God, shares or partakes of some of-a-kind-ness with him.[43] As finite, material persons cannot be the same as the infinite, incorporeal divine, we are rather *nonidentical, analogous expressions.* We are to source being, God, what an analogy is to its referent: holding an underlying of-a-kind-ness yet different in appearance and particulars.

One thing that the source of being, God, is, is distinction-amid-relation. Thus if humanity shares an of-a-kind-ness with him, we share something of this. God is at once distinct from particular beings yet "inheres" in each of us as a condition of our existence. This distinction yet inherence/relation is the way anything comes to be. Each particular thing "partakes of" (or simply is "of") distinction-amid-relation. As there is no way to be other than distinction-amid-relation, we are this way with each other as well; we are distinct in relation. *Partaking of divine distinction-amid-relation is the ground for distinction-amid-relations among persons.* The interdependence of singular persons is the nature at least of this world. (One can imagine a world where there are no distinct beings but only one marvelous blob or where there are distinct beings who are entirely hermetic, but it seems this is not our world.)

The parallel from energy/matter is useful: all beings are of energy/matter — partake of energy/matter — and each particular thing is an instance or example of what energy/matter overall can be. Similarly, all persons participate in distinction-amid-relation; we are differentiated beings constituted by relation and have reciprocal impact and responsibility. Each particular worldly instance of distinction-amid-relation is one possibility of what distinction-amid-relation overall can be. This is how persons come to be distinctly and be together.

Not unlike the *analogia entis,* the *tselem Elohim/imago Dei*[44] considers each person as of God's image — an of-a-kind-ness in nonidentical, analogic expression. Thus each time we engage another, we engage something of God and must treat the other with apt regard. And as in the *analogia entis,* the God in whose image we are made is distinction-amid-relation. On one hand, he is distinct from us and has made each of us distinct: "When a man casts many coins from a single mold, they all resemble one another, but the supreme king

---

42. Nicholas of Cusa, *De apice theoriae* (1464); *De ludo globi* (1463); *De quaerendo Deum* (1444/1445); *Reformatio generalis* (1459); and especially *De visione Dei* (1453). An excellent overview of Cusa's work is found in J. Hoff, *The Analogical Turn: Rethinking Modernity with Nicholas of Cusa* (Grand Rapids: Eerdmans, 2013).

43. Aquinas, *Summa Theologica* Ia, q. 105, art. 5.

44. These concepts from the Judaic and Christian traditions are not identical but share a number of important features.

of kings . . . fashioned each man in the mold of the first man, yet not one of them resembles another" (*m. Sanhedrin* 4:5). Yet something of his spirit or "breath" also inheres in each being.[45] God is "transcendent in relationship." Terence Fretheim notes, he "has created a world in which interrelatedness is basic to the nature of reality."[46] (In narrative form, God judged Adam alone as "not good" and created Eve; God created relationship as the structure of human living.) There is no way to "be" outside of distinction-amid-relation.

Tselem Elohim/imago Dei informs us not only that relationality is a condition of being but also that we, given free will, may choose relation. Being in God's (relational) image grants us "moral correspondence" *(dmuth Elohim/ similitude),* morality that is human and thus radically different from the divine but in correspondence with him. To the question of whether this pertains to evil persons, relationality theologies respond that it does but has been severely, tragically perverted — otherwise, there would be no moral issue. The matter before us is not how something that starts out evil, and is through-and-through evil, remains evil. It is how a person endowed with the capacity for relation perpetrates evil.

In sum, being in the image of God — partaking of his distinction-amid-relation — makes each person distinctly worthy of consideration *and* able to give it. As agents of free will, we may reject or ignore this — indeed, sin may be taken as the disregard or rupture of relation. But we retain the capacity nonetheless. Without this, humanity would not be morally accountable; without the relational capacity of distinct persons, there would be no moral issue.

The idea of co-creatorship builds on moral correspondence. We have the capacity to work analogously to God, within our human talents, to further his vision of a moral world. That is, we have sufficient moral capacity to be analogous "co-creators." The *analogia entis* explains this as the principle of "secondary causes." God, Aquinas holds, "contains" all that is possible, including the natural processes by which the world runs. Humanity, in analogous participation, acts "secondarily" to make particular things from these basic principles — that is, something like God's co-creator.

In the book that follows, humanity as persons of distinction-amid-relation analogously in God's image with the capacity for relation and co-creatorship is elaborated in:

45. The concept of God's spirit or breath as enabling life is taken from Gen. 2:7: "The LORD God formed a man from the dust of the ground and breathed into his nostrils the breath of life."
46. T. Fretheim, *God and World in the Old Testament: A Relational Theology of Creation* (Nashville: Abingdon, 2005), Kindle locations 613, 620.

Covenant: we are not only of God's relationality but also "in relation" with him, world, others.

Trinity: God's internal (triune) relationality is the image in which we are made, a triune *imago* on earth, with others.

Eucharist: each is distinctly herself with others in the body of God.

Salvation: justice will come to our human bodies and relations (before all is spirit) as we are brought closer to relationship with God, to divine relationality and love.

Each of these ideas in its way relies on the principle of mutual constitution; each pair below is mutually constituted:

- distinction/relation
- source being/analogous beings
- covenant with divine/covenant among persons
- forgiveness from God/forgiveness among persons
- immanent Trinity (God in himself)/economic Trinity (God with humanity)
- spiritual salvation/worldly justice
- belief/ethics

As they are grounded in the *analogia entis* and *tselem/imago,* theologies of relationality eschew strains of Neoplatonism that privilege the spiritual over the corporeal. They hold instead — again — to their reciprocal influence. In this bodily Neoplatonism, as I will call it, spirit/form/principle is the ground for particular beings. Particulars partake of and express form/source, which in turn would have no expression absent particulars. The material world is not a degraded realm but the realization of source being. In Adrian Pabst's words, "matter matters";[47] in Sallie McFague's, "bodies count."[48] Nor is the intimacy between principle and particular a new idea: Tertullian held that God was both

---

47. A. Pabst, *Metaphysics: The Creation of Hierarchy* (Grand Rapids: Eerdmans, 2012), p. 49.

48. S. McFague, *The Body of God: An Ecological Theology* (Minneapolis: Fortress, 1993), pp. 168-69; David Gushee similarly writes, "it is significant that Christ rose in a body. . . . Paul concludes from Christ's bodily resurrection that we too shall have bodies at our own resurrection (1 Cor. 15:42-49). Human life never ceases to be bodily, even at the resurrection. Once again, human bodiliness gains powerful affirmation." D. Gushee, *The Sacredness of Human Life: Why an Ancient Biblical Vision Is the Key to the World's Future* (Grand Rapids: Eerdmans, 2013), p. 103.

infinite thought and infinite materiality; Irenaeus, that God was the human fully alive.[49]

There is a certain optimism in the *analogia entis* and *tselem/imago*. They suggest that if we go with the distinction-amid-relation of which we analogously partake — if relationality/reciprocal consideration is not blocked — human thriving is more likely. William Desmond calls this the "incognito work" of "grounding trust."[50] Conversely, a breach of relationality goes against the ontological grain and gums up the gears. At the subatomic level, the failure to take other particles' trajectories into account would collapse all matter. Among humans, the failure to take others into account yields neglect, abuse, disease, resource grabbing, waste of talent, and societal instability.

The theology of the way things are yields an ethics of how not to mess things up — what Olthuis calls the "ethico-ontological possibility of an agent self as power-with, responsibility-with."[51] Yoram Hazony holds this theology-to-ethics to be of central biblical import: "there exists a law whose force is of a universal nature, because it derives from the way the world itself was made, and therefore from the natures of the men and nations in this world."[52]

Theologies of Relationality and Truth

There is no contradiction, however, in finding that, while relational theologies search for the way things are, for *ontologies,* no one alone possesses complete, absolute truth, as suggested above. To begin with, modern notions of truth conditions are not readily applicable to the processes of earlier theological development or to the ways ancient texts were understood by their authors and audiences. Correct and productive ideas were developed but not in the ways modern logic or science, within their specific parameters, develops them. The modern lines between reason, metaphor, and narrative, for instance, were not necessarily useful in developing theology or even law. Citing two examples (the "Christian Topography of the Entire Cosmos" of Cosmas, mid–sixth

49. See A. Funkenstein, *Theology and the Scientific Imagination* (Princeton: Princeton University Press, 1996).

50. W. Desmond, "Between Metaphysics and Politics," in *Theology and the Political: The New Debate,* ed. C. Davis, J. Milbank, and S. Žižek (Durham, N.C., and London: Duke University Press, 2005), p. 165.

51. Olthuis, "Face-to-Face," p. 137.

52. Y. Hazony, *The Philosophy of Hebrew Scripture* (Cambridge: Cambridge University Press, 2012), pp. 22, 249.

century, and the "Quaestiones Bartholomaei"), Christoph Markschies writes, "the substance of these images cannot be understood by a strict distinction between res factae and res fictae."[53]

Moreover, it is a tenet of relationality — the distinction aspect of distinction-amid-relation — that humanity has employed multiple ways of understanding what is. These include various modalities — myth, narrative — and within each modality, plural interpretations of any one idea. Joseph Soloveitchik notes that all particular things in the world are expressions of the possible. As these expressions are plural and varied, each person going through life experiences different ones and so has a different "version" of the world. Each account of it will differ from others, depending on the experience, concerns, and *telos* of the interpreter. "Teleological heterogeneity" of our ideas is part of our human condition as the world presents itself to us plurally. "Pluralism," Soloveitchik writes, "is founded on reality itself."[54] Paul Ricoeur echoes the idea in his theory of language and translation. The plurality of languages and the need for translation/explanation of ideas even within one's mother tongue are evidence for Ricoeur of our plural understandings of world.[55]

Varying descriptions of the world are needed also for different life endeavors. The scientist, Soloveitchik observes, measures time linearly; others may see time as cyclical (in repeating agricultural, generational, or ritual cycles), and still others find time's most important property to be reversibility — that atonement can undo wrongs committed. Reversibility is no less "true" for the atoner than linear time is for the scientist.[56] Each is incomplete but true or apt within its arena, and so adds to our understanding of time. This does not mean all ideas are true — we regularly concoct pernicious and mistaken ones — but rather that not only one idea is, and thus the work needed to understand the world is multiple and continual.

Theological tenets, like all human ideas, have been looked at in different modalities, as truth or metaphor for instance, and within these categories, single ideas have been plurally interpreted. The Trinity, for instance, has been seen as frustratingly arcane, the truth about God, and as a metaphoric illumination

---

53. C. Markschies, "Glaubten antike Christenmenschen an ihre Bilder für Himmel und Hölle?" in *The Metaphorical Use of Language in Deuterocanonical and Cognate Literature,* ed. M. Witte and S. Behnke, Deuterocanonical and Cognate Literature Yearbook, 2014-2015, ed. F. V. Reiterer et al. (Berlin: De Gruyter, 2015), p. 509.

54. J. Soloveitchick, *The Halakhic Mind* (New York: Free Press, 1986), p. 16.

55. See P. Ricoeur, *On Translation,* trans. E. Brennan (London: Routledge, 2006).

56. Soloveitchick, *The Halakhic Mind,* pp. 48-49.

of relationality. The three persons are ever distinct but also who they are only in relation to each other, each giving being and identity to the others. This is not to say there are no consequences to seeing Trinity as truth or image, only that the idea has in both cases enriched our understanding of what it means to be distinct in relation. Writing of the Hebrew Bible, Hazony notes that while biblical intent is often expressed in narrative and allegory, its ontology and ethics have much to tell us when we understand how the narratives and symbolism work as communicative modes. "We would still have reason to read Plato as philosophy," he writes, "even if it were to turn out that the story of Socrates were all a great fiction," and so too, one may read the Bible, where metaphors are based on and emerge from "universal characteristics of human nature and of the nature of God's creation more generally."[57]

Reprising the orthodox Jewish philosopher Soloveitchik, the American Baptist theologian Glen Stassen writes, "nor am I arguing for only one tradition as having all truth; all traditions need continuous correction."[58] The Eastern Orthodox theologian David Bentley Hart adds, "It may be that one faith is truer than any other, or contains that ultimate truth to which all faiths aspire in their various ways; but that still would hardly reduce all other religions to mere falsehood."[59] Colin Gunton, of the United Reformed Church, notes, if in being human Jesus was fallible, churches run by human beings cannot be otherwise: "If our christology takes on board the full implications of the contingency and fallibility of Jesus, what of the Church?"[60] The Catholic Lonergan makes much the same point,[61] as does his interpreter Robert Doran: "Anyone

---

57. Hazony, *Philosophy of Hebrew Scripture*, pp. 53, 23. For a discussion of narrative, metaphor, imagery, analogy, etc., and the meaning of biblical texts, see, among others, R. Alter, *The Art of Biblical Narrative* (New York: Basic Books, 1981, 2011); W. Brueggemann, *A Social Reading of the Old Testament: Prophetic Approaches to Israel's Communal Life* (Minneapolis: Fortress, 1994); R. Kearney, *Anatheism: Returning to God after God* (New York: Columbia University Press, 2009); R. Polzin, *Moses and the Deuteronomist: Deuteronomy, Joshua, Judges*, Literary Study of the Deuteronomic History (New York: Seabury Press, 1980); E. Stump, *Wandering in Darkness: Narrative and the Problem of Suffering* (New York: Oxford University Press, 2012); R. Whybray, *The Making of the Pentateuch: A Methodological Study* (London and New York: Bloomsbury T. & T. Clark, 1987).

58. Stassen, *A Thicker Jesus*, p. 14; see also, S. Hauerwas, *The Peaceable Kingdom: A Primer in Christian Ethics* (Notre Dame: University of Notre Dame Press, 1983), p. 101.

59. Hart, *The Experience of God*, p. 4.

60. C. Gunton, "The Church on Earth: The Roots of Community," in *On Being the Church: Essays on the Christian Community*, ed. C. Gunton and D. Hardy (London: T. & T. Clark, 1993), p. 61.

61. Lonergan, *Method in Theology*, p. 267.

engaging in direct theological discourse must always be engaged as well in a continual *ressourcement*" involving critique within the faith community and exchange with those outside it.

> The church itself in its concrete practice will always stand under the judgment both from within and from without of women and men of intellectual, moral, religious, and affective integrity. Elements in the culture itself can occasion a conversion on the part of the church from biased and sinful elements. . . . Failure on the part of the church to recognize the varieties of grace in history, the fact of the gift of the Holy Spirit beyond the boundaries of church affiliation, has resulted in some of the most conspicuous mistakes in the mission of the church.[62]

The same is true of biblical interpretation. "Any human book," David Gushee notes, "bears the traces of humanity, including growth and development, advances and regressions. I therefore do not embrace a 'flat Bible' but instead see peaks and valleys in the sacred texts."[63] Fretheim suggests that the "advances and regressions," including biblical philological and narrative inconsistencies, "are a plus and are revealing of a complex understanding of the development of law within the canonical shape of things."[64]

Thus, like any proposal about the human condition, theological proposals evolve, which makes them not less reliable but *more* so as they are pondered and tested over centuries by people in different circumstances as they confront the best and worst of human conduct and take into account accumulated and new knowledge. The accumulation, comparison, critique, and adjustment are how humanity gets at what there is. Incomplete knowledge is not no knowledge, and though human efforts to understand the world may be always asymptotic, asymptotic effort means that one knows something and that such knowledge accrues.

To be sure, some claim theologies don't change and so disparage them as benighted, rigid, primitive, and unadaptable; others assert that theology is unchangeable, and thus, absolute truth. But the notion of theological stasis is historically unsupported. The Christianity of ninth-century Ireland is not the same as the Christianity of twenty-first-century Korea or Moldova. The Abrahamic faiths have been seen as inimical to female self-realization, yet

---

62. Doran, *What Is Systematic Theology?* pp. 198-99.
63. Gushee, *Sacredness of Human Life*, p. 9.
64. Fretheim, *God and World*, Kindle location 3327.

Saba Mahmood's *Politics of Piety*[65] describes just such self-realization not in resistance to Abrahamic theologies but through them.

In recognition of the plurality of understanding, Ricoeur held that we must "inhabit" the words of others and invite the words of others into our understanding. This is not relativism but epistemological humility. Dialogue, *dia-elegin,* Ricoeur notes, means to welcome difference. The twentieth-century German Catholic theologian Karl Rahner called it "reciprocal inclusiveness," each plumbing her own and other beliefs not for what can be appreciated at a distance, as in a museum, but for what can be learned. He did not predict convergence or reconcilability but held that irreconcilability does not void one tradition of worthy ideas — ideas others can grasp and weave into their understanding. The Jewish philosopher Ephraim Meir calls it "interreligious theology," where each plumbs her own and other beliefs not for what can be appreciated at a distance, as in a museum, but for what can be learned. Neither predicts convergence or reconcilability but holds that irreconcilability does not void one tradition of worthy ideas that others can grasp and weave into their understanding. "Interreligious or dialogical theology," Meir writes,

> investigates both the incommensurability of religions as well as the comparability between them and creates bridges. Interreligious theology is the intellectual account of interreligious and intercultural meetings and discusses a multiplicity of aspects in "trans-difference." The uniqueness of one's religion does not prevent the lofty possibility of communication. If I am not opening myself up to the other's understanding of the Ultimate, I may miss an aspect of religiosity that is relevant to my own religious life. . . . To be in the interreligious dialogue is first of all to be there for the other in non-indifference.[66]

In particular, David Burrell notes this from his study of the cross-fertilization of the Abrahamic religions: "the presence of other believers can help the faithful in each tradition to gain insight into the distortions of that tradition: the ways it has compromised with seductions of state power, or ways in which fixation on a particular other effectively skewed their understanding of the revelation given them."[67]

65. S. Mahmood, *Politics of Piety* (Princeton: Princeton University Press, 2005).

66. E. Meir, "Levinas's Approach to the Other in Its Relevance for Interreligious Theology" (lecture at Humboldt University, Theologische Fakultaet, July 9, 2015); see also, Meir, *Interreligious Theology.*

67. D. Burrell, *Towards a Jewish-Christian-Muslim Theology* (Chichester, UK, and Malden, Mass.: Wiley-Blackwell, 2011), Kindle locations 2583-2584.

Emphasizing not only plural interpretations but plural interpret*ers*, the mid-century Jewish-French philosopher Emmanuel Levinas wrote, "the totality of the true is constituted from the contribution of multiple people: the uniqueness of each act of listening carrying the secret of the text; the voice of the Revelation as inflected, precisely, by each person's ear, would be necessary to the 'Whole' of the truth."[68]

And so, following from these proposals, Wonhee Anne Joh looks at Christian and Korean tenets in her "Christology of *Jeong*."[69] Raymond Aldred looks at the Christian Trinity alongside the aboriginal people's trinity of land, people, and spirit.[70] Vajrayana Buddhism posits a trinity in its idea of the specific self, one's eternal spirit, and one's bonds to others and nature.[71] None of these efforts collapses traditions into each other but rather explores them with their differences and echoes. To sum up, Robin Lovin writes, "The shared questions about how to live a good life give us a great deal to occupy our attention together, even when we differ on important questions about whether there is a God and how we should relate to God."[72]

The same may be said of theologies of relationality as *truth or truthful metaphor*. In either case, one never knows what of interest one might find there about the world's setup and our life together in it. As post-Newtonian science holds to many phenomena that cannot be directly measured, forms of understanding that fall outside empirical observation — such as theology and art — should not be ruled out of court. Niels Bohr, in confronting the discontinuities in matter and energy that quantum theory had uncovered, wrote that we, in describing what we cannot see or measure but have only traces of, must rely on the "complementary" accounts of the traces that we do see and experience. That is, we must rely on accounts that we know are metaphorical and partial to get at what is there: "a whole new background." Bohr wrote, "for the relationship between scientific research and religious attitude has been

68. E. Levinas, "Revelation in the Jewish Tradition," in *Beyond the Verse: Talmudic Readings and Lectures,* trans. G. Mole (Bloomington: Indiana University Press, 1994), pp. 133-34.

69. W. A. Joh, *The Heart of the Cross: A Postcolonial Christology* (Louisville: Westminster John Knox, 2006), pp. 20-26; ch. 5.

70. Aldred writes, "Consider that the primary categories of relationships for the First Peoples of North America include relationship with land or creation, relationship with people, individuals and other groups, and the relationship with the spiritual." R. Aldred, "Freedom," in *Prophetic Evangelicals,* ed. B. Benson, M. Berry, and P. Heltzel (Grand Rapids: Eerdmans, 2012), pp. 152-53.

71. Vajrayana Buddhism contrasts with the more monastic Buddhist traditions, which may detach one from a focus on life on earth.

72. R. Lovin, *Christian Ethics: An Essential Guide* (Nashville: Abingdon, 2000), p. 18.

created by modern development of physics . . . it will be attempted to show the development in our time has forced us to look into epistemological problems of a kind which recalls the common problems of the religions."[73]

Or one may take up the suggestion of James Pambrun, that one consider theological tenets such as distinction-amid-relation as hypotheses and assess how well they help in understanding the human condition and addressing its problems.[74]

What's in the Book, and What's Not

After part I, the ontological argument for distinction-amid-relation, theologies of relationality will be explored in part II, where I look at contemporary theologies nondenominationally as they have drawn and built on tradition. This is neither a general overview of Judaic and Christian thought nor a comprehensive detailing of relational approaches; both projects would take several books indeed. It is rather a look at some key voices among relational approaches so that we may get a feel for their principles. With the exception of Aquinas's *analogia entis,* the focus is on primary biblical sources and the rabbinic and early church period, as these have undergirded relational thinking since. Because this volume is interested in the contributions of relational theologies to current policy, the last set of voices is Christian and Jewish thinkers of the twentieth and twenty-first centuries.

The point is not that relational interpretations of Judeo-Christian thought are the only ones (they clearly are not). Our task is rather to look at those interpretive landscapes that help us restore distinction-amid-relation, a separability-situatedness meld. The voices — signposts on these landscapes — were culled from a range of thinkers with different starting points and genealogies. Indeed, it is part of this book's methodology to draw on a range of writers who labor in different traditions, whose work does not always map neatly onto each other's, who may not be "in conversation," or who may have disagreements. The reader will already have noted this approach in this introduction, where philosophers of various schools are cited alongside theologians from across the Judeo-Christian traditions. Yet their ideas about distinction-amid-relation

---

73. Notes dated August 26 and 27, 1953; MSS: 20 in the Niels Bohr Archive, cited in J. Honner, "Unity-in-Difference: Karl Rahner and Niels Bohr," *Theological Studies* 46 (1985): 499.

74. J. Pambrun, "The Relationship between Theology and Philosophy: Augustine, Ricoeur, and Hermeneutics," *Theoform* 36, no. 3 (2005): 292-319.

share a family resemblance, and my purpose is to point them out so that we get an idea both of relationality itself and of how different traditions contribute to it. It is a horizontal approach, aiming at reappearance, affinity, and reciprocal illumination. While affinities do not erase differences, differences need not be erased for affinities to remain important. In sum, *the methodology of this book reflects its content*: it highlights *distinction-amid-relation in the voices gathered here*. Differences and debates are elaborated when they add substantially to our understanding of distinction and relation and are described more extensively in the notes for the interested reader.

Indeed, the family resemblance running through this range of work offers support for the idea that distinction-amid-relation is ontology rather than opinion. People from different eras and intellectual and faith traditions have come to it and describe it in ways that are recognizably similar. *If distinction-amid-relation is found broadly throughout the human condition and is widely seen as basic to it, it might be because it is.*

In culling from the range of writers, I cite both scholars and practitioners at sufficient length, I hope, for the reader to get a feel for their voices, priorities, and imagery. It is my hope that both experts and others will consider their work — that it reaches beyond what Esther Meek has called "guild-approved" audiences[75] — as many of us are concerned about personal and public ethics and about economic and political policy. I do not focus on applications of relationality that exceed the scope of this book, such as relations with the environment or interfaith, interracial, and gender relations. Relational theologies are robust in these arenas and are of long standing in America's black churches — in the personalism movements and works of Rufus Burrow, Martin Luther King, Cornel West, and Willie Jennings, to mention a very few.[76] These applications of relationality demand studies of their own, as does relationality in Islam, all of which are fortunately under way.

Finally, by looking at theologies of relationality with an eye to separability, situatedness, and public policy, I am not suggesting that is their *raison d'être* or that they must show pragmatic effects to justify themselves. I am sensitive

75. E. Meek, *Loving to Know: Covenant Epistemology* (Eugene, Ore.: Wipf and Stock, Cascade Books, 2011), p. xiv.

76. See, for instance, R. Burrow, *Personalism: A Critical Introduction* (St. Louis: Chalice, 1999); W. J. Jennings, *The Christian Imagination: Theology and the Origins of Race* (New Haven: Yale University Press, 2011); M. L. King, *Where Do We Go from Here: Chaos or Community?* (Boston: Beacon Press, 1967, 2010); C. West, *Prophesy Deliverance! An Afro-American Revolutionary Christianity* (Louisville: Westminster John Knox, 1982, 2002); C. West, with C. Buschendorf, *Black Prophetic Fire* (Boston: Beacon Press, 2014).

to Hauerwas's concern that one should not treat religion as sociology or, as he put it, not "do Durkheim with an ecclesial twist."[77] Ola Sigurdson notes this tendency even in recent "postsecular" sociology,[78] which tries to *defend* religious belief by pointing to its ongoing influence. As Sigurdson notes, "their use of religion and/or theology is not very interested in religious phenomena, communities or experiences."[79] On the other hand, theological ideas are not meant to have *no* impact on our lives, to be irrelevant to the way we live in the world.

Theologies are meant, among other things, to make us reflect on our conduct and yield ethics. It is not that theologies of relationality are recruited for something else of prior, prime importance (sociological concerns), but that the something else emerges from relationality theologies, which grapple with the most fundamental condition of our lives.

77. S. Hauerwas, *Sanctify Them in the Truth: Holiness Exemplified* (Nashville: Abingdon, 1989), p. 37.

78. Germinal works in this area include J. Casanova, *Public Religions in the Modern World* (Chicago: University of Chicago Press, 1994); Taylor, *A Secular Age*; C. Taylor, *Sources of the Self: The Making of the Modern Identity* (Cambridge: Harvard University Press, 1992).

79. O. Sigurdson, "Beyond Secularism? Towards a Post-Secular Political Theology," *Modern Theology* 26, no. 2 (April 2010): 177-96, especially p. 180.

CHAPTER 2

Separability and Situatedness: Defining the Terms

This chapter reviews the terms "separability" and "situatedness," "distinction" and "relation." In life, we are persons of relationality, distinct but formed and sustained by relation. The two are mutually constitutive, with neither the base modality or of more fundamental importance. To clarify what is meant by each idea, however, we will look at one and then the other.

Situatedness takes identity as emerging from one's point in a nexus of relations. "The person," John Zizioulas states, "cannot be conceived in itself as a static entity, but only as it *relates to.* . . . [I]t is not in its 'self-existence'; but in communion that this being is *itself* and thus *is at all.*"[1] Or, in Elisabeth Moltmann-Wendel's words, "Life begins as life together."[2] Situatedness takes the group and its traditions as conceptually prior to the individual, whose sense of self, values, movements, habits, improvisations, and rebellions are formed in acculturation roughly to what the French sociologist Pierre Bourdieu has called habitus: the ongoing interactions between the self and her natural and cultural environment(s). Habitus is formative but also generative and inventive: one develops from one's environment yet is not fully determined by it as one strategizes and improvises to create new possibilities for thought and action. Bourdieu speaks of habitus as a "generative principle of regulated improvisations," a "cultural unconscious," a "set of basic, deeply interiorized master-patterns," and a "mental and corporeal schemata of perceptions, appreciations, and action."

On the situatedness view, groups are called societies precisely because

---

1. J. Zizioulas, "Human Capacity and Incapacity: A Theological Exploration of Personhood," *Scottish Journal of Theology* 28 (1975): 409.

2. E. Moltmann-Wendel, *I Am My Body: A Theology of Embodiment* (New York: Continuum, 1995), p. 43.

they have clear but not necessarily closed boundaries and membership requirements, some enduring stability, a shared purpose, and commitment to certain values and ways of doing things. Indeed, our basic conscience derives from *con-sciere*, to know with others, together. Groups of various sorts, Philip Selznick writes, "establish a common faith or fate, a personal identity, a sense of belonging, and a supportive structure of activities and relationships."[3] Once a member of such a group, by birth or agreement (explicit or implicit), one has "insider status" and value — Selznick calls it "ascriptive value."[4]

Situatedness has been looked at from minimal and maximal positions. In the minimal position, the individual person is acknowledged but the group is taken as formative. Michael Sandel takes this view when he writes, "we cannot conceive our personhood without reference to our role as citizens, and as participants in a common life."[5] His position acknowledges "personhood," while the maximal view takes persons to be so societally constituted that they do not go much beyond that constitution. The Scottish philosopher John Macmurray writes, "there can be no man until there are at least two men in communication. . . . 'I' exist only as one element in the complex 'You and I.'"[6]

The separable person is, in some contrast, a completed entity who, having been acculturated somewhere, has the physical and mental mobility to leave land, traditions, and obligations to follow the beliefs and opportunities of her choice — in short, to develop her future in ways distinct from past and neighbors. This "methodological individualism"[7] might be considered the minimal position. Sandel writes, "The priority of the self over its ends means I am never defined by my aims and attachments, but always capable of standing back to survey and assess and possibly revise them. This is what it means to be a free and independent self, capable of choice."[8] A more maximal claim is that there are only individuals and no such thing as groups. This "ontological individualism"[9] was at work in former British Prime Minister Margaret Thatcher's

---

3. P. Selznick, *The Moral Commonwealth: Social Theory and the Promise of Community* (Berkeley: University of California Press, 1992), p. 357.

4. Selznick, *The Moral Commonwealth*, pp. 190-91.

5. M. Sandel, "Justice and the Good," in *Liberalism and Its Critics* (New York: New York University Press, 1984), p. 5.

6. J. Macmurray, *Persons in Relation* (Atlantic Highlands, N.J.: Humanities Press, 1991), pp. 12, 24.

7. See C. Bird, *The Myth of Liberal Individualism* (Cambridge: Cambridge University Press, 1999), p. 9.

8. Sandel, "Justice and the Good," p. 5.

9. Bird, *Myth of Liberal Individualism*, p. 59.

famous announcement that there are only individuals and no such thing as society.[10]

Descriptions of separability and situatedness are accompanied by normative claims about the behavior and institutions that should be encouraged. Normative situatedness holds that policies, practices, and resources should support a range of societal groups — rather than allow them to sink or swim on their own — as it is groups that make society work. It is from engagement in them that people get their values and life skills. Each interaction, Esther Meek writes, entwines us in a web of responsibility, mutuality, and accountability[11] from person *to* groups and from groups to members and other groups. A more sweeping normative claim is that, as traditional communities carry extensive practical wisdom born of long experience, they should change only slowly. Persons should thus live not only in groups but in traditional groups with only cautious change.

Still another claim is that goods broadly considered important, such as clean water or basic education, should be supported by societal resources and institutions (not only by individuals as they privately can afford). This support is warranted both as a matter of ethics and because democracy falters when citizens are so occupied by survival that they cannot consider the big picture or the long term. Thinkers as diverse as Aristotle, Machiavelli, Rousseau, Edmund Burke, John Stuart Mill, Thomas Hill Green, and Hannah Arendt have noted the difficulties of contributing to the public sphere under conditions of privation. These "primary goods" or the "social minimum"[12] may be distributed more or less equally among society's members or by setting a floor for each good, below which no member is allowed to fall. In the first scheme, a prospering society will see everyone's share of the goods rise; in the second, a successful society will allow the rich to get richer as long as the floor is maintained for all.

10. M. Thatcher, in the *Sunday Times*, October 31, 1987; see http://briandeer.com/social/thatcher-society.htm.

11. E. Meek, *Loving to Know: Covenant Epistemology* (Eugene, Ore.: Wipf and Stock, Cascade Books, 2011), p. 429. Educator Parker Palmer, describing the interdependence between knowing and one's relationships, puts it poetically: "To know something or someone in truth is to enter troth with the known. . . . To know is to become betrothed, to engage the known with one's whole self, an engagement one enters with attentiveness, care, and good will. To know truth is to allow one's self to be known as well, to be vulnerable to the challenges and changes any true relationship brings." P. Palmer, *To Know as We Are Known: Education as a Spiritual Journey* (San Francisco: HarperSanFrancisco, 1996), p. 31.

12. J. Waldron, *Liberal Rights: Collected Papers, 1981-1991* (Cambridge: Cambridge University Press, 1993), pp. 250-51.

Again in some contrast, normative separability holds that public policy should focus on benefits to the individual, sometimes called value individualism.[13] The jewel in the crown is democracy and human and civil rights, as these adhere to persons regardless of background and status. The classic modern rights include the right to bodily integrity, protections from certain forms of abuse (even in detention), and the right to self-govern, through direct democracy or representative government that one can criticize and depose, with all the freedoms this entails (freedom of speech, press, assembly, and so on).

A second normative claim is that our primary liberty is negative, the absence of restraint on individual activity. Thus institutions — governmental, traditional, community, family — should recede to make way for individual choice. Negative liberty is often considered best protected by rights-based legal systems, where the mechanism for preserving freedoms is constitution and statutes rather than mores and customs. Sandel continues, "Rights-based liberalism begins with the claim that we are separate, individual persons, each with our own aims, interests, and conceptions of the good, and seeks a framework of rights that will enable us to realize our capacity as free moral agents, consistent with a similar liberty for others."[14] The political theorist and philosopher Isaiah Berlin noted the optimism in this: that women and men of different goals and beliefs can nonetheless work up a sociopolitical system of at least noninterference and possibly "the harmonizing [of] human interests" where "social harmony and progress were compatible with reserving a large area for private life over which neither the state nor any other authority must be allowed to trespass."[15]

*   *   *

In this discussion, I have not used the terms "liberal," "conservative," "individualist," "communitarian," or "collectivist." I will continue to avoid them where possible because "separability"-"situatedness" and "distinction"-"relation" are the more fundamental terms on which these more composite ideas are built. Moreover, definitions of liberalism and conservatism problematically vary considerably by era and location.

Some accounts of conservatism (the Irish-Anglo eighteenth-century

13. Bird, *Myth of Liberal Individualism*, p. 58.
14. M. Sandel, *Public Philosophy: Essays on Morality in Politics* (Cambridge: Harvard University Press, 2005), p. 151.
15. I. Berlin, *Four Essays on Liberty* (Oxford: Oxford University Press, 1969), p. 126.

philosopher Edmund Burke's, for instance) hold that the individual and her reason are limited, and so communal wisdom is needed to live peaceably and well. Other accounts (the twentieth-century philosopher Friedrich Hayek's, for one) too hold that individual reason is limited and thus communal knowledge is again needed. But Hayek excludes government from the institutions that may offer this knowledge. On his view, government should be limited precisely because it is a construction developed by human reason and not the organic practices that emerge from group living. Still other accounts of conservatism hold that individual reason is *not* limited but the best we have to rely on, and so government should be constrained and allow individuals to live as they think best. It is Hayek's end from the opposite point of departure.

To add to the confusion, this last idea — prioritizing individual reason over societal wisdom and government — is attributed also to liberalism. Yet other accounts of liberalism wish not to limit but to expand government's role in order to give the individual a leg up.

This definitional tangle being unhelpful, I will keep to "separability" and "situatedness," "distinction" and "relation," throughout the book.

CHAPTER 3

Separability and Situatedness in Mutual Constitution — an Ontology

Though separability and situatedness have been taken as opposing strains of the modern West, this chapter will argue for their mutual constitution and will look at some of the difficulties that arise when they are taken apart.

Separability and Situatedness in Mutual Constitution: Psychological and Evolutionary Arguments

Paul Tillich describes two aspects of persons that are "distinguishable but not separable." One is "the self as a self; that is, of a separated, self-centered, individualized, incomparable, free, self-determining self," "unique, unrepeatable, and irreplaceable." Yet it is only itself "because it has a world, a structured universe. . . . Only in the continuous encounter with other persons does the person become and remain a person."[1] That is, the unique character of each person develops through interactions, *yet* those exchanges occur as only each particular person could have them. On Freud's account, one recognizes one's own experiences in the seeing experiences of others; one "judges" degrees of similarity, and one "remembers" them, forging identity from interaction with the other, who is now internalized as part of the materiél of the self.[2]

---

1. P. Tillich, *The Courage to Be* (New Haven: Yale University Press, 1951, 2008), pp. 86-88, 91; Alistair McFayden describes the person as at once centered in herself yet formed, dialogically, in "every interaction in which there is change and exchange"; A. McFadyen, *The Call to Personhood: A Christian Theory of the Individual in Social Relationships* (Cambridge: Cambridge University Press, 1990), p. 7.

2. *The Standard Edition of the Complete Psychological Works of Sigmund Freud*, ed. J. Strachey (London: Hogarth, 1958), 1:331.

Freud's insight was pursued in twentieth-century attachment theory,[3] which studied the need for relationships in the emotional and linguistic development of children. Describing the earliest months of life, Daniel Stern identifies the "core self" and the "core self-with-another" — the sense of self intact-and-distinct and the self that develops from interaction and so evolves into a person capable of communication and sympathy.[4] "Each new sense of self," he writes, "defines the formation of a new domain of relatedness."[5] Looking at the adult, David Schnarch describes the "differentiated" (but not separated) self, distinct but able to engage others and sustain complex relationships, the self in relationship without erasure of singularity.[6]

Freud's suggestion that one recognizes one's experience in the experiences of others has reappeared in neuroscience,[7] which finds this mirroring in the "empathy neurons" hardwired into our neurological systems. Donald Pfaff describes five steps that constitute the microsecond decision to act cooperatively, even selflessly. First is the brain's recognition of the act about to be performed; second is the internal imaging of the person involved; and third, recalling Freud, is the "blurring" of the image of the other with one's image of oneself.[8] With this, one assesses whether the act is cooperative, the fourth step; fifth is the decision to go ahead if the act is judged to be caring.[9]

Moreover, this mirroring process, which moves us to act kindly, seems to be the evolutionary "default."[10] Sarah Hrdy notes that early *Homo sapiens* mothers able to attract generosity by themselves being generous were likely to spend more time with their offspring and be more nurturing parents, creating

3. See, for instance, the foundational work of Mary Ainsworth and John Bowlby; see also, A. Meltzoff, *The Scientist in the Crib: What Early Learning Tells Us about the Mind* (New York: Morrow, 2000); A. Meltzoff, *Words, Thoughts, and Theories* (Cambridge: MIT Press, 1997).

4. D. Stern, *The Interpersonal World of the Infant: A View from Psychoanalysis and Developmental Psychology* (New York: Basic Books, 2000).

5. Stern, *The Interpersonal World,* Kindle locations, pp. 605-12.

6. Schnarch contrasts this with "an egocentric attempt to set ourselves apart from others." See D. Schnarch, *Passionate Marriage: Keeping Love and Intimacy Alive in Committed Relationships* (New York: Henry Holt, 1997), pp. 57, 67.

7. See, among others, R. Churchland, *Braintrust: What Neuroscience Tells Us about Morality* (Princeton: Princeton University Press, 2012); D. Pfaff, *The Altruistic Brain: How We Are Naturally Good* (New York: Oxford University Press, 2014).

8. Pfaff, *The Altruistic Brain,* p. 63.

9. Pfaff, *The Altruistic Brain,* pp. 9-10, 54-62.

10. Pfaff, *The Altruistic Brain,* p. 16; see also, Y. Benkler, *The Penguin and the Leviathan: How Cooperation Triumphs over Self-Interest* (New York: Random House, Crown Business, 2011).

something of a mating contest in good will, with both female and male adults competing to show their cooperative skills.[11] Fathers too formed closer bonds with their children and developed enduring relationships with women, which reduced competition among males for sexual access, thus allowing for greater cooperation among adults[12] — a virtuous circle of cooperation.

Such cooperation structures not only dyadic exchange and family relations but also complex societal networks of what Robert Trivers calls "reciprocal altruism."[13] "Natural selection," Dorothy Cheney and Robert Seyfarth add, "therefore appears to have favored individuals who are motivated to form long-term bonds *per se* not just bonds with kin."[14] Importantly, given present relocation patterns, this motivation is active in highly mobile persons,[15] absent long-term attachment, an adaptive mechanism likely from our hunter-gatherer experience (95 percent of our evolutionary history), where one hunted or traded with people one might not again meet.[16] Nicholas Christakis and James Fowler find that, even amid the mobility and urban anonymity of the present day, generous acts prompt generous responses not only immediately but also from person to person in network fashion.[17]

Kindness and cooperation can be distorted by chemical disposition (high testosterone levels being the most frequent), survival threats (food and other shortages), and violent environments, where hippocampal pathways to generous conduct are damaged and pathways to aggressive conduct are repeated

11. S. Hrdy, *Mothers and Others* (Cambridge: Harvard University Press, Belknap Press, 2009).

12. See, for instance, F. De Waal, *The Age of Empathy* (London: Souvenir Press, 2010).

13. R. Trivers, "The Evolution of Reciprocal Altruism," *Quarterly Review of Biology* 46, no. 1 (1971): 35-57; see also, S. Bowles and H. Gintis, *A Cooperative Species. Human Reciprocity and Its Evolution* (Princeton: Princeton University Press, 2013); E. O. Wilson, *The Social Conquest of Earth* (New York: Norton, Liveright, 2013); D. Cheney, "Extent and Limits of Cooperation in Animals," *Proceedings of the National Academy of Sciences* 108, suppl. 2 (2011): 10902-9; J. Silk and B. House, "Evolutionary Foundations of Human Prosocial Sentiments," *Proceedings of the National Academy of Sciences* 108, suppl. 2 (2011): 10910-17.

14. R. Seyfarth and D. Cheney, "The Evolutionary Origins of Friendship," *Annual Review of Psychology* 63 (2012): 179-99.

15. See C. Roca and D. Helbing, "Emergence of Social Cohesion in a Model Society of Greedy, Mobile Individuals," *Proceedings of the National Academy of Sciences* (2011); retrieved from http://www.pnas.org/content/108/28/11370.full.

16. See, for instance, A. M. Hurtado and K. Hill, *Ache Life History: The Ecology and Demography of a Foraging People* (Livingston, N.J.: Aldine Transaction, 1996).

17. N. Christakis and J. Fowler, *Connected: The Surprising Power of Our Social Networks and How They Shape Our Lives — How Your Friends' Friends' Friends Affect Everything You Feel, Think, and Do* (New York: Little, Brown, 2009).

and facilitated. Yet cooperation may also be enhanced by one's surroundings, with caring relationships boosting the generosity neurochemistry even after it has been compromised by neglect and aggression[18] — and by war.[19] David Barash writes, "war — being historically recent, as well as erratic in worldwide distribution and variation in detail — is almost certainly a capacity." Capacities, he explains, are "derivative traits that are unlikely to have been directly selected for, but have developed through cultural processes." And, he continues, "capacities are neither universal nor mandatory."[20] As they emerged from cultural pressures, they may be modified by them — an argument not only about child rearing but also about economic and political policies that reduce hardship and the frustration and anger associated with it.[21]

The Ontological Correlative

The psychological and evolutionary understanding of self-amid-others is, in our terms, the ontology of relationality, with which, my students joke, science is catching up. Whatever makes everything makes everything distinct yet in relation — what Alain Badiou calls our "universal singularity."[22] The source of being is distinct from particular beings but "inheres" in each as a condition of its existence. As G. W. F. Hegel described in his *Philosophy of Right*, all particular beings exist in relation,[23] or as Jay Gupta parses, "anything comprehensible

18. See, for instance, R. Davidson, *The Emotional Life of Your Brain* (New York: Penguin Group, 2012).

19. See D. Fry, *Beyond War: The Human Potential for Peace* (Oxford: Oxford University Press, 2007).

20. D. Barash, "Is There a War Instinct?" *Aeon*, September 19, 2013.

21. See, for instance, S. Nasar, *Grand Pursuit: The Story of Economic Genius* (New York: Simon and Schuster, 2011).

22. A. Badiou and S. Žižek, *Philosophy in the Present*, ed. P. Engelman, trans. P. Thomas and A. Toscano (Cambridge: Polity Press, 2010), pp. 26-48. Robert Jenson's substantial work on the idea of "individual identity" as established and expressed in relation might be of interest as well; see, for instance, R. Jenson, *Systematic Theology*, vol. 1, *The Triune God* (New York: Oxford University Press, 1997).

23. G. W. F. Hegel, *The Philosophy of Right*, ed. A. Wood, trans. T. Knox (Oxford: Oxford University Press, 1942; original 1821), para. 182. Hegel goes on to say that, owing to humanity's relationality, a certain kind of state and civil society creates the conditions for the fullest realization of personal freedom, allowing for "the principle of subjectivity to attain fulfillment in the *self-standing* [*selbständigen*] *extreme* of personal particularity, while at the same time *bringing it back to substantial unity* and so preserving this unity in the principle of subjectivity itself" (para. 260).

involves implicit and explicit *structures of relation and interaction all the way down.*[24] As there is no way to "be" other than distinct-amid-relation, we are so also with each other; relationality is the way we are in world.

This is neither univocity, the sameness of all particular beings, nor equivocity, difference so thorough that connection is impossible.[25] Nor is it dialectic, which overcomes difference by transforming two particulars into a new third. The idea here is metaxalogical, allowing for differences within relationality and for relation that creates difference. It supposes a reciprocal relationship between the source of being and particular beings. Each particular is what it is by partaking of distinction-amid-relation, and each, as one possible instance of distinction-amid-relation, gives a bit more expression of what can be.

At bottom, this is a Neoplatonic view — but one that does not invert the Aristotelian emphasis on particulars to unduly prioritize form or the source of being. Luigino Bruni is right to note that a Neoplatonism focused on the source of being may yield withdrawal into contemplation away from world and human relations.[26] In the Neoplatonism meant here — a bodily Neoplatonism, if you will — "matter matters"[27] and "bodies count."[28] The source of being and particular beings are in continual, mutually constitutive relation.

"Constitutive" does not mean sameness. Particular beings (including persons) are not cookie-cutter replicas of either the source of being or each other. They are not in direct, mathematical proportion — not the same as source being, only smaller, so to speak. Rather, each particular being has an of-a-kind-ness with the source of being. As set out by ibn Sina, Maimonides, Thomas Aquinas, and Nicholas of Cusa (the fifteenth-century philosopher, jurist, and vicar-general in the papal states), our source of being and particular

24. J. Gupta, "Suffering Violence at Your Own Hands: Hegel on Ethical and Political Alienation" (paper presented at the 2015 Telos Conference on universal history, philosophical history, and the fate of humanity, February 13-15, 2015, New York University, New York), p. 7.

25. David Bentley Hart writes of univocity as "that of the passionate idealist or apostle of pity or merciless social engineer, who sees truth as lying only in one single grand abstraction, in service of which all the uniqueness and difference of the particular is reduced to allegory or instrumental detail." Equivocity, he declares, "is that of the tedious, solipsistic absurdist, for whom nothing means anything beyond itself." D. B. Hart, *In the Aftermath: Provocations and Laments* (Grand Rapids: Eerdmans, 2009), pp. 173-74.

26. L. Bruni, *The Wound and the Blessing: Economics, Relationships, and Happiness,* trans. N. M. Brennen (Hyde Park, N.Y.: New City Press, 2012), p. 5.

27. A. Pabst, *Metaphysics: The Creation of Hierarchy* (Grand Rapids: Eerdmans, 2012), p. 49.

28. S. McFague, *The Body of God: An Ecological Theology* (Minneapolis: Fortress, 1993), pp. 168-69.

beings share an affinity *not* in the details of how things appear but at the level of underlying structure — at the level of analogy. Particular beings are to the source of being as an analogy is to its referent: of an underlying of-a-kind-ness but distinct in particular features of appearance.

Each particular being, partaking not proportionately but analogously of the source of being, is a case of nonidentical repetition. Each particular is an analogous instance of source being — a unique expression out of all possible expressions. As Aquinas notes, each particular takes in or accepts "being" differently; Rudi de Velde parses "each thing as differently related to the same of being."[29] Not only is each particular being nonidentical, but each can change and new beings can appear, each change and new being partaking analogously of source being and each also a concrete instance of all possible expressions. Each particular, in expressing source being in a nonidentical way, reveals a bit more of what can be.

Absent Distinction-amid-Relation: Epistemological and Ethical Difficulties

Absent distinction-amid-relation and each person's analogous partaking of it, the universe would be either one fine blob (no distinct beings) or full of hermetic monads (no relation). As we have distinct beings, the blob option is out of court, and we are left with the possibility of unrelational hermetic monadism. But this presents several epistemological and ethical difficulties.

Epistemologically, the hermetic, separat*ed* self is not embedded in and formed by a system of all particulars, persons, and the source of being — a system that is in part knowable because one is amid it and *of* it. It is rather apart from its surroundings, on its own in itself and in its own mind. Such a person may know what her sensory apparatus perceives, but she cannot be sure that these sensory-mental images correspond to anything outside of her mind. It's not that she is sure there is *no* world or undergirding setup; it is rather that she, separated, cannot access it. There is a break in the connection. She can get things wrong or brilliantly right or be beset by skepticism. At least the philosophical demands of pragmatism require that ideas "fit" the surroundings, that they account for what we encounter. And this assumes that we can tell if our ideas indeed do. We must be able to know something of world to assess

29. R. de Velde, "Metaphysics and the Question of Creation," in *Veritas: Belief and Metaphysics,* ed. C. Cunningham and P. Candler Jr. (Norwich: SCM, 2007), p. 89.

if our ideas about it are correct (and if we err, the lack of fit between idea and world will become evident as things don't work as our theories predict). Yet the separated mind observing the world from within itself has not even this pragmatism to fall back on. Without a system that she is of, amid, and can know, the separated person can be sure of only her internal conjurings.

This account of mind and world got substantial airing in modern rationalist philosophies, robustly from Descartes to Kant but with antecedents in the late Middle Ages. It is as if, with modernity's increasing scientific control of the environment, there came also an increase in the importance of the mind that produces the science. Charles Taylor has called this "the immanent frame," the picture of world as independent of a larger order and unaffected by anything other than its natural laws, which humanity with reason and science can control. Francis Bacon in the sixteenth century spoke of subjecting nature to impediments and constraints; Leibniz, in the seventeenth, more frankly talked about the "rack" and "torture" until nature yielded to man. Or as Bernard Lonergan explains, because certain aspects of nature are explainable by natural laws decipherable by humanity, it was imagined that all aspects are — as though, as David Bentley Hart quips, "Physics explains everything, which we know because anything physics cannot explain does not exist, which we know because whatever exists must be explicable by physics, which we know because physics explains everything."[30]

Overlooked was the obvious point that being itself — that there is nature at all — cannot be explained from *within* nature, from the laws that govern how nature works, for it is their presence that needs explaining. As each natural phenomenon can be identified as having been caused by an antecedent one (lakes from glacial movements, glacial movements from temperature shifts, temperature shifts from gaseous reactions, etc.), explaining nature from within it ends in infinite regress. Lacking is an explanation for why there are gases and chemical interactions at all. Something transcendent to nature — perhaps Aristotle's "final cause" (aim or purpose) — need be at work, and this might not be under humanity's aegis.

Yet as scientific breakthroughs accumulated, it became ever more worthwhile to invest time and energy on this "immanent" arena (and to leave queries about "being" aside), as what humanity could effect in it substantially increased, to benefits in survival and prosperity. "Western persons," Hart writes, "quickly acquired the habit of seeing the universe not simply as something

---

30. D. B. Hart, *The Experience of God: Being, Consciousness, Bliss* (New Haven: Yale University Press, 2013), p. 77.

that can be investigated according to a mechanistic paradigm, but as in fact a machine . . . as something merely factitiously assembled and arranged from without by some combination of efficient forces, and perhaps by one supreme external efficient cause — a divine designer and maker, a demiurge, the god of the machine. It is difficult to exaggerate how profound a conceptual shift this constituted for the culture — intellectual and, in time, popular — of the West."[31] Even the aims of art, Taylor holds, shifted from reflecting world, *mimesis,* to creating a world from imagination, *poeisis.*[32]

It is not that an exit from connectedness and relationality became in fact possible, as the world is grounded in distinction-amid-relation. It is that *belief* in such an exit or disconnection became an unintended consequence of modernity's success.

At least three things followed. One, the sense of interdependence with world and its source — what David Burrell calls "an enveloping tapestry in which we can locate ourselves"[33] — diminished, and was replaced by the thrill of autonomy and lordship over nature. Two, an increased focus — time, energy, creativity — was placed on observable events that we can test and change as we like. Three, there arose a reverence for the mind's ability to determine the meaning of things — to manipulate, for instance, unpredictable nature into an obedient tool. The determiner of meaning moved from outside the mind — from things themselves and their undergirding principles — to the mind's inner processes. In this nominalist move, things are not what they are but what we say they are. They are not organized by source principles but are contingent on us. With this came an inflated sense of self-sufficiency and awe of the (internal) mind that masters (external) world — the beginnings of epistemological disembeddedness. The possibility of the "buffered" self who is "aware of the possibility of disengagement"[34] emerges.

To be sure, the understanding of humanity as separable from its source

---

31. Hart, *The Experience of God,* pp. 57-58. Kirill Chepurin discusses the early modern mechanization of world and the resulting binary — controlling reason on one side, controlled nature/world on the other — in the work of Kant, Fichte, and Hegel, where human freedom is taken not as possibilities within an ontological system but as the right to inscribe human will over matter, over world-in-itself. See K. Chepurin, "Spirit and Utopia: (German) Idealism as Political Theology," *Crisis and Critique* 2, no. 1 (2015): 327-48.

32. C. Taylor, *A Secular Age* (Cambridge: Harvard University Press, 2007), pp. 352-53.

33. D. Burrell, *Knowing the Unknowable God: Ibn-Sina, Maimonides, Aquinas* (Notre Dame: University of Notre Dame Press, 1986), p. 6.

34. Taylor, *A Secular Age,* p. 42; see also, L. Mudge, *We Can Make the World Economy a Sustainable Global Home* (Grand Rapids: Eerdmans, 2014), Kindle locations 1088-1092.

is long-standing, found in Plato's idea of our being separated from our essence and in the Judeo-Christian view of our being separated from God after the Fall. But both recognize humanity's partaking of the source of being and our dependence on world and others. We partake of and analogously express Form/principle (Plato), and we partake of and analogously express God's image (Judeo-Christian traditions). In both ontologies, separation is partial and tragic. In early modernity, by contrast, "the possibility of disengagement" grabbed our attention. Tillich continues, "The synthesis between individuality and participation . . . was dissolved."[35]

It was dissolved, both the Catholic Taylor and the Protestant Tillich hold, not only by nominalism and the new sense of self-sufficiency but inadvertently also by Protestantism. Taylor explains that, in reconceptualizing the sacred from a defined church arena to the world at large, the Reformation sacralized world but unseated our sense of a divine plan or hierarchy of things (God, sacred church, mundane world). What remained was less faith in cosmic ordering, which left the world humanity's responsibility and privilege to structure.[36] On Tillich's account, the "dissolution" of "individuality and participation" was the unintended consequence of certain of Protestantism's tenets: the emphasis on the individual's relationship with God, her obligation to come to such relationship regardless of worldly situation, and the suspicion of "the relativities and ambiguities of the human condition," which might "weaken" the individual moral obligation. Each person, using reason, was to rise above the temptations of her situation such that "man became more and more transformed into an abstract moral subject."[37] By the time of Descartes's rationalist philosophy, Tillich writes, "Man becomes pure consciousness, a naked epistemological subject; the world (including man's psychosomatic being) becomes an object of scientific inquiry and technical management."[38]

The problem with Descartes's system, as Lonergan continues, is his claim that one can deduce an infallible understanding of world by beginning with a first principle that cannot be doubted — Descartes's *cogito ergo sum,* which he thought undoubtable. From this he sought to deduce all further principles. But this idea about selecting an undoubtable first principle precedes the first principle. Before the *cogito,* it is already an idea, a proposal about how knowledge works. The idea that we need an undoubtable first premise is thus an article

35. Tillich, *The Courage to Be,* p. 106.

36. Taylor, *A Secular Age,* p. 80. For a critical review of Taylor's thesis, see M. Jay, "Faith-Based History," *History and Theory* 48 (February 2009): 76-84.

37. Tillich, *The Courage to Be,* p. 131.

38. Tillich, *The Courage to Be,* pp. 131-32.

of faith, an unproven, pre-*cogito* idea. The *cogito* is no longer a first principle, and the Cartesian system has little to stand on. Descartes in his private works may not have so thoroughly relied on rational deduction to understand world. In a June 28, 1643, letter to Elisabeth of Bohemia, he wrote, "what teaches us how to conceive the soul's union with the body is the ordinary course of life and conversation and not meditating or studying things."[39] But his published works led centuries of readers to think he had.

The epistemological limits of the separat*ed* view of humanity were noticed even as it was developing. The break-in-the-connection hypothesis found its high point in the works of Immanuel Kant, but even in his day, his friend Johann Georg Hamann saw difficulties. He noted that the Kantian vision is more mystical than the most mystical religion in its worship of invisible noumena, forms that constitute reality outside the mind but that are unreachable and unknowable by us. It is vulnerable as well to skepticism about the phenomenal world, for on the Kantian view one cannot be sure phenomena are anything but mind generating images for itself in isolation from world. I would add that Kant's claim of worldly "sense impressions" acting on mind — the ostensible point of contact between mind and world — is a first assertion of his system, his *cogito*. But it remains unsubstantiated and unsubstantiable, as the Kantian mind, with only its inner, transcendental categories, has no perch from which to "know" whether "sense impressions" come from world or are a "home screening"[40] of its own conjuring. One can base neither an ontology nor an epistemology on such unreliable "impressions," and world remains occluded from mind.

On religious views of the world, Hamann noted, God at least makes himself known to humanity through revelation and his acts in world. But the Kantian system relies on sense impressions we can never be sure are anything but the mind's self-generated images. Moreover, as we cannot know how the noumenal world acts — consistently, arbitrarily — we face an inscrutable setup indeed. To survive, Kant continues, we rely on reason, which, thankfully, all persons have universally. But this returns us to skepticism: we cannot know whether the sense impressions that reason interprets are real or our own projections and thus we cannot know if reason, building on unreliable impressions, tells us anything correct about the unreachable, unknowable world.

---

39. Retrieved from http://www.earlymoderntexts.com/pdfs/descartes1643_1.pdf. I am grateful to Mathias Greffrath for drawing my attention to this letter.

40. J. Betz, "Beyond the Sublime: The Aesthetics of the Analogy of Being (Part One)," *Modern Theology* 21, no. 3 (July 2005): 378.

This makes reason, in Kant's scheme, disconnected from world yet paradoxically the only way to know it. For Hamann and other critics, this is a triple error: one, reason does not work universally (we don't all know the same things in the same way); two, it is not the only way to apprehend world, which, three, is not unknowable. Reason is not universal because it is situated in the circumstances of the thinker, which vary through cultures, time, and place. Reason is not our only avenue to knowledge because it is but one mode of engagement with the world. As we learn also from sensory, imaginative, and emotional experience, reason cannot be anointed as the only decoder of life.[41] Finally, the world is not beyond our grasp. It is knowable because we and world together are of the same stuff, whatever constitutes all. As we are not separated from world, boxed in our minds with only suspect sense impressions, we have some access to its workings. For whatever makes everything, makes mind; mind is of it. When we think, we use the stuff of world and something of its source or undergirding principles as well. These are in play even as we think.

In the Kantian veneration of universal reason, Hamann found either noumena deified but inaccessible (and thus useless) or hermetic human reason deified in its place.[42] His corrective replaces the separated with the situated mind. Ideas and the words we use to express them are not internal symbols based on uncertain impressions from a (real, noumenal) world from which we are separated. Ideas and words are themselves real and as much a part of the cosmic order as any other real thing, as much embedded in it and amid other languages, cultures, and materiél.[43] As real, they — like all things — partake of the source of being (in Hamann's belief, God) and unfold in unending variety from it as all particulars unfold. Each idea, language, and culture is one possible instantiation of source being.

Second, precisely because each idea, language, culture, and being is but one instance of what can be, we live in a world of plurality where all these

---

41. J. Hamann, *Londoner Schriften, Historisch-kritische Neuedition*, ed. O. Bayer and B. Weissenborn (Munich: C. H. Beck, 1993; original 1758), p. 70.

42. Hamann wrote, "your universal human reason, which, going beyond mere poetic license, you have divinized into a real person; you have fabricated so many similar gods and persons through substantiation of your word-images." J. Betz, "Hamann before Kierkegaard: A Systematic Theological Oversight," *Pro Ecclesia* 16, no. 3 (Summer 2007): 305.

43. Lonergan more recently took a similar view: that what our senses experience and the linguistic, symbolic, and cultural patterns that give them meaning — experience, understanding, and judgment, in his words — are all real and part of the world; see especially, B. Lonergan, *Insight: A Study of Human Understanding*, Collected Works of Bernard Lonergan, vol. 3, ed. F. Crowe and R. Doran (Toronto: University of Toronto Press, 1992).

particulars are also situated among each other. Rational thought is situated among emotions, sensory input, and all of life experience. Each culture, language, work of art, emotion, and way of seeing, naming, and using things evolves from both "sensible *revelations*" of experience in the world and equally real engagement with "human *testimonies*," linguistic/cultural signs.[44] Each person, in describing the workings of world, "invents" but also "recollects" what others have invented; each gives and receives.[45] In this way, knowledge accumulates. Only the source of all being understands all there is.

Thus it makes little sense to talk about reason as universal because it is situated in the culture, place, and relationships of each thinker. And it makes little sense to claim reason as the sole knower of what is because it is situated amid sensory input, emotion, and other life experiences. "Everything that is in our understanding has previously been in our senses"[46] and in our life circumstances, our *Sitz im Leben*. Eternal truths, Hamann held, are "incessantly temporal."

In sum, Hamann rejected Cartesian and Kantian rationalism for reasons that recall David Hume's: we do not know world from logical progressions or from deduction based on impressions whose origin is uncertain (from world? the internal mind?). We know something of world from experiencing it and its principles. We are amid it, of its principles, and the very processes of knowing partake of the same source being that makes world. On Hart's synopsis,

> most of the things we know to be true, often quite indubitably, do not fall within the realm of what can be tested by empirical methods; they are by their nature episodic, experiential, local, personal, intuitive, or purely logical. The sciences . . . accumulate evidence and enucleate hypotheses within very strictly limited paradigms; but they do not provide proofs of where reality begins or ends, or of what the dimensions of truth are. They cannot even establish their own working premises — the real existence of the phenomenal world, the power of the human intellect accurately to reflect that

---

44. J. G. Hamann, *Writings on Philosophy and Language*, ed. and trans. K. Haynes (Cambridge: Cambridge University Press, 2007), p. 117; J. G. Hamann, *Sämtliche Werke*, ed. J. Nadler (Vienna: Herder Verlag, 1949-1957), 3:39-40.

45. Hamann wrote, "It is not a question of how can 'I' (understood as an immediately self-present cogito, a pre-textual identity) understand the text, but rather a question of how the text understands and constitutes me." See O. Bayer, *Autorität und Kritik: Zur Hermeneutik und Wissenschaftstheorie* (Tübingen: Mohr-Siebeck, 1991), pp. 19-21.

46. Hamann, *Writings on Philosophy and Language*, p. 116.

reality, the perfect lawfulness of nature, its interpretability, its mathematical regularity, and so forth.[47]

Because each of us encounters only a small number of all possible experiences, languages, and cultures, each knows only some of what's possible. Yet knowledge of the world that is partial (and different in different cultures) is knowledge of *world* (not private mental images). We have access to it, can know something of it, and *precisely because we can access it, we are obligated to it, to making our ideas account for what we encounter.*

Ironically, early modernity's worldly focus on the "immanent frame" and human reason ended by *separating* reason from world. Hamann and Hume, by contrast, situated the mind amid varied human experience, world, and its undergirding principles.

A second difficulty arising from the hermetic, separated view of humanity is ethical. For the disembedded person has no ground to assume commonality with others and little way of imagining what might be helpful to them since, knowing only the operations of her mind, she cannot know much about them. She has no call to be concerned with them, who are after all equally unconcerned with her. *Belief in epistemological hermeticism makes ethics not only unlikely but also irrelevant* (and, as seen above, contradicts evolutionary and neurological science). What follows from stand-alone particulars is what Taylor calls "the great disembedding"[48] and John Milbank calls the "unfolding of autonomy,"[49] life with little concern for one's surroundings. It is what Paul Ricoeur protested against when he wrote that our life stories are always "entwined" with those of others even as they become ours.

Like epistemological difficulties, these ethical problems too have a history in early modernity, in what I've called "the problem of autonomous doing." While science and increasing control of the environment aimed at well-being, they also allowed for the slide from what we can do to benefit well-being to what we can do, period. *Autonomous doing became a good in itself.* Taylor calls this "excarnation," the removal from our worldview of any principles or agency other than our own — save natural phenomena, which fall increasingly under our agency. Separated and convinced she is self-sustaining, this sort of person

---

47. Hart, *The Experience of God*, p. 71.

48. Taylor, *A Secular Age*, p. 146.

49. J. Milbank, "Materialism and Transcendence," in *Theology and the Soul of the Liberal State*, ed. L. Kaplan and C. Cohen (Lanham, Md.: Rowman and Littlefield, Lexington Books, 2010), p. 224.

need worry little about others or a system of which her autonomous doings might run afoul, be it rules about subatomic particles or disease transmission.

As the separated self found a place in Protestantism, so did autonomous doing, inadvertently. One stresses "inadvertently" because of the Protestant focus not on disconnected doings but on moral striving, yet striving may have been the Trojan horse. With the mandate for each person to strive toward moral conduct and God, individual striving per se became a way of life, a frequent, lauded activity and well-exercised muscle flexed — *because* it was laudable — in many of life's arenas. Advances in living standards and the relief of much misery followed. Yet from the thrill of not dying so young and of linens and teacups came the lure of continual betterment. And with striving interwoven into *ethical* behavior, its losses[50] became harder to see.

The modern fundamental error, Gupta writes, "is to take one legitimate *dimension* of it [freedom] — what Hegel variously calls the moment of identity, self-relation, or being-for-self — and to posit it as a principle for grasping its entire nature. . . . But a complete understanding of what it means to be a modern, self-determining (i.e., free) individual, will require a comprehension of how such self-determination occurs within already standing, historically evolved structures of interaction."[51]

The double avoidance of epistemological and ethical problems is the constant theme of the British philosopher Gillian Rose.[52] Building on Hegel, Rose holds to the reciprocal constitution of the free, separable person capable of singular judgments yet aware of her situatedness and thus responsible for her group's roles in history and present affairs.[53] On one hand, Rose insists on individual critical judgment as a foundation of the moral stance and opposes self-congratulatory claims of innocence. Indeed, her critique of Martin Heidegger — his search for Being and supraworldly *Gelassenheit* (release of life's particulars into all Being)[54] — is exactly that he sought a pristine spot, Being, free from the culpabilities and responsibilities of history and embed-

---

50. See nn. 105, 106 below.

51. Gupta, "Suffering Violence," p. 8.

52. See, for instance, G. Rose, *The Broken Middle: Out of Our Ancient Society* (Oxford: Blackwell, 1992); G. Rose, *Hegel contra Sociology* (London: Athlone, 1981); G. Rose, *Dialectic of Nihilism: Post-Structuralism and Law* (Oxford: Blackwell, 1984).

53. As Rose scholar Andrew Shanks calls it, "between the justifiable authority claims of effective local *Sittlichkeit* and the justifiable counter-claims of a critical secularity"; see A. Shanks, *Against Innocence: Gillian Rose's Reception of Gift of Faith* (London: SCM, 2008), p. 142.

54. See, for instance, M. Heidegger, *Being and Time*, trans. J. Macquarrie and E. Robinson (Oxford, Basil Blackwell, 1962; original 1927).

dedness — what Rose calls his "magical nihilism."[55] Yet for all her insistence on individual critical judgment (especially of one's own group), she insisted also that such judgment develops *through* one's traditions and history in openness to the traditions and history of others. Only with a critique (separability) that is situated can persons and groups work through the differences and conflicts that history has yielded.

On her account, Hegel got it right in his description of the World Historical Spirit working its way through each particular society (its material and cultural life) as the way each (situated) person comes to her (separable) particular ideas. And he was right in contending that each person's open, honest grappling ("principles of subjectivity") with differences among histories and traditions ("substantive unity") is the way ideas and cultures are moved to where *personal "subjectivity" is the value, aim, and practice of group mores (Sittlichkeit)*.[56] Our goal, on Rose's reading of Hegel, is maximal personal development unto critique of situatedness *from within* situatedness. The personal commitment to this goal and the societal institutions needed for its flourishing are mutually constituted. Societal policies and institutions must thus be stable and capable of teaching, yet ever open to critique and dissent.

Rose uses Hegel as a standard of sorts by which to assess other modern thinkers, finding for instance that Søren Kierkegaard's concerns are with a similar mutual constitution of personal singularity and community (though Kierkegaard positioned himself as Hegel's critic). The difference between them, Rose finds, is that Hegel focused on traditional situatedness *(Sittlichkeit)* and the modern state that upholds the individual's rights (regardless of her situation) while Kierkegaard focused on traditional situatedness and then directly on individual singularity. The situation of Kierkegaard's greatest concern was the church, which was, he held, to be not conformity-inducing but a globally scaled entity that, for all its institutionalization, was committed to the individual voice and critique — parallel, on Rose's reading, to Hegel's critique of situatedness from within one's situation. The individual obligation, on Rose's view of Kierkegaard, must thus be to overcome the anxiety of leaving one's comfortable community for wherever one's rigorous moral explorations lead — but these explorations must be not of just anything but of one's situated traditions and the conduct of group members.[57]

55. Rose, *Dialectic of Nihilism*, p. 77.
56. See Hegel, *The Philosophy of Right*; G. W. F. Hegel, *The Phenomenology of Spirit*, trans. J. Findley (Oxford: Oxford University Press, 1979; original 1817).
57. See, for instance, S. Kierkegaard, *The Concept of Anxiety*, in *Kierkegaard's Writings*, trans. R. Thomas (Princeton: Princeton University Press, 1980).

Rose compares Kafka and Freud also favorably to Hegel in their efforts to maintain both the separable, nonconformist, self-critical mind *and* the surrounding situation that enables and constrains it. J. G. Fichte, on the other hand, comes in for some of Rose's severest criticism for his repudiation of any productive reciprocity between self and situation. Indeed, he asserts the Absolute I (see pt. I, ch. 5), sealed off in Kantian fashion from world and obligated to arrive at moral conduct from its own abstract, reasoned imperatives.[58] While Hegel, on Rose's reading, saw the individual mind in development with situation and contributing to it, Fichte saw the mind as separated from world or in resistance to its limitations. Hegel rejected both Fichte's self-positing Absolute I and Fichte's choice of rational law alone (absent situated ethics, *Sittlichkeit*) as the mediating agent between the individual and the group and between rational justice and (ostensibly irrational) traditional mores.

Also among those Rose finds wanting are her fellow Jewish philosophers Hermann Cohen, Franz Rosenzweig, Simone Weil, and Emmanuel Levinas.[59] Rose finds Cohen unhelpful for his neo-Kantian efforts to, on her view, exempt Judaism from charges of particularism. That is, to make Jewish chosenness for the blessing of *all* people (Gen. 12:3; 26:4; 28:14) more universal than Christianity's missionizing efforts that would erase difference by welcoming all into Christianity. A believer in openness to difference from within particularity, Rose sees Cohen's universalization going rather in the wrong direction. Rosenzweig, by contrast, she faults for undue particularism. As both on her view argue for one side or the other, neither is in a position to mediate between the in-group mores of situatedness and modern human rights or between traditional groups and the nonconformist.

Weil and Levinas, though they set a high bar on personal morality, are critiqued for their unsituated view of moral standards — for asking each to follow a (high) universal standard of morality decontextualized from situation. Rose finds their moral criteria simplistic and polarizing between perpetrator and victim with inadequate self-critique by those who have been victimized. Though Weil finds situatedness important — she lambastes capitalism for destroying communities and thus making the artificial "unity" of totalitarianism attractive[60] — she also has a substantial wariness of groups and the conformist

58. See, for instance, J. S. Fichte, *The Science of Knowledge,* ed. and trans. P. Heath and J. Lachs (Cambridge: Cambridge University Press, 1980).

59. See, especially, G. Rose, *Judaism and Modernity: Philosophical Essays* (Oxford: Blackwell, 1993).

60. S. Weil, *The Need for Roots: Prelude to a Declaration of Duties towards Mankind* (New York: Routledge, 2011; French 1949; English 1952).

moral dullness they may foster.[61] Levinas too speaks of the moral dangers of situatedness, which breeds us-other thinking and the inability to take moral stances against the crowd. Their common wariness of groups (though Levinas was a critic of Weil) left moral demands to fall on the individual, who is obligated to help others universally.

This evades, on Rose's view, the messiness of groups learning amid their particular situations to take responsibility for others. It evades also the modern issue of how traditional groups express and limit their demands in light of the rights of others. Neither do they work out individual expression within traditional groups. They do not, in short, work through the difficulties of competing claims, where none is innocent yet all are worthy of consideration.

Absent Distinction-amid-Relation:
The Violence of Univocity and Equivocity

With this look at some of the epistemological and ethical problems emerging from the unrelational view, the next section will briefly sketch parallel problems in modern sociopolitical and economic history.

The Univocity of Situatedness

Absent distinct persons of inviolable dignity, situatedness becomes a fig leaf for suppression. The claim, for instance, that communities should remain fairly unchanging confuses commitment to community and commitment to only ancestral community. *Within* groups, it is a pretext to stanch political or socioeconomic change and a club for those who want to keep others — women, minorities — out of the club. *Among* groups, it yields zero-sum, us-them thinking and aggression. Sociologist Peter Berger was right to note that one who too sharply criticizes modern separability "should pause and question whether he wishes to include in the denunciation the specifically modern discoveries of human dignity and human rights."[62]

---

61. Weil writes, for instance, "What frightens me is the Church as a social structure. Not only on account of its blemishes, but from the very fact that it is something social. . . . I am afraid of the church patriotism which exists in Catholic circles." S. Weil, *Waiting for God*, trans. E. Craufurd (New York: HarperCollins, 2001), p. 21.

62. P. Berger, "On the Obsolescence of the Concept of Honor," *European Journal of Sociology* 11 (1970): 339-47.

Berger was criticizing oppression from government and other authorities. But oppression from the crowd is equally pernicious. Bias, Robert Doran notes, "can affect not only intelligence, rational reflection, and responsible deliberation, but also sensitivity, its underlying neural manifold, feelings, receptivity, and the extent of interpersonal relation and community."[63] Keith Thomas has described eighteenth-century European and American villages as dominated by "the tyranny of local opinion and the lack of tolerance displayed towards non-conformity or social deviance."[64] In these villages — where "ethnic and religious solidarity and attendant intolerance . . . provided the atmosphere"[65] — one finds also the mix of tyranny from the top and from the crowd; historian Forrest McDonald notes that "the local community had traditionally exercised absolute power over the lives of its members."[66]

Somewhat ironically, both top-down and crowd oppression were found in modernity's early calls for freedom. To be rid of the monarchical boot, Jean-Jacques Rousseau called for a society ruled by the "general will" — not the freedom of persons or the sum of all opinions (the mere "will of all") but the laws that all would consider good were they guided by a proper "legislator," who, on Rousseau's view, would have the ideas he himself had. This would be men's true will, and so the state may compel men to it, forcing them to be free, in Rousseau's famous phrasing.[67] Yet, arguing against Rousseau, the counter-Enlightenment theocrat Louis de Bonald proposed a similar form of control. People would toe the line not by dint of the "general will" but by the traditional aristocratic system, an advance evident mostly to the aristocracy. His program pithily enough would replace En-

---

63. R. Doran, *What Is Systematic Theology?* (Toronto: University of Toronto Press, 2005), p. 164.

64. K. Thomas, *Religion and the Decline of Magic* (New York: Charles Scribner's Sons, 1971), p. 527. See also, R. Hofstadter, *America at 1750: A Social Portrait* (New York: Vintage Books, 1971), p. 281.

65. B. Shain, *The Myth of American Individualism: The Protestant Origins of American Political Thought* (Princeton: Princeton University Press, 1994), p. 64.

66. F. McDonald, *Novus Ordo Seclorum: The Intellectual Origins of the Constitution* (Lawrence: University Press of Kansas, 1985), p. 289. Legal historian William Nelson adds, "all members of society [in eighteenth-century Massachusetts] shared common ethical values and imposed those values on the occasional individual who refused to abide by them voluntarily"; W. Nelson, *Americanization of the Common Law: The Impact of Legal Change on Massachusetts Society, 1760-1830* (Cambridge: Harvard University Press, 1975), p. 4.

67. J.-J. Rousseau, *The Social Contract and Discourses*, trans. G. Cole (New York: Dutton, 1950; original 1762), p. 18.

lightenment empiricism, or "the authority of evidence," with "the evidence of authority."[68]

The French Catholic conservative Joseph de Maistre proposed that people should be constrained by neither the "general will" nor aristocracy but by something of a mix: heritage. Men are born into ancient and organic nations, he declared, each with fixed authorities, customs, institutions, soul, and the right to demand the sacrifice of individuals to preserve its archaic identity. He coined the term "individualism" to excoriate what he saw as the fragmentation of the archaic society that happily had placed him at its top. Men, he held, situated in their land and traditions, do not associate into political entities (nations) of their free will but are born into a legacy for which there is no substitute or escape. Should men pervert this legacy with cowardly ideas like representative government, others will purify it with violence and the sacrifice of innocents.[69]

Hoisting de Maistre on his own petard, the democratizing nationalists of his day argued against him too with situatedness. They claimed national self-determination and suffrage by declaring the rule of the (archaic) People against aristocratic privilege like de Maistre's. In this nationalism, each man unavoidably accedes to his national group because he is no one without it. Here Rousseau's "general will" became the national collective unconscious and racial memory. It's not the aristocrats who keep you in your place but the place itself. In short, though ostensibly political enemies, de Maistre and his democratic detractors advocated a situatedness that recognizes culture only as it has been — the culture of hierarchical tradition or the archaic People. Little authority was given to actual persons who might envision a situation different from either traditional authorities or national culture.

This sort of tribal situatedness was picked up by social Darwinists, who argued — against Darwin[70] — for the superiority of one race, their own. This is situatedness not in cultural *ethnos* but in the unchangeable *ethnos* of morphological distinction. In the late nineteenth century, Vacher de Lapouge exhumed thousands of skulls from French vaults to prove his theories of racial determinism. On Ellis Island, New York's port of entry, officials studied the cranial shapes and skin pores of arriving immigrants to determine each one's place on

68. D. Klinck, *The French Counter-Revolutionary Theorist, Louis de Bonald* (New York: Peter Lang, 1996).

69. J. de Maistre, *Consideration on France*, trans. R. Lebrun (Cambridge: Cambridge University Press, 1994; original 1796); see also, R. Lebrun, ed., *Joseph de Maistre's Life, Thought, and Influence: Selected Studies* (Montreal: McGill-Queen's University Press, 2001).

70. See C. Darwin, *The Descent of Man* (New York: Penguin Classics, 2004; original 1871).

the evolutionary scale. And, as Søren Kierkegaard, John Dos Passos, and D. H. Lawrence, among others, recount, top-down oppression and crowd conformity were what countless young moderns fled when they left home to make their way in the city. In Bruni's words, groups, with considerable frequency, turn themselves into "a gigantic I," in which "the individualism of each individual is replaced by the egotism of the group."[71]

The Equivocity of Separability

If nothing else, this history suggests that we sell off separability at peril to democracy and the flourishing of persons. Yet an overload yields the separated person acting from self-interest or the separated person not acting at all, from apathy and anomie. I will develop this here in some detail, as it is our present burden and what theologies of relationality address. Michel Foucault adds that the danger of disconnection persists even when liberalism is taken up to temper the extreme univocity of totalitarianism. As Nazism and Stalinism made clear the horrors of too much state, Foucault wrote in *The Birth of Biopolitics*,[72] some hoped to prevent future oppression by constraining states and promoting individualism as society's regulatory principle.[73] But individualism may stoke separatedness, leaving few ways for citizens to work toward common projects. Society is turned into a rather nasty market with a view to personal gain over the common goods that support persons. The cure for extreme situatedness in oppressive states became the problem of extreme separability.

With this ironically comes the need for more state. Under separability gone to normative agon, legal and political power is no longer a means of accomplishing societal tasks but is necessary to check grasping connivers. Legal protections from the other, once a backup when more usual means fail to resolve conflict, are seen as a first resort — as where much of life "naturally" occurs in the effort to restrain otherwise marauding neighbors.[74] From this come an overreliance on the legal system per se — yielding litigiousness and

---

71. Bruni, *Wound and the Blessing*, p. 59.

72. M. Foucault, *The Birth of Biopolitics: Lectures at the College de France, 1978-1979*, ed. M. Senellart, trans. G. Burchell (New York: Palgrave Macmillan, 2004), p. 116.

73. Foucault, *The Birth of Biopolitics*, p. 147.

74. "[W]e moderns," David Bentley Hart notes, "tend to elevate what should at best be regarded as the moral life's minimal condition [law abidance] to the status of its highest expression, and in the process reduce the very concept of freedom to one of purely libertarian or voluntarist spontaneity." Hart, *In the Aftermath*, p. 77.

high incarceration rates — and lawyering as legalized hooliganism aimed at achieving one's ends just inside the letter of the law.

Separability and Law

The idea here is not that law is unnecessary but that it is. As law follows from societal values, it reflects them back to society and is a backup when usual means of dispute resolution fail. Good lawyering, nineteenth-century legal ethicists David Hoffman and George Sharswood note, conveys values to public and lawyers both. Lawyering, situated in the "organic whole" of society, is responsible for promoting the public good, "diffusing sound principles among the people," and for promoting justice by "counsel[ing] the ignorant, defend[ing] the weak and oppressed."[75] Precisely because law is societally situated, Sharswood wrote, the "invisible hand of reputation" — after Adam Smith — would prompt lawyers to see this as their role.[76] This does not make lawyers unconcerned about their clients' interests but suggests that interests are also responsible to society. These ideas held in the American Bar Association's 1908 Canons of Ethics and through much of the century, even on Wall Street, where, through the 1950s, lawyers were considered guardians of the law and public good.[77]

Echoing Hoffman and Sharswood, Bruni today writes, "No city could function without rules, contracts, and justice," but he continues, "as the extension of contract and the limits on personal encounters exceed a critical point, life in common becomes dismal."[78] Bruni is pointing to both overreliance on the legal system per se and the shift within the legal profession toward "autonomous self-interest":[79] lawyers as "hired guns" whose task is to get away with as much as possible by skirting the letter of the law.[80] For absent the

75. G. Sharswood, "An Essay on Professional Ethics," 32 *Annual Report of the American Bar Association,* 5th ed. (1907), pp. 53, 54.

76. Sharswood, "Essay on Professional Ethics," pp. 131-32.

77. E. O. Smigel, *The Wall Street Lawyer: Professional Organization Man?* (New York: Free Press of Glencoe, Collier-Macmillan, 1964).

78. Bruni, *Wound and the Blessing,* p. 110.

79. See R. Pearce and E. Wald, "Rethinking Lawyer Regulation: How a Relational Approach Would Improve Professional Rules and Roles," *Michigan State Law Review* (2012): 513-36; E. Wald and R. Pearce, "The Obligation of Lawyers to Heal Civic Culture: Confronting the Ideal of Incivility in the Practice of Law" (University of Denver Sturm College of Law, legal research paper series, working paper 11-27), *University of Arkansas Law Review* 34 (2011): 1-52.

80. See, for instance, L. A. Cunningham, "A Prescription to Retire the Rhetoric of

idea of law and lawyers as societally situated, laws will be followed only until lawyers think they can get away with finessing or breaking them. No democratic legal system could stanch the chaos, and even a totalitarian one would have difficulty keeping up. Neither does homogeneity of population address the problem. The idea that cooperation is more likely among people who are culturally or racially alike ignores that the victims of street crime most often belong to the same demographic group as the perpetrators; so too the victims of Wall Street yahoo-ism and its law firms.

This late-twentieth-century shift parallels the period's overall uptick in separability, and it has been prodding alarm since its inception.[81] Warren Burger, Supreme Court chief justice from 1969 to 1986, and a conservative, called the "hired gun" shift a crisis of professionalism. An array of jurists joined him to declare that "lawyers, their ethics, and their professionalism are 'lost,' 'betrayed,' in 'decline,' in 'crisis,' facing 'demise,' near 'death,' and in need of 'redemption.'"[82]

Eli Wald and Russell Pearce propose instead a "relational" view of law, which promotes better lawyering within the profession and extralegal practices that preempt an agonistic framework so that we end up resorting to litigation less. Within the law, they write, a relational view "encourages individuals and groups to select strategies and goals that seek to maximize dialogue, cooperation, trust, and reconciliation." But even where "substantive agreement and cooperation appear unlikely" — that is, where we must turn to law — "civility demands mutual respect for the human dignity of those whose opinions or actions we find deplorable."[83]

Looking to extralegal practices, economists Luigino Bruni and Stefano Zamagni note that the more business operates in an arena of promise keeping

---

'Principles-Based Systems' in Corporate Law, Securities Regulation, and Accounting," *Vanderbilt Law Review* 60 (2007): 1423.

81. For a review of the worldview and standards of legal ethics, see M. Hoeflich, "Legal Ethics in the Nineteenth Century: The 'Other' Tradition," *University of Kansas Law Review* 47 (1999): 793-99; D. Luban, "Rediscovering Fuller's Legal Ethics," in *Rediscovering Fuller: Essays on Implicit Law and Institutional Design*, ed. W. J. Witteveen and W. van der Burg (Amsterdam: Amsterdam University Press, 1998); D. Luban, *Legal Ethics and Human Dignity* (Cambridge and New York: Cambridge University Press, 2007); R. Pearce, "Rediscovering the Republican Origins of the Legal Ethics Codes," *Georgetown Journal of Legal Ethics* 6 (1992): 241-82; R. Pearce, "The Legal Profession as a Blue State: Reflections on Public Philosophy, Jurisprudence, and Legal Ethics," *Fordham Law Review* 75, no. 3 (2006): 1338-68.

82. R. Pearce, "The Professionalism Paradigm Shift," *New York University Law Review* 70 (1995): 1229, 1237 n. 35, 1254-55.

83. Wald and Pearce, "Obligation of Lawyers," p. 8.

and trust, the fewer legal and governmental controls are needed.[84] This, they write, is a matter of ontology, culture, and normative practices that allow persons and groups to work difficult problems through, a reality without which the justice system would be overwhelmed. It is not in law courts that we learn this, Larry Rasmussen writes, but it is "in relatively intact, small-scale communities with some staying power that we learn to trust, to temper individualism and restrain appetites, freely serve, hone leadership skills for work together."[85]

Separability and Anomie: Leaving People Alone

Untempered separability brings difficulties also in its claim that groups, institutions, and traditions make way for the (enterprising) individual — that such withdrawal yields the most productive person and society. On this view, Anne Wonhee Joh notes, relationship is ever suspect, and "is a threat in a culture that values individualism and separation while devaluing communal interdependence and the interconnectedness of all."[86]

Yet, wariness of relation may leave one not free and flourishing but anomic and value-less, in what Taylor has called the "malaise of immanence" and the "the spectre of meaninglessness."[87] The will, as David Bentley Hart writes, becomes "sovereign because unpremised, free because spontaneous, and this is the highest good." With unpremised will as king, its choices — choice per se — are valorized, and we are left with the "unreality of any value higher than choice, or any transcendent Good ordering desire to a higher end."[88] Able to choose but with few choices that move one, one becomes *not unsatisfied but unsatisfiable.* "The modern buffered self," J. K. A. Smith writes, "is also sealed off from significance, left to ruminate in a stew of its own ennui."[89]

Moreover, even assuming that one could develop a purpose on one's own,

84. L. Bruni and S. Zamagni, *Civil Economy: Efficiency, Equity, Public Happiness* (Bern: Peter Lang, 2007), pp. 45-75.

85. L. Rasmussen, *Moral Fragments and Moral Community: Proposal for Church in Society* (Minneapolis: Augsburg Fortress, 1993), pp. 71-72.

86. W. A. Joh, *The Heart of the Cross: A Postcolonial Christology* (Louisville: Westminster John Knox, 2006), p. 121.

87. Taylor, *A Secular Age*, pp. 309, 717.

88. Hart, *In the Aftermath*, p. 1.

89. J. K. A. Smith, *How (Not) to Be Secular: Reading Charles Taylor* (Grand Rapids: Eerdmans, 2014), p. 64; Tibor Scitovsky called this the opposite of contentment, the bored "restlessness" of unending dissatisfaction; see T. Scitovsky, *The Joyless Economy: The Psychology of Human Satisfaction* (New York and Oxford: Oxford University Press, 1976, 1992).

de novo, one would lack the networks, public policies, or institutions to realize it. One would be left with little opportunity to pursue opportunity and little help when things don't go swimmingly. To have the possibility *de facto* to pursue possibilities *de jure,* one needs support at several levels, from government to family relations.

Separability and Self-Absorption

Untempered separability also risks self-absorption. To be sure, it does not compel one to it; indeed, the idea of institutional withdrawal is to allow the individual voluntarily to engage world. But it may be difficult to see societal projects as worthwhile — or to see them at all — where the value of self-fulfillment is foregrounded.

Self-absorption is not a recent temptation but, as Tocqueville noted in the 1830s, a possibility as old as opportunity. The freedom to follow it leads men to cultivate little else, he wrote, which ends with each person "habitually busy with the contemplation of a very pretty object, which is himself."[90] Its outcomes were noted in the Sadler Committee Report on Factory Children's Labour (1832)[91] and in Thomas Piketty's masterful investigation, *Capital in the Twenty-First Century.*[92]

90. A. de Tocqueville, *Democracy in America,* ed. J. P. Mayer, trans. G. Lawrence, vol. 1 (Garden City, N.Y.: Doubleday, 1966, 1969; original 1835), p. 460; see discussion, pp. 506-10.

91. M. Williams, ed., *Child Labor and Sweatshops* (San Diego: Greenhaven Press, 1999).

92. T. Piketty, *Capital in the Twenty-First Century,* trans. A. Goldhammer (Cambridge: Harvard University Press, 2014); see also, R. Blank and W. McGurn, *Is the Market Moral?* (Washington, D.C.: Brookings Institution, 2004); Bruni and Zamagni, *Civil Economy;* D. Foley, *Adam's Fallacy: A Guide to Economic Theology* (Cambridge: Harvard University Press, Belknap Press, 2006); W. Greider, *One World, Ready or Not: The Manic Logic of Global Capitalism* (New York: Simon and Schuster, Touchstone, 1997); D. Hausman and M. McPherson, *Economic Analysis and Moral Philosophy* (Cambridge: Cambridge University Press, 1996); D. Korten, *When Corporations Rule the World* (West Hartford, Conn.: Kumarian Press; San Francisco: Berrett-Koehler Publishers, 1995); M. Lind, *The Next American Nation: The New Nationalism and the Fourth American Revolution* (New York: Free Press, 1995); D. S. Long, *Divine Economy: Theology and the Market* (London and New York: Routledge, 2000); J. Madrick, *Why Economies Grow: The Forces That Shape Prosperity and How We Can Get Them Working Again* (New York: Basic Books, Century Foundation Book, 2002); T. Palley, *Plenty of Nothing: The Downsizing of the American Dream and the Case for Structural Keynesianism* (Princeton: Princeton University Press, 1998); J. Stiglitz, *The Price of Inequality: How Today's Divided Society Endangers Our Future* (New York: Norton, 2013); L. Thurow, *The Future of Capitalism: How Today's Economic Forces Shape Tomorrow's World* (New York: Morrow, 1996).

Neither is self-absorption always the modern case. Greater concern for the commons emerged, for instance, in America of the Great Compression (1933-1966), in which many saw governmental, public-good projects not as a hindrance to individual liberty and enterprise but as a leg up for the little guy and as leveling the playing field. This view emerged first in response to nineteenth-century labor abuses, and at the turn of the twentieth century, Teddy Roosevelt (Republican) broke up the monopolies not to close markets but to allow more people in. It was furthered, under the pressures of the Great Depression, World War II, and the early Cold War, by the social insurances and public projects of his cousin Franklin Roosevelt (Democrat) and by Roosevelt's successors, Harry Truman (Democrat) and Dwight D. Eisenhower (Republican).

In 1954, Eisenhower wrote to his brother Edgar, "Should any political party attempt to abolish social security, unemployment insurance and eliminate labor laws and farm programs, you would not hear of that party again in our political history. There is a tiny splinter group, of course, that believes you can do these things. . . . Their number is negligible and they are stupid."[93]

The policies Eisenhower listed got a triple trouncing after the 1960s: first, from economic neoliberals, who found receptors for reducing public projects and market regulations in America's traditional self-reliance (see pt. I, ch. 4).[94] The second trouncing came from the "liberationist" left wing, where individualism emerged as self-expression and as libertarian wariness of government and common-good projects. Third, the civil rights movement[95] and Great Society aid programs sparked a backlash, the view that these pro-

---

93. *The Papers of Dwight David Eisenhower*, vol. 15, *The Presidency: The Middle Way Part VI; Crises Abroad, Party Problems at Home; September 1954 to December 1954*, ch. 13, p. 1386. Robert and Edward Skidelsky describe similar policies in postwar Britain, which saw "the maintenance of continuous full employment, reduction in inequality through progressive income taxes, a big extension of social security and the preservation of peace. Increases in productivity enabled real wages to rise and working hours to fall, with only very moderate inflation. . . . There were advances in health, education, women's rights"; R. Skidelsky and E. Skidelsky, *How Much Is Enough? Money and the Good Life* (New York: Other Press, 2012), p. 191.

94. Historian Andro Linklater notes the influence of the Austrian school of economics, which equates unregulated market activity with individual freedom and which thus resonates with traditional American individualism and notions of negative freedom; see A. Linklater, *Owning the Earth: The Transforming History of Land Ownership* (London: Bloomsbury, 2014).

95. Eli Wald and Russell Pearce suggest that an unintended consequence of the civil rights era, in which discrimination laws were often voided in the courts long before they were scotched by legislatures, was an increase in the use of the legal system to resolve disputes, thus contributing to the upswing in America's individualist, agonistic worldview. See Wald and Pearce, "Obligation of Lawyers," p. 22.

grams were not giving the little guy a leg up but were "handouts" to the lazy, spoiled, hippie, yippie, and black — as "big government" vitiating productive self-responsibility.

With that, much of the nation returned to its long-standing self-reliance (and concomitant suspicion of government), which, untempered by relationality, may yield us self-absorption. As noted above, the hired-gun view of law became a "crisis" in business and law. In 1984, J. L. England and S. L. Albrecht found that the rapid changes in the U.S. economy, while creating the opportunities of separability, also create — in boom and bust cycles alike — alienation, suspiciousness, distrust, and erosion of support from communities and of commitment to them. Most harmed is "the effectiveness of facilities that support informal ties such as friendliness and community spirit."[96] In 1986, Mark Baldassare found that the commons fared little better in suburbia, where residents were "pessimistic, distrustful, unwilling to tax themselves to pay for services and hostile towards newcomers."[97] Even religious institutions, Catherine Albanese wrote in 1991, became little more than malls where "clientele" shop for houses of worship based on "non-binding commitments."[98] These community-wary outcomes were by no means everywhere, but where they were, the adverse effects were substantial.

Separability in Present Politics and Economics, Brief Examples

David Frum, a Republican conservative and speechwriter for G. W. Bush, wrote for the editorial page of the *Wall Street Journal* and *Forbes* magazine, and contributed to the right-of-center Manhattan Institute and American Enterprise Institute. In 2011, he lambasted his party for failing what he called its first mandate, to provide for the common good, and for succumbing to greed. The purpose of the critiques below is not party politics, as both critics and targets are Republican, but undue separability in the nation's political and economic centers.

"In the aughts," Frum wrote, "Republicans held more power for longer than at any time since the twenties, yet the result was the weakest and least broadly shared economic expansion since World War II, followed by an eco-

96. J. England and S. Albrecht, "Boomtowns and Social Disruption," *Rural Sociology* 4 (Summer 1984): 230-46.

97. M. Baldassare, *Trouble in Paradise: The Suburban Transformation in America* (New York: Columbia University Press, 1986), pp. 101-68.

98. C. Albanese, "Forum," *Religion and American Culture: A Journal of Interpretation* 1, no. 2 (Summer 1991): 138, 141.

nomic crash and prolonged slump. In the throes of the worst economic crisis since the Depression," he continued, "Republican politicians demand massive budget cuts and shrug off the concerns of the unemployed. In the face of evidence of dwindling upward mobility and long-stagnating middle-class wages, my party's economic ideas sometimes seem to have shrunk to just one: more tax cuts for the very highest earners."[99]

The year of Frum's lambaste, Mike Lofgren, a twenty-eight-year Republican congressional staffer, accused his party[100] of economic self-absorption, militarism, and the exploitation of fundamentalist religion.[101] "The GOP cares solely and exclusively about its rich contributors," he wrote.

> After a riot of unbridled greed such as the world has not seen since the conquistadors' looting expeditions and after an unprecedented broad and rapid transfer of wealth upward by Wall Street and its corporate satellites, where is the popular anger directed, at least as depicted in the media? At "Washington spending" — which has increased primarily to provide unemployment compensation, food stamps and Medicaid to those economically damaged by the previous decade's corporate saturnalia.[102]

Commenting on the private sector, Greg Smith described the corporate culture at Goldman Sachs, where he worked for twelve years, as "toxic and destructive," concerned only with making money off clients, who are contemptuously called "muppets."[103] Umair Haque, director of Havas Media Labs,

---

99. D. Frum, "When Did the GOP Lose Touch with Reality?" *New York Magazine*, November 20, 2011.

100. M. Lofgren, "Goodbye to All That: Reflections of a GOP Operative Who Left the Cult," *Truthout* (2011); retrieved from http://www.truth-out.org/goodbye-all-reflections-gop -operative-who-left-cult/1314907779.

101. Lofgren writes, "The Republican Party is becoming less and less like a traditional political party in a representative democracy and becoming more like an apocalyptic cult, or one of the intensely ideological authoritarian parties of 20th century Europe." Against the charge of exaggeration, Lofgren notes Republican legislation that violates basic constitutional protections (such as *habeas corpus*), Republican use of the filibuster that "one could have observed 80 years ago in the Reichstag of the Weimar Republic," and Republican efforts to keep Democratic voters from the polls (by means of shorter voter registration periods, residency requirements that disenfranchise students, and "onerous" voter ID requirements).

102. To make his case, Lofgren notes that U.S. tax rates are among the lowest among countries of the Organisation for Economic Co-operation and Development, and refutes the idea that tax cuts to millionaires and billionaires automatically create jobs.

103. G. Smith, "Why I Am Leaving Goldman Sachs," *New York Times*, March 14, 2012.

called this sort of ethos a "McFuture" of quick fixes and fast personal gain.[104] Republican Party officer Mike Stafford called it "McHell."[105]

Addressing both governance and economics, Stafford and D. R. Tucker, a Republican blogger and political commentator, bemoaned party policy as the "tireless defense of struggling millionaires" (quoting John Gehring).[106] The "real roots" of American conservatism, they note, are "a concern for the common good — a political philosophy rooted in the stewardship ethic. . . . It begins with three simple premises: that recognition of the shared dignity of all human beings is the essential predicate of a just society, that rights always correspond to duties, and that we bear a collective responsibility towards one another."[107]

104. U. Haque, "Is America Giving Up on the Future?" *Harvard Business Review,* September 28, 2011.

105. M. Stafford, "Christian Resistance to the Cult of the Self," *Religion and Ethics,* March 21, 2013; Stafford identified the problem as the "cult of the self": "We are meant to live in communion and fellowship, not seeking to maximize our own self-interests while locked in remorseless competition with others."

106. http://www.huffingtonpost.com/john-gehring/the-catholic-case-against_b_1184224.html.

107. D. Tucker and M. Stafford, "A Phoenix Rising: Common-Good Conservatism," *Truthout,* April 27, 2012; retrieved from http://truth-out.org/opinion/item/8643-a-phoenix-rising-common-good-conservatism.

CHAPTER 4

Those Claimed for Separability — and Their (Sometimes Ignored) Constitution with Situatedness: A Few Examples

In the preceding chapters, I have begun to make an argument for an ontology of distinction-amid-relation and for policies that take it into account. The idea is that building into public policy both the value of the person and the interlocking relationships that constitute her make greater well-being a more viable possibility. This chapter will look at thinkers claimed to have abrogated this ontology by advocating separability over situatedness. Looking at their work as a whole and in historical context, it will suggest that they did not advocate separability but rather advocated a mutually constitutive meld. The chapter is thus *not* a comprehensive genealogy of separability per se but rather highlights a few examples of thinkers whose work has been misread under our present separability emphasis. We misread them, I suggest, at the risk of the more nuanced ideas that were proffered.

The Mutual Constitution of Separability-amid-Situatedness in Early Modernity and the Enlightenment

One might begin with Francis Bacon, who in the *New Organon* (1620) describes his inductive, empirical science not as an endeavor of the testing, controlling mind detached from its object, world, but as a means to aid humanity, as the Christian obligation to *agape* directed by humanity's needs. Thomas Hobbes is seen as a linchpin of separability for his view of person as so separated and competitive as to be ever-warring over goods and for his idea that, as primordially free, even these warring creatures have individual inalienable rights.[1]

---

1. T. Hobbes, *Leviathan*, ed. E. Curly (Indianapolis: Hackett, 1994; original 1651), pp. 74-78,

Thus he held that the state should be run by law (not royal whim);[2] should respect citizen choices in commerce, contract, professions, residence, and child rearing;[3] should address only public religious practice (not private conscience); and should curtail liberty only where one could justifiably hold that citizens themselves would do so to preserve the peace.[4]

This does sound like a bill of individualist rights; yet, for all this separability, Hobbes assumed its constitution with relation and situatedness.[5] By situatedness I do not mean that Hobbes topped off natural separability with the Leviathan sovereign who controls individual will for societal peace and order. But rather that he believed society itself depends on the internal ability to control appetite and check our fears that others will grab what we want, leading us to preemptive aggression. For all his talk of the competitive individual, Hobbes's aim was a society that works much of the time without the monarchical boot controlling competitive citizens top-down. And he considered this aim doable because, he held, each of us is capable of societally minded "virtue" fostered in educational and religious institutions. Belief in this well-tutored virtue allowed Hobbes to grant each citizen choice in commerce, contract, etc. Indeed, if people had little capacity for virtue and little appreciation of societal well-being, why would they turn over their primordial individual rights and consent to be ruled at all — why would they not prefer the risks and adventures of continual violent contest?

To be sure, Hobbes wrote that virtues are but "insignificant sounds" (*Leviathan,* ch. 4). But this reference is to the virtues in his day called "Aristotelian," which Hobbes spurned because he felt they led to chaos and undermined the law,[6] eroding the very purpose of virtue. Hobbes's disagreement with "Aristo-

---

92, 84-85, 97, 144-45, 191, 198; J. Grey, *Liberalism,* 2nd ed. (Minneapolis: University of Minnesota Press, 1995), p. 10; M. Oakeshott, "Introduction to Leviathan," in *Rationalism in Politics and Other Essays,* ed. T. Fuller (Indianapolis: Liberty Press, 1991), pp. 282-83; L. Strauss, *Natural Right and History* (Chicago: University of Chicago Press, 1953), pp. 181-82; R. Tuck, *Hobbes* (Oxford: Oxford University Press, 1989), pp. 72-74, 97.

2. Hobbes, *Leviathan,* pp. 97-98, 114.

3. Hobbes, *Leviathan,* p. 138.

4. Hobbes, *Leviathan,* chs. 16–18, pp. 101-18, 136-38, 161-62.

5. For a longer analysis of a concern with situatedness in Hobbes, Locke, Kant, and Mill, see P. Berkowitz, *Virtue and the Making of Modern Liberalism* (Princeton: Princeton University Press, 1999).

6. Considered essences separated from matter, such "Aristotelian" virtues, if they existed, could imbue men with internal, supposedly virtuous justification for disobeying the law whenever inner feelings and law conflict. Hobbes thought this bad social policy and bad science of "essences."

telity" is not a rejection of societal virtues per se, but a call for those virtues that teach one, as he wrote, to understand experience correctly, grasp the nature of man, and so near the virtues of God (see the introduction to *Leviathan*). Hobbes writes, "*justice, gratitude, modesty, equity, mercy* and the rest of the laws of nature are good (that is to say, *moral virtues*), and their contrary *vices, evil*."[7] He ends not with paeans to primordial, individual man, to societal contractual man, or to the restraining sovereign, but with the well-known mandate to *social, relational* man: "Do not that to another, which thou wouldest not have done to thyself."[8]

Among those championed (or disparaged) as early modern advocates of separability, Hobbes is superseded only by John Locke. Yet even his individualist contractarianism — his view that society is formed by contract agreements among autonomous individuals — is situated in the citizen ethic, virtues, and social norms.[9] Beginning empirically, Locke held that the mind at birth is an empty slate. Ideas come to us through sensory input that the mind fashions into concepts, which in turn form who each person is and what each does and acquires — that is, identity and property.[10] To steal or tax it without consent is a violation of the person — which is a substantial individualist focus. Yet, Locke continued, as God provides all persons with these idea-producing processes, all have equal access to understanding world and the moral life. With this universally available understanding, people realized that society (not isolation or chaos) most effectively yields well-being, and each ceded those liberties whose surrender is necessary for societal cooperation. That is, wisdom and understanding brought persons to societal living, the best form of life.

On Locke's theory of mind, not only does understanding bring persons together in society, but understanding itself emerges from situatedness in the surroundings that provide the mind's inputs.[11] We become who we are by taking in from our environments. Thus, society is responsible for organizing good ones, specifically for educating persons to the relationally minded virtues necessary to live in freedom, without constant control from the top. Those virtues, on Locke's account, are justice, courage, civility, industry, truthful-

---

7. Hobbes, *Leviathan*, pp. 100, 174-75, 180-81, 237.

8. Hobbes, *Leviathan*, p. 99.

9. C. Taylor, *A Secular Age* (Cambridge: Harvard University Press, 2007), p. 484.

10. J. Locke, *Two Treatises of Government*, ed. P. Laslett (Cambridge: Cambridge University Press, 1988; original 1690). Second treatise, pp. 287-90, 296, 298-99.

11. Locke never doubted that these were real and so was not plagued by the skeptic's worry that what we consider real might be only mental images. He believed that we become who we are through interaction, and that with which we interact is the world.

ness, liberality (toleration), and the submission of passion to reason. They are needed especially to avoid confusing imaginary (impulsive, short-term) pleasures for "real happiness"[12] and impetuous desire for "real Bliss."[13]

Virtues are to be taught by one's relations, first in the family, equally by mother and father,[14] and should the father die without having appointed a tutor, the public law must provide for the children's education.[15] Among the things to be taught is obligation to the public good and the poor — an obligation so strong that, Locke held, the poor have a claim on the wealth of others. Locke's sense of the commons was such that, he wrote, one may assert ownership of a perishable item (food) only in an amount that one can use; no person may legally claim a plot of land unless others have access to plots equal in quality and size. Religious toleration, on Locke's view, was not an individualist right but necessary for our living together in social harmony. Imposed religion, in any case, never persuades anyone of real faith — a principle of great importance to Locke. Indeed, his calls for toleration and church-state separation *(Two Treatises on Government)* are so grounded in his own Christian belief that the Scottish philosopher Alasdair MacIntyre quipped that they could not be taught in American public schools.[16]

In sum, persons in Locke's scheme are not quite disconnected, contracting entities but are individual *within* God's realm and responsible for following his vision of our life together on earth. Locke saw us, Lewis Mudge writes, as existing "under, and in virtue of, God's dominion. These persons engage one another to make and maintain contracts in their shared status as creatures of God. Their status as moral actors rests on their responsibility as individuals before God."[17]

---

12. J. Locke, *An Essay concerning Human Understanding*, ed. P. Nidditch (Oxford: Oxford University Press, 1975; original 1690), p. 266.

13. Locke, *Essay concerning Human Understanding*, pp. 266-67; see also, J. Locke, *Some Thoughts concerning Education*, in *Some Thoughts concerning Education: And, Of the Conduct of the Understanding*, ed. R. Grant and N. Tarcov (Indianapolis: Hackett, 1996), pp. 32-34.

14. Locke held that both parents were equal teachers to their children as God created men and women in his image, and both men and women were responsible for the Fall; see Locke, *Two Treatises of Government*, second treatise, ch. 6. Locke also believed in education for both boys and girls, with minor adjustments in pedagogy made for gender; see Locke, *Essay concerning Human Understanding*, p. 12.

15. Locke, *Two Treatises of Government*, second treatise, pp. 47, 309, 312; see also, Locke, *An Essay concerning Human Understanding*, in *Some Thoughts concerning Education*, p. 27.

16. J. Waldron, *God, Locke, and Equality: Christian Foundations in Locke's Political Thought* (Cambridge: Cambridge University Press, 2002), p. 44.

17. L. Mudge, *We Can Make the World Economy a Sustainable Global Home* (Grand Rapids: Eerdmans, 2014), Kindle locations 1083-1088.

By the eighteenth century, separability and innovation *for* the public good was getting a reputation on the Continent, where Voltaire became its publicist. When a nobleman derided him for changing his name (from Francois-Marie Arouet to the more refined-sounding Voltaire), he retorted that it was better to give oneself a new name than disgrace an old one. The old name had Voltaire beaten up and arrested, and upon release, Voltaire fled to England. His reports back to France (*Letters on England,* 1734) described England's openness to novelty and invention (separation from the past) and their employment in public works. Moderate democracy, where at least some commoners had the right to use their own (separable) minds to vote, benefited not only individuals, Voltaire wrote, but also the nation, increasing prosperity and political stability as citizens were less likely to protest a government in which they participated.

His compatriot, the baron de Montesquieu, came to his appreciation of separability from tradition and individual liberty through his friendship with a Chinese Christian man, through his own marriage to a Huguenot woman (which put him at odds with Catholic tenets and at risk with church authorities), and through his objections to monarchical absolutism — which put him at risk with the crown. Yet, in *The Spirit of the Laws* (1748), he notes that individual liberty, however important, may lead to tumult and thus, in efforts to restore order, to despotism. This might be avoided through a system of political checks and balances that preempts such despotism, fosters stability, and thus boosts cooperation in civil society, which increases prosperity. But this, he rued, would shift men's focus to private wealth, leading again to competitive tumult and thus to the need for restraining tyranny. Montesquieu concluded that all governments must on one hand preserve individual liberty so that persons may discover new knowledge, improve society, and govern themselves. Yet they must also prevent self-interest from luring citizens away from public service.

In sum, two of the most-touted advocates of individualist liberty, Locke and Montesquieu, assumed large roles for family, religion, public service, virtue, education, and political institutions. For all the importance of the separable mind, when eighteenth-century thinkers wrote about "natural" reason, they did not mean *untutored* reason; they meant natural in the sense of part of God-given nature. Reason capable of complexity commensurate with the complex world does not, they held, develop autonomously but with training in family, school, and society. The Scottish sentimentalist philosopher Frances Hutcheson may have proposed that a "common sense" and "moral sense" reside in all persons and that these senses glean ethical ideas from experience much as eyes and ears interpret physical stimuli. But he held that this universal sense must be educated. His compatriot Thomas Reid said much the same about a universal "moral faculty." Voltaire, in *Discourse in Verse on Man* (1739), too suggested an educational program that would foster a "philosophical spirit" so that one would use reason to contribute to the common good.[18] The French rationalist Claude-Adrien Helvétius devoted his life to freedom and progress, but these, he held, depended on educating people to a "moral self-interest" at one with the common good. So central were education and situatedness in culture to his work that he declared that if he and his valet had been switched in their cribs, his valet, given elite upbringing, would be the one writing books.

Even Adam Smith, who was so enthusiastic about the market regulating itself, did not think persons regulate themselves. Political and economic liberty, he held, require the traditional virtues of self-reflection, self-control, and responsibility for the common good so that top-down control is not needed. In both *The Theory of Moral Sentiments* (1759) and *The Wealth of Nations* (1776), Smith argues that market forces are not meant to set the mores of society but rather must be set by them — by the virtues and relations that train market forces toward their positive uses and school people in ethical conduct.[19] In markets, as in all of society, each should "endeavor, as much as he can, to put himself in the situation of the other, and to bring home to himself every little circumstance of distress which can possibly occur to the sufferer."[20]

Virtue of this sort requires education, Smith wrote. Honesty, discipline, promise keeping, deferred gratification, thrift, patience, cooperation are learned in families, communities, and churches, and without them markets collapse into a free-for-all of chaotic greed. While he noted the self-interest (such as price-fixing) that can emerge from groups (such as trade associations), he held that virtue and the presence in society of nongroup members guided self-interest toward the good of the commons.[21]

18. See also, *Essai sur les moeurs et l'esprit des nations* (1756) and the *Philosophical Dictionary* (1769).

19. See, for instance, K. Haakonssen and D. Winch, "The Legacy of Adam Smith," in *The Cambridge Companion to Adam Smith*, ed. K. Haakonssen (Cambridge: Cambridge University Press, 2006), pp. 366-94; E. Rothschild, *Economic Sentiments: Adam Smith, Condorcet, and the Enlightenment* (Cambridge: Harvard University Press, 2001); A. Sen, "What Do We Want from a Theory of Justice?" *Journal of Philosophy* 3 (2006): 215-38; A. Skinner, *A System of Social Science: Papers Relating to Adam Smith* (Oxford: Oxford University Press, 1996), especially pp. 123-44.

20. A. Smith, *The Theory of Moral Sentiments*, ed. D. Raphael and A. Macfie (Oxford: Clarendon, 1976; original 1759/1790), p. 21.

21. It is an Aristotelian view of person and society, where one may strive to be happy —

While Smith's contemporary Antonio Genovesi saw that market contracts themselves might be based on notions of reciprocity, Smith found contracts to be more self-interested and so in need of guidance by virtue. But since contracts must be written with honesty, cooperation, and care for "every little circumstance of distress" to the other, contracts would in the end be documents of reciprocal concern. The idea of taking self-gain and competition as a model for all societal endeavors is one Smith "would have found startling, had he been able to conceive it at all," Larry Rasmussen notes. It ignores what Smith prized: "the existence of noneconomic ties of trust and solidarity fostered by civil society."[22]

The Scottish historian Andro Linklater identifies Smith not as a champion of unregulated markets per se but as a champion of giving commoners an economic foothold following the land enclosures of the previous two centuries.[23] In a trickle-down of abuse, the Crown had tried to centralize land under its aegis, to which local landowners responded by enclosing the common fields where peasants had traditionally farmed, leaving them with little economic wherewithal. This, Luigino Bruni notes, was what Smith hoped to relieve. The open market was a means to give commoners thrust out of the economy by Crown and nobility a way back in. Indeed, Smith was wary of the monied classes. On one hand, he notes in his "theory of ranks," commoners are moved to act morally by the knowledge that others are watching — especially rich others, whom they admire — which has a stabilizing effect. On the other, he notes that his theory of ranks "is, at the same time, the great and most universal cause of the corruption of our moral sentiments."[24] As England's markets grew increasingly unregulated, Smith's critique sharpened: capitalism, he wrote, makes workers dull, destroys communities, vitiates morality, fosters anonymous cities, and allows the flamboyant rich to corrupt all.

In sum, while Smith thought self-interest would prod economic productivity much as curiosity prods scientific inquiry, he made two distinctions: between productive markets and greed, and between socially minded gov-

---

on Aristotle's account, content with what one *does* — but this, owing to the sorts of creatures we are, requires affirmation by others. The presence of others guides what one is happy doing, and so on Smith's view, virtues taught in families, schools, and churches and appreciated in one's surroundings will more likely become what one does.

22. L. Rasmussen, *Moral Fragments and Moral Community: Proposal for Church in Society* (Minneapolis: Augsburg Fortress, 1993), p. 48.

23. A. Linklater, *Owning the Earth: The Transforming History of Land Ownership* (London: Bloomsbury, 2014).

24. Smith, *Theory of Moral Sentiments*, p. 61.

ernment and the "will to power" of Europe's colonizing states.[25] *The Theory of Moral Sentiments* opens with this declaration of our common bonds: "How selfish soever man may be supposed, there are evidently some principles in his nature, which interest him in the fortunes of others, and render their happiness necessary to him, though he derives nothing from it except the pleasure of seeing it."[26]

The eighteenth-century philosopher who brought the separable mind and person to their apogee was Immanuel Kant, who sought to describe how individuals using autonomous reason could make moral choices independent of society and convention. Yet, in his appeal to "practical anthropology" — our varied social, political, and legal systems — situatedness returns to his scheme.

At first blush, it seems that Kant followed his predecessors neither in ideas about the mind's development nor in ideas about the need for well-tutored virtue to support the common good. He rejected the Lockean idea of the mind, blank at birth, onto which sense perceptions fall, proposing instead a priori "forms of intuition." These apprehend sensory input, from which they create the mental "impressions" that built-in categories of the mind interpret — categories of time and space, for example. As the human mind has time and space categories, time and space are applied to whatever impressions the intuition gleans from sensory input; thus we believe objects possess spatial and endurance attributes. It is impossible, however, to know whether objects in fact do, as we have no access to them but only to our categories' interpretations of the impressions intuited from the senses. Humanity is left with perceptions, impressions, and interpretations — the phenomenal world — with little link to the way things are in the noumenal (real) world.

This seems to leave humanity without free will or moral capacity. If the phenomenal world is determined by built-in mental mechanisms that obscure reality but determine how we always, repeatedly interpret it, our choices are mechanical ones on the playing field of preset rules.[27] No amount of education or culture can make us free agents, as both are the products of a delusional, rule-governed phenomenal world. Moreover, we are separated in a dismal way, severed from world and others and alone in our minds, which run on preset programs. Morality is thus impossible not only because we are not free agents but because, even if we were, we would have no way to know if others are "out

25. A. Arrighi, *Adam Smith in Beijing: Lineages of the Twenty-First Century* (London: Verso, 2007), pp. 1-68.

26. Smith, *Theory of Moral Sentiments*, p. 9.

27. I. Kant, *Critique of Pure Reason*, trans. N. Smith (New York: St. Martin's Press, 1965; original 1781), A540/B568, A550/B578.

there" (beyond our phenomenal impressions), how they experience the world, or what they would find helpful. Following from this, Kant, in "Perpetual Peace," holds that freedom could be established even by a nation of intelligent devils who embrace it merely out of strategic advantage to themselves.[28] That is, even if we create a society based in freedom, it is evidence of neither free will (as our minds are preset) nor concern for others (as we are unknowable to each other), and thus we cannot be moral (as the decision is merely self-interestedly strategic).

In spite of this grim starting point, one of Kant's chief aims was to describe a universal morality guided by reason and independent of convention — reason as "the author of its own principles independent of alien influences."[29] It was this universal, abstract "moral philosophy" that he was after. Yet he came to believe that human experience and cultural practice, "practical anthropology," are needed as well — in fact, needed twice: first, to foster in persons the virtues that quell short-term desires so we autonomously decide to make the (universal) moral choice, and then to know how to implement these universal principles in particular settings. In short, the mores and customs of practical anthropology are needed first to learn universal morality and then to apply it.

Kant's universal moral standard, the categorical imperative, requires that one take only those actions that one could wish were taken universally and that one treat people as ends, never as means, as one would want oneself to be treated — principles taken from Kant's own "practical anthropology," his situatedness in the Judeo-Christian tradition. The point of this morality is not only to foster one's own excellence but also to promote the happiness of others.[30] If this were a universal morality, all persons would embrace it. Yet in practice, people don't agree on morality, so Kant held that *the effort* to use one's reason to follow universal moral law is the important thing.[31] The effort is the "regulatory principle" that should shape personal and political behavior.

Making this effort in specific contexts is where cultural mores and customs are needed. They provide the virtues that prod us to make the moral

---

28. I. Kant, "Perpetual Peace," in *Kant's Political Writings*, ed. H. Reiss (Cambridge: Cambridge University Press, 1970), pp. 112-13.

29. I. Kant, *Groundwork for the Metaphysics of Morals*, in *The Moral Law*, ed. and trans. H. Paton (London: Hutchinson, 1948), p. 116.

30. See "Doctrine of Virtue," the second part of the *Metaphysics of Morals*.

31. Kant wrote, "It is in fact merely an *idea* of reason, which nonetheless had undoubted practical reality; for it can oblige every legislator to frame his laws in such a way that they could have been produced by the united will of the whole nation. . . . This is the test of the rightfulness of every public law." *Kant's Political Writings*, pp. 77, 79.

effort, and they indicate how the universal categorical imperative should be applied in each setting. The virtues necessary for moral choice are learned from community and society and include critical reflection on experience, prudent judgment, self-discipline,[32] and affability, sociability, courtesy, hospitality, and gentleness (when they are sincere and not mere politesse) — all aimed at public cooperation.[33] In sum, societal and cultural institutions train us in virtue so that we make the moral choice and apply it aptly, *and* the purpose of moral choice is the happiness of others and the good-flourishing of the commons.

What then of Kant's nation of strategic evil devils? Here it seems that no culturally guided virtues are needed — indeed, no virtues whatsoever — as apparently good behavior is merely self-interestedly strategic. Yet Kant held such a situation possible only under two conditions: first, if these evil citizens designed their laws so that immoral tendencies cancel each other out and all behavior that impacts on another is the same as it would be were citizens truly moral.[34] Second, if these evil devils have enough "understanding" to grasp that moral conduct is in their interest. If people, Kant argues, have sense enough to choose moral conduct even for strategic purposes, they prefer it to trickery and violence. While not the Kantian ideal, it is a sort of elementary choice for morality nonetheless, with the same needs that true morality has for virtue, community, and education (to lead "evil" people to choose morality and aptly apply it).

In this, the Enlightenment's most avid seeker of morality independent of culture could imagine no way to foster it other than to take into account the conditions and relationships in which people live. And the purpose of morality is the well-being of others and the common good.

The Constitution of Separability-amid-Situatedness in Early America

The separable mind and person got an especially good hearing in America, to which people came uprooted from land and traditional bonds. The deracination of the immigrant and her need for self-reliant initiative to survive on the unsettled continent reinforced the early modern shift toward the "immanent

---

32. I. Kant, *Groundwork of the Metaphysics of Morals,* trans. H. Paton (New York: Harper and Row, 1964), pp. 411-12.

33. See *Groundwork of the Metaphysics of Morals.*

34. Kant writes that selfish tendencies to disregard moral law "inhibit one another in such a way that the public conduct of the citizens will be the same as if they did not have such evil attitudes." Kant, "Perpetual Peace," pp. 112-13.

frame" and self-sufficiency. The nation, in this sense, is self-selected for separability.[35] But even so, America was not separability all the way down. The purpose of uprooting from homeland was not only self-betterment but also societal uplift. In overview, the American meld of separability-amid-situatedness emerged from the colonies' Protestant legacy (especially Reformed and Arminian/Methodist tenets; see also, pt. II, ch. 5), the anticentralization animus inherited from England, the dissenting churches that came to America, and the demanding conditions of the immigrant and settler experience.

The aspects of Protestantism contributing to the separable self are among the faith's core tenets: emphasis on the individual's moral obligation and relationship with God, the individual's reading and grappling with the Bible, and the priesthood of all believers. Each of these sets responsibility for belief and moral conduct in the internal drama of the singular person, however much one's community may help one not to stray. This doctrinal self-responsibility was strengthened by political factors in Europe — importantly the persecution of dissenting Protestant churches. For dissenters, reliance on oneself and one's like-minded community became a matter of survival. Escape, first within Europe and then to America, gave further value to mobility and separability's advantages. A second political boost to self-responsibility was resistance to Charles I's efforts to centralize power in the Crown (1625-1647) — resistance that boosted localism and self-reliance. "The settlers departed England," T. H. Breen writes, "determined to maintain their local attachments against outside interference, and to a large extent the Congregational churches and self-contained towns of Massachusetts stood as visible evidence of the founders' decision to preserve in America what had been threatened in the mother country."[36]

Once in America, Protestant faith, dissenter self-reliance, and anticentralization animus interacted synergistically with the rough nature of settlement. Sparse population and primitive conditions made self-reliance not so much a concept-in-formation as a condition of life. Survival on isolated farms depended on energetic do-it-yourself-ism and voluntarist association in local, ardently independent communities. But even these, as Barry Shain is right to point out, were "in tension with the overall high worth they attached to the individual."[37] American colonials, he notes, were highly mobile, litigious

35. This is true of immigrant but not slave populations, who did not self-select to come to America.

36. T. Breen, "Persistent Localism: English Social Change and the Shaping of New England Institutions," *William and Mary Quarterly*, 3rd ser., 32, no. 19 (January 1975): 3-28.

37. B. Shain, *The Myth of American Individualism: The Protestant Origins of American Political Thought* (Princeton: Princeton University Press, 1994), p. 28.

in protection of personal interest, and concerned with personal economic benefit.[38]

Under demanding survival conditions, colonials were eager to attract every helping hand willing to risk the Atlantic. One enticement was religious toleration, grounded in two sorts of separability: from Europe's history of religious persecution, and in respect of the individual mind on her own path toward God. By the eighteenth century, America's "perfect equality and freedom among all religious denominations," Tench Coxe of Pennsylvania declared, would lure the persecuted of Europe; "they will at once cry out, America is the 'land of promise.'"[39] Multifaithed immigration slowly bred multifaithed towns.

While at first this was a modest break from Europe's territorialized religions (established by the 1648 Westphalian Treaty, where the local prince determined the faith of the region), soon religious life in America became a wholesale experiment in separability from the past. This was most evident in the socioreligious innovations of the First Great Awakening (1730s-1740s) — the breakaway churches, new modes of worship, and iconoclastic ideas preached by anyone moved by the spirit.[40] Even in seventeenth-century colonies with established churches,[41] arguing that faith should be uniform and policed by authorities became an increasingly poor fit. Maryland passed its Religious Toleration Act, prohibiting the religious persecution of Trinitarian Christians, in 1649 — just a year after the Westphalian Treaty had made faith precisely a matter policed by the state. Pennsylvania, Rhode Island, and Carolina were, from their inceptions, experiments in toleration. The theocracy of Massachusetts Bay Colony by the 1660s found that it had to create the Halfway Covenant, a baptism for those who did not hold to strict belief. That religious conformity fit poorly with colonial development does not mean it was not tried; it means it did not endure.

38. Shain, *Myth of American Individualism*, p. 77.

39. M. Jensen, ed., "The Documentary History of the Ratification of the Constitution," in *Commentaries on the Constitution, Public and Private: 10 May to 13 September 1788*, vol. 18 (Madison: Madison State Historical Society of Wisconsin, 1997), pp. 278-85.

40. See M. Noll, *America's God: From Jonathan Edwards to Abraham Lincoln* (New York: Oxford University Press, 2002); for a companion look at the innovations of the nineteenth-century Second Great Awakening, see N. Hatch, *The Democratization of American Christianity* (New Haven: Yale University Press, 1989).

41. Massachusetts and Connecticut, among others. After America's earliest settlement in Jamestown nearly foundered just three years after its establishment in 1606, London dispatched Sir Thomas Gates to impose martial law and religious observance on the wayward community; nonconformity was a capital offense in seventeenth-century Connecticut and Virginia.

The doctrinal, survival, and political pulls of separability were thus substantial in early America, yet in tension with them was the simultaneous push into particularly American voluntarist forms of situatedness. The result was an American interplay and meld of separability and situatedness. The pushes to situatedness came, ironically, from the very factors that at the same time prodded separability. Rough survival conditions made not only self-reliance but also close-knit communities advisable. The dissenter's concern for religious freedom made groups of the like-minded band together to protect themselves. Protestantism sought to situate persons in communities that would help each to develop an inner moral compass and relationship with God. "For most colonial Americans," Shain notes, "serving God and leading a fulfilled human life depended on membership in a locally controlled community,"[42] where corporate bodies exercised considerable control over individual conduct and individuals adjusted to the common good.

While most prominent in seventeenth-century villages, where "the corporate community bred intolerance for every form of deviant behavior,"[43] local conformity continued into the eighteenth century. In 1734, Rev. John Barnard declared that "no man was born for himself, but for mankind."[44] The president of the theological seminary at the College of New Jersey, later Princeton, repeated in 1761, "let your own Ease, your own Pleasure, your own private Interests, yield to the common good."[45] The idea reached across the races. In 1801 the African American minister Lemuel Haynes wrote that "selfishness

---

42. Shain, *Myth of American Individualism*, p. 28.

43. O. Handlin and L. Handlin, *Liberty and Power: 1600-1760* (New York: Harper and Row, 1986), p. 91.

44. J. Barnard, *The throne established by righteousness. A sermon preached before his excellency Jonathan Belcher, Esq; his majesty's council, and the representatives of the province of the Massachusetts Bay in New England, May 29, 1734. Being the day for the electing his majesty's council there* (Boston: n.p., 1734), p. 37.

45. S. Davies, *Religion and the Public Spirit: A Valedictory Address to the Senior Class* (New York: James Parker, 1761), pp. 4-7. In 1773 the Baptist preacher John Allen echoed, "the body politic can only be in health, and prosper, when every member unites regularly, and ardently, to preserve the privileges of the whole"; J. Allen, *American Alarm . . . for the Rights and Liberties of the People* (Boston: D. Kneeland and N. Davis, 1773), p. 21. As late as 1777, the preacher Nathaniel Whitaker, staunch supporter of the revolution and no conservative, nonetheless held to the importance of community in constraining license: "perfect Liberty differs from natural, only in this, that in a natural state our actions, person and possessions, are under the direction, judgment and control of none but ourselves; but in a civil state, under the direction of others. . . . All Liberty beyond this is mere licentiousness, a liberty to sin"; N. Whitaker, *Antidote against Toryism* (Newburyport, Mass.: John Mycall, 1777), pp. 10-11.

enervates every social bond and endearment, sets men at variance, and is the source of every evil."[46]

This was not an idea only among the devout. In 1753 the *New York Mercury* held that "in all communities, as it is the highest reason, that private Convenience should give place to publick Emolument, so 'tis the Business of the Legislature, in providing the publick Good, to prescribe to all the Members of the Community, Limits and Restrictions of the Enjoyments and Conduct."[47] And it was not limited to Northeasterners and Puritan Congregationalists. The Virginia planter Landon Carter wrote that if the public good "required the suspension of 'Private Justice' or the suppression of the individual liberty of the minority that opposed it, then it was . . . 'a Thing absolutely necessary to be done' and therefore just in itself."[48] In surveying the colonial period, Gordon Wood writes that virtue, "that is, the willingness of the people to sacrifice their private desires for the good of the whole . . . represented all that men of the eighteenth century, from [rationalist revolutionary] Benjamin Franklin to [Reformed theologian] Jonathan Edwards, sought in social behavior."[49]

In sum, Protestantism and the experiences of persecution, immigration, and settlement prodded separability and situatedness simultaneously, as these noble exhortations to community-mindedness reveal. Had contribution to the public good been ubiquitous, its advocates would have had less need to continually encourage it. The frequent appeal to the "publick good" evinces its importance but also the substantial lure of new ideas and places and individual opportunity. Voluntarism meant that town members rather than elites determined local mores and could change past practice to suit changing conditions. It meant also that dissenters were *free* to move: "minorities excluded from local communities had one consolation," historian Paul Conklin writes; "they could usually find their own fulfilling niche somewhere in the vast ex-

46. L. Haynes, "Nature and Importance of True Republicanism," in *Black Preacher to White America: The Collected Writings of Lemuel Haynes, 1774-1833*, ed. R. Newman (Brooklyn, N.Y.: Carlson Publishing, 1990; original 1801), p. 85.

47. *New York Mercury*, September 17, 1753, p. 1. In 1778 the representatives of Berkshire County, Massachusetts, stated that "the common happiness is to be preferred to that of individuals." "Statement of Berkshire County Representatives," in *The Populist Sources of Political Authority: Documents on the Massachusetts Constitution of 1780*, ed. O. Handlin and M. Handlin (Cambridge: Harvard University Press, 1996; original 1778), p. 375.

48. Cited in J. P. Greene, *Diary of Colonel Landon Carter of Sabine Hall, 1752-1758*, Virginia Historical Society Documents, 1987, p. 31.

49. G. Wood, *Rising Glory of America: 1760-1820* (New York: George Braziller, 1971), pp. 5-6.

panse of America."[50] As this option increased with continental expansion, the individual gained importance as the unit of physical and economic mobility. Americans situated and resituated voluntarily and often, and America's self-conception cohered into suspicion of controlling central authorities, individualist self-responsibility, and deep commitment to local community until a move to the next one.

During the revolutionary period, colonial separability and situatedness shifted in three ways. First was a change in the definition of "community" from local to national in an effort to build support for revolution. In a 1772 *Massachusetts Spy* column, for instance, public loyalty is directed not at town but at "love of our country, resignation and obedience to the laws, public spirit."[51] The sentiment extended to the churches, which were by and large behind the revolution and the new nation. In 1783, Pastor Henry Cumings declared, "everyone ought to consider that he was born, not for himself alone, but for others, for society, for his country."[52] A second shift was the emergence of secular towns that did not demand forgoing quite so much of the tempting world as earlier, colonial ones had required. Third was the growing accent on individualist opportunity.[53] One finds murmurings at mid-century, for example, from lawyer and journalist William Livingston, who ended a 1753 discussion of liberty with the startling idea that "the Design of entering into a State of Society, is to promote and secure the Happiness of its Individuals."[54] But on the whole, "Only at the end of the eighteenth century," Shain correctly notes, "did the modern understanding of the self begin to gain acceptance."[55] In 1781, Sam Adams claimed individual (civil) liberty as the goal of political liberty overall.[56]

50. P. Conklin, "Freedom: Past Meaning and Present Prospects," in *Freedom in America*, ed. N. Graebner (University Park: Pennsylvania State University Press, 1977), p. 210.

51. The Perceptor, "Social Duties of the Political Kind," in *American Political Writing during the Founding Era, 1760-1805*, ed. C. Hyneman and D. Lutz, vols. 1-2 (Indianapolis: Liberty Press, 1983; original 1772), p. 177. Both James Otis and Sam Adams, revolutionary provocateurs, were of the mind that "the only principles of public conduct that are worthy of a gentleman or a man, are to sacrifice estate, ease, health, and applause, and even life to the sacred calls of his country"; see *The Writings of Samuel Adams*, ed. H. Cushing, vols. 1-4 (New York: Octagon Books, 1968; original 1906), p. 365.

52. H. Cumings, *Massachusetts Election Sermon* (Boston: T. and J. Fleet, 1783), p. 8.

53. See E. Countryman, *American Revolution* (New York: Hill and Wang, 1985), p. 167.

54. W. Livingston, "Of the Use, Abuse, and Liberty of the Press," in *Independent Reflector; or, Weekly Essays on Sundry Important Subjects More Particularly Adapted to the Province of New York* (Cambridge: Harvard University Press, 1963; original 1753), p. 339.

55. Shain, *Myth of American Individualism*, p. 101.

56. In an April 2, 1781, article, Adams wrote, it is "that personal Freedom and those Rights

Yet, even with the rise of separability in the adventurous nineteenth century, the meld with voluntarist situatedness remained, as Tocqueville and others have noted. Towns continued to "regulate the minor details of social life . . . and promulgate such orders as concern the health of the community and the peace as well as the morality of the citizens."[57] Henry Bellows in 1872 described the "thousands of American towns, with an independent life of their own," and decried their disruption by the railroads and industrialization.[58] Daniel Rodgers, writing of the twentieth century, notes the great value given to localism and community through the early decades, when one could still write that the individual "has not the right to demand anything of the community. . . . [He] must do what the community determines it is best for him to do."[59]

The Nineteenth-Century Constitution of Separability-amid-Situatedness: The Example of John Stuart Mill

So thoroughly is John Stuart Mill identified with separability that he is regularly faulted for mechanical utilitarianism, seeking the greatest good for the greatest number of individuals with little concern for goods in common. Yet, like his father, the philosopher James Mill, John Stuart held that the well-being of (separable) persons depends on the flourishing of societal institutions.

Mill envisions two dangers to persons, tyrannical government and the oppressive crowd,[60] which hobble "human development in its richest diversity."[61] His bulwark against both is his famous declaration, "the sole end for

---

of Property which the meanest citizen is entitled to and the Security of which is the great End of political Society."

57. See S. Adams, "Extract from a Letter from the Southward," in *The Writings of Samuel Adams*, ed. H. Cushing, vol. 4 (New York: Putnam, 1904), p. 253; A. de Tocqueville, *Democracy in America*, ed. J. P. Mayer, trans. G. Lawrence, vol. 1 (Garden City, N.Y.: Doubleday, 1966, 1969; original 1835), p. 44.

58. H. Bellows, "The Downward Tendency," *The City: An Illustrated Magazine* 1, no. 1 (1872): 38.

59. D. Rodgers, *Contested Truths: Keywords in American Politics Since Independence* (New York: Basic Books, 1987), pp. 117, 159-61.

60. J. S. Mill, "On Liberty," in *Essays on Politics and Society: Collected Works of John Stuart Mill*, ed. J. Robson (Toronto: University of Toronto Press, 1977), pp. 219-20.

61. Mill is here quoting William von Humboldt on spheres and duties of government, in Mill, "On Liberty," p. 215.

which mankind is warranted, individually or collectively, in interfering with the liberty of action of any of their number, is self-protection."[62] From this came his reputation as a separability man. Yet Mill immediately notes (as Locke and Smith had) that living well amid others who have freedoms equal to one's own requires self-restraint and virtue from all. He distinguishes between virtues that affect the self and societal ones that affect others. Both require lifelong education.[63] Conduct lacking in social virtue may be, on Mill's view, legally regulated;[64] conduct that is not in "the best interest of the agent" may be discouraged by disincentives such as sales taxes.[65]

Public policies, Mill writes, should be judged on their "utility," that which promotes happiness. But this far from individualist whim is neither desire nor self-indulgence. While one may desire both "lower and higher pleasures," it is only the higher[66] that promote happiness. Mill contrasts "miserable individuality,"[67] or doing whatever one wants, with real individuality, the ability through proper education to develop one's particular talents and skills.[68] Real "happiness" is what societal policies should promote; virtue enables us to design policies that promote it.

These virtues, Mill continues, are groomed in democracy, where the practices of self-governance *for* the commons educate citizens in the virtues needed for it.[69] He holds that all citizens should at least occasionally serve in public office,[70] and he recommends jury trials, robust local government, and voluntary associations with the public good as their mandate. These take the person out of the private sphere, "out of the narrow circle of personal and family selfishness, and accustoming them to the comprehension of joint interests, the management of joint concerns — habituating them to act from

62. Mill, "On Liberty," p. 223.

63. Mill, "On Liberty," p. 277.

64. Mill, "On Liberty," p. 280; conduct that violates both self and others (like substance abuse) may be punished by public authorities; see Mill, "On Liberty," p. 292.

65. Mill, "On Liberty," p. 298

66. J. S. Mill, "Utilitarianism," in *Essays on Ethics, Religions, and Society: Collected Works of John Stuart Mill,* ed. J. Robson (Toronto: University of Toronto Press, 1969), pp. 210-12, 218-19, 227, 230-32.

67. Mill, "Utilitarianism," p. 216.

68. Mill, "On Liberty," p. 262.

69. Monarchs or autocracies fail Mill's standard not because they violate abstract rights but because they blunt the intellectual, political, and moral capacities of citizens by depriving them of the exercise of self-rule; see Mill, "On Liberty," p. 305.

70. J. S. Mill, "Considerations on Representative Government," in *Essays on Politics and Society,* p. 404.

public and semi-public motives."[71] Mill recommends freedom of expression and public debate not as an abstract right of the separable individual but as a means to discover the best policies for society.[72] Should heated debate require regulation, Mill holds that citizens, trained by education and virtue, will distinguish between honesty and chicanery and repudiate every "mode of advocacy either want of candor, or malignity, bigotry, or intolerance of feeling manifest themselves."[73]

In addition to democratic practice as a forger of virtue, Mill identifies the family, state-backed schools, and church — all, if properly run. While he considered nineteenth-century family structures and gender roles "despotic,"[74] family, he held, could become a "real school of the virtues of freedom"[75] if women had legal equality with men. Parents who cannot afford to educate their children should be given state payments for the purpose, and should they still fail, the state should step in. But aside from this extreme situation, government should not run schools (this, he feared, would lead to excessive controversy or to dull, conformist curricula). Rather, government should mandate universal education to a certain level of achievement.[76] Church too needs to be properly run; Mill felt that many in his day were not, as they made people dull, passionless, selfish, and weak.[77] His preferred Religion of Humanity takes Jesus as its model because of his service to humankind.[78] Its main purpose is "the strong and earnest direction of the emotions and desires towards an ideal object, recognized as of the highest excellence, and as rightfully paramount over

71. Mill, "On Liberty," p. 305.

72. Mill, "On Liberty," p. 231. For the same reason, he proposed proportional representation, weighted voting, and open ballots. Proportional representation, he held, would raise the chances that citizens of high intellect and virtue would be elected to government; see Mill, "Considerations on Representative Government," p. 457. Weighted voting would give greater political power not to the propertied classes but to the "natural aristocracy" of those with greater intellect and morality, determined either by national examination or by the ranking of professions (p. 475). Open ballots would discourage self-interested voting.

73. Mill, "On Liberty," p. 259.

74. J. S. Mill, "The Subjection of Women," in *Essays on Equality, Law, and Education: Collected Works of John Stuart Mill*, ed. J. Robson (Toronto: University of Toronto Press, 1984), pp. 294-95.

75. Mill, "The Subjection of Women," p. 295.

76. Mill, "On Liberty," p. 301.

77. J. S. Mill, "The Utility of Religion," in *Essays on Ethics, Religions, and Society*, pp. 403-4; see also, Mill, "On Liberty," pp. 226-27.

78. J. S. Mill, "Theism," in *Essays on Ethics, Religions, and Society*, pp. 487-88; see also, Mill, "On Liberty," pp. 235-36, 255-57.

all selfish objects of desire."[79] The ideal toward which people should strive, Mill concluded, is enduring help to others and the provision of the public good.

The Twentieth-Century Constitution of Separability-amid-Situatedness: Examples from the Work of Hayek, Rawls, and Nozick

If Mill was taken as the champion of separability in the nineteenth century, in the early twentieth, it might be Friedrich Hayek, the Austrian philosopher and economist who loudly promoted the individual economic actor and warned against governmental regulation of society. Prices, he held, should be left to fluctuate with supply and demand, as these fluctuations provide the most complete information about the economy, allowing each person to make the decisions she sees fit. He held that people should generally be left to do as they will in their private lives, with as little state interference as possible. In his postscript to *Constitution of Liberty*,[80] titled "Why I Am Not a Conservative," he rejects the conservative idea that states should legislate morality.

Hayek based his position on his agreement with Kant that human beings lack direct access to the real (noumenal) world and impose their own mental categories on it. But Hayek added that mental categories are not universal (Kant's claim) but rather adapt evolutionarily to circumstances. Because of the large influence of culture and experience on the mind (one's situatedness, if you will), Hayek held that much of what we know is unconscious — the unarticulated assumptions and "gut" feelings come to us genetically and through adaptation and acculturation to our surroundings. The idea of relying only on conscious, rational thinking for public and economic decisions seemed to him self-limiting, as we know far more intuitively — in the "primacy of practice" — than we know consciously.

This wealth of knowledge, Hayek held, is revealed by the multiple micro-movements of the market: the rise and fall in prices and salaries tell us about the products and careers most socially in demand and thus what is worth pursuing.[81] So too in the political arena, where accumulated knowledge is found in common law and custom rather than in statute books. Particularly unproductive, he thought, are laws that redistribute wealth to increase equality

79. Mill, "The Utility of Religion," p. 422.
80. F. Hayek, *The Constitution of Liberty* (Chicago: Henry Regnery and University of Chicago Press, 1960, 2011).
81. Hayek, *The Constitution of Liberty*, pp. 159, 157.

because families able to rise in status have likely been passing on produc-tive values and practices to their children. Society will thus get better leader-ship if families are allowed to spiral up. The benefits, Hayek held, are to all: "The acquisition by any member of the community of additional capacities to do things which may be valuable must always be regarded as a gain for that community."[82]

In short, one of the staunchest champions of separate, individual choice grounded his views in situatedness and was concerned primarily for societal good. The purpose of freedom, on his account, is not to please the self but to reveal much-needed societal information and so contribute to the public well-being. Owing to this, Hayek opposed neither aid to the needy nor social insurances. He objected to the idea that the needy have legal rights to a share of other people's wealth[83] and proposed instead aid to the needy through civil society and political mechanisms — the primacy of traditional practice and institutions over legal mandate. Indeed, Hayek believed that the West suffers from a destructive tendency to undervalue its traditions, leading to policies that — unmoored from community and practice — cannot support a stable, responsible society. Though Hayek argued that persons be left free from *state* planning, he did not think persons should be left free from *planning*, at large or amok in the broader sense. He was counting on societal values and institu-tions to guide conduct and make it possible for persons and society to flourish.

In the second half of the twentieth century, the role of poster boy for separability shifted to John Rawls, owing to his scheme for designing an ideal society. Rawls's famous thought-experiment begins with one imagin-ing oneself in an "original position" where one doesn't know what abilities or socioeconomic station one will have in the society one designs. From be-hind this "veil of ignorance," one must then determine society's political and economic structures.

Though Rawls laudably wants his model society to be "fair and just," he has been charged with trying to reach this goal on a double fiction: that of cultureless, unsituated persons participating in his thought-experiment, and that of cultureless persons in the newly designed society. Alasdair MacIntyre, a Rawls critic, holds that no such cultureless neutrality exists. People do not start societies from scratch but are situated in long-standing cultures that

---

82. Hayek, *The Constitution of Liberty,* pp. 153, 151.

83. Hayek writes, "The fact that all citizens have an interest in the common provision of some services is no justification for anyone's claiming as a right a share in all the benefits"; see Hayek, *The Constitution of Liberty,* p. 165.

shape their beliefs, actions, and even hopes for change. All principles, including fairness and justice, are based on situational, cultural values. Moreover, MacIntyre continues, it is unproductive to ignore people's actual views of the good life, as we need to know what people value in order to design apt policies for them.[84] Tom Nagel additionally notes that the "veil of ignorance" cannot recognize joys and good that come from relations with others. Rawls assumes, Nagel writes, that "the best that can be wished for someone is the unimpeded pursuit of his own path."[85]

Yet the place Rawls gives to culture and relationships, especially in his later writings, is somewhat underestimated. For one thing, Rawls relies on cultural values in the thought-experiment itself. While he asks participants to refrain from assuming their *future* positions in society, they are not, while designing it, without the values they bring in from their *pasts* (before they came to the thought-experiment room). Indeed, designing fair and just policies depends on the ideas of justice and fairness that people have, ideas garnered from their values and traditions. The "original position" does not wipe the mind blank. An experiment participant who believes the best society has already been set out by tradition can recommend its wise proposals.

Moreover, it is not only the individual but also relationships and groups that may benefit from Rawls's proposal: participants may well design a society with sturdy support for such networks — especially as participants, like all real persons, live in them. MacIntyre, holding that Rawls's experiment excludes the past, finds that it cannot rectify historical injustices (like racism). Yet, being "veiled" from one's position in a future society does not erase one's knowledge of history. Experiment participants would be aware that injustice is more likely without bulwarks against it and may well erect them — bulwarks from law, mores, tradition — especially because they might be injustice's victims in the society under design.

Rawls's own ideas about society are not neutral or cultureless.[86] They rely

---

84. Rawls's thought-experiment, MacIntyre writes, is "as though we had been shipwrecked on an uninhibited island with a group of other individuals, each of whom is a stranger to me and to all the others"; A. MacIntyre, "Justice as Virtue: Changing Conceptions," in *Communitarianism and Individualism*, ed. S. Avineri and A. De-shalit (Oxford: Oxford University Press, 1992), pp. 58-59.

85. T. Nagel, "Rawls on Justice," in *Reading Rawls: Critical Studies of "A Theory of Justice,"* ed. N. Daniels (New York: Oxford University Press, 1975), pp. 9-10.

86. Michael Scherer holds that Rawls is so aware of the variety of values brought in by his society-designing participants that he makes considerable effort to guide them toward his own. Rawls does so, on Scherer's view, through rhetorical moves that make his ideas seem

on two principles: that "each person has an equal right to a fully adequate scheme of equal basic rights and liberties, which scheme is compatible with a similar scheme for all," and that "social and economic inequalities are to satisfy two conditions: first, they must be attached to offices and positions open to all under conditions of fair equality of opportunity; and, second, they must be to the greatest benefit of the least advantaged members of society" — Rawls's famous "Difference Principle."[87] These are culturally specific: they prize justice, fairness, and certain inalienable rights (rather than greater rights for the highborn); they require equality of opportunity (rather than greater opportunity for the highborn and rather than equality of results); and they require that society give the less well-off a leg up.

Rawls's efforts to foster social cooperation are also culturally specific. He understands this cooperation as not merely coordinated public activity (which could follow from dictatorial commands) but as emerging from agreed-upon cultural norms and procedures. It specifies "an idea of reciprocity and mutuality" and aims for the good of each person. Finally, this good is not quite, as Nagel held, "unimpeded pursuit of his own path" in the sense of one's path *alone*. In his view of the good, Rawls includes relationality, "attachments to other persons and loyalties to various groups and associations. . . . [W]e must also include in such a conception a view of our relation to the world — religious, philosophical, or moral."[88]

It is this appreciation for values and relations that made Rawls an irritant not only for situatedness advocates but also for separability advocates. He devises, they charge, an "original position" for the free design of society but short-circuits the endeavor by the designers' values (in the thought-experiment) and by his own. John N. Gray finds incoherent "the requirement that the contractarian method yield principles that are strictly, if not uniquely, determinate solutions."[89] In the end, Rawls's society-designing scheme proposes that we

---

utterly reasonable (considerate even of objections), thus implicitly complimenting the reader on her reasonableness, should she agree with him. See M. Scherer, "Saint John," in *Political Theologies: Public Religions in a Post-Secular World*, ed. H. de Vries and L. E. Sullivan (New York: Fordham University Press, 2006), p. 358.

87. J. Rawls, "The Basic Liberties and Their Priority," Tanner Lectures on Human Values, April 10, 1981 (Ann Arbor: University of Michigan, 1981); retrieved from http://tannerlectures .utah.edu/lectures/documents/rawls82.pdf.

88. J. Rawls, "Justice as Fairness: Political Not Metaphysical," in *Communitarianism and Individualism*, p. 196.

89. J. Gray, *Post-Liberalism: Studies in Political Thought* (New York and London: Routledge, 1993), p. 49.

imagine something new (the separability of the thought-experiment) out of our (situated) values within the parameters set by his. In this, it is a project replete with culture, that of the modern West.

Robert Nozick is considered among the staunchest defenders of the separable person, not least of all because he employs a similar term, "separateness of persons." He uses it to mean the Kantian idea that people should be treated as ends, not means. Such good treatment includes the right to property, what is acquired through free exchange among consenting adults beginning at the same just starting position. Thus, property cannot be redistributed (through taxes, for instance) even if substantial inequalities result from economic transactions. Such redistribution, on Nozick's view, would turn the better-off person into a means for the poorer person's betterment, which is on his view ethically unjustifiable. From this, Nozick defends the minimal state, which is responsible for the maintenance of free economic exchange and national security but is otherwise inactive, to allow for individual endeavor.

Yet Nozick, who so strongly defends the separable person against the *state,* relies on substantial situatedness in society. In his minimalist utopia, described in *Anarchy, State, and Utopia,*[90] each person joins the community whose norms and practices she finds preferable. If she ceases to enjoy them, she may leave to join another community or start her own. Utopia is thus not community-less but community-full, consisting "of many different and divergent communities in which people lead different kinds of lives under different institutions. . . . Utopia is a framework for utopias, a place where people are at liberty to join together voluntarily . . . but where no one can *impose* his own utopian vision upon others."[91] Nozick sets no constraints, such as Rawls's justice or fairness, other than nonimposition. He concedes that a person could choose a community where he is enslaved. But the person "may use the voluntary framework to contract himself out of it."[92]

Thus, Nozick seeks not maximum separability but choice in situatedness. This is a voluntarist, rather than inherited, notion of community, but it is situatedness nonetheless. He writes, "We *live* in particular communities. . . . Allowing us to do that is what the framework is *for.*"[93] I do not want to say that Nozick's work has more situatedness than he admits, because I think he admits it.

90. R. Nozick, *Anarchy, State, and Utopia* (New York: Basic Books, 1974).
91. Nozick, *Anarchy, State, and Utopia,* pp. 312, 329-30.
92. Nozick, *Anarchy, State, and Utopia,* p. 331.
93. Nozick, *Anarchy, State, and Utopia,* p. 332.

*　　*　　*

The point of this chapter has been to note the mutual constitution of situatedness and separability especially among those often cited as advocates of separability — at least a few examples of them. I have hoped to show that they, in various ways, recognized the importance of separability *within* mores and institutions, and importantly within responsibility for others and reciprocal consideration in the common infrastructure. The next chapter has a mirror-image purpose: to sketch the separability/situatedness meld among those often cited for situatedness.

CHAPTER 5

Those Claimed for Situatedness — and Their (Sometimes Ignored) Constitution with Separability: A Few Examples

Ask not what's inside your head but what your head's inside of.[1]

This chapter, the mirror to chapter 4, looks at ideas about situatedness and explores their mutual constitution with separability — especially among thinkers often considered one-sided advocates of situatedness. As with the previous chapter, this is not an exhaustive genealogy of situatedness but a review of work whose meld with separability has at times been overlooked — an inattention we can afford only insofar as we accept losing the nuanced ideas of distinction and change *amid* community and conservation.

The Enlightenment Constitution of Separability-amid-Situatedness: Examples from the Work of Edmund Burke and David Hume

In the eighteenth century, Giambattista Vico[2] began one of the earliest, specifically modern discussions of situatedness, an investigation that adumbrated modern anthropology in its focus on the person embedded in society. In 1725, rejecting the idea of a universal character of mankind, Vico held that human conduct should be understood in the context of heritage — the language,

---

1. W. Mace, "Gibson's Strategy for Perceiving: Ask Not What's Inside Your Head but What Your Head Is Inside Of," in *Perceiving, Acting, and Knowing*, ed. R. Shaw and J. Brandsford (Hillsdale, N.J.: Erlbaum, 1974).
2. G. Vico, *The New Science of Giambattista Vico*, trans. T. Bergin and M. Fisch (Ithaca, N.Y.: Cornell University Press, 1994; original 1725).

customs, science, economics, and politics in which one lives. These, he argued, weave into a cultural unity, which in turn forms the basis for various domains (science, economics, etc.). The basic assumptions of one domain are congruent with those of another, Vico held, because the beliefs and values of the culture undergird them all.

The man in England who most vigorously applied Vico's anthropology to politics was Edmund Burke, the Irish-Anglo philosopher who was as terrified by the French Revolution as Hobbes had been by the violence of the English. Liberty, on Burke's diagnosis, was not per se a good: "The effect of liberty to individuals is, that they may do as they please: we ought to see what it will please them to do, before we risk congratulations." He was particularly concerned about liberty given to groups who had not previously had it, as that set power in the hands of those "of whose principles, tempers, and disposition" society has little experience.[3] He was wary of both new political acts and new political actors.

Burke proposed instead reliance on past practices, as they form character, expectations, and judgment[4] — that is, not only situatedness but also the situations of one's forefathers with but slow change. Ideas, political or otherwise, developed through conscious reasoning should not be discounted, he held, but must be guided by past experience.[5] The highborn are thus best suited to govern because their experience from birth trains them in the virtues for public service: the ability to take the large view of things, to reflect and consult wise counselors, to be brave, pursue honor and duty, and administer law and justice.[6] Yet even their wisdom, taken individually, is limited, so governments would do better to rely on the accumulated wisdom of society. This "prejudice" — long-held assumptions and practices — inscribes impulses, habitual conduct,[7] and manners, which "are of more importance than laws. Upon them, in a great measure, the laws depend."[8] And laws themselves should be based not on abstract rights but on the affections and obligations of long duration.

---

3. E. Burke, "Revolution in France," in *The Works of the Right Honourable Edmund Burke,* vol. 3 (London: John C. Nimmo, 1899), p. 242.

4. See B. Frohnen, *Virtue and the Promise of Conservatism: The Legacy of Burke and Tocqueville* (Lawrence: University Press of Kansas, 1993), ch. 2.

5. Burke, "Revolution in France," p. 311.

6. E. Burke, "New to the Old Whigs," in *The Works of the Right Honourable Edmund Burke,* vol. 4 (London: John C. Nimmo, 1899), p. 175.

7. Burke, "Revolution in France," p. 347.

8. E. Burke, "Letters on a Regicide Peace, Letter 1," in *The Works of the Right Honourable Edmund Burke,* vol. 5 (London: John C. Nimmo, 1899), p. 310.

In sum, government is "not to force . . . the public inclination" but "to give a direction, a form . . . to the general sense of the community."[9]

Religion in particular, Burke felt, fosters moral conduct and social stability by teaching that God created mankind to live righteously in society; that is, it is in society that men may practice righteousness and virtue. Yet, even religion requires the guidance of tradition, and there is no use in imposing foreign religions. Burke thus opposed British suppression of Catholicism in Ireland. In one famous summation, he wrote, "We have obligations to mankind at large. . . . They arise from the relation of man to man, and the relation of man to God, which relations are not matters of choice."[10]

In addition to religion, Burke placed great value on gentlemanly virtue to preserve good societies and government. "All good things," he wrote, "depended for ages upon two principles . . . the spirit of a gentleman and the spirit of religion."[11] Gentlemanly virtue makes business honest and thus advances prosperity, and it knits society together through bonds and affection in ways that statutes cannot. All — including the highborn — must submit to virtue's codes. Importantly, it was virtue that led England to gradual political change rather than revolution. It tempers power and allows ordinary citizens to be granted liberties, for they, obligated by virtue to good behavior, when given liberties, can be trusted not to abuse them. Virtue "mitigated kings into companions, and raised private men to be fellows with kings."[12] Possessed of virtue, men may contribute to society according to their capacities and station. While commoners of low rank, lacking the requisite experience, should not have a say in government, those of higher if nonnoble rank may participate as virtue and talent can be found among them. "Woe to the country which would madly and impiously reject the service of the talents and virtues, civil, military, or religious, that they are given to grace and to serve it."[13]

Burke himself was such a commoner, a man of intellect and talent whose devotion to public service elevated him through its ranks. When the duke of Bedford attacked him for accepting a pension for his parliamentary service, Burke wrote that at every stage of his advancement, "I was obliged to show

9. E. Burke, "Letter to Sheriffs of Bristol," in *The Works of the Right Honourable Edmund Burke*, vol. 2 (London: John C. Nimmo, 1899), p. 225.

10. Burke, "New to the Old Whigs."

11. E. Burke, "Letter to a Member of the French National Assembly," in *The Works of the Right Honourable Edmund Burke*, vol. 4, p. 335.

12. Burke, "Revolution in France," p. 332.

13. Quoted in H. Mansfield Jr., *Statesmanship and Party Government: A Study of Burke and Bolingbroke* (Chicago: University of Chicago Press, 1965), p. 201.

my passport, and again and again to prove my sole title to the honour of being useful to my country. . . . I had no arts but manly arts. On them I have stood, and please God, in spite of the Duke of Bedford and the Earl of Lauderdale, to the last gasp will I stand."[14]

Here, the role of separability emerges in Burke's traditionalist politics. It is merit-based: the criterion for moving out of one's inherited station is intelligent service to the system one has inherited. Though not revolutionary, it is significant: while Burke allowed for only limited critique of the status quo (as newcomers must earn approval of those already in power), he did not preclude it. The best example is Burke himself, who criticized the duke of Bedford and his own mentor, Lord Rockingham, for their poor handling of the American colonies.[15] Burke was also key to the investigation of the East India Company for illegal transactions and the corruption of Parliament. He defended the representation of commoners in government and praised many of America's demands: "this fierce spirit of liberty is stronger in the English colonies probably than in any other people on the earth."[16]

That is, Burke supported the people who, having left their land and bucked authority, were among the eighteenth century's apogees of separability. "A state," he wrote, "without the means of some change is without the means of its conservation."[17] In sum, considering the mayhem across the Channel, Burke's insistence on order and stability may be understandable. But given this mayhem, his recognition that societies must nonetheless change is noteworthy. Burke should be taken as a moderate who found himself arguing for caution by the immoderacy of his French neighbors. Were Burke as much a situatedness insister as he is taken to be, he — a man of common rank — would not have dared to write books to insist on it.

David Hume, Burke's contemporary in Scotland, did not write directive political works as Burke did. Yet his philosophical framework relies on man's separability within situatedness. Hume begins with the limits of reason. One observes correlations of events, such as a rock hitting glass and the glass breaking, and one assumes causality, that moving rocks break glass — though one has seen only two separate events. We notice a tree at noon and a tree in

14. E. Burke, "Letter to a Noble Lord," in *The Works of the Right Honourable Edmund Burke,* vol. 5, pp. 124-25.

15. E. Burke, "The Correspondence," in *The Works of the Right Honourable Edmund Burke,* vol. 3, pp. 192-93.

16. E. Burke, *On the American Revolution: Selected Speeches and Letters,* ed. E. Barkan (New York: Harper and Row, 1966), p. 82.

17. Burke, "Revolution in France," pp. 259-60.

the same location at two in the afternoon, and from this we assume it is the same tree, though we have seen only two distinct snapshots. The philosophy Hume developed from this has led his critics to declare him a severe skeptic who doubts we can know anything beyond sequenced appearances. Or to declare him a correlational positivist who claims there *is* nothing more than sequences. Or to declare him an intuitivist, holding that theoretical logic is limited and that we intuit the way the world works through experience rather than rationalist deduction or empirical induction.

Hume, I believe, would opt for the last possibility. He recognized, for instance, that we experience our thoughts not as a series of sequenced points (now I think A, now B) and not by using reason to prove that each thought is our own. Rather, we experience thinking as continuous and continuously our own; one knows these thoughts are one's own and yesterday's are as well. We know it not from logic but from feeling and the way we live in the world: "We shall find, upon a nearer examination, that it [theoretical logic] is really confined within very narrow limits, and that all the creative power of the mind amounts to no more than the faculty of compounding, transposing, augmenting, or diminishing the materials afforded us by the sense and experience."[18]

Moreover, Hume holds, we can rely on sensory and other experience because we naturally and continually subject them to correction from other experiences and persons. This engagement and correction occur foundationally in groups, where all persons grow up, which makes *thought itself the outcome of interaction and exchange of feeling, values, and ideas.* One's sense of the world, born of engagement with it and other persons, is not the opposite of reason but rather is the primary stuff reason works with.[19] What we (reasonably) know emerges from our experiences in family, society, nature, science, law, economics, public policy, and so on. Thus we must attend to the experiences we have there as they form what we sense, what we think, our conduct, and thus society itself — which, in turn, gives us our experiences. In short, our life is a relational loop among environment, our sense of it, our thought about it, the resulting actions we take, and thus the environment we make. John Milbank writes, "unlike Locke, Rousseau or Kant he [Hume] considers that the core of political society is a matter of substantive feeling. . . . [P]olitical order depends always less on any formal procedure than on a 'political class' however

---

18. D. Hume, *An Enquiry concerning Human Understanding,* ed. L. A. Selby-Bigge and P. H. Nidditch, 3rd ed. (Oxford: Oxford University Press, 1975), p. 19.

19. J. Milbank, "Stanton Lecture 7: The Objectivity of Feeling," 2011; retrieved from http://theologyphilosophycentre.co.uk/papers/Milbank_StantonLecture7.pdf.

constituted or to whatever degree dispersed — that is a class of people able to link their personal destinies with the destiny of the whole of their society: local, national or global."[20]

Yet for all this situatedness, Hume by no means believed that all people in a group experience things the same way or think alike. When one says one's thoughts are one's own, one is speaking of the separable mind. Persons — within families as within nations — find themselves in and choose different experiences, yielding different values and conduct. Not only the similarities but also the differences constitute the dynamics of any group. Hume's discussion of intuition and experience points not to univocity or cultural determinism but to how each person comes to think and act uniquely through her particular engagement with her surroundings.

The Romantic Constitution of Separability-amid-Situatedness

Burke and Hume's critique of the unsituated mind became a central project of the Romantics in Britain and Germany. Two central arguments were made: from the value of the particular culture (situatedness) to the value of the particular person (separability), and the knowability of persons different from oneself because of our situation together in world and its source.

On the Romantic account, French notions of an internal reason that deduces, by universally logical principles, the world "out there" should be resisted. And most resisted of all should be the idea that persons, owing to universal reason, will come to the same ideas the French had. German Romantics held that the French Enlightenment ignored real, particular cultures and ways of thinking — and ignored German culture especially. Yet in their counterposing emphasis on particularist culture, the Romantics did not abandon the separable self — did not anoint culture above person. Instead, they flipped the argument on its head, arguing for the value of each person's ideas and political rights *not* because each possesses universal reason (and thus is due universal rights) but because each person is unique and is due regard for her uniqueness.

The flip worked as follows. In protesting against universal homogeneity, the Romantics championed national particularity over universal sameness and then local culture over national. But they did not stop there in the move from universal to local; they continued from group to subgroup, eventually

20. J. Milbank, "Hume against Kant: Community, Faith, Reason and Feeling," *Modern Theology* 27 (March 2011): 276-97.

coming to the individual life, *the eminence of the intimate.* Even Romantics who believed that a transcendent spirit runs through history believed that each person is a distinct, individual reflection of the transcendent and should thus develop her unique instantiation of it. In short, from a defense of situatedness in national, linguistic, and cultural groups, Romantics ended by fostering the eccentricity of the poet, artist, and nonconformist. Charles Taylor writes, "The modern subject is no longer defined just by the power of disengaged rational control but by this new power of expressive self-articulation as well   the power which has been ascribed since the Romantic period to the creative imagination."[21]

A linchpin of the Romantic vision is the critique of Johann Gottlieb Fichte by his contemporaries F. W. J. Schelling and Georg Philipp von Hardenberg, pen name Novalis.[22] Fichte, in the Kantian line, posited an "I" isolated within itself and mind. Novalis and Schelling disagreed, positing a self in engagement with world, nature, others, and the transcendent. Yet, this engagement neither homogenizes persons nor subsumes them. Each remains unique yet able to understand (different) others because all partake of transcendent being.

Fichte, beginning with Kant's idea that the mind projects its mental categories onto world, had posited a self, an I, that is a unified whole but sees the world only from its own inner perspective. There is, on his view, a World Spirit or Absolute Self, but no person can experience it other than through her individual instantiation of it — the I-am-I of holistic intuition that precedes consciousness, precedes the mind's representation of world, and yet is one's portal to it. Fichte writes, "My world is the object and sphere of my duties, and absolutely nothing more; there is no other world for me."[23] In his critique, Novalis noticed that when we think of ourselves, we often do so as if looking at ourselves from the outside. Azade Seyhan calls this the "eye" necessary for

21. C. Taylor, *Sources of the Self: The Making of the Modern Identity* (Cambridge: Harvard University Press, 1992), p. 390.

22. Novalis, "Fichte Studies," in *Cambridge Texts in the History of Philosophy,* ed. J. Kneller (New York: Cambridge University Press, 2003; original 1795-1796); G. W. F. Hegel, *The Difference between Fichte's and Schelling's Systems of Philosophy,* ed. W. Cerf and H. Harris (Albany: State University of New York Press, 1988; original 1801).

23. J. G. Fichte, *The Vocation of Man,* trans. W. Smith (LaSalle, Ill.: Open Court, 1965; originally published as *Die Bestimmung des Menschen,* 1800), p. 108; or as Dalia Nassar writes, "The moral self, he [Fichte] argues, is absolutely autonomous and does not have any relation to the natural world or the world of (empirical) activity"; see D. Nassar, *The Romantic Absolute: Being and Knowing in Early German Romantic Philosophy, 1795-1804* (Chicago: University of Chicago Press, 2013), Kindle location 3723.

the "I."[24] The notion of other beings is thus built into human consciousness; there is no hermetic self sealed off from world and others. The "I" includes unity of self but also others — how else would we see ourselves from their perspectives?

The interrelation of "I" and Other emerges, Novalis held, because being, the ground for all that is, is neither a transcendent god outside world nor the product of the subject's conjuring but rather inheres in world and everything in it — in the "I," in others, and in all else. The aim of philosophy is thus to understand the relations between the Absolute and the particular and among all particulars, both how each person and particular is part of the Absolute and how the Absolute self-expresses in each particular. Even the body, on Novalis's view, does not distinguish one from world, others, and Absolute but is "a variation of it."[25] Knowledge too is amid world, is an analogical "symbol" of world as world expresses being. "My knowledge of the whole," Novalis writes, has "the character of analogy."[26] In short, philosophy is not to understand the items in world — its products, so to speak — but *productivity,* how and why things synergistically become what they are from their ground in being. "Beginning with his 1797 *Hemsterhuis-Studien,*" Dalia Nassar writes, "relationality becomes Novalis's central concern."[27]

Given this, Novalis's critique of Kant and Fichte was twofold: he found that they underestimated the creative aspect of knowledge — how each mind works with what is in world — and second, he found that their premising philosophy on a first principle (Kant's noumena or Fichte's World Spirit) misses the interactive particularity-yet-oneness of world and being. "Why," he asks, "do we need a beginning at all?"[28] Instead, Nassar continues, "Novalis seeks to establish a system based on the relation between the part and the whole, such that each gains meaning and achieves greater distinction in its relation with and determination through the other."[29]

This is achieved, on Novalis's view, in moral conduct and art. Moral con-

---

24. A. Seyhan, *Representation and Its Discontents: The Critical Legacy of German Romanticism* (Berkeley and Los Angeles: University of California Press, 1992), p. 38.

25. Novalis writes, "I find my body determined and made effective by itself and the world soul at the same time"; see Novalis, *Philosophical Writings,* ed. and trans. M. M. Stoljar (Albany: State University of New York Press, 1997), p. 62.

26. Novalis, *Philosophical Writings,* p. 62.

27. Nassar, *The Romantic Absolute,* Kindle locations 873-874.

28. Novalis, *Notes for a Romantic Encyclopedia,* ed. and trans. D. Wood (Albany: State University of New York Press, 2007), entry 634.

29. Nassar, *The Romantic Absolute,* Kindle locations 1633-1636.

duct requires finding the ideal in every particular and realizing the ideal in each personal act in world. The bringing together of personal act, ideal (Absolute), and worldly particulars transforms the person, nature, and each person *as part* of nature. Finally, since for Novalis God is "the moral being par excellence,"[30] moral conduct — bringing the ideal to world — is the effort to bring God to world. The effort is possible only if humankind has access to world and if our knowledge of world is not separated from it (isolated in our minds) but rather amid it. In short, human knowledge is not inner, idealistic figuring but of the real world. So, Novalis reasoned, Kant's view of soul as unworldly renders it incapable of acting as a moral agent. An out-of-worldly soul can be moral only abstractly — precisely the universal, abstract moral code Kant sought to describe. Yet on Novalis's view, morality is not this Kantian formalism but action among particulars in particular worldly places.

Bringing self, world, and ideal together happens also, Novalis thought, in art, which for him includes both the imagination and philosophy (our understanding of nature and its ground in Being/Absolute). It is in imaginative play and philosophical understanding that people may come together and move toward bringing timeless Being into the temporal and material — yet without erasing the vision and understanding of each "I." Novalis "sees the world of the senses in participation with the divine reality undergirding it, a reality he attempts to disclose in his poetry."[31] While the body exists as a "variation" or *expression* of Being within world, the mind, in art/philosophy, *transforms* world. Poetry, Novalis held, could serve even political purposes, the most pressing being the critique of the autocratic Prussian state. By highlighting the importance of personal imagination, poetry on one hand shows up the limits of totalizing, centralizing monarch, and on the other, allows distinct persons to engage each other in spite of (or through) their different perspectives.

Schelling similarly criticized Fichte for imagining an "I" of self-reference and an Absolute (the ground for world) that is ever out of reach — that is only ideal and never apprehended by us in the real. Though Schelling's thought underwent several transformations, even in his earlier works[32] he understood the Absolute or transcendent ground for all as an unconditioned, self-causing cause of all which includes, structures, and harbors the potential for all that is

30. Novalis, *Notes for a Romantic Encyclopedia*, p. 198.

31. M. Martin, *The Submerged Reality: Sophiology and the Turn to a Poetic Metaphysics* (Tacoma, Wash.: Angelico Press, 2015), p. 119.

32. In *Vom Ich als Prinzip der Philosophie oder über das Unbedingte im menschlichen Wissen* (1795) *(Of the I as the Principle of Philosophy or on the Unconditional in Human Knowledge)*, for instance.

differentiated in world *and* which is *in* the structure of all — not something separate from world but that which self-realizes in world and of which all particulars partake. Thus our knowledge of world and its ground is real, not an internal conjuring, or as Schelling writes, "he who wants to know something, wants to know at the same time that what he knows is real," so "there must be something which and through which everything that is reaches existence. . . . This something should be what completes all insights within the whole system of knowledge and it should reign — in the entire cosmos of our knowledge — as the original ground [*Urgrund*] of all reality."[33]

The "original ground" is apprehended, in Schelling's view, by our "intellectual intuition,"[34] which grasps self, world, and being at once together.[35] It apprehends the Absolute *through* the particulars — much as Spinoza, Schelling wrote, understood that a mathematical sequence is its distinct numbers, the relations among them, and the sequence as a whole. Because the Absolute/Being is within particulars and because of our capacity to understand them together, we can "work back" from particulars/world to an understanding of the Absolute/Being itself.[36] Moreover, each moment of apprehending Being-and-world is not an understanding of something outside ourselves but rather, because the self too partakes of Absolute/Being, it is a moment of grasping also the self.

In his natural philosophy *(Naturphilosophie)*, world or nature assumes a greater role as the reality through which the I constitutes itself.[37] That is, the ground for world (which is in world and of which world partakes) is the ground for the self: "the system of nature is at the same time the system of our mind."[38] Moving more explicitly away from Fichte, Schelling declares in the *First Plan of a System of the Philosophy* that what we understand of nature cannot be only the product of mind. Rather, nature's underlying structure — that which yields development, limitation, and differentiation — is real and self-organizing and is the site of the emergence of the self. Whatever sets out

33. F. W. J. von Schelling, *Werke: Historisch-kritische Ausgabe,* ed. H. M. Baumgartner, W. G. Jacobs, and H. Krings (Stuttgart-Bad Cannstatt: Frommann-Holzboog, 1976-), 1/2, 85.

34. Schelling, *Werke: Historisch-kritische Ausgabe,* 1/2, 131.

35. Contra Fichte, who maintained the distinction between the I and the not-I.

36. F. W. J. von Schelling, *Schellings Sämmliche Werke,* ed. K. F. A. Schelling (Stuttgart: Cotta, 1856-1861), 1/5, 127.

37. Schelling, *Werke: Historisch-kritische Ausgabe,* 1/8, 31 — though in his *Ideas (Ideen),* Schelling at times writes that nature is the *result* of the self-organizing cause of all, and at other times, that it *itself* is self-organizing.

38. Schelling, *Schellings Sämmliche Werke,* 1/2, 39.

the way nature runs sets out the mind as well. And the system that makes nature as it is makes mind as it is. A study of nature would yield a better grasp of how the ideal or Absolute/Being — what Schelling here calls the "absolute hypothesis" — self-realizes in natural forms, including mind.[39] It would make explicit or conscious the unconscious processes of nature, through which humankind and human understanding come to be. Such a study must be done, again, by working back from our experience of world/nature to ideal/Absolute. Philosophy's task, outlined in several works but most fully in Schelling's *System of the Whole of Philosophy and of Naturphilosophie in Particular,* is to work back from experience and world to discover how the ground for the mind/knowledge and the ground for nature/world are one.

At this point, Schelling sees both art and intellectual intuition as apprehending such unity: "the aesthetic intuition simply is the intellectual intuition become objective,"[40] visible and palpable, so to speak. Finding, however, that art, as a *product* of mind, cannot express the *ground* of mind and of nature, Schelling in his later works[41] focused on reason — beyond subject/knowledge and object/nature, what he called "indifference" — as best able to apprehend Absolute or Being. Reason may grasp not only particulars and persons but particulars as expression of Absolute. While "form" differentiates particulars,[42] "archetype" is both original form/universal *and* particular. The Absolute again is the unity of ideal and real and is apprehendable by archetypal cognition, an echo of the intellectual intuition of his earlier work. Archetypal intuition abstracts from all particulars to arrive at reason — to arrive at seeing particulars as expression of Absolute[43] — and it sees the Absolute in particulars, "the indifference in the difference."[44]

Importantly in Schelling's later work, the archetypal relationship between universal and particular is not one of derivation (particulars derived *from* Absolute/Being/universal) but one of *co-formation.*[45] Our experience and art too have their roles in grasping this. Just as nature is the real expression of

39. Schelling, *Werke: Historisch-kritische Ausgabe,* 1/8, 34.

40. Schelling, *Werke: Historisch-kritische Ausgabe,* 1/9.1, 325.

41. The *Presentation of My System of Philosophy* and *Further Presentations,* for instance.

42. Schelling, *Schellings Sämmliche Werke,* 1/4, 267.

43. Schelling, *Schellings Sämmliche Werke,* 1/4, 364.

44. Schelling, *Schellings Sämmliche Werke,* 1/4, 362.

45. Schelling, *Schellings Sämmliche Werke,* 1/4, 416. "The aim," Nassar writes, "is to grasp a differentiated absolute, where the differences are inherent to the absolute, without, however, losing sight of the absolute — of the archetypal unity that underlies all things." See Nassar, *The Romantic Absolute,* Kindle locations 5279-5281.

ideal/Absolute in world, art is its ideal expression, demonstrating the unity of particular and universal, ideal and real.[46] Yet reason, finally in Schelling's view, *is* their unity.[47]

For all their exploration of the oneness of nature, mind, and Absolute/ Being, at no point do Schelling and Novalis risk eradicating the "I." Persons remain distinct while partaking of Absolute/Being in nature. We, Schelling wrote, "cannot get rid of the self."[48] In sum, Romantic ideas about self, others, nature, and God did not quash but venerated the individual mind and imagination — each an expression of our underlying, shared humanity and its divine source. The philologist Johann Gottfried Herder made a parallel case: nations are culturally and linguistically unique, each with its own spirit *(Volksgeist)*, and thus will not move on a common path. Each has the right to defend its culture against foreign conquest and cultural colonization. But culture does not subsume the individual's ideas or rights but rather fosters them.[49]

A similar case was made in Britain by the philosopher William Godwin, husband of the feminist Mary Wollstonecraft and father of *Frankenstein* author Mary Shelley. Godwin had great faith that reason would correct the inadequacies of society, yet he argued the Romantic case for education that would advance neither universal reason nor particularist culture but the talents of each person.[50] Indeed, the *Sturm und Drang* arts movement and the writers Friedrich Schiller, K. W. F. Schlegel, William Blake, Percy Bysshe Shelley, William Wordsworth, and much of the Romantic roster held, in sometimes similar, sometimes quite different ways, that while cultures are distinct and distinctly valuable, they do not overwhelm the person. Rather, it is through cultural, individual, and especially aesthetic particularities (as Novalis said of poetry) that people come together not adversarially but to appreciate difference.[51]

These ideas in America took the form of transcendentalism, whose father,

46. Schelling, *Schellings Sämmliche Werke*, 1/5, 383.

47. Schelling, *Schellings Sämmliche Werke*, 1/5, 385.

48. Schelling, *Werke: Historisch-kritische Ausgabe*, 1/3, 89C.

49. Herder in "Yet Another Philosophy of History concerning the Development of Mankind" and elsewhere; see also, I. Berlin, *Vico and Herder* (New York: Viking Press, 1976).

50. See *The Anarchist Writings of William Godwin*, ed. P. Marshall (London: Freedom Press, 1986); W. Godwin, *An Enquiry concerning the Principles of Political Justice and Its Influence on General Virtue and Happiness* (New York: Viking Press, 1993; original 1793).

51. See, for instance, P. Shelley, *Prometheus Unbound: A Lyrical Drama in Four Acts*, in *Shelley's Poetry and Prose: Authoritative Texts, Criticism*, ed. D. Reiman and S. Powers (New York: Norton, 1977), act 4, scene 4.1, verse 321; M. Heidegger, *Schelling's Treatise of the Essence of Human Thought* (Athens: Ohio University Press, 1984); W. Marx, *The Philosophy of F. W. J. Schelling: History, System, and Freedom* (Bloomington: Indiana University Press, 1984).

Ralph Waldo Emerson, sought communion among (distinct) persons, nature, and transcendent. He held, as did Romantics in Europe, that we are not subsumed or diminished by engagement with others and world. Neither are we diminished or made the same by the transcendent — what Novalis called God, expressed in our shared being, and what Emerson called "Over-Soul" or "universal soul." Rather, we become who we distinctly are by openness to world and Soul.

While Emerson is often remembered for the self-reliance of his eponymous essay,[52] he did not mean self-reliance as isolation or self-interest. Indeed, he held that each of us comes to develop and know the self through engagement with the thoughts and feelings of others: "Other men are lenses through which we read our own minds."[53] As we develop through and with others, the point of self-reliance is not to detach but, more narrowly, to resist conformity — to resist subsumption of the (distinct) person by the crowd. And the point of resisting is to open oneself to insight, spirit, and the sublime, "an influx of the Divine mind into our mind."[54]

Here we are on firm Romantic ground, the landscape sketched out by Schelling, by Novalis, and formidably by G. W. F. Hegel, who too posited a World Spirit, all physical matter, history, and ideas that interact and move world forward. On Hegel's account, World Spirit forms who we are, and each being and idea is a unique expression of it.[55] While Hegel and Emerson, like all Romantic thinkers, had their distinct ways of getting at this idea, each person, Emerson too held, is formed by and is ever open to world and its source in "universal soul" — the transcendent that guides persons and history and "is not mine, or thine, or his, but we are its."[56] As each person is a singular form of this soul, each must develop her distinct way of expressing it, her distinct way of being in world with others, our "lenses" onto the world. And so she must resist erosion of her distinction by conformity (such erosion was a concern also of Hegel). Emerson's contemporary Walt Whitman held that we

52. R. W. Emerson, "Self-Reliance," in *Essays: First Series* (1841); retrieved from http://www.emersoncentral.com/selfreliance.htm.

53. R. W. Emerson, *Representative Men,* ed. P. Schirmeister (New York: Marsilio, 1995; original 1850), p. 5.

54. R. W. Emerson, "The Over-Soul," in *Selected Prose and Poetry,* ed. R. L. Cook (New York: Holt Rinehart Winston, 1950), p. 133.

55. See especially, G. W. F. Hegel, *The Philosophy of Right,* ed. A. Wood, trans. T. Knox (Oxford: Oxford University Press, 1942; original 1821); G. W. F. Hegel, *The Phenomenology of Spirit,* trans. J. Findley (Oxford: Oxford University Press, 1979; original 1817).

56. R. W. Emerson, "Nature, 4," in *Selected Prose and Poetry,* p. 16.

need "not that half only, individualism, which isolates. There is another half, which is adhesiveness or love, that fuses, ties and aggregates, making the races comrades, and fraternizing all" — what he called, underscoring the meld of distinction and situatedness, "ensemble-Individuality."[57]

In sum, the transcendentalist argument against universalism on one hand and isolation on the other was that we are ever engaged with our specific surroundings, specific others, and transcendent. Yet we are neither made uniform by culture and transcendent, nor are we made hermetic, isolated in our differences. Rather, World Spirit or Over-Soul is expressed uniquely in each natural phenomenon, culture, language, work of art, idea, and being. Indeed, each may (uniquely) engage world and other persons (though we are distinct) *because* all are of the transcendent.

Separability-amid-Situatedness after Romanticism: The Example of Alexis de Tocqueville

One of the great ponderers of separability and situatedness in the generation after Romanticism was the French historian Alexis de Tocqueville, who despised monarchical tyranny, admired democracy, and considered antidemocracy efforts "against God Himself."[58] Yet he worried that democracy would founder either in the separability slide from liberty to self-absorption or in the situatedness demand to sacrifice individual freedoms for equality. Focus on private gain is most perilous, Tocqueville thought, when it prevents citizens from uniting to resist political or economic tyranny.[59] Sacrifice of freedoms for equality, Tocqueville's second fear, occurs through government regulations that, while reducing inequality, also limit citizen activities, losing us individual initiative, invention, and independence of vision. Writing of his travels around the United States, Tocqueville noted, "I saw very few who showed that virile candor and manly independence of thought. . . . [O]ne might suppose that all American minds had been fashioned after the same model, so exactly do they follow along the same paths."[60]

Tocqueville's solution is situatedness *for the sake* of separability and liberty.

57. W. Whitman, *Complete Prose Works* (2008); retrieved from Google e-books: MobileReference.

58. A. de Tocqueville, *Democracy in America*, ed. J. P. Mayer, trans. G. Lawrence, vol. 1 (Garden City, N.Y.: Doubleday, 1966, 1969; original 1835), p. 12.

59. Tocqueville, *Democracy in America*, pp. 506, 517.

60. Tocqueville, *Democracy in America*, p. 258.

In an echo of Smith and anticipating Mill, he held that the culture of a people must develop in them the virtues to use freedom well so that liberty does not yield self-absorption, crime, and the tyranny needed to stanch it but so that liberty and the common good serve each other.[61] Virtues are learned in interaction with family and community and importantly through religion: "One cannot establish the reign of liberty without that of mores, and mores cannot be firmly founded without beliefs."[62] In a virtuous circle, religious beliefs ground mores and practices, which bind people together in associations that resist tyranny (from authorities or the crowd) and self-absorption (undue separability).

For this reason, America's voluntary associations were of prime interest to Tocqueville. They relied on and reinforced individual liberty and initiative while directing them toward virtue and public projects. "For only freedom," Tocqueville wrote, "can deliver the members of a community from that isolation which is the lot of the individual" and enable them "to get in touch with each other, promote an active sense of fellowship" In a word, it "offers other objectives than that of getting rich."[63] As Tocqueville believed these associations flourish under limited central government, he supported American federalism. It constrains central government to relatively light direction and thus allows for "an infinite number of occasions for the citizens to act together and so that every day they should feel that they depended on one another."[64] Government stepping back is good insofar as it allows citizens to step in. Tocqueville located liberty wherever a community took on a project without central government and yet without squelching individual vision:

> Suppose that an individual thinks of some enterprise, and that enterprise has a direct bearing on the welfare of society; it does not come into his head to appeal to public authority for its help. He publishes his plan; offers to carry it out, summons other individuals to aid his efforts and personally struggles against all obstacles. No doubt he is often less successful than the state would have been in his place, but in the long run the sum of all private undertakings far surpasses anything the government might have done.[65]

61. Tocqueville wrote, "Next to virtue as a general idea, nothing, I think, is so beautiful as that of rights, and indeed the two ideas are mingled"; Tocqueville, *Democracy in America*, p. 237.

62. Tocqueville, *Democracy in America*, p. 17.

63. A. de Tocqueville, *The Old Regime and the French Revolution*, trans. S. Gilbert (Garden City, N.Y.: Doubleday, 1955), p. xiv.

64. Tocqueville, *Democracy in America*, p. 511.

65. Tocqueville, *Democracy in America*, p. 95.

A key factor in the success of voluntarist associations, on Tocqueville's view, is their concern with local, practical projects rather than "general ideas." Their procedures are developed by members themselves, are specific to the needs of the place,[66] and can be changed if they prove lacking.[67] Laws too, he held, "are the children of custom"[68] and practice, and should emerge from the relevant community.

Tocqueville recognized that America — absent religion, virtue, and association — could slip toward group conformity or self-absorption. But he found the meld of liberty and situatedness considerably sounder in the United States than in his own country. In France, the crown's undermining of corporate bodies and civil society activity in the early modern period had vitiated the public's ability to act on its own behalf.[69] Should the people, he wrote, be given a sudden chance at elections and self-rule, they would fall into chaos or repeated revolution.[70] He considered constitutional monarchy a compromise, but as the monarchy wouldn't hear of its constraint by constitution, Tocqueville found himself supporting calls for an antimonarchist republic in a nation he thought ill-prepared for it.

Separability-amid-Situatedness Mid-century: The Examples of John Ruskin, Socialism, and Germans Who Want to Be French

While in the eighteenth century progressives had supported the new open market for the access it gave commoners to opportunity, by the mid–nineteenth century some conservatives — also out of concern for commoners — opposed it. Capitalism had become deracinating and abusive; inherited rank and traditional practice, these conservatives held, fostered responsible if paternalistic care for the poor. John Ruskin, for instance, argued, against economists like

66. Tocqueville was keenly aware of the differences between the cultures and political organization of various regions in the United States.

67. He writes, "Without ideas in common, no common action would be possible and without common action, men might exist, but there could be no body social"; Tocqueville, *Democracy in America*, pp. 433-34.

68. Tocqueville, *Democracy in America*, p. 79.

69. Political and economic frustration, he believed, led to revolutionary schemes rather than pragmatic, workable reform. "A nation so unused to acting for itself was bound to begin by wholesale destruction when it launched into a program of wholesale reform"; Tocqueville, *The Old Regime*, p. 167.

70. Tocqueville, *Democracy in America*, p. 315.

Thomas Malthus and David Ricardo, that the self-interest of the new markets was not natural, indeed no more natural than generosity. People's interests and wants are no more in perpetual competition than in continual agreement. Interests and wants, Ruskin held, are not a matter of nature but of culture: should competition be taught, competition will follow, but so too will consideration. Societal flourishing is a matter of what people in communities are acculturated to value and want.

Thus the development of wants — preferred items and practices — must be based on moral principle as well as economics,[71] on "justice," not only "expediency," as "intended by the Maker of men."[72] From this a just society will follow. Profit may be had, but justice does not allow for profit *maximization* at the expense of fair wages and prices, labor and sanitation codes, etc. Justice demands that the market be governed by valor and virtue — Ruskin's echo of Locke, Smith, Burke, and Tocqueville — which the poor too have and for which they should be respected. For models of such virtue, Ruskin looked to the codes of honor in the professions (the military, law, medicine, and the priesthood), which commit members to goals above self-interest. He looked also to the artisan, who has pride in his work and respect from clients and community. Throughout his life, Ruskin developed a vision of beauty, goodness, and justice in daily living to counter the brutality and aesthetic coarsening in both bourgeois and factory life. *It was an argument from situatedness — acculturation by morality, religion, and aesthetics — for the sake of personal dignity and well-being.*

While Ruskin is considered a situatedness advocate from the right, the socialism of his day was its advocate from the left. The socialist analysis so situated persons in their economic class — correctly, if you like it, unduly, if you don't — that they seemed to have little wiggle room for individual action. Yet, the socialism of the mid-nineteenth century (if not its later, totalitarian versions) reserved a considerable role for the distinct, separable self. It regarded class as formative but not dispositive, and it aimed at economies obligated to the flourishing of each person — each different from the next and free to develop herself anew, unconstrained by Europe's traditions and conventions. Indeed, mid-century socialism sought to give workers control over their labor so that they would be economically secure enough to develop themselves

71. J. Ruskin, *"Unto This Last" and "Munera Pulveris"* (London: George Allen and Sons, 1911), p. 91.
72. Ruskin, *"Unto This Last" and "Munera Pulveris,"* pp. 23, 61.

without a "predetermined yardstick"[73] — a break from their economic pasts and from societal conventions, considerable separability indeed.

Moreover, while mid-century socialism held that workers and capitalists are defined by their class positions, it also declared that workers can escape them and revolt. Marx considered a workers' revolt to be a historical "necessity," but his term finesses the requirement that each worker must actively break with her past, adopt a new, socialist analysis of her circumstances, and take political action to change society from old to new — all actions of a self distinct from past and status quo. If Marx's claim about the "necessity" of change were correct, he could have simply waited for it to happen and need not have impoverished himself writing his books.

In 1870, the Franco-Prussian War put separability and situatedness at the center of European political debate. Alsace-Lorraine, long contested between France and Germany, was about to be shunted back to Germany owing to its military victory. The German government made a situatedness case for its land claims: the people speak German; the children sing "O Tannenbaum" on Christmas, and so, as the culture is German, the people — and their mineral-rich land — belong to Germany. French conservatives, also believing in the primacy of land and culture, should have been persuaded by the German argument but for one problem: the people of Alsace-Lorraine wanted to remain French, seeking apparently to separate from their heritage. The French were not in an enviable position. To keep the land, they had to recognize the separability claims of the Alsatians, who were demanding in German that they stay French. But this violated the French conservatives' values of situatedness and tradition.

The ensuing political muddles can be seen in the writings of the historian and political theorist Ernest Renan. At the beginning of his career, Renan was a conservative, anti-Semitic racial-determinist who blamed France's military defeats on the Enlightenment's disregard of tradition and heritage. Yet the declaration of loyalty to France by Alsace-Lorraine moved him to a new definition of nation; it was no longer a bond of blood and culture but a "large-scale solidarity" characterized "in the present by a tangible fact, namely, consent.... We have driven metaphysical and theological abstractions out of politics. What then remains? Man, with his desires and his needs."[74] That persons can decide

73. K. Marx, *Grundrisse*, ed. M. Niklaus (Harmondsworth, U.K.: Penguin, 1973; original 1858), p. 488.

74. E. Renan, "What Is a Nation?" in *Becoming National: A Reader*, ed. G. Eley and R. Suny (New York: Oxford University Press, 1996; original 1882), p. 53.

against culture for a new national belonging — considerable separability — was thus valorized by France's champion of situated cultural roots.

The Constitution of Separability-amid-Situatedness in the "Structural" Sciences

The French conundrum was the paradox of the day. On one hand, separability — broadening economic and political rights that broke with the past and protected persons regardless of background — was everywhere. On the other, the new sciences of anthropology, sociology, and psychology were discovering mankind's situatedness in past, tribe, and culture. William James developed his sociopsychology from the pragmatist claim that people determine the truth of an idea from its results, from what happens when it is put into effect.[75] If water here boils at 100 degrees Centigrade as best as we can measure, then the claim that it does is true. Over time, one notices patterns of effects and develops certain expectations of how things work: water everywhere boils at 100 degrees Centigrade. But expectations — what we call knowledge — depend on the patterns one has noticed during one's experiences in one's era and society. Truth, James concluded, is not absolute but cultural. An idea is considered correct *in a given situation* if it accounts for new observations while preserving as much as possible of what is already considered true.

This is a situatedness perspective that reaches back to Burke, Hamann, and Herder, and like these thinkers, James understood it in tandem with separability. As each person makes judgments based not only on her culture but also on her individual experience, her judgments will differ somewhat from those of her neighbor. Like the Romantics, James begins with the differences between cultural groups and ends with individual judgment, which he held is of significant value and entitled to legal protection.

What James proposed in psychology became the prevailing position of structural anthropology and sociology, a few examples of which I'll review here. *Lebensphilosophie* (philosophy drawn from life) held that life cannot be understood by analyzing theoretical, philosophical claims; we must look at life as it's lived in specific times and places. This living gives us our thoughts; our

75. See *The Works of William James*, ed. F. Burkhardt, F. Bowers, and I. Skrupskelis (Cambridge: Harvard University Press, 1975-1988); W. James, *Writings: 1902-1910: "The Varieties of Religious Experience"; "Pragmatism"; "Some Problems of Philosophy"; "A Pluralist Universe"; "The Meaning of Truth"; "Essays,"* ed. B. Kuklick (New York: Library of America, 1988).

philosophies do not stand outside experience, pronouncing about it, but are situated in it. Edmund Husserl and Friedrich Nietzsche wrote that it is life — not philosophical analysis — that "gives" (Husserl) and is the proper topic of investigation. Wilhelm Dilthey held that the way to understand thought is to understand how it works in context, in living, its *Wirkungszusammenhang*. Oswald Spengler emphasized the study of ordinary life, "our common life together" — familiar, often habitual, unreflected upon, and aimed at common projects that enable us to get on. Language, he continued, following Hamann and Herder, is not a system for representing the world — as though language "steps back" outside world — but is what occurs as we live and do things together.[76]

The French sociologist Émile Durkheim contested the contractarian claim that society emerges when individuals contract to come together for their benefit. This sort of self-interest, he held, would produce instability. Since groupings are called societies precisely because they are relatively stable, he looked for the structures that form the social glue.[77] Internalized and often unconscious, these beliefs and habitual practices are the underpinnings of articulated rules. Legal systems, for instance, emanate from society's shared fears about what or who is dangerous and shared values about what or who should be protected.[78] Even suicide, Durkheim wrote in his famous study,[79] though seemingly an individual choice, reflects culture. The very notion of suicide as a private choice made from despair is a Western idea and contrasts with the suicide aimed at preserving the honor of one's clan. A principal problem of modern, mobile life, Durkheim held, is the raveling of the "mechanical solidarity" that emerges from these internalized yet shared beliefs and practices. He saw socialism's appeal not so much in common property as in the search among workers (uprooted from traditional communities and put into factories) for the protections and at-home-ness of social bonds and projects.

In their work *Primitive Classification*,[80] Durkheim and his nephew Marcel

---

76. O. Spengler, *Man and Technics: Contribution to a Philosophy of Life* (Honolulu: University Press of the Pacific, 2002), pp. 20, 27, 50-58.

77. E. Durkheim, *Rules of Sociological Method*, trans. W. Halls (London and New York: Free Press, 1982; original 1895); E. Durkheim, *Elementary Forms of the Religious Life*, trans. K. Fields (London and New York: Free Press, 1995; original 1912); E. Durkheim, *The Division of Labor in Society*, trans. W. Halls (London and New York: Free Press, 1997; original 1893).

78. See Durkheim, *Rules of Sociological Method*.

79. E. Durkheim, *Suicide: A Study in Sociology*, trans. J. Spaulding and G. Simpson (London and New York: Free Press, 1997; original 1897).

80. E. Durkheim and M. Mauss, *Primitive Classification*, trans. R. Needham (Chicago: University of Chicago Press, 1967; original 1903).

Mauss declared that not only are values and conduct culturally contingent but so too are our mental categories. Over a century after Kant claimed that we see the world through them, Durkheim and Mauss added that even these are not universal but depend on culture and experience (as Hayek [see pt. I, ch. 4] would also come to say).[81] Durkheim's contemporary Ferdinand de Saussure added that if thought is dependent on culture, it is unthinkable absent a culturally developed language that gives it form. Absent language, there is nothing to "think," no concepts, no words to put them into. Language, he declared, is a system of symbols agreed upon by the language-using group.[82] Only this (tacit, evolving) group agreement can grant meaning ("signification") to the noises ("sound images") one uses to communicate. Saussure's view of language as group agreement about symbols was put to use mid–twentieth century by the anthropologist Claude Lévi-Strauss, who held that societal relations are also based on agreement about cultural symbols: male-female, sacred-profane, etc. These binary pairs, he believed, form the basic underpinnings of all societies, with one of the pair considered "unmarked" and normative, the other, "marked" and a deviation ("man," for example, being normative, "woman" being judged against masculine traits as lacking them).

In the generation after Saussure, Ludwig Wittgenstein —elaborating the entire thrust of *Lebensphilosophie* — described language and thought not as mental, logical systems but as what occurs in living, as *Lebensformen* (ways of life), *gewönliche Leben* (ordinary life), or simply *unser Leben* (our life).[83] Our beliefs about anything, Wittgenstein wrote, and the confidence that we can use them as a basis for action come not from analytical proof in "philosophy" but from living.[84] In the same interwar years, the Polish physician Ludwik Fleck published his study of syphilis, demonstrating the influence of "thought-style" on even the supposedly "factual" sciences.[85] Thought-style — the way of thinking of one's cultural environment — is learned dialogically, through

---

81. This too was a bow to Hamann, Herder, and the Romantics, who had found that language and thought are cultural; see J. Moran and A. Gode, *On the Origin of Language* (Chicago: University of Chicago Press, 1986); C. Taylor, "Language and Human Nature," in C. Taylor, *Human Agency and Language: Philosophical Papers* (Cambridge: Cambridge University Press, 1985), 1:215-47.

82. F. Saussure, *Course in General Linguistics* (London: Duckworth, 1983; original 1916).

83. L. Wittgenstein, *Philosophical Investigations* (Oxford: Blackwell, 1958), especially pp. 122, 174.

84. L. Wittgenstein, *On Certainty* (Oxford: Blackwell, 1969), pp. 7, 9

85. L. Fleck, *Genesis and the Development of a Scientific Fact* (Chicago: University of Chicago Press, 1981; original 1935).

engagement with others. It includes one's ideas about such basic categories as time, space, notions of causality, and what counts as "facts." Thus, while syphilitic symptoms remain fairly constant over time, differing descriptions of them reveal the thought-style of the diagnosing culture. When syphilis was considered evidence of sin, priests were in charge of it and cures were doctrinal. When it was considered evidence of licentiousness, civil regulatory agencies were in charge, and the cure shifted to isolation from proper society in insane asylums.

In this, Fleck anticipated the work of Michel Foucault and was in line with his own contemporary, Michael Polanyi. Through his work in chemistry, economics, and philosophy, Polanyi came to believe that science too, like all knowledge, emerges from the values, mental habits, and interests one has and has inherited. Learning, he wrote, is discovery: one attends to clues in the environment for a pattern that might make things work — an explanation, formula, or person. This effort relies on a series of *beliefs:* that there is something yet to find, that the not-yet-known thing is knowable, that one will be able to find it. In this process, "creative intuition" makes minute judgments about what hunches to pursue while "creative imagination" is what one does with the clues one finds. "Integration" is the moment of apprehending the new pattern, like the camera lens bringing blurred images into focus. One does all this, Polanyi holds, under the normative guidelines, thinking "practices," and predispositions acquired from one's culture (including scientific subculture). We thus notice some things but not others, think along certain lines but not others.

Polanyi concluded that, if one does not understand the cultural situatedness of learning, one might take science as "objective" and the "best" measure of truth to the denigration of what cannot be proved through its procedures — religious or moral tenets, for instance. This leaves us choosing scientific, mathematical, and economic formulas to determine how to treat each other, an idea Polanyi found dangerous. If persons are "sacred," he wrote, limits against abuse follow; if they are not, one may immiserate some for the benefit of the majority or powerful minority. This, Polanyi wrote, is what makes capitalism secular — the absence of transcendent values that one cannot tweak to suit oneself.

Among those influenced by Polanyi was the postwar philosopher of science Thomas Kuhn (also accused of plagiarizing Polanyi's work). Science, on Kuhn's view, as on Polanyi's, is not only the pursuit of new ideas but also the elaboration of accepted ways of thinking and paradigms. The questions asked and the ways of arriving at answers emerge from the scientific culture of the day — and this, Kuhn held, is characterized by significant "bandwagon" effects, where scientists confirm and embellish received wisdom. Only when evidence unexplainable by existing theory reaches a tipping point are scientists moved to find a new theory, what Kuhn famously called the paradigm shift.[86]

One of the last architects of the structuralist approach — the study of society's situating structures — before it underwent something of a paradigm shift of its own, was the sociologist Talcott Parsons. He acknowledged the individual actor with personal goals, individual decision-making, and a wide berth of free will. Yet he saw these as constrained by cultural and historical context. He tried to discover a macrosystem that explains both societal constraint and the wiggle room it allows, including to sociologists like himself.[87] Much as Fleck, Polanyi, and Kuhn held that natural scientists work within cultural patterns, Parsons said the same of social scientists. His own work inadvertently proved his point. He saw cultures as moving from less toward greater adaptation to the environment, from less toward greater variety of societal institutions, and from less to greater inclusion and toleration — in short, from less toward something like an idealized version of postwar America.[88] This was criticized as unwitting cultural chauvinism, but the critique confirmed Parsons's basic premise that no one, including sociologists, escapes her culture.

The description of our situatedness in history and culture was structuralism's purpose and is its legacy to us. But as with Enlightenment and Romantic thinkers, it did not inspire structuralists to disregard the separable person. Their study of the situated person yielded neither totalitarian politics nor the fatalistic idea that we are stuck with the past and the status quo. Most structuralists indeed were progressives concerned about individual rights and opportunities. The purpose of even the earliest structuralist texts was often to make us aware of cultural constraints so that we might lift them for greater liberty, equality, and well-being. William James, we recall, argued that not only group but also individual beliefs are of such value that they warrant legal protection. Like Tocqueville's argument, it is a situatedness brief for separation. Perhaps obviously, the structuralists also appreciated the separability that allowed them to develop the new scientific study of situatedness.

---

86. T. Kuhn, *The Copernican Revolution* (Cambridge: Harvard University Press, 1957); T. Kuhn, *The Essential Tension* (Chicago: University of Chicago Press, 1979); T. Kuhn, *The Structure of Scientific Revolutions* (Chicago: University of Chicago Press, 1996).

87. T. Parsons, *Social Structure and Personality* (New York: Free Press, 1964); T. Parsons, *Theories of Society: Foundations of Modern Sociological Theory*, ed. K. Naegele (New York: Free Press, 1965); T. Parsons, *Economics and Society: A Study in the Integration of Economic and Social Theory* (New York: Routledge, 1999).

88. T. Parsons, *The System of Modern Societies* (New York: Prentice-Hall, 1971).

Post-Structuralism: The Example of Michel Foucault

The situated person was the concern also of the post-structuralists, who beginning in the 1960s and 1970s sought not to describe society's visible institutions and practices but to discover the unarticulated assumptions undergirding them. They investigated, for example, not only a society's legal system but also how it conceptualizes criminality: as the result of a sinful will, economic hardship, or a difficult childhood?

Pierre Bourdieu's description of habitus in part I, chapter 2 is one such investigation. His work parallels the investigations of Michel Foucault, who famously emphasized that assumptions and beliefs set up societal structures, and these structures — families, schools, hospitals, prisons, and politics — determine how information and power are distributed and thus how things happen and to whom. For example, beliefs about what learning is, what counts as knowledge, and what sorts of beings children are determine how we set up schools, which in turn determine who gets a good education (according to our definition of "good" and "education"). Our ways of thinking do not explain the world, Foucault held; they are what must be explained.

Foucault begins with knowledge structures or epistemes, not what people do but how they explain it — not schools but pedagogical theory, not emotional behavior but psychiatry. Epistemes, he continues, do not recognize that they too are part of the culture they're describing. Departing from structuralism, Foucault holds that epistemes do not operate as a coordinated system but rather overlap in congruent and conflicting ways both among and within societal groups.[89] In his later, more political books or "genealogies,"[90] Foucault describes the relations between epistemes and power. Every sort of power requires a certain body of knowledge (episteme) that makes the power distribution credible and acceptable. Modern legal systems, for instance, contain

---

89. Foucault's studies of epistemes are found in the books known as his "archeologies"; see M. Foucault, *Madness and Civilization: A History of Insanity in the Age of Reason* (New York: Vintage Books, 1988); M. Foucault, *The Order of Things: An Archeology of Human Sciences* (New York: Vintage Books, 1994); M. Foucault, *Archeology of Knowledge and the Discourse on Language,* trans. A. Sheridan (New York: Pantheon Books, 1982); M. Foucault, *The Birth of the Clinic: An Archeology of Medical Perception,* trans. A. Sheridan (New York: Vintage Books, 1994).

90. M. Foucault, *Discipline and Punish: The Birth of the Prison,* trans. A. Sheridan (New York: Vintage Books, 1995); M. Foucault, *The History of Sexuality: An Introduction* (New York: Vintage Books, 1990); M. Foucault, *The Use of Pleasure* (New York: Vintage Books, 1990), among them.

institutions and practices (courts, police procedures) that legal theory (epistemes) discusses. But both the practices and epistemes circulate the premise (directly and tacitly) that this specific legal system is necessary to prevent crime and other systems (like community shaming) are inadequate. Thus the present system appears inevitable and best.

Importantly, the discourses available to a person — the knowledge and the power they give — influence what she can achieve. Access to dominant discourses — higher education, grasp of the law — affords greater success. Discourses are most easily observed in times of "breaks," unusually rapid shifts in the way knowledge and power are distributed. These moments bring to the surface both dominant discourses and competing or emerging ones. In *Discipline and Punish,* for example, Foucault describes the early modern "break" or change from monarchical power to more diffuse, civic forms of social control. This politico-legal change required a parallel shift in discourse from control by agents of church and crown to civic control through internalized ideas of "normal" behavior, of "common sense and decency," and the informal peer pressure that keeps people to it. On Foucault's view, the discourse and mores of "normality" are themselves part of the power shift from nobility to civil society.

Yet, for all his focus on cultural situatedness, Foucault did not claim an immobilized person, fixed by discourses. In his later work, a deterministic account is resisted by the recognition that, as every society has many, even contradictory discourses, conduct is informed by their interplay. Each person, based on her singular set of experiences, puts discourses together differently. Her understanding of world and her conduct will thus also differ from those of her neighbors. Moreover, the microdifferences in each person's behavioral repertoire prod changes in discourses themselves. Small shifts and recombinations accumulate and change discourses and conduct. One of Foucault's well-known examples is the development of homosexuality, which shifted from a kind of action, buggery, to a kind of person, homosexual. The shift allowed for persons who thought of themselves as having this identity, which in turn enabled newly self-aware "homosexuals" to work politically against prejudice and discrimination — which in turn altered the social discourse about homosexuality.

In sum, persons are formed by their discourses but construct them as well. Post-structuralists do not suggest that persons do not make choices and discoveries (within quite broad limits). As they are of the modern West, such determinism would violate the value they themselves place on separability. Indeed, the purpose of post-structuralist theory is liberty. It hopes to call attention to the ways in which beliefs and culture maintain power hierarchies so that those with less power can demand its redistribution. *In describing situatedness, it hopes for separability from situatedness's confines.*

Separability-amid-Situatedness in the Work of Charles Taylor, Michael Sandel, and Alasdair MacIntyre

The argument for situatedness grounds the work of Canadian philosopher Charles Taylor,[91] who begins his work with a study of Hegel's World Historical Spirit, the synergy of nature, cultures, things, and persons that moves history forward.[92] Hegel — and Taylor — are concerned that modernity leads to the homogenization and thinning of distinct cultures, obliterating the varieties that are so important to Spirit's unfolding and that develop in persons culturally specific morality. As there is, on Hegel and Taylor's account, no unsituated person or unsituated moral sense, erosion of culture comes to erosion of moral conduct. Of specific concern to Taylor is the erosion of the sort of culture that fosters the morality of free persons. "The free or autonomous moral agent," Taylor writes, "can only achieve and maintain his identity in a certain type of culture."[93]

As Locke, Mill, Smith, and Tocqueville argued, freedom endures where people have the virtues to support it — to conduct themselves responsibly, honestly, and with concern for the common good. In this way, freedom doesn't devolve into self-interested competition (or crime) and into the consequent controls needed to keep it from becoming society-wide chaotic greed. Virtue also moves citizens to sustain the societal institutions (schools, religions, family, voluntary associations, political groups) that teach persons to value freedom and to act so that it may endure. "I am arguing," Taylor writes, "that the free individual of the West is only what he is by virtue of the whole society and civilization which brought him to be and which nourishes him."[94]

Taylor finds unuseful political theories that laud individual freedom but fail to attend to the societal structures that undergird it. His complaint is that these theories take individual choice per se as freedom but do not advance

91. See C. Taylor, *The Ethics of Authenticity* (Cambridge: Harvard University Press, 1992); Taylor, *Sources of the Self*; C. Taylor, *Modern Social Imaginaries* (Durham, N.C.: Duke University Press, 2003); C. Taylor, *A Secular Age* (Cambridge: Harvard University Press, 2007).

92. C. Taylor, *Hegel* (Cambridge: Cambridge University Press, 1975).

93. C. Taylor, "Atomism," in *Philosophy and the Human Sciences: Philosophical Papers*, vol. 2 (Cambridge: Cambridge University Press, 1985), p. 205.

94. Taylor, "Atomism," in *Philosophy and the Human Sciences*, p. 206.

the particular choices that yield free societies. Thus, free people, lacking the acculturation and virtues that sustain freedom, will make choices but not necessarily ones that preserve liberty. If choice per se is good, if all choices are equally good, the choice for freedom and its infrastructure has no ground to argue for itself. Why, if all choice is good, not choose to suspend civil rights in the name of efficiency? The sustenance of freedom, Taylor argues, requires situatedness in a culture that prizes and protects it:[95] "since the free individual can only maintain his identity within a society/culture of a certain kind, he has to be concerned about the shape of this society/culture as a whole."[96]

The "society" we must concern ourselves with, Michael Sandel holds, in continuing Taylor's line, is not merely living among others but commitment that is part of personal identity — affections, aims, and obligations that we feel are "the way we are" and that we work into our behavior and institutions. "Community must be constitutive of the shared self-understandings of the participants and embodied in their institutional arrangements."[97] He contrasts this with the deontological view, where identity is seen as belonging to the individual prior to her ontology, "the possessions of a self given prior to its ends,"[98] prior to a person's context, its goals and practices. Sandel finds such an identity unlikely because persons do not emerge prior to contexts that give them goals, values, and ways of getting there. And were the existence of such a deontological person possible, she would have nothing from which to decide goals or behavior — no values, memories, traditions, not even ones to rebel against. This person is not free but suspended in a void. "The deontological self, stripped of all possible constitutive attachments, is less liberated than disempowered."[99]

Yet, while Sandel doubts that unsituated persons could construct goals *de novo*, he holds that persons can, using their values, assess and modify beliefs, practices, and societal norms. Here he works separability into his situatedness scheme: the person's capacity to think and do things differently from past and others. He supports the rights and opportunities that allow her to do

95. Taylor writes, "Primacy-of-rights theories in other words accept a principle ascribing rights to men as binding unconditionally, binding, that is, on men as such. But they do not accept as similarly unconditional a principle of belonging or obligation"; see C. Taylor, "Atomism," in *Communitarianism and Individualism,* ed. S. Avineri and A. De-shalit (Oxford: Oxford University Press, 1992), p. 30.

96. Taylor, "Atomism," in *Philosophy and the Human Sciences,* p. 207.

97. M. Sandel, "Justice and the Good," in *Liberalism and Its Critics* (New York: New York University Press, 1984), p. 167.

98. Sandel, "Justice and the Good," p. 169.

99. Sandel, "Justice and the Good," p. 170.

so, including a rights-based legal system, education — especially the skills of self-examination and societal critique — and the economic means to change oneself and society.

As with Tocqueville, the Romantics, and the post-structuralists, this is situatedness that aims at a certain separability — not dropping into anomie or self-absorption but making distinct choices amid society and being able to evaluate society in light of new ideas and circumstances. A similar argument appears in the work of Scottish philosopher Alasdair MacIntyre, who begins by arguing for the "embedded self": "we all approach our own circumstances as bearers of a particular social identity. I am someone's son or daughter, someone else's cousin or uncle; I am a citizen of this or that city."[100] MacIntyre thus holds to the "discovery" notion of the self, where finding one's identity and values means discovering the "stories" of one's roles and the larger societal stories in which they are embedded. This discovery includes one's moral sense, which too is not hatched by each person anew but emerges from engagement with the "stories," attitudes, values, and practices of her culture — and from discussion in the *polis*.

Importantly, the requirement of *public* discussion preempts self-absorbed conduct destructive of the common good. It sets the development of procedures and standards for policy not within one's or one group's private benefit but amid a wide range of those involved. "What such a shared understanding provides is precisely the kind of standard independent of, not only individual desires, preferences and will, but also of the interests of particular groups within the community, but appeal to which rational debate on practical questions can be carried on."[101]

People come to their standards and procedures for the *polis* by trying to survive together under the conditions in which they live, by engaging in common endeavors, and by working out what is needed. In a virtuous circle reminiscent of Tocqueville and Mill, the process of working together teaches people the skills needed to do so. These skills, on MacIntyre's view, distinguish a *polis,* capable of self-awareness and self-critique, from a *volk,* which proceeds from heritage unreflectedly.[102] MacIntyre contrasts *polis* with the individualist view, which pictures life as unconnected spheres — work divided from home, public conduct from private — and which breaks down complex actions into unconnected

100. A. MacIntyre, *After Virtue: A Study in Moral Theory* (London: Duckworth, 1981), pp. 204-5.

101. A. MacIntyre, "Community, Law and the Idiom and Rhetoric of Rights," *Listening: Journal of Religion and Culture* 5 (1991): 99.

102. A. MacIntyre, "Politics, Philosophy, and the Common Good," in *The MacIntyre Reader,* ed. K. Knight (Notre Dame: University of Notre Dame Press, 1998), pp. 234-52.

components. One's conduct at work is assessed as if unlinked to consequences in the larger economic sphere; policy is unmoored from those affected by it. This makes societal functioning impossible because these spheres and complexities are in fact interwoven, and principles that take this into account are needed to guide one throughout society's interdependent arenas. First among these principles, MacIntyre holds, is that human life is not disconnected but life in common.

Like Taylor, MacIntyre is concerned that, with its increasingly individualist emphasis, the West is losing the ontology that makes the West possible — the idea of a shared future and goals and agreement on the virtues needed to achieve them.[103] It is, on his view, a failure across the political spectrum. He lambastes "liberal, conservative, radical, or socialist" proposals: "the tradition of the virtues is at variance with the central features of the modern economic order and more especially its individualism, its acquisitiveness, and its elevation of the values of the market to a central social place."[104]

Yet, this is not the whole of MacIntyre's story. While he writes of the "embedded" self, this "does not entail that the self has to accept the moral *limitations* of the particularity of those forms of community.... Rebellion against my identity is always one possible mode of expressing it."[105] Here MacIntyre recognizes the (separable) person able to act in ways different from her place and past. If this were not the case, her conduct would not be labeled rebellious. Like Sandel, he prizes her ability to judge and adjust the status quo. In the end, MacIntyre writes, "In order to flourish, we need both those *virtues that enable us to function as independent and accountable practical reasoners and those virtues that enable us to acknowledge the nature and extent of our dependence on others.*"[106]

Absent some possibility of independent reasoning and change, MacIntyre, like Burke and Marx, might not have written his books. There would be no point to his critique of the West if the West could not change and separate from the fatal separability he describes. But MacIntyre is not fatalistic. He bothers to write so that we reject self-absorption and choose care of the commons that fosters the self. *Indeed, he is counting on our separating from our present separability — counting on separability to take the West back to its situatedness.*

---

103. A. MacIntyre, "The Virtues, and Unity of a Human Life and the Concept of Tradition," in *Liberalism and Its Critics*, pp. 141-42.

104. A. MacIntyre, "Justice as Virtue: Changing Conceptions," in *Communitarianism and Individualism*, p. 64.

105. MacIntyre, *After Virtue*, p. 205.

106. A. MacIntyre, *Dependent Rational Animals: Why Human Beings Need the Virtues* (London: Duckworth, 1999), pp. 155-56.

CHAPTER 6

Concluding Thoughts on Separability and Situatedness

"It ain't what you got. It's who you know and what they got."[1]

In *We Have Never Been Modern*,[2] Bruno Latour notes that, while Western modernity presents separability as a linchpin achievement, it has always been inseparable from situatedness amid society and transcendent. To Latour's observations this volume has added an ontology of distinction-amid-relation: Latour found a separability-situatedness meld in the modern period because the meld is our usual human condition. In certain times and places, we take it into account in our practices and institutions; in others, less so. But significant univocality, be it of separability or situatedness, is out of whack with the human situation.

The previous two chapters reviewed the work of thinkers considered advocates of one or the other "side" but who, on close reading, proposed a meld. There are arguments against my claim, one being that some of modernity's influential thinkers were in fact one-sided, and to be sure, some have been. The point of the preceding chapters, however, was to identify those who did not think in such binary terms. By noting the historical circumstances, we can distinguish between thinkers who argued one-sidedly and those who championed one position to offset strong demands from the other, their arguments being a pull toward the middle and meld.

---

1. *Maid in Manhattan* (motion picture), directed by W. Wang, produced by R. Baratta and E. Goldsmith-Thomas (Los Angeles: Columbia Pictures/Sony Pictures Entertainment, 2002).

2. B. Latour, *We Have Never Been Modern*, trans. C. Porter (Cambridge: Harvard University Press, 1991, 1993).

Locke, one of the misread, defended individual "property"[3] not as self-absorbed accumulation but rather as life and liberty.[4] He aimed at defending the earnings of commoners from aristocratic appropriation and held that the life of liberty was conditioned on societally minded virtues taught in family, church, and community. Adam Smith argued for greater economic separability to broaden opportunity for commoners, who had been abandoned and impoverished by the land enclosures of the preceding centuries.[5] However critical of capitalism, Luigino Bruni nonetheless writes, "the wound that Smith saw and wanted to avoid by recourse to the mediation of the market is . . . the wound I receive from power asymmetry."[6] Moreover, Smith required that markets be situated in and checked by societal affections and responsibilities (virtues). While his contemporary Antonio Genovesi held that contracts themselves could be based on relationality (Smith was less convinced), both men identified reciprocal concern as necessary to the success of markets and human living.[7]

In the nineteenth century, John Stuart Mill's defense of liberalism did not aim for individualist disregard of society but aimed against the abuses of hierarchy in the public and familial spheres. Under the tutelage of his wife, Harriet Taylor, Mill supported the cooperative movement in England, which developed business models on the reciprocal concern among stakeholders. If capitalists worked in their businesses, he argued, and if workers owned part of them, class conflict would evolve into new forms of cooperation and business enterprise. His support for women's rights emerged from the same concern to eradicate unjust hierarchies.

To be sure, ideas have legs, and one might correctly argue that the ideas of Locke, Smith, and Mill evolved into present, undue separability. But mutation is not origin. Our present separability is a situation these earlier moderns would neither recognize nor recommend. They argued for greater separability in a context of substantial situatedness, which they applauded and relied on.

3. See, for instance, W. Hamacher, "The Right Not to Use Rights," in *Political Theologies: Public Religions in a Post-Secular World*, ed. H. de Vries and L. E. Sullivan (New York: Fordham University Press, 2006), pp. 671-90.

4. J. Locke, *Two Treatises of Government*, ed. P. Laslett (Cambridge: Cambridge University Press, 1988; original 1690), paras. 124, 123.

5. See, for instance, A. Linklater, *Owning the Earth: The Transforming History of Land Ownership* (London: Bloomsbury, 2014).

6. L. Bruni, *The Wound and the Blessing: Economics, Relationships, and Happiness*, trans. N. M. Brennen (Hyde Park, N.Y.: New City Press, 2012), p. 18.

7. Bruni, *Wound and the Blessing*, p. 64.

In parallel fashion, those discussed in chapter 5 argued not for maximum situatedness but to forestall the raveling separability that left few responsible for the poverty following land foreclosures and the appalling exploitation of early capitalism. They took aim at those economics, at the chaos of the French Revolution, and at the "solution" to that chaos in imperialist, Napoleonic dictatorship that would impose itself on much of Europe. Similarly, many present-day arguments for situatedness seek not to hobble the individual but to ensure well-being and opportunity against the self-absorption described by Greg Smith and David Frum, among others (see pt. I, ch. 3). Just as the policies of Locke, Smith, Mill, and Rawls would not yield anomie or greed if taken seriously, the proposals of Burke, the Romantics, MacIntyre, and post-structuralists would not yield oppression. None today would roll back our bills of rights or require that people remain in the communities or traditions of their forefathers, as Burke himself did not. Indeed, key to Taylor and MacIntyre's critique is that we are losing situatedness in the cultures and capacities that enable the separability of freedom.

Another complaint against my position is to concede my point about authorial intent but to hold that at issue is not intent but consequence. Once an idea, however well-meaning, is unleashed, it may be used for one position or the other of the binary choice. It is true that ideas influence the future in unforeseeable ways, but perhaps this is the point. They are unforeseeable, and thus reading original texts as accurately as possible is needed to forestall later misreads and importantly the projection of later beliefs onto earlier ones. Just as Burke, Ruskin, and Taylor do not condemn us to only ancestral station, so Locke, Smith, and Rawls do not condemn us to no station whatsoever. It is the projection of present-day separability onto Smith that establishes him as the guru of greed. In a society less separability-minded than our own, he might be read for his communal theory of moral development and for moral limits on the market.

The impulse to validate new ideas (such as present separability) by projecting them back into history (thus hopefully adding to their gravitas) is itself a maneuver of incautious separability. It unmoors us from the past as it was and loses us the sagacity of earlier precepts that don't conform to current trends. What's sacrificed can be illustrated by the history of the term "liberty," widely considered both code for separability and its politico-legal protector.[8] Samuel Huntington, for instance, holds that the meaning of the term

---

8. Among classic academic texts, see D. Himmelfarb, "Freedom, Virtue, and the Founding Fathers: A Review Essay," *Public Interest* 90 (Winter 1988): 15-120, here p. 117; I. Kramnick,

has more or less remained constant, and thus we can take its present, high-separability gloss as the meaning it always had. He writes, though "ideals such as liberty and equality acquire different meanings through their application in new contexts, the core meaning of the value remains."[9]

Setting aside "liberty" in the medieval and ancient worlds and looking only at the modern, the word has nonetheless pointed to very different ideals and practices. Override them with present-day meanings, and we lose the others. As we've seen, until the mid–nineteenth century, "liberty" was thought to be not roaming individual will but the privilege of using carefully tutored reason for virtue and the common good. In a letter most likely by Henry Brooke (1759), "Perfect Liberty" is defined as "the Latitude of voluntary Conduct informed by Reason, and limited by Duty."[10] Even the revolutionary advocate of liberty Sam Adams in 1770 asked, "where did you learn that in a state or society you had a right to do as you please? . . . Be pleased to be informed that you are bound to conduct yourselves as the Society with which you are joined."[11]

After the Revolution, when many British conventions were thrown off, this duty-bound notion of liberty was not. Jonathan Boucher explained in 1797, "true Liberty, is a liberty to do every thing that is right, and being restrained from doing any thing that is wrong. So far from our having a right to do every thing that we please, under a notion of liberty, liberty itself is limited and confined."[12] The Federal Farmer in 1787 declared that very few rights "are natural and inalienable, of which even the people cannot deprive individuals." To the contrary, he claimed, most rights associated with liberty — including trial by jury and *habeas corpus* protections — were constitutional, thus societal, and could thus be altered or rescinded by society.[13] Even freedom of religion

---

Republicanism and Bourgeois Radicalism: Political Ideology in Late Eighteenth Century England and America (Ithaca, N.Y.: Cornell University Press, 1990), p. 198.

9. S. Huntington, *American Politics: The Promise of Disharmony* (Cambridge: Harvard University Press, 1981), p. 23.

10. H. Brooke, *Liberty and Common-sense to the People of Ireland, Greeting* (London: J. William, 1759/1760), letter 2, p. 6; Ambrose Searle echoed the sentiment; see A. Searle, *Americans against Liberty; or, An Essay on the Nature and Principles of True Freedom*, 2nd ed. (London: J. Mathews, 1776), p. 8.

11. *The Writings of Samuel Adams*, ed. H. Cushing, vols. 1-4 (New York: Octagon Books, 1968), p. 5.

12. J. Boucher, *On Civil Liberty, Passive Obedience, and Non-Resistance*, in *A View of the Causes and Consequences of the American Revolution: In Thirteen Discourses, 1763-1775* (New York: Russell and Russell, 1967; original 1797), p. 511.

13. Federal Farmer, Letter VI, in *The Anti-Federalist*, ed. Herbert Storing (Chicago: University of Chicago Press, 1985; original 1787), p. 70.

was assumed to apply to believers whose strong faith led them to duty and ethical conduct. Finally, liberty of this era included some of the individual rights associated with liberty today, but these applied only to certain persons, distinguished by property, gender, profession, and race.

Though liberty in the nineteenth century came to mean greater individual mobility and nonconformity, still in 1839, Michael Chevalier noted, as his compatriot Tocqueville had, "the system of government in this country is therefore, not so much a system of absolute liberty and free will, as a system of equality . . . [that] takes the character of a strong rule by the majority." The majority he refers to is not 51 percent of unconnected individuals but the town, county, and state councils and church committees that had significant sway over the individual person.[14] Twenty years later, in the buildup to and during the Civil War, the South held that it was defending the independence of these corporate bodies (not individuals) against the tyranny of central government. The North saw its mission similarly, holding that the Confederacy was factional and unconcerned with the good of the societal whole.

Comparing these meanings of liberty to each other and to meanings commonly used today suggests, if nothing else, the unusefulness of imagining a univocal understanding of liberty through American history, much less through the history of the modern West. In such impoverished univocity, the range of the term's application is lost, including the many applications that assumed values and duties without which persons would not have been trusted to act on their own, at liberty. It was the values and responsibilities to the commons that conditioned living in freedom.

As liberty has for much of modernity been enmeshed with responsibility and relationality, Jean-Claude Michea's critique of its excessive form — "liberalism" in his words — may too easily let us off the hook. He holds that the undue separability of "liberalism" was an unavoidable, historical progression through modernity starting from the assumptions of Hobbes and Locke. But if excessive "liberalism" does not derive from the seventeenth century but appears only later in the modern period, after centuries of separability-situatedness melds, it may be the result not of organic progression but of a recent, active hacking away at situatedness. In short, of more recent and nefarious doings.

In *The Realm of Lesser Evil*, Michea describes the West today as heir to a five-hundred-year-old separability: the individual rights of early political lib-

---

14. M. Chevalier, *Society, Manners, and Politics in the United States* (New York: Augustus M. Kelley, 1966; original 1839), pp. 336-37.

eralism (Locke, Montesquieu) yielded the individual selfishness of today's neo-liberal economics. Those thinkers who held to liberalism's mutual constitution with situatedness did so, on Michea's account, only as they were impelled by the vestiges of premodern forces. They were in any case pursuing a lost cause because, Michea writes, "the soulless world of contemporary capitalism is the only historical form in which this *original liberal doctrine* could be realized in practice."[15] The slide from early political liberalism to today's neoliberal economics was inescapable: early moderns unwittingly slipped self-absorbed greed in with the Trojan gift of political rights.

Michea's critique of the present day is serious, yet matters may be worse than he says. If today we are mere heirs of a mess, we are at least not culpable; perhaps we are fine fellows who wish to fix it. However, we may not have inherited a mess but made one. If many modern thinkers have for five hundred years proposed a variety of separability/situatedness melds *against* forces pushing to undue separability, then today's separability is not the result of unfortunate heritage and bad *Bildung*. It is cultural violence, hacking off half of our history — the mutual constitution with situatedness — for an undue separability that had not been before. This possibility gains credence when we recall the many advocates of liberalism and separability who assumed such a meld — in the seventeenth through twentieth centuries (ch. 4 above) and among recent Republicans like Dwight Eisenhower, David Frum, and Mike Stafford (ch. 3). *If separability-amid-situatedness is the West's history, those who ignore it are not following tradition but dismembering it.*

The second half of this book will look at one framework, relationality in the Judeo-Christian traditions, that may help preserve this separability-amid-situatedness heritage and may help foster the well-being of distinct persons, even those rather different from oneself, amid or through reciprocal consideration-worthiness.

---

15. J.-C. Michea, *The Realm of Lesser Evil: An Essay on Liberal Civilization*, trans. D. Fernbach (Malden, Mass.: Polity Press, 2009), p. 2, emphasis mine.

PART II

Theologies of Relationality

Separability-amid-Situatedness or Distinction-amid-Relation in Theological Voice

Faith must inhabit the world and give back to God the being he has not.[1]

As we turn to theologies of relationality themselves — to distinction-amid-relation in theological voice — it's perhaps worth reprising that this book investigates contemporary theologies nondenominationally as they have drawn and built upon tradition. This investigation is neither a general overview of Judaic and Christian thought nor a comprehensive genealogy of relationality but rather a look at some of the key voices of the relational approach. With the exception of Thomas Aquinas's *analogia entis*, those voices are mostly in primary biblical sources and the rabbinic and early church period, as these undergird relational thinking since. As this volume is interested in the guidance relational theologies offer to current public policy, the last set of voices is Christian and Jewish thinkers of the twentieth and twenty-first centuries.

The point is not that relational interpretations of Judeo-Christian thought have been the only ones; the point is, rather, to look at signposts on the landscape of those interpretations that are relational. It is of course my selection of signposts; other writers would make different choices. The voices here, while all contributors to relationality, are not limited to one tradition or school but emerge from a number of starting points and standpoints. It is part of this book's methodology to draw on this wide range of writers whose work may

---

1. Stanislas Breton, cited in R. Kearney, "Sacramental Aesthetics," in *Transcendence and Phenomenology*, ed. P. Candler and C. Cunningham (London: SCM, 2007), p. 354.

not be "in conversation" or neatly congruent and may in places conflict. Yet their ideas about distinction-amid-relation share a family resemblance, and the emphasis here is on the affinity and illumination among them. While differences are not smoothed over by ideas in common, they need not be for common positions to remain clear and important; neither are common ideas erased by differences and debates (which are given more attention in the notes for the interested reader). The methodology of this book, then, reflects its *telos* to show a range of (distinct) ideas in relation.

That key ideas about distinction-amid-relation run throughout this broad array of writings offers some evidence that they are ontology and theology rather than personal opinion: people from different eras and intellectual and faith traditions have come to them and describe them similarly. If distinction-amid-relation is found so broadly and is seen so widely as a correct description of our basic condition, it might be because it is. This is not to say that groups and cultures understand our human circumstances in the same ways. Indeed, the plurality of our efforts to discover how the world works is part of how the world works. Yet the thing about which our approaches and understanding are plural is world. The suggestion here is that the distinction-amid-relation is basic to it.

I have just said that though our approaches to discovering our ontology are many, the thing we are aiming at is ontology The inverse is also central to theologies of relationality: though we are aiming at ontology, our plural efforts are critical to getting at it, as no one alone suffices. Though we in the modern era are used to relying on the empirical sciences for knowledge of what is, imagery, allegory, metaphor, and narrative also contribute substantially. "What is obvious in knowing is, indeed, looking," Bernard Lonergan wrote in his critique of relying only on scientific observation for truths about world. "But empiricism amounts to the assumption that what is obvious in knowing is what knowing obviously is."[2] It is a tenet of Lonergan's and of *distinction-*amid-relation that plurality of interpretation —the use of science, art, humanities, and theology — is needed to discern what is. "There must be rejected," Robert Doran writes in his work on Lonergan, "the possibility of some single definitive *Summa* of theological understanding."[3] Even to the question of why there is plurality there are plural responses. The alternative is absolutism, the

2. *The Lonergan Reader,* ed. E. Morelli and M. Morelli (Toronto: University of Toronto Press, 1997), p. 245.

3. R. Doran, *What Is Systematic Theology?* (Toronto: University of Toronto Press, 2005), p. 145.

dead end of knowledge. "If divinity is unknowable," Richard Kearney writes, "humanity must imagine it in many ways. The absolute requires pluralism to avoid absolutism."[4]

The Bible opens with this idea in its plural accounts of creation. "It is of the essence of what we mean when we speak of something as being biblical in character," Yoram Hazony writes, "that it presents its truth by means of a diversity of views."[5] The rabbis added that each line of the Torah has seventy interpretations; Ibn Rushd (Averroës) argued against absolutist notions of God and for a critical interpretation of religious texts. As each person sees the world from her perspective, plural, possibly correct ideas will emerge; for instance, Newton's and Leibniz's independent proofs of the calculus are each correct yet different. Emmanuel Levinas saw plurality as following from humanity's role as God's co-creator, each person bringing forth certain aspects of creation's possibilities, of what can be.[6] Or, as General George Patton noted, "If everybody is thinking alike, then somebody isn't thinking."[7]

While multiple approaches may be simultaneously correct, plurality of effort helps also with those that are incorrect. David Kraemer notes that what we have of the divine is in texts, which require interpretation, and this "was (and remains) a profoundly human activity. . . . Humans are, by definition, imperfect; it is this that distinguishes them from God. Human interpretations must also, therefore, be imperfect, and even, on frequent occasions perhaps, wrong."[8] It is the accumulation of efforts that gets at an understanding of world

---

4. R. Kearney, *Anatheism: Returning to God after God* (New York: Columbia University Press, 2009), Kindle location 137. "No human," he continues, "can be absolutely sure about absolutes" (Kindle location 314). Writing even about orthodoxy, Graham Ward notes that our knowledge of world and God comes from our texts of revelation understood on "the basis of faith." And faith "is a courageous groping towards promises in Christ that may or may not have been understood." It is "an endless formulation and reformulation," an "ongoing set of interrelated activities," and a "process" completed "only when time and creation itself come to their completion. . . . When it stops being a process of discernment and it starts being an ideology then orthodoxy is reified; and reification is always possible and, when it occurs, always dangerous." G. Ward, "Receiving the Gift," *Modern Theology* 30, no. 3 (2014): 84.

5. Y. Hazony, *The Philosophy of Hebrew Scripture* (Cambridge: Cambridge University Press, 2012), p. 227.

6. E. Levinas, "Revelation in the Jewish Tradition," in *Beyond the Verse: Talmudic Readings and Lectures*, trans. G. Mole (Bloomington: Indiana University Press, 1994), p. 133.

7. G. S. Patton Jr., *Quotes;* retrieved from http://www.goodreads.com/author/quotes/370054.George_S_Patton_Jr_, first quote.

8. D. Kraemer, *The Mind of the Talmud: An Intellectual History of the Bavli* (New York: Oxford University Press, 1990), p. 121.

and our circumstances, as the multiplicity itself is one way each perspective self-corrects and deepens.[9]

Moreover, in one's investigations, one need not embrace all facets of an idea to learn from some of them. This is especially important when reading premodern texts where passages are redacted from asynchronous sources and where philosophical concepts are often anthropomorphized and woven into allegories and narratives.[10] Readers have understood these as illuminating imagery and truth and — though these two readings are quite different activities — in both instances have learned much about the human condition.

On the theological view, to claim complete truth is self-divination and idolatry. We must thus content ourselves with a certain epistemological humility, with the possibility that quite different positions will be as right as (or righter than) our own, that our beliefs will be confirmed, falsified, or amended, and importantly, that *aporia* today will be resolved in ways we cannot yet configure. This book says a few things about distinction-amid-relation, but these are but a bit of what can be known about it. As Ronald Thiemann reminds us, "Not only does the Christian gospel make no a priori denial of the possibility of God's self-revelation to persons in different times and places, it alerts Christians to the continuous possibility that God's revelation is likely to appear where we least expect it."[11] The idea is shared by the Chief Rabbi of the United Hebrew Congregations of the Commonwealth, Lord Jonathan Sacks; "truth emerges," Sacks writes, "from the quite different process of letting our world be enlarged by the presence of others who think, act, and interpret reality in ways radically different from our own."[12]

---

9. Daniel Migliore writes, "Christians will engage in testing other religious communities in the light of the gospel, even as Christians must be willing to have their doctrines and practices tested by others." D. Migliore, "The Trinity and the Theology of Religions," in *God's Life in Trinity,* ed. M. Volf and M. Welker (Minneapolis: Augsburg Fortress, 2006), p. 116.

10. For a discussion of the various interpretations of anthropomorphized images, see, for instance, A. Gottstein, "The Body as Image of God in Rabbinic Literature," *Harvard Theological Review* 87 (1994): 171-95; C. Markschies, "God's Body: A Neglected Dimension of Ancient Christian Religion and Theology" (paper presented at a meeting of the North American Patristics Society, Chicago, 2014).

11. R. Thiemann, "Beyond Exclusivism and Absolutism," in *God's Life in Trinity,* ed. M. Volf and M. Welker (Minneapolis: Augsburg Fortress, 2006), p. 128.

12. J. Sacks, *The Dignity of Difference: How to Avoid the Clash of Civilizations* (London: Continuum, 2007), p. 23.

Distinction-amid-Relation in Theological Voice

On the Judeo-Christian account of distinction-amid-relation, all beings come to be by partaking of God, the source of being, the reason why there is anything at all (something rather than nothing) and why there are the particular things that are. Richard Taylor gets at this in his story of a man out for a walk who comes upon a large translucent sphere in the middle of a wood. He would naturally wonder what it is and how it got there — which might be aptly asked, Taylor notes, about anything at all, about everything we come upon.[13] The answer, Ian Barbour suggests, is the "structuring cause" of all unfolding possibilities or "designer of a self-organizing process,"[14] something like the cause of causes or condition for what is now and what may become.[15] Not simply one more and the largest of earthly causal factors, it is the *causa in esse* (ground for being itself) rather than *causa in fieri* (a force that effects change or becoming but not being itself). It is the prime cause of all possibility and the world's unfolding (rather than secondary causes that have effects within an already existing setup).

German theologian Christian Link speaks of the world as a "parable" of God and as a place where traces of God may be found.[16] He cannot be found in the characters, scenery, or parable plot any more than Shakespeare can be found in his plays (not even at the beginning of the tale). Yet he is there throughout and the reason for their existence. Franz Rosenzweig called it "the eventfulness of the limitless possibilities that will come to exist, the

13. R. Taylor, *Metaphysics* (Englewood Cliffs, N.J.: Prentice-Hall, 1992), pp. 100-103.

14. I. Barbour, *When Science Meets Religion: Enemies, Strangers, or Partners?* (San Francisco: HarperSanFrancisco, 2000), p. 164.

15. On the same theme, Milbank writes, "the higher cause is a 'flowing into' the entire lower causal scenario, such that it conditions, at a qualitatively higher level, *both* the lower effect *and* the lower cause, just as the sun's heat has already determined in large part the shapes taken by the surface of the earth which allows plants to grow within it." See J. Milbank, *Beyond Secular Order: The Representation of Being and the Representation of the People* (Chichester: Wiley Blackwell, 2014), p. 42; see also pp. 42-49. Robert Sokolowski's (and later David Burrell's) dubbing this view of God as the "Christian distinction" intends to distinguish it from the Platonic idea of many divine forces and from certain Neoplatonic claims of the necessity of creation (by force of matter rather than from God's will). However, this overlooks this view of God in the Judaic tradition; see R. Sokolowski, *The God of Faith and Reason: Foundations of Christian Theology* (Washington, D.C.: Catholic University of America Press, 1995); D. Burrell, "The Christian Distinction Celebrated and Expanded," in *Faith and Freedom: An Interfaith Perspective* (Oxford: Blackwell, 2004).

16. C. Link, *Die Welt als Gleichnis: Studien zum Problem der natürlichen Theologie* (Munich: Kaiser, 1976).

not-nothing that is the 'divine essence in all infinity' prior to there being a distinct something or a distinct nothing."[17] Importantly, it is, after kabbalah and F. W. J. Schelling, that which self-externalizes, not what precedes what is, but what is realized as it yields what is. It makes sense, David Bentley Hart writes, "to ask what illuminates an object, but none to ask what illuminates light."[18] It also makes little sense, he notes, to reject the notion of an undergirding structure (or ground for there being something rather than nothing) in an attempt at "scientific" truth since the reason that there are phenomena to scientifically study at all is that structuring ground. "If one refuses to believe in God out of one's love of the truth, one affirms the reality of God in that very act of rejection."[19]

This idea of God amends the emanationist theory of the third-century philosopher Plotinus, who held that the universe "comes forth," overflows, or emanates from the One source of all being. His idea was at once attractive to theologians of the Abrahamic traditions but also problematic in its description of an automatically emanating creation, rendering creation an inevitable result of natural phenomena, removing divine decision, and making emanated beings the same as the One from which they mechanistically emanated.[20] Addressing this idolatrous notion, the medieval Islamic philosopher ibn Sina highlighted the radical, immutable "distinction" between the One source and all else — no automatic overflowing of sameness. He did so by reworking Aristotle's discussion of existence (being at all) and essences (the features that make something what it specifically is). While material beings exist *and* have essences/specific features, the One source has no such binary: essence and existence are one, the Islamic idea of divine unity, *tawhid*.

With this radical distinction, ibn Sina removed the possibility of seeing the One source as mechanistically outpouring into beings such that One source and beings are the same nature. Maimonides continued the idea, writing that, unlike humans, in God, "essence and existence are perfectly identi-

---

17. Elliot R. Wolfson, *Giving beyond the Gift: Apophasis and Overcoming Theomania* (New York: Fordham University Press, 2014), Kindle location 2812.

18. D. B. Hart, *The Experience of God: Being, Consciousness, Bliss* (New Haven: Yale University Press, 2013), p. 143.

19. Hart, *The Experience of God*, p. 250.

20. The emanationist notion flies in the face also of each divine decision for change and intervention, for instance, in noticing in Genesis that "it is not good" that Adam is alone and in thus creating Eve. See T. Fretheim, *God and World in the Old Testament: A Relational Theology of Creation* (Nashville: Abingdon, 2005), Kindle location 1092.

cal."[21] Aquinas held that in God, existence is an "act" that transcends the binary of unchanging, eternal being and changing essences or features.

The development of this Muslim, Jewish, and Christian thought secures two principles: one, that in God, existence is an act, not a passive, automatic emanation, and two, that since God is the unity of being and essences, his act self-expresses both as well, both being and all possible (changing) essences. In a word, this is creation (not automaticity), the divine act of self-expressing. While Aristotle had seen the universe's basis as whatever exists in *itself,* ibn Sina, Maimonides, and Aquinas saw world as *partaking* of the One source that self-unfolds being and differentiated beings. In Aquinas's words, "the very existence of creatures is to-be-related to their creator."[22]

Said another way, as a condition of being at all, humanity partakes of the source of all existence and differentiation — or, more poetically, we are in his image. What we partake of is distinction-amid-relation. On one hand, we partake of the One source of being in order to exist at all, yet this source is radically distinct and different from us. While it self-expresses in yielding world, it remains radically other. We partake of a source — we are in a "partaking" relationship — that is yet ever distinct. This distinction yet partaking/relation is the way anything comes to be. The *structure* of being is thus distinction-amid-relation.

From the human perspective, we partake of or are in the image of this self-expressive unfolding. From the "perspective" of the source of being, it kenotically self-empties or expresses itself in material beings as a timeless "donative outgoing" that is or "harbors" the potential for all particular beings in all their singular differences.[23] Each person is a singular expression of this source, an instance of what can be; each particular being, item, language, and culture gives a bit more concrete expression to all that can be. Maurice Merleau-Ponty writes, "There is a sort of impotence of God without us, and Christ attests that God would not be fully God without becoming fully man. . . . Transcendence no longer hangs over man; he becomes, strangely, its privileged bearer."[24]

21. M. Maimonides, *Guide for the Perplexed,* trans. A. H. Friedländer (New York: Dover, 1956), bk. 1, ch. 57.

22. Aquinas, *Summa Theologica* 1.45.3.

23. J. Milbank, "Christianity and Platonism in East and West," in *Divine Essence and Divine Energies: Ecumenical Reflections on the Presence of God in Eastern Orthodoxy,* ed. C. Athanasopoulos and C. Schneider (Cambridge: James Clarke, 2013), p. 177.

24. M. Merleau-Ponty, *Signs,* trans. R. McCleary (Evanston, Ill.: Northwestern University Press, 1964), p. 71. Kearney parses Merleau-Ponty's text, "to equate God with a timeless, otherworldly Being that is sovereign cause of itself and has no desire for nature or humanity

Augustine got at this — the expression of the source of being in particular beings — by looking at God, persons, and language. He noted that a person uses words to refer to the meaning that something has for her. One person may be "cousin" to family but "mathematician" to colleagues. Yet, she is also more than these features and their unique combination. The "more" is what of the source of being is "innermost" in her, which she can always potentially express more of and become something beyond what she at present is. The distinction between a person's topical features and the "more" is what Aquinas called the difference between one's characteristic "essences" and one's being-from-God "existence." In the twentieth century, Rosenzweig distinguished between "personality" and the "self" that resists pigeonholing and is irreplaceable.[25] The British Catholic theologian Nicholas Lash (following Hermann Cohen and Martin Buber) calls relating to features an I-It encounter, engaging the "more" as I-Thou, God's presence in the other.[26]

Yet God's being "innermost" in persons, a commonality among us, does not collapse us into each other or into the divine, in idolatry or pantheism. The differences characteristic of each being are part of what it means to be of God; his donative self-expression is, in world, distinction and differentiation. Each person is of this "donative outgoing" yet her distinct self, as a child is "of" her parents and could not come into being on her own yet is not conflatable with them or with siblings, who too are of the same parents. Indeed, the more each is uniquely herself, the more she is a singular expression of the source of being.[27] Hart calls this "one very delightful consequence . . . the more we become the particular beings that we are, the more we show forth (precisely through our 'infinite difference' from God) the being of God."[28] Or, as Paul Tillich wrote, "By affirming our being we participate in the self-affirmation of being-itself."[29]

— as Descartes and the rationalists did — is to reject the sanctity of the flesh"; see Kearney, *Anatheism*, Kindle location 2073.

25. See E. Santner, *On the Psychotheology of Everyday Life: Reflections on Freud and Rosenzweig* (Chicago: University of Chicago Press, 2001), pp. 72-80; for a summary of these distinctions, see S. Ticciati, "The Castration of Signs: Conversing with Augustine on Creation," *Modern Theology* 23, no. 2 (April 2007): 161-79.

26. N. Lash, *Easter in Ordinary: Reflections on Human Experience and the Knowledge of God* (Notre Dame: University of Notre Dame Press, 1988), pp. 202, 214, 221-31, 283; for his discussion of Buber, see chs. 13 and 14.

27. See Milbank, "Christianity and Platonism," pp. 198-99.

28. D. B. Hart, *In the Aftermath: Provocations and Laments* (Grand Rapids: Eerdmans, 2009), p. 173.

29. P. Tillich, *The Courage to Be* (New Haven: Yale University Press, 1951, 2008), p. 181.

The source of being, God, expresses himself in particular beings despite the radical differences of corporeality/incorporeality, finitude/infinitude. The kabbalist concept of Ein Sof, the without-end, describes the One source from which there are the many differentiated beings: "the (non) essence of the One must be reckoned from the absolute incommensurability of individual entities."[30] In Aquinas's words, "In all things, God himself is properly the cause of universal being which is innermost in all things . . . in all things God works intimately."[31] God self-expresses in particulars also without being exhausted — an idea drawn from the Judaic and theurgic Neoplatonist traditions, where being is the ever-outpouring activity of its source. "From His transcendence beyond all," the Church Father Dionysius the Areopagite writes, "He is brought down to that which is in all, in accordance with this ecstatic and supersubstantial power of remaining."[32]

As we are differentiated beings, partaking of the One source of being is a case of *nonidentical repetition*. We express something of source but not by becoming miniature replicas of it, not proportionally, not with the same features, only smaller. We partake of it as an analogy expresses its referent, with different features but an undergirding of-a-kind-ness, thus preserving Augustine's *maior dissimilitudo* (God's alterity) within *tanta similitudo* (of-a-kind-ness). As Aquinas importantly described in his *analogia entis* (analogy of being): since causes yield resembling outcomes (resembling at the underlying level), humanity, caused by the source of being, God, is of an underlying resemblance to him.[33] God is immanent and intimate but ever beyond, distinct amid relation.[34] John Milbank notes, "each creature . . . is always in the direct presence of God, but equally, for the same reason, this presence is never direct, but always mediated by the participation of created structures."[35] The outpouring of being

---

30. Wolfson, *Giving beyond the Gift*, Kindle locations 6344-6346.

31. T. Aquinas, *Summa Theologica*, trans. Fathers of the Dominican English Province, vols. 1-5 (Westminster, Md.: Christian Classics, 1948; original 1265-1274), Ia, q. 105, art. 5.

32. *Divine Names* 4.13, Patrologia Graeca 3:712 A-B; cited in D. Bradshaw, *Aristotle East and West: Metaphysics and the Division of Christendom* (Cambridge and New York: Cambridge University Press, 2007), p. 181.

33. As Eph. 4:6 expresses the idea: "one God and Father of all, who is over all and through all and in all." Unless otherwise indicated, direct quotations from the Bible in this book come from the New International Version (NIV), 2011 edition.

34. As Graham Ward has pointed out, absent this distinction, there is no *gift* in the creation of particulars and persons, just the necessity, the "divine emanation," and thus there is no relationality, just auto-process, and no gift or giving for humanity to analogously express in relations with God or among persons; see Ward, "Receiving the Gift," p. 80.

35. Milbank, "Christianity and Platonism," p. 194.

goes, analogically and mediated, from God "all the way down," in Milbank's words, and participation by creatures goes "all the way up."

Analogia entis pertains not only to matériel but also to energy: while the source of energy may be eternal and unchanging, in the physical world it yields change (seasons, chemical interactions) — an idea found in Platonic ideas of causality, Aristotelian ideas about action, and the Judeo-Christian traditions, especially the Eastern Church.[36] David Bradshaw's reading of John of Damascus, monk and priest of the Eastern, Syrian church, is helpful. "For John, the divine *energia* is not simply the divine activity *ad extra* but God himself as he is participated by creatures."[37]

In sum, as both beings and processes are of the donative source of being in God and express possibilities of what can be, there is much in the world to unfold — what John Betz calls "a positive infinity."[38]

In this worldly unfolding, God, the cause of causes, sets up the basic principles, the presence of oxygen and nitrogen, for instance, while persons plant seeds and so "secondarily" cause grain to grow. This Thomist idea of "secondary causes" was developed also by the medieval Islamic philosophers al-Ash'ari and al-Ghazali, who saw humanity as "performing" what God creates. It is seen as well in the Judaic principles of co-creatorship and *tselem Elohim/imago Dei*. The *tselem/imago* holds that humanity is made — partakes of — God's image too in analogic of-a-kind-ness. Co-creatorship holds that humanity, analogously partaking of God's image, works in this world with human capacities, secondarily, to further his vision in nature and history.[39] Indeed, the point of the *tselem/imago* is that we have the capacity to do so, the "moral correspondence" *(dmuth Elohim, similitude)* to act in correspondence with the divine. As God is distinction-amid-relation, we have the moral capacity to act with regard for each person's distinction and our simultaneous interdependence. "Human beings," Terence Fretheim writes, "are not only created in the image of God (this is who they are); they are also created to be the image of God (this is

---

36. See J. Milbank, "Only Theology Saves Metaphysics," in *Veritas: Belief and Metaphysics,* ed. C. Cunningham and P. Candler Jr. (Norwich: SCM, 2007), p. 498; see also, Milbank, "Christianity and Platonism," p. 175.

37. Bradshaw, *Aristotle East and West,* p. 209.

38. J. Betz, "Beyond the Sublime: The Aesthetics of the Analogy of Being (Part Two)," *Modern Theology* 22, no. 1 (January 2006): 33.

39. "When we contingently but authentically make things and reshape ourselves through time," Milbank writes, "we are not estranged from the eternal, but enter further into its recesses by what for us is the only possible route." J. Milbank, *Being Reconciled: Ontology and Pardon,* Radical Orthodoxy (New York: Routledge, 2003), p. ix.

their role in the world)."[40] In Rahner's terms, humanity may be "asymptotically moral," possessing "asymptotic approximation" to divine vision.[41]

Partaking of divine distinction-amid-relation (in his image) is thus the ground for distinction-amid-relation among persons. "Everything may be what it is and not another thing," Colin Gunton writes, "but it is also what it uniquely is by virtue of its relation to everything else."[42] This, Douglas John Hall notes, is the import of the Bible, which is "relational through and through: this record of a people's history; these complex narratives of the often dramatic relationships . . . the whole presentation of truth in the one source they took to be absolutely and finally binding (sola Scriptura) was relational."[43] Martin Buber's conclusion is thus not surprising: "The individual is a fact of existence insofar as he steps into a living relation with other individuals."[44]

Paul noted this in his view that persons relate to each other through being of the (divine) spirit.[45] "As Paul sees human relations," Bruce Chilton writes, "one person can only know what another thinks and feels on the basis of their shared 'spirit.' 'Spirit' is the name for what links one person with another, and by means of that link we can also know what God thinks and feels."[46] As creatures of free will, we can ignore God's spirit in world as a "link" with others —we can ignore "stepping into a living relation" — but things don't go well when we do, as we then run against the divine ontology.

Merleau-Ponty[47] and others have been concerned that the concept of analogous participation in self-unfolding God compromises free will such that we can express only what has been predetermined by him.[48] Merleau-Ponty had

40. Fretheim, *God and World in the Old Testament*, Kindle location 1294-1295.

41. K. Rahner, "The Theology of Power," in *Theological Investigations*, vol. 4 (London: Darton, Longman and Todd, 1966), pp. 401, 402.

42. C. Gunton, *One, the Three, and the Many* (Cambridge: Cambridge University Press, 1993), p. 173.

43. D. J. Hall, *Imaging God: Dominion as Stewardship* (Grand Rapids: Eerdmans, 1986), pp. 113-14.

44. M. Buber, *Between Man and Man* (New York: Routledge, 1993), p. 203.

45. See, for instance, 1 Cor. 2:11: "For who knows a person's thoughts except their own spirit within them?"

46. J. Neusner and B. Chilton, *Jewish and Christian Doctrines* (New York: Routledge, 2000), p. 177.

47. M. Merleau-Ponty, *The Phenomenology of Perception*, trans. C. Smith (London: Routledge, 2002); M. Merleau-Ponty, *The Primacy of Perception and Other Essays* (Evanston, Ill.: Northwestern University Press, 1964).

48. David Abram suggests that the idea of participation, discussed by the early French anthropologist Lucien Lévy-Bruhl, is helpful in understanding what Merleau-Ponty was getting at; see D. Abram, *The Spell of the Sensuous: Perception and Language in a More-Than-Human*

little difficulty with the notion that certain life conditions (laws of nature, for instance) constrain our actions — what he called relative contingency, the idea that contingencies (whatever is changeable) are confined to certain natural limits. He was more concerned that the notion of a cause of causes limits "absolute or ontological contingency," our discussion of the meaning of existence. It teleologically directs our investigations to "God"; our discussions of life's cause and meaning must end with him. Yet it is not clear that this is so. Assuming a source of being exists, it has not stopped challengers, including Merleau-Ponty, from declaring that it doesn't, from declaring that life's causes and meaning end nowhere or natural phenomena have no ground. If one believes the source of being is God, he too has not stopped us from discounting him. It seems we need not fear we have less freedom than the (divine) setup has set up.

Those who don't recognize a source of being may thus freely continue with their understanding of world. But those who do are justified in holding that they may come to know something about that source because we and world are of it and are its analogous expression. First, as our perceptions and thinking are of the source of being, it is not external to us when we think but is itself in play. Mediated through humanness, it is "involved" in the thinking, so to speak. Hart notes that were this not the case, it would be difficult to understand how the conscious-less matter of neurological cells and processes could make the leap to conscious thought and the experience of subjectivity.[49] As by themselves no number of repetitions of conscious-less operations could produce conscious mind, whatever allows for the being of everything allows for thought and subjectivity — though the biological component parts have none. Moreover, this cause of causes grounds not only thought but the way thought is, the structure and features of thinking. Just as being is inherent in particular beings (in order for anything to be at all), the structuring cause inheres in — or is the grammar of — the particular sort of thought and consciousness that we have. It is in play as we think. As we have access to our own thoughts, we have some access to it. We are aware of our thinking *as it is being structured* by whatever structures everything and we know something of the structuring cause as we think at all and think about it. The cause of causes is, Hart writes, "the ground both of the subjective rationality of mind and the objective rationality of being, the transcendent and indwelling Rea-

---

World (New York: Vintage Books, 1996); L. Lévy-Bruhl, *How Natives Think* (Princeton: Princeton University Press, 1985), ch. 2; A. Nordlander, "The Wonder of Immanence: Merleau-Ponty and the Problem of Creation," *Modern Theology* 29, no. 2 (April 2013): 104-23.

49. See Hart, *The Experience of God*, pp. 152-272.

son or Wisdom by which mind and matter are both informed and in which both participate."[50]

Second, we can work backward, so to speak, gleaning from world to its source. "In the Hebrew Scriptures," Hazony notes, "God's wisdom and truth are, in principle, recognizable as such by human beings, according to the standards of the present world."[51] And, Jacob Neusner adds, the narratives and allegories of God's communication to us occur over and over in human life and are "paradigms" for the world's undergirding principles,[52] which are graspable with observation of world and history. We are not working in the dark, trying to parse world yet unsure if our experience in fact informs us about it. We may rely on our experience of nature and history as it teaches us about world. And should we err, later experience and thinking correct us.

Theologies of relationality, however, do not ignore the phenomenology of the last century, roughly from Edmund Husserl and Martin Heidegger on, that points to the radical otherness of being's source — alterity that suggests it is nonsense to discuss God, the "nonpresence beyond presence and absence," as Rosenzweig and Jacques Derrida called it, by observing world and history. Equally incoherent, on this view, is the idea that we can know anything about the cause of causes or its "grammar" by extrapolating from human experience, or using anthropomorphisms, metaphor, reason, or narrative. Nor do relational theologies ignore the negative, apophatic theologies (in Aquinas, Maimonides, and kabbalah), which repeat the point.[53] Jean-Luc Marion writes of the "idolatry" of "imagining oneself to have attained God and to be capable of maintaining him under our gaze, like a thing of the world."[54] Alexander Altmann and Leo Strauss similarly note that if religion

---

50. Hart, *The Experience of God*, pp. 234-35.

51. Hazony, *Philosophy of Hebrew Scripture*, pp. 231, 236.

52. This is a frequent theme in Neusner's work; see, for instance, Neusner and Chilton, *Jewish and Christian Doctrines*, p. 111.

53. The important difference between post-Heideggerian phenomenology and apophatic theology is as follows: the post-Heideggerian views hold that the source of being is an absence that can never be present — not the temporary absence of that which *could* be present but the ever absence of what can never be present. Apophatic theology holds that the source of being has a presence of some sort that humanity cannot apprehend; see Wolfson, *Giving beyond the Gift*, Kindle locations 6659-6660; T. J. Altizer, "The Impossible Possibility of Ethics," in *Saintly Influence: Edith Wyschogrod and the Possibilities of Philosophy of Religion*, ed. E. Boynton and M. Kavka (New York: Fordham University Press, 2009), p. 46. For a look at an apophatic analysis of attributing gender traits to God, see C. Keller, "The Apophasis of Gender: A Fourfold Unsaying of Feminist Theology," *Journal of the American Academy of Religion* 76 (2008): 905-33.

54. J.-L. Marion, "In the Name: How to Avoid Speaking of 'Negative Theology,'" in *God,*

is what humanity can fully grasp and express, then what, in Strauss's words, "could prevent one from taking the last step, i.e. to assert that God Himself is a product of the human mind . . . ?"[55]

Relational theologies, facing the paradox of alterity that humanity nonetheless intuits, observe that it is the case: our experience of finitude, time, and materiality has enabled the image of infinitude, eternity, and that for which the categories of finite/infinite and corporeal/incorporeal are irrelevant. The wholly-other no-thing beyond presence/absence leaves "traces," in Derrida's words, apprehendable to humanity.

Given that we have "traces" but only traces, one conclusion is that we ought not to make too much of them by inflating trace into metaphor and narrative and so squeezing the self-unfolding source of being into anthropomorphic categories. We must understand, Elliot Wolfson writes, "that vision entails seeing that one cannot see, apprehending that one cannot apprehend."[56] Heidegger felt constrained to describe Being as enabling time and as what is absent in the very givenness of its presence. Wolfson rejects *doxa*, God-talk, representation ("even the representation of nonrepresentability"),[57] and discussion of revelation.[58] He suggests that the idea of God's "gift" (of being) be scotched owing to the anthropomorphisms of "giver," gift, and "recipient." He recommends instead "givenness"[59] and describes the source of being as "unthought otherness," an approach to God that "is not anti-theological or atheistic but is a/theological."[60]

An alternate approach to the paradox of radical-otherness-yet-intuited begins with the recognition that humanity cannot think about the source of being (or anything else) in ways "beyond" our capacities. Yet this is no detraction. "We can speak," Rahner writes, "about transcendental experience only by means of what is secondary to it" — his "Christology within an evolutionary

---

the Gift, and Postmodernism, ed. J. Caputo and M. Scanlon (Bloomington: Indiana University Press, 1999), p. 34.

55. L. Strauss, *Spinoza's Critique of Religion* (New York: Schocken Books, 1965), p. 8.

56. Wolfson, *Giving beyond the Gift*, Kindle locations 286-287. Abraham Joshua Heschel wondered even if using symbolism to speak of the divine implied that God had not successfully communicated to humanity and thus whether symbolism is an "authentic category"; see A. J. Heschel, *Man's Quest for God: Studies in Prayer and Symbolism* (New York: Scribner, 1954), pp. 142-43.

57. Wolfson, *Giving beyond the Gift*, Kindle locations 7468-7469

58. See M. Henry, *The Essence of Manifestation*, trans. G. Etzkorn (The Hague: Martinus Nijhoff, 1973), p. 41.

59. Wolfson, *Giving beyond the Gift*, Kindle locations 476-483.

60. Wolfson, *Giving beyond the Gift*, Kindle location 8141.

view of the world."[61] Because "the transcendent experience of the radical nature of the Spirit is mediated through categorical objects" — what Rahner calls "complementary dependence"[62] — the ontology of world *is* that we use our human faculties to understand the radically other One even if the effort will be ever asymptotic. Indeed, absent capacity to grasp something of the cause of causes, the notion of moral conduct in correspondence with it is void, and humanity ceases to be morally accountable. Maimonides is well known for his caution against "imagining" in metaphor and anthropomorphism — God "speaks," or "loves," for instance — what we cannot know about the divine source. Yet he does not conclude that effort to understand that God's meaning or our moral accountability is pointless. He prescribes the synergistic activities of guided study and the praxis of aligning conduct with what is learned to get at what we can of God's vision.

Al-Ghazali, Maimonides, and Aquinas held that our "guide" in this is the very source of being, who is "intimate" within us as a condition of our being. Aquinas analogizes that just as sense impressions take on meaning when interpreted by human intellect, so the "prophetic visions" (sacred texts) become meaningful when study is supported by grace, God intimate within us. Thus we may reach an understanding of the source of all that is greater than human reason alone yields (*Summa Theologica* 1.12.13). The use of human language to understand sacred texts, while not literally applicable to the cause of causes, is permissible as long it is understood analogically. That is, we may speak of God "giving" or "loving." On Maimonides' view, David Burrell writes, our minds "will never be freed 'from the grip of imagination,' nor can our intellects ever claim to have grasped 'objective reality.' Indeed, with the help of our friends, we shall always be freeing whatever discourse we employ from unintended implications which imagination will spontaneously supply, just as we shall ever be directing our critical faculties to more adequate conceptualizations, as the history of science palpably reminds us."[63]

Yet this is not wasted effort in either theology or science but what we should be doing to grasp what we can, however asymptotically, of world and its source. In the words of Graham Ward, "God does not hide Godself — the gift of Godself is given absolutely." We are careful in our God-talk, he notes,

61. K. Rahner, *Foundations of Christian Faith: An Introduction to the Idea of Christianity*, trans. W. V. Dych (New York: Seabury Press, 1978), pp. 71, 178, 181, 192, 298, 301.

62. K. Rahner, "Experience of the Spirit and Existential Commitment," in *Theological Investigations*, vol. 11 (London: Darton, Longman and Todd, 1974), pp. 16, 28.

63. D. Burrell, *Towards a Jewish-Christian-Muslim Theology* (Chichester, UK, and Malden, Mass.: Wiley-Blackwell, 2011), Kindle locations 2215-2219.

to avoid mystical escapism and delusional absolutisms that lead to oppression and violence. But we are not silenced entirely because we know something of God, the self-expressing cause, from what he expresses: world (including our experience and knowledge) and revelation (sacred texts). Because the grammar of all that exists is of the cause of causes, we can "work back" from world, revelation, and human experience to source. And this allows us to use cataphatic discourse to say what we have understood.[64]

In sum, on this view, we know about world and the source of being because we are respectively in it and of it, as the *analogia entis* and *tselem/imago* suggest. And as we are of it, what we employ to understand it (logic, narrative, music) is itself analogous expression of it. Mediated through human modalities, it is so to speak involved in the process of human understanding. As Johann Georg Hamann wrote, our ideas, imagery, language, culture are themselves real, analogous expressions of self-unfolding God. Even wrong thinking occurs within the limits of being (we may err about microbes but we do not think bodies are in five dimensions). And continued thinking slowly rights it. In short, there is nothing misguided, as apophatic theology suggests, about relying on image and narrative to think not literally but *analogically* about the source of being since the world that was yielded by God's self-expression is that we do so.[65]

Kearney notes that it is especially metaphor and poetics that show us the world outside quotidian take-for-granted-ness and thus allow us to really notice it — to think about the astonishing fact of its being at all (something rather than nothing) and its source.[66] He is building on strong tradition. The idea that

---

64. Ward, "Receiving the Gift," p. 82.

65. Richard Kearney proposes one way to proceed — a "way of seeking and sounding the things we consider sacred but can never fully fathom or prove" — in *Anatheism*, Kindle location 267; see also, R. Alter, *The Art of Biblical Narrative* (New York: Basic Books, 1981, 2011); W. Brueggemann, *A Social Reading of the Old Testament: Prophetic Approaches to Israel's Communal Life* (Minneapolis: Fortress, 1994); K. J. Clark, *Return to Reason: A Critique of Enlightenment Evidentialism and a Defense of Reason and Belief in God* (Grand Rapids: Eerdmans, 1990); Hazony, *The Philosophy of Hebrew Scripture*; J. Levenson, *The Hebrew Bible, the Old Testament, and Historical Criticism: Jews and Christians in Biblical Studies* (Louisville: Westminster John Knox, 1993); R. Polzin, *Moses and the Deuteronomist: Deuteronomy, Joshua, Judges*, Literary Study of the Deuteronomic History (New York: Seabury Press, 1980); E. Stump, *Wandering in Darkness: Narrative and the Problem of Suffering* (New York: Oxford University Press, 2012); R. Whybray, *The Making of the Pentateuch: A Methodological Study* (London and New York: Bloomsbury T. & T. Clark, 1987).

66. "Poetics," he writes, "in short, makes us strangers to the earth so that we may dwell more sacramentally upon it." Kearney, *Anatheism*, Kindle location 474.

metaphor and narrative are ways of speaking about "unthought otherness" was the conclusion, for instance, of John and Charles Wesley, who supported their Christology and reliance on biblical text by holding that humanity can come to understand something of God's vision by studying the "oracles," texts, imagery, and parables brought by Jesus. Precisely these human forms of thinking lead one to God. Rosenzweig, who wrote about the divine as "nonpresence beyond presence and absence," nonetheless held to the use of images as long as we do not fix the divine to any one but recognize that they are ever our partial understandings in a metaphorical process that relies on our experience and interpretation.[67] It was the approach also of Martin Buber, who wrote,

> The designation of God as a person is indispensable for all . . . who, like myself, mean by "God" him that, whatever else he may be in addition, enters into a direct relationship to us human beings through creative, revelatory, and redemptive acts, and thus makes it possible for us to enter into a direct relationship to him. . . . The concept of personhood is, of course, utterly incapable of describing the nature of God; but it is permitted and necessary to say that God is also a person.[68]

In closing this section, we note that using human capacities to understand the unknown but intuited is the approach also of science, where experimental hunches and intuitions are expressed in metaphor and anthropomorphic images — as philosophers of science since Michael Polanyi and Thomas Kuhn have noted. Pierre de Fermat's last mathematical theorem was "intuited" in 1637 with apparently no way to know it, as the necessary math had not yet been invented. Fermat left no explanation, only his sense that it was the case. His theorem continued to be intuited but was yet unknowable for 357 years, until Andrew Wiles in 1994 solved it using math unknown in Fermat's day.

Rahner was aware of the parallel between theological and scientific approaches, writing, "It may be true, therefore, that Christian statements . . . make use of conceptual models of a mythological kind. . . . On this point it

---

67. L. Batnitzky, *Idolatry and Representation: The Philosophy of Franz Rosenzweig Reconsidered* (Princeton: Princeton University Press, 2000), pp. 20-24, 32, 53.

68. M. Buber, *I and Thou*, prologue and notes translated by W. Kaufmann (New York: Charles Scribner's Sons, 1970), pp. 180-81. Levinas too held to the rightness and need for metaphor to hear "the voice of God"; see E. Levinas, *Oeuvres 1: Carnets de captivité suivi de Écrits sur la captivité et Notes philosophiques diverses,* ed. R. Calin, preface and notes by R. Calin and C. Chalier, general preface by J.-L. Marion (Paris: Éditions Grasset & Fasquelle, 2009), pp. 432-33.

seems that, as a matter of ultimate principle, a difference of this kind, between the perceptual model and the reality to which it relates, is present even in modern physics. . . . In all this the situation is, as we have said, not such that a reality referred to could be expressed in non-image form and without the aid of such conceptual models."[69]

Analogy of Being: Man and the Divine Man

Aquinas develops his ideas about humanity analogously partaking of the divine in his discussion of man and the divine man. As the humanity of Jesus partakes of God, so does the humanity of all persons — "all the way up," to recall Milbank. In turn, as the One, source of being, inheres analogously in the humanness of Jesus, so it inheres in each of us — "all the way down." This "inhering," Aquinas holds, is not two systems, divine and human, running in parallel, but rather the unfolding of being intimately in each particular being.

Aquinas first considers Jesus: when Jesus acts, it is not a divine plus a human action, as two horses might pull a barge. That would make the actions of each parallel but separable (a view associated with the sixteenth-century philosophers Francisco Suárez and Luis de Molina). Rather, the nature of Jesus is a more enmeshed affair where the divine is expressed *through* the human — a case of influence rather than concurrence.[70] This, Aaron Riches notes, is *enhypostatos*. The human nature of Jesus has no hypostasis (subsistence) on its own (it is "anhypostatic") but "subsists only and always as the human nature of the Son of God, the second person of the Trinity (it is thus 'enhypostatic' in him)."[71] Analogously, Aquinas wrote, just as the humanity of Jesus occurs only as it partakes of God, the humanity of persons too occurs only as it analogously partakes of him: "all beings," Aquinas wrote, "apart from God are not their own being, but are beings by participation."[72] Riches parses, "the human nature of Christ only 'is' in union with the person of the Word, while creation [world, persons] only has 'being' in relation to the being of God in which it

69. K. Rahner, "Ideas for a Theology of Death," in *Theological Investigations*, vol. 13 (London: Darton, Longman and Todd, 1975), pp. 172-73.

70. This was also the view of John of Damascus; see U. M. Lang, "Anhypostatos — Enhypostatos: Church Fathers, Protestant Orthodoxy and Karl Barth," *Journal of Theological Studies* 49 (1998): 630-57.

71. A. Riches, "Christology and Anti-Humanism," *Modern Theology* 29, no. 3 (July 2013): 331.

72. Aquinas, *Summa Theologica* I, q. 44, art. 1.

participates."[73] In short, humanity too is enhypostatic in God; we are beings insofar as we analogously partake of him. We are not creatures that could be were there no divine being, creatures that might be of *natura pura.*[74]

As we've noted, from our perspective we partake of God; from God's, he self-expresses in eternal "donative outgoing." Riches notes that receiving the donation of being from another is expressed in the figure of the Virgin Mother, whose reception of divine being literally makes for new being, a new person. He notes also that the idea of persons as distinct but dependent on the donation of being contrasts with two modern ideas: that distinction requires no commonality between entities (Descartes's finding) and that freedom requires human actions to have no underlying or presupposed *telos.*[75]

The prohibition on commonality, Riches writes, problematically overlooks the possibility of *analogous* expression, which is neither separateness nor commonality but influence. We are neither the same as the source of being nor lack all commonality with him, but rather "are" through the influence of God analogously in us. The prohibition on underlying *telos* prohibits recognition of the systemic order in which we live, where certain things work and others do not. But this, Riches observes, is at odds with world. We are remarkably not in randomness but in systems of time and nature (that express the principles of their being). Our freedom is constrained by these undergirding systems that possibilize our being. Humanity is also oriented toward these systems (by natural selection and whatever set it up) — what Aquinas called grace.

One of the features of our world, Riches writes, is that each of us is a par-

73. A. Riches, "Christology and the *Duplex Hominis Beatitudo:* Re-sketching the Supernatural Again," *International Journal of Systematic Theology* 14, no. 1 (January 2012): 61.

74. In addition to Aquinas, Riches notes also the work of Cardinal Pierre de Bérulle, contemporary and teacher to Descartes, who also held that persons aren't "substances" save in relation to that which is all, God, and to the becoming-more, the realization of potential, that participating in the unfolding source of being allows. "It is not merely that the human being receives his being from another in whom he must participate in order 'to be'; but his perfectibility — the real reality of his humanness — involves a second receptivity to another . . . we can say that for Bérulle (as for Thomas Aquinas), the 'subsistence' of the human being arises from relation to the Alpha of God-the-source and the Omega of God-the-vocational-destiny." Riches, "Christology and Anti-Humanism," p. 229.

75. The requirement of no undergirding *telos* is what Servais Pinckaers calls William of Ockham's "freedom of indifference." These two linchpins of modernity are identified in D. Schindler, "The Embodied Person as Gift and the Cultural Task on America: *Status Quaestionis,*" *Communio: International Catholic Review* 35 (2008): 411, 412; see also, S. Pinckaers, O.P., *The Sources of Christian Ethics* (Washington, D.C.: Catholic University of America Press, 1995), p. 242.

ticular being "distinguishable" but "inseparable" from the source of being — in his words, "distinction-within-unity." Our being at all is "distinction-within-unity; we are 'enhypostatic' in it. At the core of our existence," he concludes, "there is no escape from gift" (of being, from the source of being, to beings),[76] and no escape from distinction-amid-relation.

What We Relate to in Distinction-amid-Relation: Bodily Neoplatonism in Theological Voice

To summarize the view from relationality so far: each singular person is of the source "structuring causality," which is radically distinct from material beings but, as it self-expresses in yielding world, particulars and persons are of it to be at all. This distinction from self-unfolding cause yet relation to it is the way anything comes to be. As there is no other way to "be," we are distinct yet in relation with other persons and world. To complete the relational circle, being in relation to others is also relationship to the source of being, God. It both expresses the structuring, original distinction-amid-relation, and is a moment of engagement with what-of-the-structuring cause inheres in them. A student I know recently said, "There is a setup to the world; I'm in it, so that setup sets me up too, and when you relate to me, you're relating to the setup that sets me up."

This view of self-unfolding being and material beings entails a reappreciation of Neoplatonic tradition away from the polarizing divisions of being/beings, spirit/matter — what Milbank calls "Platonising *in a bad sense*."[77] On this account of Plato, his description of beings taking their forms from original being/form is reinterpreted to prioritize form/transcendent over the particular and material.[78] Yet privileging being over beings — and likening only our mental/spiritual faculties to revered being — leaves the mind to

---

76. Riches, "Christology and the *Duplex Hominis Beatitudo*," p. 69.

77. Milbank, *Beyond Secular Order*, p. 33.

78. This section looks at the Christian discussion of the relationship of bodies to source of being; the Judaic discussion can be followed, for instance, in P. Brown, "Late Antiquity," in *A History of Private Life*, vol. 1, *From Pagan Rome to Byzantium*, ed. P. Aries and Georges Duby, trans. A. Goldhammer (Cambridge: Harvard University Press, Belknap Press, 1987), pp. 235-311; P. Brown, *The Body and Society: Men, Women, and Sexual Renunciation in Early Christianity*, Lectures on the History of Religion, vol. 13 (New York: Columbia University Press, 1988); and D. Boyarin, *Carnal Israel: Reading Sex in Talmudic Culture* (Berkeley and Los Angeles: University of California Press, 1993).

make decisions about material life from a rather abstracted perch. A more bodily reading of Plato, as I've called it, preserves the importance of both the unfolding source of being and material beings. Not only do particulars partake analogously of form/being, but each singular being gives expression to its self-expressing source. *In short, beings are good for being too.* Or, to reprise Merleau-Ponty, "transcendence no longer hangs over man; he becomes, strangely, its privileged bearer."[79]

All persons are its bearer, just as — if we follow Riches — Jesus was its bearer. Indeed, the unfolding source of being expressing itself in human beings is one principle of the incarnation. The source of being inheres intimately, analogously, as influence in each of us as in Jesus. In short, "Platonising *in a bad sense*" is trounced by the incarnation. "At the most basic level," Hart notes, "the belief that God himself had really assumed human flesh at once dispelled a certain antique reserve with regard to the body" — a body that is, he continues, "the real vehicle of divinization in Christ, as essential to our humanity as the rational will."[80] The spirit and mind are not above body; they are as they are by being en-bodied. Each person, Thomas Torrance writes, "is not body and mind but body of his mind and mind of his body, a unitary whole. . . . It will not allow us to go along with the dualist outlook that cuts the universe in two, a physical half and a spiritual half, and then argues that the former is a closed mechanistic system governed by rigid laws of nature, and that the latter is only a subjective realm which is not open to intelligible, let alone scientific, apprehension."[81]

James K. A. Smith's study of Augustine shows the Church Father to be not despairing of the fallen body but far more inclusive of it. Augustine notes that as we are finite, live in time, and require language to communicate (rather than live in "union" with the divine), we are not in a state of grace.[82] Yet, humanity was not sinful at creation but became so upon Adam's decision to ignore God's principles. Prior to that, humanity was sinless yet finite, material, and

---

79. Merleau-Ponty, *Signs*, p. 71. Kearney parses Merleau-Ponty's text, "to equate God with a timeless, otherworldly Being that is sovereign cause of itself and has no desire for nature or humanity — as Descartes and the rationalists did — is to reject the sanctity of the flesh"; Kearney, *Anatheism*, Kindle location 2073.

80. D. B. Hart, *Atheist Delusions: The Christian Revolution and Its Fashionable Enemies* (New Haven: Yale University Press, 2009), p. 210; see also p. 144.

81. T. Torrance, "The Goodness and Dignity of Man in the Christian Tradition," *Modern Theology* 4, no. 4 (July 1988): 310, 311, 322.

82. J. K. A. Smith, *The Fall of Interpretation: Philosophical Foundations for a Creational Hermeneutic* (Downers Grove, Ill.: InterVarsity, 2000), p. 141.

language-using.[83] Thus, humanity's materiality cannot be per se sinful. The separation of sinful body and sinless spirit does not stand theologically. Augustine notes that in Genesis, God called the material world "good" and "very good." He continues, "Matter participates in something of the ideal world, otherwise it would not be matter. . . . [A]ll existence as such is good."[84]

The alternative to bodily Neoplatonism is self-absorption. Catherine Keller notes that a denigration of particular beings in favor of being tends to an unethical neglect of worldly responsibilities, as it leaves earthly life as a mere corridor to "real," spiritual life.[85] It leaves (elevated) mind/spirit distant from (degraded) world, oddly ignorant, impotent, and unable to do much about it. Yet, on a bodily Neoplatonic account, we are analogously of donative, structuring causality, and so may learn a bit about it and the world that is of it. Mind is together with/in world and responsible for it. This, G. K. Chesterton said, is the only view congruent with experience and common sense.[86]

In Relation or on One's Own: The Example of the Sublime

The self-absorption of "Platonising *in a bad sense*" is found as well in modernity's many efforts — from Kant and Nietzsche to postmodern deconstructionists — to distinguish between the beautiful (items of excellent form, proportion, etc.) and the sublime (what shatters standing notions of form). Both the Kantian and deconstructionist approaches, Betz notes, rely on a disconnection of beings from the source of being, an unhelpful lack of analogical, relational thinking. The Kantian version comes to self-absorption that is hopefully channeled into ethics; the deconstructionist version, to self-absorption devolving into nihilism. In both cases, humanity is seen as separated from world and self-unfolding cause, unable to know anything of it and left only what we happen to make of things or happen to make up.

Kant begins with the imagination, holding that its usual task is to provide images for the mind's faculty of understanding, to help the mind understand

---

83. Indeed, Smith notes, if during the prelapsarian period humanity was not finite, temporal, and language-using, humanity would be presuming to be divine.

84. Augustine, *De vera religione*, in *Augustine: Earlier Writings*, trans. J. Burleigh (Philadelphia: Westminster, 1953; original 390), 11.21.

85. C. Keller, *On the Mystery: Discerning Divinity in Process* (Minneapolis: Fortress, 2008), p. 6.

86. G. K. Chesterton, "The Ethics of Elfland," in *Orthodoxy* (London: Bodley Head, 1957), pp. 66-103.

concepts. But in the case of the beautiful, the imagination is not impressed into this service but has "free play." Something is considered beautiful not because of anything about it but because it is an occasion for the mind's "free play" — the first level, Betz notes, of self-absorption, an occupation with one's internal conjurings, what he calls "a home-screening of one's own subjectivity." Betz writes, "The philosophical value of beauty lies in that it adumbrates yet greater capacities and power of the subject itself as *deux artifex*."[87] In this, Betz recalls Charles Taylor's description of the early modern fascination with mind — a fascination in play here in Kant's effort to underscore the freedom and autonomous capacities of the individual mind, in this case, to create beauty.

The autonomous mind is Kant's aim in his discussion of the sublime as well. By shattering the usual notions of form and excellence, the sublime shows the limits of nature and even imagination. To understand the sublime, we must turn to reason — also, Betz notes, an accolade to oneself. In the beautiful, one's imagination is applauded; in the sublime, one's reason — all told, a self-referential affair. The sublime "presents the subject with an enthralling sense of its own superiority *over* nature . . . reason's ability to legislate for itself and practically to fashion the world in its own image"[88] — again, an echo of the "immanent frame" and the early moderns' lauding of their own intellect. Rather than seeing oneself enfolded in world and structuring cause, one sees reason as a force over world and the cause of whatever it wills. In Betz's words, instead of believing in the donative being of the triune God, Kant takes faith in his trinity of imagination, understanding, and reason.

The Kantian triune god-self was radicalized in Nietzsche's "will to power." For while Kant's aim is self-determining reason that autonomously chooses beauty and morality, Nietzsche's aim is simply self-determination — or "unlimitation," as Jean-Luc Nancy writes. Nancy's work is taken up by Betz to illustrate postmodern deconstructionism, the study of all possible meanings of words and symbols as they are used in all possible personal and cultural circumstances. While in ontologies based on our enfoldedness in world and being, interpretations of world may be many, but the thing about which interpretations are many is world. One cannot say just anything, and limits to what can be said are set by what we encounter (not by the "free play" of the subjective mind). Deconstructionism turns its attention precisely toward this

---

87. J. Betz, "Beyond the Sublime: The Aesthetics of the Analogy of Being (Part One)," *Modern Theology* 21, no. 3 (July 2005): 378.

88. Betz, "Beyond the Sublime (Part One)," pp. 386, 384, 385, 387.

free play of meaning. The deconstructionist sublime, unlike Kant, reveals not the importance of reason but arbitrariness. For it shatters not only previous notions of excellence but also the notion of excellence itself — anything that would guide one to select one reading of a word/symbol over another. All are possible and equal on the landscape of one's imagination.

Though deconstructionism was intended to present the wide range of human expression and so respect humanity's varied perspectives, it ended with randomness, the unending and unendable arbitrary creating and discarding of one idea after the next — what Betz calls the autonomy of nihilism, "imago nihili."[89] Amid such a revel of indeterminacy at the level of meaning, it is difficult to imagine anything other than indeterminacy at the level of conduct, values, or standards. For not only are evil intentions possible choices, but intentionality itself is also just one possibility among many. On the deconstructionist view, the sublime "not only transcends political abuse but dethrones intentionality altogether."[90] One is left with the ethical quagmire of relativism — all actions are equal — and ontological depression. Deconstructionism moors us in immanence — a same-level-of-everything-ness, all ideas and choices equal to all others — with no call or means to discern among them. Among the results are indifference, boredom, and the inability to establish a moral code amid the global deconstructed clutter.

Postmodern deconstructionists, who are in fact neither nihilists nor self-absorbed hedonists, are concerned about justice for unheard voices. Derrida, for instance, well-intentionedly declares that the very premise of language is the "promise" of relationality — that someone grasps what one says (about justice, for instance) because one's utterances are comprehensible to others.[91] Other people's thoughts and their source in God may be ultimately unknowable, he holds, but we nonetheless hope that we can communicate and better life. "The operative distinction for Derrida," John Caputo explains, "is not between [transcendent-rich] religious faith and [transcendent-less] philosophical

---

89. Betz, "Beyond the Sublime (Part One)," pp. 395, 398; Betz notes that Heidegger's efforts to distinguish Being per se from beings also end in self-absorption because "Being, for its emphatic alterity, is ultimately nothing other than the revelation of the Being of beings' — which is the odd univocity running through all postmodern talk of ontological 'difference'" (p. 395).

90. Betz, "Beyond the Sublime (Part One)," p. 400; see also, J. Milbank, "Sublimity: The Modern Transcendent," in Transcendence: Philosophy, Literature, and Theology Approach the Beyond, ed. R. Schwartz (London and New York: Routledge, 2004), p. 271.

91. Derrida here builds on Martin Heidegger's "die Sprache spricht" (language talks) and more precisely on Paul de Man's "die Sprache verspricht" (language promises).

reason but between a more deeply lodged structural faith, more indeterminate then determinable, and the determinate faiths of the concrete messianisms."[92]

Moreover, both Derrida and Caputo note, no person is adrift in a deconstructionist sea of meanings but is rather situated in the language and values of "wherever we are," and is guided by them in her belief and practice. From this come the promise and hope of understanding, relationship, and justice.

Yet Derrida relies on this hope absent any setup that would make it more probable than marauding evil. He relies, as Caputo rightly notes, on "indeterminacy," ruling out of court the idea that one way of attaining understanding or justice might be better than another. He cannot determine any standard of "better," for he holds all possibilities to be equal and resists any determinate setup where certain things work better than others. Unanswered in Derrida's account is how, in a landscape of indeterminacy, one determines that justice has been abrogated when multiple meanings of it proliferate. Where slavery is the norm and given positive meaning, one has no means to reject it. If the solution, after Caputo and Derrida, is that slavery violates the values of "where we are," how did "where we are" get where it is? How did it get its values from amid all possible (equal) ones? Kearney is right to note that Derrida, while hoping for a just "messianic" future, "hovers in the antechamber of messianism,"[93] unable to recommend any particular course of action to bring justice closer.

In addressing these concerns, Betz suggests that neither beauty nor the sublime refers solely to what each person conjures up but are aspects of world and its donative, unfolding source. Beautiful things, excellence of worldly form, partake of this source and tell us something about it. The sublime, in shattering worldly form, suggests what of self-expressing source is beyond human comprehension. That humanity can experience the sublime, Betz writes, and apprehend something of what is beyond comprehension is grace, God's gift of self-opening to the world.

Analogy of Being: Objections and Debate

The "natural theology" of the *analogia entis* — that humanity from creation *by its nature* partakes of the source of being — was famously criticized by

---

92. J. Caputo, "What Do I Love When I Love My God? Deconstruction and Radical Orthodoxy," in *Questioning God*, ed. J. Caputo, M. Dooley, and M. Scanlon (Bloomington and Indianapolis: Indiana University Press, 2001), p. 296.

93 Kearney, *Anatheism*, Kindle location 1540.

Karl Barth, who was less optimistic about humanity's capacities since the Fall to analogously express divine being or moral vision. He thus held to revealed theology, where the principles given by God through Christ and Scripture are what humanity must rely on since our own capacities are so damaged by our wrongdoings. In the debate between Barth and the German-Polish Jesuit Erich Przywara, the latter argued that the gift of being of God is "double," coming both from *analogia entis* and from *analogia fidei* (revelation/justification and faith).[94] On his view, the grace of God's self-revelation in Christ continues and perfects the grace of creation.[95]

Barth, by contrast, was concerned that the argument from creation suggests a too-closeness between humanity and God. It does not account for humanity's fallenness and so presumes we can know about God's world and vision through analogous likeness *(imago)* rather than by relying on Scripture. In coming to his position, Barth began with Kant's idea that God is not knowable by reason, which starts with impressions or intuitions of the world, which are then interpreted by the mind's categories of understanding (space, time, etc.). As incorporeal God does not present anything to the intuition or provide sensory impressions, God does not give our mental categories anything to work with and so is not knowable to them. God then disappears from Kant's work and reappears only later, in his discussion of morality: God is the giver of the moral law, which the autonomous person using reason can recognize and embrace.

As God plays only this small role in Kant's scheme, Barth held, theology should not try to build upon it but should begin with a different premise altogether: that God exists ("God is God," as Barth put it)[96] and is unknowable. Barth thus eliminated the need for Kant's proof that God is unknowable by reason — this he took as his premise — and asserted that we know of God instead through Christ in Scripture. He disagreed with Przywara's idea that "every creature's being is a participation in the being of the immanent yet utterly transcendent God who stands in constant relationship with it."[97] Our knowledge of God, Barth held, emerges not from our partaking of him but

94. See K. Johnson, "Reconsidering Barth's Rejection of Przywara's *Analogia Entis*," *Modern Theology* 26, no. 4 (2010): 636; see also, Betz, "Beyond the Sublime (Part Two)"; K. Oakes, "The Question of Nature and Grace in Karl Barth: Humanity as Creature and as Covenant-Partner," *Modern Theology* 23, no. 4 (November 2007): 595-616.

95. Cited in Johnson, "Reconsidering Barth's Rejection," p. 637.

96. See T. Stanley, "Barth after Kant?" *Modern Theology* 28, no. 3 (July 2012): 423-45, especially pp. 435-37.

97. Johnson, "Reconsidering Barth's Rejection," p. 636.

from God's reconciling with us and revealing his vision through Christ — all of which occurs over and against humanity's sinfulness.

Supporters of each position over time filled out their views. Przywara, Hans Urs von Balthasar, Gottlieb Söhngen,[98] among others, held to the *analogia entis* on the grounds that it follows from the *imago*. Yet, they continued, the *analogia entis* is also in context with the *analogia fidei*, apprehension of God and his vision through revelation in Christ. *Analogia entis*, Przywara writes, is a "unity-in-tension"; it "signifies that what is decisive in 'every similarity, however great' [between humanity and the divine], is the 'ever greater dis-similarity.' It signifies, so to speak, God's 'dynamic transcendence,' i.e., that God is ever above and beyond 'everything external to him and everything that can be conceived.'"[99] Balthasar called the *analogia entis* "a 'suspended middle' between the absolute transcendence of the God of Calvin, Kierkegaard, and Barth, and the absolute immanence of the God of Schleiermacher, Ritschl, and Harnack."[100]

Betz holds that this "suspended middle" is in fact two suspensions: one, between earthly beings and divine being, and two, between oneness with God (God "in" us) and difference from him (God beyond us). Partaking of the unfolding source of being *analogously* is the "suspended" way between both sets, where God is neither one with humanity nor entirely beyond us but expressed through us, through influence rather than concurrence or what Betz calls "correlated otherness."[101]

Betz notes that not only our being but also our understanding — of world, others, and the source of being — has the form of "correlated otherness." Our understanding of God is not direct or proportional to his knowledge of himself but analogous, a correlated otherness. Betz writes of "an illumination of the one *in* the other, which is to say, that the event of truth *is* analogy."[102] This recalls the image of Moses being able to know only God's "back," not directly God's wisdom but something of-a-kind-ness with it. Truth is cannot-be-represented being and knowledge expressed in representable beings and human-correlated knowledge. This is much like Jesus, Betz points out, who is the unrepresentable divine being and Word, wisdom, in a representable person.[103]

98. G. Söhngen, "Analogia Fidei," *Catholica* 3 (1934): 176-208.

99. E. Przywara, *In und Gegen: Stellungnahmen zur Zeit* (Nürnberg: Glock und Lutz, 1955), p. 278.

100. H. U. von Balthasar, *The Theology of Karl Barth: Exposition and Interpretation*, trans. E. T. Oakes (San Francisco: Ignatius Press, 1992).

101. Betz, "Beyond the Sublime (Part Two)," pp. 22, 24.

102. Betz, "Beyond the Sublime (Part Two)," p. 24.

103. Betz, "Beyond the Sublime (Part Two)," p. 32.

The same is true for our understanding of nature and others. We are different from both but correlated with them. Thought is not at one with nature/others, yet neither is it mental images severed from them. It is mind-in-world, mind amid nature and others. Thought, world, and others are correlated as all partake of the self-expressing source of being. To reprise Paul, each can know what another thinks on the basis of our shared "spirit." Or, as Hamann wrote, our ideas partake of and express the source of being as any real thing does. Through this correlation, through this shared partaking, we have the possibility of understanding something of world. Przywara coined the term "relationology" for our shared analogical partaking of God, which enables us to know something of him and each other.[104]

Barth, for his part, determined that, absent some form of analogy as part of humanity's nature or being, we would be hard pressed to know if our interpretations of Scripture are true. How would we distinguish true ones from rubbish absent analogous of-a-kind-ness with God to tell us something about him, knowledge we can rely on to distinguish bad from good ideas? Absent this, we have only our interpretations of Scripture to judge our interpretations. For all his efforts to distance himself from Kant, Barth backed himself into the Kantian quandary, where one's thoughts — including thoughts about revelation — are sealed off from what they ponder (God, world) and have only themselves to consider.

Barth adjusts this through the strong Christology of his mature work, *Church Dogmatics* III. Whatever we know about ourselves, world, and God, we know through God's self-revelation in Christ, his determination *ab initio* to reconcile with humanity, teach us, and save us through Jesus. As everything we know emerges from this act of grace, we must start from there. Barth retains analogy, but what humanity analogously partakes of is not divine donative being but this reconciling/saving/teaching act.[105] Because of this act of grace, we can rely on or trust our understanding of Scripture — just as, on the *analogia entis*, partaking of the divine source allows us to trust our understanding of it and world. Should we err, God's continuing grace will right us. On Barth's account, we cannot know about God, his moral vision, or world because we directly if analogously partake of being. But we can know about these things

---

104. See "Phänomenologie, Realogie, Relationologie," in E. Pryzwara, *Analogia Entis: Metaphysics; Original Structure and Universal Rhythm* (Grand Rapids: Eerdmans, 2014; original 1932).

105. This discussion continues; see Betz, "Beyond the Sublime (Part One)"; Betz, "Beyond the Sublime (Part Two)"; Johnson, "Reconsidering Barth's Rejection," pp. 632-50; Oakes, "Question of Nature and Grace," pp. 595-616.

because God *ab initio* is in saving relation with us, giving us his lessons and redeeming us through revelation in Jesus. It is this we can trust to teach us about God and world.

Analogy and Relation: An Example from Nicholas of Cusa

Much of the ontology outlined above was intimated half a millennium ago by Nicholas of Cusa (1401-1464), philosopher, jurist, and vicar-general in the papal states, who preempted many of modernity's fraught divisions between mind/world and science/theology. Subverting the mind/world binary, Cusa held that humanity's many ways of mind, of apprehending world — through the senses, reason, science, and religion — are not confined to internal states but are themselves real world items. Anticipating Johann Georg Hamann, Kant's friend and critic (pt. I, ch. 3), he held that our ways of knowing are just as real, just as much of God, as are material objects of knowledge. Subverting the science/theology divide, Cusa held that these various ways of knowing are not in opposition but are complementary. As alone each is limited, we must explore all modes of understanding. Imagination and belief in particular prevent reason from spinning up notions that may be internally consistent but unmoored from life as we live it.[106] In this, Cusa echoed the argument of the medieval Sufi ibn Arabi, who held, as Robert Dobie explains, that human efforts to understand world, God's vision, and "the meaning of revelation" involve not only reason but also "the faculty of imagination, the ability to strike similitudes for what transcends reason."[107]

Cusa began his call for multiple ways of knowing by noting that, while no one sees what another sees, each person knows that she doesn't because she hears others describe things in ways she could not. From the synesthesia of seeing (by oneself) and listening (to others), she recognizes that the world is constituted of multiple perspectives. As one's own view is not the defining or all-encompassing one, one understands that one must learn from the views of others and attempt to grasp what the all-encompassing view of the cause of all might be. "The mind sees that its own possibility is not the Possibility of all possibility.... [I]t sees that it is not Possibility itself but is an image of Possibility

106. B. McGinn, "Seeing and Not Seeing: Nicholas of Cusa's *De visione Dei* in the History of Western Mysticism," in *Cusanus: The Legacy of Learned Ignorance*, ed. P. J. Casarella (Washington, D.C.: University of America Press, 2006), pp. 26-53.

107. R. Dobie, *Logos and Revelation: Ibn 'Arabi, Meister Eckhart, and Mystical Hermeneutics* (Washington, D.C.: Catholic University of America Press, 2010), p. 27.

itself."[108] From his recognition of perspectival multiplicity, Cusa rejected the invention of perspective in art, which he felt hobbles rather than advances knowledge by suggesting that there is but one angle from which to see things — and then hubristically dictates what it is. Cusa objected not only to seeing from one angle but also to the emphasis on seeing per se, oculocentrism, absent the more interactive act of listening to other points of view.

The problem of unifocal oculocentrism, Johannes Hoff explains, took front seat in the seventeenth century, when the physical eye of mono-focalism became the philosophical "I" of the *cogito* and rationalism. Descartes's "I" believes that what it sees is all there is to be seen. On this view, the world is a knowable object, encompassable by one's own vision, adequately described by one's words, and manageable by one's will.[109] Hoff again echoes Taylor's critique of the early modern view of mind and its reign over world. Plurality of perspective is reduced. Things are narrowed to fixed characteristics, measurable and describable by the I/eye, the same everywhere and presumably described the same by all.[110]

Cusa would have thought Cartesian philosophy strange. For on his account, knowledge is not input (the same the world over) encountering mind (the same logic in all persons) but rather is composed of many perspectives and modalities. Cusa also would have found strange the Kantian alternative, where the mind projects its internal categories onto the world and thus can't be sure its sense impressions are real (or its own projections) — can't be sure of contact with world to describe, measure, or manage.

Cusa held instead that our multiple ways of knowing are not confined to mind (Kant's claim) but are real, are about the real, knowable world and its source, and work together to accumulate knowledge. He captures this in his description of iconic images: "I stand before the image of Your Face, my God — an image which I behold with sensible eyes. And I attempt to view with inner eyes that truth which is pointed to by the painting."[111] (Note the echo of ibn Arabi's idea that "The act of interpretation allows the human self to cross over . . . from the visible to the hidden . . . from the less real to the more real . . . through a thoroughly rigorous rational analysis of the text supplemented by a creative imagination that is able to go beyond rational categories to perceive

---

108. Nicholas of Cusa, *De aspice theoriae* (1464), n. 24, 2-4.

109. J. Hoff, *The Analogical Turn: Rethinking Modernity with Nicholas of Cusa* (Grand Rapids: Eerdmans, 2013), p. 151.

110. Hoff, *The Analogical Turn*, p. 64.

111. Nicholas of Cusa, *De visione Dei* (1453), c. 10 n. 38, 6-10.

the higher meanings intimated by the symbolic nature of the 'two books' of creation and the Qur'an.")[112]

The first point in Cusa's reference to icons is that the truth of the divine source of being is in physical, visible items (a painting) that we encounter through physical, sensory experience. The symbols in iconic paintings are physical things (canvas, paint), apprehendable to the senses (sight, touch), yet they express the immaterial (God), apprehendable to the "inner" eye. The symbols are real and material yet express what is immaterial, and our ideas about them are real, worldly things yet understand what is beyond world (God). Using the corporeal, we come to the incorporeal source of all. Both symbols and our ideas are real owing to their partaking of the cause of causes, to which they also give expression. Cusa explained this also through a second example, numbers.[113] They are abstract concepts that we think, but they are not confined to abstraction or our thinking. They are also real entities, owing to their partaking of the world's source, and one can do real things with them.

Cusa explains his second point, our multiple ways of understanding, by noting that uncovering earthly, analogous traces of the source of being happens through all "inner eyes," all modes of mind and feeling, none of which can be forgone. For what is clear at the sensory level may be unclear intellectually, and vice versa. The human processes of uncovering these traces are varied because God is the minimum that is in each particular (for it to be at all) and is the maximum that all beings are in.[114] For Cusa, as for Aquinas before him, this does not make God the direct cause of earthly objects/events but the cause of a setting-up "actuality," which in turn yields local causes and things. Because the unfolding source of being is "in" all worldly things and because each person experiences only some of them (and experiences even one thing in ways different from others), we need all ways of knowing by all people — sensory, scientific, artistic, theological — to understand world and its source. Our efforts are complementary.

Love, on Cusa's view, is the most important mode of understanding as it partakes of divine "seeing." God envisioned world, created what he envisioned, and loves what he sees/created. Thus humanity, created in his "sighted" image (in the image of God who can "see"), may analogously see and love. Love is the way to know that is closest to God's way.

112. Dobie, *Logos and Revelation*, p. 47, 55.

113. See J. Milbank, "*Mathesis* and *Methexis*: The Post-Nominalist Realism of Nicholas of Cusa" (forthcoming).

114. Nicholas of Cusa, *De ludo globi* (1463), II, n. 62.

In sum, there is on Cusa's account no unbridgeable trifurcation of mind, world, and eternal source. Every activity of the mind is within the self-expressing source of being (is enfolded, *complicatio,* in God), and every activity expresses it (unfolds, *explicatio,* in the world). While no mode of thinking or even all modes and persons together have an encompassing view of divine being, each adds to what we know and what is expressed. While not every idea we come to is true, neither are all false; we correct false with true by continuing to explore and uncover what Hoff calls "traces of the invisible [truth] in the visible."[115]

In a move unanticipated and unappreciated by the Holy See, Cusa applied his ontology to church politics, notably in his proposal for reform of the curia, *Reformatio generalis.* Just as multiple perspectives contribute to our grasp of truth, he proposed, so the multiple perspectives of missionaries from Christendom's periphery should contribute to the running of the Vatican.[116] This led to some discord between Cusa and Pope Pius II; Cusa threatened to leave office. Neither Cusa's reforms nor his threat to resign came to pass. He died in 1464 on the road to a crusade of minor importance.

115. Hoff, *The Analogical Turn,* p. 171.

116. "Since the eye, which sees the blind spot of the others, does not see its own blind spot, it cannot visit itself. For this reason it has to submit itself to another visitor, who visits, corrects, and cleanses it in order to make sure that it is suitable to visit the members of the body." Nicholas of Cusa, *Reformatio generalis* (1459), n. 6, 21-24.

CHAPTER 2

The Separable Self in Theologies of Relationality: Covenant

If it is my claim that theologies of relationality maintain distinction-amid-relation, we should ascertain whether they do. Relationality, after all, sounds very communal; from which tenets is distinction/separability developed and sustained? The next four short chapters will look at separability in theologies of relationality as it is found in notions of the *tselem Elohim/imago,* in religious arguments for freedom of conscience, and in the Reformed tradition. But I will start with perhaps the least likely place to find separability: in the theory and practice of covenant.

Covenant, to begin, is a relationship of reciprocal concern, the commitment by each to give for the flourishing of the other, generously, not *quid pro quo.* It is a form of relationship in which each party is distinct and through which each becomes more of the distinct person she is. The gift of commitment — of having one's needs and concerns taken as consideration-worthy — is how distinct persons flourish whether in childhood or business.

Though the relational aspect of covenant is often and rightly emphasized, covenant also requires, as philosopher Esther Meek notes, "diversity at the same time as there is reciprocity."[1] Both the Judaic and Christian traditions hold that covenant is made by parties who are not only distinct but also free. Absent distinction, beings are collapsed into each other and cannot *inter*relate in covenant — cannot bring to each other the gift of attention and assistance. Absent freedom, they cannot choose to join together in mutual commitment and pursuits. In such a case, concern for the other is not gift but unappealable duty. Abraham, for instance, must agree to covenant with God, as must the

---

1. E. Meek, *Loving to Know: Covenant Epistemology* (Eugene, Ore.: Wipf and Stock, Cascade Books, 2011), p. 335.

Hebrew tribes at Sinai. In the Christian tradition, Jesus asks that believers leave their families to follow him in the new covenant. This is radical separation in a day when living outside one's land and clan risked survival. Each disciple must determine freely to do so, a decision that relies on the separability of mind/belief as well as physical person.

Covenant thus relies on the distinct person in two ways: each is distinct from the unfolding source of being, God, and each is separable from other persons, including family/community, so that she can decide her faith for herself. Dietrich Bonhoeffer, the German theologian executed for his protest against the Nazis, wrote that "the idealist goal of totality," as he called it, "must be overcome." He proposed instead "a concept which preserves the concrete individual concept of the person as ultimate and willed by God."[2] God wills beings distinct from himself not in opposition to his desire for covenant but for its sake, for absent distinction there is no relation, no covenant, no reciprocal care.[3] Charles Marsh's gloss on Bonhoeffer notes that even in discussing the church's identity as a community,

> Bonhoeffer refuses to decimate the inner integrity of the person in his explication of the Christological axiom, "Christ existing as community." . . . Christ in no way occasions the diffusion of the individual into a communal monism. . . . Even though there is an unavoidable teleological structure in the relation of individual and community, *inasmuch as life with others capacitates the person's genuine humanity, the integrity of the particular individual remains indispensable.*[4]

From the idea that only distinct persons may freely form relations, it follows that in covenant, no party may be coerced. There can be no faith forced from above, the crowd, or convention. Covenant must be considered, accepted, and maintained by people in a position to refuse. The capacity to say yes — not *pro forma* but in real consent — requires the capacity and conditions to say no. The reverse is also the case: the capacity to say no must coexist with the capacity and conditions to really say yes. Each partner in covenant must be

2. D. Bonhoeffer, *Sanctorum Communio,* trans. R. G. Smith (London: Collins, 1963), p. 28.

3. "The reasons for God's choosing man," the Swiss theologian Hans Urs von Balthasar notes, "lie in his love, free and groundless. It promotes as response the free, reciprocal love of the chosen, because free love can only be answered with love given freely"; H. U. von Balthasar, *Engagement with God,* trans. R. J. Halliburton (San Francisco: Ignatius, 2008), p. 20.

4. C. Marsh, *Reclaiming Dietrich Bonhoeffer: The Promise of His Theology* (New York and Oxford: Oxford University Press, 1994), pp. 140-41, emphasis mine.

capable of informed consent — of understanding covenant and its implications — and must have the information to be so informed (the terms of covenant clearly explained). Each must also have the emotional wherewithal to sustain relationship; that is, to take the other as consideration-worthy, to give for her well-being, and to accept the gift of consideration (advice, support) in return *without* losing the distinct self that allows one to embrace covenant to begin with. For if one partner loses herself in the covenantal relationship, there is no longer covenant, as this sort of bond requires at least two.

CHAPTER 3

The Separable Self in Theologies of Relationality: *Imago Dei* and *Similitude*

A second arena in which we find separability in relational theologies is the *tselem Elohim* or *imago Dei*. This intricate body of Judeo-Christian and Sufi theology holds that each person, made in God's image, is of — analogously partakes of — the self-expressing source of being and is of unique value regardless of worldly station. Genesis 1:26-28 introduces the idea,

> So God created mankind in his own image [*b'tsalmo*],
> in the image of God [*tselem*] he created them;
> male and female he created them. (v. 27)[1]

It continues throughout the biblical period into the rabbinic period: "when a man casts many coins from a single mold, they all resemble one another, but the supreme king of kings . . . fashioned each man in the mold of the first man, yet not one of them resembles another. Therefore, each person is obliged to say, 'the world was created for my sake'" (*m. Sanhedrin* 4:5). Prohibitions against violence are grounded in this principle (Gen. 9:6), which extends not only to murder but also to nonfatal violations (rape, torture) with few exceptions (self-defense, regulated acts of criminal justice).[2]

Emmanuel Levinas captures the *tselem/imago* in his notion of "face" — encounters of regard between persons: "Through his use of *face*," Philip Rolnick writes, "Levinas presents an embodied encounter with beings who

---

1. It is repeated in Gen. 5:1, "When God created mankind, he made them in the likeness of God."

2. D. Gushee, *The Sacredness of Human Life: Why an Ancient Biblical Vision Is the Key to the World's Future* (Grand Rapids: Eerdmans, 2013), p. 51.

cannot be subsumed under a concept."[3] Each person is unsubsumable and inviolable because she is a unique expression of God and thus uniquely of value. Levinas's compatriot, Simone Weil, held that each person be "read" as her unique self. Every person is distinct and, when abused, is uniquely damaged and wronged. "Justice," she writes, is "to be ever ready to admit that another person is quite different from what we read when he is there (or when we think about him). . . . Every being cries out silently to be read differently."[4] There is, on her account, no general concern, compassion, or charity but only attention to the specific other, whose distinction from oneself is inviolable.

In the New Testament, explicit mention of *tselem/imago* is found in fewer than a dozen places, but, as Stanley Grenz has noted, "the New Testament cannot be understood in its fullness without taking into consideration what is declared in its pages about the *imago dei*."[5] It is found, for instance, in 1 Corinthians 11:7, "A man ought not to cover his head, since he is the image and glory of God" (which continues, problematically for many, "but woman is the glory of man"). Christian tradition holds that the humanity of Jesus too is the image of God, which triangulates the *imago*. Human persons and the humanity of Jesus are in God's image, but persons are also in Jesus' image, as he is the divine (Trinitarian) person of God (see, for instance, "the glory of Christ, who is the image of God" [2 Cor. 4:4, 6], and "The Son is the radiance of God's glory and the exact representation of his being" [Heb. 1:3]).

In early Christian theology, the notion of Jesus as humanly *in* God's image and also divinely *as* God's image was not immediate orthodoxy. It emerged gradually from the idea that through the person of Jesus something of God became manifest on earth. F. F. Bruce explains this early formulation: "To say that Christ is in the image of God, is to say that in him the nature and being of God have been perfectly revealed — that in him the invisible has become visible."[6] The notion that Jesus conveys something of God (but *is* not God's image) was supplanted in patristic writings that distinguished between Jesus in God's image and Jesus *as* God's image, as the image in which

---

3. P. Rolnick, *Person, Grace, and God* (Grand Rapids: Eerdmans, 2007), p. 51.

4. S. Weil, *La pesanteur et la grace* (Paris: Plon, 1947); published as *Gravity and Grace*, trans. E. Craufurd (London: Routledge and Kegan Paul, 1952; London and New York: Routledge Classics, 2002), pp. 134-35.

5. S. Grenz, *The Social God and the Relational Self* (Louisville: Westminster John Knox, 2001), p. 203.

6. F. F. Bruce, *The Epistles to the Colossians, to Philemon, and to the Ephesians*, New International Commentary on the New Testament (Grand Rapids: Eerdmans, 1984), pp. 57-58.

humanity is formed[7] — as "the divine form (morphe), the pattern according to whom those who are stamped with the divine image are conformed."[8] That is, the donative source of being, God, mediated through humanness, is Jesus, in whose (divine-human) form we each uniquely partake. The idea was reinforced in the translation from the Hebrew *tselem* to the Greek *eikon*, which denotes not only image but also prototype and close expression of the original, God.

This benign-sounding concept, undergirding the value of each person, has also had its share of controversy. On functional/structural readings, humanity, as a result of being in God's image, has special capacities and privileges to use the world's resources. The classic proof text is Genesis 1:26: "Then God said, 'Let us make mankind in our image, in our likeness, so that they may rule over the fish in the sea and the birds in the sky, over the livestock and all the wild animals, and over all the creatures that move along the ground.'" D. J. A. Clines writes that being in God's image "comes to expression not in the nature of man so much as in his activity and function. This function is to represent God's lordship to the lower orders of creation."[9]

There is considerable debate, however, about "lordship" and whether biblical passages constitute agreement or critique.[10] Mesopotamian and North African traditions held kings to be quasi-divine persons who may act as God acts with lordship over the planet. Interpreting the Bible to mean something similar suggests that not only kings but all persons, owing to their being in God's image, may too act as God acts with lordship privileges. This equates being in God's image with being quasi-divine. Yet claiming persons, however much in God's image, as quasi gods is difficult to square with the corpus of biblical texts. The idea violates the basic tenets of monotheism[11] and constitutes idolatry, the gravest of biblical sins. If persons are not quasi gods, we may not arrogate to ourselves whatever of the divine powers we see fit. We may act analogously, secondarily, and the Bible specifies how we may do so — acting covenantally among persons, for instance, and resting on the Sabbath as God rested. The *imago* may thus be not a continuation of surrounding traditions

7. See, for instance, Grenz, *The Social God*, p. 217.

8. M. Talbot, R. Lints, and M. Horton, *Personal Identity in Theological Perspective* (Grand Rapids: Eerdmans, 2006), p. 81.

9. D. J. A. Clines, "The Image of God in Man," *Tyndale Bulletin* 19, no. 1 (1968): 101.

10. For an overview of this discussion, see Grenz, *The Social God*, pp. 186-203.

11. The Hebrews of the biblical period were often not monotheists but monolatrists, believing in one God for our people (though other peoples have different gods). Nonetheless, even here, persons were not considered quasi or minor deities.

but a distinction from them.[12] This reading of the *imago* — that it entails caring for the planet as God does — has been the ground for recent biblically based environmental protection.

Functional/structural readings are unclear also as to which human functions or capacities would prove likeness to God. Associated with Irenaeus and Augustine, among others, they emphasize spirit, reason, and free will. Yet Douglas John Hall, among others, notes the historical contingency of this list.[13] As it reflects the cultural values of early church writers, questions about its groundedness in the Bible and its long-term morality arise: Should persons lacking these features — infants, people in comas — have inferior status, dignity, and rights? Also problematic is the treatment of those animals that have been found to possess features once thought to be characteristic only of persons.[14]

In part to address these issues, Karl Barth, Emil Brunner, and Hendrikus Berkhof, in the first half of the twentieth century, and Jürgen Moltmann and others in the latter half, developed interactional readings of the *imago*.[15] It is not human reason that most expresses God's image but the capacity for responsible relationship. Relationships may be horizontal, person-to-person, or vertical: from person to God or from person to animal[16] and planet. Yet, this again opens the issue of persons who cannot sustain such relationships (persons in comas, for example). Unwilling to remove such persons from the likeness of God, Dietrich Bonhoeffer held that as Jesus recovered all humanity into the image of God, all persons are so, even those who are unable to agree to the idea or who discount it. Dignity and worth thus inhere in all. "In Christ's incarnation," he wrote, "all of humanity regains the dignity of bearing the image of God. Whoever from now on attacks the least of the people attacks Christ, who took on human form and who in himself has restored the image of God for all who bear a human countenance."[17]

Claus Westermann and others have taken up Bonhoeffer's point. "No

12. See G. Wenham, *Genesis 1-15*, ed. D. Hubbard, G. Barker, and J. D. W. Watts, Word Biblical Commentary, vol. 1 (Waco: Word, 1987), pp. 30-31; T. Jacobsen, "The Eridu Genesis," *Journal of Biblical Literature* 100 (1981): 513-29.

13. D. Hall, *Imaging God: Dominion as Stewardship* (Grand Rapids: Eerdmans, 1986), p. 91.

14. D. Miller, "Responsible Relationship: *Imago Dei* and the Moral Distinction between Humans and Other Animals," *International Journal of Systematic Theology* 13, no. 3 (2011): 323-39.

15. Miller, "Responsible Relationship," pp. 328-31.

16. Barth noted that people are not in a position to ascribe inferior status to other creatures since we cannot know what it means to be them but only to be human.

17. D. Bonhoeffer, *Discipleship*, Dietrich Bonhoeffer Works, vol. 4 (Minneapolis: Fortress, 2003), p. 285.

particular quality of man is meant [in the *imago*]," Westermann writes, "but simply being man."[18] Gushee concurs, "all distinctions between human beings and persons are purely speculative, lack grounding in biblical revelation, and have proven hugely dangerous. . . . These definitions can and do differ dramatically and have often been skewed by self-interest and degrading ideologies."[19] On this reading, contra functionalist and structuralist readings, it is not in particular qualities but in each person's very being that something of God analogously yet singularly inheres. Each is distinctly of value, a unique "coin," as the *Sanhedrin* authors wrote.

Tselem and *Dmuth*, *Imago* and *Similitude:* Humanity's Moral Capacity

Separability and distinction lie also in humanity's moral capacity, which can't be passed off to collective, state, or priest. The image of God has two renderings, *tselem/eikon/imago* and *dmuth/homoiosis/similitude*.[20] The *tselem/imago* pertains to one's nature and the nature of the other, the recipient of our actions, who is deserving of regard as one in whom God's image inheres. *Dmuth/similitude* is a moral potential and pertains to us as actors. Emerging from the theology of analogy and secondary causes, it holds that, as each partakes of God (in his image) and acts secondarily, each has the "moral correspondence" to do so — to act not as God acts but analogously, secondarily. This is what makes each morally accountable. L. Harold De Wolf writes, it is a person's "nature" *(imago)* to have "categories of moral distinction" *(similitude)* that reflect God's image as it is distinctly in her.[21] If the *imago* is *metexis*, distinction within analogical likeness to God, *similitude* is *mimesis*, the capacity for analogous moral conduct.[22]

Imago and *similitude* together suggest that, because each person is of God's image, each is of unique worth *and* uniquely able to treat others as persons of

18. C. Westermann, *Creation,* trans. J. Scullion (Philadelphia: SPCK and Fortress, 1974), p. 59.

19. Gushee, *Sacredness of Human Life,* p. 45.

20. For a discussion of these terms, see, for instance, A. Hoekema, *Created in God's Image* (Grand Rapids: Eerdmans, 1986).

21. L. H. DeWolf, *A Theology of the Living Church* (New York: Harper, 1953), pp. 205, 207.

22. Hans Urs von Balthasar similarly writes, "My behavior toward all other people, even toward strangers, is conditioned by this knowledge that I am unique, for it is this that established me as a person and shows itself in all actions for which I am responsible"; H. U. von Balthasar, *Engagement with God,* trans. R. J. Halliburton (San Francisco: Ignatius, 2008), p. 24.

unique worth.[23] The concept of the distinct person is substantial here. "To the extent that I am a unique self," James Olthuis writes, "no one else can replace me in my responsibility."[24]

In the Judaic tradition, this includes care for the widow, orphan, stranger, and enemy, which each of us does uniquely yet analogously to God — indeed, in two analogies: to God's eternal concern for the downtrodden and in analogy to God's redemption of the downtrodden Hebrews from Egypt (Deut. 24:22; Lev. 19:33). In both analogies, human justice is in correspondence with divine action — not a quasi divinity that allows persons to arrogate what they choose of the divine but an arena of moral correspondence set out in the biblical text. Absent such correspondence, the Hebrews might have been rescued from slavery but would subsequently have little capacity to act justly on their own, and persons would not be morally accountable — not only to specific laws but also, Nicholas Wolterstorff notes, to the structural sense of justice that runs through the Hebrew Bible.[25]

In the Christian tradition, Ephesians 4:32 shares the Hebrew Bible's analogical structuring of the *imago/similitude:* "Be kind and compassionate to one another, forgiving each other, *just as* in Christ God forgave you."[26] The analogy is bolder in the Pauline doctrine of the two Adams (1 Cor. 15:21; Rom. 5:12-19; et al.).[27] Paul holds that the last man/Adam, the man named Jesus, brings the first Adam/humanity more fully to express God's image as it is singularly in each person. As each expresses more of God's image, each may act correspondingly with God's vision and so realize more of her humanity. Each

23. John captures this in 14:12: "Whoever believes in me will do the works I have been doing, and they will do even greater things than these." The sister concept in Sufi Islam holds that one may see the face of God in the other (like the *imago*), thus entering a space where one may act as sacred friend and servant to her *(similitude).*

24. J. Olthuis, "Face-to-Face: Ethical Asymmetry of the Symmetry of Mutuality?" in *The Hermeneutics of Charity: Interpretation, Selfhood, and Postmodern Faith; Studies in Honor of James H. Olthuis,* ed. J. K. Smith and H. I. Venema (Grand Rapids: Brazos, 1996, 2004), p. 140.

25. Not only from Exodus to Deuteronomy but Psalms (see 106:3 or 12:5, for instance) and the prophetic literature (Isa. 28:17; 42:1-4); see N. Wolterstorff, *Justice, Rights and Wrongs* (Princeton: Princeton University Press, 2008), pp. 78-79.

26. Luke 17:21 similarly reads, "the kingdom of God is in your midst," that is, God's kingdom of righteousness is not only in the world to come but also on earth, in each person's capacity to behave righteously.

27. Aaron Riches explains the doctrine of two Adams as follows: "Christ's solidarity with the human race does not detract from his divinity. On the contrary, the divinity of Christ's Person establishes the condition by which his perfect intimacy with humanity is possible"; A. Riches, "After Chalcedon: The Oneness of Christ and the Dyothelite Mediation of His Theandric Unity," *Modern Theology* 24, no. 2 (April 2008): 202.

emerges "in the truth and wholeness of his humanity" through Christ, who "saves and divinizes us by his life, death, and Resurrection."[28] God through Christ "divinizes," that is, brings each person closer to him — again, not as a minor deity but more fully in his image as each is uniquely made. In the words of Pope John Paul II: Christ *fully reveals man to himself* and brings to light his most high calling."[29] In sum, in the Judaic tradition, each uniquely in God's image may act correspondingly; in the Christian, each, through Jesus, is brought more fully into her unique expression of God's image and thus may more fully act correspondingly.

The moral capacity of the distinct person is continued in the writings of the pre-Nicene father Justin Martyr: "In the beginning he [God] made the human race with the power of thought and of choosing the truth and doing right."[30] But it is Irenaeus who most explicitly developed it in distinction from the *imago*. While the *imago*, he writes, is retained after the Fall, *similitude* is damaged. Thus, absent the Holy Spirit (God's ongoing earthly presence), persons would lack moral capacity: absent spirit, we are left "of an animal nature," "an imperfect being, possessing indeed the image [of God] in his formation (*in plasmate*), but not receiving the similitude through the Spirit."[31] It is the Spirit, on Irenaeus's account, that guides each child (in God's image) to mature *similitude* and personal accountability.[32]

Augustine, as we've seen, is associated with the structuralist view, though this is not an uncontested view of the bishop of Hippo. On the structuralist reading of his works, it is the faculty of reason that is of God's image and allows for moral correspondence. Augustine begins with the structure of reason, which, because it analogically partakes of the source of being, can grasp

28. International Theological Commission, "Select Questions on Christology," in *International Theological Commission: Texts and Documents, 1969-1985*, ed. M. Sharkey (San Francisco: Ignatius, 1989), p. 192.

29. John Paul II, *Redemptor hominis* (1979); retrieved from http://www.vatican.va/holy _father/john_paul_ii/encyclicals/documents/hf_jp-ii_enc_04031979_redemptor-hominis_en .html, para. 8, quoting *Gaudium et spes*, para. 22.

30. Justin Martyr, *Apology* 1.28, in *The Ante-Nicene Fathers*, ed. A. Roberts, J. Donaldson, and A. C. Coxe (Peabody, Mass.: Hendrickson, 1994; original 155-157), p. 172.

31. Irenaeus, *Against Heretics (Adversus haereses)* 5.6.1, in *The Ante-Nicene Fathers*, p. 532 (original ca. 180); see also, http://www.newadvent.org/fathers/0103506.htm.

32. Similar to Paul and Irenaeus, Clement of Alexandria held that humanity may be made in God's image but that persons, beginning with Adam, achieve similitude only as they reach the sort of perfection available to humanity — when they become "holy and righteous and wise by Jesus Christ"; see Clement of Alexandria, *Stromata (Miscellanies)* 6.12, in *The Ante-Nicene Fathers*, p. 502.

something of it: numerical principles, ratios, the structure of beauty, and so on. Augustine then notes that Paul called for humanity to be renewed in the mind, and Augustine parses that to be reason, the mind that grasps God's principles. "We are renewed in the spirit of our mind . . . according to the rational mind, wherein the knowledge of God can exist." Each person's soul, Augustine continues, is too "made after the image of God in respect to this, that it is able to use reason and intellect in order to understand and behold God."[33] And moral capacity, on his account, emerges from reason as well. At the end of the nineteenth century, Charles Hodge summarized the structuralist view of Augustine: "According to Augustine, image [*imago*] relates to the *cogito veritatis*, and likeness [*similitude*] to the *amor virtutis*: the former to the intellectual, and the latter to the moral facilities."[34]

Thomas Aquinas, continuing the Augustinian emphasis, held that, of the three ways in which God's image inheres in each person, reason is primary. Reason is given by God to direct each toward him — toward employing one's moral capacities for care among persons, peace, and justice. Reason makes it possible for each person to grasp this divine intention, makes God knowable, and thus each is able to act in correspondence with him. God has extraordinarily bound himself "to the created intellect, as an object made intelligible to it."[35] Like many medieval thinkers, Aquinas held that a good deal of the *imago/similitude* was lost in the Fall, but not everything.[36]

In the early modern era, Luther less optimistically held that no postlapsarian person possesses the reason or moral capacity to reach salvation. "From the image of God, from the knowledge of God, from the knowledge of all other creatures, and from a very honorable nakedness man has fallen into blasphemies, into hatred, into contempt of God, yes, what is even more, into enmity against God."[37] This is the case, Luther held, for each person and is specific to each. Given that, moral conduct on one's own recognizance is impossible.[38]

---

33. Augustine, *On the Trinity (De Trinitate)* 12.7.12, in *The Nicene and Post-Nicene Fathers*, ed. P. Schaff and H. Wace, ser. 1, vol. 3 (Peabody, Mass.: Hendrickson, 1994), 3:159, 3:186.

34. C. Hodge, *Systematic Theology*, vols. 1-3 (New York: Scribner, Armstrong, and Co., 1872-1873), 2:96.

35. T. Aquinas, *Summa Theologica*, trans. Fathers of the Dominican English Province, vols. 1-5 (Westminster, Md.: Christian Classics, 1948; original 1265-1274), I, q. 12, art. 4; 1:52.

36. K. Gardoski, "The *Imago Dei* Revisited," *Journal of Ministry and Theology* 11, no. 2 (2007): 5-37.

37. M. Luther, *Lectures on Galatians (Galatervorlesung)*, in *Luther's Works*, ed. J. Pelikan and H. Lehmann, trans. J. Pelikan, vols. 1-55 (St. Louis: Concordia, 1955-1986), 1:142.

38. Miller, "Responsible Relationship," p. 328.

One might, Luther thought, have reason and free will but use them wrongly, as Satan does[39] — or "Satan" may be the condition of using them wrongly. Using them rightly, on Luther's account, is the gift of grace.

Calvin more positively saw possibilities for moral conduct and thus reflection of God's image in each person. He considered the world to be a reflection of God's righteousness, and persons, made in God's image, to be the brightest mirror. The soul most of all reflects God, but so too does the body, made also by God. At creation, Calvin held, each person's capacities, *similitude,* were in line with the *imago,* with what of God inheres singularly in each. Though distorted by the Fall, it can begin anew in Christ: "The regeneration of the godly indeed, as it is said in II Cor. 3:18, is nothing else than the reformation of the image of God in them."[40] While "beginning anew" is by God's grace, each person's response also plays a role. As one acts morally *(similitude),* the *imago* intensifies; thus acting morally is the responsibility of each of us. In the present world, one sees the presence of God among elect persons as they already are reformed in God's spirit. The rest of us, on Calvin's account, will have to wait until God's kingdom comes.

The theologies discussed thus far, from Paul to the Reformation, are heirs of the structuralist view and privilege reason as the feature in each person most in God's image and most enabling of corresponding moral conduct. Charles Hodge worked out a structuralist logic of sorts: "God is a Spirit, the human soul is a spirit. The essential attributes of a spirit are reason, conscience, and will. . . . In making man after His own image, therefore, God endowed him with those attributes which belong to His own nature as a spirit. . . . If we were not like God, we could not know Him."[41] Also at the turn of the twentieth century, the Anglican Bishop Moule of Durham, the Scot Presbyterian scholar James Orr, and the American Baptist William Newton Clarke took similar positions: "If the two [humanity and God] were not alike [the *imago*], there could be neither revelation nor science; God would not manifest himself to man, and man could not understand the works of God. But in fact man finds his own mind a counterpart to the Creator's."[42] At mid-

39. M. Luther, *Lectures on Genesis (Genesisvorlesung),* in *Luther's Works,* trans. G. Schick (St. Louis: Concordia, 1958), 1:60.

40. J. Calvin, *The Epistles of Paul the Apostle to the Galatians, Ephesians, Philippians, and Colossians,* ed. D. W. Torrance and T. F. Torrance, trans. T. H. L. Parker (Edinburgh: Oliver and Boyd, 1965), p. 191.

41. Hodge, *Systematic Theology,* 2:96-97.

42. W. Clarke, *An Outline of Christian Theology* (Cambridge: John Wilson, 1894), p. 171.

century, Paul Tillich continued, "Man is the image of God because his *logos* is analogous to the divine *logos*."[43]

Approaches to *similitude* that place less emphasis on reason appeal instead to each person's correspondence with divine relationality, paralleling the relational parry to structural views of the *imago*. As God acts from love and commitment, the relational *similitude* goes, so may each of us in his image analogously act. The Danish philosopher Søren Kierkegaard may seem like an unlikely source for this, owing to his focus on Christian interiority. But he also held that the core of Christianity is God's love and that each distinct, introspective person manifests correspondence with God's love in her own loving relations. "As Christianity's glad proclamation is contained in the doctrine about man's kinship with God [*imago*], so its task is man's likeness to God [*similitude*]. But God is love; therefore we can resemble God only in loving."[44] Kierkegaard is echoed by Paul Ramsey, who holds that, as Jesus' life and teachings center on love, being in his image means each of us correspondingly centering our lives. "Jesus' pure humility and prompt obedience to God and his actions expressing pure and instant love for neighbor; they were in fact the same thing, the same image, the very image of God. . . . There is no obedience, no response to God, there are no religious duties beyond this: Thou *shalt* love."[45]

Emil Brunner and Hendrikus Berkhof, having developed interactional accounts of the *imago*, continued with relationality in their discussions of *similitude*. Brunner held that the "formal" *imago* — features that separate persons from animals and remain after the Fall — is not reason but each person's capacity for relationship. The "distinctive quality of human existence," he wrote, is "that its 'structure' is 'relation': responsible existence, responsive actuality." The "material" *imago*, Brunner continued, too is relational, the ability and responsibility in each of us to respond to God and neighbor. Here Brunner's terms echo those of *similitude*, the moral capacity to so respond. The "nature" of each of us, Brunner wrote, is "responsibility from love, in love [formal *imago*], for love [material *imago*]."[46]

Berkhof coined the term "respondable" to explain the link between each person uniquely in God's image and each as uniquely responsible for corre-

43. P. Tillich, *Systematic Theology*, vols. 1-3 (Chicago: University of Chicago Press, 1951), 1:259.

44. S. Kierkegaard, *Works of Love: Some Christian Reflections in the Forms of Discourses*, trans. H. Hong and E. Hong (New York: Harper and Row, 1962), p. 74.

45. P. Ramsey, *Basic Christian Ethics* (New York: Charles Scribner, 1950), p. 259.

46. E. Brunner, *Man in Revolt: A Christian Anthropology*, trans. O. Wyon (London: Lutterworth, 1939), pp. 98-99.

sponding moral action. It is not just any sort of response that is in God's image but rather love of God and other persons. "Man is not made," Berkhof wrote, "just for responding-as-such, but for responding to the Word, that is, to God's love. Love can only be responded to with reciprocal love." Underscoring again the link between each singular *imago* and each as singular moral actor, he continues, "In love, man becomes himself."[47]

More recently, Jürgen Moltmann, also following his relational account of the *imago* with relational *similitude*, wrote, "Human beings will only fulfill their special task as 'the image of God' if they recognize the community of creation in which and from which and with which they live."[48] Such is the mandate and responsibility of each of us. Terence Fretheim further holds that God is counting on it. As each of us in God's image has the capacity to treat others correspondingly, so it is hoped, Fretheim writes, that each person of free will does so. God then places Godself "at the service of . . . creaturely creativity."[49]

*   *   *

I would like to conclude with a brief look at the work of John Hughes,[50] who illuminates the *imago/similitude* through his study of work. He asks two questions: Why do we work and why do we rest? Beginning with the latter, he wonders why we do not work the unfortunate into the ground for profit. The capacity to be concerned about them cannot be only the pragmatic concern that brutalized workers don't work well; after all, elites can always impress more of the poor. Nor can it be only a humane concern; why be humane? If we are humane in principle, what accounts for our principles?

The answer is what Hughes calls the "hidden theological heart" in critiques of labor abuse: the command for each of us to rest on the Sabbath — and not only to rest but to rest analogously *as* God rests. Hughes observes the frequency of the biblical analogy between divine creation/rest and human work/rest.[51] He notes that even Karl Barth — so cautious about any *analogia entis,* any analogy between humanity and God — nonetheless allows for "some sort of *analogia actionis.*" Once the proper walls against idolatrous sameness

---

47. H. Berkhof, *Christian Faith* (Grand Rapids: Eerdmans, 1979, 1986), p. 188.

48. J. Moltmann, *Ethics of Hope,* trans. M. Kohl (Minneapolis: Fortress, 2012), p. 62.

49. T. Fretheim, *God and World in the Old Testament: A Relational Theology of Creation* (Nashville: Abingdon, 2005), pp. 34-35.

50. J. Hughes, *The End of Work: Theological Critiques of Capitalism* (Malden, Mass., and Oxford: Blackwell, 2007).

51. Hughes, *The End of Work,* p. 5.

between God and humanity are in place, Barth holds that being in God's image indeed guides each person's conduct: "Jesus' response to the question of the sons of Zebedee, that we, like Christ, should be lords of all by serving all (Matt. 20:25) reveals how we *can* in fact become an imitator, *mimetes* of God (Eph. 5:1) and even co-workers, *synergos* of the Kingdom (Col. 4:11) doing the works of God, *ergon, tou Theou* in his field and vineyard."[52] Being in God's image and acting correspondingly as his *mimetes* and *synergos* are for Barth the ground of moral conduct.

Hughes applies this *mimesis* to his question about work and rest: God rested, analogously each of us does *(imago),* and each, possessed of *similitude,* allows her workers to rest. Moreover, Hughes argues, we know we have correspondence with the divine not only because we are concerned about others but also because we work for reasons beyond utility,[53] pursuing "useless" beauty. This too is analogous to God, who created world for no practical reason but as artists create, for the "sheer delight" of it and the "love of the thing made."[54] In sum, our own impractical efforts to excel beyond survival — to act as artists — demonstrate the analogical being of each of us with the divine.

---

52. Hughes, *The End of Work,* p. 14.

53. Hughes notes that even producing only for utility begs the question: Useful for what? Why care about the outcome; by what standard does one do so? Utility itself, then, is based on a prior set of values.

54. Hughes, *The End of Work,* p. 226.

CHAPTER 4

The Separable Self in Early Modern Theology: Freedom of Conscience

Theological principles of separability and distinction grounded arguments for freedom of conscience a century or more before the secular Enlightenment. One claim for such freedom was that, as each is made unique in God's image, each must come to him in her own way. Though one might err, no one made in God's image may be violated. While discussion may be used to persuade people of missteps, true beliefs will prevail because they are true. Indeed, humanity, made in God's image, can be trusted to come to them over time. A second distinction claim of early modernity was that coming to God in covenant must be freely chosen by each person. Coerced obedience is not covenant but servitude, and religious behavior by convention is not belief. *Individual* freedom of conscience is therefore a condition of faith. A third was that, while made in God's image, each person's and all humanity's knowledge is incomplete. As only God knows the truth, persons may not judge the beliefs of others. Each, even if with help from community, must work out her way to God.

Thus the idea, sturdy since Augustine, that persecuting heretics was a task of the church — the idea that each could not decide her path to God — came under question. The Catholic humanist Desiderius Erasmus was an early critic. But a more forceful writer of this period was Sebastian Franck, the sixteenth-century spiritualist who declared that even the followers of the radical Jan Hus and the Anabaptists were true Christians. With this flourish, he nearly voided the concept of Christian heresy, a kindness for which Europe was unready.[1] The separable, deciding mind was contemplated also among pietists, both out of doctrinal commitment to each person's individual relationship with God

---

1. See the *Chronica* and *Paradoxa ducenta octoginta,* in J. Lecler, *Toleration and the Reformation* (London: Longmans, Green; New York: Longmans, 1960; original 1534), 1:175, 176.

and out of fear of persecution by the official churches. Stanley Grenz writes, "the Pietists shifted the locus of true Christianity from baptism to personal conversion, from the objective to the subjective, from the external to the internal . . . a move that opened the way for the eventual advent of the modern self that seeks to marshal inner resources in the task of self-mastery."[2] As Charles Taylor and Paul Tillich noted, the pietist emphasis emerged from and contributed to the early modern shift toward the importance of the individual mind (pt. I, ch. 3).

A generation after Franck, Sebastian Castellio,[3] in *Concerning Heretics* (1554), deconstructed heresy from a sin into a disagreement among well-meaning individuals, each of whose efforts to near God have merit (if not complete truth). He was among the first to distinguish between individual faith (for God to judge) and action (for magistrates to judge), and he warned that continued state policing of belief would perpetuate not faith but persecution. Patience and education, he wrote, are Jesus' ways, and "left free," truth will emerge.[4] Persons will come to it. Castellio died, somewhat fortunately, before Calvin could try and burn him for heresy. But Calvin was not as far from Castellio as he thought — Calvin's enmity being in part a strategic political response to Castellio's rising influence in the Reformed church. As Calvin de-emphasized the role of the church as intercessionary between God and person, the individual comes to the fore as the agent responsible for rejecting sin and nearing God.

By the seventeenth century, calls for both group worship rights and individual freedom of conscience had gained significant footing in Britain. Quakers and the democratizing, populist Ranters and Levellers argued that individual belief could be judged only by God, and thus freedom of conscience was due to each person regardless of faith, an idea for which the Leveller John Lilburne was famously whipped. His colleague William Walwyn argued for freedom of conscience in nearly full modern voice: erroneous views would fade in time as they failed the test of debate, a precursor to the "marketplace of ideas."[5] Richard Overton dared to call for religious toleration even for Muslims and Jews.[6] This exceeded the petitions of even the era's great poet John

2. S. Grenz, *The Social God and the Relational Self* (Louisville: Westminster John Knox, 2001), p. 83.

3. S. Castellio, *Concerning Heretics and Whether They Should Be Persecuted, and How They Should Be Treated*, ed. and trans. R. Bainton (New York: Octagon Books, 1965; original 1554), p. 129.

4. Castellio, *Concerning Heretics*, especially pp. 123, 129, 132-35, 222-25, 251-53.

5. See *A New Petition of the Papists* (1641).

6. He also demanded freedom from church taxes, freedom of the press, the right of all

Milton, who, in *A Treatise of Civil Power in Ecclesiastical Causes* (1659), argued for freedom of conscience on classic *sola Scriptura* grounds: each person must rely on Scripture — not magistrate or priest — to find her faith, and no human official may judge it.

Writing in the American colonies, Roger Williams found his arguments for individual conscience unappreciated by theocratic Massachusetts, which expelled him in the winter of 1635-1636. His idea that colonial churches were insufficiently separated from the Church of England and that the Crown had to purchase — not steal — land from the Indians did not help his cause. In his *Bloudy tenent of persecution for cause of conscience* (1644), Williams held that Jesus' teachings distinguish between the political and religious arenas: government pertains to the former (the defense of individuals, property, and peace), and churches pertain to spiritual matters. Yet, Williams continued, one's spiritual path must in the end be decided by oneself with help from God.[7] With this he left the Puritan confession, his adult rebaptism making him a father of the American Baptist church. He rhetorically asks, "How can he [the magistrate] give judgment of a false church, a false ministry, a false doctrine, false ordinances, and with a civil sword pull them down, if he have no spiritual power, authority, or commission from Christ Jesus for these ends and purposes?"[8] Williams concludes by holding doubly that persons should be free to choose their beliefs and churches should be free from the state.[9]

Williams can be seen as a republican *avant la lettre* and his *Bloudy tenent* as a forerunner of John Locke's summation of the toleration literature, *A Letter concerning Toleration* (1689).[10] Both writers effected political outcomes. One was the charter of Rhode Island, which Charles II granted to Williams in 1663. It guaranteed not only group worship rights but full religious liberty to

---

believers to participate in government, prisoners' rights, rights to trial, free public education and housing, and care for the poor, especially their right to keep their land. See R. Overton, "An Appeal to the Free People," in *Leveller Manifestoes of the Puritan Revolution*, ed. D. Wolfe (New York: T. Nelson and Sons, 1944; original 1647), pp. 154ff.; see also Overton's *The Arraignment of Mr. Persecution* (1645); C. Marshall, *Crowned with Glory and Honor: Human Rights in the Biblical Tradition*, Studies in Peace and Scripture, vol. 6 (Telford, Pa.: Cascadia Publishing House, 2002), p. 148.

7. R. Williams, *The bloudy tenent of persecution for cause of conscience*, in *The Complete Writings of Roger Williams* (New York: Russell and Russell, 1963; original 1644), pp. 153-60, 250, 343.

8. Williams, *The bloudy tenent*, pp. 193-95.

9. Williams, *The bloudy tenent*, pp. 79-81.

10. J. Locke, *Letter concerning toleration*; retrieved from http://www.let.rug.nl/usa/documents/1651-1700/john-locke-letter-concerning-toleration-1689.php.

individuals: "all and everye person and persons may, from tyme to tyme, and at all tymes hereafter, freelye and fullye have and enjoye his and theire owne judgments and consciences, in matters of religious concernments."[11] It was Williams who also gave America its famous "wall" between church and state. Complaining about church-state collusion in Massachusetts, he wrote that such mingling punctured "a gap in the hedge or wall of Separation between the Garden of the Church and the Wilderness of the World."[12] When Thomas Jefferson repeated the phrase in 1802, he was cribbing from Williams.

Locke's religio-political impact in the colonies came through his contribution, together with his employer the earl of Shaftesbury, to the Fundamental Constitutions of Carolina (1669).[13] Locke and Shaftesbury argued that persecution is an offense to God; thus the American Indians should be justly treated, and not only toleration but, as the Ranters and Levellers had argued, religious freedom should be granted to every person, including Jews and dissenters: "that civil peace may be maintained amidst diversity of opinions . . . the violation whereof, upon what presence soever, cannot be without great offence to Almighty God, and great scandal to the true religion which we profess." The document continues, "No person whatsoever shall disturb, molest, or persecute another for his speculative opinions in religion, or his way of worship." In Williams and Locke, the distinct person and separable mind are clear and protected.

Locke's later work, *A Letter concerning Toleration,* was written under the double shadow of the Huguenot persecution in France and Locke's own exile to Holland, where he fled to escape the wrath of the British Crown after his employer Shaftesbury had imprudently criticized it. Expanding on Castellio, Lilburne, and especially Williams, Locke distinguishes between government, which is to secure "civil goods" (life, liberty, security, health, and property), and church, "a free and voluntary society" where individual persons of like minds gather for matters of the soul. While persons, he held, must agree about

11. Yale Law School, Charter of Rhode Island and Providence Plantations — July 15, 1663, in the Avalon project, Documents in law, history and diplomacy, Lillian Goldman Law Library (2008); retrieved from http://avalon.law.yale.edu/17th_century/ri04.asp, para. 2; see also, J. Wilson and D. Drakeman, eds., *Church and State in American History: Key Documents, Decisions, and Commentary from the Past Three Centuries,* 3rd ed. (Boulder, Colo.: Westview Press, 2003), pp. 30, 31.

12. Williams, *The bloudy tenent,* p. xxiv.

13. Yale Law School, The Fundamental Constitutions of Carolina: March 1, 1669, in the Avalon project, Documents in law, history and diplomacy, Lillian Goldman Law Library (2008); retrieved from http://avalon.law.yale.edu/17th_century/nc05.asp.

their form of government to conduct daily life, they will disagree about God. And as it is disagreeing, fallen persons who found churches, it is inevitable that "every church is orthodox to itself; to others, erroneous or heretical." Thus no one of us persons of limited, partial knowledge can judge the other; only God can judge belief. In yet another plea for the separable mind (even an erroneous one), Locke wrote, "every one should do what he in his conscience is persuaded to be acceptable to the Almighty."[14]

The Quaker William Penn published his *Great Case of Liberty of Conscience* in 1670 and, in his Pennsylvania Charter of Privileges (1701), granted freedom of conscience (among other liberties) to the colony. He reprised the idea that only God could arbitrate faith and that each person be allowed her distinct views:

> I do hereby grant and declare, That no Person or Persons, inhabiting in this Province or Territories, who shall confess and acknowledge One almighty God, the Creator, Upholder and Ruler of the World; and profess him or themselves obliged to live quietly under the Civil Government, shall be in any Case molested or prejudiced, in his or their Person or Estate, because of his or their conscientious Persuasion or Practice, nor be compelled to frequent or maintain any religious Worship, Place or Ministry, contrary to his or their Mind.[15]

---

14. He continues, "no man can so far abandon the care of his own salvation as blindly to leave to the choice of any other, whether prince or subject, to prescribe to him what faith or worship he shall embrace. For no man can, if he would, conform his faith to the dictates of another. All the life and power of true religion consist in the inward and full persuasion of the mind."

15. William Penn, Pennsylvania Charter of Privileges, October 18, 1701; retrieved from http://www.constitution.org/bcp/penncharpriv.htm.

CHAPTER 5

The Separable Self: The Reformed Tradition and Its Influence in America

My last discussion of separability and distinction in relational theologies will focus on the Reformed Protestant tradition. In its emphasis on the individual bond with God and each person's mandate to lifelong moral conduct, the Reformed tradition began to formulate a notion of *self*-responsible moral striving (noted briefly in pt. I, ch. 3). Relationship to God and moral living are, on this view, not the sorts of things others can do for you, however helpful community and church may be. One's own conscience must come to God and morality. Puritans, historian William Haller notes, "were taught to follow by intense introspection the working of the law of predestination within their own souls." The "theater" of this "drama of sin and repentance," Haller writes, was "the human breast."[1] Though on the Reformed doctrine of predestination, salvation is given in grace, the Puritans, among others of the Reformed faiths, hoped that the intensely individual introspection of one's soul was evidence of it. This is the separable person at prayer.

Certain theological emphases followed, one being the Reformed doctrine of "eternal security," in which those who have true faith in Jesus have the gift of perseverance-in-faith until death. This sign of salvation shifts the accent from community and singles out the person who has such perseverance, reflecting the increased emphasis on the individual over the intercessionary church. A second was the Calvinist tenet that those who act as God wills them to act may take their good deeds as a sign that God works through them — another bow to personal conduct. Pietistic doctrine also held that the individual's fervent feelings could near one to God. That is, personal inner devotion plays a role not

1. W. Haller, *The Rise of Puritanism* (Philadelphia: University of Pennsylvania Press, 1972), p. 157.

only in developing worldly moral conduct but also in salvation itself (in contrast to belief that in this life one can be saved *in spe,* hope, but not *in re,* reality).

While each Reformed soul may have worried whether her perseverance-in-faith-unto-death, good acts, and fervent feelings were indeed signs of salvation, this ferocious introspection evinced a shift toward individual interiority. Ironically, though Reformed theology appears to remove the (predestined) individual from the calculus and leave all to God's grace, it fostered a self-investigation that contributed to the modern separable subject.

Its reworking of the sacred did much the same. What in medieval theology was a circumscribed arena apart from the worldly and profane opened up to became a potential of all life endeavors. The sacred was now everywhere. To compress a complex religio-sociology: if what each person does in the realm of the sacred is to strive to follow God, and the sacred is everywhere, then each of us is to strive everywhere. Individualist striving — originally the asymptotic reach of the introspective, self-responsible person toward God — became a characteristic of the person everywhere. Similarly, if Jesus meant that each Christian develop her calling and talents within the church, and the church is everywhere, then each Christian is responsible also for developing her unique talents everywhere. The separable subject was set to work.

Haller and others like Colin Campbell[2] take the "Romantic" Protestantism of introspection to be at odds with the Protestantism of efficient economic rationalization discussed by Max Weber after his 1904 visit to America,[3] where the Reformed tradition had substantial religio-cultural influence. Yet the Romantic and industrious aspects of the faith worked in tandem. The introspective, self-critical, self-responsible person motivated by inwardly generated striving toward God yielded both inwardly generated moral uplift and inwardly generated striving in the public sphere. Both emerged from and reinforced modernity's separable self.

In America, as we've seen (pt. I, ch. 4), these aspects especially of Reformed Protestantism interacted synergistically with do-it-yourself survivalism, anti-authoritarianism, and the dissenter's suspicion of hierarchy. Taken together, they forged a religio-political logic somewhat different from that in Europe's territorialized religions. While in Europe there were two terms, church and state — both tending toward societal organization by institution — in America

2. C. Campbell, "The Romantic Ethic and the Spirit of Modern Consumption" (1987); retrieved from http://www.writersservices.com/wbs/books/Romantic_ethic.htm.

3. See M. Weber, *The Protestant Ethic and the Spirit of Capitalism,* trans. T. Parson (New York: Charles Scribner's Sons, 1958).

there were three: church, state, and experimental, anti-authoritarian civil society full of energetically self-responsible initiators. The results in separability were evident by the First Great Awakening of the 1730s-1740s. With remarkable trust in the individual mind, preachers told congregants to rely not even on their churches but rather on their own "self-examination." Preachers declared the "absolute necessity for every Person to act singly."[4] And they did, experimenting with new forms of worship, prayers, and churches, outdoor camp meetings, and iconoclastic theological tenets preached by any newcomer spiritually moved to do so.[5] Moreover, as breakaway preachers attracted adherents from traditional churches, it became obvious that choice of church was one each individual would make.

Americans experimented perhaps most consequently with Arminianism, popularized in England and America by the brothers John and Charles Wesley. Arminianism reimagined Reformed theology to further accent the individual's role in salvation. While free will allows persons to sin, prevenient grace (grace in this life) allows us also to choose the moral path. And if one does, if one so chooses, one is saved. The critical step thus inheres in each person.

Rather traditionally, the Wesleys understood forgiveness, return to the image of God, and the defeat of the power of sinfulness as God's gift, as "the one thing needful" (Luke 10:42), and as impossible without Jesus' death and God's grace. With our faith in him, Christ works *for* us in justification, the first moment of turning to God, or new birth. He continues his work *in* us in sanctification, which returns us increasingly to the image of God in our thoughts and actions.

Yet a number of influences shifted the Wesleys away from Calvinist predestination toward a "relational understanding of salvation,"[6] where each person, in affiliation and partnership with God, plays a substantial role. Among those influences were the brothers' intensely personal conversion experiences, their faith in love as the "image and nature" of God (contra the more juridical emphasis of double predestination), and the influence of Moravianism, especially the importance of personal belief to receiving God's pardon. These led

4. G. Wood, "American Religion: The Great Retreat," *New York Review of Books* 53, no. 10 (June 8, 2006): 61.

5. See M. Noll, *America's God: From Jonathan Edwards to Abraham Lincoln* (New York: Oxford University Press, 2002); for a companion look at the innovations of the nineteenth-century Second Great Awakening, see N. Hatch, *The Democratization of American Christianity* (New Haven: Yale University Press, 1989).

6. J. R. Tyson, *The Way of the Wesleys* (Grand Rapids: Eerdmans, 2014), Kindle location 1067.

the Wesleys to focus less on the inheritance of sin, about which one can do little, and more on sins committed in the course of this life, which each person can address (John Wesley calling this sin "properly so-called").

In their work on justification and sanctification, the Wesleys held that God's spirit at justification not only works for us, with persons being rather passive, but also brings us into a relationship with him where each person's role is substantial. In sanctification, his spirit deepens the bond, making each person more Christlike and able to move toward her own salvation. "God worketh in you," John Wesley wrote in "On Working Out Our Own Salvation," "therefore you *can* work. . . . God worketh in you; therefore you *must* work; you must be 'workers together with him' (they are the very words of the Apostle); otherwise he will cease working." Also in "On Working Out Our Own Salvation" — a title of considerable self-initiation — he continues, "Since he [God] worketh in you of his own good pleasure . . . it is possible for you to fulfill all righteousness. It is possible for you to 'love God, because he hath first loved us.'"[7]

Thus, while holding to the idea that God's grace enables salvation, the Wesleys believed that each person, by dint of grace, becomes a partner in continuing it — that this partnering is what grace enables. "He will not save us," John Wesley wrote, "unless we 'save ourselves from this untoward generation'; unless we ourselves 'fight the good fight of faith, . . . and labour by every possible means, to *make our own calling and election sure*'" (emphasis mine).[8] Charles Wesley, in *Hymns on God's Everlasting Love*, echoes: "But all that *will* receive Him *may*."[9]

The idea that each of us may work to ensure her election sparked considerable opposition. Yet the Wesleys held that this is what's done in the five spiritual disciplines, boldly called the "means of grace," underscoring that each of us possesses, by reason of God's grace, the means to furthering it (see the "Large Minutes"). "The Scripture Way of Salvation" details these means as "works of piety" (prayer; studying Scripture, through which God's spirit works; the Lord's Supper; fasting; and Christian conference) and "works of mercy"

---

7. http://wesley.nnu.edu/john-wesley/the-sermons-of-john-wesley-1872-edition/sermon-85-on-working-out-our-own-salvation/. See also Charles Wesley's Oxford sermon "Awake, Thou That Sleepest," where he affirms, "brethren, we are called to be 'an habitation of God through his Holy Spirit,' and through his Spirit dwelling in us 'to be saints.'"

8. http://wesley.nnu.edu/john-wesley/the-sermons-of-john-wesley-1872-edition/sermon-85-on-working-out-our-own-salvation/.

9. C. Wesley, J. Wesley, and G. Osborn, *The Poetical Works of John and Charles Wesley* (Andesite Press, 2015), p. 4.

(feeding the hungry, clothing the naked, entertaining the stranger, visiting prisoners and the sick, instructing the ignorant, awakening the sinner). Works of mercy are meant not only for those nearby but also for the "world parish," for which one has *personal* responsibility (see the Methodist "General Rules"). One has similar personal responsibility for good stewardship of the planet (see John Wesley's "The Good Steward").

By these means of grace, the Wesleys held, one might come to Christian perfection or "entire sanctification," a Christian maturity free from intentional sin (sin "properly so-called"). Such worldly perfection is "loving God with all our heart, mind, soul, and strength. This implies that no wrong temper, none contrary to love, remains in the soul; and that all the thoughts, words, and actions are governed by pure love" (from John Wesley's "Thoughts on Christian Perfection").[10] This does not mean that one no longer errs, but that the will is "perfected" and has no intention to do wrong even if one makes mistakes in this mortal life. Some disagreement arose between the brothers, as Charles grew to see perfection as a slow-developing maturity that occurred only at life's end while John saw it as possible throughout life, even in one moment, a flash of gift from God. John thought Charles set the bar too high; Charles thought John allowed for unconsidered fanaticism. Yet the concept of Christian perfection in this world prevailed and continued into Methodism, with John setting out its eleven principles in *A Plain Account of Christian Perfection*.

In something of a corollary to one's personal role in salvation, the Wesleyan and Arminian traditions also democratized grace. The doctrine of Jesus' unlimited atonement holds that Christ died for all, not just the elect.[11] The universality of grace holds that all may be saved by it. Taking the two doctrines together gives each person access to God's love and to the means of grace and salvation. In his effort to democratize these means, Charles Wesley innovatively held that God had predestined the *means* by which people would be saved (faith, prayers, works of piety and mercy) but not the persons who would be. Thus again, each one of us may take the step to turn to faith and the means of grace, as John wrote in "Free Grace," "The grace or love of God, whence cometh our salvation, is free in all, and free for all." If a person is not

---

10. See also, *A Plain Account of Christian Perfection As Believed and Taught by the Reverend Mr. John Wesley from the Year 1725 to the Year 1777.*

11. So opposed to predestination had the Wesleys become that in 1740, Charles said of the "predestination party" among Methodists, that "the poison of Calvin has drunk up their spirit of love"; see also John Wesley's sermon "Free Grace" and Charles's "The Cry of Reprobate" in *Hymns of Everlasting Love* for their detailed critique of Calvinism's ruination of both God's love and our eagerness to do good works.

saved, Charles continued, it is not for lack of God's love and offer of salvation but because of the person's individual rejection of it.

The strict Calvinists among the colonials thought this focus on individual will and capacity had gone too far, and Jonathan Edwards, among America's most influential colonial ministers, preached against it. But in America, home to such considerable reliance on the can-do, self-responsible person, his opposition got somewhat lost in the bustle. After serving his congregation for over two decades, he was relieved of his duties in 1749 in a dispute about who counts as a church member. Edwards held that only those graced with a full conversion experience should be allowed full church privileges. But this was too exclusionary for the people of Northampton, Massachusetts, who had had a variety of religious experiences; people wanted their own ones to count. And it was too dependent on God's grace: earnest individual effort was not given its due. Even Edwards's grandfather had held that baptism was sufficient for full church privileges, and Edwards had to step down to make room for greater church flexibility and greater recognition of individual effort.

After the Revolution and through the antebellum period, Reformed Arminian-based Methodism saw explosive growth. The number of churches rose from 20 in 1770 to 19,883 in 1860, a 994.1 multiple of increase. The number of Baptist churches, with their strong emphasis on the individual conscience, rose from 150 in 1770 to 12,150 in 1860, an 81 multiple of increase. In the same period, the more traditional, grace-based Congregationalist churches increased by a factor of 3.6, Anglican by a factor of 6.0, German Reformed by 4.7, Dutch Reformed by 4.4, and Roman Catholic by a factor of 51, owing to increased immigration from Ireland.[12] By the Second Great Awakening (1820-1850), the Methodist and Baptist churches alone accounted for two-thirds of American Protestants. Rodney Clapp writes, "By underscoring the importance of making a decision for Christ, Charles Finney [among the most influential Second Awakening preachers] and other revivalists helped along the sanctification of *choice*."[13]

Clapp critiques the individual emphasis as a forerunner of the greed and consumerism of the twentieth century. But this may confuse separability

12. See R. Carwardine, "Methodist Ministers and the Second Party System," in *Rethinking Methodist History: A Bicentennial Historical Consultation,* ed. R. Richey and K. Rowe (Nashville: Kingswood Books, 1985); T. Smith, *Revivalism and Social Reform: American Protestantism on the Eve of the Civil War* (New York: Abingdon, 1957), p. 22; C. Goss, *Statistical History of the First Century of American Methodism* (New York: Carlton and Porter, 1866), p. 106.

13. R. Clapp, "Why the Devil Takes VISA: A Christian Response to the Triumph of Consumerism," *Christianity Today,* October 7, 1996.

with excessive separability. Reformed doctrine, with its concern about moral conduct, was keen to identify problems of individualist self-absorption. John Wesley, for instance, was wary (as Montesquieu had been) of beliefs that would "produce both industry and frugality; and these cannot but produce riches. But as riches increase, so will pride, anger, and love of the world in all its branches. . . . What way, then, (I ask again,) can we take, that our money may not sink us to the nethermost hell?"[14]

His answer to the evils of wealth — Clapp's concern — was its direction toward the public good. Through the nineteenth century, America's voluntarist churches created associations in every area of civil life. The largest U.S. government operation of the antebellum era, for instance, was the postal service, but by mid-century, religious associations (many of them Methodist and Baptist) had double the employees and twice as many facilities, and raised three times as much money.[15] They were active in public education, temperance, and overseas liberation movements; they protested sexual trafficking, Chinese foot-binding, and Indian suttee. Some were radically progressive: anti-Federalist, Jeffersonian, Jacksonian populists, against bankers and landlords, pro-squatter, and supportive of women preachers and black churches.[16]

At the turn of the twentieth century, Dwight L. Moody, the most popular evangelical preacher of the day, lambasted businesses for paying their workers starvation wages and set up schools for young women and men (in that order). Millions of the devout, notably evangelical Baptists and Methodists, supported the populist leader William Jennings Bryan in his pro-worker, pro-farmer platform and three bids for the presidency (1896, 1900, 1908). Under the leadership of Walter Rauschenbusch, they developed the Social Gospel, which ran programs for the poor and provided an early critique of laissez-faire capitalism. "Nations do not die by wealth," Rauschenbusch noted, "but by injustice." The church, in its "prophetic role," was obligated "to act as the tribune of the people."[17]

Where Clapp is right is in the critique of separability detached from relations of reciprocity and commitment to the public good — a detachment that relational theologies, explored in the chapters ahead, seek to preempt.

14. J. Wesley, "Thoughts upon Methodism," August 4, 1786, London; retrieved from http://www.imarc.cc/one_meth/vol-02-no-02.html, para. 11.

15. Noll, *America's God*, pp. 182, 200-201.

16. See Hatch, *Democratization of American Christianity*.

17. W. Rauschenbusch, *Christianity and the Social Crisis* (1907); the book was rereleased as *Christianity and the Social Crisis in the 21st Century: The Classic That Woke Up the Church* (New York: HarperOne, 2007); see pp. 265, 284 for quotations. The book's rerelease in 2007 contained commentaries by Cornel West, Jim Wallis, and Richard Rorty, who is Rauschenbusch's grandson.

CHAPTER 6

Theologies of Relationality:
A Few Notes from the Judaic Tradition

This sketch of relationality in the Judaic tradition, as with the Christian theologies that follow, is not meant as an overview of Judaic tradition or as an exhaustive review of relationality as it has developed through three thousand years of Judaic thought. It is rather a brief look at some of the central voices who contribute to an ontology that reciprocally constitutes separability and situatedness, distinction and relation, and so might productively ground our political and economic ethics. The chapter will focus on primary sources from the Bible and the rabbinic period, parallel to the early Church Fathers, as they ground relationality thinking since. Throughout, the aim is to explore the *structure and philosophy* undergirding the narrative, poetry, etc. As current economic and political policy is of prime interest, the last set of voices is Jewish thinkers of the twentieth and twenty-first centuries. The idea is not to show that relational interpretations of Judaic thinking have been the only ones but rather to look at signposts on the landscape of those that are.

It is part of the book's methodology, as we've seen, to present a wide range of thinkers whose work is not neatly congruent and who may disagree on certain points. Yet their ideas about distinction-amid-relation share a family resemblance, and while shared elements do not erase differences, differences need not be eliminated for the ideas in common to remain robust. As throughout the book, the method is horizontal, pointing to affinity and reflection among ideas as they appear in various schools of thought. Current debates are explored as they reveal important features of distinction-amid-relation (for instance, debates about the contractual or covenantal nature of God's bond with Israel and about its particularist or universalist intent). Given the space constraints of one chapter, what follows is but an indication of the wealth of contributions to relationality from the Judaic tradition.

The first idea to be explored is the ontological nature of covenant. The relationship between God and persons and among persons structures world and what occurs in it. Unlike collectivist notions of relationship, it is a bond among distinct beings that — however different the parties — is characterized by the gift of reciprocal consideration and commitment, giving for the flourishing of the other. Unlike contract, in which one protects one's interests, it is a bond to protect the relationship. The reciprocal relationship is basic to the workings of the world. Covenant is based not only on reciprocity but also on the trust that reciprocity is here the case. Stephen Geller notes that the person in relation to God and others is a central Judaic concern from the Deuteronomic period on (eighth to sixth centuries B.C.E.).[1]

Covenants of reciprocity among equals are easily imagined, as are covenants with asymmetric terms between unequal parties. The innovation of the Judaic covenant, however, is its bond of reciprocity between unequals. The structure of covenant — the *idea* behind it — is that God extends an offer that humanity is free to accept, ignore, or refuse. In some sense this must be the case, for if the superior party gives but seeks nothing in return, we have charity, not covenant. Should the superior only take from the subordinate, we have coercion. "The covenant itself," Lenn Goodman writes, "rests on (and thus cannot create) the freedom of the covenantors to accept God's law."[2]

Covenant is less a discrete act and more an outlook into which particular circumstances, decisions, and actions are set. From the extensive work on the Judaic covenant I shall highlight a few points.

The Relationality of Covenant: The Gift of Reciprocal Commitment

Certain readings of the Hebrew Bible,[3] some Christian and some Jewish,[4] have taken the Judaic covenant as legalistic and contractual. Michael Horton, for

1. S. Geller, "The Sack of Shechem: The Use of Typology in Biblical Covenant Religion," *Prooftexts* 10, no. 1 (1990): 12-13.

2. L. Goodman, *On Justice: An Essay in Jewish Philosophy* (New Haven: Yale University Press, 1991), pp. 41-42. Goodman goes on to say that it is "through history, not through covenant," that Israel becomes a community, but this sits oddly with the text and tradition. These hold that it is acceptance of the covenant at Sinai that creates the nation, as the covenantal bond with God creates also covenantal bond among persons.

3. My thanks to Rabbi Avinoam Paul Sharon for his discussion of several source texts.

4. See, for instance, M. Goldberg, *Jews and Christians: Getting Our Stories Straight* (Eugene, Ore.: Wipf and Stock, 1985, 2001), pp. 213-22.

instance, describes two Hebraic covenants: the one of promise, made to Noah, Abraham, and David, is a unidirectional offer of uncontingent love from God to humanity. The second, made to Moses, is contingent on terms and is heritable upon term fulfillment. Horton holds that while Judaism continued with the Mosaic covenant of stipulations, Christianity followed the Abrahamic/ Davidic covenant of love.[5] Horton's term-fulfillment condition can certainly be found in the First Testament. Exodus 19:5-6 is representative: "Now if you obey me fully and keep my covenant, then out of all nations you will be my treasured possession." This seems *quid pro quo*. Deuteronomy 29:1 is perhaps more so: "These are the terms of the covenant the LORD commanded Moses to make with the Israelites in Moab, in addition to the covenant he had made with them at Horeb."

Yet covenant in the Judaic tradition is not heritable upon term execution. It has been open to humanity for millennia in spite of repeated breaches, open to all since the Noahite covenant and to the Hebrews since the Mosaic. The Judaic covenant is, Yoram Hazony writes, "a new metaphor for understanding man's relationship with God, which arises precisely from the fact that man, who is free to choose, is not in God's pocket. . . . [T]hose who turn to him of their own, placing themselves in his service, are described as obtaining something that mere obedience could never have obtained — God's love."[6] Contracts may specify many conditions, but love is not the sort of thing they can mandate. In covenant, stipulative aspects might appear (as a parent might stipulate that a child clean her room or study). The Mosaic code is to help the Hebrews realize righteousness with God and neighbor so that "all peoples on earth will be blessed through you" (Gen. 12:3; 28:14; cf. 26:4). Yet covenant is not stipulative in motive or *telos* (one doesn't have children *so that* they clean their rooms).

There are a number of points to Hazony's insight: the novelty of the bond, its grounding in freedom, and the reciprocity of commitment and love. The idea of care and trust between humanity and the divine was a departure from Egyptian and Babylonian cosmogonic myths, which depicted gods as mytho-

---

5. M. Horton, *Covenant and Salvation: Union with Christ* (Louisville: Westminster, 2007), p. 20; see also pp. 12-32.

6. Y. Hazony, *The Philosophy of Hebrew Scripture* (Cambridge: Cambridge University Press, 2012), p. 94; Louis Newman, of Carleton College, similarly notes, "covenant comes to embody a unique and multi-faceted relationship between Israel and its God. That God — depicted sometimes as sovereign ruler, other times as lover, still other times as parent — remains throughout a God bound by a covenantal relationship to Israel"; see L. Newman, "Covenant and Contract: A Framework for the Analysis of Jewish Ethics," *Journal of Law and Religion* 9, no. 1 (1991): 89-112.

poetic rather than intimate and evolving. It departs as well from certain strains of Neoplatonism that consider God within frameworks of timeless, distant form.[7] "A cosmogonic myth is beyond discussion," Henri Frankfort writes. "It describes a sequence of sacred events, which one can either accept or reject. But no cosmogony can become part of a progressive and cumulative increase of knowledge."[8] Where gods are mythopoetic or noninteractive forms, the relationship does not change as humanity responds and so does not play a role in epistemological or ethical development.

Addressing Hazony's second point, covenant's grounding in freedom, one interesting proposal has been that contract, with its clear terms, might set God and man on more of an even keel. If God unilaterally establishes covenant, mankind may not have much choice about accepting the deal. Jon Levenson worries that "Israel at Sinai is [in] no position to decline."[9] Yet Israel is free to

---

7. This was noted by Dietrich Bonhoeffer in his correction of "the anti Semitism that ignores Hebraic emphasis on the dynamism of God's action in real history and pays attention only to allegedly timeless principles of Greek philosophy. Hebraic thought moved out of mythological thinking and instead focused on God's action in history"; see Glen Stassen's commentary on Bonhoeffer in Stassen, *A Thicker Jesus: Incarnational Discipleship in a Secular Age* (Louisville: Westminster John Knox, 2012), p. 46; see also, K. Stendahl, *Paul among Jews and Gentiles* (London: SCM, 1976); E. P. Sanders, "The Covenant as a Soteriological Category and the Nature of Salvation in Palestinian and Hellenistic Judaism," in *Jews, Greeks, and Christians*, ed. R. Hamerton-Kelly and R. Scroggs (Leiden: Brill, 1976), pp. 11-44; E. P. Sanders, "On the Question of Fulfilling the Law in Paul and Rabbinic Judaism," in *Donum Gentilicum*, ed. E. Bammel (Oxford: Oxford University Press, 1978), pp. 103-26; E. P. Sanders, "Patterns of Religion in Paul and Rabbinic Judaism: A Holistic Method of Comparison," *Harvard Theological Review* 66 (1973): 455-78; E. P. Sanders, *Paul, the Law, and the Jewish People* (Philadelphia: Fortress, 1983); E. P. Sanders, *Paul and Palestinian Judaism: A Comparison of Patterns of Religion* (Philadelphia: Fortress, 1977); J. D. G. Dunn, *The Partings of the Ways: Between Christianity and Judaism and Their Significance for the Character of Christianity* (London: SCM, 1991); J. D. G. Dunn, "How New Was Paul's Gospel? The Problem of Continuity and Discontinuity," in *Gospel in Paul: Studies on Corinthians, Galatians, and Romans for Richard N. Longenecker*, ed. L. A. Jervis and P. Richardson (Sheffield: Sheffield Academic Press, 1994); N. T. Wright, "Israel's Scriptures in Paul's Narrative Theology," *Theology* 115, no. 5 (2012): 323-29; N. T. Wright, "Paul and the Patriarch: The Role of Abraham in Romans 4," *Journal for the Study of the New Testament* 35 (2013): 207-41; D. Rudolph, "Paul's 'Rule in All Churches' (1 Cor 7:17-24) and Torah-Defined Ecclesiological Variegation," *Studies in Christian-Jewish Relations* 5 (2010): 1-23; J. M. Barclay, *Pauline Churches and Diaspora Jews* (Tübingen: Mohr Siebeck, 2001).

8. H. Frankfort and H. A. Frankfort, *Before Philosophy* (Harmondsworth, U.K.: Penguin, 1959), p. 251.

9. J. Levenson, *Creation and the Persistence of Evil: The Jewish Drama of Divine Omnipotence* (Princeton: Princeton University Press, 1988), p. 143; Jon Levenson is the Albert A. List Professor of Bible at Harvard's Divinity School.

decline, as the prophets complain. David Hartman finds the view of covenant as backing humanity into a golden cage to be unnecessary. Offers of care, he notes, do not secure return feeling or commitment, as many a disappointed suitor has learned. Covenant — Hazony's third point — is a request for a reciprocal bond.

Servility and lack of reciprocity will also not stand theologically, as this would remove from the picture free will and human capacities for understanding and judgment "in God's image" — and it would suppose that God wants this. But then, why forge a covenant if humanity is a doll to be programmed? "What marks the Jewish tradition," David Burrell writes, "is an untrammeled insistence on human beings' free response — whether negative or positive — to the gift of Torah, which already comprises a divine invitation to respond ... so inviting each successive generation to continue shaping it by their response in turn."[10] It is important to understanding the structure of covenant that biblical protagonists act as independent, initiating partners unto arguing with God. Jacob is given the name that becomes the nation, Israel, after wrestling with him: "Your name will no longer be Jacob, but Israel, because you have struggled with God and with humans and have overcome" (Gen. 32:28).[11] Humanity not only has, Moses Maimonides said, but "should have the ability to do whatever [it] wills or chooses among the things concerning which [it] has the ability to act."[12]

The Gift of Analogical Partaking of the Divine: Co-creatorship

The reciprocity of the Judaic covenant follows from the idea that humanity, analogously in God's image, may understand something of the workings of the

10. D. Burrell, *Towards a Jewish-Christian-Muslim Theology* (Chichester, UK, and Malden, Mass.: Wiley-Blackwell, 2011), Kindle locations 1099, 1101.

11. Similarly, Noah is able to steer a moral course independent of others and revelation, righteous on his own recognizance. Other initiators include Rebecca, Jacob (as a shepherd, he was a symbol of the independent life, not tied to the large agricultural-irrigation systems controlled by government), and David (shepherd). Abraham and Moses (shepherds) argue with God and win; David defies God's command (to annihilate Amalek) and argues with God about the killing of one of his men. Isaiah, Jeremiah, Ezekiel, Habakkuk, Jonah, and Job all question God's idea of justice; see Gen. 18:17-33; Exod. 32:9-14; Num. 14:11-20; 16:19-23; Judg. 6:13; 2 Sam. 6:8-12; Isa. 40:6-8; Jer. 2:9, 29; 4:10; 12:1-4; Ezek. 9:8; Jon. 3:10–4:3; Hab. 1:1-4; 1:12–2:1; Job 13:13-16.

12. M. Maimonides, *Guide for the Perplexed,* trans. A. H. Friedländer (New York: Dover, 1956), bk. 3, ch. 17.

world and so within human capacities further God's vision as his co-creator. Our being in God's image, *tselem/imago,* grants us the moral capacity *(dmuth Elohim, similitude)* to be co-creators. This too is structural to the workings of the world. In Terence Fretheim's words, humanity is as needed for the development of creation as is rain; prototypically, it is Adam who is given the job of naming the animals and assessing them. "Creation," Fretheim writes, "includes the activity of creatures (human and nonhuman) in and through which God works to create in ever new ways. . . . That power-sharing divine move continues into the post-fall world, evident throughout the Old Testament"[13] — indeed, immediately postfall, in Eve's declaration that *she,* with God's help, created the next man (Gen. 4:1). Fretheim further notes that the Hebrew verb *bara,* the first word used for God's creative act in Genesis, is used also to denote God's work through human history, where human action contributes to what occurs, in particular our ability to evaluate worldly conditions and human circumstances. Thus, "the creative activity of the human, in particular, has the potential of significantly enhancing the ongoing life of the world and every creature therein, indeed, bringing into being that which is genuinely new."[14]

Humanity's understanding of God's vision and responsibility for furthering it underpins Moses' declaration that prophets are to be judged by whether their report of God's words holds true in the world (Deut. 18:21-22) — which assumes that we can somewhat correctly grasp and assess worldly happenings. Jeremiah assumes that people can, by observing world, understand God's ethics and, as partners, further it:

"Stand at the crossroads and look;
　　ask for the ancient paths,
ask where the good way is, and walk in it." (Jer. 6:16)

The Mishnah and Jerusalem Talmud (Yerushalmi) see the world as ordered and the task at hand as understanding that order to follow it in daily and religious life so that things will go well.[15] Though it is God's order, the grammar

13. T. Fretheim, *God and World in the Old Testament: A Relational Theology of Creation* (Nashville: Abingdon, 2005), Kindle locations 345, 720.

14. Fretheim, *God and World in the Old Testament,* Kindle locations 461-462.

15. Jacob Neusner writes in his overview of the Mishnaic and Yerushalmi ontologies, "The world is composed of nature and supernature. The laws that count are those to be discovered in heaven and, in heaven's creation and counterpart, on earth. Keep those laws, and things will work out"; see J. Neusner and B. Chilton, *Jewish and Christian Doctrines* (New York: Routledge, 2000), p. 26.

of the cause of causes, God's human partners further his vision on earth and have a hand in its future.

Importantly, Emmanuel Levinas takes co-creation to pertain not only to the physical world but also to the meaning of covenant itself. What humanity has of covenant, Levinas writes, is sacred text, which requires interpreters. God (in offering text) and each person (in pondering it) literally — and literarily — construct covenant together. "It is as if the multiplicity of persons . . . were the condition for the plenitude of 'absolute truth'; as if every person, through his uniqueness, were the guarantee of the revelation of a unique aspect of truth. And some of its points would never have been revealed if some people had been absent from mankind."[16] This pertains, on Levinas's view, not only to the biblical era but always, daily.

The Gift of Irrevocability

Covenant, freely and reciprocally given and marked by collaborative trust, is, in distinction from contract, irrevocable (somewhat as the parental bond continues even when a child gets rebellious or into trouble). Indeed, irrevocability is part of what makes covenant a lasting, not passing, feature and ontological, structural to world. It is the ontology undergirding the earliest Genesis tales, spoken to all humankind. As Adam and Eve eat the forbidden fruit, God sends them from paradise yet does not abandon them; he clothes them, remains with them and their children, protecting Cain even after his murder of Abel so that humanity may continue. When in the Noah story, humanity's wrongdoings so overflow that nature overflows in response, covenant remains, as God promises, "This is the sign of the covenant I am making between me and you and every living creature with you, a covenant for all generations to come: I have set my rainbow in the clouds, and it will be the sign of the covenant between me and the earth" (Gen. 9:12-13). As Karl Löning and Erich Zenger write, "the creator God has a relationship of love and faithfulness toward the earth and says a fundamental and irrevocable 'yes' to this earth and these human beings."[17]

The idea repeats with Abraham: "I will establish my covenant as an everlasting covenant between me and you and your descendants after you for

16. E. Levinas, "Revelation in the Jewish Tradition," in *Beyond the Verse: Talmudic Readings and Lectures*, trans. G. Mole (Bloomington: Indiana University Press, 1994), p. 133.

17. K. Löning and E. Zenger, *To Begin with, God Created . . . : Biblical Theologies of Creation*, trans. O. Kaste (Collegeville, Minn.: Liturgical Press, 2000), p. 119.

the generations to come, to be your God and the God of your descendants after you" (Gen. 17:7). And with Isaac and Jacob: "I will not leave you until I have done what I have promised you" (Gen. 28:15). In Exodus, God five times repeats to Moses that he will uphold his covenant (Exod. 2:24; 3:6, 15; 6:3, 8), which he does even when the Hebrews do not.

Particular note should be made of the conversation between Moses and God at the burning bush (Exod. 3:14), in which God identifies himself as "I will be as I will be" and as the maker of covenant with the patriarchs. "I will be" is the first identification, indicating its importance; the letter of recommendation from the patriarchs follows. The Hebrew *ehyeh asher ehyeh* uses the future tense — "I *will* be" — suggesting that God's covenant will not extinguish, pointedly as the burning bush does not.[18] Paul Ricoeur takes up the idea and reads the text as "I am who may be" or "I am who will be with you."[19] The purpose of the burning-bush encounter is to move from the Abrahamic family to covenant with nation so that all nations may eternally be blessed. This obligation is foreshadowed in Genesis, when Joseph, at the time of famine, takes care not only of his family but of all Egypt. It is elaborated at Sinai, where God not only assures physical survival (the "promised land") but also provides guides to living that are understandable as just to all humankind. "The revelation of Exodus 3," Richard Kearney writes, is of a "salvific God" who will "prise open the moral universal horizon of a 'Promised Land.' Here God commits himself to a kingdom of justice if his faithful commit themselves to it too."[20]

The assurance of God's inextinguishable commitment to justice on earth continues into the prophetic books, whose chief plaint is that the Israelites breach it, straying into idolatry (breach with God) or abuse (breach with neighbor). Yet God's commitment endures; he "will freely pardon" (Isa. 55:7). In Isaiah 54:7-10, God expresses his constancy in the cadences of a coy lover:

"For a brief moment I abandoned you,
    but with deep compassion I will bring you back.
In a surge of anger

---

18. If the more traditional translation, "I am as I am," were correct, the Hebrew would be *Ani asher ani.* For the correct use of the future tense in English, see R. Alter, *The Five Books of Moses: A Translation with Commentary* (New York: Norton, 2008), p. 321.

19. A. LaCocque and P. Ricoeur, "From Interpretation to Translation," in *Thinking Biblically: Exegetical and Hermeneutical Studies,* trans. D. Pellauer (Chicago: University of Chicago Press, 1998), p. 331.

20. R. Kearney, "The God Who May Be," in *Questioning God,* ed. J. Caputo, M. Dooley, and M. Scanlon (Bloomington and Indianapolis: Indiana University Press, 2001), p. 160.

> I hid my face from you for a moment,
> but with everlasting kindness
> I will have compassion on you. . . .
> Though the mountains be shaken
> and the hills be removed,
> yet my unfailing love for you will not be shaken
> nor my covenant of peace be removed."

The emotional intensity of this passage is not idiosyncratic but appears throughout the Bible and is structural to the concept of covenant, bond with God and among persons, as undergirding world.

Covenant: The Spirit of the Donor, the Spirit of the Gift

Yet another structural feature of world is gift as a medium of covenant. Gift works to create and maintain covenant because it carries the intention and commitment — the spirit — of the donor to the recipient. The idea is explicit in the creation story, where God breathes his spirit into Adam, giving the gift of being (Gen. 2:7). *Tselem Elohim/imago* means that something of God's spirit has been given, in gift, to us. When God promises Abram that his descendants will be a great nation, Abram hasn't so much as one child. The rabbinic commentary in *Genesis Rabbah* reads God's promise of nation as the gift of one who sees a possibility to one who doesn't. God takes Abram outside his tent to look at the innumerable stars, the number of Abram's supposed descendants. But as it is daylight, seeing the "stars" outside the tent cannot be literal but rather a "seeing outside" of Abram's limited perspective. This glimpse into an unimaginable future is the first gift showing the intention and spirit of God. The second is the inserted *h* in Abram's new name, Abraham. The letter *h* in Hebrew signifies God; it is a synecdoche for his spirit and commitment that have now been given to Abraham and that are now literally and literarily "in" his name and life.

The commandments too are a gift establishing covenant between one who sees and those who do not. God's spirit of righteousness and care is given to the nation through the gift of the commandments to help it carry out what God knows it can (be righteous and a means to the blessing of humanity). The idea appears again in the biblical metaphor of husband bestowing gifts, unasked, to his wife, and she, to him. Hosea 2:19-20 depicts God as a lover bearing again the gift of righteousness, justice, love, compassion, and faithfulness.

That spirit carried in gift creates covenant is the principle described by the early-twentieth-century French sociologist Marcel Mauss in his work on gift-exchange societies.[21] Gift, he writes, is freely given and unrequired yet establishes bonds among persons because something of the spirit of the donor rests within it. The recipient is entrusted with care of this spirit and reciprocates by giving back something of his own spirit, not at once but in the course of time and relationship. In a gift-exchange society such as the ancient Hebrews had, a gift from God, carrying God's spirit to persons, is a breathtaking idea. Not just any chieftain but God — the source of all — entrusts his spirit to humanity and hopes we give of our spirit in return.

It is thus a part of the ontology of the world that a covenant-making, gift-giving God has made us in his image to have the capacity also to give of our spirit and so create covenant with him and among each other. Among the most important gifts from the Hebrews to God — in addition to generosity to the needy and stranger — was the dedication of land to him and bringing the fruits of the land to the temple. It is a particularly eloquent moment of gift exchange. For God's gift to humanity is being itself and, in ancient Canaan, the land that allows for survival, for being. In turn, the Hebrews return the gift by bringing back to God gifts from the land, from their means of survival. This exchange of gifts, being/land from God back to God, creates covenant — but not because the items are needed. An incorporeal God after all does not eat the crops that are brought. As in all gift-exchange societies, it is not the value of the items that creates bond but the act of the gift. *Giving to God is not obeisance or special pleading but the gift* to him *of accepting the reciprocity of covenant.*

Another gravely important gift to God is charity, gifts to other persons. The spirit of the giver, through the gift of charity, is given both to charity's recipients and to God. That charity is gift to God is made explicit in the vow uttered when donating the charitable gift. This vow is made by the human donor, not God, again highlighting that we, in God's image, have something of his capacity to give gifts in covenant. The idea is illustrated in the covenant between God and Jacob; it is Jacob, not God, who dedicates the area as Beth-El, house of God (Gen. 28:18-19). Madeleine Kochen writes, "In the Rabbinic imagination, animal sacrifice (along with Temple gifts) was the quintessential obligatory 'return gift' to God. . . . The capacity of giving back to God what is his/hers represents the power people have to make things holy."[22] Humanity,

---

21. M. Mauss, *The Gift: The Form and Reason for Exchange in Archaic Society*, trans. W. D. Halls (London: Routledge, 1990); original 1925, *Essai sur le don: Sociologie et anthropologie*.

22. M. Kochen, "'It Was Not for Naught That They Called It *Hekdesh*': Divine Ownership

in God's image, has the capacity to give such gifts and, in reciprocal covenant, has the responsibility to do so.

Covenant: The Möbius Strip

In the medieval concept of *hekdesh,* property given as charity, we have something odd: a gift from person to person is designated as gift from person to God. Kochen outlines "two categories of obligation built into the very notion of property: those owed to God directly and those in which the obligations to God are deflected and directed toward other humans."[23] Kochen is referring to the mutual constitution of covenant between persons and God and among persons. Being in covenant with God entails covenant with those in whom God's spirit analogously inheres; bond with God is expressed through covenant among persons. The two covenants are a Möbius strip, if you will, the bracelet-type band sketched independently by the nineteenth-century mathematicians August Möbius and Johann Listing, where each surface folds over and becomes the other as it goes round the loop.

The idea of this Möbius-like interdependence is structural to the concept of covenant and inheres in the Ten Commandments: the first three pertain to humanity's bond with God, and the rest,[24] flowing seamlessly, to relations among persons. Interdependence structures the bond between God and Abraham as well: it includes both bond with God and the promise of family, an arena of covenantal care among persons and the prime mode of its transmission as parents teach children to care about others. Until the Abrahamic covenant, *Genesis Rabbah* 49 notes, there had been individuals, like Noah, capable of bond with God and righteousness to others, but there had been no means to transmit this interhuman capacity. The Abrahamic covenant creates both, those in covenant with God and with others — or, more accurately, those whose covenantal regard for others in part constitutes covenant with God.

The twined covenants are illustrated as well in the binding of Isaac. A common reading is that through his obedience to the extreme demand to sacrifice his son, Abraham demonstrates faith in his covenant with God. Yet God prohibits this violence, as covenant among persons may not be broken

---

and the Medieval Charitable Foundation," in *The Bar-Ilan Conference Volume,* ed. J. Fleishman, Jewish Law Association Studies, vol. 18 (Liverpool: Jewish Law Association, 2008), p. 137.

23. Kochen, "It Was Not for Naught," p. 137.

24. They are: respect for parents; a day of rest for all workers, including slaves; and injunctions against murder, theft, lying, envy, and adultery.

both for its own importance and because it constitutes bond with God. On a more relational reading, Abraham knows from the start that God does not demand such violence — such perversion of covenant among persons — and that God will provide a sacrificial substitute, precisely as Abraham tells Isaac and his servants.[25] A related reading notes that, as human sacrifice was customary in the surrounding cultures, God's request to sacrifice Isaac would not have seemed unusual to Abraham. His faith lay not in agreeing to the ordinary (to the sacrifice request) but to the unusual — to stopping the sacrifice midact, as it would violate covenant between Abraham and Isaac and thus between Abraham and God. On this view, the lesson lies not in Abraham faithfully agreeing to sacrifice but in Abraham understanding that covenant is in keeping relationship alive.[26]

A more probing relational view suggests that Abraham *fails* his bond with God as he fails his bond with Isaac — that is, in failing to act as a moral, covenantal agent and protest against Isaac's sacrifice (as he protested against the destruction of Sodom and Gomorrah). Indeed, God makes the sacrificial request sound ridiculous by emphasizing that Isaac is Abraham's *only* son, his *beloved* son (Gen. 22:2). Once Abraham misses the cues, fails to protest, and prepares the sacrifice, he fails covenant with God *as* he breaks the bond with his son. He acts not as a moral agent in covenants of reciprocal responsibility but as a servant. Thus Abraham loses both intertwined bonds at once. God never again speaks to Abraham but sends a representative, an angel, to stay the knife. The angel acknowledges that Abraham meant to do right and promises that Abraham's descendants will grow into a nation, as God does not revoke covenant. But the special relationship between God and Abraham is past.

God turns to Isaac, who demonstrates the entwined covenant in establishing a covenant with Avimelech (Gen. 26:28-29). Avimelech concludes the

---

25. "Abraham says twice, quite explicitly, that there will be no sacrifice of Isaac: First, he tells the youths that 'the lad and I will go there and prostrate ourselves and return to you,' the Hebrew verb for 'return' (nashuv) being conjugated, unmistakably, in the plural. And then again, when Isaac asks Abraham what they will do for a sheep since they have not brought one, Abraham tells the boy precisely what is going to happen: 'God will see to the sheep for an offering himself, my son. . . .' The meaning here is unmistakable. For Abraham, there is one and only one thing that is worthy of remembering here and passing on to future generations: this is the fact that he had held fast to the conviction that God would provide the ram so that there would be no human sacrifice — and that God had indeed come through for him, providing a ram in place of his son, as Abraham had believed he would"; Hazony, *Philosophy of Hebrew Scripture*, p. 118.

26. The argument, for instance, of Rabbi Joseph Hertz, Chief Rabbi of the United Hebrew Congregations of the British Empire from 1913 to 1946.

moment with a pronouncement not about the human bond but about God: "Now you [Isaac] are blessed by the LORD." The moment of covenant between persons is a moment of covenant between Isaac and God. Numbers 5:6 repeats the notion of intertwinedness: "Any man or woman who wrongs another in any way *and so is unfaithful to the LORD*, that person is guilty." As bond with God is carried out in relations among persons, violation of persons wounds covenant with God. The theme moves to Exodus, where the wrongs of Egypt — hierarchy, force, slavery — violate persons and God alike. "The tradition, by way of the exodus," Walter Brueggemann writes, "makes a connection between YHWH, the Lord of the exodus, and the neighbor."[27]

And it is the prophets' central theme. Amos and Proverbs denounce the hypocrisy of obeying ritual while abandoning the needy, as if one could maintain bond with God absent bond among persons.[28] God through Amos derides Israel:

> "I hate, I despise your religious festivals;
>   your assemblies are a stench to me. . . .
> But let justice roll on like a river,
>   righteousness like a never-failing stream!" (Amos 5:21-24)

Isaiah too declares that redemption (covenant with God) comes with righteousness and justice for the poor (covenant with others) (Isa. 1:17, 23, 27). In Micah, aggression toward others constitutes waywardness from God (7:2-7), as it does in Hosea 1:7.[29] Consistently, the prophets urge Israel toward covenant with God as realized in covenant among persons, importantly in forging peace (Ezek. 34:25; Isa. 65:25; 9:7; Zech. 9:10; and Mic. 4:3/Isa. 2:4). It emerges as well in what Robert Gibbs calls the extensive "social ethics" of the rabbinic era (see below), where failure of covenant with the needy is again breach of

27. W. Brueggemann, *Journey to the Common Good* (Louisville: Westminster John Knox, 2010), p. 42.

28. "To do what is right and just / is more acceptable to the LORD than [ritual] sacrifice" (Prov. 21:3). These complaints are echoed by Pope Francis: "There is a kind of Christianity made up of devotions reflecting an individual and sentimental faith life which does not in fact correspond to authentic 'popular piety.' Some people promote these expressions while not being in the least concerned with the advancement of society or the formation of the laity, and in certain cases they do so in order to obtain economic benefits or some power over others." *Evangelii gaudium,* Rome, November 24, 2013; retrieved from http://www.vatican.va/holy_father/francesco/apost_exhortations/documents/papa-francesco_esortazione-ap_20131124_evangelii-gaudium_en.html, para. 70.

29. See W. Brueggemann, *A Social Reading of the Old Testament: Prophetic Approaches to Israel's Communal Life* (Minneapolis: Fortress, 1994), ch. 15.

covenant with God.[30] The Mishnah, for instance, establishes two realms of wrongdoing, between persons and God and among persons. Where God has been wronged, sins are repaired by addressing him in prayer. Where persons have been wronged, repair requires forgiveness from the victim first and then from God, as both bonds have been rent.[31]

The Möbius intertwinedness is found as well in a striking observation by the great medieval commentator Rashi, who reads the words of Isaiah, "I cannot be God unless you are my witness." Rashi glosses, "I am the God who will be whenever you bear witness to love and justice in the world." God can be God when persons are loving and just to each other. In Abraham Joshua Heschel's twentieth-century echo, *"righteousness is not just a value; it is God's part of human life."*[32] Covenantal relations among persons *are* where covenant with God is in the human realm. Irving Greenberg twines the two covenants this way: he sees covenant as God's invitation to become beings in his image, to act in his image — analogously, with human capacities — as covenantally as God acts. God attempts to repair covenantal bonds that are broken, so we, in God's image and as covenantal partners, need repair them as well. For these broken bonds are bonds also with God.[33]

Levinas's diagnosis of doubly broken bonds is a flaw in the way we think about thinking, which we take to be commensurate with reason. This works well enough for laws of nature as they are rule-governed and so may be investigated using logic that also is. But it does not work well, on Levinas's account, with other aspects of life such as emotions, ethics, or the alogical generosity of covenantal regard. "But does not the difficulty come from our habit of understanding reason as the correlative of the possibility of the world?"[34] An overreliance on reason, Levinas continues (as Hume, Hamann, the Romantics, et al. had), hobbles our understanding of what lies outside rule-governed calculation — including the possibility of covenant with an invisible God and both visible and invisible (distant) others, a double loss. Levinas holds that, as the "glory of the Infinite" happens in and through the human, social world, regaining bond with God will take us to bond with others.[35] Yet covenant

30. R. Gibbs, "Returning/Forgiving: Ethics and Theology," in *Questioning God*, p. 78.

31. See *m. Yoma* 8:9.

32. A. J. Heschel, *The Prophets* (New York: Harper Perennial Classics, 2001), p. 255.

33. I. Greenberg, *For the Sake of Heaven and Earth: The New Encounter between Judaism and Christianity* (Philadelphia: Jewish Publication Society, 2004), p. 28.

34. Levinas, "Revelation in the Jewish Tradition," p. 146.

35. E. Levinas, *Otherwise Than Being or Beyond Essence*, trans. A. Lingis (Dordrecht: Kluwer Academic Publishers, 1991), p. 152.

with God also emerges from covenant with neighbor. Relationship with God "can be traced back to the love of one's neighbor . . . the responsibility for one's neighbor and taking upon oneself the other's destiny, or fraternity. The relation with the other person is placed at the beginning."[36]

In summary, in the ontology of the biblical and rabbinic texts, the world is structured by irrevocable entwined covenants between person and God and among persons — what Fretheim calls "the interconnectedness of moral order and cosmic order": "wherever righteousness is practiced by human beings in the sociopolitical spheres, that act is in tune with the creation, and it fosters the proper integration of social and cosmic orders."[37] Covenant is characterized by commitment, care, and the priority of preserving not interests but relationship, the covenant itself. Owing to our being of God's image and in covenant with him, we have the capacity to act as co-creators and to participate in reciprocal gift exchange where each gives of his spirit in the Möbius strip of regard.

Covenant: Particularist Components, Universal "Problem Set"

> Covenant-talk is particular in nature. . . . But the teaching offered by the Hebrew Scriptures goes beyond covenant-talk and seeks to instruct us as to the underlying reasons for the covenant. And in so doing it has recourse to concepts of a general nature . . . such concepts require no prior commitment to the historic Jewish alliance with the God of Israel to be understood. Thus while they were written for the instruction of the Jews, there is no reason why the standpoint and argument they make should not be heard and debated among all nations.[38]

The Judaic covenant cannot be understood as particularist but rather as "particularist and. . . ." Though developed in an era when most gods were tribal and indeed particular, Daniel Breslauer notes, "The Jewish covenant assumes that monotheism — the God of the covenant — must be accessible to all humanity, not just to Jews."[39] It concerns the fundamental questions of human living, is understandable without group membership, and may be studied and

36. Levinas, "Revelation in the Jewish Tradition," pp. 146-47.
37. Fretheim, *God and World in the Old Testament*, Kindle locations 3028-3029, 190-191.
38. Hazony, *Philosophy of Hebrew Scripture*, p. 99.
39. S. D. Breslauer, "Toward a Theory of Covenant for Contemporary Jews," *Covenant* 1, no. 1 (November 2006).

debated as part of the global discussion of our human circumstances. This is demonstrated early in the biblical text as God speaks to non-Hebrews and makes covenants with them that become the basis and structure of future covenantal bonds. All persons are expected to know the moral law for the well-being of the world and its creatures; the righteous follow it (Enoch, Noah) and violators are punished (Cain, residents of Sodom, etc.). "The opening chapters of Genesis," Fretheim notes, "make universal claims for this God. These Genesis chapters portray a God whose universal activity includes creating, grieving, judging, saving, electing, promising, blessing, covenant making, and law giving. And we are not yet to Israel!"[40]

In the Abrahamic story, God's covenant with Abraham declares that "all peoples on earth will be blessed through you" (Gen. 12:3). Whatever God's bond with the children of Abraham, it is to bless all humankind, an idea illustrated also in Abraham's family. Though the Abrahamic covenant continues through Isaac, his half brother Ishmael too becomes a great nation and flourishes. The covenant is to see to its blessing as well. The point is repeated in covenant with Isaac: "through your offspring all nations on earth will be blessed" (Gen. 26:4), and again in Isaac's family. Though the covenant is continued through Jacob, his brother Esau too founds a great family and is the hero of the brothers' reconciliation, overcoming understandable anger at Jacob and greeting him with welcome and generosity (Gen. 33:4). And the idea reprises with Jacob, "All peoples on earth will be blessed through you and your offspring" (Gen. 28:14). Amos makes the point in mirror-image — not that the world's peoples will be blessed through Israel (making Israel the first portal of blessing) but that Israel is blessed as other nations are: "'Are not you Israelites the same to me as the Cushites?' declares the LORD" (Amos 9:7).[41]

Fretheim summarizes: "God's actions in and for Israel thus occur within God's more comprehensive ways of acting in the larger world and are shaped by God's overarching purposes for that world. . . . *the particularity of God's*

---

40. Fretheim, *God and World in the Old Testament*, Kindle location 658.
41. The blessing to all peoples is reaffirmed in Micah:

> The remnant of Jacob will be
>   in the midst of many peoples
> like dew from the LORD,
>   like showers on the grass. (5:7)

The "dew" and "showers" parallel the blessing noted in Genesis. Thus, the descendants of Jacob will bring these blessings to others.

work in and through Israel remains intact amid the universality of God's work among the nations."[42]

The theme continues in the three central commandments of the faith: love God (Deut. 6:5, for instance), love neighbor (Lev. 19:18, among many others), and love the stranger, the *non-Israelite* (Exod. 22:21; Lev. 19:34; 23:35-39; among others). When Jesus repeats the mandate to love God and neighbor and then tells the story of the good Samaritan, a spurned stranger, he is reprising this triptych (Luke 10:27-35). And the theme emerges further in the rabbinic tradition, for instance, in the concern for the non-Jew in economic arrangements (see below) and in the emphasis on saving every life. "The person who saves one life," the Talmudic authors write, "saves a world," that is, every life regardless of faith. The importance of each life is found in the Mishnah *Sanhedrin* 4:5 (ca. 220 C.E.),[43] in the Jerusalem Talmud,[44] as well as in Maimonides (1138-1204),[45] among other medieval sources. The rabbinic view in *Sanhedrin* 105a states more explicitly, "all the righteous of the nations of the world have a place in the world to come," a principle Maimonides affirmed.[46]

The midrash in the *Mikhilta de-Shimon* (bar Yochai)[47] explains that the

---

42. Fretheim, *God and World in the Old Testament*, Kindle locations 776-777, 3619.

43. This is the version of the text found in both the Kaufman and Parma manuscripts of the Mishnah.

44. Retention of the universalist passage is interesting here as the Jerusalem Talmud is later than its Babylonian sister text, which contains a more particularist version of the passage, and copyists of the era tended to "correct" the Jerusalem manuscripts to make them accord with Babylonian versions. In this case, the Jerusalem Talmud is not "corrected" but holds to the original universalist principle. The more particularist Babylonia version, "The person who saves one [Jewish] life saves a world," appears to reflect the limited context of the Babylonian passage: it pertains to the ethics of giving witness testimony in murder cases *within* the Jewish community. The context is narrow because at the time of the writing of the Babylonian Talmud, Jewish criminal courts no longer existed, as Jews were under Roman imperial rule. The rabbis discussed these issues as legal exercise and matter of principle, and the criminal court imagined here (as an exercise in ethical principles) would have had — had it existed at all — jurisdiction in cases only among those of the Jewish faith, according to Roman law. Ephraim Urbach explains that the word "Jewish" is simply the case for this narrow context, and he notes specifically that the insertion of the word was not intended to alter the original universalist principle of saving all lives; see E. Urbach, "Kol Ha'Meqayyem Nefesh Ahat . . ." (Development of the version, vicissitudes of censorship, and business manipulations of printers; in Hebrew with English summary), *Tarbiz* 40 (1971): 268-84.

45. Maimonides, Mishnah Torah, *Hilkhot Sanhedrin* 12:3.

46. *Laws concerning Repentance*, ch. 3, sect. 5; see also, Maimonides, *Commentary to the Mishnah, Sanhedrin 10:2*.

47. In his comment on Exod. 19:2.

Torah was given not in any country but in the open desert to ensure that it belongs to all because its principles derive from the conditions of all and are relevant to all — "the Torah speaks the language of human beings."[48] What is offered in these texts is not only a national story, as Leon Kass notes, not "what happened but what *always* happens"[49] to men, women, families, tribes, and states under conditions of prosperity, strife, subjugation, and importantly, when justice is and is not pursued. Both Fretheim and Hazony hold that "The law is given because God is concerned about *the best possible life for all* of God's creatures. . . . the law stands in the service of a stable, flourishing, and life-enhancing community (the community language is important). Sinaitic law sketches a vocation to which Israel is called for the sake of the neighbor and the creation,"[50] and thus biblical narratives and law should be read "as a philosophical argument for the importance of Israel's covenant with God not only for the Jews but also for 'all the nations of the earth.' . . . [The biblical author] wished to persuade his readers that there exists a law whose force is of a universal nature, because it derives from the way the world itself was made."[51]

While much of the biblical law written at the time of the Babylonian exile (586 B.C.E.) aims at preventing the southern tribes from disappearing into the Babylonian population (as had the northern tribes into the Assyrian population), the Talmud sees much else in the Bible as pertaining to the good of all humanity.[52] The law is assumed to be understandable by human reason, much as the laws of any nation are. The extensive poor laws are grounded in universal conditions for well-being and in recognition of our interdependence. "The attempt to gain insight into the will of the God of Israel ceases, in other words, to be an attempt to gain insight into what will be good for the Jews alone, and becomes an investigation into the nature of the moral and political order in general — an investigation of the kind the Greeks gave the name of *philosophia*."[53]

48. This is a frequent Talmudic principle; see, for instance, *Nedarim* 3a.

49. L. Kass, *The Beginning of Wisdom: Reading Genesis* (New York: Free Press, 2003), pp. 10, 54.

50. Fretheim, *God and World in the Old Testament,* Kindle locations 2974-2975, 3205.

51. Hazony, *Philosophy of Hebrew Scripture*, pp. 22, 249.

52. See, for instance, *b. Megillah* 14a.

53. Hazony, *Philosophy of Hebrew Scripture*, pp. 22, 58; see also, Z. Maghen, "Dancing in Chains: The Baffling Coexistence of Legalism and Exuberance in Judaic and Islamic Tradition," in *Judaic Sources and Western Thought,* ed. J. Jacobs (New York: Oxford University Press, 2011), pp. 217-37.

As the building blocks of *philosophia,* the stories and parables of the Hebrew Bible are not historical records of value for their facticity nor are they blueprints to be mimicked. They are problem sets, a compendium of personal and societal dilemmas through which readers are to derive a code of conduct applicable to all (even if particularist ritual is not). In these narratives, wretched behavior is to be examined for what it reveals about the human condition, lessons that emerge often much later in the text when the long-term consequences can be seen.[54] One of Genesis's major lessons, the perniciousness of jealousy, begins in the book's early story of Cain and Abel but does not come to its point about reconciliation until some forty-six chapters later, in the passage on Joseph's rescue of the brothers who earlier had betrayed him.

The idea of untangling problem sets emerges from the principles of covenantal reciprocity and co-creatorship. We make the text as we work to grasp its meaning. Moreover, untangling and interpretation would have been the approaches taken by the texts' contemporaneous audiences, as the pre-Hellenic Near East did not employ the abstract, philosophical language and analytical structures of later Greco-Roman texts. Writers conveyed principle through narrative, poetry, and symbol (often redacted from multiple sources), with the usual problems of overcompression, meanderings, interruptions, conflicting accounts, hyperbole, and so on. "The Hebrew Bible," Geller notes, "unlike the New Testament, does not possess the ready vocabulary and dialectic of the developed Hellenistic tradition that are so evident in the Pauline epistles."[55] Absent a hermeneutics that unpacks and decodes narrative and symbol, readers are vulnerable to what Alfred North Whitehead calls "the fallacy of misplaced concreteness"[56] or, in Catherine Keller's words, "fallacious factualism."[57] Rowan Williams, former archbishop of Canterbury, called it the "wrong end of the stick,"[58] as the biblical point is neither accuracy nor mimicry but inquiry.

---

54. See M. Sternberg, *The Poetics of Biblical Narrative* (Bloomington: Indiana University Press, 1985).

55. S. Geller, "Manna and Sabbath: A Literary-Theological Reading of Exodus 16," *Interpretation* 59, no. 1 (January 2005): 12.

56. A. N. Whitehead, *Science and Modern World* (New York: Macmillan/Free Press, 1967), p. 51.

57. C. Keller, *On the Mystery: Discerning Divinity in Process* (Minneapolis: Fortress, 2008), p. 15.

58. Rowan Williams, *Being Christian: Baptism, Bible, Eucharist, Prayer* (Grand Rapids: Eerdmans, 2014), p. 31.

Within the problem set of the First Testament, particularist violence against other tribes is among the events most problematized by the text itself.[59] 2 Kings 9, for instance, records that Jehu murders Joram, King Ahab, Queen Jezebel, and nearly all associated with them seemingly at the behest of the prophet Elisha — that is, seemingly a recommendation from God. Yet two generations later, these events are decried as horrid (Hos. 1), making the text not a suggestion to mayhem but a caution about the long-term consequences of political violence even when pursued ostensibly for good causes. Even more problematized within the text are the Deuteronomic conquest narratives. These mythic, not historical, tales[60] were written in the seventh and sixth centuries B.C.E., over half a millennium after the events they depict, and were clear fictions to the readers of the day.[61] The Canaanite tribes were neither conquered nor killed but continued to live where they always had in the land. Relations between the Hebraic tribes and their Canaanite neighbors were overall good: David and Solomon established treaties with them, and Solomon invited the Canaanite Tyrians to build the temple.

Importantly, these tales were problematized already at the outset of this Deuteronomic passage by the opening requirement that the Hebrews sue for peace before commencing any war (Deut. 20:10).[62] Moses, immediately refusing God's command to war against the Amorites, explains his disobedience, according to rabbinic commentary, by telling God that he learned to sue for peace from God's own commandment. God is hoist on his own petard, and suing for peace wins the day; both the rabbinic code and Maimonides[63] require it. Deuteronomy further constrains particularist violence by prohibiting it even against the Hebrews' worst enemies, the Egyptians. Though they enslaved the Hebrews and pursued genocidal policies, the Bible commands that by the third generation after the exodus, Egyptians "may enter the assembly of

59. See, for instance, J. Berman, *Narrative Analogy in the Hebrew Bible: Battle Stories and Their Equivalent Non-Battle Narratives* (Leiden: Brill, 2004).

60. See G. Wenham, *Story as Torah: Reading Old Testament Narrative Ethically* (Grand Rapids: Baker Academic, 2004), especially ch. 4.

61. Either the entire conquest narrative is fictitious and the Hebrews settled relatively peacefully amid the existing tribes, or small, scattered wars occurred amid the gradual settlement, as there were wars among the non-Hebraic tribes.

62. For more detailed analysis of the Deuteronomic wars of conquest, see M. Pally, "The Hebrew Bible Is a Problem Set," in *Die Gewalt des einen Gottes: Die Monotheismus Debatte*, ed. R. Schieder (Berlin: Berlin University Press, 2014).

63. See *The Laws of Kings* 6:1.

the LORD" (Deut. 23:7-8). The mandate to kill the Amalekites, who attacked the Hebrews when they were exposed and helpless in the desert, too went undone (Exod. 17). The Amalekites remained in the region, and centuries later King David, who pursues them when they carry off the inhabitants of Ziklag as slaves, refuses to attack them once he rescues the hostages and lets them ride off (1 Sam. 30).

Summing up the Judaic position on particularism, Eugene Borowitz writes, "We cannot avoid the *dialectic of duty* imposed on us by our people's Covenant with God, which teaches us of God's covenant with all human beings."[64] Jacques Derrida similarly notes, "I am Jewish," meaning "I am testifying to the humanity of human beings, to universality, to responsibility for universality."[65] He saw the Jewish ritual of male circumcision as a cut in the body of one person that opens one to others.[66] (On this view, the absence of female circumcision in Jewish law is coherent, as women are already open to others, in the sex act and child bearing.) For Levinas, "universalist singularity" is the "primordial event in Hebraic spirituality."[67] "To be with the nations is also to be for the nations." The "paradox of Israel," he continues, is that of an "exceptional message" nonetheless "addressed to all."[68]

The paradox continues in Christianity, which too holds that the church/covenantal community has a special role, expressed in the Eucharist and *ekklesia*, for the benefit of humanity. The *ekklesia* is open to all in both the Judaic and Christian traditions, both of which provide mechanisms for inclusion and conversion. The Christian tradition, however, requires conversion for salvation whereas Judaism does not. The blessing of the covenant shall go to all the nations regardless of faith. Both traditions understand themselves as being drawn from our human condition and as enabling of its future.

---

64. E. Borowitz, "The Dialectic of Living in Covenant," in *Renewing the Covenant: A Theology for the Postmodern Jew* (Philadelphia: Jewish Publication Society, 1991), p. 232.

65. J. Derrida, "A Testimony Given," in *Questioning Judaism: Interviews by Elisabeth Weber*, trans. R. Bowlby (Stanford: Stanford University Press, 2004), p. 41.

66. J. Derrida, "Shibboleth for Paul Celan," in *Word Traces: Readings of Paul Celan*, ed. A. Fioretos (Baltimore: Johns Hopkins University Press, 1994), p. 68.

67. E. Levinas, *In the Time of the Nations*, trans. M. Smith (London: Athlone, 1994), p. 144.

68. E. Levinas, *Beyond the Verse: Talmudic Readings and Lectures* (New York: Bloomsbury, 1994), p. 199.

Covenant and Ethics: Examples from Biblical and Rabbinic Thought

To love Yahweh is to do justice to the poor and oppressed.

Peruvian theologian and Dominican
priest Gustavo Gutiérrez[69]

Though it was not a form of the Hebrew Bible or Talmud to make explicit the theology undergirding ethics, there is extensive record of the kind and extent of one's ethical obligations based on the entwined covenant with God and among persons. Regarding the difficult case of the enemy, the Hebrews are to consider them compassionately — even, as we've seen, the enslaving Egyptians, who are to be accepted into "the assembly of the LORD" by the third generation after the exodus (Deut. 23:7-8). The rabbinic laws of war, Maimonides, and Nachmanides (1194-1270) require that the residents of besieged cities be allowed to leave unharmed, and, as noted above, the rabbinic code and Maimonides require suing for peace before any war may begin.[70] The Babylonian Talmud holds that when the angels began to sing at Egypt's defeat at the Red Sea, God became angry, as the drowning Egyptians too were his children.[71] The story echoes *Genesis Rabbah* 32:10, which notes that, during the Noahite flood, God cried for all those — however sinful — who were lost in the drowning waters.

From enemy the Bible moves to stranger. Exodus 22:21, among the earliest written passages in the Pentateuch, mandates, "Do not mistreat or oppress a foreigner, for you were foreigners in Egypt." Leviticus 25:35-37 places such emphasis on aid to the stranger that it cites this type of care as the model for treatment of the Hebrew poor:

"'If any of your fellow Israelites become poor and are unable to support themselves among you, help them as you would a foreigner and stranger, so they can continue to live among you. Do not take interest or any profit from them, but fear your God, so that they may continue to live among you. You must not lend them money at interest or sell them food at a profit.'"

69. G. Gutiérrez, *A Theology of Liberation* (Maryknoll, N.Y.: Orbis, 1973), p. 194.

70. Sifre Bemidbar 157, s.v. "Vayishlach otam" (on Num. 31:7); Maimonides, *The Laws of Kings (Hilchot Melachim)* 6:4; see also Nachmanides' *Additions to Sefer Hamitzvot*, Mitzvah 5, where he mandated that one "behave well in war even with enemies at the time of war."

71. S. Buber, ed., *Midrash Aggadah*, Agadischer Commentar zum Pentateuch nach einer Handschrift aus Aleppo (Vienna: AUT, 1894), Exod. 14:28-29; see also, *Exodus Rabbah (Vilna)*, ch. 23, b. Megillah 10:2.

The words "fear your God" in the middle of this text about strangers reprise the link between bond with God and the poor: responsibility to the latter emerges from and constitutes responsibility to the former.

In Leviticus 17–26, the Holiness Code mandates that farmers leave the corners of the fields for Hebrew and other resident poor (as nonresident strangers would be too far away to participate in the harvest). Even more striking for the era are the mandates that strangers be incorporated into the economy so that they do not become poor to begin with. "The foreigner residing among you must be treated as your native-born. Love them as yourself, for you were foreigners in Egypt" (Lev. 19:34). The passage ends again with the link from care among persons to covenant with God: "I am the LORD your God." Deuteronomy continues the doubled theme: in 10:18-19, God "loves the foreigner residing among you, giving them food and clothing. And you are to love those who are foreigners, for you yourselves were foreigners in Egypt."[72]

Beyond the Pentateuch, Psalm 146:9 reprises,

The LORD watches over the foreigner
    and sustains the fatherless and the widow.

In his image and in covenantal partnership as co-creators, so are the Hebrews to do. Extending even land rights to the stranger, the Second Temple prophet Ezekiel exhorts, "You are to allot it [the land] as an inheritance for yourselves and for the foreigners residing among you and who have children. You are to consider them as native-born Israelites; along with you they are to be allotted an inheritance among the tribes of Israel" (47:22).

These examples regarding enemy and stranger fall within the vast body of law and ethics of covenantal responsibility. A quick review will note the prohibition against the return of runaway slaves (Deut. 23:15-16) and the taking of interest from the poor (Exod. 22:25).[73] Deuteronomy 23:19 prohibits the taking of interest altogether. Deuteronomy 24:19-22 requires that one leave the field corners for the poor; Deuteronomy 14:22, 28-29 requires tithing "so that the Levites (who have no allotment or inheritance of their own) and the foreigners, the fatherless and the widows who live in your towns may come and eat and be satisfied." After six years of service, slaves are to be manumitted

---

72. Deut. 24:17 continues, "Do not deprive the foreigner or the fatherless of justice," and in 27:19, "Cursed is anyone who withholds justice from the foreigner, the fatherless or the widow."

73. Exod. 22:26-27 specifies that if a garment is taken as a loan pledge, it must be returned by sunset so that the poor have it to cover themselves in the night chill.

(Exod. 21:2; Deut. 15:12). Deuteronomy 15:12-15 adds that they are not to leave empty-handed but well supplied with livestock, grain, and wine. The *shmitah* (every seventh year) and *yovel* (Jubilee, every fiftieth) require that the land lie fallow, servants rest, and debts be relieved (Lev. 25:4-6; Deut. 15:1-2). Deuteronomy 15:7-10 cautions that, in the year before the *shmitah,* people may not refuse loans to the poor on the grounds that debts will soon be canceled: "Be careful not to harbor this wicked thought. . . . Give generously to them and do so without a grudging heart." The Jubilee additionally requires that land that has been sold (usually for debt relief) be returned to its original owners (Lev. 25:13).

The extensive alms provided by the temple in Jerusalem are noted in *m. Shekalim* 6:5 and Flavius Josephus's *Antiquities of the Jews* 19.294.[74] After the temple's destruction, through the rabbinic and medieval periods, extensive networks of synagogues gave aid to both the local and transient poor.[75] So effective were these that Julian, in enjoining the Galatian high priest Arsacius to improve the poor relief, noted that the Jews and Galileans did a far better job than did Rome. "It is disgraceful," Julian wrote in 362 C.E., *"that, when no Jew ever has to beg, and the impious Galilaeans support not only their own poor but ours as well, all men see that our people lack aid from us."*[76] In this period, the biblical laws on interest were amended to go, as Robert Maloney writes, "far beyond the biblical prohibition."[77] Among rabbinic views was the idea that usury is so heinous that eschewing it is a condition of covenant with God: "I, the Lord your God, have brought you out of Egypt on the condition that you accept the commandments against usury."[78] Others held usurers to be on a par

---

74. http://www.gutenberg.org/files/2848/2848-h/2848-h.htm.

75. See L. Levine, *The Ancient Synagogue: The First Thousand Years* (New Haven: Yale University Press, 2000), especially pp. 132-33, 372-73, 580-602.

76. M. Stern, *Greek and Latin Authors on Jews and Judaism: From Tacitus to Simplicius* (Jerusalem: Israel Academy of Sciences and Humanities, 1980), pp. 549-50 = no. 482; see also, G. Hamel, *Poverty and Charity in Roman Palestine: First Three Centuries C.E.* (Berkeley: University of California Press, 1990), p. 321.

77. R. Maloney, "Usury in Greek, Roman and Rabbinic Thought," *Traditio* 27 (1971): 79-109; see also, S. W. Baron, *A Social and Religious History of the Jews,* vol. 2 (New York: Columbia University Press, 1960), p. 250; *Baba Mezi'a* 5.8.114; *Baba Mezi'a* 5.1ff., 11; Philo, *De virtutibus,* in *Philo, Complete Works,* Loeb Classical Library (Cambridge: Harvard University Press, 1929), pp. 86-87.

78. Siphra on Lev. 25:38, Maloney's translation, in Maloney, "Usury in Greek, Roman and Rabbinic Thought," p. 105. The Mishnah portion of the Talmud tractate *Baba Mezi'a* 5, 11 lists the commandments violated by usury: they "transgress the command 'Thou shalt not give him thy money upon usury,' and 'Take thou no usury of him,' and 'Thou shalt not be to him

with robbers; lending even at low interest is at times equated with idolatry and bloodshed.[79] The Jewish philosopher Philo held that taking interest "[shows] the marks of a slavish and utterly illiberal soul transformed into savagery and the nature of wild beasts."[80] Prohibitions not against usury but against interest per se are found in the Mekhilta commentary on Exodus (second century c.e.) and in the Tosefta[81] to the Talmud tractate *Baba Mezi'a,* among other texts.

In late antiquity, concern for the non-Hebrew needy diminished as tensions developed between Jewish and Christian groups, and charging interest to non-Jews was permitted. Yet, even with increasing sectarian tensions, rabbinic leaders held that if the Gentile poor are present when aid is distributed to the Jewish needy, the Gentiles are to be helped as well.

Relationality and Ethics: Examples from Recent Judaic Thought

In closing, I will turn to the last century and mention just a few contributions to relational ontology. The paragraphs below are not meant as summaries of the authors' works but as examples of the links they make among partaking of God, covenantal commitment with him, co-creatorship, and covenant/gift among persons.

In looking at the turn of the twentieth century, it might appear that the neo-Kantian Hermann Cohen, like his intellectual forerunner, saw little connection between the noumenal, ideally moral world and the phenomenal

---

as a creditor,' and 'Neither shall ye lay upon him usury,' and 'Thou shalt not put a stumbling-block before the blind, but thou shalt fear thy God. I am the Lord.'" Also along these lines, the Talmudic passage in the tractate *Sukkah* 29a, b notes, "The possessions of the householders have been delivered to the [Roman] empire because of four faults: on account of those who retain in their possession bills which have been paid (in the hope of claiming them again); on account of those who lend money on usury; on account of those who had the power to protest against wrongdoing and did not protest; and on account of those who publicly declare their intention to give specified sums for charity and do not give."

79. "Come and see the blindness of those who lend at interest," a *gemara* in both the Jerusalem and Babylonian Talmud notes. Quoting Rabbi Jose, it continues, "Get together witnesses, a notary, quill and ink, and then write down and seal (a contract): 'So-and-so has denied the God of Israel'" (quoted from the Babylonian version), Maloney's translation in Maloney, "Usury in Greek, Roman and Rabbinic Thought," p. 103.

80. Philo, *De virtutibus,* pp. 86-87; see also Philo, *De specialibus legibus,* in *Philo, Complete Works,* Loeb Classical Library (Cambridge: Harvard University Press, 1929), pp. 2.74-77.

81. A text parallel to the Mishnah that often serves as its supplement.

world of human experience.[82] Yet Cohen did not propose such a totalizing break. Ontologically, he held to more fluidity between these realms as the source of being is expressed in/through particular beings.[83] Ethically, he held that systematic, philosophical morality concerns humanity's universal ideals while religion concerns the Thou, the individual in a particular, phenomenal historical moment.[84] Though each of us is distinct and lives in a distinct historical setting, he continued, one cannot remain constrained by one's individual/societal perspective but rather must extend oneself toward universal ideals. As each person recognizes herself as "Thou" — with a particular background and personal moral flaws — she may, through prayer and atonement (religion), strive to moral improvement. But this striving entails engaging universal ideals of morality, and these, for Cohen, are what we mean by God. In short, religion reaches to each specific person and turns her toward universal ideals/God. This is the double "correlation" (in Cohen's words) between person and God: one atones for specific wrongdoings *in* striving toward universal ideals/God. In turn, by engaging ideals/God as one uniquely can, one constitutes herself as a distinct Thou.

Franz Rosenzweig, writing in Germany after World War I, rejected his friend's Kantian faith in universal principles, holding that they had led to the ruin of Europe.[85] In response to the failure of universal reason, Rosenzweig developed an interactional view of God, world, and humanity, what Elliot Wolfson calls universality "reshaped continuously in light of the entanglement of the web of particularity."[86] God, world, and humanity are joined,

---

82. Especially in his *Ethics of Pure Will*; see H. Cohen, *Ethik des reinen Willens. System der Philosophie*, vol. 2 (Berlin: Bruno Cassirer, 1904, 1907).

83. A. Sh. Bruckstein, "On Jewish Hermeneutics: Maimonides and Bachya as Vectors in Cohen's Philosophy of Origin," in *Hermann Cohen's Philosophy of Religion: International Conference in Jerusalem 1996*, ed. S. Moses and H. Wiedebach (Hildesheim: Georg Olms Verlag, 1997), p. 38.

84. H. Cohen, *Die Religion der Vernunft aus den Quellen des Judentums* (Leipzig: Fock, 1919); ET: *Religion of Reason: Out of the Sources of Judaism*, trans. S. Kaplan (New York: Frederick Unger, 1919).

85. Indeed, Rosenzweig held that Cohen's *Religion of Reason*, recognizing the substantial role of particulars and religion in human life, was a departure from his earlier work on universal, philosophical morality, in Cohen's *Ethics of Pure Will*, for instance; see Cohen, *Ethik des reinen Willens*. Alexander Altmann also rejected Cohen's system for its understanding of God as a universal ideal insufficiently connected, in Cohen's theory, to world and particulars; see A. Altmann, *The Meaning of Jewish Existence: Theological Essays, 1930-1939*, ed. A. Ivry, trans. E. Ehrlich and L. Ehrlich (Hanover, N.H.: University Press of New England, 1991), p. 15.

86. E. Wolfson, *Giving beyond the Gift: Apophasis and Overcoming Theomania* (New York: Fordham University Press, 2014), Kindle locations 1667-1668.

Rosenzweig held in *Star of Redemption*,[87] through creation, revelation, and redemption — the six together making the six-sided Star of David. He began with God's *ex nihilo* creation of world and humanity and grappled with the problem of understanding what *nihilo* might mean given that there was, at the moment of creation, at the very least God and thus potentiality. Book 2 sought to overcome the problem of a static, separate triad — God, world, and humanity — by holding that they are always-already in relation.

In creation, the world is in potentiality in God, who then makes it actual. Revelation brings God to humanity and continues to unfold potentiality (God self-reveals). It also brings humanity to God: humanity understands something of his generative potentiality, God's self-revelation. And it brings humanity to the world — we grasp something of the divine structure of world and God's vision for it — so that we apprehend what we must do. That is, humanity need not wait for God's redemption but — with the understanding gleaned from God's revelation — we must "anticipate" and "drive toward" redemption.[88] Action that is taken in this world yet which drives toward God, toward redemption, is humanity's existential and ethical task. Without such human activity, there is, Rosenzweig believed, no proper future, just the past trudging along endlessly and pointlessly. In sum, God has created world and humanity, reveals something of himself and his created world to humanity, and redeems world with humanity's effort.

Abraham Joshua Heschel worked with a similar set of interdependent concepts: the words of God's revelation must move into human feelings, experience, and importantly, action in world. Our deeds in relation to world and others, as they follow God's commandments, are essential in moving toward God — Heschel's version of the twined covenants. In his "depth theology," exploring the interdependence and tensions between dogma, faith, and worldly response, Heschel wrote, "A Jew is asked to take a *leap of action* rather than a *leap of thought*."[89]

Levinas, with the substantial task of imagining an ethics in the wake of the Second World War, sought to make vivid and unavoidable each person's ethical responsibility, each person's "ethical adventure of the relationship to

---

87. F. Rosenzweig, *The Star of Redemption*, trans. W. W. Hallo (New York: Holt, Rinehart and Winston, 1971; original 1921).

88. See also E. Bloch, *Principle of Hope*, trans. N. Plaice, S. Plaice, and P. Knight (Cambridge: MIT Press, 1959).

89. A. J. Heschel, *God in Search of Man* (New York: Farrar, Straus and Giroux, 1997), pp. 183, 283.

the other person."[90] He turns to the reciprocally constitutive covenant: nearing God happens through nearing neighbor, in pursuing justice for the other.[91] This intertwined commitment is for Levinas not a "figure of speech" but a description of God, "who approaches precisely through this relay to the neighbor — binding men among one another with obligation, each one answering for the lives of all the others." This "relay to the neighbor" is "the highest possible theological knowledge one can have."[92] It is realized not by holding to general good will but in accepting — as Gillian Rose also wrote (pt. I, ch. 3) — one's specific responsibilities as they demand particular responses. Each is in a "pluralism that does not merge into unity."[93] The universe may have plural cultures and contexts, but one takes responsibility where one is.

Levinas finds this responsibility possible because we live in time, which allows us to see another without projecting onto her our own view of things — a concern too of Levinas's contemporary and compatriot Simone Weil (pt. II, ch. 9). "Knowing" another makes her one's object, "reduces the other to presence and co-presence." But time, allowing two to exist in the same moment, does not violate her personhood. Time, "in its diachrony, would signify a relationship that does not compromise the other's alterity."[94] In *Ethics and Infinity,* Levinas continues, "access to the face [of the other] is straightaway ethical. You turn yourself toward the Other as toward an object when you see a nose, eyes, a forehead, a chin, and you can describe them. The best way of encountering the Other is not even to notice the color of his eyes! When one observes the color of the eyes one is not in social relationship with the Other. The relation with the face can surely be dominated by perception, but what is specifically the face is what cannot be reduced to that. . . . it is what forbids us to kill."[95]

Taking responsibility for another need not objectify her or subsume her into oneself, but must allow for her singularity. In turn, taking such responsibility does not collapse one's own identity into the other but makes each one her unique self. "My very uniqueness," Levinas writes, "lies in the responsibil-

---

90. E. Levinas, *Time and the Other,* trans. R. Cohen (Pittsburgh: Duquesne University Press, 1987), p. 33.

91. E. Levinas, *Totality and Infinity: An Essay on Exteriority* (Dordrecht: Kluwer Academic Publishers, 1979), p. 78.

92. E. Levinas, *In the Time of the Nations,* trans. M. Smith (London: Athlone, 1994), p. 171.

93. Levinas, *Time and the Other,* p. 42.

94. Levinas, *Time and the Other,* pp. 30-31.

95. E. Levinas, *Ethics and Infinity: Conversations with Philippe Nemo,* trans. R. Cohen (Pittsburgh: Duquesne University Press, 1985), pp. 85-86.

ity for the other man."[96] On Levinas's account, *personal responsibility is what makes one a person.*

One is not free, on his view, *not* to be in relation, not to take responsibility for the singular "face" of the other.[97] His critique of Martin Heidegger, somewhat like Rose's, hangs on the idea that Heidegger set ontology and being over ethics and relation. Levinas found this self-defeating, as it thins experience with persons in world and thus depletes the experience that makes one a person. And since relations with others is where nearing God happens, engagement with God too is thinned.[98] Like James Olthuis, who wrote, "To the extent that I am a unique self, no one else can replace me in my responsibility,"[99] Levinas writes, "to follow the Most-High is also to know that nothing is greater than to approach one's neighbour."[100]

As Martin Buber's theology of the I-Thou encounter is well known,[101] I shall here highlight only three points relevant to relationality. First, in contrast to the I-Thou (recognizing the singularity of the other and what of God is in her) stands the I-It, projecting generalities or assumptions onto another, an abrogation of covenantal bond, as Levinas and Weil too wrote. Second, as I-Thou is the only sort of encounter one can have with God, relationship with God is the ground for I-Thou among persons each time it occurs — each time one takes the time to recognize the divine in a person. Yet, echoing the twined covenant, these moments of I-Thou with others are also how we come to I-Thou with God. "God appears when people truly meet others."[102] Third, not only must each reach toward the I-Thou bond, persons must live in the

96. Levinas, "Revelation in the Jewish Tradition," p. 142.

97. While Levinas is forthright on the dyadic responsibility as inseparable from relation with God, recent readings by John Milbank among others have found it to be less clear about networks of interaction and the communal practices that promote the dignity and well-being among members. This stems in part from Levinas's finding, in Maimonides' *Guide for the Perplexed* (3.54), that the ethical ideal for humanity emerges from God's actions in the world, which Levinas calls the "law of nonreciprocity" or the "asymmetry" demanded by the relation with the other. See E. Wyschogrod, *Crossover Queries: Dwelling with Negatives, Embodying Philosophy's Others* (New York: Fordham University Press, 2006), p. 288.

98. E. Levinas, *Proper Names*, trans. M. Smith (Stanford: Stanford University Press, 1996), p. 137.

99. J. Olthuis, "Face-to-Face: Ethical Asymmetry of the Symmetry of Mutuality?" in *Knowing Other-Wise: Philosophy at the Threshold of Spirituality*, ed. J. Olthuis (New York: Fordham University Press, 1997), p. 140.

100. Levinas, *Beyond the Verse*, p. 142.

101. M. Buber, *I and Thou* (Eastford, Conn.: Martino Fine Books, 2010; original 1923), p. 59.

102. Breslauer, "Toward a Theory of Covenant for Contemporary Jews."

sorts of communities where this type of relationship is fostered. "Society is naturally composed not of disparate individuals but of associative units and associations between them."[103]

Steven Schwarzschild begins his discussion of relationship and ethics from a different perch: the covenantal promise of Messiah. In covenant, God promises the Messiah's arrival, a future time of righteousness, while humanity promises covenantal regard and ethical reckoning among persons in the present. The human effort is ever asymptotic as we never achieve messianic justice, but it is critical as an organizing principle of human life. The point of the messianic idea is not only that the Messiah arrives but that the idea of his arrival is with us now. A person of a covenantal mind lives as if the Messiah were coming each day,[104] as in the Maimonidean Thirteen Principles: "I believe with full faith in the coming of the Messiah, and, though he tarry, I anticipate him, nonetheless, on every day, when he may come."

Schwarzschild, like Rosenzweig, takes "anticipate" as activity, as ethical conduct that nears us to the justice of messianic time. Both soulful contemplation of the Messiah and bodily, physical action are obligations of "anticipate," for covenant entails an "embodied soul/ensouled body."[105] The unfolding source of being inheres in bodily beings (we are ensouled bodies), which in turn express the source of being (God in us is embodied soul). (Compare with Thomas Torrance, who wrote, each person "is not body and mind but body of his mind and mind of his body, a unitary whole";[106] see pt. II, ch. 1.) As both soul and body are necessary to covenantal fulfillment, we are to contemplate and to bring into our conduct the possibility that we might find ourselves in God's kingdom.

This, Schwarzschild held, is the way to moral decision. Without it, the world may be good or horrid, but there is no ethics, as ethics requires willed

103. Cited in G. Alperowitz, "Building a Living Democracy," *Sojourners* 19, no. 6 (July 1990): 15.

104. For Jacques Derrida on the "irreducible paradox" of the "waiting without horizon or expectation" of the messianic nonarrival/ever-arriving, see, for instance, J. Derrida, "Specters of Marx," in *Futures of Jacques Derrida*, ed. R. Rand (Stanford: Stanford University Press, 2001), p. 168.

105. The German-Israeli philosopher Gershom Sholem also emphasized the this-worldly locus of Messiah and redemption, "a process that takes place publicly, on the stage of history and in the medium of the community; in short, which essentially takes place in the visible world, and cannot be thought of except as a phenomenon that appears in what is already visible." See G. Scholem, "Zum Verstaendnis der messianischen Idee," *Judaica* (1963): 7-8.

106. T. Torrance, "The Goodness and Dignity of Man in the Christian Tradition," *Modern Theology* 4, no. 4 (July 1988): 310, 311, 322.

direction of action. "When men ask themselves how to behave or, indeed, what the standards are to be of their proper behavior, the Messianic end defines the mean by which that end can and is to be attained."[107]

Schwarzschild's account is a twined project: while God promises messianic righteousness, each person must act to bring it about. Because God brings the messianic future, "humanity and its morality are a necessary but not a sufficient condition for the attainment of the life of the world to come." But because humanity must act to bring it near, God's work too "is a necessary but, for ethical reasons, not in turn a sufficient condition."[108] Without our endeavors, God could bring the world to good, but humanity would have no opportunity for *moral* conduct, as this requires our decision and action.

In sum, Schwarzschild describes something like a "messianic imaginary" (as Cornelius Castoriadis, Benedict Anderson, and Charles Taylor have spoken of social and political imaginaries). Castoriadis holds that "the imaginary of the society [the way we picture the way things are] . . . creates for each historical period its singular way of living, seeing and making its own existence."[109] Schwarzschild's "messianic imaginary" is one such way of seeing the world in which God's commitment to bring messianic justice commits us to bring it as well. It moves humanity to repair uncovenantal conduct and restore covenantal bonds. It is to "repair and heal the world through (by means of) the kingdom of God" *(Letakken olam bemalchut shaddai)*.[110]

The works of Eugene Borowitz bring together much in the preceding ideas. He begins with the goal "to restore a proper tension between our autonomy and social responsibility. . . . I too equate all human dignity with self-determination, but only within the context of a covenant with God that gives us our personal significance and makes all God's covenant-partners an essential element of our selfhood." The self of "dignity," "self-determination," and "personal significance" emerges from relation with God and others. "The self gains its inestimable worth neither by the self-evident nature of its quality nor our willing it, but by being covenanted to God. It cannot then demand a Kantian or Sartrean radical autonomy or self-legislation. . . . We employ our

107. S. Schwarzschild, "On Jewish Eschatology," in *The Pursuit of the Ideal: Jewish Writings of Steven Schwarzschild*, ed. M. Kellner (Albany: State University of New York Press, 1990), p. 218.

108. Schwarzschild, "On Jewish Eschatology," p. 228.

109. See B. Thompson, *Studies in the Theory of Ideology* (Berkeley: University of California Press, 1984), p. 6, see also, B. Anderson, *Imagined Communities* (London: Verso, 1991), pp. 6, 4.

110. Schwarzschild, "On Jewish Eschatology," p. 229.

will rightfully when God serves as its limiting condition, better, as co-partner in decision making."

Borowitz repudiates "the self as a monad. God makes us individuals but also an inseparable part of humanity. Our finitude also makes each of us necessarily dependent upon others." Borowitz concludes, *"We therefore stand under a religio-moral charge to live in communities and to exercise our personal autonomy with social concern."*[111] As communities and their concerns change, Borowitz writes, our "moral charge" is interpretive[112] so that "acts through which the covenant is lived are appropriate to that generation's situation."[113] This is not to say that people may devise moral codes to their liking — that they may say just anything — but that covenantal principles find their application in changing conditions.

Absent this, one would have to conclude either that God intends no change in persons or world such that a static covenant is eternally relevant. Or that God intends a static covenant to become irrelevant in the face of human and natural change. Indeed, Borowitz's work itself is a case of covenant in context. It considers Judaic ethics along with those ideals of the modern West that he finds consonant with it: "dignity," "self-determination," and "personal significance" with "social concern."

*   *   *

At this point in our look at relational theologies, it might be useful to summarize our ideas thus far. Each of us is at all only as each distinct one of us partakes of the unfolding source of being and only as that being, while radically distinct from us, is expressed in us. Thus distinction-amid-relation is what it means to "be." As there is no other way to be, this is the way we are with each other as well. We are distinct from each other but in relation.

One way to speak of partaking of the source of being is to say we are in God's image. One way to speak of relation is covenant, the bond between God

111. Borowitz, "The Dialectic of Living," pp. 221-22.

112. E. Borowitz, *Exploring Jewish Ethics: Papers on Covenant Responsibility* (Detroit: Wayne State University Press, 1990); see also, E. Borowitz, *A New Jewish Theology in the Making* (Philadelphia: Westminster, 1968), pp. 63-64; E. Borowitz, *Renewing the Covenant: A Theology for the Postmodern Jew* (Philadelphia: Jewish Publication Society, 1991); and E. Borowitz, "Covenant," in *Judaism after Modernity: Papers from a Decade of Fruition* (Lanham, Md.: University Press of America, 1999), pp. 195-204.

113. E. Borowitz, "The Chosen People Concept as It Affects Life in the Diaspora," *Journal of Ecumenical Studies* 12, no. 4 (Fall 1975): 566.

and persons, expressed *to* all in the Noahite covenant and to the Hebrews *for* the blessing of all in the Abrahamic covenant. Just as the donative source of being inheres in particular beings, so covenant with the source of being is expressed in covenant among persons. Just as each particular expression of God shows a bit more of what can be, each particular expression of covenant shows a bit more of what it too can be. There are multiple interpretations of covenantal relations, yet the relations about which interpretations are multiple must remain covenantal.

In the terms of this book, this "covenantality" is reciprocal consideration-worthiness, reciprocal regard and responsibility among persons (nearby and increasingly across the globe). Reciprocal regard brings our attention to the underlying concerns of others, to ask "why the other side is for the other side" so we may address our problems and build our future together with fair input from all involved. Absent this, we may be led by our fears, as Hobbes said, to quick fixes and uncreative, short-term thinking that we believe ensure safety and gain. The world's persistent problems even amid the enormous wealth of the planet suggest that our fixes and thinking are indeed short-term, which is why we are here suggesting an ontology that keeps covenant in mind and policy.

CHAPTER 7

Distinction-amid-Relation in Trinity

The Divine Paradox: Persons and *Perichoresis*

Having discussed, in the preceding chapter, Judaic notions of partaking of God (in his image) and the importance of covenant with him for our covenantality with others, it might do well to continue with these ideas as developed in the Christian tradition, starting perhaps with the Christian idea of Jesus as the new covenant. After all, "The New Testament," Stanley Hauerwas writes, "is in many ways a midrash [interpretive commentary] on the Hebrew Scriptures through which we Christians try to understand better what it means to be part of God's people in light of God's presence to us in Jesus of Nazareth."[1] Yet, as the concept of Trinity captures so much of the Christian understanding of partaking and relationality, I will start instead with it and continue with other Christian tenets in the chapters that follow. As it is these ontological ideas that I am after, my emphasis here, as in previous chapters, is in the way various writers, schools, and traditions illuminate and enrich them, their commonalities and cross-references. Though differences among certain positions are evident, they are not here the major focus unless they help us understand the principles of distinction-amid-relation.

Ironically, given the importance of the Trinity, the idea has had a bit of a spotty history. Among liberal nineteenth-century Protestant thinkers, it was found too implausible not only for reason but also for faith. Albrecht Ritschl held, for instance, that Christianity is primarily concerned with values rather than with the inner nature of God, to which humanity has no access. Friedrich

---

1. S. Hauerwas, *The Peaceable Kingdom: A Primer in Christian Ethics* (Notre Dame: University of Notre Dame Press, 1983), p. 70.

Schleiermacher, anticipating later apophatic theologies, too held that speculating about the nature of God with concepts (like Trinity) that are outside human experience is incoherent and damaging to theology: "We have only to do with the God-consciousness given in our self-consciousness along with our consciousness of the world; hence we have no formula for the being of God in Himself as distinct from the being of God in the world, and should have to borrow any such formula from speculation, and so prove ourselves disloyal to the character of the discipline at which we are working."[2]

At bottom, what rankled these thinkers was not only humanity's lack of access to the triune God but also the paradox of Trinity itself. That the divine is a paradox was already true in the Judaic concept of God, who is transcendent and incorporeal yet immanent on earth and in relation with all persons. Moreover, the Hebraic Tetragrammaton (YHWH) contains the words for "was," "is," and "will be," presenting not only a paradox but a triune one: God exists outside time yet also in the real past, present, and future. The trope of three-in-one appears throughout Judaic theology: the (one) central commandment of love is triply directed toward God, neighbor, and stranger; the (one) creation occurs in two sets of three days; the patriarchs of one people are three; the three visitors who tell Abraham he will have a son become one voice at the moment of annunciation (Gen. 18); the one people of Israel is four sets of three tribes; and finally, God is addressed, in Judaic doxology, as "Holy Holy Holy." (And, if I may stretch the idea, it took roughly three centuries for this Judaic triadic form to be overlaid with Christian content, which is heir also to Greek triads, notably Plotinus's formulation of God as the One, the Divine Mind, and the Word-Soul.)[3]

---

2. F. Schleiermacher, *The Christian Faith*, ed. H. R. Mackintosh and J. S. Stewart, 2nd ed. (Edinburgh: T. & T. Clark, 1999; original 1830/1831), p. 748.

3. Robert W. Jenson discusses in greater detail the idea that the triune life is God of the past, the present, and the future, in R. W. Jenson, "Appeal to the Person of the Future," in *The Futurist Option*, ed. R. W. Jenson and C. E. Braaten (New York: Newman Press, 1970). Some readings distinguish the Judaic from Christian traditions by holding that the former expresses the divine paradox through the mode of time (past, present, and future), the latter, through space (the Trinitarian persons and the body of the divine-man Jesus). Yet the Christian paradox is not without time; it resolves the *aporia* between transcendence and immanence through Jesus' time on earth: through Jesus, God moves into time for a time yet is at all times. Neither is the Judaic paradox without space. It resolves the *aporia* between transcendence and immanence through God's presence in all places and in specific spaces such as the temple. Moreover, both traditions hold that God is partially knowable to humanity, and this knowability must be in a form humanity can grasp: time is a human experience through which we can grasp the eternal, unending time-ness of God. Perhaps most importantly, in both traditions time

Divine paradoxes, however, have encountered renewed interest over the last thirty or so years when, as Stanley Grenz notes, Trinitarian interrelatedness came to be seen as "the final touchstone for speaking about human personhood."[4] The Trinity has a good deal to say in particular about distinction-amid-relation and thus offers much for our project of melding separability and situatedness in public policy. In the Trinity, Hans Urs von Balthasar writes, "the principles of individuality and community are at work together simultaneously, so that the Person makes demands and imposes conditions on the community, and the community does likewise in respect of the Persons. For only in this sense can God in fact be 'Love.'. . . In the Godhead, therefore, individuality and community have a common origin."[5] James Torrance further calls for a human trinity of sorts: "the person not just as an individual but as someone who finds his or her true being-in-communion with God and with others, the counterpart of a Trinitarian doctrine of God."[6]

This does not mean that God's triune nature becomes material but, as Aquinas wrote,[7] that the Trinitarian persons, who mutually constitute each other and the Godhead as a whole, teach us also about the human condition. The triune God is after all what humanity partakes of. Jonathan Wilson-Hartgrove correctly writes, "The God who is three persons in community creates humanity in the image of community."[8]

Two shifts in early church thinking were especially important for the development of Trinity. One was the Roman Church's description of the Trinity not as three *hypostases* (or *sub-stantia*, the substance *underlying* each real thing) but as the Latin *personae*, persons with distinct, nonexchangeable features. This allowed for more durable distinction among the Trinitarian persons. Philip Rolnick, among others, suggests that the concept of "person"

---

is a mode of relationality — as two beings may exist at the same time and come to relationship together — while space is a mode of distinction, as one space cannot be occupied by two beings at once. Existing in space (distinct) yet in time allows humanity to understand distinction-amid-relation.

4. S. Grenz, *The Social God and the Relational Self* (Louisville: Westminster John Knox, 2001), p. 57.

5. H. U. von Balthasar, *Engagement with God*, trans. R. J. Halliburton (San Francisco: Ignatius, 2008), pp. 30-31, 41.

6. J. Torrance, "The Doctrine of the Trinity in Our Contemporary Situation," in *The Forgotten Trinity*, ed. A. Heron, vol. 3 (London: BC/CCBI Inter-Church House, 1991), p. 15.

7. See, for instance, *Summa Theologica* Ia, q. 40, art. 2.

8. J. Wilson-Hartgrove, *New Monasticism: What It Has to Say to Today's Church* (Grand Rapids: Brazos, 2008), p. 61.

emerged in the first place with early church discussions of Trinity.[9] As this distinction may run the risk of tritheism, fathers of the Western Church took pains to emphasize the Trinity's unity. For the Eastern Church, however, this ran the risk of obscuring God's relational nature, which requires distinction in order to relate, and the Cappadocian Fathers replied by accentuating the concept of *perichoresis* — the second key early church development.[10]

Perichoresis imagines the three Trinitarian persons "in a dance around," where each is who he is in relation to ("dancing" with) the others. These relations constitute the whole of the "dance" in which the three persons are (in contrast to the *filioque*, where the Spirit proceeds from the Father and Son). "Person," John Milbank notes, is a relational term (while "essence" or "substance" is not). "Yet," he notes, drawing on Aquinas, "this does not entirely collapse the persons into the relations, because 'person' is here rather the point of equipoise between relation and substance . . . (*ST* [*Summa Theologica*] I, q. 29, a. 4 resp.)."[11] The Trinitarian persons in mutual constitution as Godhead are also mutually constitutive of humanity: we partake of the "image of community," and so have the capacity for communal relations.

Though *perichoresis* is taken to be about "partners" in the Trinitarian dance, it may also be thought of in terms not of dancers but of the dance itself. In a ballet, the movements are separate and distinct, yet in interaction they make the dance. Without the specific character of each movement in relation to other movements, each gesticulation is but a random jab. It is not a movement *in* a dance because, as an isolated gesture, it is not in a process

---

9. P. Rolnick, *Person, Grace, and God* (Grand Rapids: Eerdmans, 2007), pt. 1.

10. This is not to say that the Cappadocians maintained a settled unanimity on the Trinity. See, for instance, Najeeb Awad's discussion of differing emphases in the writings of Basil of Caesarea and Gregory of Nazianzus. Basil, Awad writes, held more to the idea that the Father alone is the uncaused Godhead, from which the Son and Spirit are caused, a view that suggests more of a "patro-centric," quasi-hierarchical arrangement. Gregory, on Awad's account, held to the more "reciprocally koinonial" view, where the Father is the origin *(arche)* of the Son and Spirit but not the source/principle *(aitios)*: "the Father is the person who unites the three hypostases as one ousia, and not the one who represents the divine ousia alone." It is thus "the totality of the three persons' equal inter-relationality" that is the *monarchia* of the Trinity. On Awad's analysis, Gregory has the more perichoretic vision; see N. Awad, "Between Subordination and Koinonia: Toward a New Reading of the Cappadocian Theology," *Modern Theology* 23, no. 2 (2007): 196, 198, also 194-98. See also T. A. Noble, "Paradox in Gregory Nazianzen's Doctrine of the Trinity," in *Studia Patristica*, ed. E. A. Livingstone (Leuven: Peeters, 1993), p. 97.

11. J. Milbank, "Christianity and Platonism in East and West," in *Divine Essence and Divine Energies: Ecumenical Reflections on the Presence of God in Eastern Orthodoxy*, ed. C. Athanasopoulos and C. Schneider (Cambridge: James Clarke, 2013), p. 177.

of constituting a dance for each movement to be part of. Each motion is but a toe's poke in the air, not an arabesque. In a dance, however, each lift and pivot in relation to all others transforms each one of them from a random gesture into a gesture *of* the dance *because* movement-in-relation makes a dance for all gestures to be part of. As each movement gives the others the "identity" of being not a poke but a dance movement, each is not depleted by this giving but is given identity itself and enriched.

Analogously, as the Cappadocians imagined it, the identity of each Trinitarian person and the relations among them make each what it is — a person of the Godhead — and also constitute the Godhead of which each is a part. No single person alone could be a person in a Trinity as, absent their relations, there is no Trinity in which to be a (Trinitarian) person. The Trinitarian persons are at once distinct, each with "its own particular distinguishing notes," as Gregory of Nyssa wrote in keeping with the dance imagery.[12] Yet, though distinguished from the others, each is equal in constituting the triune unity. Describing Gregory of Nazianzus's understanding of Trinity, Najeeb Awad writes that "He is, in fact, founding the relations that are constitutive for the distinction between the three persons on a tri-union of a completely equal presentation of the 'ousia,' in such a way that does not allow any possible suggestion of hierarchical subordination of any one of the divine persons by virtue of origination."[13] Moreover, as in dance, each gives the others the identity of a Trinitarian person without loss but with repletion, as he himself gains identity in the Trinitarian event.

The early-twentieth-century Russian philosopher, priest, and mathematician Pavel Florensky describes this as the person or "self" emerging as it "incorporates its I in the I of another," in the "not-I," in the "Thou"[14] (as his contemporary Hermann Cohen also said; pt. II, ch. 6). One becomes most fully oneself, most replete, in incorporating oneself in another and another in oneself. Or in the words of Edith Stein, the German Jewish philosopher who converted to Catholicism and became a Discalced Carmelite sister, for the persons of the Trinity, "'I am' is identical in meaning with 'I give myself totally to you,' 'I am one with you,' and so also identical with 'we are.'"[15]

---

12. Gregory of Nyssa, *Ad petrium*, in *Saint Basil: The Letters*, trans. R. J. Deferrari, vol. 2, *Epp.* 197-227, Loeb Classical Library (London: Heinemann, 1961), pp. 207-9.

13. Awad, "Between Subordination and Koinonia," p. 195.

14. P. Florensky, *The Pillar and Ground of Truth*, trans. B. Jakim (Princeton: Princeton University Press, 1997), p. 67.

15. E. Stein, *Endliches und Ewiges Sein* (Leuven: Nauwelaerts; Freiburg: Herder, 1950), p. 324.

More recently, Daniel Bell Jr. and Aaron Riches have elaborated the notion of donative repletion, where in giving, one becomes not drained but fulfilled. Riches writes, "On this view, personhood is analogically grounded in the pattern of the trinitarian perichoresis, which means that 'self'-renunciation *for* the Other is not a kenosis that exhausts the 'I.'" Rather, "there occurs a reverse restoration of I. . . . And this unlocks the paradox of theosis: becoming deiform involves receiving all one is from another in the 'dialogue of love.'"[16] Because God is the Trinitarian persons becoming replete as they give to each other, becoming analogously more like God is to become more of oneself in the act of giving.

In his discussion, Bell, like Anselm, rejects the binary between caring for oneself and caring for another, where help to another means loss to oneself and attention to the self deprives a neighbor. *Perichoresis* proposes instead that "we can give ourselves as a gift of love to our neighbors without end and without loss (Matt. 22:19; Mark 12:31)." This allows one, Bell continues, to "overcome" the "modern illusion of the isolated, alienated self (or postmodern dissolute self)" and "the masculine fantasy of an absolute self-possession." Life may instead be "lived as donation, as the ceaseless giving (and receiving) of the gift of love, life as participation in the dance of charity that is the Trinity."[17] In this, the self is not deprived but enhanced.

Trinity: Examples of Early Sources and Interpretation

The biblical sources for Trinity most cited are 1 Corinthians 12:4-6: "There are different kinds of gifts, but the same Spirit distributes them. There are different kinds of service, but the same Lord. There are different kinds of working, but in all of them and in everyone it is the same God at work." 2 Corinthians 13:14 is more clearly Trinitarian: "May the grace of the Lord Jesus Christ, and the love of God, and the fellowship of the Holy Spirit be with you all." Even more explicit is Matthew 28:19: "Therefore go and make disciples of all nations, baptizing them in the name of the Father and of the Son and of the Holy Spirit." Joseph Sittler cautions, however, that early Christian thinkers did not immediately come to the oneness of God and Jesus. Initially, they wrote not

16. A. Riches, "After Chalcedon: The Oneness of Christ and the Dyothelite Mediation of His Theandric Unity," *Modern Theology* 24, no. 2 (April 2008): 214.

17. D. Bell Jr., "A Theopolitical Ontology of Judgment," in *Theology and the Political: The New Debate*, ed. C. Davis, J. Milbank, and S. Žižek (Durham, N.C., and London: Duke University Press, 2005), p. 221.

about one substance but about "being *of* one substance."[18] As late as the fourth century, the *homoousios* of the Nicene Creed (325) regarded Christ not as one with the Father but as "of one substance with the Father."

A shift can be found first in Origen but more clearly among the Cappadocian Fathers, who argued for the triune God from soteriology: the *telos* of incarnation, crucifixion, and redemption, they held, is that humanity is forgiven and brought near to God. In Athanasius's famous phrasing, "God became man that man might become god." As only God can bring beings to himself, neither Son nor Spirit would be able to bring humanity to God were they too not God. The three must be one-in-God.

Athanasius held that the third Trinitarian person, the Spirit, is all that the Father and Son are but is neither of the two. Regarding the Son, he writes, "They are two, for the Father is Father and is not also Son, and the Son is Son and is not also Father; but the Nature is one . . . and thus there is one God and none other but he. . . . [T]he same things are said of the Son as are said of the Father, except his being said to be 'Father.'"[19] Extending this to the Spirit, Athanasius writes that if the Son is of the Father, and the Spirit is of God, then the Spirit has the same relation to both Father and Son, who are God: "If the Son is of the Father and is proper to his Being, the Spirit who is said to be of God must be proper to the Son."[20] Relations between Son and Spirit are the same as those between Father and Spirit since nothing can be said of the Father that cannot be said of the Son.

Athanasius's work had significant influence on the agreement, at the Council of Alexandria (362), to use the term *ousia* to mean one Being and *hypostasis* to mean each Trinitarian person. "While hypostasis lays stress on concrete independence, ousia lays it on intrinsic constitution. . . . Athanasius taught that in God one and the same identical 'substance' or object, without any division, substitution, or differentiation of content, is permanently presented in three distinct objective forms."[21] Two of them, Son and Spirit, are (from the human perspective) "ways" to God, who is also Son and Spirit. The three are what God is when he says, "I am" — an idea in place by the time of

18. J. Sittler, *Gravity and Grace: Reflections and Provocations* (Minneapolis: Augsburg, 1986), pp. 36-37, emphasis mine.

19. Athanasius, *Contra Arianos (Oration against the Arians)* 3.5.

20. Athanasius, *Ad Serapion (Letter to Serapion)* 1.25; 3.1; 4.1ff.

21. G. Prestige, *God in Patristic Thought* (London: SPCK, 1950), pp. xxix, 168ff., 188; see also, T. Torrance, *Theology in Reconciliation: Essays towards Evangelical and Catholic Unity in East and West* (London: Geoffrey Chapman, 1975), pp. 218-31; Torrance, "Doctrine of the Holy Trinity," pp. 398-405.

the Council of Constantinople (381), where one finds Godhead described as "three persons one being."

The equality of Trinitarian persons was Augustine's belief as well: no two are greater than one, nor are the three together greater than any one alone. He who has been sent (Son) is no less than he who sends (Father). Importantly, the Trinity is not an Aristotelian substance, as that would prioritize substance over relation. But neither is relation prioritized over substances with distinction, which, on Augustine's view, is necessary for agapic giving. As the Trinity is *agape*, giving for the sake of the other, it requires "another" to give to.

We see this otherness, on Augustine's account, as each Trinitarian person exists differently in time. The Father is all time at once; Augustine calls the Father memory, where all things always are. The Son, also all time at once, was nonetheless temporal, in "the realm of the passing away," like the understanding in the present moment that does not last. This does not mean that the Father and Son are in different times but that they are distinct in one: the eternal God (both Father and Son) encompasses all that has passed and is passing. What has not yet passed is in the ongoing presence of Son and Spirit on earth.

In parsing Augustine, Anthony Baker notes that the work of the Spirit, eternal yet in time on earth, brings together the Father, Son, and humanity. We partake of the triune God and analogously express him in earthly ways, each expressing him a bit differently, thus yielding a world of varied expressions. Spirit engages these (human, worldly) expressions of God and is the way of God to encounter them. The earthly, human expressions are "the endless Response of creation to God, [which set] in motion an infinite number of differences. . . . Christ as Word is all that needs to be said; but all is *not yet said*. The Spirit is this *saying* of creation, vocalizing the word of God as responses to God's first utterance."[22]

All is not yet said because the Father does not do all the talking, so to speak. On Augustine's account, the talking includes each person's response to the triune God, each person's way of living out Trinitarian distinction and relation, its difference without violence. The Trinity demonstrates that difference among persons does not equate with strife, nor are sameness and conformity the requirements of peace. Baker continues, "The Trinity is a non-violent community, characterized by excessive love through temporal distance. *Christian theology, therefore, poses the possibility of non-identical peace.*"[23] The practical

---

22. A. Baker, "Violence and the Trinity: A Wesleyan Reading of Milbank's Augustinianism," *Wesleyan Theological Journal* 36, no. 1 (Spring 2001): 124, 125, 126.

23. Baker, "Violence and the Trinity," p. 127, emphasis mine.

possibility of such peace is made real in each human expression — each instance on earth — of Trinitarian nonviolent difference, or nonoppositional difference, as James Olthuis wrote.

One reason persons can pursue Trinitarian nonidentical peace, Augustine held, is that humanity can know something about it. Just as the mind, in God's image, knows the structures of the world's undergirding principles (numbers, ratio, beauty), so too the mind, because it is of the Trinitarian God, also understands something of him.[24] For instance, love, on Augustine's view, is triune: the lover, the beloved, and the act of loving. As the triune nature of love is found in God and as humanity is analogously in God's image, humanity may understand something of (relational) love and so may love in (re)turn. We, in God's image, may grasp something of God; the mind, Augustine writes, is "able to remember and understand and love him by whom it was made."[25]

Augustine also saw limits to the human mind, given its radical difference from God, and held that it apprehends Trinity only as in a mirror or as enigma. Gregory of Nyssa was more optimistic. He saw the Trinitarian persons as "continuous and uninterrupted community" that disallows the "interposition of some outside thing" or any "void, in the form of an interspace."[26] God may thus reveal himself through the one Godhead or through one or the other Trinitarian person, and humanity may grasp both the one and the triune forms of revelation. Gregory writes, "the individuality of the persons of the Godhead, as they have been handed down in our faith, is made known to us."[27]

Thomas Aquinas too was optimistic, holding that God self-reveals the unity and distinction of Trinity, both apprehendable by humanity.[28] God's act of creation, on Aquinas's account, involves both coming-into-being and the individuation of beings that are yet in relation. God's gift to humanity is being, individuation, and relationality. The twelfth-century thinker Richard of St.

24. In this, Augustine was not the first. He was building, for instance, on the idea of the triadic structure of both persons and world as adumbrated in the Neoplatonism of Plotinus and Iamblichus. Origen too had believed that persons are triadic unities — on his view of body, soul, and mind — that shadow the Trinity.

25. Augustine, *De Trinitate* 15.4.15, in Patrologia Latina 42 (vol. 1, pt. 5); see also, Augustine, *The Trinity (De Trinitate)*, in *Works of St. Augustine*, trans. E. Hill and J. E. Rotelle (Hyde Park, N.Y.: New City Press, 2012).

26. Gregory of Nyssa, *Ad petrium*, p. 209.

27. Gregory of Nyssa, *Ad petrium*, pp. 207-9.

28. T. Aquinas, *Scriptum super libros sententiarum magistri Petri Lombardi*, ed. R. P. Mandonnet (Paris: Lethielleux, 1929), d. 2, q. 1, a. 3; d. 22, q. 1, a. 3; T. Aquinas, *Quaestiones disputatae de potentia Dei*, ed. P. Pession (Turin: Marietti, 1965; original 1259-1268), q. 10, a. 5; see also, A. Pabst, *Metaphysics: The Creation of Hierarchy* (Grand Rapids: Eerdmans, 2012), p. 256.

Victor too saw humanity's relationality as a consequence of the social nature of God, not only dyadic but also triune relationality opening to community and networks of relations. As humanity is in God's (relationally networked) image, networks of relations are also humanity's nature. "Relations amongst created beings," Adrian Pabst writes, "intimate in some sense, approximately and imperfectly, divine relationality within the Trinity."[29] Or, as Aquinas put it: "persona est relation."[30]

In the early modern era, Calvin, in his *Institutes,* completed his four-part proof of the divinity of Jesus with a discussion of Trinity, which substantially influenced the broad range of Reformed traditions. The distinctiveness of each Trinitarian person does not suggest, on Calvin's view, primacy or succession but eternal interdependence. "For although we affirm that there is a *principium divinitatis* in the Father in respect of order and position *(ratione ordinis et gradus),* yet we declare it a detestable invention that Being belongs to the Father alone, as though he were the deifier of the Son."[31] Parsing Calvin, Thomas Torrance refers to Calvin's distinction between subsistence/*hypostasis* (Trinitarian persons in relation, *existere ad alios*) and being/*essentia* (being-in-itself, *esse in se ipso, a se ipso*).[32] We use the terms "Father," "Son," and "Spirit" to describe *hypostasis,* persons in relation. If the Son is discussed in terms of being the son of the Father, then "Son" is the appropriate word. But in discussion not of this relationship but of *essentia,* the being of God, the Son is the same being as is the Father. Echoing Athanasius, Gregory Nazianzen, and Augustine, Calvin writes, "In each *hypostasis* the whole divine Nature is understood, it being assumed that each has his own subsistent property."[33] Calvin says the same of the Spirit: it is a *hypostasis* of God, a Trinitarian person in relation, but also divine being.[34]

Calvin uses the concept *in solidum* (as a whole) to highlight Trinitarian oneness. Holding to the whole in each and each as one and the whole, "The

---

29. Pabst, *Metaphysics,* p. 301.

30. R. Walls, "The Church: A Communion of Persons," in *Christ in Our Place: The Humanity of God in Christ for the Reconciliation of the World,* ed. T. Hart and D. Thimell (Eugene, Ore.: Wipf and Stock, 1989), pp. 104-5.

31. J. Calvin, *Institutes of the Christian Religion,* ed. J. McNeill, trans. F. Battles, vols. 1-2 (Philadelphia: Westminster, 1960; original 1536), 1.13.24. Hereafter *Institutes.*

32. T. Torrance, "Calvin's Doctrine of the Trinity," *Calvin Theological Journal* 25, no. 2 (1990): 188; see also, T. Torrance, *Trinitarian Perspectives: Toward Doctrinal Agreement* (Edinburgh: T. & T. Clark, 1994), pp. 69-71.

33. Calvin, *Institutes* 1.13.19; 1.13.23.

34. Calvin, *Institutes* 1.13.20.

in solidum concept enables Calvin to give firm expression to the intrinsically interpersonal cohesion of the Three in One and One in Three, in which there is no confusion or separation between the Persons."[35]

Trinity: Hegel and a Few Discussions from the Last Century, Linking the Immanent and Economic Trinity

One of the most significant considerations of Trinity in the modern era is in the work of G. W. F. Hegel, his idea of Absolute Spirit, the interaction of all ideas, things, and nature that moves history forward and yields ultimate truth.[36] The dialectical process by which it moves forward is triune, as each thesis and its opposite antithesis form a synthesis that moves us to a higher understanding. As this process continues through history, truth slowly becomes a bit clearer.

Beyond the structural echo to the Trinity, Hegel's three-part system — when viewed "religiously," as he put it — sees Absolute Spirit as the triune God's self-revelation through time (though Hegel did not mechanically equate Absolute Spirit and God). Hegel describes three moments of the divine. The first is essential or pure being, God in himself. Second is explicit self-existence: God as he moves into/creates something other than himself — world — which Hegel called the Son, who is at once pure being yet separate from it. The "Spirit of bare thought has become actual."[37] Third is self-consciousness, God returning to himself with self-conscious knowledge/experience of how humanity knows him. With the resurrection (God's experience of world and return from it), immaterial, timeless God "along with" material world moves through time toward truth, the *telos* of human history and the three moments of the divine.

At the turn of the twentieth century, British social Trinitarianism, recalling Richard of St. Victor, returned to the emphasis on the triune and thus the communal nature of divine relationality. In 1900, Wilfred Richmond wrote, "God is a fellowship, a communion of Persons," and, he continued, so are human persons in his image: "Personality, in the form in which it is supposed to be most intensely and unmistakably real, is a communion, a fellowship of

---

35. Torrance, "Calvin's Doctrine of the Trinity," p. 192.

36. G. W. F. Hegel, *The Phenomenology of Mind*, trans. J. Baillie (New York: Harper and Row, 1967; original 1807).

37. Hegel, *The Phenomenology of Mind*, p. 781.

Persons."[38] J. R. Illingworth wrote similarly in 1907, "A person is as essentially a social, as he is an individual being," and "the co-equal persons within the Godhead . . . [enable] us to think of God, as, if the term be guarded from any tritheistic connotation, a social being, or society."[39] George Gordon archly remarked that God is either an "eternal egoist" or an "eternal socialist." Gordon chose the latter because, as humanity is in God's image, only a "social" God provides a "ground and hope of humanity."[40]

Continuing the idea at mid-century, Wolfhart Pannenberg, a student of Karl Barth, noted that the very concept of the Trinity connotes a "social" God. He meant not only the social relations within the Trinity, of which humanity partakes, but relations between God and humanity.[41] This began the substantial discussion of God's internal Trinitarian relations (immanent Trinity) and Trinitarian persons in relation to humanity (economic Trinity). After all, Pannenberg observed, two of the three Trinitarian persons, Son and Spirit, are in the world in engagement with us. To have Trinity at all, there is relation both within Trinity and a bringing of world to the Godhead. Pannenberg noted that not only does the Father give of himself to the Son but the "worldly" Jesus glorifies the Father such that this glorification is *within* the Father. Relation to world is within his identity. God *is* both his immanent and economic relations, or as Nicholas Lash writes, "We have relationships; God *is* the relations that he has. . . . God, we might say, is relationship without remainder."[42]

The robust link between the immanent and economic Trinity continues in the work of Pannenberg's compatriot, Karl Rahner. If the two were not closely linked, Rahner argued — if God in himself (immanent) were not knowable from God's communication to us (economic) — we would have no way to know about God. Our ideas about him would be mere human imaginings. Yet, Rahner holds, God in himself is (in part) knowable owing to revelation, his communication with us, and salvation: "In the Trinity, in the economy and

---

38. W. Richmond, *Essay on Personality as a Philosophical Principle* (London: Edward Arnold, 1900), p. 17.

39. J. R. Illingworth, *The Doctrine of the Trinity* (London: Macmillan, 1907), pp. 142-43.

40. G. Gordon, *Ultimate Conceptions of the Faith* (Boston: Houghton and Mifflin, 1903), p. 374.

41. See W. Pannenberg, *Jesus — God and Man*, trans. L. Wilkins and D. Priebe, 2nd ed. (Philadelphia: Westminster, 1977); W. Pannenberg, *Systematic Theology*, trans. G. Bromiley, vols. 1-3 (Grand Rapids: Eerdmans, 1991-1998); W. Pannenberg, *Theology and the Kingdom of God*, ed. R. J. Neuhaus (Philadelphia: Westminster, 1969); W. Pannenberg, *Basic Questions in Theology*, ed. G. H. Kelm, vols. 1-2 (Philadelphia: Fortress, 1971).

42. N. Lash, *Believing Three Ways in One God: A Reading of the Apostles' Creed* (London: SCM, 1992), p. 32.

history of salvation and revelation we have already experienced the immanent Trinity as it is in itself."[43] Rahner famously continues, "The 'economic' Trinity is the 'immanent' Trinity and the 'immanent' Trinity is the 'economic' Trinity."[44]

Rahner was concerned that disproportionate focus on inner Trinitarian unity — on the internal relations among Trinitarian persons as they are *ab initio*, without world, so to speak — would downplay God's self-revelation through Jesus. And this would set God at quite a distance from us. Pannenberg, as we've seen, responded to the problem by saying that Jesus and Spirit, the "worldly" Trinitarian persons, are *ab initio* God in relation with humanity. Thus, any downplaying of God's *ab initio* decision to be in such relation significantly problematizes two of the three Trinitarian persons. Rahner responded a bit differently to the problem of immanent and economic relation, setting out what became known controversially as Rahner's rule: as God made the human form able to receive his self-revelation through Jesus, God may "become" human (in "economic" relation with humanity) while remaining unchanging and eternal (the immanent Trinity).[45] God is at once unchanging *actus purus* and yet, in incarnate form, affected by history. In this, Rahner hoped to preserve an intimacy between God's internal relationality and relation with us. He hoped also to resolve the debate over whether God being in world renders the immanent Trinity not eternal but changeable and thus not divine.

Rahner did not resolve it. Readers like Khaled Anatolios worry that his approach brings eternal God and Jesus' humanity unduly near each other, so that attributes of the historical Jesus (mutability, for instance) could seep upward, so to speak, toward the divine.[46] Anatolios's work poses similar questions for Catherine Mowry LaCugna, whose view of salvation substantially closes the gap between God and humanity. As the salvation of a single person, she holds, requires the efforts of the many, there is only *oikonomia*, only economy, only God in himself *in* relation to us many human persons. God's relations with humanity, the economic Trinity, she writes, are "the concrete realization of the mystery of *theologia* [discussion of God in himself] in time, space, history, and personality." She

---

43. K. Rahner, *Grundkurs des Glaubens: Einfuehrung in den Begriff des Christentums*, 6th ed. (Freiburg, Germany; Basel, Switzerland; Vienna: Herder, 1978); translations from *Foundations of Christian Faith: An Introduction to the Idea of Christianity*, trans. W. Dych (New York: Crossroad, 1982), p. 142.

44. K. Rahner, *The Trinity*, trans. J. Donceel (New York: Seabury Press, 1970, 1997), p. viii.

45. K. Rahner, *Foundations of Christian Faith: An Introduction to the Idea of Christianity*, trans. W. V. Dych (New York: Seabury Press, 1978), pp. 220, 223.

46. K. Anatolios, *Retrieving Nicaea: The Development and Meaning of the Trinitarian Doctrine* (Grand Rapids: Baker Academic, 2011).

continues, "God for us [she specifies: to love, save, and redeem — the economic Trinity] is who God is as God [the immanent Trinity]."[47] God's communication of love to us *is* the earthly expression of inner Trinitarian love.

Anatolios has two complaints. The first, as we've seen, is that LaCugna's near conflation of God-for-us and God-as-God threatens God's immutability. As with Rahner, if God's identity, self-expressing being in itself, is hitched to relations with humanity, he cannot remain immutable in the face of changing relations with us. LaCugna holds that it is God's "being for us" that is immutable, but this does not satisfy concerns like Anatolios's. He also finds that LaCugna's only-*oikonomia* voids all statements about God save what *we* grasp of his self-revelation (the economic Trinity). LaCugna would accept the charge, noting (as did Kant, Schleiermacher, and Barth, in very different ways) that humanity has no access to God aside from his communication. And since what God communicates is love, God "for us," we in his image must be for others as well. "The doctrine of the Trinity," LaCugna writes, "is not ultimately a teaching about 'God' but a teaching about God's life with us and our life with each other."[48]

To sum up the issue: humanity must have knowledge of the triune God from his revelation, communication to us, or our ideas about God are our own fantasies. Yet the idea of too-proximate a relation between God and humanity threatens the radical difference between God and the human. If there is only economic Trinity, only God in relation with us, then God — precisely because of his relation to us — may be affected by those relations, and thus is his eternal immutability threatened.

In this debate, Miroslav Volf and Jürgen Moltmann worry more about undue distance than proximity, and work to link God-in-himself and God-with-humanity. Volf suggests that as humanity knows God from his self-revelation, we may move from revelation toward knowledge of God's inner nature. God in himself moves toward humanity in revelation through Jesus, which allows humanity to know something of God. Our thoughts about God are *not imagination but relation.*[49] Volf describes this as a "movement — from *immanent Trinity* to *economic Trinity.*"[50]

---

47. C. LaCugna, *God for Us: The Trinity and Christian Life* (San Francisco: HarperSanFrancisco, 1992), pp. 223, 305.

48. LaCugna, *God for Us,* p. 228.

49. Volf writes, "if we were not entitled to make claims about the immanent Trinity on the basis of the economic Trinity's engagement with the world, then in the encounter with the economic Trinity, we would not be dealing with who God really is"; see M. Volf, "Being as God Is," in *God's Life in Trinity,* ed. M. Volf and M. Welker (Minneapolis: Augsburg Fortress, 2006), p. 4.

50. The full quote is: "the terms *immanent Trinity* and *economic Trinity* do not designate

Moltmann begins by rejecting what he sees as Augustine's privileging of mind/soul, overshadowing emotional and bodily experience in relations with God.[51] Conceiving a more intimate relationship between immanent and economic Trinity, he notes that the economic Trinity is also triune. God is in relation with us in creation,[52] in crucifixion/salvation, and in sanctification.[53] Each of these acts-for-us (economic Trinity) is the purview of a (immanent) Trinitarian person: creation (Father), salvation (Son), and sanctification (Holy Spirit) — even as these are a common act. On Moltmann's account, when the "economic" work of the Son (salvation) and Spirit (sanctification) is complete, *agape* and peace will reign. What God now "economically" communicates to us and what God "immanently" is will be one.[54] The inner relations of the triune God — *agape,* gift — will be our relations with each other and the state of the world. Moltmann concludes that God's presence on earth in Jesus (salvation) and Spirit (sanctification) — the economic Trinity — *is* the inner immanent life of the triune God.

The Move from Trinity to Community and Church

This, Ted Peters writes, was "perhaps the biggest step yet away from the substantialist unity of God toward a relational unity in which the divine threeness is given priority."[55] Moltmann is happy to go there as he feels that the substantialist (and less relational) interpretation of Trinity as a divine mon-

---

two related but different aspects of a statically conceived divine being. Rather, their unity in itself comprises a movement — from *immanent Trinity* to *economic Trinity* and finally to the *Trinity in glory,* that is, the Trinity in the world to come when the economy of salvation will have been completed." Volf, "Being as God Is," pp. 4-5.

51. In Moltmann's view of Augustine, "the human being's likeness to God is seated at the summit of the soul. . . . But that is not what the biblical account of creation says. It is not the bodiless individual that is the image of God and is supposed to correspond to God; it is the human being together with other human beings; for 'male and female he created them' "; see J. Moltmann, *Ethics of Hope,* trans. M. Kohl (Minneapolis: Fortress, 2012), p. 220.

52. J. Moltmann, *God in Creation: A New Theology of Creation and the Spirit of God,* trans. M. Kohl (San Francisco: Harper and Row, 1985), pp. 98-103.

53. See J. Moltmann, *The Crucified God,* trans. R. Wilson and John Bowden (New York: Harper and Row, 1973), p. 244.

54. J. Moltmann, *Trinity and the Kingdom,* trans. M. Kohl (San Francisco: Harper and Row, 1981, 1991), p. 161.

55. T. Peters, *God as Trinity: Relationality and Temporality in the Divine* (Louisville: Westminster John Knox, 1993), p. 103.

archy "generally provides the justification for earthly domination — religious, moral, patriarchal or political domination — and makes it a hierarchy, a 'holy rule.'"[56] In short, God-as-monarch is used to justify man-as-monarch — a critique found also in liberation theologies. Leonardo Boff, for instance, holds that disproportionate emphasis on Trinitarian unity risks a view of God as dominating and a view of world as laboring under an oppressive, unchangeable status quo. Boff notes instead that Jesus rejects "the structure that constitutes the mainstay of our world: power as domination."[57] He understands Trinity not as a monarchy over world but as intrinsic movement (*perichoresis*), the ebb and flow of *agape* in the divine community for the human community.[58]

The highlighting of community, from Richard of St. Victor through the British social Trinitarians, emerges again in Moltmann's unorthodox alternative to the monarchical Trinity. Moltmann suggests the human *community as a whole* to be the entity that is in God's triune image. As God is the unity of multiplicities, so humanity in his image is the unity of multiple persons. It is this multiplicity-in-unity — the comm*unity* — that is the image of God.[59] Though this risks the loss of individual distinction, Moltmann intends his idea — as did Boff and liberation theologians Ivone Gebara and Gustavo Gutiérrez — as a block against abuse: "human beings can correspond to this triune God not through domination and subjugation but only through fellowship and life-furthering reciprocity. It is not the human being as a solitary determining subject who is God's image on earth; it is the true human community."[60]

John Zizioulas looks for community with more buttresses for the individual person. He begins by observing that the Church Fathers' idea of God emerged in study together in "ecclesial community," and thus they understood God — in whose image we are — too as communion. "There is," Zizioulas holds, "no true being without communion," which he takes as *"an ontological category"*; there is no person outside it. Human persons, analogously to the triune God, strive toward ecstatic communion that exceeds personal boundaries. But, Zizioulas continues, we strive for such communion while preserving the unique, *hypostatic* person that each is. "It is not in its 'self-existence' but in

---

56. Moltmann, *Trinity and the Kingdom*, pp. 191-92.

57. L. Boff, *Passion of Christ, Passion of the World: The Facts, Their Interpretation, and Their Meaning Yesterday and Today*, trans. R. Barr (Maryknoll, N.Y.: Orbis, 1988), p. 15.

58. See, for instance, L. Boff, *Holy Trinity, Perfect Community*, trans. P. Berryman (Maryknoll, N.Y.: Orbis, 2000).

59. Moltmann, *Ethics of Hope*, p. 220.

60. Moltmann, *Ethics of Hope*, p. 68.

communion that his being is *itself* and thus is at all. Thus communion does not threaten personal particularity, it is constitutive of it."[61] Zizioulas concludes, *"the person cannot exist without communion; but every form of communion which denies or suppresses the person, is inadmissible."*[62]

Esther Meek and Colin Gunton reprise the twinedness of distinction and communion. First, "there must be diversity at the same time as there is reciprocity," in Meek's words. In Gunton's: "Trinitarian love has as much to do with respecting and constituting otherness as with unifying."[63] Yet they recall that distinct entities are impossible absent their relations. "The doctrine of the Trinity," Gunton writes, "allows us to say two things of utmost importance: that God and the world are ontologically distinct realities; but that distinctness, far from being the denial of relations, is its ground."[64] Gunton then moves to the church community, which he holds follows Trinitarian community. "The Church is called to be the kind of reality at a finite level that God is in eternity."[65] He proposes an "ecclesiology of perichoresis," of persons in a "dance" with each other, with "no permanent structure of subordination, but in which there are overlapping patterns of relationships so that the same person will be sometimes 'subordinate' and sometimes 'superordinate' according to the gifts and graces being exercised."[66]

Gunton rightly notes the importance of nonhierarchical, relational *perichoresis* for American church history, with its emphasis on grassroots participation and anti-authoritarianism.[67] He is concerned about Neoplatonic tendencies to prioritize ideal over real churches, "a platonising conception of the invisible Church, which operates as ontologically prior — because it is the *real* Church — to the 'mixed' historical community." Gunton identifies this Platonizing with Augustine's emphasis on spirit over body, as do Moltmann and others such as James Houston. While this analysis has been questioned (by John Milbank and John Betz, among others), it's worth noting

61. J. Zizioulas, "Human Capacity and Incapacity: A Theological Exploration of Personhood," *Scottish Journal of Theology* 28 (1975): 409.

62. J. Zizioulas, *Being in Communion: Studies in Personhood and the Church*, Contemporary Greek Theologians, vol. 4 (Crestwood, N.Y.: St. Vladimir's Seminary Press, 1985), p. 18.

63. E. Meek, *Loving to Know: Covenant Epistemology* (Eugene, Ore.: Wipf and Stock, Cascade Books, 2011), p. 206.

64. C. Gunton, "The Church on Earth: The Roots of Community," in *On Being the Church: Essays on the Christian Community*, ed. C. Gunton and D. Hardy (London: T. & T. Clark, 1993), p. 67.

65. Gunton, "The Church on Earth," p. 78.

66. Gunton, "The Church on Earth," p. 77.

67. Gunton, "The Church on Earth," p. 71.

that its questioners also value community and relationality. They challenge not the importance of relationality but only the idea that you can't get there from Augustine.

*   *   *

I have attempted to set out some concepts in relational approaches to *imago* and Trinity because of their contribution, as tenet or metaphor, to an ontology of distinction-amid-relation robust enough to frame public policies of reciprocal consideration-worthiness. My closing is from Adrian Pabst: "Being created in the image and likeness of God describes our share in the relationality of the Trinitarian economy. In the work of Dionysius the Areopagite . . . creation and individuation are construed as our elevation to union with God."[68]

---

68. Pabst, *Metaphysics*, p. xxxii.

CHAPTER 8

Distinction-amid-Relation in the Christian Covenant: The Gift of *Agape*

Having looked in the previous chapter at relationality in the Trinity, we continue in this chapter with tenets of distinction-amid-relation that may serve as a ground for our policies, beginning with the Christian covenant. Like the Judaic covenant, the Christian covenant is a bond beyond the binary of separability or situatedness. Neither is it the contractualist idea that we begin as individuals and then come together in a social contract, nor is it the collectivist idea that group/nation/*ethnos* supersedes persons, who may be sacrificed for it. In both traditions, covenant proposes mutual constitution: it is in covenantal relations that we become distinct persons, and it is as distinct persons that we come to be in covenantal relation. Covenant is characterized by the gift of reciprocal consideration and commitment, giving for the flourishing of the other. It brings our attention to our impact on others and responsibility for them as we live together in the private and public spheres.

"The Church," Pope Francis notes, "which shares with Jews an important part of the sacred Scriptures, looks upon the people of the covenant and their faith as one of the sacred roots of her own Christian identity (cf. *Rom* 11:16 18)."[1] Continuities between Judaic and Christian covenantal thought have traditionally been associated with the Reformed tradition (see below). But they have also been explored in the now nearly century-long revisiting of Pauline theology as it had been interpreted by German scholarship of the nineteenth and early twentieth centuries.[2] While the emphases of Ferdinand Baur, the

---

1. Francis, *Evangelii gaudium,* Rome, November 24, 2013; from http://www.vatican.va/holy_father/francesco/apost_exhortations/documents/papa-francesco_esortazione-ap_20131124_evangelii-gaudium_en.html, para. 249.

2. A fine overview can be found in M. Harding and A. Nobbs, eds., *All Things to All Cultures: Paul among Jews, Greeks, and Romans* (Grand Rapids: Eerdmans, 2013).

Religionsgeschichtliche Schule, Otto Pfleiderer, Albert Eichhorn, and most prominently Rudolf Bultmann[3] fell on the *sola fide* as Paul's central tenet and on his ostensible break with the Judaic "legalistic works-righteousness," Albert Schweitzer's work[4] on continuities between Judaic and Pauline thought, along with work by Claude Montefiore, George F. Moore, and William D. Davies,[5] among others, disputed both claims of Judaic legalism and its rejection by Paul.

Ernst Käsemann,[6] for instance, while holding to the Pauline emphasis on *sola fide*, held also to the Jewish prophetic context of Paul's messianism. Paul's understanding of Messiah was in accord with, not in opposition to, the Judaic covenantal (not legalistic, works-fulfillment) promise of Messiah. Krister Stendahl similarly writes, "For the Jew, the law did not require a static or pedantic perfectionism but supposed a covenant relationship in which there was room for forgiveness and repentance and where God applied the measure of grace."[7] E. P. Sanders[8] reprises the point, noting that Judaic law is the *fulfillment*

---

3. See especially, C. F. Baur, "Die Christuspartei in der korinthischen Gemeinde, der Gegensatz des petrinischen und paulinischen Christenthums in der ältesten Kirche, der Apostel Petrus in Rom," *Tübinger Zeitschrift für Theologie* 4 (1831): 61-206; C. F. Baur, *Paul the Apostle of Jesus Christ: His Life and Works; His Epistles and Teachings; A Contribution to a Critical History of Primitive Christianity* (London: Williams and Northgate, 1873; original 1845, 1866); O. Pfleiderer, *Das Urchristentum* (Berlin: G. Reimer, 1887); A. Eichhorn, *The Lord's Supper in the New Testament*, trans. J. Cayzer (Atlanta: Society of Biblical Literature, 2007; original 1898); for Bultmann, see R. Bultmann, *Theology of the New Testament*, trans. K. Grobel, vols. 1-2 (New York: Scribner, 1951, 1955).

4. A. Schweitzer, *Die Mystik des Apostels Paulus* (Tübingen: Mohr Siebeck, 1930).

5. C. Montefiore, *Judaism and St. Paul: Two Essays* (London: Max Goschen, 1914); C. Montefiore, "Rabbinic Judaism and the Epistles of St. Paul," *Jewish Quarterly Review* 13 (1900-1901): 161-217; G. Moore, *History of Religions: Judaism*, International Theological Library, vol. 2 (Edinburgh: T. & T. Clark, 1914); G. Moore, "Christian Writers on Judaism," *Harvard Theological Review* 14 (1921): 197-254; G. Moore, *Judaism in the First Centuries of the Christian Era: The Age of the Tannaim*, vols. 1-3 (Cambridge: Harvard University Press, 1927-1930); W. Davies, *Paul and Rabbinic Judaism: Some Rabbinic Elements in Pauline Theology*, 4th ed. (London: SPCK; Philadelphia: Fortress, 1980; original 1948).

6. E. Käsemann, "The Beginnings of Christian Theology," in *New Testament Questions of Today*, ed. E. Käsemann (London: SCM, 1969), pp. 108-37; E. Käsemann, *Commentary on Romans*, trans. G. W. Bromiley, 4th ed. (Grand Rapids: Eerdmans, 1980); E. Käsemann, "Justification and Salvation History in the Epistle to the Romans," in *Perspectives on Paul* (London: SCM, 1971), pp. 60-78.

7. K. Stendahl, "The Apostle Paul and the Introspective Conscience of the West," *Harvard Theological Review* 56 (1963): 20; see also, K. Stendahl, *Paul among Jews and Gentiles* (London: SCM, 1976).

8. E. P. Sanders, "The Covenant as a Soteriological Category and the Nature of Salvation in Palestinian and Hellenistic Judaism," in *Jews, Greeks, and Christians*, ed. R. Hamerton-Kelly

of covenant, a gift from God given to the Hebrews after its embrace; a legalistic, works *quid pro quo* is not required before covenant, in order to earn it. Paul's point, Sanders explains, was to emphasize covenant's universal application — not to propose a form of covenant that had not existed in Judaic theology. Sanders's view is elaborated by James Dunn[9] and again by N. T. Wright,[10] who holds to the centrality of covenant in both Judaic and Pauline thought. What Paul wishes to emphasize, Wright suggests, was not that the Jews had only legalisms but that the Messiah of the covenant, of God's gift, had arrived and thus that God's promise of redemption for all nations was now begun.[11]

---

and R. Scroggs (Leiden: Brill, 1976), pp. 11-44; E. P. Sanders, "On the Question of Fulfilling the Law in Paul and Rabbinic Judaism," in *Donum Gentilicum*, ed. E. Bammel (Oxford: Oxford University Press, 1978), pp. 103-26; E. P. Sanders, "Patterns of Religion in Paul and Rabbinic Judaism: A Holistic Method of Comparison," *Harvard Theological Review* 66 (1973): 455-78; E. P. Sanders, *Paul, the Law, and the Jewish People* (Philadelphia: Fortress, 1983); E. P. Sanders, *Paul and Palestinian Judaism: A Comparison of Patterns of Religion* (Philadelphia: Fortress, 1977).

9. J. D. G. Dunn, "Works of the Law and the Curse of the Law (Galatians 3:10-14)," *New Testament Studies* 31, no. 4 (1985): 523-42; J. D. G. Dunn, *Jesus, Paul, and the Law: Studies in Mark and Galatians* (London: SPCK, 1990); J. D. G. Dunn, *The Partings of the Ways: Between Christianity and Judaism and Their Significance for the Character of Christianity* (London: SCM, 1991); J. D. G. Dunn, "How New Was Paul's Gospel? The Problem of Continuity and Discontinuity," in *Gospel in Paul: Studies on Corinthians, Galatians, and Romans for Richard N. Longenecker*, ed. L. A. Jervis and P. Richardson (Sheffield: Sheffield Academic Press, 1994); J. D. G. Dunn and A. M. Suggate, *The Justice of God: A Fresh Look at the Old Doctrine of Justification by Faith* (Grand Rapids: Eerdmans, 1994); J. D. G. Dunn, *The Theology of Paul the Apostle* (Grand Rapids: Eerdmans, 1998).

10. N. T. Wright, *The Climax of the Covenant: Christ and the Law in Pauline Theology* (Edinburgh: T. & T. Clark, 1991; Minneapolis: Fortress, 1992); N. T. Wright, "Israel's Scriptures in Paul's Narrative Theology," *Theology* 115, no. 5 (2012): 323-29; N. T. Wright, *Justification: God's Plan and Paul's Vision* (Downers Grove, Ill.: IVP Academic, 2009); N. T. Wright, "New Perspectives on Paul," in *Justification in Perspective: Historical Developments and Contemporary Challenges*, ed. B. L. McCormack (Grand Rapids: Baker, 2006); N. T. Wright, *Paul: In Fresh Perspective* (Minneapolis: Fortress, 2005); N. T. Wright, "Paul and the Patriarch: The Role of Abraham in Romans 4," *Journal for the Study of the New Testament* 35 (2013): 207-41; N. T. Wright, "Romans," in *New Interpreter's Bible*, ed. L. Keck (Nashville: Abingdon, 2002); N. T. Wright, "Romans and the Theology of Paul," in *Pauline Theology*, vol. 3, ed. D. M. Hay and E. E. Johnson (Minneapolis: Fortress, 1995), pp. 30-67.

11. The expectation of a Messiah who would redeem the oppressed was a well-established strain in Judaic thought dating back to Isaiah (especially in the trope of the suffering servant in chapters 51 and 53 et al.) and others in the first temple period through to the time of Paul. Various versions of the idea included apotheosis (man become divine) and theophany (God's coming to world), both common in Jewish thinking. Some, like Paul, took Jesus to be this Messiah; see, for instance, D. Boyarin, *The Jewish Gospels: The Story of the Jewish Christ* (New York: New Press, 2012).

These and other contemporary scholars — Pamela Eisenbaum, David Rudolph, Magnus Zetterholm, Mark Given, John M. Barclay, Brendan Byrne, Michael Bird, D. A. Carson, Richard Bauckham, and Larry Hurtado,[12] among others — note that Judaic and Christian traditions of the first century c.e. held to the soteriological centrality of covenant. Covenant promises redemption in both. While Käsemann and Greg Forbes hold that *sola fide* means that Christ's atonement in crucifixion is the way of salvation, it does not follow from this that Judaic tradition has nothing of God's mercy, grace, and offer of redemption — only that it did not include Jesus in its story. The distinction between intertestamental Judaic and Christian thought was not between law and faith but between salvation through bond with God/from God's covenantal promise and salvation through bond with God in Jesus.

Importantly, in covenant in both traditions, one protects relationship; in contract, one protects interests. Michael Williams recalls the quip of O. Palmer Robertson, that asking for a definition of God is like asking for a definition of mother.[13] But Williams himself has a helpful definition. He notes that in both the First and Second Testaments, covenant has stipulative conditions but not stipulative motivation or purpose. The analogy from parenting (mentioned

---

12. P. Eisenbaum, *Paul Was Not a Christian: The Original Message of a Misunderstood Apostle* (New York: HarperOne, 2009); D. Rudolph, "Paul's 'Rule in All Churches' (1 Cor 7:17-24) and Torah-Defined Ecclesiological Variegation," *Studies in Christian-Jewish Relations* 5 (2010): 1-23; M. Zetterholm, *Approaches to Paul: A Student's Guide to Recent Scholarship* (Minneapolis: Fortress, 2009); M. Given, ed., *Paul Unbound: Other Perspectives on the Apostle* (Peabody, Mass.: Hendrickson, 2010); J. M. Barclay, *Pauline Churches and Diaspora Jews* (Tübingen: Mohr Siebeck, 2001); B. Byrne, "Interpreting Romans Theologically in a Post–'New Perspective' Perspective," *Harvard Theological Review* 94 (2001): 227-41; M. F. Bird, "When the Dust Finally Settles: Reaching a Post–New Perspective Perspective," *Criswell Theological Review* 2 (2005): 57-69; M. F. Bird, "Justification as Forensic Declaration and Covenant Membership: A Via Media between Reformed and Revisionist Readings of Paul," *Tyndale Bulletin* 57, no. 1 (2006): 109-30; M. F. Bird, "What Is There between Minneapolis and St. Andrews? A Third Way in the Piper-Wright Debate," *Journal of the Evangelical Theological Society* 54, no. 2 (2011): 299-310; D. A. Carson, "Summaries and Conclusions," in *Justification and Variegated Nomism: The Complexities of Second Temple Judaism*, vol. 1, ed. D. A. Carson, P. T. O'Brien, and M. A. Seifrid (Grand Rapids: Baker, 2001); R. Bauckham, *God Crucified: Monotheism and Christology in the New Testament* (Carlisle, U.K.: Paternoster, 1998); R. Bauckham, "Paul's Christology of Divine Identity," in *Jesus and the God of Israel: God Crucified and Other Studies on the New Testament's Christology of Divine Identity*, ed. R. Bauckham (Grand Rapids: Eerdmans, 2008), pp. 182-232; L. Hurtado, *Lord Jesus Christ: Devotion to Jesus in Earliest Christianity* (Grand Rapids: Eerdmans, 2003).

13. M. Williams, *Far as the Curse Is Found: The Biblical Drama of Redemption* (Phillipsburg, N.J.: P&R Publishing, 2005), p. 45.

above, in the discussion of the Judaic covenant) applies here: parents may have stipulative rules but not stipulative motives or *telos,* and while we know boys and girls will misbehave, we don't stop having children.[14] Indeed, the parental imagery is vivid in the incarnation: God's Son is sent to the world out of God's love for humanity, also his children. Covenantal love, Johann Georg Hamann wrote, is the source of God's willingness to become incarnate on earth and to "talk" with us in the grace of "communicated being" in forms we can grasp — through nature, reason, and biblical narrative. On Hamann's view, "covenant and creation are parallel,"[15] both acts of divine love. And Hamann adds, with his characteristic humor, God's love is also the reason he subjects himself to critiques of his writings by "the high priests in the temple of good taste."[16]

In the Christian covenant as in the Judaic, humanity both is *of* the image of God (though analogous and distinct) and, as distinct, relates covenantally to him. If one partner loses herself in the relationship, covenant ceases, as this sort of bond requires at least two. Esther Meek calls this "covenantal ontology": "The consummate Christian experience, I believe, is not God *is* us, but God *with* us."[17]

The sections below will look first at the divine partner in this relationship, and then at the human.

God in Covenant: A Covenantal Ontology

"The astonishing revelation of the biblical tradition," Thomas Torrance writes, "is that God does not wish to exist alone." God "has freely brought into being alongside of himself and yet in utter distinction from himself another upon whom he may pour out his love, with whom he may share his divine Life in covenant-partnership." Torrance draws on Augustine, who held that the very purpose of the *imago* is to bring people to this bond — an early expression of

---

14. Thomas Torrance emphasizes, "In the steadfastness of his Covenant Love God refuses to let him [humanity] go but holds on to him and redeems him from the evil that menaces his reality and integrity as a child of God"; see T. Torrance, "The Goodness and Dignity of Man in the Christian Tradition," *Modern Theology* 4, no. 4 (July 1988): 314.

15. O. Bayer, *A Contemporary in Dissent: Johann Georg Hamann as a Radical Enlightener,* trans. R. Harrisville and M. Mattes (Grand Rapids: Eerdmans, 2012), Kindle location 1070.

16. J. G. Hamann, *Sämtliche Werke,* ed. J. Nadler (Vienna: Herder Verlag, 1949-1957), p. 205; J. G. Hamann, *Londoner Schriften, Historisch-kritische Neuedition,* ed. O. Bayer and B. Weissenborn (Munich: C. H. Beck, 1993; original 1758), p. 68.

17. E. Meek, *Loving to Know: Covenant Epistemology* (Eugene, Ore.: Wipf and Stock, Cascade Books, 2011), p. 283.

imago and covenant in mutual constitution. The "relic" (Augustine's word) of God's image in each person gives her the capacity to respond to God covenantally, to love correspondingly to the way God loves. Torrance continues: the "basic covenant-partnership between God and mankind" is what it means to be in God's image.[18] *God seeks covenant with humanity; our being in the image of a covenantal God makes it possible.* For Torrance, this is ontological, the way things are,[19] and though he believes fallen humanity cannot by itself keep covenant, we are helped by God's spirit and so "have a relation to God which is continuously given and unceasingly sustained by the creative presence and power of the Spirit."[20] The Spirit is the ongoing reach of God toward covenant with humanity. Or, in Luther's wonderful phrase, covenant is a "marvelous exchange" *(commercium mirabile)* of love between God and humanity.

One finds God's "wish" not to exist alone in Jürgen Moltmann's work as well: "In his heart God has this passionate longing, not just for any random 'Other' but for 'his' Other.... And that is man, his image."[21] It is also what Karl Barth points to in saying that God freely obligates himself to his creation: "in respect of the existence of a theatre, an instrument and object of His love distinct from Himself and His own sphere and powers, in respect of the existence of a partner with whom He willed to ally Himself.... With this instrument, in relation to this object and in fulfillment of the covenant with the partner."[22] Or, in Adam Kotsko's words, "The point of the 'unilateral' divine will would then be precisely to engender a humanity precisely enabled to enter into a genuine relationship with God, meaning that it is finally not unilateral at all."[23]

God's longing for "his other" expresses itself in *kenosis,* the emptying of the self for/into another. "It comes," Richard Kearney writes, "from God being full and wanting to empty his divinity in order to be more fully in dialogue with the human.... It's Eckhart's idea of *ebullutio,* this 'bubbling over,' this

18. T. Torrance, "The Goodness and Dignity of Man in the Christian Tradition," in *Christ in Our Place: The Humanity of God in Christ for the Reconciliation of the World,* ed. T. Hart and D. Thimell (Eugene, Ore.: Wipf and Stock, 1989), p. 372.

19. David Kelsey calls being in God's relational image "ontologically contingent gift"; see D. Kelsey, "Wisdom, Theological Anthropology, and Modern Secular Interpretation of Humanity," in *God's Life in Trinity,* ed. M. Volf and M. Welker (Minneapolis: Augsburg Fortress, 2006), p. 53.

20. Torrance, "The Goodness and Dignity," p. 319.

21. J. Moltmann, *Trinity and the Kingdom,* trans. M. Kohl (San Francisco: Harper and Row, 1981, 1991), pp. 45-47.

22. K. Barth, *Church Dogmatics* III/1, ed. G. W. Bromiley and T. Torrance, trans. J. W. Edwards, O. Bussey, and H. Knight, 2nd ed. (Edinburgh: T. & T. Clark, 1958), pp. 181-82.

23. A. Kotsko, *The Politics of Redemption* (London: T. & T. Clark, 2010), p. 180.

excess or surplus of desire. Not a surplus of being but of desire"[24] — again, God's wish. Hamann too sees relationship with God as both *theosis* (union with God) and *kenosis* (reciprocal receptivity between humanity and God). Though the human and divine are radically other, Hamann holds, worldly life is nonetheless replete with God's *kenosis* and desirous bond.

Catherine Keller takes the unorthodox view that God's desire includes even *eros,* an idea she shares with philosopher Paul Ricoeur and Nicholas of Cusa, who took love to be erotic desire, friendship, and charity at once. Keller rejects the distinction between *eros* (self-interested love) and *agape* (love for the sake of the other), echoing Anselm's rejection of the binary between care for oneself and care for another: "A relational theology does not accept the polarization of self love and love of the other: the divine Eros invites a co-ordination of self and its influent others."[25] The biblical commandment, she observes, is to love one's neighbor *as* oneself. One's being and desires are not per se evil but of God's desire, as one observes from his desire for covenant.[26]

The Triune God in Covenant

As God is the relationality of the Trinitarian persons, covenant may be understood as an expression of just such relationality. Within God immanent-in-himself, the persons of the Trinity give the gift of being to each other, each constituting the identity of the others, and the round of gift-giving constitutes the whole. Yet relational God gives being not only within himself but also to humanity.

God makes to humanity a triune gift: being itself, being in God's (relational) image, and himself in Jesus. But Jesus is not any gift (like an inert object); he is a gift of a person who is himself relational (a relational Trinitarian person), indeed a person who can tell us about relationality. Through his lessons and ministries, Jesus demonstrates relationality in ways we understand. Thus we are helped to form relations of commitment and care with God and others. In this, Jesus is the new covenant, both relationality in himself *and* a new way to come to bond with God and other persons. Dietrich Bonhoeffer

24. R. Kearney, "Philosophizing the Gift," in *The Hermeneutics of Charity: Interpretation, Selfhood, and Postmodern Faith; Studies in Honor of James H. Olthuis,* ed. J. K. Smith and H. I. Venema (Grand Rapids: Brazos, 2004), p. 56.

25. C. Keller, *On the Mystery: Discerning Divinity in Process* (Minneapolis: Fortress, 2008), p. 113.

26. Keller is not alone in this: Alfred North Whitehead called God's desire "the Eros of the Universe," an appetite for beauty and intensity of experience and relationship.

writes, "His being Christ is his being for me, *pro me* [as Luther said]. The *core* of the person [Jesus] himself is the *pro me*."[27] In sum, *by giving humanity relational being* (imago) *and a relational being (Jesus), God gives humanity the capacity for relationship, covenant,* the capacity to care about others analogous to God's care for us. Volf nabs the idea: "Christ's gift makes each of us a 'Christ.'"[28]

Categorical difference between God and humanity remains, but as Luther held, there is a "marvelous exchange."[29] Paul's lesson to the Athenians brings together these gifts from God: the gift of being, of being in God's relational image (thus capable of relationship with God and others), and the gift of God's desire for relationship with us. Paul declares, "God did this [made the world and humanity as they are] so that [persons] would seek him and perhaps reach out for him and find him, though he is not far from any one of us. . . . As some of your own poets have said, 'We are his offspring'" (Acts 17:27-28).

Persons in Covenant with God

Thus far, this is the world's setup, its ontology, and God's desire. Covenant asks for humanity's response. "What's the point," Kearney asks, "in God desiring and having nobody to answer the divine desire?"[30] A "yes," an answer of acceptance, requires humanity's trust that it is covenant — agapic giving for the other — that is on offer in spite of the asymmetry of the divine-human relationship. It is, Sallie McFague writes, "more like a child's innate trust than like an adult's calculated risk."[31] Both Origen and Aquinas were getting at this trust in their discussions of the "friendship of God," where God and humanity are in interreliance.[32] The eighteenth-century theologian Jonathan Edwards spoke of the "affection" between God and humanity.[33] In the last century,

27. D. Bonhoeffer, *Christ the Center,* trans. E. H. Robertson (New York: Harper and Row, 1978), p. 47.

28. M. Volf, "Being as God Is," in *God's Life in Trinity,* ed. M. Volf and M. Welker (Minneapolis: Augsburg Fortress, 2006), p. 11.

29. *Luther's Works,* vol. 31, ed. J. Pelikan and H. T. Lehmann (Philadelphia: Fortress, 1957), p. 351; see p. 224 n. 16.

30. Kearney, "Philosophizing the Gift," p. 56.

31. S. McFague, *Literature and the Christian Life* (New Haven: Yale University Press, 1966), p. 128.

32. T. Aquinas, *Summa Theologica,* trans. Fathers of the Dominican English Province, vols. 1-5 (Westminster, Md.: Christian Classics, 1948; original 1265-1274), Ia-2ae, q. 83, art. 2.

33. J. Edwards, "Religious Affections," in *The Works of Jonathan Edwards,* vol. 2, ed. J. E. Smith (New Haven: Yale University Press, 1959), p. 101.

Moltmann and John Frame wrote, respectively, that the relationship between God and humanity is one of "friends"[34] and that the aim of knowing God is "friendship."[35] John Webster uses the term "fellowship" to indicate the "unbridgeable gulf" between God and humanity "that is the essential condition of their relations in time."[36]

Trust unto openness to covenant and commitment are what it means to be response-able, in Keller's wordplay. If one takes it up, God answers back with com/passion (again, Keller), not feeling as humanity feels but *with us* as we feel. As we've seen, since the patristic fathers, this idea has prodded debate about God's mutability: Can the source of being God, through relations with humanity, be changed by humanity's response?[37] Aquinas proposed that God feels love for humanity but not as persons feel, and so he is not changed as persons are changed by love. Keller updates: no one needs, she points out, a friend, parent, or therapist who falls apart whenever she does. We need relationship with someone who has some distance and view of the bigger picture, though with a sense for our joy and pain.[38]

Persons in Covenant with Persons

As humanity made in God's image is given relational being and *a* relational being in covenant (Jesus), we have the capacity to respond to God and others covenantally. Our covenantal response is in turn how we become ourselves. These ideas will be taken up in our chapter on ethics, but here a summary of the basic premises is captured by Robin Lovin's comment, "we need opportunities for self-correction and renewal that come from thinking through our plans in light of the way that others are working toward the same goal."[39] Moving covenantally with others — in this book's terms, reciprocal consideration-worthiness — is what allows for justice. This is not a ceding of one's own views

34. Moltmann, *Trinity and the Kingdom*, p. 221.

35. J. Frame, *The Doctrine of the Knowledge of God* (Phillipsburg, N.J.: P&R Publishing, 1987).

36. J. Webster, "God's Perfect Life," in *God's Life in Trinity*, ed. M. Volf and M. Welker (Minneapolis: Augsburg Fortress, 2006), p. 150.

37. See J. Hallmann, *The Descent of God: Divine Suffering in History and Theology* (Minneapolis: Fortress, 1991).

38. Keller, *On the Mystery*, p. 127.

39. R. Lovin, *The Descent of God: Divine Suffering in History and Theology* (Minneapolis: Fortress, 1991), pp. 35, 39.

or concerns but Lovin's "thinking through" them considering the concerns and thinking of others. We may refuse to do this, but then we don't get justice. "Without the persistent stretch of our relationality," Keller holds, "there is *no sustainable motion from eros* [our desire] *to justice.*"[40]

When one is of a covenantal mind, responding to God and others is a disposition toward the world. It is not only for eschatological and salvific purposes but a *modus operandi* for this world, daily, ordinarily. It is the underlying ontology that allows us to take the concerns of others into account, to work through one's own aims and fears by working with those of others — what John and Paul called God's Spirit within each person.[41] Importantly and unorthodoxly, Rahner universalizes the idea: God communicates with and helps all people to this *modus operandi,* even those who have not accepted covenantal ontology — though, Rahner holds, the church is a thick medium for development of covenantal thinking. Because of this, he insists that theology be *kerygmatic,* suitable for ordinary people and pertinent to daily life.

Covenant in the Reformed Tradition

The emphasis on the distinct self in the Reformed tradition (pt. II, ch. 5) is in no contradiction with its emphasis on covenant, which became the basis for political federalism or societies based on the *foedus* (covenant), including the United States. On the Reformed view, it is the responsibility of each (distinct) person in God's (relational) image to contribute to the covenantal body. Covenants are what bind together the family, church, and guild, which in turn make up the larger covenanted entities of town and nation. Reformed theology finds this a "symbiosis" between the divine bonds (within Trinity, between Trinitarian God and humanity) and human bonds in society.[42] Once the idea of *a covenant among persons guided by covenant with God* was in place, it was applied broadly by Reformed thinkers, in secular as in theological and ecclesiological arenas. In a covenantal community, each person remains in the group by consent (just as free consent is a condition of bond with God), makes her unique contribution, and serves as a check on slippages into noncovenantal

40. Keller, *On the Mystery,* p. 115.

41. P. Burke, *Reinterpreting Rahner: A Critical Study of His Major Themes* (New York: Fordham University Press, 2002), p. 254.

42. See C. McCoy and J. W. Baker, *Fountainhead of Federalism: Heinrich Bullinger and the Covenantal Tradition* (Louisville: Westminster John Knox, 1991), p. 52.

conduct in others (as others serve to check her). In the same pattern, each societal group checks others and the federated nation.

The springboard thinker of Reformed covenantal thinking, Heinrich Bullinger, was leader of the Zurich Reformed church from 1531 to 1575, principal author of the First Helvetic Confession (1536), and author of the Second Helvetic Confession (1566). He traced covenant from God and Adam to the Judaic patriarchs, which is the same covenant, he held, as the covenant taught by Jesus and Paul. "Why does the apostle Paul declare more than once that he invents no new doctrine but teaches the whole of Christianity on the authority of the Old Testament? . . . Paul openly testified that he had taught nothing other than what the prophets had predicted would come to pass (Acts 26:22)."[43] Bullinger's understanding of testamental continuity is grounded in Augustine: "The just ones who preceded the advent of our Lord Jesus who humbly came in the flesh believed in him who was to come in the same way that we believe in him who came. The times are different, but not the faith."[44] This is not to say that those before Jesus knew of his (later) time on earth but that the God in whom they believed was, at a point in history, incarnate in Jesus.

Bullinger held that the Mosaic laws were instituted to help the Hebrews uphold covenant with God, but he held also that justice, love, and mercy (not law) are the *telos* of the Judaic covenant as they are of all covenants and as the prophets insisted. He quotes Tertullian citing Isaiah 1:11-17: " 'The multitude of your sacrifices — what are they to me?' says the Lord. I have more than enough of burnt offerings. . . . Learn to do right; seek justice. Defend the oppressed. Take up the cause of the fatherless; plead the case of the widow."[45] Since Jesus' incarnation, Bullinger believed, the faithful are saved *in the same manner* as those who preceded Mosaic law were saved: by their faith. Baptism and Eucharist are signs of this faith in the time of the postincarnation covenant.[46]

Bullinger's claim that there is but one covenant from Adam to Abraham

---

43. H. Bullinger, *De Testamento seu foedere Dei unico et aeterno* (Tiguri, in aedibus C. Frosch, 1534).

44. H. Bullinger, "A Brief Exposition of the One and Eternal Testament or Covenant of God" (1534), in *Fountainhead of Federalism*, p. 119.

45. We have seen similar lambastes in Amos 5:21-24, in Prov. 21:3, and in Ps. 82:3-5. Bullinger also remarked on the Hebraic and Christian commonality in suffering to come to faith: "There is no reason for me to relate," Bullinger writes, "any details about Moses, Joshua, Samuel, David, and all the other distinguished figures. No single one of them would suffice as an example in enumerating their many hardships, calamities, and labors undertaken for the same of the Lord. . . . Truly the priests and prophets of the ancient church deserve to be made examples for Christian martyrs." Bullinger, "A Brief Exposition," pp. 117, 118, 119, 122, 129.

46. Bullinger, "A Brief Exposition," p. 132.

to Jesus was not universal in his day. While Zwingli posited a similar idea, he did not mark the reciprocity of the bond between God and humanity as Bullinger had. In Basel, Johannes Oecolampadius posited two covenants, an old one and a new one, as did Wolfgang Musculus in Bern, who held to an earlier covenant with Noah and a later one with Abraham. Others held to a covenant of works (conditioned on obligation fulfillment) and one of grace (unconditional). Unlike Bullinger, Calvin distinguished between the "carnal" covenant or law of Israel and the spiritual covenant of the New Testament. Also contra Bullinger, Calvin's double predestination left little room for covenantal reciprocity. On Bullinger's nonpredestinarian view, once baptized into covenant, one reciprocates by fulfilling it, and if one does, one is among the elect. Partaking of God (*imago*) gives one the capacity to embrace and fulfill covenant, but one's own free decision to do so also plays a role.

Bullinger's idea of one covenant that, if reciprocated, shows election broaches at least the possibility of salvation for all.[47] But it was the Dutch Cornelius Wiggertz who drew out the idea's universalist implications. Wiggertz's work was a source for Arminian theology, with its emphasis on humanity's capacity, by prevenient (this-worldly) grace, to become a partner in continuing it. There is not, on this view, unappealable predestination but rather covenantal reciprocity, where in living a moral life, one is saved. As John Wesley wrote: "God worketh in you, therefore you *can* work. . . . God worketh in you; therefore you *must* work; you must be 'workers together with him' (they are the very words of the Apostle); otherwise he will cease working."[48] On this point, Zacharias Ursinus in Germany was yet more emphatic than Wiggertz. Ursinus held that God's promise to Abraham reflects the covenant begun with humanity at creation and proffers salvation to all those of faith and moral conduct (see his Major Catechism of 1561/1562).

Moving still in universalist directions, Caspar Olevianus, Ursinus's colleague in Heidelberg, held that covenant was not with Adam (humanity) *at* creation, as Ursinus had it, but rather covenant was *with* creation. Covenant on

---

47. Taking another step in the direction of universality, the Dutch Reformed Gellius Snecanus held that the key elements of covenant — mutual commitment between humanity and God and among persons — were laid out in the covenant with Abraham that all humankind may follow it. He wrote, "In these few works [of mutual covenant] is included whatever pertains to true faith and love, both towards God and towards humanity. The sum of the entire Scripture and of piety consists in these two conditions of the divine covenant." See E. von Korff, *Die Anfänge der Föderaltheologie und ihre erste Ausgestaltung in Zürich und Holland* (Bonn: Emil Eisele, 1908), p. 41 n. 52.

48. See Wesley, "On Working Out Our Own Salvation."

this view structures humanity's relations not only with the divine and others but with the world itself. Like Wiggertz and Ursinus and contrary to the more mysterious grace of high Calvinism, Olevianus concluded that salvation comes to all those who act covenantally with God and others.

In the Reformed Tradition: Covenant and Politics

This section describes an early modern application of covenantal theology to public policy. Partaking of and in covenant with (relational) God enables covenantal relations — reciprocal consideration-worthiness — among persons *and* in the societal structures that we build. Covenantal policies and institutions in turn express the relational nature of the self-expressing being God and of our covenant with him.

Johannes Althusius, who studied law as well as theology in Cologne and Basel, was among the first to develop a theory of covenantal thinking in politics. Persons individually are created helpless, he believed, but have been given a "symbiotic" relational nature so that they live with each other in covenant as they live with God.[49] As such covenantal structures are essential to human life, politics is the art of creating them, "the art of associating *(consociandi)* men for the purpose of establishing, cultivating, and conserving social life among them."[50] It is the creation of associations, institutions, and policies of conduct so that the societal task of human upkeep may be done, and it is the division of power so that it is done covenantally, without concentration or abuse. The "fundamental law" of the nation or commonwealth "is nothing other than certain covenants *(pacta)* by which many cities and provinces come together and agree to establish and defend one and the same commonwealth by common work, counsel, and aid."[51]

Althusius contrasts himself with Jean Bodin, who held that the endurance

49. Althusius writes, "Truly, in living this life no man is self-sufficient (autarkh), or adequately endowed by nature. For when he is born, [he is] destitute of all help, naked and defenceless. . . . Nor in his adulthood is he able to obtain in and by himself those outward goods he needs for a comfortable and holy life, or to provide by his own energies all the requirements of life. The energies and industry of many men are expended to procure and supply these things. Therefore, as long as he remains isolated and does not mingle in the society of men, he cannot live at all comfortably and well while lacking so many necessary and useful things. As an aid and remedy for this state of affairs is offered him in symbiotic life." See J. Althusius, *The Politics of Johannes Althusius: An Abridged Translation of the Third Edition of* Politica methodice digesta, atque exemplis sacris et profanis illustrata, trans. F. Carney (Boston: Beacon Press, 1964; original 1603), chs. 1; 3–4.

50. Althusius, *The Politics of Johannes Althusius,* ch. 1.

51. Althusius, *The Politics of Johannes Althusius,* ch. 19.

of nations can be guaranteed only by sovereignty that is eternal (not established by dissolvable pacts) and vested in a chief magistrate or prince. Althusius countered that sovereignty lies in the network of covenantal bonds. It is not the parties alone but the parties *in covenanted relation* that is sovereign: "Bodin clamours that these rights of sovereignty cannot be attributed to the realm or the people because they come to an end and pass away. . . . I maintain the exact opposite, namely, that these rights of sovereignty, as they are called, are proper to the realm to such a degree that they belong to it alone."[52] While magistrates may administer, "It is not a collection of individuals but a covenanted whole that has the rights of sovereignty."[53] Moral law or "common law," Althusius held, is found in the Ten Commandments, which are the principles of covenantal obligation to God and to neighbor. These are interpreted into "proper laws" that specify how the Decalogue applies to each community. Althusius's final point is his most radical: because sovereignty lies in the covenanted community, not in individual leaders, it is possible for magistrates to be removed should they violate their covenant with the community, its laws, or God's.

Among those who worked on covenantal politics after Althusius, one of the most inspired was Johannes Cocceius, who lived between two banner years. He was born the year of the publication of Althusius's *Politics* (1603) and died the year of the Fundamental Constitution of Carolina (1669), authored by two sponsors of covenantal religio-politics, the earl of Shaftesbury and John Locke. Like Bullinger, Cocceius, who studied Hebrew and rabbinic literature as well as Greek and Latin, held to one covenant of love, community, and faithfulness. It is found in the communal body of the divine (immanent Trinity, Father and Son) as in world, to which this covenant has come, Cocceius believed, in phases. The first was covenant with Adam, given out of grace but contingent on obligation fulfillment. The postlapsarian covenant, also given in grace, is also contingent, but not on works; it is contingent on faith and is fulfilled by Jesus. This covenant, on Cocceius's view, runs between God and persons, between persons and nature, and among persons.

Importantly, Cocceius wrote, one understands this three-part pact by reading Scripture within an interpreting community. As people live interdependently (symbiotically) and develop thoughts and conduct in community, one cannot learn about covenant with God without the experience of covenantal exchange among persons. Here we find again covenant with God and among persons in mutual constitution. Because we partake of and are in covenant with a relational

---

52. Althusius, *The Politics of Johannes Althusius,* ch. 9.
53. McCoy and Baker, *Fountainhead of Federalism,* p. 60.

God, we can "be" only in relation with God and others. Covenant with God expresses itself in covenant among persons; reciprocally, covenant among persons is of covenant with God. *Because* human covenant is of covenant with God, we come to understand bond with God in life in covenant with others — an echo of the twined Judaic covenant that Cocceius carefully studied.

As people live and study Scripture in differing communities and circumstances, Cocceius believed each person would understand Scripture differently — an anthropological perspective that adumbrates the Romantics (Hamann, Herder, Schelling, Schleiermacher, et al.) and structuralist sociologists by two and more centuries. Multiple interpretations of Scripture will emerge, Cocceius held, as God works differently in different contexts — a creative, evolving process under God's vision in which God and humanity participate. (Here Cocceius foreshadows Absolute or World Historical Spirit in Hegel's *Phenomenology of Spirit* and *Philosophy of Right*.)[54] Absent interpretive changes that reflect varying circumstances and God's way of working in them, the Bible would become irrelevant in the face of new conditions. Coceeius writes, "there is no law that orders the person who comes after to be content with the things his predecessors have learned, thought, perceived, and explained. . . . It is good that the same things be said from the Scriptures by many mouths lest it might appear that nothing else could be learned from the Bible."[55] Resistance to variety and change is, on his account, an aspect of pride and fallenness because it presumes one's present interpretation is absolute truth, which humanity does not have.

Over the following century, the Reformed view of covenant saw effects in the political organization of Reformed communities in Germany, England, Scotland, and the British colonies. The Mayflower Compact (1620), signed en route to America, declares the new colony a covenant in the mode of Althusius and Cocceius, a covenant of persons bound together as they are bound to God: "We, whose names are underwritten . . . solemnly and mutually in the Presence of God and one another, covenant and combine ourselves together into a civil Body Politick, for our better Ordering and Preservation, and Furtherance of the Ends aforesaid; And by Virtue hereof do enact, constitute, and frame, such just and equal Laws, Ordinances . . . for the general Good of the Colony."[56]

---

54. G. W. F. Hegel, *The Philosophy of Right*, ed. A. Wood, trans. T. Knox (Oxford: Oxford University Press, 1942; original 1821); G. W. F. Hegel, *The Phenomenology of Spirit*, trans. J. Findley (Oxford: Oxford University Press, 1979; original 1817).

55. In his *Summa theologiae ex scrituris repetita*, cited in McCoy and Baker, *Fountainhead of Federalism*, p. 76.

56. Mayflower Compact (1620); retrieved from http://www.let.rug.nl/usa/documents /1600-1650/mayflower-compact-1620.php.

Althusius's and Cocceius's themes are all present: the New World would be part of the covenantal-historical process, guided by God and implemented by men in free covenant with him and each other. Laws are developed by the governed for the common good (the well-being of humanity, which is helpless alone) as guided by God's principles.

A decade later, John Winthrop, in "A Model of Christian Charity," declared that his nascent community hung together by bonds to each other, world, and God. "There is likewise a double Lawe by which wee are regulated in our conversation towardes another, the lawe of nature and the lawe of grace."[57] His explanation of the "condition of mankind" is Althusius's anthropology: "*so that* every man might have need of others, and from hence they might be all knitt more nearly together in the Bonds of brotherly affection." These bonds constitute the sovereign group, and in them, "wee must loue one another with a pure hearte fervently. Wee must beare one anothers burthens. We must not looke onely on our owne things, but allsoe on the things of our brethren." Thus, in community governance, "the care of the publique must oversway all private respects, by which, not only conscience, but meare civill pollicy, dothe binde us."[58]

As Althusius had specified, political representatives were legitimate only as long as they fulfilled their covenantal duties to the group. In 1630, when the magistrates of Massachusetts Bay attempted to make themselves into a permanent body, the citizens responded with term limits. To ensure that covenant was upheld, the Body of Liberties was enacted in 1641, with many of its provisions later written into the U.S. Bill of Rights. These were deemed essential not only to protect individual conduct but also to preserve covenant and commonwealth.

At the end of the century, John Locke published his syntheses of the covenantal literature in *Two Treatises of Government* and *A Letter concerning Toleration*. They reflect covenantal ideas about both church and secular government, unsurprisingly for a man raised in a Reformed Puritan household

---

57. The passage continues, "By the first of these lawes man as he was enabled soe withall is commanded to love his neighbour as himself. Upon this ground stands all the precepts of the morrall lawe, which concernes our dealings with men. To apply this to the works of mercy; this lawe requires two things. First that every man afford his help to another in every want or distresse. Secondly, that hee perform this out of the same affection which makes him carefull of his owne goods. . . . The Lawe of nature would give no rules for dealing with enemies, for all are to be considered as friends in the state of innocency." J. Winthrop, *A modell of Christian charity,* Collections of the Massachusetts Historical Society, 3rd ser., 7:31-48 (Boston, 1630, 1838); retrieved from http://history.hanover.edu/texts/winthmod.html, pp. 34-35.

58. Winthrop, *A modell of Christian charity,* especially pp. 45, 34, 39-40.

who had to flee the country to avoid the wrath of a monarch. Church, for Locke, is a covenanted body that men enter freely, out of love for its precepts and each other. "A church, then, I take to be a voluntary society of men, joining themselves together of their own accord in order to the public worshipping of God."[59] Locke followed Cocceius in recognizing the plurality of scriptural interpretations, as God works differently in different worldly conditions. Thus, as no one interpretation is absolute truth, no one can be sure of it, and none may be persecuted for believing uncommon or unpopular ideas whose rightness or wrongness cannot be determined by human others.

Locke held that the state too is a covenanted body: "a society of men constituted only for the procuring, preserving, and advancing their own civil interests."[60] Thus, both church and state are compacts — one for spiritual matters, which may not be settled by human sanctions, the other for civil flourishing, which may require sanctions by community representatives so that daily life may proceed. Should a magistrate or monarch violate the terms of covenant among persons or with God, he may be removed.

The U.S. Declaration of Independence relies on Althusius's and Locke's idea that sovereigns may be deposed for covenant violations and on Locke's criteria for doing so. The Virginia Declaration of Rights (1776) — forerunner of the Bill of Rights and written by Thomas Jefferson and the Baptist John Leland — declares Virginia to be a covenant of inalienable rights and duty to advance the common good. Covenantal thinking undergirds the idea of government by "we the people" in compact with each other (1789). American Constitutional protections of freedom of religion are based on Cocceius's and Locke's recognition of the plurality of scriptural interpretation and thus of the incoherence of punishing interpretations that, in fact, no one can definitively prove wrong. The division of government into three branches and into federal and state powers follows covenantal principles of checks and balances. As Althusius might have said, "That all power is vested in, and consequently derived from, the people. . . . That government is, or ought to be, instituted for the common benefit."[61]

---

59. J. Locke, *Letter concerning Toleration* (1698); retrieved from http://www.let.rug.nl/usa/documents/1651-1700/john-locke-letter-concerning-toleration-1689.php.

60. Locke, *Letter concerning Toleration*.

61. Virginia Declaration of Rights (1776); retrieved from http://www.let.rug.nl/usa/documents/1776-1785/the-virginia-declaration-of-rights-1776.php.

CHAPTER 9

The Christian Covenant: A Möbius Strip Expressed in Baptism, Learned from Incarnation

> Love of the neighbor includes within it the love of God and together they constitute the Borromean knot . . . characterized by the fact that each loop holds together the other two; to cut one is to unravel the connection between the other two. . . . [T]he subject loves the neighbor only by means of the love of God, and loves God only by means of loving the neighbor.[1]

> Know that the Lord walks among the pots and pans helping you both interiorly and exteriorly.[2]

The Twined Covenant: A Möbius Strip

"Everything that exists is covenantally charactered," Esther Meek writes,[3] and everything that is covenantally charactered is, as we've seen, twined-ly so: partaking of divine relationality enables us to respond not only to God in covenant but also to each other, and each instance of *agape* or covenant among persons is an expression of divine relationality and covenant with us. Covenant with God and covenant with others are of a piece. "It is *divine* love," Robert Doran

---

1. K. Reinhard, "Toward a Political Theology of the Neighbor," in *The Neighbor: Three Inquiries in Political Theology*, ed. S. Žižek, E. Santner, and K. Reinhard (Chicago: University of Chicago Press, 2005), p. 72.

2. Teresa of Avila, *The Collected Works*, vol. 3, trans. K. Kavanagh and O. Rodriguez (Washington, D.C.: ICS Publications, 1980), 5.8.

3. E. Meek, *Loving to Know: Covenant Epistemology* (Eugene, Ore.: Wipf and Stock, Cascade Books, 2011), p. 401.

writes, "that has been poured into our hearts. It is with divine love that we love God. . . . It is with divine love that we love our neighbours as ourselves." This love, he holds, is the love that God is (and is among the Trinitarian persons),[4] given to humanity in sanctifying grace and yielding "charity" or covenantal *agape* among persons. He speaks of *"a penetration of God's action to the level of our sensitivity and spontaneous intersubjectivity and even physiology,"*[5] so that "the dynamic state of being in love gives in a habitual fashion to acts of love of God and neighbour."[6] Bernard Lonergan first developed the theme in his distinction between the habit of grace and the state of grace, the latter of which is among persons, the "just" who, because of the love of the Father and Son in the Holy Spirit, are given sanctifying grace and "are thereby just and upright."[7]

Importantly, this love, Doran continues, "is offered to all, and while it is manifested more or less authentically in the many religions of humankind and apprehended in as many different manners as there are different cultures, the gift itself as distinct from its manifestations is transcultural."[8]

While love of others is of God's love, conversely, rejecting the twined covenant, as we of free will may do, is fallenness. Cornelius Plantinga calls refusal of covenant — being together, for the other — the "vandalism of *shalom*" (from the root *shalem*, "whole").[9] The breach of being-for is a distortion of the planet's covenantal workings and sets the entire system under stress. The covenantal parties are God, humanity, and cosmos — a triune Möbius strip, so to speak. At present, humanity, on Plantinga's view, is the party in breach, lacking in covenantal, *agapic* commitment.

Since the seventeenth century, objections to this natural ontology — where it is humanity's *nature* (in God's image) to have the capacity for covenant — have arisen from revealed theology. Its point is that the principles revealed by God through Christ and Scripture are untweakable to suit the pressures of the day while our natural dispositions too easily stray; thus its insistence on revelation.

---

4. Doran summarizes this Trinitarian love as follows: "As the Holy Spirit is the uncreated internal term of the actively spirating love of Father and Son, so the habit of charity is the created external term of the actively spirating *being*-in-love that is sanctifying grace. This is fundamentally what it means to be *recipients* of the mission of the Holy Spirit." R. Doran, *What Is Systematic Theology?* (Toronto: University of Toronto Press, 2005), p. 44.

5. Doran, *What Is Systematic Theology?* p. 120.

6. Doran, *What Is Systematic Theology?* p. 44; see also p. 77.

7. B. Lonergan, *De Deo trino, Pars systematica,* trans. M. Shields (Rome: Gregorian University Press, 1964), pp. 257-58.

8. Doran, *What Is Systematic Theology?* pp. 108, 109.

9. C. Plantinga Jr., *Not the Way It's Supposed to Be: A Breviary of Sin* (Grand Rapids: Eerdmans, 1995), pp. 12-18.

Yet it might also be the case that covenantal ontology is not rival to but in coop-eration with revelation, as Erich Przywara argued against Karl Barth (pt. II, ch. 1). Aquinas's important phrase, "Nothing created is so far from God as not to have Him in itself,"[10] suggests that God, whose covenantal relationality inheres in all persons, also reveals something of this relationality as part of his relational being. His relationality both forms us (in his image) and is among those things that are revealed (in the relationality of Trinitarian person Jesus). We in turn know of God's relationality from both sources: partaking of it (*imago*, ontology) and covenant, revealed in the First Testament, and in Jesus' words and life in the Second. It is a matter not of contest but of complement. "The cognition of God in all things," Jürgen Moltmann writes, "can only be a 're-cognition' of the God who has first of all disclosed himself in his revelation."[11]

James Loder gives an account of covenantal twined-ness from psychology. Infants learn to love, he notes, through intimate, face-to-face encounters with parents, which enable them to understand the love of others and respond to it. "I suggest that what is established in the original face-to-face interaction is the child's sense of personhood and a universal prototype of the Divine Presence . . . a *cosmic, self-confirming impact from the presence of a loving other*."[12] As a child draws on her parents' genetic donation and love to develop her sense of self and ability to love, so each of us partakes of God's image and (revealed) covenantal love for the development of personhood and the capacity to respond in covenant.

This in modern voice echoes the famous double insight of 1 John 4:7-21: in loving others we understand God's love (as in loving our children, we come to understand our parents' love) *and* God's love enables us to love others (as the parents' love enables the child to love them and, later, others). John writes, "No one has ever seen God; but if we love one another, God lives in us and his love is made complete in us" — much as the love of parents "living in" children enables them to love others. John continues, "Whoever claims to love God yet hates a brother or sister is a liar. For whoever does not love their brother and sister, whom they have seen, cannot love God, whom they have not seen." Here John anticipates the psychological point that, as it is relationship with parent and caretakers that enables a child to love, aggressive, hostile behavior suggests some earlier, painful break in the caretaker-child bond. Analogously, as it is agapic, covenantal relation with God that enables one to love, aggressive,

10. T. Aquinas, *Summa Theologica*, trans. Fathers of the Dominican English Province, vols. 1-5 (Westminster, Md.: Christian Classics, 1948; original 1265-1274), I, q. 8.

11. J. Moltmann, *Ethics of Hope*, trans. M. Kohl (Minneapolis: Fortress, 2012), p. 138.

12. J. Loder, *Transforming Moment*, 2nd ed. (Colorado Springs: Helmers and Howard, 1989), p. 163.

hostile behavior suggests some break in the bond with him. John says (1 John 4:19), "We love because he first loved us" (as we love because we were loved by our parents) and "Anyone who loves God must also love their brother and sister" (4:21). In Miroslav Volf's words, "God gives out of God's own proper resources; we can give only because we have been given to by God."[13] Rahner's summation of our twined covenants is worth noting: "God who *is* Love (1 Jn 4:16) has loved us, not so that we might love him in return but so that we might love *one another* (1 Jn 4:7, 11). . . . [W]hoever does not love the brother whom he 'sees,' also cannot love God whom he does not see, and that one can love God whom one does not see only *by* loving one's visible brother lovingly."[14]

The twined-ness of covenant is the underpinning of debates about circumcision and baptism, especially since the Reformation and challenges against paedo-baptism by Anabaptists. Both rituals can be seen as marks of belief (relationship with God) since Jews and Christians perform them in conversion ceremonies, to mark a turn of the spirit.[15] But as this reading would preclude performing these rituals with infants (who cannot attest to belief), the rituals are also seen as marks of group belonging, which includes infants and (in several biblical narratives) males who are circumcised without mention of their beliefs (the men of Abraham's household, his son Ishmael, and his sons by Keturah). Yet, belonging is also insufficient as an explanation of either ritual since Christian and Jewish tradition expects belief from converts, and a declaration of no belief ("I want to be circumcised/baptized and belong to your group but care not a bit about your beliefs or practices") is equally incoherent. The Christian reference to baptism as a "circumcision of the heart," a concept developed also by Jeremiah, suggests the shared Judeo-Christian nature of the belief/belonging problem.

Resolution may be found in the mutual constitution of belief (relation with God) and belonging (with others). Belief develops amid belonging. Love and covenant with God, as John and Loder note, emerge through engagement with others, through education in the faith's beliefs, but importantly through

---

13. M. Volf, "Being as God Is," in *God's Life in Trinity*, ed. M. Volf and M. Welker (Minneapolis: Augsburg Fortress, 2006), p. 8.

14. K. Rahner, "Reflections on the Unity of the Love of Neighbour and the Love of God," in *Theological Investigations*, vol. 6, *Concerning Vatican Council II*, trans. K.-H. Kruger and B. Kruger (New York: Crossroad, 1982), pp. 235, 247.

15. Pierre Marcel, for instance, writes that the import of circumcision, though a physical act, is spiritual. Thus, "the efficacy of the sacraments of the Old Testament is identical with that of the sacraments of the New, because equally they are signs, seals, and confirmations of the good will of God for the salvation of men." P. Marcel, *The Biblical Doctrine of Infant Baptism* (London: James Clarke, 1953), p. 86; see also p. 90.

the experience of trust and care.[16] We learn to trust and care from those who behave caringly toward us. Baptism and circumcision reflect this loop: one circumcises/baptizes children because of the expectation that as they grow up amid community relationships, through the experiences of belonging, they come to understand relationship/belonging with God. Similarly converts, to arrive at the conversion moment, have had sufficient engagement with the community to bring them to it, to want to belong to it and God.[17]

In sum, circumcision and baptism are symbols of belief-amid-belonging because of their interplay. Conversion is different from born-into circumcision/baptism in acknowledging only that older persons may, through engagement with others and their ideas, come to belief different from that of their natal communities. At the turn of the twentieth century, B. B. Warfield recognized that Christians baptize "on presumption and not on knowledge" that children will come to belief through belonging in community. That they love and belong to God is presumed from a "good presumption that they belong to God's people."[18]

The Twined Covenant: Brief Examples

The twined bond between God and humanity and among persons is seen early in Christian writings, for instance, in Jesus' reliance on Isaiah, who calls for

16. Instances of being struck by mystical, direct contact with the divine, seemingly absent relations with others, fall into two categories. Where a person belongs to one faith and comes to belief in another, the person's earlier engagement with the new faith (even if hostile) can be the engagement that prods, however mediatedly, new belief. Saul of Tarsus is one such person. Instances where there is no circumcision/baptism and *no* contact with the faith — as was the case with some Jewish children raised by Christians to save their lives in World War II — are also rare. As the rituals of circumcision/baptism emerged from usual group experience over time, they may be adapted to address exceptional circumstances.

17. The interplay between belonging and belief is seen also in instances where a person has grown up in a faith community but, for health or other reasons, has not been circumcised or baptized. If those rituals become possible, they are performed without the preparatory education needed for converts because the person, living in the community, has formed relations with others and has developed as much understanding of God as any other community member has. Conversely, if a person who is not a member of the faith arrives in a community and declares a relationship with God, the community nonetheless has preparatory requirements (classes, conversations with religious leaders) to ensure belief before conversion rituals are arranged.

18. B. B. Warfield, "The Polemics of Infant Baptism" (1899); retrieved from http://www.the-highway.com/InfantBaptism_Warfield.html.

both love of God *and* love of the downtrodden. It's this Isaiah whom Jesus cites when describing God's own kingdom, which also includes covenant among persons (justice, peace, and healing) and between persons and God (repentance, joy in fulfilling God's vision, God's presence, and redemption). Among Church Fathers, the twined nature of covenant is in Irenaeus: "to love Him above all, and one's neighbor (now man is neighbor to man) . . . do reveal one and the same God."[19] In Augustine, these ideas emerge still more clearly, for instance, in his reading of Romans 5:5, "God's love has been poured out into our hearts through the Holy Spirit, who has been given to us." Augustine parses, "So it is God the Holy Spirit proceeding from God who fires man to the love of God and neighbor."[20]

On Adam Kotsko's view, this entwined vision dimmed among medieval scholars such as Anselm, who, he holds, emphasized bond to God over bond to others. Anselm's view of sin, on Kotsko's account, is a matter between a person and God and less a matter among persons — to the disadvantage, it turns out, of God.[21] Kotsko writes, "The outgoing and loving God of the patristic account who desires relationship with humanity has been replaced by a God who is remarkably self-involved, trapped in a problem of his own devising [humanity's inability to pay for its grave sins]. . . . One might say, then, that the shift away from a social-relational scheme and toward an individualistic one is not simply bad for our relationship to creation or to one another — it's bad for God as well."[22]

Kotsko's view is not uncontested,[23] but regardless of whether it is the correct reading of Anselm, other medieval thinkers did not share this view of a "self absorbed" God. Saint Francis of Assisi retrieved the twinedness of covenant in holding that love of God must be also love of world, which brings even the "lower orders" toward the divine.[24] And, as we've seen, Aquinas gives a robust account of the twined covenant, holding that God's love and charity

---

19. Irenaeus, *Against Heresies (Adversus haereses)*, ed. A. Roberts and J. Donaldson (Grand Rapids: Eerdmans, 1989; original ca. 180), p. 478.

20. Augustine, *The Trinity (De Trinitate)*, trans. E. Hill (New York: New City Press, 1991), 15.31.

21. A. Kotsko, *The Politics of Redemption* (London: T. & T. Clark, 2010), pp. 123-49, especially pp. 143-44.

22. Kotsko, *The Politics of Redemption*, p. 149.

23. David Bentley Hart, for instance, is in substantial opposition; see pt. II, ch. 13 of this volume.

24. M. Scheler, "The Sense of Unity with the Cosmos," in *The Nature of Sympathy* (London: Routledge and Kegan Paul, 1954), p. 87.

toward humanity promote covenantally inclined persons capable of two sorts of "friendships," with God and others, including love, charity, solidarity, trust, and concern for the common good.[25] The two friendships share much on Aquinas's account, and without both, one can have neither virtue nor happiness. Happiness on his view is relational and covenantal, the fellowship that the blessed share with God and among themselves.[26] It is possible because of God's "friendship" for humanity and is of analogous nature to it.

One of the prime expressions of the entwined covenant can be found in Luther's declaration that "a Christian lives not in himself, but in Christ and in his neighbor. . . . By faith he is caught up beyond himself into God. By love he descends beneath himself into his neighbor."[27] It is found as well in the simple words of the Lord's Prayer: "God, forgive us . . . as we forgive others." In this passage, forgiveness among persons is the first act accessible to humanity. It is to this generosity among persons that we refer when we request God's forgiveness.

In the last century, Simone Weil's theology was unorthodox but provocative in its expression of covenantal twining. Responsible care for others, she writes, is so intertwined with bond to God that care for others occurs when God moves *through* individual persons. She begins with affliction, a state of continuing, severe distress that deadens one into a thing.[28] Rebarbative to others and unable to defend itself, affliction is God's absence from the world. Weil takes this as the usual state of affairs as, she believes, humanity is motivated by self-absorbed competition for survival. The exceptional moment is the gesture of compassion when God moves through one person toward the afflicted other, when Christ acts *in* the giver[29] — the bond between God and person literally making a bond between persons. "God is absent from the world," she writes, "except in the existence in this world of those in whom His love is alive. . . . Their compassion is the visible presence of God here below."[30]

25. As Adrian Pabst writes, "The horizontal and the vertical models of relationality in Thomas are intimately connected." A. Pabst, *Metaphysics: The Creation of Hierarchy* (Grand Rapids: Eerdmans, 2012), p. 248.

26. See D. Schwartz, *Aquinas on Friendship* (New York: Oxford University Press, 2007).

27. M. Luther, *The Freedom of a Christian (De libertate Christiana),* in *Martin Luther: Selections from His Writings,* ed. J. Dillenberger (Garden City, N.Y.: Anchor Books, 1961), p. 80.

28. Weil's work in the factories of the 1930s gave her much of the material and insight from which she wrote about being ground by the mechanics of necessity to a sort of living death.

29. S. Weil, *Waiting for God* (New York: HarperCollins, 1951), p. 93; see also, S. Weil, *The First and Last Notebooks* (London: Oxford University Press, 1970; original 1950), p. 327.

30. S. Weil, "La connaissance surnaturelle," trans. R. Rees, in *First and Last Notebooks,* p. 103.

When persons offer compassion, they "project" themselves into an afflicted other — lose themselves in what Weil calls "decreation," both nothingness and divinity. Thus "it is not really their own being, because they no longer possess one; it is Christ himself." Compassion, she writes — "only Christ has done it."[31]

Weil's notion of compassion is covenantal and agapic, not passing charity but an opening, *kenosis,* toward the afflicted that leaves one "naked, without clothes or protection, exposed to every blow."[32] Importantly, it is inhibiting one's assumptions about the other and giving her the dignity of being attended to. Weil defines justice and love as "being open to the unexpected," to the singularity in the other.[33] The result of this precise attention, what Weil calls the "sacrament" of compassion,[34] is that it brings dignity and perhaps voice to the downtrodden but — again highlighting covenantal twinedness — also brings God to the giver. We are compassionate when Christ acts through us, and compassion to others brings us to God: "compassion itself is the effect and sign of being united to God by love."[35]

Weil's imagery continues provocatively; she doesn't hesitate to write of being inhabited, consumed, or eaten by God, which may seem to collapse into pantheism or to an ecstatic state where persons are not accountable for their actions. But Weil disallows this in her discussion of responsibility: because we are of God, the abuse of persons in God's image is as "impossible" and outrageous as the crucifixion, the abuse also of a person in God's image. The only possible response is to take responsibility for relieving the duress. In her famous image of humanity as a fly in a bottle ever straining to break free and reach the light (of God), she writes that even if one never escapes, "one must stay pressed against the glass."[36]

In the generation after Weil, Hans Urs von Balthasar and Stanley Hauerwas again used the analogy from parenting to illustrate covenant's twining. "We cannot return our parent's love," Hauerwas writes, "except as we receive

---

31. S. Weil, *Gateway to God,* ed. D. Raper (London: Collins, Fontana Books, 1974), p. 94.

32. Weil, *First and Last Notebooks,* p. 95.

33. S. Hollingsworth, "Simone Weil and the Theo-Poetics of Compassion," *Modern Theology* 29, no. 3 (July 2013): 216. Edith Stein, Weil's Jewish contemporary who converted to Catholicism and became a Discalced Carmelite nun, Saint Teresa Benedicta of the Cross, places similar stress on the singularity of the other. "Empathy," she writes, "is the experience of foreign consciousness"; E. Stein, *On the Problem of Empathy* (Washington, D.C.: ICS Publications, 1989), p. 11.

34. Weil, *Gateway to God,* p. 95.

35. Weil, *First and Last Notebooks,* p. 327.

36. Weil, *First and Last Notebooks,* p. 292.

it and love others similarly."[37] So too with God's covenantal commitment: we return it to him in caring analogously for others. Balthasar expands: "After a mother has smiled at her child for many days and weeks, she finally receives her child's smile in response. . . . God interprets himself to man as love in the same way: he radiates love, which kindles the light of love in the heart of man."[38] This love is meant for response to God and others, as Balthasar notes in his discussion of the Ten Commandments: "on the two tables of the Law the Commandments concerning man's relationship to God . . . pass straight on to those concerning his relationship to his neighbor. . . . To God he [humanity] owes his very being, so it is written on the first table of the Law. On the second, his sense of indebtedness [to God] is given practical expression in the social, political, and legal sphere of man's existence."[39]

To this loop between God and person and among persons in the "social, political, and legal sphere," Balthasar adds the notion of *kenosis*. God's opening to humanity enables us to open to each other, which in turn opens us to God.[40] "It would be impossible to conceive of man maintaining a so-to-speak vertical and religious relationship toward God within the terms of the covenant and of his adopting a quite different law of behavior toward his fellow men."[41] Rather, Balthasar writes, covenant proposes that "because God forgave me while I was still his enemy (Rom 5:10), I must also forgive my fellow men even while they are enemies (Mt 5:43-48); because God has given to me without counting the costs. . . . I must surrender any worldly calculation of the relationship between almsgiving and compensation (Mt 6:1-4; 6:19-34); the standard that God lays down becomes the standard that I must lay down."

What God does for persons we must do amongst ourselves. This standard is, on Balthasar's account, the *Christian categorical imperative,* his answer to Kant: the covenantal mandate to "enter every situation as a representative of the whole and of the comprehensive idea of love."[42]

37. S. Hauerwas, *The Peaceable Kingdom: A Primer in Christian Ethics* (Notre Dame: University of Notre Dame Press, 1983), p. 27.

38. H. U. von Balthasar, *Love Alone Is Credible,* trans. D. C. Schindler (San Francisco: Ignatius, 2004), p. 76.

39. H. U. von Balthasar, *Engagement with God,* trans. R. J. Halliburton (San Francisco: Ignatius, 2008), pp. 22-23.

40. H. U. von Balthasar, *Theo-Drama,* vol. 3, trans. G. Harrison (San Francisco: Ignatius, 1992), pp. 149-57; see also, H. U. von Balthasar, *A Theology of History* (New York: Sheed and Ward, 1963, 1992), p. 25.

41. Balthasar, *Engagement with God,* p. 22.

42. Balthasar, *Love Alone Is Credible,* pp. 112-13, 119.

The Twined Covenant: Learned from Incarnation

The idea of a reciprocally constitutive covenant is unavoidable in the idea of the incarnation. Since the Chalcedonian Definition of God's nature (451 C.E.), the antinomy of God and man has been declared overcome in Jesus, a being "perfect in divinity" and "perfect in humanity" and "truly God and truly man." Or, as Sallie McFague writes, *"The body of God must be fed."*[43] This is not one creature subsuming the other or a dialectic that synthesizes a new third being but two natures that are unconfusable, unchangeable, indivisible, and inseparable (the famous Chalcedonian four negatives) — what Balthasar calls *"the concrete universal,"*[44] the one source of being that is also particular.

Thus covenantal relations with God are at once covenant with a man. One does not get one bond without the other — a situation that is eternal because, as Balthasar notes, *God did not cease being human after the crucifixion.* He continues to be God and man, all being, all knowledge, and all particulars that can ever be. "God has become man, and he will never again lay aside this humanity; the Son's humanity, and everything . . . [that] will eternally flow forth from it, will forever be our open access to the Father."[45]

For the Russian Orthodox Sergius Bulgakov, the incarnation can be understood through the concept of Sophia. John declared, "the Word was made flesh" (John 1:14), and Bulgakov takes the Word to be Sophia, eternal divine wisdom, preceding even creation.[46] It — God's wisdom — is the "Proto Image" in which bodily humanity was created *(imago).* It is the "common-ness" between God and humanity, what "correlates" the divine and human worlds

---

43. S. McFague, *The Body of God: An Ecological Theology* (Minneapolis: Fortress, 1993), p. 170.

44. H. U. von Balthasar, "Characteristics of Christianity," in *Explorations in Theology,* vol. 1, *The Word Made Flesh* (San Francisco: Ignatius, 1989), p. 170.

45. H. U. von Balthasar, *The Glory of the Lord: A Theological Aesthetics,* vol. 1, *Seeing the Form,* ed. J. Fessio, S.J., and J. Riches, trans. E. Leiva-Merikakis (San Francisco: Ignatius; New York: Crossroad, 1982), pp. 235, 251-52, 330.

46. In this, John and Bulgakov echo the rabbinic teaching that Torah precedes creation and is the vision for it; see *Genesis Rabbah* 1; the text cited to support the idea that Torah means wisdom is Prov. 3:19, "By wisdom the LORD laid the earth's foundations." For a discussion of this tradition in light of post-Heideggerian phenomenology, see E. Wyschogrod, "Trends in Postmodern Jewish Philosophy: Contexts of a Conversation," in *Reasoning after Revelation: Dialogues in Postmodern Jewish Philosophy,* ed. P. Ochs, R. Gibbs, and S. Kepnes (Boulder, Colo.: Westview Press, 1998), especially pp. 127ff. Wyschogrod recognizes that creation is not only *kenosis* but also the original instance of limitless being creating something of analogous being to itself that is limited.

and what accounts for analogous human Sophia/wisdom. Linking Bulgakov's approach to the mysticism of Jacob Boehme, Michael Martin notes that, as the correlation of the divine and human, Sophia/Word/divine wisdom is not only the "common-ness" of God and humanity but also the site, so to speak, of divine-human longing. It is both humanity's yearning for God and God's yearning for humanity: "the human soul's desire for Sophia is correlative to Sophia's desire for the human soul. Nowhere is this reciprocity more evident than in Boehme's considerations of the Incarnation of Christ."[47]

Because Sophia/Word/divine wisdom is the "bridge" between God and humanity, what "unites God and man,"[48] it is the bridge between God and Jesus' humanity as well. It is the site of connection between Jesus' divine and human natures. Jesus at once *is* divine Sophia/wisdom yet, as human, has the same common-ness and "correlation" with divine wisdom/Sophia that other persons have.[49] When we call Jesus the divine-human, we are saying that Word/Sophia/divine wisdom remains but has also been made human/flesh. "Sophia, as the *divine-humanity,* is precisely the ontological foundation of the Divine Incarnation that makes it understandable as 'the Word was made flesh' (John 1:14)."[50] In Jesus both human and divine wisdom inhere owing to their "communication" (Bulgakov's term) in the incarnation. Sophia/Word/divine wisdom is in Jesus the site of divine-human oneness.

Sophia is also the site of humanity's bond with God. In "correlating" the divine and human wisdoms, it allows for apprehension of God; in being a "bridge," it allows for relationship with him. It allows for bond with God and with the God-man who is Sophia/divine wisdom yet whose care for other persons is analogously possible for each of us. Bulgakov traces Sophia through Jesus' ministries[51] and notes that, as people encountered and

---

47. M. Martin, *The Submerged Reality: Sophiology and the Turn to a Poetic Metaphysics* (Tacoma, Wash.: Angelico Press, 2015), p. 49.

48. S. Bulgakov, *The Lamb of God,* trans. B. Jakim (Grand Rapids: Eerdmans, 2008; original 1933), p. 445.

49. See Bulgakov, *The Lamb of God,* especially pp. 1-88, 193-212, 261-320, 443-47.

50. Bulgakov, *The Lamb of God,* p. 445.

51. On Bulgakov's account, in Jesus' prophetic ministry, divine truth is told in the manner of the prophets and includes Jesus' works and miracles, which were also possible to other prophets. The priestly ministry is meant not only to redeem humanity from sin but also to elevate persons to divine humanity, to a divine-human wisdom, which was God's vision for humanity from the time of creation. Though humanity and God are radically different and kept distant by sin, God — by creating humanity — commits both to redeem us and to elevate us to the divine humanity he knows we are capable of. The royal ministry continues until Christ's reign on earth is realized and the kingdom of God begins.

learned from him, they encountered both divine wisdom and the human wisdom that enables us to act in a "corresponding" way. We are helped to act correspondingly because Jesus, though being divine wisdom/Word/Sophia, may also speak to humanity in ways we can understand. When we attend to Jesus' words, we attend at once to God and to another (comprehensible) person. Gerhard Sauter writes, "God reveals Godself to humanity. God shows us at the same time both how God acts and what God does. This activity has a name: Jesus Christ."[52] Rahner similarly writes, "The eschatological climax of God's historical self-communication . . . is called Jesus Christ."[53] God's self-communication must be of what God is (or our ideas are only of our own imaginations — the problem of the immanent and economic Trinity). But it also must be a form that we can grasp. Karl Barth puts it this way: Jesus is "the decision as to what God's purpose . . . is, not just for Him [Jesus] but for every man."[54]

To summarize the ideas so far regarding incarnation: this form of God's self-explanation furthers the *imago, similitude,* and covenant (humanity in God's relational image, in covenant with a relational God, and capable of corresponding covenantal behavior). Undergirding these three instances of relationality and the incarnation is the importance of what happens to persons in this world. We are to act covenantally, with *agape,* toward each other on earth as God acts toward us. If we fail in this world, we breach bond with both, as noted in the famous text, "Whatever you did for one of the least of these brothers and sisters of mine, you did for me" (Matt. 25:40). This attention to humanity on earth (not only in the world to come) is in part what the incarnation is for, part of its purpose. In the passage where Jesus speaks of bringing the kingdom of God to the world, he quotes the Aramaic version of Isaiah. Yet in the original Hebrew, as Bruce Chilton rightly notes, God comes to this world not to sweep all into the next world but to intervene on humanity's

---

52. G. Sauter, *What Dare We Hope? Reconsidering Eschatology* (Harrisburg, Pa.: Trinity, 1999), p. 75.

53. K. Rahner, *Grundkurs des Glaubens: Einfuehrung in den Begriff des Christentums,* 6th ed. (Freiburg, Germany; Basel, Switzerland; Vienna: Herder, 1978); translations from *Foundations of Christian Faith: An Introduction to the Idea of Christianity,* trans. W. Dych (New York: Crossroad), pp. 435-36. Patrick Burke parses, "God is not merely man's eternally asymptotic goal, but rather he gives himself in his own reality in self-communication to man"; P. Burke, *Reinterpreting Rahner: A Critical Study of His Major Themes* (New York: Fordham University Press, 2002), pp. 292-93.

54. K. Barth, *Dogmatics in Outline,* trans. G. T. Thompson (New York: Harper and Row, 1959), p. 89.

behalf here. Thus in the kingdom that Jesus brings, God comes to humanity to bring his righteousness also here.[55]

One appreciates the importance of this idea for those who developed their ethics in conditions of great risk. André Trocmé, the French minister who saved thousands of Jews from the Nazi deportation, wrote copious notes and preached two sermons on Matthew 22:39, emphasizing that care for all humanity (including Jews) is of a piece with love for God who became human. Dietrich Bonhoeffer grounded his arguments against Hitler also on the twined covenants as united in the incarnation.[56] He begins, "God loves human beings. God loves the world. Not an ideal human, but human beings as they are; not an ideal world, but the real world."[57] We know this, he continues, in part because "God becomes human, a real human being."[58] Then he comes to his point: as we partake of the God who so loves humanity that he became human, so must we love humanity. "Inasmuch as we participate in Christ, the incarnate one, we also have a part in all of humanity. . . . The incarnate one transforms his disciples into brothers and sisters of all human beings. The 'philanthropy' (Titus 3:4) of God that became evident in the incarnation of Christ is the reason for Christians to love every human being on earth as a brother or sister."[59] This is not, on Bonhoeffer's account, a lesson for the end times but for all times.

---

55. B. Chilton, *Pure Kingdom: Jesus' Vision of God* (Grand Rapids: Eerdmans, 1996), pp. 11ff.

56. D. Bonhoeffer, *Ethics*, trans. C. C. West, D. W. Stott, and R. Krauss, Dietrich Bonhoeffer Works, vol. 6 (Minneapolis: Fortress, 2005), pp. 173, 174, 179, 180, 182, 184-95.

57. Glen Stassen similarly writes, "The good is not an unchanging ideal high above the [Platonic] cave of actual life: the good is the living God. God has become present in the cave, in the actual history where we live, in the incarnation of Jesus Christ." G. Stassen, *A Thicker Jesus: Incarnational Discipleship in a Secular Age* (Louisville: Westminster John Knox, 2012), p. 44.

58. Bonhoeffer, *Ethics*, pp. 47-75, 83, 84.

59. D. Bonhoeffer, *Discipleship*, Dietrich Bonhoeffer Works, vol. 4 (Minneapolis: Fortress, 2003), p. 285. Bonhoeffer elaborates, "I have come to understand more and more the profound this-worldliness of Christianity. The Christian is not a homo religiosus, but simply a man, as Jesus was a man. . . . It is only by living completely in this world that one learns to have faith. . . . By this-worldliness I mean living unreservedly in life's duties, problems, successes, experiences and perplexities. In so doing we throw ourselves completely into the arms of God, taking seriously, not our own sufferings, but those of God in the world — watching with Christ in Gethsemane." D. Bonhoeffer, *Letters and Papers from Prison*, trans. R. Fuller et al., enlarged ed. (New York: Simon and Schuster, 1979), pp. 369-70. See also, D. Bonhoeffer, *Letters and Papers from Prison*, trans. I. Best et al., Dietrich Bonhoeffer Works, vol. 8 (Minneapolis: Fortress, 2010), p. 486.

Also in Bonhoeffer's view, the lessons of God having become human — of God being ever human, as Balthasar notes — are not only personal but also societal. As Jesus engaged the public issues of the day, so must we who are of him and in relationship with him. Bonhoeffer writes, "Community with God is not without social community, nor is social community without community with God."[60] Or, as the eighteenth-century pastor Samuel Davies put it, "unless you conscientiously observe the duties of social life, you cannot enter the kingdom of heaven."[61]

It is worth reading Richard Kearney's moving summation of the twined covenants: "This is a deus capax who in turn calls out to the homo capax of history in order to be made flesh, again and again — each moment we confront the face of the other, welcome the stranger. . . . A capacitating God who is capable of all things cannot actually be or become incarnate until we say yes."[62] *God cannot come to world to bring justice until we are just.* In *Anatheism*, Kearney continues with echoes to Bonhoeffer: "The only Messiah still credible after the death camps would be one who wanted to come but could not because humans failed to invite the sacred stranger into existence."[63]

It is also worth reading together Kearney, Barth, and the medieval Jewish commentator Rashi. Barth: "He who has once realised the fact that God was made man cannot speak and act inhumanly."[64] Rashi: God is God "whenever you [humanity] bear witness to love and justice in the world." Kearney: "God can't create the kingdom unless we create the space for the kingdom to come. . . . [T]ransfiguring is not just something God does to us: it's also something that we do to God. And we transfigure God to the extent that we create art, we create justice, we create love. . . . God gives to us a transfiguring promise: we give it back to God as a transfigured world."[65]

60. Cited in E. Feil, *The Theology of Dietrich Bonhoeffer* (Philadelphia: Fortress, 1985), p. 8.

61. Cited in L. Trinterud, *The Forming of an American Tradition: A Re-examination of Colonial Presbyterianism* (Philadelphia: Westminster, 1949), p. 194.

62. R. Kearney, "Paul's Notion of Dunamis: Between the Possible and the Impossible," in *St. Paul among the Philosophers*, ed. J. Caputo and L. Alcoff (Bloomington and Indianapolis: Indiana University Press, 2009), pp. 142-57, especially pp. 143, 155.

63. R. Kearney, *Anatheism: Returning to God after God* (New York: Columbia University Press, 2009), Kindle location 1463.

64. Barth, *Dogmatics in Outline*, p. 138.

65. R. Kearney, "Philosophizing the Gift," in *The Hermeneutics of Charity: Interpretation, Selfhood, and Postmodern Faith; Studies in Honor of James H. Olthuis*, ed. J. K. Smith and H. I. Venema (Grand Rapids: Brazos, 2004), pp. 54, 58.

A Few Notes about Covenant and Sin

To refuse to invite God to world and so transfigure it is what's called sin. As we ignore commitment and covenant with other persons, we cannot have them with the divine person. "Our sin and alienation," Glen Stassen writes, "are alienation from God, as well as from God's creatures — other humans and the creation itself."[66] In Robin Lovin's words, sin "keeps us turned in upon ourselves. . . . Looking out for yourself, we think, is just what normal people do."

As sin/separation from God is separation from others, justification with God is embrace of commitment to others. This is also learned from the incarnation, which overcomes the sin of isolation in "showing us, in Jesus, what life is like when it is lived in love for God and for other people."[67] From Jesus the idea continues in Paul, whose statement of salvation by faith may seem to sidestep relations with other persons. Yet it is followed by the declaration, "For we are God's handiwork, created in Christ Jesus to do good works, which God prepared in advance for us to do" (Eph. 2:10). John's avowal of faith is followed by the note, "Anyone who does not do what is right is not God's child, nor is anyone who does not love their brother and sister" (1 John 3:10). In James (2:8), we read that keeping the ritual law (bond with God) without caring for neighbor is as good as not keeping any law: "If you really keep the royal law found in Scripture, 'Love your neighbor as yourself,' you are doing right."

This is neither a calculus of works nor a sequential rendering of justification, first with God and then with neighbor. To be sure, Luther, in *Freedom of a Christian*, holds that if a tree is good (right relations with God), its fruit will follow (right conduct with others). Yet the source text in Matthew 7:17 ("every good tree bears good fruit . . .") is also read to mean not sequence but simultaneity: not that a tree must become good *before* it yields good fruit (one must have reconciled relations with God *before* one turns to humanity) but that the tree and fruit being good occur at once. Indeed, the fruit being good is part of what makes the tree so. Analogously, one's covenantal, agapic relations with others are part of what make relations with God covenantal.

Moreover, attempting to earn justification through good works is not *agape* or covenant but strategic self-absorption. " 'Love for God's sake,' " Rahner writes, "does not mean love of God alone in the 'material' of our neighbour merely seen as an opportunity for pure love of God, but really means the love

---

66. Stassen, *A Thicker Jesus*, p. 150.

67. R. Lovin, *Christian Ethics: An Essential Guide* (Nashville: Abingdon, 2000), p. 75.

of our neighbour himself."[68] Commitment to others is not a technique to get at God. Nor does one do good deeds with *upright* intentions and *then* find bond with God. Both moves, strategic and sincere, rely on an "if . . . then" construction — if one is good to others (calculatedly or earnestly), then one nears God. Yet the twined covenant is not if-then but reciprocally constitutive. In summary Rahner writes, "love of neighbour is given in St Matthew as the only explicit standard by which man will be judged (Mt 25:34-46), and that the cooling down *of this* love is represented as the content of 'lawlessness' among the afflictions of the last days (Mt 24:12)."[69]

Paul Untwining the Covenants? A Few Notes in Protest

Theologies that hold to the twined-ness of covenant distinguish themselves from traditions that separate covenant among persons from covenant with God/salvation/justification — a split that usually locates the interpersonal in Jesus and the salvific in Paul. On the latter view, the institutional church after Jesus worked out policies considerably less revolutionary than Jesus' were. The late-nineteenth-century theologian Ernst Troeltsch influenced a century of scholars with his work on the shift in church policies from Jesus' radical ethics to political accommodationism appropriating Stoic natural law and its forbearance with the status quo. Troeltsch held that, as the church gained upper-class adherents and sociopolitical power, it came to support the hierarchies of the day and its own church elites.[70] Paul, on this view, was the beginning of the shift to the more inner, spiritual emphasis of reconciliation with God that left relations among persons and socioeconomic/political structures as they were.

Yet the direction of bond with God away from dealings among persons is not, in recent scholarship, a Pauline intention. Paul, like Jesus, holds that God's love reveals itself when persons love neighbor, stranger, sinner, and enemy. Paul too says that God's vision emerges not only in the private arena (care of the family and slaves) but also in the societal and political, in care for the poor, in treatment of enemies, and in the rejection of violence. Moreover, Paul's mandates even for the private arena were sociopolitically radical.[71]

68. Rahner, "Reflections on the Unity," p. 244.
69. Rahner, "Reflections on the Unity," p. 234.
70. See, for instance, E. Troeltsch, *The Social Teaching of the Christian Churches* (Louisville: Westminster John Knox, 1992; original 1912).
71. Claims have also been made that the apostolic *Haustafeln* in any case came not from Jesus but from existing Jewish law and Stoic philosophy; see F. C. Baur. Arguments restoring

The *Haustafeln* (instructions for Christian households in Col. 3:18–4:1; Eph. 5:21–6:9; and 1 Pet. 2:13–3:7, for instance) not only admonish wives to submit to husbands, children to obey their parents, and slaves to obey their masters. Husbands too are required to love their wives "as Christ loved the church and gave himself up for her" (Eph. 5:25-33). Fathers are told not to "exasperate your children" (Eph. 6:4), and masters to "treat your slaves in the same way. Do not threaten them, since you know that he who is both their Master and yours is in heaven, and there is no favoritism with him" (Eph. 6:9).

Importantly, the ethical intent of the *Haustafeln* emerges not only from their content but also from their relational structure. They are written in pairs, husband-wife, parent-child, and master-slave. This contrasts with contemporary Stoic philosophy, where morality was anchored in individual status: because one was a slave owner or father, one behaved in certain ways. The moral demand of the *Haustafeln* is grounded in the pair, in relationship. Rather than directing us to the spiritual realm (to the neglect of public life), the Pauline *Haustafeln* declare that ethics emerges precisely from relation. It is relation that is the structural basis for conduct.

This reading of Paul allows for more continuity between Paul and Jesus and more reciprocal constitution of bond with God and among persons. Jesus' earthly care for others *is* God's care for us; it is divine *agape* in a form humanity can understand. The man who taught covenantal, agapic love of neighbor is the God with whom one seeks spiritual communion. Paul and Jesus, whatever the differences in circumstances, do not gainsay each other: relationship with God and *agape* toward others are interdependent.[72] Indeed, Paul makes this a structural aspect of Christianity. While relation with God (justification) may rest on faith (Rom. 3:28), salvation rests on *agape* with others: "If I have the gift of prophecy and can fathom all mysteries and all knowledge, and if I have a faith that can move mountains, but do not have love, I am nothing. If I give all I possess to the poor and give over my body to hardship that I may boast, but do not have love, I gain nothing" (1 Cor. 13:2-3).

The interplay of bond with God and among persons helps to resolve the apparent distinction in Paul's writings between Abraham (ostensibly a man of faith, love of God) and Moses (ostensibly, of legal relations among persons). The corpus of the First Testament does not support this divide, as there are

---

Haustafeln to Jesus' vision can be found in E. Hoskyns and N. Davey, *The Riddle of the New Testament* (London: Faber and Faber, 1947, 1957).

72. J. Yoder, *The Politics of Jesus* (Grand Rapids and Cambridge: Eerdmans, 1972, 1994), pp. 103-6.

covenantal and obligation-fulfillment aspects to both men's bonds with God. Abraham has rules to follow as well as faith, and Moses the lawgiver has leaps of faith throughout Scripture, beginning at the burning bush. A close reading of Paul fails to support the distinction as well. The law *(nomos)* and faith *(pistis)* are not riven but brought together in his idea that covenant with God is the antecedent ground and *telos* of law. As one cannot behave generally but only through concrete acts, covenant with God is expressed through specific rituals, and covenant with neighbor, through specific conduct among persons. The rules of ritual and conduct do not prevent covenant and commitment but enable them (as the rules of finger placement do not prevent one from playing the violin but enable it). This is true for the Mosaic as it had been for the Abrahamic perspective.

Moreover, in opening their faith to the Gentiles and leaving the Mosaic law, Christians *did not abandon* all rituals and rules in a faith of pure interiority absent behavioral expression — or in a faith run amok in every possible expression. The early church created *new rituals and rules* to express bond with God and neighbor — as the Pauline epistles to the emergent churches describe, and as every church has established since.

In sum, Paul does not set *pistis* against *nomos*. He distinguishes between acts that emerge from faith/love/covenant and those that do not. His point is that if one acts from covenantal commitment, one does not calculate one's actions according to legal or contractual stipulation but takes into account the other's concerns and needs — as the Pentateuch, prophets, and Talmud tirelessly prescribe (pt. II, ch. 6). To reprise a point of ethics among the thousands in the biblical and rabbinic texts, manumitted slaves are not to be released empty-handed or according to the letter of the law, but with generous supplies (Deut. 15:12-15).

*   *   *

Here we come again to covenant's application to public policy. The agonistic framework of law, however necessary as a last-case scenario, is not the first case, not where most of life begins. To the extent that we start from our covenantal bonds of mutual concern and responsibility, we will have the outlook and creativity to make not only our problem solving but also the societal structures we set up from the start more conducive to well-being.

CHAPTER 10

Covenant's Irrevocability

To be sure the church is often unfaithful [but God is not]: God refuses to let that unfaithfulness be the last word. God creates and sustains a peaceable people in the world, generation after generation.[1]

The covenant between God and persons is, as we've seen, irrevocable. The donative source of being, God, of whom we partake and that makes us as we are, continues unendingly to constitute us as distinct beings in relation. In poetic as in theological terms, this is God's commitment and covenant.

Perhaps the most important point for relationality readings is this: How would one's conduct change if one took God's commitment seriously? As God eternally constitutes us as distinct-amid-relation, in moments of covenantal breach, how would the ongoing-ness of distinction-amid-relation alter what one does *next*? Persons, groups, and countries err. But key to being of an eternally relational God and eternally in relationship (covenant) with him is that we are eternally relational and so need not continue to err. Each (distinct) one of us can in the next moment act from relational regard. This in some sense was the question facing Paul and Augustine, who had had less than exemplary early lives. Turning to our practice and policy, where our record of uncovenantal conduct is substantial, the idea of irrevocability, being ever of a relational God and thus ever relational, asks if we will be covenantal in our next round of policy.

Jürgen Moltmann gets at this in his linking of irrevocability to *imago*. He

---

1. S. Hauerwas, *The Peaceable Kingdom: A Primer in Christian Ethics* (Notre Dame: University of Notre Dame Press, 1983), p. 98.

writes that while *similitude* is a person's moral capacity to behave covenantally to God and others — at which humanity regularly fails — the *imago* is God's donative *kenosis* to humanity, at which he obviously never fails but has also determined never to revoke. Moltmann writes,

> [I]f we understand the two relationally: Then the image of God *(imago)* means God's relationship to human beings: God puts himself in such a relationship to the human being that the human being becomes his image on earth. Likeness to God *(similitude)* then describes the human being's relationship to God. Sin is able to distort the human being's relationship to God in such a way that human beings in place of God make created things their idols, but it cannot destroy God's relationship to human beings. . . . The dignity of the human being is to be found in this objective relationship of God to human beings; it is therefore non-disposable, inalienable, and indestructible.[2]

While Moltmann has confidence in the *imago* and covenantal irrevocability, others have been less optimistic about the *imago*'s sturdiness after the Fall. Nonetheless, even Calvin — who held to the predetermined damnation of all but the elect — held to irrevocability: "the Celestial Creator himself, however corrupted man may be, still keeps in view the end of his original creation."[3] The neo-Calvinist tradition takes ongoing covenant as even more robust, notably in the doctrine of common grace developed by Abraham Kuyper (theologian and prime minister of the Netherlands, 1901-1905). Kuyper builds on the Noahite covenant, in which God promises never again to destroy the world, to ever sustain it and (fallen) humanity within it. Common grace, he holds, emerges from this enduring promise. Even when we strive to do all we can to sustain covenant and yet fail, the covenantal relationship is of a sort that remains.

The incarnation — God becoming human in spite or perhaps because of humanity's breaches — further reveals the unbreakable covenantal bond. Karl Barth characteristically holds to this in his Christology, in which humanity exists at all owing to God's decision to continue his bond with us through Christ — a commitment that is *ab initio* and eternal. Not only human dignity, as Moltmann writes, but also our continuing existence and nature itself are, on Barth's view, from this divine, enduring steadfastness. In his discussion of

---

2. J. Moltmann, *Ethics of Hope*, trans. M. Kohl (Minneapolis: Fortress, 2012), pp. 226-27.
3. J. Calvin, *Commentary on Genesis*, in *Calvin's Commentaries*, vol. 1, trans. J. King (Grand Rapids: Baker, 1981), p. 296.

Barth, John Thompson writes, "God has from all eternity chosen to be the God of man and to have him in fellowship with himself. . . . Its effect in time is manifest in a covenant of grace broken by man but reconstituted by God's act of reconciliation in Jesus Christ."[4] Thomas Torrance, as we've seen, noted "the astonishing revelation of the biblical tradition," that "God does not wish to exist alone,"[5] to which we can add, for eternity.

Importantly, the twined-ness of covenant too is unending, which redoubles the claim on public life. God's eternal commitment to us yields God's eternal community among us. As we unendingly partake of (relational) God and are in inviolable covenant with him, there is no way to be other than in covenantal relation. And so there is eternally no other way to be with each other, with the reciprocity and commitment that this entails. Gerhard Sauter writes that through Jesus' incarnation and Paul's lessons — efforts from God to reach us, to maintain covenant — persons are drawn at once to God and to relations in community. "Gentiles," he writes, "become co-heirs of the promises made to the people of God. . . . Whoever has been declared an heir is now a member of the *household of God*. Being an heir means *inviolable 'belonging.'*"[6] Some readers of Sauter's passage may detect the particularist claim that God's eternal commitment yields human commitment only within the church. And it is true that God's bond to us is in mutual constitution with bonds within the church community. But not only within one's home church. As with the Judaic covenant, the purpose of relations within God's community is to act in covenantal regard for the world.

Seemingly a boon, irrevocable divine commitment has made uncomfortable many who know they will live up neither to covenant with God nor to covenant among persons. They feel they are falling short in both arenas — something like a bigamist mucking up both marriages. Guilt ensues, both for falling short and for being cared about anyway, and then one finds it even harder to trust that one could be cared about. In short, in a downward spiral, we fail to act covenantally, feel ashamed, fail to trust that covenant could be offered anyway, and in that failure, breach covenant again. It is part of covenant's irrevocability that God's commitment remains nonetheless. Glen

4. J. Thompson, "Christology and Reconciliation in the Theology of Karl Barth," in *Christ in Our Place: The Humanity of God in Christ for the Reconciliation of the World,* ed. T. Hart and D. Thimell (Eugene, Ore.: Wipf and Stock, 1989), p. 208.

5. T. Torrance, "The Goodness and Dignity of Man in the Christian Tradition," in *Christ in Our Place,* p. 372.

6. G. Sauter, *What Dare We Hope? Reconsidering Eschatology* (Harrisburg, Pa.: Trinity, 1999), pp. 58-59, emphasis mine.

Stassen writes, "we still fear that we will disobey and distrust and be hostile once again, and therefore will be rejected. We fear trusting in God. Therefore, we need God to receive our hostility in the cross and show that it does not cancel the offer of presence and incorporation."[7]

God, in spite of a breach as stunning as the crucifixion and all the other breaches made daily before and since, nevertheless asserts that he will not abandon us, will not stop making it possible for us to "be." As being at all is being distinct in relation, we continue, because of his unending commitment, to be in covenantal relation to him and each other.

---

7. G. Stassen, *A Thicker Jesus: Incarnational Discipleship in a Secular Age* (Louisville: Westminster John Knox, 2012), p. 166.

CHAPTER 11

Grace

Divine commitment to constitute us and be in relation, in covenant, is irrevocable because whatever has made everything has made it so. This is God's grace, *chesed* or *chen* (Hebrew), *charis* (Greek). On relational accounts, grace is the continuation of being and of a particular form of being — distinct in relation — that allows us to respond to the source of our being, God, and to others. In light of this, God's rejection of wrongdoing manifests not breach of his covenant but evidence of it. Like the incarnation, it is a communication, in a form humanity can grasp, about what goes with and against the ontological grain — a productive anger that a student of mine called *analogia ire*. Drawing again from parenting, parental anger emerges from concern for the child. The child learns from parental anger what is harmful and analogously can begin to make judgments on her own. Analogously, humanity learns from God's "anger" about what does and doesn't work in the cosmos.

In exploring grace, I'll begin with Karl Barth, who, holding God to be at bottom unknowable, gets at the relationality of grace, as we've seen, through his Christology. Though humanity, Barth writes, "can know about God only because and to the extent that He gives Himself to us to be known," God has indeed made himself known through revelation in Christ. God's "work is a grace," Barth writes, "a free divine decision"[1] to engage with us. Jesus *is* God's activity of care, his becoming human out of commitment to us. Jesus is also *evidence,* so to speak, of God's care; absent this care, why would God bother to become incarnate? And Jesus teaches us *about* God's care through his lessons and ministries. We have seen the christological argument before in

---

1. K. Barth, *Church Dogmatics* III/1, ed. G. W. Bromiley and T. Torrance, trans. J. W. Edwards, O. Bussey, and H. Knight, 2nd ed. (Edinburgh: T. & T. Clark, 1958), p. 371.

Barth's mature work on the *analogia entis,* where he holds that what humanity is begins with God's decision to care for us (reconcile) through Jesus. The divine decision to be with us constitutes us as we are. We have seen it also in Barth's *analogia actionis,* where humanity learns through Jesus' lessons to be "memetes" of God, to act concernedly toward others as God acts toward us.

Writing about Barth, Ronald Thiemann points out that "The wonder of grace is that God uses that unconstrained self-determination to bind Godself eternally to human beings through the person of Jesus Christ." God is thus both hidden to us, what we cannot grasp, and open to us through Jesus. Thiemann continues, God's mystery, on Barth's account, "is every bit as much a part of God's self-giving in Jesus Christ as is God's self-revelation."[2] Yet the grace of the matter is that we may rest assured that God does make himself known.

The meld of mystery and revelation asks for humility about our knowledge of God yet confidence in his grace to sustain our being and make the world's workings known. This confidence is hope, not a passing expectation but a disposition, a way of living based on the idea that we are graced with God's continuing sustenance.[3] "The great hope," Barth writes, "which God sets before men compels them to demonstrate against the course of this world. To rejoice in *hope* means to know God in hope without seeing him."[4] Hope of grace entails responsibility. As God in grace sustains us, we are with analogous grace to sustain each other and world. As we are able to learn about God's vision through the grace of his communication/revelation, we are responsible for acting secondarily in grace, with analogous covenantal reciprocity toward others.

We may reasonably come to this hope because of grace's endurance, bringing together the ideas of grace and irrevocability. God continues to constitute human life and, through his self-revelation, to guide us even when we fail. Robin Lovin writes that God acts

> primarily as the gracious One who accepts us despite our failures to live up to what the moral life requires of us, and who restores our hope for the future despite our inability to take back what we have already done or make up for what we have failed to do in the past. . . . If we accept the grace God offers, we are freed from the weight of our past and our hope is restored.

2. R. Thiemann, "Beyond Exclusivism and Absolutism," in *God's Life in Trinity,* ed. M. Volf and M. Welker (Minneapolis: Augsburg Fortress, 2006), p. 126.

3. Gerhard Sauter describes hope as the future one "lives in" now, the future we form by our present actions.

4. K. Barth, *The Epistle to the Romans,* trans. E. C. Hoskyns (London: Oxford University Press, 1933; original 1919), p. 457.

If we refuse it, our moral life is apt to become a self-deceptive exercise in justifying our mistakes and blaming our failures on others.[5]

The notion of God's grace as continuing to constitute us and be in relation with us contrasts, Timothy Dearborn notes, with four classic notions of grace: *dualistic or double predestination* (God determines who will and will not believe in him and thus who will and will not be saved); *universalistic predestination* (God has decided that it's possible that all may believe in him); *dualistic synergism* (God has decided that salvation depends on the human choice to believe in him); and *universalistic synergism* (God has decided that salvation depends on human choice but all people will in time come freely to him).

Dearborn holds that these approaches suffer from a "monotheistic" rather than a Trinitarian view of grace. On the "monotheistic" view, grace is something of a standing attribute of God, an unchanging stance toward humanity — God makes all the decisions — rather than part of a living relationship with us. He writes, "it makes God's being in *una substantia* [one substance] the foundational characteristic of God, rather than God's being one in communion."[6] Lacking in this "mono" notion is God's active grace, active relationship, with each person and each person's analogous obligation to act with grace toward others. By contrast, Dearborn emphasizes, the Trinitarian grace is neither an unchanging characteristic of God nor tritheism; nor is it modalism (three modes or standing ways of being within one deity). It is rather that the *relations* among the Trinitarian persons — not the three "stations" but their mutual constitution — make each what he distinctly is and make the divine unity. "The threeness of the unity of God," he writes, "are linked together in such a way that the threeness is not dissolved into the unity nor the unity divided by the threeness."[7]

Following Trinitarian grammar, as God is internally relational, his *kenosis*, opening to us, constitutes us as relational — which is his act of grace every moment that he continues to do so. "Every aspect of God's dealings with humanity is an expression of his grace, for it is a manifestation of God's being-in-relationship, his call to humanity to enter into that relationship, and his disclosure of the consequences of humanity's refusal to live in communion with

5. R. Lovin, *Christian Ethics: An Essential Guide* (Nashville: Abingdon, 2000), p. 125.

6. T. Dearborn, "God, Grace and Salvation," in *Christ in Our Place: The Humanity of God in Christ for the Reconciliation of the World,* ed. T. Hart and D. Thimell (Eugene, Ore.: Wipf and Stock, 1989), pp. 266, 277.

7. Dearborn, "God, Grace and Salvation," pp. 288-89.

God and one another."[8] The grace of relationship is extended by God through Jesus to man, by the God-man to God, and by humanity, through spirit, to God — a Trinity of relational pairs that Dearborn calls onto-relational. Grace is "from the Father to the incarnate Son in the Spirit; from the Son on behalf of humanity in the Spirit to the Father; from humanity in the Spirit through the Son to the Father."[9] As with the Trinity, the three relationships are discrete but interdependently form each other and the whole of grace.

Anthony Baker adds to Trinitarian logic the logic of the *imago,* intimated in Dearborn's account. As God is himself eternal relationality, his act of grace is that humanity in his image is analogously relational and expresses God's relationality. "God's own mediated agency is the very fabric of our being, and our being, in turn, as Meister Eckhart supposed, is mediated divinity."[10] Baker notes that this grace — from a relational God to persons analogously relational — is a divine-human cooperation. Attempts to sever God's work in the world from humanity's posits, on Baker's view, hubristic autonomy in humanity and disinterestedness in God. The severing of "God's work and ours amount[s] to the granting of a basic independence to the creature and a lack of charitable sharing to God, thus mortally wounding the Christian accounts of creation, the *imago dei,* and the Holy Trinity" — all reflecting God's relationality and relation with us — "with one swipe."[11]

Rather than inflict this triune wound, Baker looks to Aquinas's notion of operative and cooperative grace to show the divine-human cooperation that is the totality of grace. While God constitutes humanity to be relational (operative grace), we have a cooperative moment as we *willingly* respond to God. "Our will is 'moved' by God's operation towards a desire for union with him who is our final cause; but this help is also cooperative, in that it is the will that is so affected, and no will is free if it is simply caused and not also in some sense self-causing."[12] As we are of God's relationality in his image, we may be "moved" to relationship with God, but we in his image also move ourselves. Absent this cooperative moment, there is no free will, no decision to respond to God; there is only automatic programming.

Baker proceeds from cooperative grace between persons and God to cooperation among persons. Here he echoes Rashi's "God is God whenever

---

8. Dearborn, "God, Grace and Salvation," pp. 272-73.

9. Dearborn, "God, Grace and Salvation," p. 284.

10. A. Baker, "Poesis and Immediacy: A Reply to Davis," *Political Theology* 10, no. 1 (2009): 167-76; see also, p. 175.

11. Baker, "Poesis and Immediacy," p. 171.

12. Baker, "Poesis and Immediacy," p. 171.

you [humanity] bear witness to love and justice in the world" and Richard Kearney's "God can't create the kingdom unless we create the space for the kingdom to come."[13] Church, on Baker's account, is both sorts of cooperation — between God and persons and among persons — both made possible by grace with operational and cooperational moments. Our cooperation means that, as we are in time and live in different places and cultures, the forms of our relations with God and others too will differ. It means that our notions even of church differ, and, Baker notes, are at times constructed of "fetishistic substitutions"[14] that are humanity's ways of trying to grasp the divine. Yet the church community is also grounded in divine, operational grace: God's constitution of humanity in his image, his covenantal commitment to us, and his rupture into the world to communicate with us and so bring us to his vision.

Humanity's cooperation with God is the historical process of expressing these three — the *imago*, God's covenantal commitment to us, and incarnation/communication — in human terms as we live together. As we grasp what they tell us about the world, we may incorporate this knowledge into our relationships and practices. Church, in Baker's summation, is a human project but one suffused with a God whose being is relational thrice: in (immanent) Trinitarian communion, in the incarnation (relation with humanity), and in all subsequent moments of grace on earth. To the idea that cooperation between God and humanity (in contrast to divine monopoly or unidirectionality) must be rent by a who-is-running-the-show tension, Baker notes that this ignores both divine and human relationality. Cooperation or mediation between God and humanity does not yield competition but a recognition that God is relational, relational with us, for us, and is partnered by humanity's analogous relationality. "All is divine operation," Baker holds, "and all is thoroughly mediated through creaturely cooperation."[15]

Baker's emphasis on cooperation in grace finds an echo in Catherine Keller's work. She calls the grace of relationality call-and-response, a *reciprocal grace*. God begins by offering us in grace something of his relational being, of his understanding of the world, and of his commitment to our well-being (in communication/revelation in ways we can grasp). In grace, God constitutes us as relational to be *in response*. Our capacity to respond to God is, on this

---

13. R. Kearney, "Philosophizing the Gift," in *The Hermeneutics of Charity: Interpretation, Selfhood, and Postmodern Faith; Studies in Honor of James H. Olthuis*, ed. J. K. Smith and H. I. Venema (Grand Rapids: Brazos, 2004), pp. 54, 58.

14. C. Davis, J. Milbank, and S. Žižek, eds., *Theology and the Political: The New Debate* (Durham, N.C., and London: Duke University Press, 2005), p. 424.

15. Baker, "Poesis and Immediacy," p. 172.

view, part of grace. Keller writes, "The power of God, if it is a response-able power, *empowers* the others — to respond. In their freedom. God's will is indeed God's will! But the term *will* derives from *voluntas,* from which also comes 'voluntary,' which means not control but *desire.* What God *wants.* . . . Grace — fishy as it seems to predestinarians — needs our cooperation. It is not a power over us, but an empowerment of us."[16]

David Platt comes to similar ideas. In his discussion of "the centrality of grace in the life of faith," he writes, "the Word of God accomplishes the work of God." That is, "the faith God has graciously given to you begins to produce radical fruit from you."[17] As Keller would say, the grace of faith enables one to respond. Platt continues, what God gives in grace — constituting us of his relationality and communicating with us in relationship (to save us from erring and when we have erred) — renders us relational, capable of covenantal bonds with God and others. He describes this interlooping: "True faith in Christ inevitably produces great work for Christ. . . . And all of it is by grace. The basis for our salvation — Christ — is a gracious gift from God. The means of our salvation — faith — is also a gracious gift from God. And the fruit of our salvation — works — is indeed a gracious gift from God. . . . *The Gospel saves us to work.*"[18]

One of the most radical renderings of grace came from the mid-twentieth-century German theologian Karl Rahner, who too underscored its reciprocal aspects and substantially universalized them. While his earlier writing acknowledged the classic distinction between God's grace and humanity's response, his later work accented a greater inter-twined-ness, where humanity's capacity to answer God's grace is also a moment of it. Human capacity for reciprocity is a part of what grace is.

Rahner calls humanity "the event of God's grace," the moment and site, so to speak, where God's grace — to constitute and communicate — expresses itself. Rahner moves from the idea of God giving *to* humanity in grace to the idea of humanity *being* the grace of God as he constitutes beings and sustains relationship with them. Importantly, he continues, as the offer and acceptance of grace change one's subjectivity, one's sense of self and way of living, it may occur in any moment or experience, not only in the religious. Rahner universalizes grace and takes its sacredness into the world.

16. C. Keller, *On the Mystery: Discerning Divinity in Process* (Minneapolis: Fortress, 2008), pp. 89, 149.

17. D. Platt, *Radical Together: Unleashing the People of God for the Purpose of God* (Colorado Springs: Multnomah, 2011), pp. 45, 30.

18. Platt, *Radical Together,* p. 30, emphasis mine.

Rahner wrote extensively on this "uncreated grace," God's direct *kenosis* through the Holy Spirit to each person, a divine opening to persons in quotidian life offered universally regardless of confession (just as he wrote of God's universal offer of covenant). "Every human being," he writes, "is really and truly exposed to the influence of divine, supernatural grace which offers an interior union with God and by means of which God communicates himself *whether the individual takes up an attitude of acceptance or of refusal toward this grace.*"[19] Following from this, Rahner holds that acts of generosity — even those not done out of faith or love of God but from "natural" motives — are salvific because God, so desiring agapic relation, universally enables all persons to express it.[20] In his overview of Rahner, Linus Ibekwe concludes,

> The view on the *universality of grace* is Rahner's own innovation. . . . [O]n the basis of God's universal salvific will grace is seen to be abundant. God is abidingly present and persistently inviting all to the banquet. All of life, even in its most secular corners, is embraced by the presence of God offering Himself to human beings. Thus, the walls erected between Church and world, between Christianity and other religions, between the sacred and the secular collapse.[21]

Over the course of his writing, Rahner shifted also in his view of grace and revelation. Whereas he earlier spoke of grace as internal to each person and revelation as public word, he later envisioned the two reciprocally. Neither is inner or outer, first or subsequent. While each person inwardly experiences God, a moment of grace, these personal experiences contribute to public recognition of his presence — to revelation. And such public recognition may inform personal experience.

The universality of grace — for all persons and possible in all moments of life, both Rahner emphases — was taken up by Richard McBrien, who caused substantial controversy in the Catholic Church for his accent on plurality and universality. McBrien writes,

19. K. Rahner, *Theological Investigations,* trans. K.-H. Kruger (Baltimore: Helicon Press, 1966), p. 141, emphasis mine.

20. See K. Rahner, "Reflections on the Unity of the Love of Neighbour and the Love of God," in *Theological Investigations,* vol. 6, *Concerning Vatican Council II,* trans. K.-H. Kruger and B. Kruger (New York: Crossroad, 1982), p. 239.

21. L. Ibekwe, *The Universality of Salvation in Jesus Christ in the Thought of Karl Rahner* (Würzburg: Echter Verlag, 2006), p. 299.

Everywhere where the word God is given flesh, given concrete expression in good deeds, God's grace, which is Jesus Christ, is present. This grace is part of the historical condition of human existence. It is universally available. And it is intrinsic to ordinary, everyday human experience. Since human existence is social as well as individual, however, grace has a social as well as an individual dimension. Therefore, it has an impact on communities, institutions, and social structures in every sphere of human life.[22]

Several points here extend Rahner's thought: that God's grace — his communication and commitment to us — is expressed in deeds of goodness universally,[23] and importantly, the impact on daily and public life of taking universal grace seriously.

To sum up the ideas of this chapter: our being of God and our bond with him given in grace are both a relationship *and an ikon or template for our relationships:* "See that you also excel in this grace of giving. . . . For you know the grace of our Lord Jesus Christ" (2 Cor. 8:7, 9). In the words of Glen Stassen, "the Christian life is not just hard human effort to live up to high ideals; nor is it just a bunch of duties. . . . We are allowed, privileged, and invited to respond to the call of Jesus to follow him as he shows us how to act in the way that fits with what God is doing in our midst."[24] This is not "cheap" grace, as Stassen calls it, with no requirements for the way we live, but neither is it gray, grinding duty. God may have a vision for humankind, but he also gives us a leg up in getting there. That leg up is grace — in Stassen's words, both "christomorphic grace," all that Jesus was and taught, and "participative grace,[25] our capacity to learn and respond.

---

22. R. McBrien, *Catholicism* (London: HarperCollins, 1994, 2000), p. 179.

23. Catherine Mowry LaCugna echoes, "we become by grace what God is by nature, namely, persons in full communion with God and with every creature"; see C. LaCugna, *God for Us: The Trinity and Christian Life* (San Francisco: HarperSanFrancisco, 1992), p. 1.

24. G. Stassen, *Living the Sermon on the Mount: A Practical Hope for Grace and Deliverance* (Hoboken, N.J.: Jossey-Bass/Wiley, 2006), p. 16.

25. G. Stassen, *A Thicker Jesus: Incarnational Discipleship in a Secular Age* (Louisville: Westminster John Knox, 2012), p. 152.

CHAPTER 12

Crucifixion

In the crucifixion, Jesus is at once a tortured Jewish prophet, God, and God's commitment to humanity, Christ the Messiah. Among the many readings of this problematic simultaneity is the disturbing idea that crucifixion — this awful/awesome point of such pain — means *agape* or covenant, God's eternal support of life and commitment to humanity. The point and difficulty of the crucifixion are that, as Thomas F. Torrance writes, "The Cross of Christ is a window into the Divine Heart."[1]

The crucifixion proposes that it is the screaming magnifier of the *imago* done with the same dedication to humanity. Not only is humanity in God's image but God is willing to enter into ours at the most painful moment out of bond with us and commitment to saving us from breaching it — and to save us though we have breached it. Dietrich Bonhoeffer described it as *eintreten* (to enter): on the cross, God enters into humanity, already in his image, thus making more emphatic his care for the human life he has constituted.[2] Jesus, the God-person, steps into the place of all persons (*Stellvertretung*, "substituting"), like a soldier taking another's place at the front. The idea has not been lost on Jewish scholars. Irving Greenberg writes, "As a Jew, I had hesitated to

---

1. T. Torrance, "The Goodness and Dignity of Man in the Christian Tradition," in *Christ in Our Place: The Humanity of God in Christ for the Reconciliation of the World*, ed. T. Hart and D. Thimell (Eugene, Ore.: Wipf and Stock, 1989), p. 377.

2. Delores Williams looks at the notion of *eintreten* in her work on black women's roles of surrogacy, as mammies, wet nurses, and sexual surrogates; see D. Williams, "Black Women's Surrogacy Experience and the Christian Notion of Redemption," in *Cross Examinations: Readings on the Meaning of the Cross Today*, ed. M. Trelstad (Minneapolis: Augsburg Fortress, 2006), p. 28; see also, D. Williams, *Sisters in the Wilderness: The Challenge of Womanist God-Talk* (Maryknoll, N.Y.: Orbis, 1993).

use language of God suffering, because it seems to be a Christian patent. But it's not so. I came to see this has been a central belief of the Jewish people — that God shares our pain. Indeed Christianity was never more Jewish than when it expressed it in those terms — that God suffers with humans."[3]

Glen Stassen investigates the theme of entering *(erchomai)* as a lesson taught by the crucifixion and elsewhere in the Gospels, especially in Mark, where it is a repeating theme. As in the crucifixion, God enters into the most miserable of human conditions to bring sufferers to him. In Capernaum (Mark 1:21–3:12), Jesus enters into the world of outcasts — a leper, a sick woman, a paralyzed man, a tax collector — touches them, eats with them, forgives and heals them, and so brings them from their marginal status into his compassion. The process of entering repeats, Stassen writes, in Mark 5, with the courageous but impoverished, hemorrhaging, unclean woman, and it repeats again with Jairus's dying daughter. Jesus enters into their situations, touches and heals. And it continues with Jesus entering Jerusalem, seat of the highest-flying sinners, where he enters into all their places, sins, and guilt, and in his suffering saves even them. The cross, Stassen continues,

> is Jesus Christ's act to enter into Jerusalem, as he had entered into the midst of the lives of people throughout the Gospel — the very perpetrators of injustice, violence, betrayal, and denial — to confront their wrong and to offer even them the opportunity to repent and be included in his mission, in community with him. Jesus does this amazing act of compassion and sacrifice because it is God's will to deliver them and us. In what Jesus does, God is acting because of God's judgment on the injustice, domination, violence, greed, denial, and exclusion, and because [of] God's compassion to redeem, to deliver from alienation.[4]

Importantly, Jesus does this — works to save us from breaking commitment to God and others — not only by "paying" for our breaches. On the relational view, the crucifixion is not only a restitutionary balance sheet but also, John Goldingay notes, "gift."[5] It is a breathtaking demonstration of God's care and commitment so that humanity can understand it, analogously respond,

3. I. Greenberg, "Easing the Divine Suffering," in *The Life of Meaning: Reflections on Faith, Doubt, and Repairing the World*, ed. B. Abernethy and W. Bole (New York: Seven Stories, 2002), p. 69.

4. G. Stassen, *A Thicker Jesus: Incarnational Discipleship in a Secular Age* (Louisville: Westminster John Knox, 2012), p. 165.

5. J. Goldingay, "Old Testament Sacrifice and the Death of Christ," in *Atonement Today*, ed. J. Goldingay (London: SPCK, 1995), pp. 6-8.

and so uphold covenant and *agape*. Shifting the accent from sin-accounting to *agape* and gift, Goldingay sees Christ's death not as payment in an "intrinsically hierarchical and/or contractual web of relationships" between humanity and God, but as God giving to us, in *agape,* a path and model of how to live in *apape*. Reaching it may be ever asymptotic as humanity is imperfect and fallen, but in the crucifixion God has made a supreme effort to help us.

In Bonhoeffer's words, "the secret, however, of this judgment, this suffering and this dying, is the love of God for the world, for human beings."[6] In his gloss of Bonhoeffer, Stassen reprises the twined-ness of the bonds between God and persons and among persons: the crucifixion shows us not only God's love, "It connotes being-with-each-other and being-for-each-other, entering into the other's reality and even into the other's guilt."[7] Doing this for each other, in God's image and under the tutelage of the crucifixion, follows from God doing it for us. In a nearly parallel passage, Torrance writes, "God loves us more than he loves himself. Such is the immeasurable worth, the infinite value, that God puts upon man in the price he has chosen to pay in order to share with him his own divine Life and Love. In view of what God has done for man . . . we are unable to set any limits on the worth of our fellow human beings."[8]

Stassen moves his discussion of "being-for-each-other" to community and society, a central theme in relational accounts. "They and we crucify him, but he continues to work to restore community."[9] In healing the discarded, Jesus brought them not only to himself but also into social acceptance. His ministries and miracles are often societal, concerned with outcasts — not a divine or individual but a sociocultural designation — and their reincorporation into society. The point is to disturb the sociopolitical status quo and prod us to rethink our cultural and societal (not only individual) mores and practices. In the crucifixion, Jesus made the gift of love-unto-sacrifice not for *an*other person but for all as we live together. Miroslav Volf has called this the "social significance of divine self-giving." He writes, "God does not abandon the godless to their evil but gives the divine self for them in order *to receive them into divine communion* through atonement," and then Volf adds, "so also should we."[10]

In its societal aspect, the crucifixion — the juxtaposition of might and the

---

6. D. Bonhoeffer, *Ethics*, trans. C. C. West, D. W. Stott, and R. Krauss, Dietrich Bonhoeffer Works, vol. 6 (Minneapolis: Fortress, 2005), pp. 88-95.

7. Stassen, *A Thicker Jesus*, p. 153.

8. Torrance, "Goodness and Dignity," p. 378.

9. Stassen, *A Thicker Jesus*, p. 165.

10. M. Volf, *Exclusion and Embrace: A Theological Exploration of Identity, Otherness, and Reconciliation* (Nashville: Abingdon, 1996), p. 23, emphasis mine.

trampled — is political in the original sense of the word, power's distribution within and among groups. "It is precisely here at the nexus of Empire and the cross that hybridity and exile are useful lenses," Gabriel Salguero, president of the National Latino Evangelical Coalition, writes. "The cross is not the glorification of suffering. It is the recognition of the horrors of suffering particularly with regard to the innocent and most vulnerable. The solidarity expressed by the crucifixion of Christ is not an affirmation of violence but God's 'emphatic no' to the horrors of the torturing, othering, and execution of the least of these."[11]

I'll close with this observation by M. Douglas Meeks, which, in using economic discourse, parallels Salguero's political one in moving from God-to-person to person-to-person to person-to-persons as we live together economically and politically.[12] (More detailed discussions of politics and economics are found in pt. II, ch. 16, and the conclusion.) Meeks sees in the crucifixion the suggestion that engagement and exchange even in economics may be based not on the tally sheet of debt (profit, utility, or benefit maximization) but on the idea that tallying is not the point — on the idea that the quality of our future life together is the point and depends on the ontology, mores, and practices of reciprocal regard.

In this, Meeks says, using the imagery of the crucifixion, what Antonio Genovesi, Alexis de Tocqueville, John Stuart Mill, Robert Skidelsky, Luigino Bruni, Joseph Stiglitz, William Greider, and Michael Lind, among others, have said in economics. "In the cross," Meeks writes,

> God cancels the possibility of debt itself and therefore debt economy as the source of obligation and security. If God accounts us as having no debt, the possibility of our being restored to God's economy of graceful giving is opened up. In this sense God's redeeming work transforms the economy of debt into the economy of grace. . . . To be the *homo economicus* in God's economy of grace means that we are shaped by God's giving rather than by maximizing utility.[13]

Evoking *homo economicus* is not incidental to Meeks's work. His quite serious economic proposal is that policy be designed following God's economy of giving and *for*-giving.

11. G. Salguero, "The Cross," in *Prophetic Evangelicals*, ed. B. Benson, M. Berry, and P. Heltzel (Grand Rapids: Eerdmans, 2012), pp. 129, 130.

12. See also, G. Agamben, *The Kingdom and the Glory: For a Theological Genealogy of Economy and Government* (Stanford: Stanford University Press, 2011).

13. M. D. Meeks, "The Social Trinity and Property," in *God's Life in Trinity*, ed. M. Volf and M. Welker (Minneapolis: Augsburg Fortress, 2006), p. 20.

CHAPTER 13

Resurrection and Salvation

The promise of the messiah allows humanity to have *"the memory of the future."*[1]

Not Abacus but Beckoning:
Covenantal Promise in This World as in the Next

Closely linked to the crucifixion, resurrection, redemption, and salvation are, on relational readings, both spiritually salvific, a matter between persons and God, and an expression of divine commitment to us as we live *with each other* in the world. Our living with reciprocal concern and commitment is part of God bringing salvation. While it has been my method in this book to pursue affinities among relational ideas from different traditions, I have pointed to certain controversies, such as that between *analogia entis* and *analogia fidei* or between natural and revealed theologies, when they are especially helpful in understanding relationality. Likewise, I open this chapter with a long-standing debate on the nature of redemption and salvation.

Like Dietrich Bonhoeffer and John Goldingay in the previous chapter, Daniel Bell Jr. holds that it is gift,[2] which he distinguishes from the restitutionary view of atonement/redemption and its emphasis on our debt to God

---

1. J. Zizioulas, *Being in Communion: Studies in Personhood and the Church,* Contemporary Greek Theologians, vol. 4 (Crestwood, N.Y.: St. Vladimir's Seminary Press, 1997), p. 180.

2. See also, H. U. von Balthasar, *The Glory of the Lord: A Theological Aesthetics,* vol. 1, *Seeing the Form,* ed. J. Fessio, S.J., and J. Riches, trans. E. Leiva-Merikakis (San Francisco: Ignatius; New York: Crossroad, 1982), pp. 248, 249; J. Milbank, *Beyond Secular Order: The Representation of Being and the Representation of the People* (Chichester: Wiley Blackwell, 2014), pp. 79ff.

so grave that it cannot be repaid other than by God/Jesus himself. "In this commonplace reading of Christ's work," Bell writes, "death — the sacrifice that is the loss of life, the suffering that is redemptive — is the unmistakable fulcrum of salvation. Moreover, the unspoken subtext of this account is fear — the fear of eternal damnation." On this reading, fear and death are the linchpins, but, Bell continues, "the commonplace reading is also a profound distortion of Christ's work. Christ's work of atonement is the gift, not of death, but of resurrected life."[3]

Substitutionary or restitutionary accounts have traditionally regarded Jesus' death as payment for human wrongs so great that God, in his justice and righteousness, cannot let them pass (as parents cannot let children run amok), yet in his dedication to us, he cannot let them bring us to damnation. Thus God becomes sinless in the form of Jesus so that the sacrifice of this divine-human innocence generates a repository of redemption. (The dual nature of Jesus, as we've seen, was already substantial in Irenaeus's and Athanasius's accounts of redemption.)[4] As Jesus himself needs no redemption, the redemption passes on to humanity and our debt and sin are canceled. Church Fathers used the imagery of slavery, bondage, and servitude to illustrate humanity's need for redemption from the taskmaster of sin and thus for restitution. Saint Basil, among other Cappadocians, used prison ransom imagery, holding in *Homily on Psalm 48*[5] that humanity is captive to sin and, like prisoners, must be redeemed by the divine man. Origen and Augustine wrote of the devil himself holding humanity captive: "Men were held captive," Augustine explains, "under the devil, and served devils; but they were redeemed from captivity. . . . The Redeemer came, and gave a price; He poured forth His blood, and bought the whole world."[6]

In some contrast, Gregory of Nyssa, while holding to the Fall as human-

---

3. D. Bell Jr., "The Politics of Fear and the Gospel of Life," in *Veritas: Belief and Metaphysics*, ed. C. Cunningham and P. Candler Jr. (Norwich: SCM, 2007), p. 445.

4. See Irenaeus, *Aversus haereses* 5.1; http://www.newadvent.org/fathers/0103.htm; Athanasius, *Oratio adversus Arianos* 59 and 60. Athanasius held as well that the crucifixion was *necessary* as the only path to the redemption of mankind: "The Word, perceiving that not otherwise could the corruption of men be undone, save by death as a necessary condition"; see *The Incarnation of the Word* 9; http://www.ccel.org/ccel/athanasius/incarnation.pdf. The view from necessity was not embraced by all Church Fathers; Saint Gregory Nazianzen, for instance, did not take it up, though he did allow Basil's prison ransom interpretation.

5. Basil, *Exegetic Homilies*, trans. Sr. A. C. Way, Fathers of the Church, vol. 46 (Washington, D.C.: Catholic University of America Press, 1963).

6. Augustine, *Enarratio in Psalmos* 96, v. 5; http://www.newadvent.org/fathers/1801.htm; biblical sources for this include 1 Cor. 6:20; 7:23; Gal. 3:13; 4:5; 1 Pet. 1:18; 1 Tim. 2:5, 6.

ity's agreement with the devil, came to focus less on restitution and more on God's grace in redemption. He saw atonement and redemption following from the generosity of the incarnation. God had, in becoming human, tricked the devil into murdering not just a man but the divine man. Thus humanity's debt to the devil and the devil's "rights" over an indebted humanity were annulled, freeing man to turn to God.[7] This emphasizes less the agony of the crucifixion, the "payment," and makes God's grace and humanity's nearing God more the point.

Among the medieval views of redemption, Anselm's has generated substantial discussion. He held that the devil, as God's creation, could not have rights over humanity, also God's creation. And God, as creator of both, could not be obliged to trick the devil or buy his rights — a necessity that might pertain to equals but not to God and a creature of his own making.[8] Relying less on ransom imagery and more on a "satisfaction" model (from Roman law), Anselm held that "every sin must be followed either by satisfaction or by punishment."[9] Satisfaction, on his view, is not only the cessation of wrongdoing but also righting it beyond mere law fulfillment, asymptotically toward infinity to address infinite God. Humanity cannot on its own do this as it cannot redress sin by giving God something he does not have; worse for us, all we have comes from God.[10] Thus God faces the possibility that sin cannot be redressed and his world will remain unjust, an unacceptable condition, or he himself must submit something of infinite worth, the God-man in the incarnation.[11] As with Irenaeus, God becomes a sinless person, Jesus, so that the sacrifice of this innocence redeems all that is owed God, thus healing and repairing God's order[12] and opening up the possibility of redemption and life.

For many who accept this interpretation of Anselm, God's justice is disturbingly more prominent than his compassion. Yet on the view of David Bentley Hart, among other relationality thinkers, this interpretation of Anselm is itself sinful — a construction of God's justice absent his mercy. Hart holds instead that Anselm upends his traditional interpreters. If, as classic

---

7. As Nyssa explained it, the devil or death (on alternate readings) was lured by the "bait" of Christ's humanity and was defeated by his divinity; see Gregory of Nyssa, *The Great Catechism*, in *The Nicene and Post-Nicene Fathers*, vol. 5, ed. P. Schaff and H. Wace (Peabody, Mass.: Hendrickson, 1903), p. 494.

8. See *Cur Deus Homo* 1.7; http://www.ewtn.com/library/CHRIST/CURDEUS.HTM.

9. *Cur Deus Homo* 1.15.

10. *Cur Deus Homo* 1.24.

11. See especially the preface to *Cur Deus Homo.*

12. *Cur Deus Homo* 1.15; 2.4.

interpretations have it, humanity's efforts to atone are useless and only Jesus' sacrifice is salvific, one might as well not atone. As penitence is a waste of time, Anselm should have no use for it. But, Hart continues, this is not what we find. Anselm does not scotch atonement but gives it an important role consistent with a merciful God. Atonement is not punishment for sin by an uncompassionate God but the apt posture of a person already redeemed by a forgiving one. Atonement does not precede redemption but follows from it. It is "simply a thankful piety that responds to (and is the result of) an unmerited and transforming grace."[13] In short, Hart's reading of Anselm finds God to be not a calculating jurist but merciful and already forgiving owing to God's triune nature, itself relationality and love. Jesus' death is not payment or ransom for humanity's sin; it rather invokes a blessing and forgiveness from a gracious, committed God.

Moreover, Hart reexamines the meaning of "sin" in Anselm's text. On traditional interpretations, it is a failure to respect God's "honor," making God seem rather narcissistic. But Hart notes that in Anselm's medieval context, "honor" does not mean pride but one's position in a network of relations and commitments: "One's honor lay not only in the obeisance one received, but in the social covenant one upheld and to which one was obliged."[14] Thus, humanity's sin is not in injuring the pride of a self-absorbed deity but in failing the covenantal relations in which both God and humanity participate. Yet God forgives, "when humanity fails to take up the creature's side of the divine covenant, the righteousness that condemns is also the love that restores by surmounting even human disobedience and creation's lawful subjection to death, to take up the human side on humanity's behalf."[15]

In sum, God's offer of redemption, as truth or metaphor, is not an abacus but a beckoning. Here again is Bell: "The atonement is not about infinite debt and totalized judgments, but about the instantiation of the gift that enables us to return to our source."[16]

This sets resurrection and salvation within the covenantal promise. They are the divine end of the agreement, part of what God promises in that agapic bond: that Jesus, resurrected, will return to humanity, save it from breaking

---

13. D. B. Hart, "A Gift Exceeding Every Debt: An Eastern Orthodox Appreciation of Anselm's *Cur Deus Homo*," *Pro Ecclesia* 7 (1993): 341.

14. Hart, "Gift Exceeding Every Debt," p. 346.

15. Hart, "Gift Exceeding Every Debt," p. 344.

16. D. Bell Jr., "A Theopolitical Ontology of Judgment," in *Theology and the Political: The New Debate*, ed. C. Davis, J. Milbank, and S. Žižek (Durham, N.C., and London: Duke University Press, 2005), p. 213.

covenant, and bring his kingdom to this world and then to the next. "But in keeping with his *promise* we are looking forward to a new heaven and a *new earth,* the home of righteousness" (2 Pet. 3:13).

The inclusion of "earth" again highlights the interweaving of spiritual salvation with God's commitment to world. God brings righteousness not only in the messianic world of spirit but also to this one. Instances of our regard and commitment to others are instances of this divine bringing. We should note that concern for this world cannot be taken for granted as part of the messianic portfolio. A Messiah might, after all, evaporate our corrupted universe into never-having-been so that something wholly other could begin. Yet the idea that messianic return brings righteousness to *earth,* Dale C. Allison notes, had substantial antecedents in mid-antiquity Judaism, where earthly events were often taken as the start of the apocalypse, messianic arrival, and God's new kingdom. When natural or historical events conformed to expectations of the end times, some took those events as the beginning of the end and of God's new reign. "Events in history were thought sufficiently close to eschatological expectations so as to encourage some Jews to believe that certain of those expectations had come and were coming to pass."[17]

The early Jewish Christians thought similarly. The notions of a suffering Messiah, his divinization (apotheosis), and God's arrival to redeem earth (theophany) had all been themes within Judaism (in Isaiah, Daniel, and the books of Enoch, for instance).[18] As end-times events were thought to occur on earth, when a suffering Messiah figure indeed appeared on earth, divinized to redeem humanity, people had good reason to see these events as end-times moments. "If he [Jesus] had preached the imminence of tribulation and resurrection, and if he had suffered and died and had been seen again alive, his friends would have concluded that his end belonged to the end of the age."[19] After the apocalypse on earth would come God's kingdom also to earth. Allison writes, "Jesus and his disciples were more than Platonists. They hoped that the eschatological promises would be realized not only beyond history but within it, that the transcendent order would merge with the mundane order — and soon."[20]

17. D. Allison Jr., *The End of the Ages Has Come: An Early Interpretation of the Passion and Resurrection of Jesus* (Minneapolis: Fortress, 1985), p. 170.

18. See, for instance, D. Boyarin, *The Jewish Gospels: The Story of the Jewish Christ* (New York: New Press, 2012); L. Hurtado, *Lord Jesus Christ: Devotion to Jesus in Earliest Christianity* (Grand Rapids: Eerdmans, 2003).

19. D. Allison Jr., *The End of the Ages Has Come: An Early Interpretation of the Passion and Resurrection of Jesus* (Minneapolis: Fortress, 1985), pp. 170-71.

20. Allison, *End of the Ages,* p. 177.

One sees the interdependence of salvation-in-spirit with redemption-of-world in Pauline theology, unsurprisingly as it conforms to the Judaic tradition in which Paul was educated. On Paul's view, Jesus is both spiritual salvation with God and bodily redemption.[21] That it is Jesus' *body* that is resurrected points to the importance of bodily life, this world, in God's scheme. It is human bodies that will be resurrected as well (see 1 Cor. 15, for instance). Indeed, the material world will not only be redeemed but it will be redeemed first, before all is spirit. Jesus is the last Adam, a person in history and nature who inaugurates redemption of body until such time as all is spirit: "If the Spirit of him who raised Jesus from the dead is living in you, he who raised Christ from the dead will also give life *to your mortal bodies* through his Spirit who lives in you" (Rom. 8:11). The human story does not begin with a body-in-world, Adam, and end with worldless spirit. It ends with a series of body- and world-rich events: the incarnation, crucifixion, Jesus' bodily resurrection, and ours. The two bodies-in-world — Adam and Jesus — bookend the human story.

It is the story of both persons and *polis,* as the human condition is not only material but also relational and societal. This appears too in our discussion of the crucifixion: from God-to-person to person-to-person to person-to-persons. Indeed, it is a lesson of resurrection/salvation that bodies in our human societies are of key importance in the divine vision. If bodily life is important, so are our (bodily) lives together. John Milbank writes,

> Paul adds the precondition for a more democratic version of the ancient politics of the city, namely, corporeal resurrection. For if the body also is immortal, then the body is also potentially the site of a perfect harmony and goodness. This means that the once "baser" passions and the once subordinate categories of humanity can now fully participate in political processes; *all* of one's life as an individual (erotic, domestic, and economic as well as politically deliberative) can now become part of political life, while all stages, genders, and ranks of human life are fully brought within the scope of the highest friendship and love (agape), which is political in the most precise sense (1 Cor. 13).[22]

---

21. See Bruce Chilton's discussion in J. Neusner and B. Chilton, *Jewish and Christian Doctrines* (New York: Routledge, 2000), ch. 8.

22. J. Milbank, "Paul against Biopolitics," in *Paul's New Moment: Continental Philosophy and the Future of Christian Theology,* ed. J. Milbank, S. Žižek, and C. Davis (Grand Rapids: Brazos, 2010), p. 47.

Salvation, *Imago, Similitude,* and Will:
God's Forgiveness as the Gift of Forgiving Others

Salvation, begun in this world and continued in the next, follows from the *imago* and *similitude*. We, of God's (relational, covenantal) being, have the capacity to act covenantally so we, of the eternal God, may partake of something of his eternal life as we act with analogous covenantal *agape*. 1 Corinthians 15:49 puts it succinctly: "Just as we have borne the image of the earthly man, so shall we bear the image of the heavenly man." We will partake of something of the eternal man.

Among church writings, Maximus the Confessor's doctrine of dyothelitism was an early support for salvation as following from *imago*. Upheld in 1979 by the (Catholic) International Theological Commission, it holds that two wills, divine and human, are involved in humanity's redemption and salvation.[23] The human is Jesus' will (in his humanity), but it is also each of our wills. Given that we partake of the divine image, we partake of the divine will to redeem humankind; in God's image, we too will redemption. Given *similitude,* we also have the moral capacity to will ourselves to act with *agape* and so move toward redemption (though we do not achieve it by human effort). We can think again of Aquinas's "cooperative grace," through which we willingly respond to God and move toward him and salvation. The Swiss theologian and contemporary of Karl Barth, Emil Brunner, called the *imago* a matter of "word" (God's vision and will) *and* our "answer."[24]

Interestingly, Calvin, for all his concern with the predestination of the saved, held that we should pray that all humanity is redeemed, and he relied on the *imago* to make his case. "We pray for the salvation of all whom we know to have been created after the image of God, and who have the same nature with ourselves; and we leave to the judgment of God those whom he knows to be reprobate."[25] On Calvin's account, while God knows who is irredeemably fallen, none of us does, and thus we must act toward all in God's image as persons worthy of God's salvific promise.

Finally, Milbank importantly highlights that God's forgiveness and re-

23. International Theological Commission, "Select Questions on Christology," in *International Theological Commission: Texts and Documents, 1969-1985,* ed. M. Sharkey (San Francisco: Ignatius, 1989), pp. 185-206.

24. E. Brunner, *Man in Revolt: A Christian Anthropology,* trans. O. Wyon (London: Lutterworth, 1939), p. 98.

25. J. Calvin, *Commentary on the Gospel according to John,* trans. W. Pringle (Grand Rapids: Baker, 1996), p. 173.

demption of humanity become, through the *imago/similitude*, our forgiveness of one another. As beings in his image, we have the capacity to forgive analogously as he forgives — and not only at the end of time but always, daily. This human-to-human forgiveness is so important on Milbank's view that, when done, it is sufficient to bring God to forgive us. When we in the image of a forgiving, redeeming God forgive others, it is a brief for God to forgive and redeem us. *God,* Milbank writes, *forgives humanity with the gift — the moral capacity — to forgive others.*

This is not quite two forgivenesses, God's to us, ours to each other. It is rather that God's forgiveness of humanity *is* our capacity to forgive one another. Moments of forgiveness among persons are of God's forgiveness of humanity. And it is our this-worldly, daily forgiving that brings salvation: *"divine redemption* is not God's forgiving us, but rather his giving us *the gift of the capacity for forgiveness.*"[26]

Salvation in This World as in the Next: A Few Examples

Milbank is pointing again to the importance of bodily life, this world, to God. It will not only be redeemed first, before all is spirit, but what happens here before messianic times of salvation is of grave importance. Worldly life throughout history and life in salvation are distinct but not separate. Gerhard Sauter describes salvation as not only at "the end" but also in the present. He proposes a discussion of salvation that "does not ask questions about what comes 'afterward' [in the next life] or encourage spiritual versions of the future" but one that "offers, rather, an incomparably intensive awareness of the present; what is present does not 'pass away,' but stands in relation to eternity."[27]

In various forms, this twined-ness of worldly life and salvation runs through relationality theologies of the last century. Aaron Riches writes, "Christians live a reality that is both 'already but not yet'; they live in the violence of the present age but they do so as citizens of another *polis,* the peaceable Kingdom that abides the 'end' of history."[28] The purpose of this other *polis* is not to escape into that world but to *inform* this one, our present life. In some

---

26. J. Milbank, *Being Reconciled: Ontology and Pardon,* Radical Orthodoxy (New York: Routledge, 2003), pp. 66-67, emphasis mine.

27. G. Sauter, *What Dare We Hope? Reconsidering Eschatology* (Harrisburg, Pa.: Trinity, 1999), p. 19.

28. A. Riches, "Hannah's Child: A Life Given and Therefore Lived," *Modern Theology* 28, no. 2 (April 2012): 332.

sense, this must be the case, for a salvation that had to do only with messianic times would have little influence on life as we live it. Relation with God would be irrelevant to relations in world. "If Jesus Christ," Thomas Torrance notes, "is risen only in spirit — whatever that means! — then he is, so to speak, but a ghost with no relevance to men and women of flesh and blood in history. If Jesus Christ exists only at the right hand of the Father, then we have little ground for hope in this life. It is *the risen humanity of Christ* that forms the very center of the Christian's hope, for this *is the ground and basis of the Christian's own renewal and indeed of the renewal of all creation.*"[29]

John de Gruchy sees this interrelation especially in Jesus' healing missions, which are both worldly and salvific. They assist people in this world, are evidence of salvation, and move toward it. "The New Testament," he writes, "regards Jesus' and the early Christian community's *healing* ministry as integral to the proclamation of the kingdom of God, a sign of the salvific purposes of God." That people take care of one another in this committed way is a sign of and the beginning of God's salvation. "Healing was a sign that the kingdom of God had broken into history in Jesus, and it pointed towards the liberation of humanity from the bondage of decay, and its restoration in Christ at the end of time."[30]

To develop the idea that salvation is not only a future point but also interdependent with actions in the world, Jürgen Moltmann employs a distinction between his views and Karl Barth's. Barth certainly saw the connection between salvation and life in this world, but, on Moltmann's reading, he also saw the crucifixion and resurrection as "finished," after John 19:30: "When he had received the drink, Jesus said, 'It is finished.' With that, he bowed his head and gave up his spirit." Thus, on Moltmann's reading of Barth, when Christ returns, he will come with the salvation that has already occurred.

Moltmann proposes instead that we look at resurrection from the long-term view, what he calls "messianic dimensions," where only "the beginning of the coming consummation of salvation has already taken place in the coming of Christ."[31]

What remains to be done, Moltmann suggests, is that humanity must respond.

29. T. Torrance, "Karl Barth," *Union Seminary Quarterly Review* 12, no. 1 (1956): 30, emphasis mine.

30. J. de Gruchy, "Salvation as Healing and Humanization," in *Christ in Our Place: The Humanity of God in Christ for the Reconciliation of the World*, ed. T. Hart and D. Thimell (Eugene, Ore.: Wipf and Stock, 1989), p. 34.

31. J. Moltmann, *Ethics of Hope*, trans. M. Kohl (Minneapolis: Fortress, 2012), pp. 37-38, 181.

Humanity's Response

Salvation, on Moltmann's view, as yet incomplete, continues to occur as humanity realizes Isaiah's promises to the downtrodden. Jesus says he is of God's spirit — is the God of salvation — but he does not say that he "then" aids the needy in a sequential process. He says rather that he is of God's spirit *because* he gives aid:

> "'The Spirit of the Lord is on me,
>   because he has anointed me
>   to proclaim good news to the poor.
> He has sent me to proclaim freedom for the prisoners
>   and recovery of sight for the blind,
> to set the oppressed free,
>   to proclaim the year of the Lord's favor.'" (Luke 4:18-19)

Analogously, we in God's image move toward salvation *as* we too aid these needy. It is not a sequential or causal process — our aiding the needy leads to salvation — but a melded one in which righteousness and justice in this world are part of the larger horizon of salvation. On Moltmann's view, this has begun and continues not as an ideal bumped upstairs to messianic times but daily: "The kingdom is not merely an ethical ideal of righteousness and justice and peace. It is that too, but in its fullness it is earthly and bodily and is experienced with the senses."[32]

Moltmann submits and Karl Rahner elaborates the mutual constitution of worldly life and spiritual salvation. While Moltmann sees salvation as emerging through the uplifting of the world's needy, Rahner holds that human relations in this world *have a hand* in determining the next. Redemption and salvation require a decision "here and now" for God, which humanity realizes in care for others. The spiritual is *constituted by* the corporeal. As Ted Peters summarizes, Rahner asks that we "reconceive the relationship between time and eternity so that what happens in the history of salvation [on earth] becomes constitutive of the content of eternal life."[33]

More recently, Peter Heltzel, Bruce Benson, and Malinda Berry "think together" spiritual salvation and Jesus' teachings in and for this world. They

---

32. Moltmann, *Ethics of Hope*, p. 54.

33. T. Peters, *God as Trinity: Relationality and Temporality in the Divine* (Louisville: Westminster John Knox, 1993), p. 102.

offer the paradoxical-sounding "*theological* account of Jesus' Jewish, *human* flesh" (emphasis mine).[34] Jesus' work — his giving in his ministries and his giving in death — is, again, not only salvific as debt payment but also points us to God's commitment to save us from breaking covenant. At the same time, Jesus' giving points to the results of our breaches, which we must analogously "save."[35]

Good as this sounds, Allison notes that this is also "the difficulty." God may seek covenantal righteousness on earth, but he "waits upon humanity." We too must act. "Just as the salvation of the individual is God's work but at the same time requires a believing response . . . so the arrival of the kingdom of God on earth can only be conceived of as a work of God that will not be established unless humanity participates."[36]

In investigating what such human response and participation might mean, Christian Collins Winn employs the distinction between apocalyptic and prophetic eschatology. In the former, the break between this era and the messianic is "catastrophic and disruptive and the key component will be the divine inbreaking or intrusion." It allows for hope: regardless of the brutality and injustice of the day, Jesus' radical intercession will come. In prophetic eschatology, the messianic promise of redemption in this world and the next is part of reciprocal covenant. "The role of human covenantal fidelity through works of justice and mercy is paramount."[37] God's human partner in covenant, Winn writes, does not bring eternal salvation but builds in this world "parables" of God's righteous, salvific vision: "we are not called or empowered to build the kingdom," which only God can do, "but to construct and live our lives as communities and individuals which can be described as parables of the kingdom."[38] Building these is the human response to God's messianic promise. Any instance of it creates a messianic possibility: "any longing for love, justice

---

34. Part of their purpose in developing this theology is "connecting it to the suffering of black and brown human flesh in the Americas as a vigorous expression of a prophetic, intercultural evangelicalism." Peter Heltzel, personal communication, February 7, 2015.

35. Heltzel, Benson, and Berry write, "The death of Jesus on the cross becomes the site of our redemption from sin" — that is, Jesus' bodily death brings humanity's spiritual redemption. At the same time, "his resurrection provides a horizon of hope for our witness to the just and peaceable kingdom" — here, Jesus' bodily/spiritual resurrection brings hope for justice and peace in this (bodily) world and the (spiritual) next. See B. Benson, M. Berry, and P. Heltzel, eds., *Prophetic Evangelicals* (Grand Rapids: Eerdmans, 2012), p. 5.

36. Allison, *End of the Ages*, pp. 177-78.

37. C. Winn, "Kingdom," in *Prophetic Evangelicals*, p. 86,

38. Winn, "Kingdom," p. 91.

or new life, regardless of its Christian imprimatur, can become 'the strait gate through which the Messiah might enter.'"[39]

Winn's idea of response and parable is on the same landscape with a number of (distinct, differing) others: Aquinas's cooperative grace, Rashi's "I am the God who will be whenever you bear witness to love and justice in the world," and Balthasar's Christian categorical imperative. We can think also of Richard Kearney's "God can't create the kingdom unless we create the space for the kingdom to come,"[40] Keller's call-and-response grace, and Rahner's view of salvation as a process that has begun and seeks humanity's justice on earth. Echoing Winn's literary image of "parables" is the image of the Messiah "at hand" (Mark 1:15), peace and justice pressing forth their arrival, and the active "anticipating" of the Messiah found in the Maimonidean Thirteen Principles. It echoes Steven Schwarzschild's suggestion that humanity act as if peace and justice will arrive today; they just might.[41] In Moltmann's similar words, "in Christ the kingdom has already come so close — it is actually 'at hand' — that people no longer have just to expect it, but in community with it can also already actively 'seek' it, and should and can make its righteousness and beauty the goal of the way they shape the world and life."[42]

Living in this way shapes world. If we act with the covenantal regard and righteousness that God has given, then they have begun on earth. In the messianic promise, Sauter writes, "God *has* come so close that we can no longer avoid asking who we *are* before this God."[43] He explains, "The decisive question is whether future generations will also be subject to the same suffering that has until now constituted so much of human existence."[44] Sauter's question echoes Paul's idea of the *ekklesia,* the emerging church communities that sought to aid the suffering and where even women and slaves could be members. These "contrast communities" or "means" to more trusting, agapic living (Walter Benjamin's and Giorgio Agamben's terms) would live by the

---

39. Winn, "Kingdom," p. 93; W. Benjamin, "Theses on the Philosophy of History," in *Illuminations: Essays and Reflections* (New York: Schocken Books, 1968), p. 264.

40. R. Kearney, "Philosophizing the Gift," in *The Hermeneutics of Charity: Interpretation, Selfhood, and Postmodern Faith; Studies in Honor of James H. Olthuis,* ed. J. K. Smith and H. I. Venema (Grand Rapids: Brazos, 2004), pp. 54, 58.

41. Stanley Hauerwas writes, "It is from Israel's continuing willingness to wait for the Messiah that we learn better how we must wait between the times. The church and Israel are two people walking in the path provided by God." S. Hauerwas, *The Peaceable Kingdom: A Primer in Christian Ethics* (Notre Dame: University of Notre Dame Press, 1983), p. 107.

42. Moltmann, *Ethics of Hope,* p. 55.

43. Sauter, *What Dare We Hope?* p. 118.

44. Sauter, *What Dare We Hope?* pp. 9-10.

values of God's kingdom, *pistis,* faith, trust, and fidelity. They would be *koinonia,* which Paul expands from a partnership or community of interests to an international support network.[45]

Living by trust may sound naïve, but the alternative of legal/police systems is as prone to corruption and miscarriages of justice. To be just and fair, political and judicial leaders must be dedicated to the just care of the *polis.* Paul insightfully recognized that it is the trust and commitment that are ground for the rest.[46]

This is what Moltmann calls not the resurrection of the dead but the *resurrection of life.*[47] The horizon of salvation, of a future and *telos* beyond quotidian living, serves as a regulatory principle drawing humanity to a *present* covenantal regard. It does so in part by allowing for a reassessment of the hegemony of immanence and fear of death. With the view from immanence — from the workings of the status quo and immediate world — we are ruled by fear of want. This was Hobbes's diagnosis of the source of aggression: we grab and bludgeon out of fear that others will grab from us first. We assume, within the world of immanence, that mutual grabbing is the only thing going on, the only thing that ever goes on. In Daniel Bell Jr.'s words, we seek the "fantasy of absolute security, the pursuit of which only entrenches us more deeply in insecurity, terror and fear."[48]

Yet a horizon of different things going on, the ontology and mores of trust and mutual regard, allows for a shift from fear to reciprocity.[49] Luke Bretherton calls it "an eschatological horizon that takes account of the future already achieved in Christ and thereby posits an end of the agonistic rivalry between traditions and opens up the possibility of a peaceful communion."[50] That is,

---

45. B. Blumenfeld, *The Political Paul: Justice, Democracy, and Kingship in a Hellenistic Framework* (London: Continuum, 2001), pp. 110-11.

46. Blumenfeld, *The Political Paul,* pp. 151, 112-20; see also Milbank, "Paul against Biopolitics," pp. 46, 72.

47. Moltmann, *Ethics of Hope,* p. 101.

48. Bell, "The Politics of Fear," p. 450.

49. Thomas Torrance writes, "The Christian Church that believes in the resurrection of Jesus Christ from the dead has no right to despair of 'this weary world of ours' or to be afraid of its utter dissolution into nothing. Jesus Christ is risen from the dead and completely victorious over all the mighty demonic forces of destruction that threaten our world. In him we can lift up our heads and laugh in the face of fear and disaster." Torrance, "Karl Barth," p. 30.

50. L. Bretherton, *Hospitality as Holiness: Christian Witness amid Moral Diversity* (Farnham, U.K., and Burlington, Vt.: Ashgate, 2006), p. 87; Bell similarly sums up, "we are liberated from all that would prevent us from giving. . . . We are freed from captivity to an economic order that would subject us to scarcity, competition-domination, and debt, that would distort

if one ventures to trust others, they may risk responding not in competitive maneuvers and in return of trust.

This has effects, as suggested above, if the horizon of salvation is taken as truth or metaphor, and it is one way to think about the example of the logging firm in the introduction to this volume. There the question is asked: What would the negotiations look like if all involved believed — in the way we believe we breathe — that taking account of the other's concerns is simply what's done? The suggestion here is that a horizon of a more trusting setup to which we are moving is one way to believe it.

And so the eschaton changes the *polis*.[51] The covenantal promise of salvation changes our conduct in the present, as Philip Goodchild notes: "What there is now is dependent upon what we believe there will be: our eschatology determines our mode of being."[52]

---

human desire into a proprietary and acquisitive power. We are released from the agonistic logic of rights that envisions only a world where atomistic individuals compete from access to the goods necessary for the pursuit of private ends"; Bell, "Theopolitical Ontology of Judgment," pp. 215, 222.

51. Alain Badiou, for instance, writes, "it is [in the] here and now that life takes revenge on death, here and now that we can live affirmatively, according to the spirit, rather than negatively, according to the flesh, which is the thought of death." A. Badiou, *Saint Paul: The Foundation of Universalism*, trans. R. Brassier (Stanford: Stanford University Press, 2003); see also, Blumenfeld, *The Political Paul*, pp. 124-39, 248.

52. P. Goodchild, "Capital and Kingdom," in *Theology and the Political*, p. 143.

CHAPTER 14

Eucharist

In the chapter on resurrection, redemption, and salvation, the body of Christ is at once his body and the symbol of our bodies. It is the body of the divine man yet, in coming to earth, it marks the importance of what happens to our bodies in this world and the next. So too is the Eucharist, the bread symbolizing the body of Christ. It is Christ's body but also the site of our bodies in bond with God and others. It expresses *koinonia,* church community as a *network of relations in relation with God.*

Partaking of the eucharistic bread binds each person to God — indeed, makes the body of Christ constitutive of the person's body. "You are," Calvin wrote, "made a member of him [Christ], indeed one with him." For Calvin, it is the union in particular that allows for salvation: "his righteousness overwhelms your sins; his salvation wipes out your condemnation; with his worthiness he intercedes that your unworthiness may not come before God's sight. Surely this is so: We ought not to separate Christ from ourselves or ourselves from him. Rather we ought to hold fast bravely with both hands to that fellowship by which he has bound himself to us [Rom. 8:10]."[1]

Yet, the book of Romans that Calvin cites continues with a discussion of the relations among the many in Christ's body — a focus on the community into which persons are incorporated by the Eucharist:

> For just as each of us has one body with many members, and these members do not all have the same function, so in Christ we, though many, form one body, and each member belongs to all the others. We have different gifts,

---

1. J. Calvin, *Institutes of the Christian Religion,* ed. J. McNeill, trans. F. Battles, vols. 1-2 (Philadelphia: Westminster, 1960; original 1536), 3.2.24.

according to the grace given to each of us. If your gift is prophesying, then prophesy in accordance with your faith; if it is serving, then serve; if it is teaching, then teach; if it is to encourage, then give encouragement; if it is giving, then give generously; if it is to lead, do it diligently; if it is to show mercy, do it cheerfully. (Rom. 12:4-8)[2]

Parsing this along with passages in Acts and Corinthians, Hans Urs von Balthasar remarks on the distinctness of each person in God's body/community but notes also that each becomes a singular person through it, in commitment to others as others have to that person:

In the Church, therefore, each member is a person insofar as he assumes the unique role to which God by his grace had called him, in order that he may be truly a person, through serving the interests of the community as a whole. St. Paul's image of the Body and its many members illustrated this principle and has to stand the test of the most difficult situations (cf. Acts 21:17-30) and to hold good in the face of the almost disastrous tensions that arise from time to time between the "stronger" and the "weaker" brethren (see Rom 14-15; 1 Cor 8). . . . [T]he act of sharing must be at the very center of the Church's life and being.[3]

Balthasar's comment captures a number of ideas, the most basic being that, upon partaking of the Eucharist, upon accepting relationship with the *resurrected* Christ, one becomes part of his body *on earth*, the church household founded on reciprocity of commitment.[4] "Is not the bread that we break," Paul

---

2. In his gloss on Paul, Miroslav Volf analogizes from eucharistic communion to human communion, preserving the unique persons in both. "We were created for communion with one another, not just with God. Christ came not just to live in us, or even just to live through us. He came to make us into one body — his body, the church." Yet Volf continues, "Each member of the body is endowed with what the apostle Paul called 'spiritual gifts' — roles and abilities that the Holy Spirit gives to each for the benefit of other (1 Cor. 12:1-30; 14:1-40). . . . The reciprocal exchange of gifts expresses and nourishes a community of love." M. Volf, "Being as God Is," in *God's Life in Trinity*, ed. M. Volf and M. Welker (Minneapolis: Augsburg Fortress, 2006), p. 11.

3. H. U. von Balthasar, *Engagement with God*, trans. R. J. Halliburton (San Francisco: Ignatius, 2008), pp. 33-34; see also, p. 47, where Balthasar speaks of removing "the dualism between prayer and works, between contemplation and action. . . . [T]he source of grace at which I as an individual must first of all drink is nothing less than God's total involvement, everything he does in fact for the salvation of the world."

4. Catherine Keller and Sallie McFague note that this is not pantheism, God in all, but,

asks the Corinthians, "a participation in the body of Christ? Because there is one loaf, we, who are many, are one body, for we all share the one loaf" (1 Cor. 10:16-17). The former archbishop of Canterbury Rowan Williams describes this double incorporation — each person in God, each with others in God — by calling humanity "the guests of Jesus," the guests of his corporate body. "We are there because he asks us, and because he wants our company. At the same time we are set free to invite Jesus into our lives and literally to receive him into our bodies in the Eucharist."[5] Yet, like Calvin's and Balthasar's glosses, Williams continues with the communal: "Celebrating the Eucharist not only reminds us that we are invited to be guests; it also reminds us that we are given the freedom to invite others to be guests as well. . . . [T]he Eucharist is not, in Christian practice, a reward for good behaviour; it is the food we need *to prevent ourselves from starving as a result of our own self-enclosure and self-absorption,* our pride and our forgetfulness."[6]

A second idea in Balthasar's work on Eucharist is that, once in the body/community of Christ, distinction-amid-relation is the ontology of that body. Distinct beings form in relationship, indeed a trinity of them. One is among (distinct) persons within the community. (Colin Gunton notes that the Pauline emphasis on "the plurality of the Church's gifts and graces"[7] parallels the Trinity, where the distinct persons of God too have distinct identities and "talents.") Next are the relationships between community and God, and finally are the relationships between each community and those outside it. Each distinct relationship calls for a certain response: to God, persons and communities offer trust, fidelity, prayer, and worship (as there is no need to offer God material goods). To persons, we offer trust and generosity both material and immaterial.

As in covenant and Trinity, these relations constitute each other. We have seen that God, in making us in his (relational, Trinitarian) image, makes us relational with each other. We have seen too that God in covenant and commitment to us constitutes us as caring beings capable of covenant and commit-

---

they suggest, more like "panentheism," all is *in* the "body" God; see C. Keller, *On the Mystery: Discerning Divinity in Process* (Minneapolis: Fortress, 2008), p. 53; see also, S. McFague, *The Body of God: An Ecological Theology* (Minneapolis: Fortress, 1993).

5. R. Williams, *Being Christian: Baptism, Bible, Eucharist, Prayer* (Grand Rapids: Eerdmans, 2014), p. 43.

6. Williams, *Being Christian*, pp. 46, 53, emphasis mine.

7. C. Gunton, "The Church on Earth: The Roots of Community," in *On Being the Church: Essays on the Christian Community,* ed. C. Gunton and D. Hardy (London: T. & T. Clark, 1993), p. 75.

ment to others. In parallel, Eucharist, God's care for us in his body/community, enables us to care for others in community. In turn, the concern within and among communities is expression of our being in the care and commitment that is God's body. In short, our covenantal relations with each other in community emerge from and reflect back God's drawing us into his corporate body. Balthasar writes, "In the Church, therefore, there exists no other difference between the celebration of the sacraments [bond with God] and our everyday existence [with others], save that between the source and its issue."[8]

The interconstitution of relations with God and others is what Anthony Baker calls the specifically *Trinitarian* "obsession with charity," giving to others. Baker holds that human community and commitments of giving are formed from two sources: our partaking (in God's image) of Trinitarian plurality-amid-unity *and* God giving us the gift of Eucharist, of being in his community. Being of Trinitarian distinction-amid-community and being distinct in the eucharistic community enable us to give in human community. First, like all gifts, God's gift to us of the eucharistic community per se models gifting. Second, as a gift from God to many persons together as community, it models community. Third, the Eucharist is also a particular gift: it is the celebration of God's giving himself for humanity's sake. It is the gift of God's self-giving. As persons in the body/community of Christ perform the Eucharist, they receive *a gift that is itself God's self-giving.* This may, in turn, Baker notes, be "echoed in the excessive giving and receiving among members of the body."[9]

It is because of the importance of reciprocal giving in the eucharistic community that Paul chastens the Corinthians for quarreling among themselves and then expecting to partake of the Eucharist, symbol of God's gift of himself in crucifixion (1 Cor. 11:18-19). The Corinthians are at cross-purposes with the cross because they, as a communal body based on God's giving, cannot refuse to give to any part of that body. In the traditional formulation, the eye cannot neglect the hand. The first step, Paul tells them, is peacemaking, without which there can be no nearing God (and no partaking of his body, Eucharist). Paul goes on to chasten not only those who quarrel but also those who eat while others are hungry and then expect to partake of the Eucharist — who thus "despise the church of God" (11:22). Those who partake of the Eucharist in this "unworthy manner" eat and drink judgment against themselves (11:27, 29).

It is a radically equalizing idea in that no part of the community is supe-

---

8. Balthasar, *Engagement with God*, p. 34.

9. A. Baker, "Violence and the Trinity: A Wesleyan Reading of Milbank's Augustinianism," *Wesleyan Theological Journal* 36, no. 1 (Spring 2001): 129.

rior or more consideration-worthy than any other. Discussion of this principle's socioeconomic consequences is extensive in relational theologies (see pt. II, ch. 16), including in the works of Baker, Balthasar, and M. Douglas Meeks, who sets the discussion of economics squarely "in the Eucharistic existence gifted at the spreading of the Lord's table." The point of the Eucharist, of being together in the body/community of Christ, Meeks notes, is not only to meet the physical needs of others (which could presumably be done by writing a check) but also to create bonds of mutual commitment and regard. Meeks writes,

> Whereas commodity exchanges are anonymous, the emphasis in giving as God gives is in the persons brought into relationship, not on the objects that are exchanged. Gift giving creates communal relationships of interdependence. A commodity transaction ends the relationship as soon as goods are exchanged. . . . For the household of God, the tendency of property to create domination is to be overcome in *oikos* (household) relationships of mutual self-giving in which possessions are used for the realization of God's will in the community.[10]

Karl Rahner, in his work on the Eucharist, again highlights its universal applicability (as he did in his work on grace and salvation). The Eucharist, he holds, is the renewal of the death of Jesus, which is an offer of love and redemption for all. Thus, the reenactment of his death in the Eucharist meal too has meaning and possibility for all. More recently, John Franke has noted that a univocal, exclusionary church is impermissible not only in ethics but also from Christian theology: "the plurality of the church is not simply a fact, but is also the very intention of God. As [Justo] González concludes: 'Simply and boldly stated, what this means is that the opposite of a pluralistic church and a pluralistic theology is not simply an exclusivistic church and a rigid theology, but a heretical church and a heretical theology!'"[11]

---

10. M. D. Meeks, "The Social Trinity and Property," in *God's Life in Trinity*, ed. M. Volf and M. Welker (Minneapolis: Augsburg Fortress, 2006), p. 20.

11. J. González, *Out of Every Tribe and Nation: Christian Theology at the Ethnic Roundtable* (Nashville: Abingdon, 1992), pp. 25-26, cited in J. Franke, "Church," in *Prophetic Evangelicals*, ed. B. Benson, M. Berry, and P. Heltzel (Grand Rapids: Eerdmans, 2012), pp. 142, 139.

CHAPTER 15

Communities of Covenant: The Gift of Gift Exchange

In calling church communities *koinonia* — networks of trust and support — Paul was using the language of gift exchange. Relations of gift exchange — the ontology behind it, its practices, and its institutions — come to the heart of this book. These networks of giving, over sometimes extensive distance, were discussed at the turn of the twentieth century by Marcel Mauss[1] (mentioned in pt. II, ch. 6) and more recently by Lewis Hyde,[2] John Milbank, Jacques Godbout, and Alain Caillé. The gifts exchanged within and among groups, while often unnecessary to survival, forge and sustain relationships of long-term commitment and support. The glue of the commitment is not the item but the "spirit" of the donor that inheres in it, the donor's concern and trust. To refuse the gift is to refuse relationship. To accept is to welcome the bond and the commitments that go with it. Implicitly, it is a pledge to make a similar gift of one's "spirit," of one's trust and concern, at a later time. Mauss writes, "to make a gift of something to someone is to make a present of a part of oneself. . . . One clearly and logically realizes that one must give back to another person what is really part and parcel of his nature and substance."[3]

Beyond the dyadic relationship between donor and recipient, gift exchange establishes societal and political bonds of mutual concern and voluntary, reciprocal obligation. Each gift in the giving loop recalls and reinforces earlier gifts — the memory of giving — that sustain the bonds across the

1. M. Mauss, *The Gift: The Form and Reason for Exchange in Archaic Society*, trans. W. D. Halls (London: Routledge, 1990); original 1925, *Essai sur le don: Sociologie et anthropologie*.

2. L. Hyde, *The Gift: Imagination and the Erotic Life of Property* (New York: Vintage Books, 1983).

3. M. Mauss, *The Gift: Form and Function of Exchange in Archaic Societies* (New York: Routledge, 1990), p. 12.

network. "The gift's memory," Godbout and Caillé write, "is the memory of the social bond, the mnemonic traces left by past gifts."[4] They contrast this to modern gift-giving, where a private bond may be fostered but does not bring with it societal pledge. Indeed, modern gift-giving may set the two persons apart from their respective groups, as they have formed a dyadic bond exclusive of others. A modern gift, Godbout and Caillé note, "serves to individualize that person *from* society and not, like the archaic gift, to reinforce his individualism *within* society."[5] In creating private bonds with the potential to destabilize the larger group, modern gift-giving may have an effect opposite to gift exchange.

Classic gift exchange is summarized by John Milbank as having four key features:[6] (1) delay of return (immediate return feels like payment, not gift); (2) nonidentical repetition (the returned item is never the same as the initial one); (3) recipient orientation, where the gift aims at gratifying not the giver but the recipient (found not only in the societies studied by Mauss et al. but also in Thomas Aquinas and Simone Weil, for instance, who see aid to others not as a general act but as one appropriate to the recipient and relationship);[7] and (4) asymmetrical reciprocity, wherein a gift from A to B generates a gift from B to C, then from C to D, etc., and may return to A only much later, after many gifts have traveled through the giving loop, thus sustaining it.

Milbank, Godbout, and Caillé recognize that gift exchange can occur among elites or privileged classes within larger groups that, excluding some from the giving loop, are discriminatory and hierarchical. They may have stultifying mores that suffocate individuals and permit "no permanent and structured relationship with a stranger, for if it cannot turn him into an ally, no concrete and personal gift relationship is possible."[8] Godbout and Caillé note that those in feudal gift-exchange communities were bound by their inherited station "in a subordinate position and that the market freed both individuals and the community itself from such submissive relationships."[9] Yet they

4. J. Godbout and A. Caillé, *The World of the Gift*, trans. D. Winkler (Montreal: McGill-Queen's University Press, 1998), p. 202.

5. Godbout and Caillé, *World of the Gift*, p. 146.

6. J. Milbank, "Can the Gift Be Given? Prolegomena to Any Future Trinitarian Metaphysic," *Modern Theology* 11, no. 1 (1995): 119-61.

7. T. Aquinas, *Summa Theologica*, trans. Fathers of the Dominican English Province, vols. 1-5 (Westminster, Md.: Christian Classics, 1948; original 1265-1274), 2-2, q. 26, the order of priorities in charity, and q. 27, art. 3; S. Weil, *La pesanteur et la grace* (Paris: Plon, 1947), published as *Gravity and Grace*, trans. E. Craufurd (London: Routledge and Kegan Paul, 1952; London and New York: Routledge Classics, 2002), pp. 134-35.

8. Godbout and Caillé, *World of the Gift*, p. 143.

9. Godbout and Caillé, *World of the Gift*, p. 151.

observe also, as Adam Smith and more so Antonio Genovesi did, that the freeing opportunity of modern markets was possible *because* those markets were embedded in networks of mutually responsible relationships and mores of trust and honesty (fostered by gift, as they are today). Godbout and Caillé continue, "For a long period the market frees people primarily from personal bonds of economic dependence. It opens up the circulation of things and provokes a producer-consumer split but, despite that, does not alter other social relationships. . . . The market has little influence on the system of primary relationships: the family, kinship, the village It sets one free from subservience to the lord but at the outset it barely affects community ties."[10]

It is when bonds and mores of trust and honesty are ruptured that societies and markets devolve into competitive fear, cheating, and greed: "whereas the gift puts in place and supports a free social bond, the market frees us by pulling us out of the social bond; in other words, its freedom consists in freeing us from the social bond itself." Or, as Godbout and Caillé continue, "the great gift of modernity is the *exit.*"[11]

It might be argued that undue exit is unproductive but, with present-day mobility, difficult to prevent. And if it is difficult to prevent, we may be unable to regain the honest, trusting practices that are maintained when one's relationships are close by (and closely watching). But gift-exchange societies maintained their commitments and trust without close watching, across impressive distances and infrequent contact. In short, *modern societies, with airplanes, Skype, IM, etc., cannot claim impossible what was done in canoes.*

God gifts humanity with the capacity to gift, to receive, and to return.

10. Godbout and Caillé, *World of the Gift*, p. 156.
11. Godbout and Caillé, *World of the Gift*, pp. 191, 162.

CHAPTER 16

The Ethics of Relationality: Prophetic Voice, Incarnational Discipleship, Communities of Trust

It was religion that got us on the buses for the Freedom Rides. We were in Selma that day because of our faith.[1]

In . . . President Obama's first month in office, he signed executive orders that sought to dismantle the practice of torture that had become normalized during the Bush/Cheney administration; however, he has not been thorough enough in investigation nor tough enough in prosecutions. . . . Joining with other people of faith, prophetic evangelicals must continue to call the United States to accountability.[2]

The polity is nothing less than the public space in which God calls us to be human in that we call each other to come together in justice.[3]

Teleological Freedom and Untweakable Ethics: Belief Constitutes Conduct Constitutes Belief

The claim of this book has been that ontologies and theologies of relationality yield an ethical framework for economic and political policy. The theological

---

1. John Lewis, among the leaders of the 1965 civil rights march in Selma, Alabama; see J. Meacham, *American Gospel: God, the Founding Fathers, and the Making of a Nation* (New York: Random House, 2006), p. 192.

2. D. Gushee, "Shalom," in *Prophetic Evangelicals*, ed. B. Benson, M. Berry, and P. Heltzel (Grand Rapids: Eerdmans, 2012), p. 74.

3. R. Jenson, *Systematic Theology*, vol. 2, *The Works of God* (New York: Oxford University Press, 1999), p. 79.

voice has been taken as truth, metaphor, revelation, or illustration of the human condition. I am not suggesting here, as before, that there is no difference between belief and metaphor, only that in both cases, these principles — from the Judaic covenant to Jesus' ministries — have provided insight to a wide range of people in the discussion of ethics in policy. They have suggested important guiding frameworks — an ontology — without which we would lack both motive and a standard by which to choose one policy over another. For this reason, while some of what follows is written for and about the ethics of church communities, the principles apply to political and economic ones.

Stanley Hauerwas adds another reason to attend to ontology: that worldview and action are not separable. Our responsibilities, he writes, are not a "second step" in a sequential process from belief to behavior, but rather, beliefs and conduct work together. *Living ethically is belief constituting conduct that informs belief.*[4] Beliefs constitute the creative development of practices and policies that live out and feed back into our beliefs. "Our convictions embody our morality; our beliefs are our actions."[5] In the Judaic tradition, Emmanuel Levinas works through the idea: "I speak of responsibility as the essential, primary and fundamental structure of subjectivity. . . . Ethics, here, does not supplement a preceding existential base; the very node of the subjective is knotted in ethics understood as responsibility."[6]

Those who believe that God rejects violence, Hauerwas notes, do not decide, case by case, whether to engage in it. Rather, he writes, "their being nonviolent means they must use their imaginations to form their whole way of life consistent with their convictions."[7] They must develop a way of living

---

4. Ian Smith notes this as a central theme of the later Pauline letters, Ephesians, Philippians, Colossians, and Philemon: "theology dictates practice. . . . Christians are to conduct their earthly lives in the light of liberation from the power of evil and cosmic reconciliation. This reconciliation is to be seen primarily within the church, between Jew and Gentile ([Col.] 3:11) evidenced through forgiveness (3:13) and love (3:14); the church is to be a society where the peace of Christ rules (3:15)." I. K. Smith, "The Later Pauline Letters," in *All Things to All Cultures: Paul among Jews, Greeks, and Romans*, ed. J. Harding and A. Nobbs (Grand Rapids: Eerdmans, 2013), pp. 302, 317-18.

5. S. Hauerwas, *The Peaceable Kingdom: A Primer in Christian Ethics* (Notre Dame: University of Notre Dame Press, 1983), p. 93. David Platt concurs: "so-called faith without acts prompted by that faith is a farce. Real faith always creates fruit"; D. Platt, *Radical Together: Unleashing the People of God for the Purpose of God* (Colorado Springs: Multnomah, 2011), pp. 29, 38.

6. E. Levinas, *Ethics and Infinity: Conversations with Philippe Nemo*, trans. R. Cohen (Pittsburgh: Duquesne University Press, 1985), pp. 96-97.

7. Hauerwas, *The Peaceable Kingdom*, pp. 16, 125.

based on their beliefs that, through living it, develops their beliefs. Robin Lovin similarly notes that beliefs neither precede nor follow action. To precede would mean that people receive God's guidance (belief) entirely before they act, as though belief could develop absent experience. To follow would mean that we find out beliefs only at life's end, upon God's final judgment, rendering belief irrelevant to conduct and ethics during our lives. Lovin observes that belief and ethics occur together in what Dietrich Bonhoeffer called the worldly "divine mandates": government, the judiciary, and legislatures; education; arts/culture; business/work; family/friends; and religious institutions. In these arenas we act from our ethics and we learn about ethics by acting in them. "We learn something about the Word of God," Lovin writes, "in and through our participation in these mandates as well as in the Word proclaimed to them." Against the idea that faith should be protected from worldly corruptions, Lovin continues, "Faith that is insulated from the full range of human interactions may be weak and incomplete, and it may easily become confused with the prejudices that just happen to be strongest in those places where I think my faith is safest."[8]

In sum, beliefs, conduct, and character are mutually constitutive in something like a trinity of ethics: beliefs constituting conduct become identity, which in turn forms both beliefs and conduct in the public as well as private sphere: "Political discourse," John Milbank writes, "displays, in a pale theoretical fashion, the homology of ontology with action."[9] This chapter will look at some ethical principles emerging from our ontology; an introduction to specific economic and political policies will continue in the concluding chapter.

There is little question that an ontology and theology of distinction-amid-relation with its responsibility to reciprocal consideration-worthiness and relational networks limit nonteleological or absolute freedom.[10] This negative liberty or freedom as absence of restraint is, as Paul Tillich wrote, "what it makes of itself . . . because anything more would restrict the absolute freedom of the self."[11] From its perspective, any parameters for behavior are "perceived as promoting a particular prejudice and as interfering with individual freedom."[12]

---

8. R. Lovin, *Christian Ethics: An Essential Guide* (Nashville: Abingdon, 2000), pp. 106, 102.

9. J. Milbank, *Beyond Secular Order: The Representation of Being and the Representation of the People* (Chichester: Wiley Blackwell, 2014), p. 10.

10. Milbank, *Beyond Secular Order*, p. 131.

11. P. Tillich, *The Courage to Be* (New Haven: Yale University Press, 1951, 2008), p. 151.

12. Francis, *Evangelii gaudium*, Rome, November 24, 2013; retrieved from http://www.vatican.va/holy_father/francesco/apost_exhortations/documents/papa-francesco_esortazione-ap_20131124_evangelii-gaudium_en.html, para. 64.

Relationality theologies acknowledge that they set parameters, for the absolute freedom to abrogate distinction or relation may be exercised only insofar as one is prepared to accept the social hostility, loss of talent, poverty, disease, and policing necessary to control societal instability.

The relational view proposes instead a *teleological freedom* with obligations to the distinct other, to the relational networks that make us who we are, and to the common good.[13] The idea of "situated freedom"[14] was afoot in rabbinic thought and in the medieval Islamic philosophy of al-Ghazali, who held that human freedom is not mere unconstrained action as we live in a setup with world and others, of which we must take account. Freedom is the ability to discern among options, temptations, and attractions and to take action that yields productive living within our setup. When we do this through study and by aligning our actions with our understanding of God's vision,[15] we draw — al-Ghazali, Maimonides, and Aquinas continued — on his guidance, which is internal to us as our existence is a matter of partaking his "act of being." This act, Aquinas wrote, is "more intimately and profoundly interior to things than anything else" (*Summa Theologica* 1.8.1). We are thus not unconstrained, context-less beings but "moved movers," capable of agency and of being moved to *moral* agency by the God of whom we partake. We may refuse this guidance, this grace, but then outcomes run against the ontology we're in.

Kant's friend and critic Johann Georg Hamann thought of this situated freedom as Aristotelian citizen responsibilities — to participate in judgment *(krisis)* and governance *(arche)* for the good of the *polis* — but Hamann extended them from Aristotle's tiny elite to all citizens, making teleological freedom an *anthropological category* pertaining to all persons. Each is her own

---

13. As Bernard Lonergan pointed out in his discussion of human freedom and decision taking, "what is intelligible, intelligent and reasonable is not arbitrary"; *The Lonergan Reader,* ed. E. Morelli and M. Morelli (Toronto: University of Toronto Press, 1997), p. 281. Former archbishop of Canterbury Rowan Williams describes this freedom as the ability to shape "our lives and our human environment in the direction of God's justice, showing in our relationships and our engagement with the world something of God's own freedom, God's own liberty to heal and restore"; R. Williams, *Being Christian: Baptism, Bible, Eucharist, Prayer* (Grand Rapids: Eerdmans, 2014), p. 16. In the Catholic tradition, these principles undergirded Pope Leo XIII's important *Rerum novarum* (1891), which decried the condition of workers and the poor and called for fair wages, the right to voluntary unions, and fair increases in time off.

14. D. Burrell, *Towards a Jewish-Christian-Muslim Theology* (Chichester, UK, and Malden, Mass.: Wiley-Blackwell, 2011), Kindle location 805.

15. Faith *(tawhid)* in the Islamic tradition and practice *(tawakkul)* are reciprocal, as understanding God's words comes with study that informs conduct guided toward God's vision, which in turn furthers understanding.

legislator, Hamman suggested, but each is at the same time neighbor to her "subjects."

To the question of determining the responsibilities of teleological freedom, James K. A. Smith notes, after Augustine, that human beings have no direct access to each other's thoughts or concerns and thus we require language to cover the gap between "the incommensurability between subjective interiorities."[16] As words require interpretation, a plurality of interpretations and misinterpretations results. Undecidability among them, Smith observes, is a condition of human life: "There is, if you will, a possibility for misunderstanding built into the very fabric of human life; there is the possibility of misunderstanding in Eden."[17] But, Smith continues, plurality of interpretations does not mean their *equality*. Guidelines and limits on interpretation are set by the one *interpreted*. Interpretations must account for what they encounter. As the critique of nominalism and rationalism noted, interpretations cannot be projections but must "fit" and work in the world. Thus, Smith writes, "while every interpretation of the world is just that, an *interpretation* of the world, it is also simultaneously an interpretation of the *world*."[18]

In our responsibilities and ethics, it is the other who shapes what can be said and done. Like Emmanuel Levinas and Simone Weil, Smith holds that it is "the face of the other . . . that makes me ethically responsible and demands justice."[19] To the argument that cultural differences preclude any ethics save relative, local ones, Smith holds that bottom-line, inviolable obligations are set by the twined covenant with God and among persons. Ethical standards are not every individual preference or norm, which for much of history would have included slavery. They are not, as Susannah Ticciati writes, a game where the person best rhetorically equipped "wins."[20] They are accountable to our ontology and the source of being, God, who, as Ticciati notes, is in all our encounters as we are all of his being/image. One can, given free will, ignore this, but the standard itself is not amendable to one's current interests. *Thus covenantal, agapic relationality resists both relativism* (it is what any cultural groups says it is) *and self-absorption* (it is what I say it is): "If it seems to you," Augustine writes, "that you have understood the divine scriptures, or any part

16. J. K. A. Smith, *The Fall of Interpretation: Philosophical Foundations for a Creational Hermeneutic* (Downers Grove, Ill.: InterVarsity, 2000), pp. 145-46.

17. J. K. A. Smith, *The Fall of Interpretation*, p. 157.

18. J. K. A. Smith, *The Fall of Interpretation*, pp. 169, 171.

19. J. K. A. Smith, *The Fall of Interpretation*, pp. 169, 175.

20. S. Ticciati, "The Castration of Signs: Conversing with Augustine on Creation," *Modern Theology* 23, no. 2 (April 2007): 161-79.

of them, in such a way that by this understanding you do not build up twin love of God and neighbor, then you have not yet understood them."[21]

Kenneth Reinhard develops the idea of "neighbor" for political ethics. He notes that politics pertains to the state (group), the symbolic order (law, justice), and the political Other (abstract beings to whom law and justice apply). But treating persons as abstract others erases distinctiveness. A mechanistic justice emerges, but not a workable society with distinct persons and relationships. What's needed is a way to treat people not only in the political abstract but also as "neighbors," a societal role that involves regard and commitments beyond law. By contrast, love relationships, Reinhard notes, have the inverse problem. They are based in love far in excess of law, but this intensity does not reach the public sphere.

To have a *political* ethics, we must be able to treat others less hermetically than we treat lovers and less abstractly than in the law code — indeed, as neighbor, a point of equipoise and mediation more concerned than law is and more attuned to the commons than is dyadic love. Neighbor is "the seam where the equality and sameness of the political encounters the singularity and difference of love."[22] Reinhard envisions the loop from politics to love back to politics as a Möbius strip, serendipitously echoing the Möbius strip of relational theologies, the relationality of God constituting relationality with God and among persons that in turn expresses bond with God. Neighbor is the turn where politics, situatedness in the public, recognizes the distinctness of individuals and where separable individuals recognize the situatedness of all in the political order.[23]

A prime feature of societal ethics is the gift of dignity. In Reinhard's terms, our practices, policies, and application of law must mediate between abstractions and the distinct dignity of each. "The most significant thing in life that can happen to our neighbor," Hans Urs von Balthasar writes as well, "is his being laid claim to and taken seriously as a person."[24] Having the *de jure* right to education, for instance, does not give one the dignity of a good education until educational policies make it accessible to people in their specific circum-

21. Augustine, *On Christian Doctrine (De doctrina Christiana)*; retrieved from http://www9.georgetown.edu/faculty/jod/augustine/ddc1.html. Original 397/426.

22. K. Reinhard, "Toward a Political Theology of the Neighbor," in *The Neighbor: Three Inquiries in Political Theology*, ed. S. Žižek, E. Santner, and K. Reinhard (Chicago: University of Chicago Press, 2005), p. 64.

23. Reinhard, "Toward a Political Theology," p. 67.

24. H. U. von Balthasar, *Engagement with God*, trans. R. J. Halliburton (San Francisco: Ignatius, 2008), pp. 55, 83.

stances. This applies to one's near neighbor and, given the global movement of people and goods, to those outside: "our involvement," Balthasar continues, "on behalf of the stranger whom we do not know, whoever he may be . . . can be no less than our involvement on behalf of those of our own household."[25]

Ethics: Sources

The idea of freedom guided by the divine *telos,* the well-being of (distinct) persons through relation, runs throughout Judeo-Christian texts, beginning with the Pentateuch and extending into the Prophets (pt. II, ch. 6) and Gospels. Peter Brown's study of poverty in the Roman Empire[26] notes that rabbinic and early Christian ethics were responding to a similar cultural milieu, to values, and to intertestamental literature.[27] The idea that bishops, as stewards of church funds, were responsible for aiding the needy echoes Rav Yosef's idea that he, as rabbi and steward, is "the hand of the poor" (*b. Bekhorot* 36b).[28] The soup kitchens and poor tables of Basil of Caesarea parallel Rabbi Yehuda ha-Nasi's provision for the poor (*b. Bava Batra* 8a) and Rav Huna's declaration, "Let all who are hungry come and eat" (*b. Ta'anit* 20b). As historian and priest Robert P. Maloney notes, "the Fathers, in particular Clement of Alexandria, Basil, and (through Basil) Ambrose, quote verbatim from the Jewish literature on usury"[29] (see pt. II, ch. 6).

In the Second Testament, the importance of care throughout society — reciprocal consideration, especially for the needy — emerges even before Jesus' birth, in the annunciation, and again at the time of his baptism. As Luke describes (Luke 1:52-53), Mary speaks to her cousin Elizabeth immediately after the annunciation:

> "He [God] has brought down rulers from their thrones
>   but has lifted up the humble.
> He has filled the hungry with good things
>   but has sent the rich away empty."

25. Balthasar, *Engagement with God,* p. 53.

26. P. Brown, *Poverty and Leadership in the Later Roman Empire* (Hanover, N.H.: University Press of New England, 2002), p. 31.

27. See S. Schwartz, *Imperialism and Jewish Society, 200 B.C.E. to 640 C.E.* (Princeton and Oxford: Princeton University Press, 2001).

28. See also, A. Gray, "Redemptive Almsgiving and the Rabbis of Late Antiquity," *Jewish Studies Quarterly* 18 (2011): 146-48.

29. R. Maloney, "Usury in Greek, Roman and Rabbinic Thought," *Traditio* 27 (1971): 109.

This, Mary foresees, is what God will do with his time on earth. Ruth Padilla-DeBorst notes that Mary's life is itself an instance of lifting up the humble, as she, a poor subject in an imperial backwater, is nonetheless chosen by God for a profound role in humanity's future. "In the Roman Empire, she is an absolute nothing. . . . But in God's eyes, she is an active and valuable agent of God's mission."[30]

In Mark (1:29-34), the interwoven scenes of Jesus' baptism (bond with God) and the healing of the afflicted (bond with others, among them Simon's mother-in-law) highlight the interconstitution of the relationships. In Luke's account (3:10-18), John, as prelude to Jesus' baptism, exhorts the crowd to give to the needy, tax collectors to forgo collecting, and soldiers to stop extorting money and bearing false witness. Following the account of Jesus' baptism are numerous passages on his attention to the downtrodden, among them: the healing of the masses (Matt. 4:23-24; 8:16-17) and of the Canaanite woman's daughter, the giving of life to the widow's son (Luke 7:11-17), the feeding of the crowd of five thousand, the parable of the Good Samaritan, Jesus' inclusion of women into his closest circle, and his rescue of the adulterous wife (John 8:7).

In addition to narratives on aid to the needy are those of Jesus' service, which require personal relationship and invert societal hierarchies. When Jesus ends his forty-day fast, he does not feed himself but serves those around him. He washes his disciples' feet, which he does again at the Last Supper, declaring, "the greatest among you should be like the youngest, and the one who rules like the one who serves." Even God incarnate serves: "I am among you as one who serves" (Luke 22:25-27). Mark reprises, "whoever wants to become great among you must be your servant, and whoever wants to be first must be slave of all. For even the Son of Man did not come to be served, but to serve" (Mark 10:43-45).

Beyond accounts of Jesus' ministries and service are his lessons, such as the parable of the merciless servant, a manumitted slave who refuses to forgive the debts of another slave and who is then punished when, once again in debt, he is arrested and sold back into slavery (Matt. 18:23-25, 35). Luke 6:35-36 contains the famous injunction to "love your enemies, do good to them, and lend to them without expecting to get anything back." The mandate to "Sell your possessions and give to the poor" (Luke 12:33) is often read as an injunction only to those called to monastic orders, the "councils of perfection." The rest

---

30. Cited in J. Harrison, "Paul among the Romans," in *All Things to All Cultures*, p. 123. As Robert Jensen portrays her, Mary is "the 'arch prophet' who intercedes for the people of God"; Jenson, *Systematic Theology*, 2:202-3.

need only tithe. Yet Jesus was not content with 10 percent. "Woe to you Pharisees, because you give God a tenth of your mint, rue and all other kinds of garden herbs, but you neglect justice and the love of God" (Luke 11:42). Like the familiar trope in the Hebrew Bible, the call to giving is twined with bond with God. Apart from the Gospels, the *Didache, the Teaching of the Twelve Apostles* (late first or early second century) teaches, "Never turn away the needy; share all your possessions with your brother, and do not claim that anything is your own."[31] *The Shepherd of Hermas* (first or second century, considered canonical by Irenaeus) continues, "visit widows and orphans, and neglect them not; and spend your riches and all your displays, which ye received from God, on fields and houses of this kind."[32]

Together, the life and lessons propose not only a personal ethics but also an overhaul of the public sphere, which so exercised the authorities that they resorted to irregular means to be rid of it. As political sedition was the only charge over which the Roman prefect Pontius Pilate could preside, had he not thought Jesus' threat was political, he would have had no standing to try him, as mere heretics or prophets were outside his purview. At trial, Jesus did nothing to dissuade Pilate but rather aggravated his fears of a political challenge. Jesus claimed both divine connection and the presence on earth of a power greater than Caesar's.[33] As the Caesars starting from Augustus (who reigned from 27 B.C.E. to 14 C.E.) claimed foundationality (links to Rome's mythic founders Remus and Romulus) and connection to the divine, Jesus might well have sounded like a political threat. Murray Smith writes, "the expectation of Christ's return" was "cast in language designed to radically subvert Roman imperial claims. . . . In doing so, they pit Jesus against Augustus, the deified 'son' of the divine Julius Caesar, who was in the first century widely believed, by virtue of his *apotheosis,* to be ruling the world from the heavens in the presence of his father."[34] John Howard Yoder echoes,

---

31. http://www.ewtn.com/library/SOURCES/DIDACHE.TXT.

32. http://folk.uio.no/lukeb/books/theo/The%20Shepherd%20of%20Hermas.pdf.

33. John Dominic Crossan writes, "There was a human being in the first century who was called 'Divine,' 'Son of God,' 'God,' and 'God from God,' whose titles were 'Lord,' 'Redeemer,' 'Liberator,' and 'Savior of the World.' . . . And most Christians probably think that those titles were originally created and uniquely applied to Christ. But before Jesus ever existed, all those terms belonged to Caesar Augustus. To proclaim them of Jesus the Christ was thereby to deny them of Caesar the Augustus." J. Crossan, *God and Empire: Jesus against Rome, Then and Now* (San Francisco: HarperSanFrancisco, 2007), p. 28; see also, J. Crossan, *The Historical Jesus: The Life of a Mediterranean Jewish Peasant* (New York: Harper One, 1991, 1993).

34. M. Smith, "The Thessalonian Correspondence," in *All Things to All Cultures,* p. 294. Creston Davis and Aaron Riches continue: "Paul is making a royal proclamation: Jesus is

"the events in the temple court and the language Jesus uses were not calculated to avoid any impression of [nonviolent] insurrectionary vision." Jesus was, Yoder continues, "the bearer of a new possibility of human, social, and therefore political relationships."[35]

Pauline ethics, as we've seen (pt. II, ch. 9), has generated more debate.[36] Some readings find him more spiritually and less politically focused (those of Ernst Troeltsch and Ferdinand Baur in the nineteenth century, for instance, Rudolf Bultmann and others in the twentieth). Others find him substantially economic and political but coded to avoid appearing subversive to Roman authorities. Still other readings note that Roman governments of the period (mid–first century c.e.) were relatively open and did not require substantial encoding of political messages (save those of insurrection). Some obfuscation, on this account, may have been used by Paul to avoid tensions *within* the church, as some early members remained loyal to the quasi-divine Caesar, and talk of a different God-on-earth might have been to them unacceptable.

Two things about early Christian political ethics, however, are clear: neither Jesus nor Paul advocated violent revolution or disobedience to Roman law, yet both proffered a transformational and supersessionary vision — saying at least that Roman rule is earthly, limited, and ending while Christ's is the cause of causes, eternal, and has already begun. These ethics look from the present into a future where the church reflects God's vision of personal and societal righteousness in this world and prepares for his kingdom's full realization, transforming again this world according to God's already-declared reign.

The work of Joseph Cardinal Bernardin (archbishop of Cincinnati, 1972-1982; of Chicago, 1982-1996) emphasized the continuous thread from God, to each of us, to others in our common political life. He wrote:

Lord! And this announcement of the Lordship of Christ is simultaneously an announcement that Caesar is not"; C. Davis and P. A. Riches, "The Theological Praxis of Revolution," in *Theology and the Political: The New Debate*, ed. C. Davis, J. Milbank, and S. Žižek (Durham, N.C., and London: Duke University Press, 2005), p. 29.

35. J. Yoder, *The Politics of Jesus* (Grand Rapids and Cambridge: Eerdmans, 1972, 1994), pp. 49, 50, 52.

36. See, for instance, N. Elliot, *The Arrogance of Nations: Reading Romans in the Shadow of Empire* (Minneapolis: Fortress, 2008); Harrison, "Paul among the Romans"; J. Harrison, *Paul and the Imperial Authorities at Thessalonica and Rome: A Study in the Conflict of Ideology* (Tübingen: Mohr Siebeck, 2011); R. Horsley, ed., *Paul and Empire: Religion and Power in Roman Imperial Society* (Harrisburg, Pa.: Trinity, 1997); R. Jewett, *Romans: A Commentary* (Minneapolis: Fortress, 2007); S. Kim, *Christ and Caesar: The Gospel and the Roman Empire in the Writings of Paul and Luke* (Grand Rapids: Eerdmans, 2008).

[A] common element that links [our moral] concerns is our conviction about the unique dignity of each human person. . . . The person is the clearest reflection of the presence of God among us. To lay violent hands on the person is to come as close as we can to laying violent hands on God. To diminish the human person is to come as close as we can to diminishing God. . . . *From our recognition of the worth of all people under God flow the responsibilities of a "social morality."*[37]

Discipleship and the Prophetic Role: The Moral Task Is Not in Being Right but in Making the Solution So

In putting ontological relationality and divine *telos* into ethical practice, two approaches widely discussed are discipleship — learning from Jesus' life for application to present conditions — and the prophetic role of "speaking truth to power," speaking publicly against injustice. Each has been applied, as the civil rights movement illustrates, in political and economic contexts.

The Prophetic Role

To begin, the prophetic role of "speaking truth to power," making injustice public, does not mean gaining control of government or employing mechanisms of aggression, which government does in its monopoly on legal force. As David Hollenbach has noted, religious groups work not to control or usurp governmental power but to maintain ethical standards and conduct.[38] They should eschew, Tony Campolo advises, a priori backing of political parties and should advocate instead for policies nonpartisanly, advancing the position, case by case, that best realizes Jesus' teachings. David Gushee's litmus test for Christian political involvement is "whether we have the capacity to say no to our favorite party or politician."[39]

---

37. J. Cardinal Bernardin, *Consistent Ethic of Life* (Kansas City, Mo.: Sheed and Ward, 1988), pp. 28-29.

38. See, for instance, D. Hollenbach, *The Common Good and Christian Ethics* (New York: Cambridge University Press, 2002); D. Hollenbach, "Sustaining Catholic Social Engagement: A Key Role for Movements in the Church Today," *Journal of Catholic Social Thought* 10 (2013): 431-47; special issue on "Social Movements in Context."

39. D. Gushee, *The Future of Faith in American Politics: The Public Witness of the Evangelical Center* (Waco: Baylor University Press, 2008), p. 50.

Indeed, conflation of church with government or political party comes rather too close to the sort of politics proposed by Carl Schmitt, where, to bolster governmental authority, sovereign political power is likened to the sovereignty of God.[40] Against such idolatrous conflation, Karl Barth warned that no political rule can be said to represent God's kingdom, a position today with wide agreement. Among the many like Gushee and Campolo who assent, Oliver O'Donovan writes, "Pending the final disclosure of the Kingdom of God, the church and society are in a dialectical relation, distant from each other as well as identified."[41]

Miroslav Volf describes this "dialectical relation" as the mandate "to divert without leaving,"[42] neither becoming government nor avoiding societal problems but transforming them into what Pope Francis calls "cultures of encounter."[43] Volf suggests two approaches: bringing injustice to public attention (even at political risk) and then developing and publicizing alternatives.[44] "*The task of prophetic ministry,*" Walter Brueggemann concurs, "*is to nurture, nourish, and evoke a consciousness and perceptive alternative to the consciousness and perception of the dominant culture around us.*"[45]

On Brueggemann's account, the first alternate consciousness was Moses' against the pharaoitic worldview of power and the "annulment" of others.[46] It continued through the Pentateuch, Jeremiah, Lamentations, Isaiah, and Jesus, whose first effort, as in Volf's analysis, was to puncture the numbness of the status quo so that we may recall that God is "for us"[47] and, knowing he has our backs, we may risk being for each other, especially under political threat. Lest

---

40. See, for instance, L. Bretherton, "Coming to Judgment: Methodological Reflections on the Relationship between Ecclesiology, Ethnography and Political Theory," *Modern Theology* 28, no. 2 (April 2012): 167-96.

41. O. O'Donovan, *The Desire of the Nations: Rediscovering the Roots of Political Theory* (Cambridge: Cambridge University Press, 1996), p. 251.

42. M. Volf, *A Public Faith: How Followers of Christ Should Serve the Common Good* (Grand Rapids: Brazos, 2011), pp. 7, 89.

43. Francis, *Evangelii gaudium*, para. 220, citing the United States Conference of Catholic Bishops, "Pastoral Letter: Forming Conscience for Faithful Citizenship," November 2007, para. 13.

44. Lewis Mudge suggests that religious communities may be especially suited to this as they identify state or civil society "carriers" of good practices; see L. Mudge, *We Can Make the World Economy a Sustainable Global Home* (Grand Rapids: Eerdmans, 2014), Kindle location 1829.

45. W. Brueggemann, *The Prophetic Imagination* (Minneapolis: Fortress, 2001), p. 3.

46. Brueggemann, *The Prophetic Imagination*, pp. 22, 4-19, 37.

47. Brueggemann, *The Prophetic Imagination*, p. 16.

this seem idealistic, Monica Duffy Toft, Daniel Philpott, and Timothy Samuel Shah, in their study of religion and democratization, note that in 62 percent of democratization efforts between 1972 and 2009, religious actors were actively engaged (73 percent in the Americas, 67 percent in Asia), and in thirty of those forty-eight efforts, religious groups took leading roles.[48]

In their book *Prophetic Evangelicals,* Peter Goodwin Heltzel, Bruce Ellis Benson, and Malinda Elizabeth Berry refer to this alternate consciousness as *shalom* (peace, wholeness).[49] *Theologically,* it highlights the effects of salvation (bond with God) on our present conduct on earth (with others). "Salvation is truly good news," Vincent Bacote writes in the same volume, but "[w]hen salvation is understood almost exclusively as the reconciliation of individuals to God . . . it minimizes our understanding of the incarnation and the resultant implications for creation."[50] Our covenantal regard and commitment to each other are part of what our salvation means. Looking at salvation with this consciousness alters our conduct in the world. *Methodologically, shalom* draws on the prophetic tradition of public lambaste against greed, neglect, and injustice — and of making the alternate consciousness public. For Heltzel, Benson, and Berry, it draws also on contemporary critical theories (including postcolonial, gender, etc.). As a *practice, shalom* makes public alternatives to suffering. It reanimates Amos 5:21-24, the prophet's rejection of empty ritual and his demand for righteous *acts.*

Acting in the prophetic mode to call attention to injustice and to its alternatives requires the patience and trust to work with people who are sociologically and ideologically different from oneself. And this, Luke Bretherton notes, is itself a purpose of the prophetic role: not only to protest injustice done to others but also to befriend and work with them. *Covenantal, agapic relations are thus the* telos *and method of the prophetic role:* one develops such relations in the process of working with others to develop them. Both Bretherton and Richard Kearney call this openness to different others "hospitality," as does Levinas: "This book," he writes in *Totality and Infinity,* "will present subjectivity as welcoming the Other, as hospitality."[51] Bernard Lonergan and

---

48. M. D. Toft, D. Philpott, and T. Shah, *God's Century: Resurgent Religion and Global Politics* (New York: Norton, 2011), p. 95.

49. "We understand shalom," they write, "as primarily the presence of justice among everything and everyone from close friends to entire nations"; see Benson, Berry, and Heltzel, *Prophetic Evangelicals,* p. 8.

50. V. Bacote, "Creation," in *Prophetic Evangelicals,* pp. 54, 56.

51. R. Kearney, *Anatheism: Returning to God after God* (New York: Columbia University Press, 2009), Kindle location 1304; Levinas, *Totality and Infinity,* p 27.

Robert Doran call it the "learning church" and the "mutual self-mediation that results from an encounter and dialogue of persons with different horizons."[52]

Its importance appears early in the Bible as Abraham, confronted by three strangers, treats them without suspicion as guests, choosing invitation over fear. The apostles who gather at the crucifixion and resurrection identify themselves also as those who partook of Jesus' hospitality, who "ate and drank with him" (Acts 10:41). Paul Ricoeur's "linguistic hospitality" invokes the same idea: all acts of dia-logue are moments of welcoming difference, endeavors to translate oneself to a different other, to be listened to and to listen. The hospitality of dia-logue is to do more than acknowledge; it is to move through difference to attention and regard, to "charity and gift."[53]

"The Christian practice of hospitality," Bretherton writes, "is often, because of its priorities, deeply prophetic, calling into question the prevailing economic, social, or political settlement. . . . Welcoming the stranger reorientates us to ourselves, our neighbor and to God by raising a question mark about the 'way we do things round here.'"[54] It broadens who comes into decision-making and policy development. By way of example, Joel Hunter, of President Barack Obama's President's Advisory Council on Faith-Based and Neighborhood Partnerships, 2009-2010, said this about the church he pastors:

> We partner with governments all over the world. Locally, when we have convocations on torture, creation care, and poverty, I ask for broad leadership: the bishop of the Catholic Church, the head of the Islamic Society, a rabbi. . . . We specifically invite the African American church, other churches, and faith communities into much of what we do. . . . Same is true

52. R. Doran, *What Is Systematic Theology?* (Toronto: University of Toronto Press, 2005), pp. 57, 198. Lonergan and Doran hold that the work of theology and the church occurs in the exchange between those within the church community and the various "cultural matrices" outside it: "The church is, or should be, and willy-nilly has always been, a learning church, a church whose own constitutive meaning is, within the limits imposed by truly dogmatic meanings, changed by interaction with various cultural matrices" (Doran, p. 57).

53. Ricoeur discusses five features: an ethics of hospitality (openness to the narratives of another); ethics of narrative flexibility; ethics of narrative plurality (recognition that one's own, while not abandoned, is enriched and revised by those of others); transfiguring of the past as one learns from others what one's own narratives didn't reveal; and pardon, the move requiring great patience that yields remembrance of harms done yet reciprocal generosity among those involved. See P. Ricoeur, "Reflections on a New Ethos for Europe," in *Paul Ricoeur: The Hermeneutics of Action*, ed. R. Kearney (London: Sage, 1996), pp. 5-14.

54. L. Bretherton, "A Postsecular Politics? Inter-faith Relations as a Civic Practice," *Journal of the American Academy of Religion* 79, no. 2 (2011): 360.

for our missions in other countries. . . . Westerners have a view of the Gospel that's very different from someone in South America, China or Africa. We need that kind of cross-pollination.[55]

In the words of Episcopal priest Robert Farrar Capon, the prophetic role is the effort to "look the world back to grace,"[56] both to expose injustice and to propose solutions. A prophet, Abraham Joshua Heschel wrote in his writings on racism, "is a person who is not tolerant of wrong done to others, who resents other people's injuries. He even calls upon others to be champions of the poor."[57] The prophetic responsibility is what Dorothy Day meant by *nonsovereign service* (the ethics not of power but of aid and commitment) in her antiwar, antipoverty Catholic Worker Movement. It is what Pastor Greg Boyd calls not power over others but "power under," in their support. And what Glen Stassen calls "transforming initiatives" or paradigm shifts that unexpectedly transform an injustice or fight into a way out.[58]

Incarnational Discipleship

Transforming initiatives begin, Stassen suggests, with "incarnational discipleship." If the prophetic role is the mandate to publicize injustice and develop alternatives, "discipleship" is their creative implementation.[59] "Incarnational"

55. Interview with the author, May 13, 2009; for an overview of churches with similar priorities, see M. Pally, *The New Evangelicals: Expanding the Vision of the Common Good* (Grand Rapids: Eerdmans, 2011), ch. 8.

56. R. Capon, *The Supper of the Lamb: A Culinary Reflection* (New York: Harcourt, Brace, 1967), p. 3.

57. A. J. Heschel, "Religion and Race," in *The Insecurity of Freedom: Essays on Human Existence* (New York: Noonday Press, 1967), p. 92.

58. For a description of churches that take this as their prime mission, see Pally, *The New Evangelicals*, especially ch. 8.

59. In a formulation parallel to discipleship and prophetic role, Miroslav Volf sees Christian ethics as a two-step process, "ascent" and "descent." In the first phase, analogous to discipleship, one learns of God's vision through engagement with texts, traditions, interpretations, and inspirational figures, and through spiritual and emotional engagement with God. The second phase, "descent," analogous to the prophetic role, is the creative moment, where one, alone and with others, brings his vision to the world. "For a religion to maintain its prophetic character, ordinary believers and their leaders must replicate in their own way both the 'ascent' and the 'return' of the great founding figures. . . . The work of medical doctors, garbage collectors, business executives and artists, stay-at-home parents and scientists needs to be inserted into God's story of the world." Volf, *A Public Faith*, pp. 9, 17.

means that this process is guided by the principles expressed in Jesus' life and lessons: "a thick, historically-embodied, realistic understanding," Stassen writes, "of Jesus Christ as revealing God's character."[60] Or, in the words of the former archbishop of Canterbury Rowan Williams, "the Bible is not simply saying, 'Here is a story,' but 'Here is your story.'"[61] Shane Claiborne of the new monasticism movement says, "I am following the Homeless Rabbi."[62]

The importance of the *imago,* covenant, and incarnation — God becoming human because of the importance of humanity — here comes into full force. Through them God's commitment and lessons become our ethics. Jesus is, Thomas Torrance writes, "*our* fellow-man, as *our* brother, for it is *our* actual human being and nature that have been taken up in him."[63] Sallie McFague concurs: "it is both the concrete, physical availability of God's presence ('became flesh') and the likeness to ourselves, a human being ('lived among us'), that matter."[64] Stassen cites Bonhoeffer: "Man was created a body, the Son of God appeared on earth in the body, he was raised in the body, in the sacrament the believer receives the Lord Christ in the body, and the resurrection of the dead will bring about the perfected fellowship of God's spiritual-physical creatures. The believer therefore lauds the Creator, the Redeemer, God, Father, Son and Holy Spirit, for *the bodily presence of a brother.*"[65]

On Stassen's view, it was this "brother" that enabled Bonhoeffer to avoid collaboration with the Nazis, to which many of his church brethren succumbed.[66] André Trocmé, as we've seen, relied on the lessons of the Sermon

60. G. Stassen, *A Thicker Jesus: Incarnational Discipleship in a Secular Age* (Louisville: Westminster John Knox, 2012), p. 16.

61. Williams, *Being Christian,* pp. 29 30.

62. S. Claiborne, *Irresistible Revolution: Living as an Ordinary Radical* (Grand Rapids: Zondervan, 2006), p. 169.

63. T. Torrance, "The Goodness and Dignity of Man in the Christian Tradition," *Modern Theology* 4, no. 4 (July 1988): 317.

64. In McFague's description of incarnational ethics, the parables, or deconstructive phase, overturn "oppressive, dualistic hierarchies." The healing stories, or reconstructive phase, "focus attention on bodily pain and bodily relief." The prospective phase, "Jesus eating with sinners . . . suggest that all are invited to the banquet of life." S. McFague, *The Body of God: An Ecological Theology* (Minneapolis: Fortress, 1993), pp. 168-69.

65. D. Bonhoeffer, *Life Together,* trans. J. W. Doberstein (New York: Harper, 1954), p. 20, emphasis mine.

66. Bonhoeffer, Stassen writes, "not only spoke out early, but organized others to gather a church leadership that would be faithful to the way of Jesus rather than to the way of militaristic nationalism"; Stassen, *A Thicker Jesus,* p. 22. Gushee, in his study of those who saved Jews during the Holocaust, found that many understood Jesus in his historical, Jewish context and

on the Mount to save thousands of Jews from Nazi deportation. The white Southern Baptist Clarence Jordan wrote his *Cotton Patch Translation of the New Testament* as a reimagining of Jesus' story for the American South of the 1930s. Among his other efforts against racism, Jordan set up an interracial cooperative farm in which the workers of both races earned ownership. Both the American civil rights movement and the South African anti-apartheid movement were based on the ethics of inclusion and justice found in Jesus' life and lessons. Explaining her ethics of nonsovereign service, Dorothy Day again invokes incarnation, Jesus' life on earth: "It is with the voice of our contemporaries that He [Jesus] speaks, with the eyes of store clerks, factory workers, and children that He gazes; with the hand of office workers, slum dwellers, and suburban housewives that He gives. It is with the feet of soldiers and tramps that He walks, and with the heart of anyone in need that He longs for shelter. And giving shelter or food to anyone who asks for it, or needs it, is giving to Christ."[67]

Incarnational *Discipleship*

Discipleship — creative change to bring Jesus' vision into the world — requires understanding the incarnation not as a blueprint to mimic, as this would render it irrelevant in circumstances different from Jesus' own. He is vision and model,[68] "thus providing norms for guiding our lives."[69] Karl Rahner, as we've seen before, universalizes the idea: Jesus "remains an example worthy of emulation for all men."[70] Following Jesus' life and vision is doable, we are assured, because of the incarnation itself. Jesus, while divine, was fully human, prone to doubts, temptations, and failings. Perhaps not his (divine) miracles but his lessons and practices are analogously doable and are not to be bumped upstairs into unattainable ideal. In Rowan Williams's words, Jesus is "not only someone

---

saw God's vision as reaching to all of life and their particular lives; D. Gushee, *Righteous Gentiles of the Holocaust: Genocide and Moral Obligation*, 2nd ed. (St. Paul: Paragon House, 2003).

67. D. Day, *Selected Writings* (Maryknoll, N.Y.: Orbis, 1992), pp. 94-95.

68. K. Rahner, *Foundations of Christian Faith: An Introduction to the Idea of Christianity*, trans. W. Dych (New York: Crossroad, 1978), p. 251.

69. Stassen, *A Thicker Jesus*, p. 16. As Hans Urs von Balthasar writes, "If we who constitute the living community of the Church share a common life in the source [God], then we are striving to allow to be operative in our own community the kind of divine society that Jesus Christ has opened for the world as a whole." Balthasar, *Engagement with God*, p. 51; see also, p. 40.

70. L. Ibekwe, *The Universality of Salvation in Jesus Christ in the Thought of Karl Rahner* (Würzburg: Echter Verlag, 2006), p. 12.

who *exercises* hospitality; he *draws out* hospitality from others. By his welcome he makes other people capable of welcoming."[71] Following that is discipleship.

Incarnational discipleship, then, is a practice — not salt and light but, Stassen writes, "salt, light, and *deeds*."[72] Underscoring the application to political and economic policy, Stassen details two pairs of deeds in particular. One pair, within the church community, starts with the activities by which groups constitute themselves — meeting, studying together, discussing problems, and implementing solutions (church structure and finances, *de facto* and *de jure* practices of inclusion/exclusion, methods of study, etc.). The partner in this pair is the resulting public-sector activities: church contribution to the larger community and cooperation with other civil society groups. The second pair of deeds occurs in church-state relations, where one sector provides another with resources or presents a challenge. An example would be government partnerships with faith-based social services that, under Bill Clinton, G. W. Bush, and Barack Obama, afforded such agencies increased access to public funds.[73] In turn, faith groups are resources for communities and governments as they serve as laboratories for new ideas and provide education, job training, health care, and environmental protection services alongside public-sector agencies.[74]

To be open to this sort of discipleship is, on Bretherton's account, again hospitality. It is openness to the ideas and practices of those who are socioeconomically and ideationally different and to the interpersonal work necessary to take them into account — both those in need and other groups in service provision. And it requires befriending them. While some aid and funds-distribution programs work well absent relationships (like income tax credits), many programs don't; they become bureaucracy. And even those that in implementation don't require relating, need in the development phase to be worked through by persons and groups with varied experience and exper-

71. Williams, *Being Christian*, p. 42.

72. G. Stassen, *Living the Sermon on the Mount: A Practical Hope for Grace and Deliverance* (Hoboken, N.J.: Jossey-Bass/Wiley, 2006), p. 60. This might mean, on his view: "Anyone who makes wealth in this society is benefitting from the education that the society gives to workers and consumers, from the society's justice system supported both by the legal system and police and the character and consent of the governed, from the transportation systems provided in large part by people and government working together, and from the natural resources that are a gift from God. . . . Benefitting from all this creates a covenant obligation by the wealthy to the community"; Stassen, *A Thicker Jesus*, p. 119.

73. See, for instance, Bretherton, "Coming to Judgment," pp. 173ff.

74. See Pally, *The New Evangelicals*, pp. 122-23.

tise who are open to each other, can come to understand each other, and can incorporate each other's perspectives into the final proposal. Thus, just as the effort to speak in the prophetic voice creates the covenantal, agapic relationships needed to do so, so the effort to follow incarnational discipleship creates the relationships needed for its practice. *Agape is telos and method of both.*

Trust and the Role of Community

The relationships that are needed for and develop through discipleship — for creative, sophisticated policy development — start in communities (families, schools, community associations, religious institutions, economic groups, and manifold forms of the body politic). When Tocqueville and John Stuart Mill wrote that civic participation is learned from doing it — from living in societies where those practices are taught and done — they were reprising the discipleship notion that one learns it from relations with those who study and practice it. Neither the worldview nor the implementation of reciprocal consideration-worthiness develops in individuals in isolation, absent communities where this consideration is indeed the mores and practice. A just social order, David Bentley Hart writes, would "recognize that there can be no simple partition between the polity of the soul and the polity of the people, and that there is in fact a reciprocal spiritual relation."[75] And one learns more of discipleship the more the group is committed to it, the more one is committed to the group, and the more the group endures to form practices of regard/care and ways of transmitting them.

Or, as Lovin notes, consideration and commitment among persons come not only because "[God] first loved us" (1 John 4:19) but because other people have loved us as well: they have helped us form goals, rules to work toward them, and the virtues without which rules would become rigid, irrelevant to changing conditions, or mistakenly taken as ends in themselves.[76]

Lonergan holds to just this in his view that all our distinct ideas — traditional, ethical, including the most innovative — emerge from a "dialectics" of each person's singular "original meaningfulness" and the "sedimented" values,

---

75. D. B. Hart, *In the Aftermath: Provocations and Laments* (Grand Rapids: Eerdmans, 2009), p. 80. Stanley Grenz writes about "the divinely given human calling to be the image of God as a social reality"; S. Grenz, *The Social God and the Relational Self* (Louisville: Westminster John Knox, 2001), p. 15.

76. See R. Lovin, *Christian Ethics: An Essential Guide* (Nashville: Abingdon, 2000) throughout, but especially chs. 4 and 5.

practices, and ways of thinking of our communities — and then the dialectics of both with transcendent vision. Doran summarizes, "The first point is that human meaning, whether technical, social, or cultural, develops and expands in human collaboration."[77] As with Hume and Hamann, society's "sedimented" discourses include not only articulated principles (legal, philosophical, political) but also its unarticulated sensibilities, daily practices, biases, tonalities, and emotions. The dialectics includes each person and her church community, but also the church community's exchange with the surrounding "cultural matrices" and secular discourses. This layered exchange will, on Lonergan's view, yield concepts and relationships that are *trans*cultural (that attract agreement and unite people regardless of cultural background) and *inter*cultural (that allow communication while holding to cultural differences).

Ethics building in community and policy, as with any teleological freedom, limits and enhances individual choice. New possibilities emerge as one's vision and capacities expand beyond what one alone can do and beyond the satisfaction of private aims. Limitations follow because one's actions must account for others. Yet these limitations, Lovin notes, lead also to new ideas and persons: "we also need to be part of a community that will challenge us to extend our vision to include new people and live our virtues in new ways."[78] When a community cannot extend its vision, it falls into what Alasdair MacIntyre calls "epistemological crisis." Stassen adds, "Both MacIntyre and [Charles] Taylor are saying . . . [t]hat we cannot simply insist on the rightness of our tradition as if it were absolute and unchangeable authority."[79] This is neither freedom nor tradition but fossilization.

Communities, to develop policy, thus need shared history and a sense of trust and common future but also members whose loyalty moves them to adjust the status quo to conserve undergirding values. The complex effort of *change-to-conserve* provokes tough debate (whether to desegregate the workplace/school/church, admit women to the profession/ministry, work with secular/church groups, etc.), but absent such debate, we risk ossifying ethics as though it were not meant to address circumstances different from those of ancient texts.

Fostering groups of trust and change — or trust in response to change — is essential to discipleship itself, an idea prominent in the Pauline writings: "The major theme of these letters," Ian Smith notes, "is that the church as a com-

---

77. Doran, *What Is Systematic Theology?* p. 159.
78. Lovin, *Christian Ethics*, pp. 32, 115, 123.
79. Stassen, *A Thicker Jesus*, p. 7.

munity, as well as Christians as individuals need to work out the practical and everyday implications of what it means to be united with Christ in his death and resurrection. Christians are to be those who reflect the reconciliation and new life achieved in these Easter events."[80] Karl Barth and Dorothee Soelle, writing under the moral collapse of World War II, stressed (in implicit critique of collaboration) that the realization of God's vision is brought about by specific communities responding to specific circumstances — not just "a cluster of individuals who share only a relationship with God or with the church conceived as an authoritative institution,"[81] as Adam Kotsko writes in his summary. Soelle argued, "If Christ provisionally represents us before God, this means that the company of believers [in God's image] must also stand in for someone before God. For the Church, this someone can only be the world."[82]

Volf gets at the role of community in discipleship from a problem inherent, ironically, in its *fulfillment,* the limits of human capacity that were noticed early on by Origen. Volf writes, "Like God we should give to the needy without any distinction. . . . Then must we, like God, give to everyone? If so, our responsibility could never be fulfilled; and the choice to give to one person would be a choice to sacrifice all others." His solution to human limitation lies in community: "We are finite beings. . . . There is only 'one man,' God-man, whose gift is meant for all — Jesus Christ (Rom. 5:15-21). . . . [I]t is not a responsibility of any single individual to give to everyone. Giving to everyone is the responsibility of God and all human beings collectively."[83]

Hauerwas, much of whose work looks at community in ethics, describes Christianity as a communal, performative act. It is what one does with one's day. It is being "embedded in a community of practices that make those beliefs themselves work and give us a community by which we are shaped. Religious belief is not just some kind of primitive metaphysics, but in fact it is a performance just like you would perform *Lear.*"[84]

To his idea that living ethically, discipleship, is belief-constituting-conduct-constituting-belief, Hauerwas adds that this loop occurs substantially

80. Smith here is focusing on Ephesians, Philippians, Colossians, and Philemon; I. K. Smith, "The Later Pauline Letters," p. 302.

81. A. Kotsko, *The Politics of Redemption* (London: T. & T. Clark, 2010), p. 15.

82. D. Soelle, *Christ the Representative: An Essay in Theology after the "Death of God,"* trans. D. Lewis (Philadelphia: Fortress, 1967), p. 112.

83. M. Volf, "Being as God Is," in *God's Life in Trinity*, ed. M. Volf and M. Welker (Minneapolis: Augsburg Fortress, 2006), p. 10.

84. S. Hauerwas, "Bonhoeffer: The Truthful Witness," *Homiletics online* (2004); retrieved from http://www.homileticsonline.com/subscriber/interviews/hauerwas.asp.

with others in community. Such communities and practices "give us ways to go on when we are not sure where we are."[85] They help us with the wisdom and resources to face complexities without the fear and frustration that push us to quick fixes, to obscure root causes, blur the big picture, and blind us to the concerns of others who are also involved. Said another way, they help us avoid undue separability or situatedness. The more, on Hauerwas's view, one is in a community that ethically ponders problems and solutions — again, discipleship — the more one may come to creative, productive results. Importantly, such communities serve as models to other communities. We start "first by having the patience amid the injustice and violence of this world to care for the widow, the poor, and the orphan. . . . [I]t is our conviction that unless we take the time for such care neither we nor the world can know what justice looks like."[86]

These are Hauerwas's "communities of trust," with all that entails in developing ongoing reciprocal commitment — in shedding unconscious prejudgments, practices of suspicion and competition, in-group-ism, etc. "The first task of the church is to exhibit in our common life the kind of community possible when trust, and not fear, rules our lives."[87] Importantly, Hauerwas notes, it is the process of forming such communities that creates the trust and care that are its goals: one forges trust by the common endeavor to build a community of trust.

Thus we have *agape,* trust, and covenantal regard as *telos* and method in triune form: in the prophetic voice, in incarnational discipleship, and in their realization in community.

Trust is also needed thrice, first *within* institutions/associations, as Adam Smith and Antonio Genovesi noted about markets. We cannot live, work, or trade together where backstabbing is the norm. The mores of honesty and trust are "freedom's essential living space,"[88] in Jürgen Moltmann's words. They are the condition for freedom of ideas and action and thus of creativity, innovation, and productiveness.

Trust is needed as well between institution and community. A case in point was the 2014 rise in polio cases in Pakistan that followed from Pakistani loss of trust in immunization teams after the United States used healthcare programs as a front for intelligence gathering. Third, trust is needed

85. S. Hauerwas, *The State of the University* (Oxford: Blackwell, 2007), p. 40.

86. Hauerwas, *The Peaceable Kingdom,* p. 100.

87. S Hauerwas, *A Community of Character: Towards a Constructive Christian Social Ethic* (Notre Dame: University of Notre Dame Press, 1981), pp. 11, 84, 85.

88. J. Moltmann, *Ethics of Hope,* trans. M. Kohl (Minneapolis: Fortress, 2012), p. 210.

also among institutions, Hauerwas notes, especially those of different classes, races, and faiths that lack the history and habits of working together. Here we come again to Bretherton's "hospitality" and Joel Hunter's practice of making service projects interracial, interreligious, and interclass efforts. "The moral challenge," Gushee writes, "most often, is to learn to broaden the boundaries of that universe so that they extend to include not just my parents and children and fellow tribesmen but also strangers and aliens and even enemies."[89] Gushee further observes that we must make every effort not to pit one institution or group against another (e.g., domestic poor against foreign poor), but to, as inventively as possible, devise public policies of across-the-board consideration-worthiness.

The international stage raises its own problems of trust, and Reinhold Niebuhr was right in noting, in *Moral Man and Immoral Society,* that persons may find trust and overcome self-interest more easily than do nations, owing to issue complexity and the mandate to protect the in-group. Yet networks of cooperating nations too have fostered transnational mores where trust is what's done and is presumed unless grave counterevidence emerges. Even substantial tensions are worked through without aggression because all recognize the importance of the long-term trust and bonds. The British Commonwealth, European Union, NATO, among others, come to mind.

On one hand, Heltzel, Benson, and Berry share ground with Hauerwas. They begin as he does with the idea that Christianity is performative in protesting injustice, in promoting "public engagement,"[90] and in providing alternatives using known strategies (used by Gandhi or Martin Luther King, for example) and new "improvisations." They hold these to the dialogic standards of careful listening and conversation within communities and with outsiders, importantly both those in power and those in need. On the other hand, Hauerwas comes in for some critique as Heltzel, Benson, and Berry wonder if his vision of a "contrast community" that models ethics in its internal relations risks a too-thin engagement with people outside it. "For Hauerwas," they write, "it is ethically adequate for the church to struggle to embody peace as a distinct community in its own right. However, people both within the church and outside of church continue to be victims of violence, posing ongoing ethical problems that Christian ethics must address."[91] Historically speaking, the

---

89. D. Gushee, *The Sacredness of Human Life: Why an Ancient Biblical Vision Is the Key to the World's Future* (Grand Rapids: Eerdmans, 2013), p. 68.

90. Benson, Berry, and Heltzel, *Prophetic Evangelicals*, p. 32.

91. Benson, Berry, and Heltzel, *Prophetic Evangelicals*, pp. 24, 25.

charge is something of a compliment to Hauerwas, as it comes from the relational stance that he has long advanced. If nothing else, it reflects self-critique among those who take seriously prophetic and discipleship obligations and take communities of trust as their most likely implementers.

Another area of the "disciple's" self-critique, applicable to church and public institutions, is wariness of comforting simplifications. Balthasar notes the "obligation of studying carefully the complexities of a situation, and of accepting it as such. On no account must [a person] behave like one of those frightful simplifiers."[92] Hunter has similarly noted, "Here's what I think the enemy is: the luxury of being simplistic, of not understanding how complex problems are and how much cooperation is required to solve them."[93] Hunter advises that one "eschew 'group-think' " and be wary of "the human readiness to believe that benefits to oneself are benefits for all."[94] Picking a tough example, Boyd points to the abortion debate: "It has been hard in my environment [nondenominational evangelical church in the Midwest] to help people see the complexities of the situation. A person could vote for a candidate who is not 'pro-life' but who will help the economy and the poor. Yet this may be the best way to curb the abortion rate. So precisely because a Christian is pro-life, he or she might vote for a candidate who is not 'pro-life.' "[95]

Yet a third arena for self-awareness and criticism is the use of self-righteousness and pressure in a means-ends calculus. Volf is particularly concerned about the passion for good becoming oppressive: "the adherents of prophetic religion will let faith dictate the ends to be achieved . . . but fail to allow faith to determine the means to achieve those ends (opponents are not even respected let alone treated with benevolence and beneficence)."[96] Cautions against aggression, from sanctimonious imposition to violence, are seen in the Deuteronomic mandate to sue for peace before engaging in war. They continue in the prophetic and Pauline lambastes not only against violence[97]

---

92. Balthasar, *Engagement with God*, pp. 89, 93.

93. Interview with the author, May 13, 2009.

94. Interview with the author, May 13, 2001.

95. Interview with the author, May 4, 2009.

96. Volf, *A Public Faith*, p. 18.

97. Among Church Fathers, Tertullian declares, "How will a Christian man war, nay, how will he serve even in peace, without a sword, which the Lord has taken away? . . . The Lord . . . in disarming Peter, unbelted every soldier" (*On Military Service*, in *The Sacred Writings of Tertullian: Extended Annotated Edition*, trans. P. Holmes and S. Thelwall [Altenmuenster: Jazzybee/Juergen Beck Verlag, 2012], ch. 19). Origen reprises Isa. 2:4, calling us to turn swords into pruning hooks (*Against Celsus* 5.33, retrieved from http://www.newadvent.org/fathers/04165.htm). The second-century theologian Athenagoras reprises, "We cannot endure

but also against condescension and the self-righteous hypocrisy of following the letter of the law while neglecting the mandate to be of aid to others.

They continue importantly in Jesus' lessons and Paul's vision of reconciliation, which mandates not only avoiding contempt and aggression but active repair: "All this is from God, who reconciled us to himself through Christ and gave us the ministry of reconciliation" (2 Cor. 5:18). The obligation to repair and reconcile recalls the lesson from covenantal irrevocability: If God's commitment to us and ours to each other are irrevocable, how, after breach of that commitment, would that affect what one does *next?*

In the last century, Yoder's work — which has had significant influence on emerging/emergent churches and new monasticism movements[98] — offers a two-step look at aggression. Yoder speaks to churches, but his principles have much to say about all participation in the public arena. He begins with the mandate that Christians accept their sociopolitical positions, a stance that arises from the biblical view of earthly powers as fallen but necessary to check crime and chaos. There is no exception made even for oppressive states in Paul's linchpin passage on government (Rom. 13:1-7): "Everyone must be subject to the governing authorities." Yet Yoder's notion of "subordination" to power is, like Jesus', not ordinary but "revolutionary." It tolerates neither passivity nor weakness in the face of injustice but holds that — because of the *imago, similitude,* covenant, and the incarnational lessons of the "divine brother" — one may always speak in the prophetic voice and act in discipleship.

In times of relatively just government, Yoder holds, Christians are to live as "contrast societies," promoting the dignity, freedom, and equality of each person (1 Cor. 7:20; John 17:15-16). By quiet modeling — here Yoder and Hauerwas are close — community practices of equality and service spread.[99] In Boyd's words, Christians are "resident aliens" with an outsider's look at the status quo. "The Kingdom," Boyd writes, "has always thrived — and really, has

---

even to see a man put to death, though justly" (*A Plea for the Christians,* in *Ante-Nicene Fathers,* 2:147). Arnobius of Sicca (third century C.E.) admonishes that we avoid aggression even if it means taking the blows ourselves: "we should rather shed our own blood than stain our hands and our conscience with that of another" (*Against the Heathen,* in *Ante-Nicene Fathers,* 6:415).

98. See, for instance, Claiborne, *Irresistible Revolution;* S. Claiborne and T. Campolo, *Red Letter Revolution: What If Jesus Really Meant What He Said?* (Nashville: Thomas Nelson/ HarperCollins, 2012); J. Wilson-Hartgrove, *New Monasticism: What It Has to Say to Today's Church* (Grand Rapids: Brazos, 2008); Pally, *The New Evangelicals.*

99. Miroslav Volf holds as well that "conversations with non-Christians presuppose Christian readiness to listen and learn." Christians, he continues, do not tyrannically impose or "sell" their views but rather point to wisdom and live as Jesus lived so that others can, so to speak, get a feel for what it might be like; see Volf, *A Public Faith,* pp. 86, 106-8.

only thrived — when it was on the margins of society."[100] There the church community exercises not power but authority (after the German sociologist Max Weber). As power achieves its aims by sanction, it may provoke backlash, and, in any case, abrogates the ethics of nonaggression. Authority moves by moral suasion, by the persuasiveness one has when one works *from* a community's deepest principles — so that one has legitimation, gravitas, and trust — and from there moves toward the future and the common good.

In times of unjust government, Yoder continues, where government demands that Christians violate their principles or itself grossly violates them, noncooperation is an effective block[101] (as the Danes and Albanians demonstrated in making it impossible for the Nazis to deport Jews). It was the strategy of Gandhi and, during the Soviet era, of Adam Michnik in Poland and Václav Havel in Czechoslovakia: small changes in daily life that gum up the works.

When nonviolent protest is ineffective, Christians have the harsher option of leaving as, Yoder notes, Mary and Joseph fled when the Hebrew infants were murdered and as Bonhoeffer recognized when he wrote, "At any moment [the Christian community] may receive the signal to move on."[102] One wonders if he was thinking of the effect on Nazism if large numbers of German Christians had in the 1930s left the country.

This sort of thing is extremely difficult, but as relationality theologians point out, the aim is not to make life easy, just better.

---

100. G. Boyd, "Don't Weep for the Demise of American Christianity," April 8, 2009; retrieved from http://www.gregboyd.org/blog/dont-weep-for-the-demise-of-american -christianity/.

101. A position taken also by Joel Hunter; see J. Hunter, *A New Kind of Conservative* (Ventura, Calif.: Gospel Light, 2008), p. 182, and much of his argument throughout; see also, J. Hunter, *Right Wing, Wrong Bird: Why the Tactics of the Religious Right Won't Fly with Most Conservative Christians* (Longwood, Fla.: Church Press, 2006).

102. D. Bonhoeffer, *Discipleship*, Dietrich Bonhoeffer Works, vol. 4 (Minneapolis: Fortress, 2003), pp. 250-51.

PART III

Conclusion

Review of Major Tenets

The aim of this book has been to suggest, beginning simply, that individuals and societies thrive when policies and practices see to both the unique value of each person and the interconnectedness of persons, that is, to our separability and situatedness. A condition of our being is that we are distinct yet we partake of the unfolding source of being, the reason for there being something rather than nothing. This source of being is distinct from particular beings but "inheres" in each of us as a condition of our existence. This distinction yet inherence/relation is the way things are. As there is no other way to "be," we become our (distinct) selves in relation to others as only each of us can uniquely have those relations.

Absent an understanding of our ontology, we have difficulty accounting for what we encounter, both the principles of the world and the problems that emerge when we ignore them. We founder on relativism: all policies and practices are of equal merit because they are accountable only to those who already believe them (they are not judged on their outcomes). Or we founder on self-absorption: proposals that I or my group like are best, for they are accountable only to me or my group. The plurality of efforts to understand how the world works is part of how the world works; each teaches us a great deal, as no single account is complete. But the thing about which there are multiple efforts is our human condition. We are obligated to it, from chemical interactions to our societal interdependence, and efforts to ignore it often yield tragic results.

Developmental psychology and evolutionary biology teach us the same curriculum: we are "wired" for cooperation and reciprocal giving — or, in this book's terms, relationality, separability-*amid*-situatedness, distinction-*amid*-relation. While undue situatedness yields top-down oppression and conformity pressures, and undue separability yields self-absorbed greed and anomie, policies that take the two in mutual constitution proffer a life together that is more conducive to well-being than the binary alternatives.

Part I describes this ontology, and part II offers its theological ground, beginning with analogic participation, the *imago,* and covenant. On the *analogia entis,* causes yield resembling results, and so each of us, caused by the "structuring cause," God, partakes of an of-a-kind-ness with him. We partake not identically, as finite persons cannot be identical to the source of being; rather, we are each a distinct, nonidentical but analogous expression of this of-a-kind-ness. Poetically, we are in God's image, *tselem Elohim/imago Dei.* The self-expressing being, God, is distinct from us but "inherent" in all — he is the minimum, as Nicholas of Cusa wrote, that is in each particular and the maximum that all beings are in.[1] Thus, being of his distinction-amid-relation makes us analogously distinct yet in relation. We are in the image of and in covenant with relational God, and so relationality is the condition of our being and being with each other.

Thus we must take each other's concerns into consideration and into responsibility — taking the concerns of others to be as consideration-worthy as our own. Reciprocal consideration-worthiness brings out two things: common needs, goals, and interests, and differences, which — if we are to avoid the ills of separat*edness* — need to be approached by asking, in Joel Hunter's words, "why the other side is for the other side."[2] This does not require ceding one's own views or granting all that's wanted. It means each reciprocally getting at the other's underlying concerns (fears, needs, hopes) — even or especially if they are difficult to articulate — so that they may be brokered into practices and policies with contributions from all involved. While we might begin with those near us, the present mobility of persons, goods, microbes, and ideas suggests that the relations we need to attend to reach across the globe.

Absent such understanding, we may be led by our fears, as Hobbes wrote, to quick fixes and uncreative, short-term (often competitive and aggressive) thinking that we believe ensures safety and gain. This is not to say that the world is amok with undue separability, undue situatedness, or quick-fix belligerence. But when we do neglect distinction-amid-relation, we do less well than when we account for it — which is why this volume proposes an ontology

---

1. Nicholas of Cusa, *De ludo globi* (1463), II, n. 62.
2. J. Hunter, *A New Kind of Conservative* (Ventura, Calif.: Gospel Light, 2008), pp. 84-85.

and theology to keep it in mind and in policy. *The theology of the way things are yields an ethics of how not to mess things up.*

In part II, I have looked at how distinction-amid-relation and reciprocal consideration are expressed in several theological concepts: covenant, the *imago,* Trinity, grace, crucifixion, salvation, Eucharist, and ethics. To do so, I have brought together a number of thinkers nondenominationally as they have drawn and built on tradition. These thinkers work in different schools of thought; some may not engage others while some engage in disagreement. Yet their ideas about relationality share a family resemblance, and differences among them need not be eliminated for their common ideas to remain robust and important. In keeping with my purpose to investigate relationality as it is enriched by different traditions, I have aimed at affinity and reflection among these approaches — how they illuminate each other — so that relationality itself may be better understood. I have discussed debates between traditions when they have been useful in explaining the idea of distinction-amid-relation. That is, the methodology of this book reflects its content: it highlights distinction-amid-relation in the voices gathered here.

The family resemblances running through the range of writers mentioned here offer support for my premise that distinction-amid-relation is an ontology (rather than personal opinion). People from different eras and intellectual and faith traditions have come to it and described it in ways that are recognizably similar. If distinction-amid-relation is found broadly throughout human ponderings and is widely seen as our ontology, it might be because it is.

This means that distinction-amid-relation, precisely because it is a condition of being, is found not in one philosophical or theological approach but in many, in each a bit differently, as the theologians discussed here attest. No account of relationality is complete because each of us experiences the world differently, and thus no single account of any part of it is complete. "Teleological heterogeneity" and "pluralism," Joseph Soloveitchik writes, are "founded on reality itself."[3] Yet we learn from each account as it contributes to our knowledge from its perch. In the twelfth century ibn Rushd (Averroës) argued both against absolutist notions of God and for a critical interpretation of religious texts. In this century, Glen Stassen wrote (and I concur), "nor am I arguing for only one tradition as having all truth; all traditions need continuous correction."[4]

---

3. J. Soloveitchick, *The Halakhic Mind* (New York: Free Press, 1986), p. 16.

4. G. Stassen, *A Thicker Jesus: Incarnational Discipleship in a Secular Age* (Louisville: Westminster John Knox, 2012), p. 14; see also, S. Hauerwas, *The Peaceable Kingdom: A Primer in Christian Ethics* (Notre Dame: University of Notre Dame Press, 1983), p. 101.

In sum, the differences among accounts of relationality suggest at least three things: that differences in approach do not expunge common ground; that the common ground amid differences supports relationality as ontology; and though it may be our ontology, none has complete knowledge of it, and so we must learn from the differences. These are features of our *study* of relationality, but they are features also of our distinct-yet-relational lives: differences among persons do not expunge common ground, the common ground suggests relationality as our ontology, and we must learn from our differences to better grasp — and to better — life.

Not only is relationality developed through many traditions, but some have taken these traditional ideas as truth, others as metaphor or illustration of our human circumstances. This is not to say that the differences between truth and metaphor have no consequences, but that in both cases, these ideas have enriched our understanding of human life and hold us to standards of reciprocal consideration-worthiness substantially conducive to human flourishing. *As we would continue to plumb Plato's philosophy were the dialogues with Socrates "untrue" and "mere" narrative, so we may ponder relational theologies.*[5] Or, combining the suggestions of James Pambrun and Karl Rahner, we may consider these theological ideas as hypotheses, investigate them in light of what happens when they are applied, and so assess how well they help in understanding our human condition.[6]

Covenant in Practice in America's Covenantal Communities

One method of assessing relationality might be to look at America's covenantal communities from the colonial era through the nineteenth century, as their members were committed to relationships and the commons as a matter of principle. Those that began with commonality of dream (be it apocalyptic communitarianism or socialist Fourierism) but did not sustain it or sustain agreement on quotidian practices raveled quickly. One might say that, in spite of grand schemes, they suffered insufficient situatedness. Those that lacked outlets for individual expression foundered as well. One might say that, in spite of strong communal practices, they had insufficient separability born of rather

---

5. Y. Hazony, *The Philosophy of Hebrew Scripture* (Cambridge: Cambridge University Press, 2012), pp. 53, 23.

6. J. Pambrun, "The Relationship between Theology and Philosophy: Augustine, Ricoeur, and Hermeneutics," *Theoform* 36, no. 3 (2005): 292-319.

pessimistic anthropologies and theologies. Not trusting that their values would endure absent detailed and usually top-down controls, they abrogated Stanley Hauerwas's "communities of trust." By contrast, the communities that endured over generations had clear values and common practices yet also significant venues for individual expression even amid highly regulated daily routines.

One example of the first sort of foundering — initial vision but low situatedness — is the Owenite community at New Harmony, Indiana (1825-1827). Though Robert Owen had amassed wealth and reputation from his experimental community in New Lanark, Scotland, and though his American followers had the benefit of moving into an already-settled region,[7] the community lasted only two years. Owen did not lack for details about his future community, but as his "new empire of peace and goodwill" was open to "the industrious and well-disposed of all nations," the roughly eight hundred who came, of varied classes and backgrounds, had little practice in getting on with each other and no beliefs or experience to unite them in common purpose. Their successive communitarian constitutions were open to many interpretations and got them — five in one year, splitting the group into four separate sections where members "continued strangers to each other in . . . all their pretence of co-operation."[8] This is not to say that Owen and his followers made no contributions to the nation; substantial ones were made especially in education and women's rights.[9] Yet by 1830, lacking a common goal and the practices of working together, the dozen or so Owenite communities had all closed.

The socialist community in Skaneateles, New York (1843), had a similar problem of insufficient situatedness. Founder John Collins's injunction to "believe what you may, but act as well as you can" attracted a wide range of laudable and unscrupulous people with little means to build common purpose or practice. Though Collins rid the group of its worst cheaters, this did not square with his belief in complete voluntarism; when he left two years later, the group disbanded. The Hopedale community of Christian socialists (1841) had more commonality of vision in its practical Christianity (abolition, women's rights, pacifism, and aid to the poor as the path to salvation). Moreover, it aimed to

7. The settlement was built and sold to Owen by the Rappite Quietist community.

8. M. Holloway, *Utopian Communities in America: 1680-1880* (Mineola, N.Y.: Dover Publications, 1966), pp. 105, 106.

9. Owenite William Maclure inaugurated kindergartens, trade schools, free education for both sexes, and the Pestalozzian educational system, later adopted throughout the United States. Owen's son, Robert Dale Owen, as representative in the Indiana state legislature, secured universal free public education and greater rights for women to control their wages and property.

grant each member work and "a suitable sphere of individual enterprise and responsibility, in which each one may by due self-exertion elevate himself to the highest point of his capabilities."[10] But it lacked common practices, especially in governance; its reforms of 1847 came too late, and the community soon failed when the Draper brothers, owning three-quarters of the community's stock, withdrew it to invest in their own manufacturing company and future fortune.

Fourierism garnered substantial enthusiasm in antebellum America with its detailed economic plans (communal living and accounts, highest pay for the least pleasant work), federated internal organization, and free choice of occupation and movement among internal groups. Albert Brisbane, a student of Fourier, brought the ideas to the United States in the 1840s; Horace Greeley gave them substantial coverage in the *New York Tribune,* and over forty communities were started. Yet only three lasted for more than fifteen months; another three, for more than two years.

A central cause of demise was again the problem of a varied population with insufficient common practices. Unusually, the North American Phalanx in New Jersey lasted from 1843 to 1854, owing to its requirement of a one-year probationary period prior to admission, which gave its members greater commonality of vision and mores. Disagreements over religious practice fractured it, and after a fire destroyed the mills and workshops, there was little will to continue. The Wisconsin Phalanx lasted from 1844 to 1850 also by implementing an admissions system but fell prey to loss of vision, its members selling their land and buildings for individual profit. Brook Farm, lasting five years, 1841-1846/47 (the last two under Fourierism), flourished modestly (seventy to eighty members) as long as members agreed on its wage-paying, cooperative (not communist) system. The importation of Fourier's communal economy yielded early enthusiasm, but its detailed regulations were inorganically imposed and soon rejected, absent evolution from the practices and values of the group. Commonality of vision was fractured and incoming members fractured it further; the group disbanded within a year of its main phalanstery building catching fire.

In brief, though the founders of these communities may have had clear ideals, member disagreement about them or about daily living undermined the endeavors. Loss of situatedness in ontology, purpose, or practice was an effective raveler. Communities of substantial regulation did little better, however, as high discipline maintains routine but hobbles individual contribution and

10. Holloway, *Utopian Communities in America,* p. 122.

community adaptability. The late-seventeenth-century religious/communist Labadist community practiced strict asceticism, separation but equality of the sexes, a rigid daily agricultural routine and regulation so careful as to account for each slice of bread. Their leader, Peter Sluyter, could not, however, keep up the requisite self-denial, allowing himself tobacco, a hearth, and finally the slave trade. In 1698, the community switched to private ownership. It disbanded after Sluyter died (1722), having failed to develop an economy in which individuals could innovate (to suit conditions) and any governance procedures where individuals other than Sluyter could step up and lead.

In some contrast to communities that either lacked commonality or strictly imposed it were associations that agreed on vision and daily praxis yet fostered individual initiative. Several of these emerged from the pietist traditions, which as a matter of theological principle uphold the importance of each person (and her personal relationship with God) along with commitment to the church community. The most impressive of these are the Inspirationists of the Amana communities, which began in the early 1840s and whose members remain together today in a community of roughly 1,400 persons.

Of German pietist tradition,[11] they were devoted to study, sobriety, self-examination, and separation from the world, but not asceticism.[12] Children of both sexes were educated until age sixteen in reading, writing, math, music, and practical skills. Quiet religious meetings and the reading of Scripture and Amana religious publications were frequent. Taking the Eucharist was rare and performed only when one of the group's leaders — God's "instruments" — felt it appropriate. The annual self-critique, conducted in small groups, held the society's values in place, but if a group was not ready, self-critique was not forced but postponed until it was. Applicants to the community were required to provide recommendations, which the society solicited, and then waited for a two-year probationary period.

Religious life and membership were, then, communal and regulated but not punitive or imposed. Importantly, the community encouraged members to contribute ideas and innovations to community living and so adapted to economic change, agreeing, for instance, to industrialize their production. They chose a communal rather than individual-enterprise model, grew or made most of what was needed, and shared common property (eating hall,

11. Following the teachings of Philipp Spener, Eberhard L. Gruber, and Johann F. Rock.

12. The Amanians ate simply but well; marriage was not uncommon, and families lived in houses of their own, though wedlock was not considered especially laudable, young couples having to work their way back into the higher spiritual strata.

factories, school, store, and tavern). But when it was productive to do so, they also bought and sold products from other farms and towns. All members received an annual sum for personal items and purchased what they liked. Government was representative; each member had a voice.[13] Women ran the committee for household management; those over thirty who were unmarried or widowed could also vote. By 1908, the Amana Society had 26,000 acres of land, 1,800 members, and more than $1.8 million in assets.[14]

Amana's decision in 1932 to change its communal economy into a joint-stock, profit-sharing corporation further evinced its ability to adapt — to deal with the collapsing, Depression-era farm market and to allow individuals to thrive. Their description of this change flags the importance of both the commons and individuals: "What finally propelled the change was a strong desire on the part of residents to maintain their community. By 1932, the communal way of life was seen as a barrier to achieving individual goals, so rather than leave or watch their children leave, they changed. They established the Amana Society. . . . Private enterprise was encouraged. The Amana Church was maintained."[15] As an example of personal initiative, when George Foerstner recognized the need for beverage coolers that emerged with the end of Prohibition, he used his Amana savings to start the Electric Equipment Company in 1934 and sold the company to Amana two years later. In 1947 it began manufacturing and selling the first upright freezers, and in 1949 it was sold to an investment group organized by Foerstner. Under the name of Amana Refrigeration, Inc., it made refrigerators and air conditioners until 1965, when it was sold to the Raytheon Corporation.

Perhaps the most important communities after Amana to meld communal living and individual initiative were the Ephrata Cloister, the Harmony Society of George Rapp, and the Shaker community. Though famed for their regulated daily living, the Shakers developed an impressive range of industries and inventions to which members could devote their ingenuity and talents. They were an ascetic, celibate community of men and women[16] grouped into "families" and "societies." Family elders constituted the governing bodies that held nearly absolute control, appointing the various society officers and their

13. Thirteen annually elected trustees elected a president and administered the community's secular affairs; decisions required unanimous trustee consent.

14. B. Shambaugh, *Amana: The Community of True Inspiration* (Iowa City: State Historical Society of Iowa, 1908), p. 89.

15. http://amanacolonies.com/pages/about-amana-colonies/history.php.

16. After their belief in the bisexuality of God, as both men and women are made in his image.

own successors. Nearly every aspect of life — from what to do each hour to what color to paint the bed frames — was controlled. The careful admissions process involved a year of preparation; upon acceptance — which radically was granted to Jewish and black applicants — property was relinquished, marital ties severed, children given to communal care,[17] and the complete confession of sin was begun, a process that often took several years.

During its peak (1830-1860), the Shaker community had five thousand people. Though members did leave, the community continued to attract new ones. Its appeal, despite strict daily regulation, was owed in part to the religious fervor of the Second Great Awakening, in part to its quiet modeling of abolitionist and antiwar ethics, and in part to the opportunities it offered for inventiveness. The Shakers invented or substantially improved tools such as the saw, mower-and-reaper, printing press, planting machine, tongue-and-groove machine, pea-shelling machine, metallic pen, cut nails, and spinning heads. The quality of their crops, medicinal herbs, and seeds was known nationally, as was the design and construction of their furniture, which remains of substantial value today. Shaker numbers began to dwindle in the late nineteenth century owing to a decline of revivalist fervor and competition from mass-produced products. Unlike the Amanians, the Shakers were unwilling or unable to incorporate technological innovation into their production, narrowing their economy and the arenas for personal talent. In 1900, roughly one thousand Shakers remained; by 1940, about one hundred. In 2012, the Sabbathday Lake Shaker Village remained the last group, with three members.

The Ephrata Cloister (1735), our second example of a communal/individual meld, was a celibate community of male and female German pietists, ascetics who observed a strict daily routine and the Saturday Sabbath. They foresightfully set no date for their millenarian hopes, which allowed them to continue without disappointment for nearly two centuries. In spite of strict regulations, their industriousness and creativity were directed into farming and industry, and when their efforts produced substantial, tempting wealth, the members unusually shifted to less remunerative but nonetheless creativity-encouraging religious projects. Commitment to their underlying vision helped the community survive the scandal of their leader's inappropriate interest in the group's young female members, and the group successfully redirected their energies into the publication of beautifully crafted religious books and church music. That is, communal purpose gave them the trust to endure scandal

---

17. Children and parents saw each other once a year in the presence of an elder.

but also to encourage personal creativity. In 1786, the cloister moved from its communal economy to private property ownership and slowly away from its mandate to celibacy. In 1814, Ephrata was incorporated as the German Seventh Day Baptist Church; congregations worship still today, though the last member of the cloister itself died in 2008.

A last example of melding shared vision/practices with individual initiative is the Harmony Society, founded by George Rapp in 1805. Composed of (German Lutheran) Quietist farmers, it was not ascetic and adopted a communal economy not from ideology but for pragmatic reasons. By agreement, they adopted celibacy in 1807, and in 1818 burned the records of each person's contribution to the common pool. Likely because of this trust, the group, like the Ephrata Cloister, survived scandal. In 1831, Bernard Mueller persuaded a portion of the community to readopt marriage and other worldly pursuits. By agreement again, a third of the group left with a goodwill gift of $105,000 — without damage to the founding community. Because of the group's commitment to theological tenets, economic principles, and good governance (by Rapp and his adopted son Friederich), little need for daily, top-down regulations emerged, leaving the Rappites to more or less govern themselves. Though millenarian disappointment and Rapp's death at age ninety began a gradual diminishment in members, the group lasted until the start of the twentieth century.

Amana, the Shaker community, the Ephrata Cloister, and the Harmony Society for a time got right the meld of individual contribution and commitment to group — or at least got it right for their time and purposes. They seemed also to know why they had developed it. A certain self-awareness about visionary purpose and pragmatic practice appears to have contributed to community endurance. It was only, for instance, when the Rappites' worldview itself collapsed that they lost their reason for remaining together. They lived in expectation of the second coming, and when it didn't arrive, the group lost anything to be committed to.

Similar fates befell other groups, suggesting that it is not only separability-amid-situatedness that is important but also the ontological framework that supports it. As this faded, so did the communities. The Bethel (Missouri) and Aurora (Oregon) communities (1844-1881), founded by Wilhelm Keil, began with agreement on values and practices yet also offered possibilities for personal initiative. They endured for two generations, developing a prosperous, mixed communal-private economy[18] with light quotidian regulation. Over

---

18. The mixed economy required that each person work in the group's farming and indus-

time, however, they lost sight of an overarching vision beyond daily prosperity, and both dissolved after Keil's death.

The Zoarites (1817), like the Harmony Rappites composed of German Quietists, were on firm economic footing after 1827, when the new Erie Canal brought a boom in trade. In the early 1830s, they developed a system of governance involving elected trustees and appointed supervisors, all accountable to the group's adult members. The community instituted a one-year probationary term for applicants who, on acceptance, donated their money, but not property, to the common pool. They had Sunday meetings but no public prayer, baptism, Eucharist, ceremonies, or church hierarchy. In short, the group had substantial agreement on church, economic, and quotidian practices as well as on governance that brought all persons into the decision-making process. But over time, as was true of the Bethel and Aurora communities, the religious vision became increasingly amorphous, which, historian Mark Holloway suggests, led to the community's gradual decline after eighty-one years.[19]

The Oneida community, in spite of its fame for unorthodox sexual relations, had a similar trajectory. It began with John Humphrey Noyes's efforts to improve upon marriage, which yielded, on his view, multiple (stressful) pregnancies for women and high infant mortality, yet little physical outlet for romantic love. His solution, which he grounded in Scripture and called male continence and complex marriage, allowed consensual sexual relations within a covenantal community (monogamy was frowned upon as selfish) and prescribed *coitus interruptus* for all occasions not intended for pregnancy.[20]

Noyes's community of "Perfectionists" (1848) thrived for several decades with ample room for individual initiative in its economy, governance, and intellectual life. Committee meetings were open to all; proposals were implemented only if they earned general approval. Long-term projects were determined at the annual meeting; all could propose them. Women had rights equal to those of men; talented young people were sent outside the community for special training, including to university. Disputes were resolved through

---

trial projects but also allowed for private housing and gardens, marriage, change of occupation, purchases with money earned from work in free hours.

19. Holloway, *Utopian Communities in America*, p. 99.

20. Progeny was to be arranged by community elders "to produce the usual number of offspring to which people in the middle class are able to afford judicial moral and spiritual care, with the advantage of a liberal education." See J. H. Noyes, *Essay on Scientific Propagation* (Oneida, N.Y., 1875).

mutual criticism, where faults and merits were discussed with a small group of trusted friends yet without authoritarian or punitive mechanism. By 1878, the group had grown to over three hundred members — farmers, lawyers, tradespersons, clergy, physicians, and teachers — who employed nonmember workers as well. It produced its own newspaper, the *Circular*, and the central Manor House had central heating, baths, an up-to-date kitchen, and a library of 5,000 volumes, including works of Darwin, Aldous Huxley, and Herbert Spencer.

Yet, for the later generations of Oneidans, the biblical grounding for the community's practices and thus its undergirding vision faded. Some found the group's sexual arrangements too unorthodox; others expressed frank agnosticism. Dissent worsened when Noyes attempted to transfer leadership to his unpopular son. The group reinstituted marriage in 1879 and shifted from a communal economy to joint-stock ownership in 1881. Unlike members of the Amana colony, who retained their religious vision and adapted their economy and inventions around it, the Oneidans lost their grounding vision, and families started to leave.

In sum, the covenantal communities of greatest endurance and vitality were those with agreed-upon (sometimes strict) governance and quotidian practices yet with outlets for individual initiative — all of which were supported by a clear ontological/theological frame (Amana, the Shaker community, and Ephrata). These groups were known locally and at times nationally for their skills and honest dealings, and their standard of living was often higher than that of their neighbors. "Nor was the communal life dull. The variety of employment, personal interest in every aspect of the community, and the opportunity for group amusements were features unknown to, and envied by, the isolated farmer. So much so that the hotels kept at Amana, Zoar, and some of the Shaker societies were frequently used by neighbours for their pleasure as well as for business."[21]

At least two communities with severe constraints on personal life (Ephrata, Shaker community) were nonetheless among the most enduring, as long as outlets remained for what members produced, invented, or refined — religious books and music for Ephrata, a wide range of tools and furniture for the Shakers. When these outlets constricted in the Shaker community, neither faith and discipline nor daily/governance practices protected it from the lure of opportunities elsewhere. Where these did not constrict, as with the Amana colony, the community endured.

21. Holloway, *Utopian Communities in America*, p. 224.

*   *   *

I suggest this understanding of the successes and failures of American covenantal communities as a hypothesis; other socioeconomic, political, and religious factors were no doubt involved. One might argue against my idea that short-lived communities did not have the time to strengthen ideals or develop avenues for individual initiative. That is, the lack of a communal-individual meld may have been the result of quick demise, not its cause. But this leaves open the question of short duration — why did they quickly founder? And it is difficult to argue that lack of agreement on vision/practices and lack of individual opportunity had nothing to do with community endurance.

At present, a range of economists and political scientists seems to think such triune commitment — to vision, practices for the commons, and individual development — important for real possibilities of greater well-being. Their approach might be summed up as follows: capitalist markets rely basically on capital/credit, material resources, human resources (skills, information), and their transfer. These may be organized both for individual initiative and profit and for the structures that allow individuals to become who they are. This is worth doing because no individual thrives alone but rather in a mix with what she is given by other persons and her educational, socioeconomic, and political networks.

This approach would not change market relations (supply and demand, etc.) but *would change relations within the market, prioritizing them*. This change, a relational settlement of individual distinction and the covenantality of our circumstances, would alter economic transactions by configuring them as part of common goals, negotiated means, and mutual regard. As Christian Felber notes, echoing Genovesi and Smith, the first principles of economics are "dignity, solidarity, sustainability, justice, and democracy; as well as values which allow relationships to succeed: trust, empathy, appreciation, cooperation and sharing."[22]

What follows are a few examples drawn from economic and political writers and community and religious leaders.[23] Many build on the well-known

---

22. C. Felber, *Change Everything: Creating an Economy for the Common Good* (London: Zed Books, 2015), Kindle location 3296; similarly, "It is not," Baron Robert and Edward Skidelsky write, "human beings who need adapting to the market; it is the market that needs adapting to human beings"; R. Skidelsky and E. Skidelsky, *How Much Is Enough? Money and the Good Life* (New York: Other Press, 2012), p. 158.

23. Among them, R. Blank and W. McGurn, *Is the Market Moral?* (Washington, D.C.: Brookings Institution, 2004); L. Bruni and S. Zamagni, *Civil Economy: Efficiency, Equity, Public*

notion of stakeholder-ship and subsidiarity in politics and economics. Subsidiarity here is meant in its basic suggestion that societal responsibilities be distributed to the institutions best able to shoulder them — industrial, educational, labor, and other civil society associations as well as local, regional, and national government. This distribution creates not only vertical administration between local and central powers but also horizontal networks to address what small communities alone cannot (negotiations with foreign countries, funding large research hospitals).

This was the practice for much of American development, as Tocqueville, among others, has noted: "The township is the first in order, then the county, and lastly the state. . . . Town meetings are to liberty what primary schools are to science; they bring it within the people's reach, they teach men how to use and how to enjoy it."[24] But the idea reaches back to antiquity, for instance, in biblical wariness of the Mesopotamian and Egyptian centralized empires and the introduction of an early form of federalism, each state located within a unified nation governed by a limited monarch who is not to consider himself better than his fellow Israelites (Deut. 17:20). Today, a neo-Tocquevillian distribution of societal tasks might better foster civil society *and* markets while a lack of subsidiarity hobbles community ability to meet local needs and renders large governments, no longer in conversation with regional or sector-wide institutions, unable to recognize local innovations, capacities, and requirements.

The reader will be familiar with some of the proposals below, as the point here is not that these suggestions are *un*known but rather that they *are* known.

Happiness (Bern: Peter Lang, 2007); D. Foley, *Adam's Fallacy: A Guide to Economic Theology* (Cambridge: Harvard University Press, Belknap Press, 2006); W. Greider, *One World, Ready or Not: The Manic Logic of Global Capitalism* (New York: Simon and Schuster, Touchstone, 1997); D. Hausman and M. McPherson, *Economic Analysis and Moral Philosophy* (Cambridge: Cambridge University Press, 1996); D. Hicks and M. Valeri, eds., *Global Neighbors: Christian Faith and Moral Obligation in Today's Economy* (Grand Rapids: Eerdmans, 2008); M. Lind, *The Next American Nation: The New Nationalism and the Fourth American Revolution* (New York: Free Press, 1995); J. Madrick, *Why Economics Grow: The Forces That Shape Prosperity and How We Can Get Them Working Again* (New York: Basic Books, Century Foundation Book, 2002); J. Milbank and A. Pabst, *The Politics of Virtue: Britain and the Post-Liberal Future* (forthcoming); D. Seebeck and T. Stoner, *My Business, My Mission: Fighting Global Poverty through Partnerships* (Grand Rapids: Faith Alive Christian Resources, 2009); Skidelsky and Skidelsky, *How Much is Enough?*; J. Stiglitz, *The Price of Inequality: How Today's Divided Society Endangers Our Future* (New York: Norton, 2013). I would also like to thank John Ashmen, Greg Boyd, Tony Campolo, Joel Hunter, Tim McFarlane, Ed Morgan, and Tri Robinson for showing me how these ideas work on the ground.

24. A. de Tocqueville, *Democracy in America*, bk. I, pp. 59, 78; retrieved from http://www2 .hn.psu.edu/faculty/jmanis/toqueville/dem-in-america1.pdf.

Yet, under our present separability, we don't quite believe — in the way we believe we breathe — that accounting for distinction and interrelatedness yields better outcomes than the alternatives. As ethicist Lewis Mudge and others have noted, many of these suggestions have been discussed at various high-level meetings around the world, with disappointing results. It's not that the economic suggestions are lacking but that the ontology is, and thus political will and implementation.

One political idea is to bring democratically run civil associations (professional, labor, educational, religious)   those that democratically represent their members and are accountable to them — into political debate at the structural level, and in some instances into policy making. The aim is to get out of the agonistic frame by bringing groups *regularly* into policy conversation so that they don't write each other off as the Other but learn why others hold the positions that they do. Felber proposes community conventions nationwide to discuss basic legislative priorities for the nation and to vote periodically on basic plans for finance, education, public services, etc. After all, he notes, "In a genuine democracy the interests of the sovereign people and its representatives are identical."[25]

This integrative policy structure is in some sense the political equivalent of stakeholder economics, which integrates into corporate planning each new proposal's broad consequences (to management, employees, surrounding communities, environment, etc.). Such integration entails a more broadly based sharing of risk and reward. This might include, for instance, closing loopholes that allow firms to pay little in taxes earmarked for public benefit (education, infrastructure). Such loophole closing would spread the costs and benefits of these projects among citizens, small businesses, and larger corporations. The situation that Mark Baldassare found, where well-off suburban residents were "pessimistic, distrustful, unwilling to tax themselves to pay for services,"[26] should be simply embarrassing. Broad-based sharing of risk and reward would mandate business contribution — to medical clinics or parks, for instance, commensurate with profit gains and losses — to the localities that sustain them. It would require corporations to contribute substantially to the cleanup of their externalities (e.g., pollution). In the field of finance, it might call also for linking managers' profits to the gains and losses of their clients or to manager contribution to the gross domestic product.

25. Felber, *Change Everything*, Kindle location 3370.
26. M. Baldassare, *Trouble in Paradise: The Suburban Transformation in America* (New York: Columbia University Press, 1986), pp. 101-68.

A related idea, proposed by John Milbank and Adrian Pabst,[27] is the development of regional stock markets whose lending is tailored to regional industries and whose money flows are somewhat shielded from global money speculation. (These flows themselves might be more productive if they did not favor short-term speculation over society-building projects such as infrastructure development, scientific research, etc. Various proposals since the 1970s include the Tobin and Spahn taxes to prevent currency speculation, taxes on financial transactions, and Special Drawing Rights [SDRs], the latter two aimed at raising funds to assist developing economies. As these have been extensively discussed, I won't elaborate on them here.)

Regional stock markets might work in tandem with banks modeled after state banks and credit unions. Each stock market and bank would be dedicated to the needs of a region or economic sector made up of professional or industry associations. Associations would train individual businesses in financial stewardship, in how to benefit from stock market investments and bank loans, in best practices, and in product, labor, and environmental standards. As membership would convey benefits and services, it would be attractive to individual businesses. In turn, industry associations might oblige individual businesses to participate (as they can, given resources) in relevant societal projects, from apprenticeship programs to pollution reduction. Importantly, associations would coordinate programs among schools, technical colleges, and businesses as well as provide job placement services for graduates and those who retrain later in life. They might assist also in welfare-to-work programs where aid recipients are trained in school and/or job settings, after which each would be required to take a job or lose benefits.

On Milbank and Pabst's idea, several associations would operate in each business sector to avoid monopoly, and membership in at least one would be required for a business operating license. Adherence to high standards and responsibility for externalities would garner awards, preferred product labels, and preferred status for loans from the banks working with the industry associations. Mudge adds that corporate annual reports review not only profits but also the company's impact on health, safety, the environment, local household income, education, etc.[28] — an idea echoed in Felber's Common Good Balance Sheet, which assesses enterprises for their production of socially useful products and services, contribution to public services, cooperation with

27. Milbank and Pabst, *The Politics of Virtue.*
28. L. Mudge, *We Can Make the World Economy a Sustainable Global Home* (Grand Rapids: Eerdmans, 2014), Kindle locations 1697-1698.

other enterprises and educational institutions, and environmental protection. "Economic success," he writes,

> would no longer be measured by (monetary) exchange value indicators in terms of means (profit, return on investment), but rather by (non-monetary) use value indicators in terms of goals (satisfaction of needs, quality of life, the common good). At the macro level (of the national economy) the GDP, as a success index, would be replaced by the Common Good Product. At the meso level (the level of enterprises) the financial balance sheet would give way to the Common Good Balance Sheet. At the micro level, the success of investments would be measured in the ethical instead of financial return on investment, and applications for loans would be subject to a Common Good audit.

High marks on the Common Good Balance Sheet would include lower rates on taxes, loan interest, and customs as well as preferential status in public project bidding and research grants. "In this way ethical, environmentally friendly and regional products and services would become less expensive than unethically produced ones, and ethical enterprises would assert themselves on the market."[29]

On the sector-tailored financial plan, these sector banks would share financial risks and rewards along with their investors. Working within a sector would allow them to offer sector-specific incentives (for research, for instance) and tailor loans to sector-specific needs (e.g., sector-specific safety gear). Having loan applicants already trained (by the sector-wide associations) in financial stewardship and best practices would curb irresponsible lending especially in combination with banking regulations that favor societally-productive projects over high-risk speculation.

Related ideas for the finance industry are those discussed since the 2008 crash, such as raising the reserve requirements and limiting leveraging or the amount of investing that can be done with borrowed money. Another suggestion is forbidding headquarter shifts to no/low-tax countries so that corporations can operate in and impact several nations yet pay taxes to none. Yet another is the development of loan repayment schedules that convert debt into equity, such as lease-to-buy programs. Still others are arrangements that, in cases of repayment failure, avoid foreclosure and eviction, given their devastating societal and economic effects. Israeli foreclosure law, for instance, in

---

29. Felber, *Change Everything,* Kindle locations 3301-3315.

2008 was amended to require that banks, in demanding foreclosure, find reasonable alternate housing[30] for families, giving banks considerable incentive to work out a solution where families stay in their homes. Against the concerns of critics, Israeli banks, following the change in law, remained solidly profitable.

For developed economies that are finding it difficult to offer full employment, Robert and Edward Skidelsky suggest a society-wide basic income commensurate with unemployment benefits and limited to certain expenditures like food, housing, education, and start-up investment. This would allow those who work less (those caring for children or elderly parents, for example) and those who work in societally valuable but low-paying positions (teaching, high-quality crafts) to do so, easing overall unemployment. They suggest it would also give the poor and working classes a leg up, especially as this basic income would be funneled into areas like education and business start-up. Felber adds that a basic income could also be used to finance time off from work for all citizens for one year in every ten, also easing unemployment, on his estimate, by 10 percent.[31]

Proposals for funding a basic-income program vary, and include taxes on luxury goods, capital gains, and investment transactions; yields from governmental but privately managed investment trusts; and sale of pollution permits.[32] Economist Robert Frank suggests a tax on luxury goods specifically to fund common goods (pollution and traffic reduction, city parks, better policing, medical research, retirement insurances, etc.).[33] While there is likely little political will in the United States for this sort of funding policy, perhaps the idea could be reworked with an emphasis on a basic income for education/job training, health care, and business development.

Among the gravest economic problems internationally is the well-known race-to-the-bottom in the developed world in combination with the decimation of agriculture and industry in developing nations. On one hand, low-tech and increasingly high-tech jobs flow to low-wage countries, destroying the incomes and working conditions of the middle classes in developed ones. On the other, developed countries flood developing ones with agricultural and manufactured goods, hobbling the development of both in poorer nations. Yet

---

30. By law, "reasonability" is determined not by the foreclosing bank but by the execution of judgments registrar, a person qualified to serve as a magistrates court judge and appointed by the minister of justice upon the recommendation of a statutory appointments committee.

31. Felber, *Change Everything,* Kindle location 3356.

32. Skidelsky and Skidelsky, *How Much Is Enough?* p. 200.

33. R. Frank, *Luxury Fever: Money and Happiness in an Era of Excess* (Princeton: Princeton University Press, 2000), pp. 211-16.

economies that are today "developed" grew under eighteenth- and nineteenth-century protectionist policies, which suggests that we consider Michael Lind's proposal that firms in developed economies invest in developing ones but must also sell there.[34] This would allow those firms to make substantial profits and bring jobs and technological skills to emerging economies, yet it would preserve agricultural and manufacturing jobs in developed nations, thus maintaining middle-class incomes and conditions.

These suggestions are but a brief indication of the ideas that have emerged from relationality and reciprocal consideration-worthiness. Many others are under discussion; some will be shelved for poor results, and all need modification, combination, and tailoring to specific circumstances. Ones with productive outcomes should become "a benign contagion of good practice."[35]

At bottom, domestic and (linked) global economic problems should be addressed as were the issues in the logging-firm example at the beginning of this book. Beginning with the recognition that all parties have an interest in producers, consumers, and resources surviving to the next generation, what would the outcomes look like if all involved believe — again, in the way we believe we breathe — that we find out "why the other side is for the other side" and take that as worthy of consideration. No one leaves the discussion until all have contributed substantially to the solution and until an idea is developed where no one's concerns are abandoned.

But this returns us to a key tenet of this book: ontology affects conduct. Given the present focus on separability, we need a way back to the evolutionary, ontological, and theological principle of distinction-amid-relation — *to an ontology where the proposals above do not look naïve or strange* but rather reasonable for short- and long-term development. It was only a few decades ago that a Republican president wrote, "Should any political party attempt to abolish social security, unemployment insurance and eliminate labor laws and farm programs, you would not hear of that party again in our political history. There is a tiny splinter group, of course, that believes you can do these things.... Their number is negligible and they are stupid."[36]

---

34. M. Lind, *The Next American Nation: The New Nationalism and the Fourth American Revolution* (New York: Free Press, 1995).

35. Milbank and Pabst, *The Politics of Virtue*.

36. *The Papers of Dwight David Eisenhower*, vol. 15, *The Presidency: The Middle Way Part VI; Crises Abroad, Party Problems at Home; September 1954 to December 1954*, ch. 13, p. 1386; retrieved from http://www.usmessageboard.com/threads/dwight-d-eisenhowers-1954-letter-to -his-brother-edgar.266267/. Robert and Edward Skidelsky describe similar policies in postwar Britain, which saw "the maintenance of continuous full employment, reduction in inequality

Distinction-amid-relation may in the end be the easier path, as it seems to go with the grain of the way things are — or at least that's the idea of recent biology and in many of the cultures in which human beings live:

- Zoroastrianism: "Do not do unto others whatever is injurious to yourself" (Shayast-na-Shayast 13:29).
- Buddhism: "Treat not others in ways that you yourself would find hurtful" (*Udana-Varga* 5:18).
- Jainism: "Just as sorrow or pain is not desirable to you, so it is to all which breathe, exist, live or have any essence of life" (H. Jacobi, *Ācāranga Sūtra, Jain Sutras Part I, Sacred Books of the East* [1884], vol. 22, sutra 155-56).
- Jainism: "One should treat all creatures in the world as one would like to be treated" (Mahavira, Sutrakrtanga).
- Sanskrit: "Hence, (keeping these in mind), by self-control and by making *dharma* (right conduct) your main focus, treat others as you treat yourself" (*Mahābhārata Shānti-Parva* 167:9).
- Baha'i: "And if thine eyes be turned towards justice, choose thou for thy neighbor that which thou choosest for thyself" (*The Hidden Words of Bahá'u'lláh,* part II).
- Confucianism: "Zi Gong asked, saying, 'Is there one word that may serve as a rule of practice for all one's life?' The Master said, 'Is not reciprocity such a word?'" (*The Analects, Wei Ling Gong* 15.24).
- Confucianism: "Do not do to others what you do not want done to yourself" (Confucius, *Analects* 15:23).
- Isocrates: "Do not do to others that which angers you when they do it to you" (*Nicocles or the Cyprians,* Isocrates 3.61; see also, 1.14; 2.24; 4.81).
- Hinduism: "This is the sum of duty: do not do to others what would cause pain if done to you" (*Mahabharata* 5:1517).
- Taoism: "Regard your neighbor's gain as your own gain, and your neighbor's loss as your own loss" (*T'ai Shang Kan Ying P'ien* 213-218).
- Islam: "None of you [truly] believes until he wishes for his brother what he wishes for himself" (*An-Nawawi's Forty Hadiths* 13, p. 56).
- Islam: "Seek for mankind that of which you are desirous for yourself, that you may be a believer" (Sukhanan-i-Muhammad, Teheran, 1938).

---

through progressive income taxes, a big extension of social security and the preservation of peace. Increases in productivity enabled real wages to rise and working hours to fall, with only very moderate inflation. . . . There were advances in health, education, women's rights." Skidelsky and Skidelsky, *How Much Is Enough?* p. 191.

- Hebrew Bible: "Love your neighbor as yourself" (Leviticus 19:18).
- Talmud: "What is hateful to you, do not do to your fellow: this is the whole Torah; the rest is the explanation; go and learn" (*b. Shabbat* 31a).
- Christian Bible: "So in everything, do to others what you would have them do to you, for this sums up the Law and the Prophets" (Matthew 7:12).
- Christian Bible: "Do to others as you would have them do to you" (Luke 6:31).

Bibliography

Abram, D. *The Spell of the Sensuous: Perception and Language in a More-Than-Human World.* New York: Vintage Books, 1996.

Adams, J. Letter to Mercy Warren. In J. Adams, S. Adams, and J. Warren, *Warren-Adams Letters,* edited by W. C. Ford. Vols. 1-2. Boston: Massachusetts Historical Society, 1917; original 1776.

Adams, J., S. Adams, and J. Warren. *Warren-Adams Letters.* Edited by W. C. Ford. Vols. 1-2. Boston: Massachusetts Historical Society, 1917.

Adams, J. L. *Voluntary Associations: Socio-Cultural Analyses and Theological Interpretation.* Edited by J. R. Engel. Chicago: Exploration Press, 1986.

Adams, N., and C. Elliott. "Ethnography Is Dogmatics: Making Description Central to Systematic Theology." *Scottish Journal of Theology* 53 (2000): 339-64.

Adams, S. "Extract from a Letter from the Southward." In *The Writings of Samuel Adams,* edited by H. Cushing, vol. 4. New York: Putnam, 1904.

————. *The Writings of Samuel Adams.* Edited by H. Cushing. Vols. 1-4. New York: Octagon Books, 1968.

Agamben, G. *The Time That Remains: A Commentary on the Letter to the Romans.* Translated by P. Dailey. Stanford: Stanford University Press, 2005. Original *Il tempo che resta: Un commento alla lettera ai Romani.* Bollati Boringhieri, 2000.

————. *The Kingdom and the Glory: For a Theological Genealogy of Economy and Government.* Stanford: Stanford University Press, 2011.

Agrippa. Letters of Agrippa I-XI. Letter VII. In *The Anti-Federalist,* edited by H. Storing, pp. 227-53. Chicago: University of Chicago Press, 1985; original 1787.

Albanese, C. "Forum." *Religion and American Culture: A Journal of Interpretation* 1, no. 2 (Summer 1991).

Aldred, R. "Freedom." In *Prophetic Evangelicals,* edited by B. Benson, M. Berry, and P. Heltzel, pp. 143-59. Grand Rapids: Eerdmans, 2012.

Allen, J. *American Alarm . . . for the Rights and Liberties of the People.* Boston: D. Kneeland and N. Davis, 1773.

Allison, D., Jr. *The End of the Ages Has Come: An Early Interpretation of the Passion and Resurrection of Jesus.* Minneapolis: Fortress, 1985.

―――. *Constructing Jesus: Memory, Imagination, and History.* Grand Rapids: Baker Academic, 2010.

Alperowitz, G. "Building a Living Democracy." *Sojourners* 19, no. 6 (July 1990): 11-23.

Alter, R. *The Art of Biblical Narrative.* New York: Basic Books, 1981, 2011.

―――. *The Five Books of Moses: A Translation with Commentary.* New York: Norton, 2008.

Althusius, J. *The Politics of Johannes Althusius: An Abridged Translation of the Third Edition of* Politica methodice digesta, atque exemplis sacris et profanis illustrata. Translated by F. Carney. Boston: Beacon Press, 1964; original 1603. Retrieved from http://www.constitution.org/alth/alth.htm.

Altizer, T. J. "The Impossible Possibility of Ethics." In *Saintly Influence: Edith Wyschogrod and the Possibilities of Philosophy of Religion,* edited by E. Boynton and M. Kavka, pp. 31-47. New York: Fordham University Press, 2009.

Altmann, A. *The Meaning of Jewish Existence: Theological Essays, 1930-1939.* Edited by A. Ivry. Translated by E. Ehrlich and L. Ehrlich. Hanover, N.H.: University Press of New England, 1991.

Anatolios, K. *Retrieving Nicaea: The Development and Meaning of the Trinitarian Doctrine.* Grand Rapids: Baker Academic, 2011.

Anderson, B. *Imagined Communities.* London: Verso, 1991.

Appleby, J. *Inheriting the Revolution: The First Generation of Americans.* Cambridge: Harvard University Press, Belknap Press, 2000.

Aquinas, T. *Scriptum super libros sententiarum magistri Petri Lombardi.* Edited by R. P. Mandonnet. Paris: Lethielleux, 1929.

―――. *Summa Theologica.* Translated by Fathers of the Dominican English Province. Vols. 1-5. Westminster, Md.: Christian Classics, 1948; original 1265-1274.

―――. *Quaestiones disputatae de potentia Dei.* Edited by P. Pession. Turin: Marietti, 1965; original 1259-1268.

―――. *In librum Boethii de Trinitate expositio.* 1992; original ca. 1256-1259. See q. 5, art. 4, co. 2.

Arendt, H. *The Origin of Totalitarianism.* New York: Harcourt Brace, 1973.

Aristotle. *The Nichomachean Ethics* [ἠθικὰ Νικομάχεια]. Edited by L. Brown. Translated by D. Ross. New York: Oxford University Press, 2009.

Arnold, E. *Why We Live in Community.* Farmington, Pa.: Plough Publishing, 1995.

―――. *God's Revolution: Justice, Community, and the Coming Kingdom.* Farmington, Pa.: Plough Publishing, 2002.

Arrighi, A. *Adam Smith in Beijing: Lineages of the Twenty-First Century.* London: Verso, 2007.

Asad, T., W. Brown, J. Butler, and S. Mahmood. *Is Critique Secular? Blasphemy, Injury, and Free Speech.* Berkeley: University of California Press, 2009.

Astell, M. *Political Writings.* Edited by P. Springborg. Cambridge Texts in the History of Political Thought. New York: Cambridge University Press, 1996; original 1694-1705.

Athanasopoulos, C., and C. Schneider, eds. *Divine Essence and Divine Energies: Ecu-*

menical Reflections on the Presence of God in Eastern Orthodoxy. Cambridge: James Clarke, 2013.

Augustine. *On Christian Doctrine (De doctrina Christiana).* Original 397/426. Retrieved from http://www9.georgetown.edu/faculty/jod/augustine/ddc1.html.

———. *Soliloquies.* Translated by R. Cleveland. Boston: Little, Brown, 1910; original 386/387. Retrieved from http://files.libertyfund.org/files/1153/0579_Bk.pdf.

———. *De vera religione.* In *Augustine: Earlier Writings,* translated by J. Burleigh. Philadelphia: Westminster, 1953; original 390.

———. *The Trinity (De Trinitate).* Translated by E. Hill. New York: New City Press, 1991.

———. *On the Trinity (De Trinitate).* In *The Nicene and Post-Nicene Fathers,* edited by P. Schaff and H. Wace, ser. 1, vol. 3. Peabody, Mass.: Hendrickson, 1994.

———. *The Trinity (De Trinitate).* In *Works of St. Augustine,* translated by E. Hill and J. E. Rotelle. Hyde Park, N.Y.: New City Press, 2012.

Awad, N. "Between Subordination and Koinonia: Toward a New Reading of the Cappadocian Theology." *Modern Theology* 23, no. 2 (2007): 181-204.

Bacon, F. *The Advancement of Learning and the New Atlantis.* Oxford: Clarendon, 1974; original 1605/1626.

———. *The Essays or Councils Civil and Moral.* Oxford: Oxford University Press, 1999; original 1625.

———. *The New Organum.* Edited by M. Silverthorne and L. Jardine. Cambridge: Cambridge University Press, 2000; original 1620.

Bacote, V. "Creation." In *Prophetic Evangelicals,* edited by B. Benson, M. Berry, and P. Heltzel, pp. 50-58. Grand Rapids: Eerdmans, 2012.

Badiou, A. *Saint Paul: The Foundation of Universalism.* Translated by R. Brassier. Stanford: Stanford University Press, 2003.

Badiou, A., and S. Žižek. *Philosophy in the Present.* Edited by P. Engelman. Translated by P. Thomas and A. Toscano. Cambridge: Polity Press, 2010.

Baggot, M. "The Positive Potential of Religion for Democracy." May 5, 2014. Retrieved from http://www.telospress.com/the-positive-potential-of-religion-for-democracy/.

Bailyn, B. "Religion and Revolution: Three Biographical Studies." *Perspectives in American History* 4 (1970): 140-43.

Baker, A. "Violence and the Trinity: A Wesleyan Reading of Milbank's Augustinianism." *Wesleyan Theological Journal* 36, no. 1 (Spring 2001): 113-33.

———. "Poesis and Immediacy: A Reply to Davis." *Political Theology* 10, no. 1 (2009): 167-76.

Baker, D. *The Subject of Desire: Petrarchan Poetics and the Female Voice in Louise Labe.* West Lafayette, Ind.: Purdue University Press, 1996.

Baldassare, M. *Trouble in Paradise: The Suburban Transformation in America.* New York: Columbia University Press, 1986.

Balthasar, H. U. von. *A Theology of History.* New York: Sheed and Ward, 1963, 1992.

———. *The Glory of the Lord: A Theological Aesthetics.* Vol. 1, *Seeing the Form.* Edited by J. Fessio, S.J., and J. Riches. Translated by E. Leiva-Merikakis. San Francisco: Ignatius; New York: Crossroad, 1982.

———. "Characteristics of Christianity." In *Explorations in Theology,* vol. 1, *The Word Made Flesh.* San Francisco: Ignatius, 1989.

———. *Theo-Drama.* Vol. 3. Translated by G. Harrison. San Francisco: Ignatius, 1992.

———. *The Theology of Karl Barth: Exposition and Interpretation.* Translated by E. T. Oakes. San Francisco: Ignatius, 1992.

———. *Love Alone Is Credible.* Translated by D. C. Schindler. San Francisco: Ignatius, 2004.

———. *Engagement with God.* Translated by R. J. Halliburton. San Francisco: Ignatius, 2008.

Barash, D. "Is There a War Instinct?" *Aeon,* September 19, 2013. Retrieved from http://aeon.co/magazine/society/human-beings-do-not-have-an-instinct-for-war/.

Barbour, I. *When Science Meets Religion: Enemies, Strangers, or Partners?* San Francisco: HarperSanFrancisco, 2000.

Barclay, J. M. *Pauline Churches and Diaspora Jews.* Tübingen: Mohr Siebeck, 2001.

Baring, E., and P. Gordon, eds. *The Trace of God: Derrida and Religion.* New York: Fordham University Press, 2014.

Barnard, J. *The throne established by righteousness. A sermon preached before his excellency Jonathan Belcher, Esq; his majesty's council, and the representatives of the province of the Massachusetts Bay in New England, May 29, 1734. Being the day for the electing his majesty's council there.* Boston: n.p., 1734. Retrieved from http://www.belcherfoundation.org/John%20Barnard%20The%20Throne%20Established%20by%20Righteousness.pdf.

Baron, S. W. *A Social and Religious History of the Jews.* Vol. 2. New York: Columbia University Press, 1960.

Barth, E. *An Embassy Besieged: The Story of a Christian Community in Nazi Germany.* Eugene, Ore.: Cascade, 2010.

Barth, K. *The Epistle to the Romans.* Translated by E. C. Hoskyns. London: Oxford University Press, 1933; original 1919.

———. *Church Dogmatics.* Vol. III/1. Edited by G. W. Bromiley and T. Torrance. Translated by J. W. Edwards, O. Bussey, and H. Knight. 2nd ed. Edinburgh: T. & T. Clark, 1958.

———. *Dogmatics in Outline.* Translated by G. T. Thompson. New York: Harper and Row, 1959.

———. *Church Dogmatics.* Vol. I/1, *The Doctrine of the Word of God.* Edited by G. Bromiley and T. Torrance. Translated by G. Bromiley. 2nd ed. Edinburgh: T. & T. Clark, 1976.

———. *The Christian Life.* Translated by G. Bromiley. Grand Rapids: Eerdmans, 1981.

———. *Protestant Theology in the Nineteenth Century: Its Background and History.* Translated by B. Cozens and J. Bowden. London: SCM, 2010.

Barton, D., M. Hamilton, and R. Ivanic, eds. *Situated Literacies: Reading and Writing in Context.* London: Routledge, 2000.

Basil. *Exegetic Homilies.* Translated by Sr. A. C. Way. Fathers of the Church, vol. 46. Washington, D.C.: Catholic University of America Press, 1963.

Batnitzky, L. *Idolatry and Representation: The Philosophy of Franz Rosenzweig Reconsidered*. Princeton: Princeton University Press, 2000.

Bauckham, R. *God Crucified: Monotheism and Christology in the New Testament*. Carlisle, U.K.: Paternoster, 1998.

———. "Paul's Christology of Divine Identity." In *Jesus and the God of Israel: God Crucified and Other Studies on the New Testament's Christology of Divine Identity*, edited by R. Bauckham, pp. 182-232. Grand Rapids: Eerdmans, 2008.

Baum, M. *Against the Wind: Eberhard Arnold and the Bruderhof*. Rifton, N.Y.: Plough Publishing, 1998.

Baur, C. F. "Die Christuspartei in der korinthischen Gemeinde, der Gegensatz des petrinischen und paulinischen Christenthums in der ältesten Kirche, der Apostel Petrus in Rom." *Tübinger Zeitschrift für Theologie* 4 (1831): 61-206.

———. *Paul the Apostle of Jesus Christ: His Life and Works; His Epistles and Teachings; A Contribution to a Critical History of Primitive Christianity*. London: Williams and Northgate, 1873; original 1845/1866.

Bayer, O. *Zeitgenosse im Widerspruch: Johann Georg Hamann als radikaler Aufklärer*. Munich: Piper, 1988.

———. *Schöpfung als Anrede: Zu einer Hermeneutik der Schöpfung*. Tübingen: Mohr Siebeck, 1990.

———. *Autorität und Kritik: Zur Hermeneutik und Wissenschaftstheorie*. Tübingen: Mohr Siebeck, 1991.

———. *Vernunft ist Sprache: Hamanns Metakritik Kants*. Stuttgart: Frommann-Verlag, 2002.

———. *A Contemporary in Dissent: Johann Georg Hamann as a Radical Enlightener*. Translated by R. Harrisville and M. Mattes. Grand Rapids: Eerdmans, 2012.

Beach, W., and H. R. Niebuhr, eds. *Christian Ethics: Sources of the Living Tradition*. New York: Ronald Press, 1955.

Beccaria, C. *On Crimes and Punishments and Other Writings*. Cambridge: Cambridge University Press, 1995; original 1764.

Becker, G. *The Economic Approach to Human Behavior*. Chicago: University of Chicago Press, 1976.

Beiner, R. *Political Judgment*. London: Methuen, 1983.

Bell, D., Jr. *The Cultural Contradictions of Capitalism*. New York: Basic Books, 1976.

———. "A Theopolitical Ontology of Judgment." In *Theology and the Political: The New Debate*, edited by C. Davis, J. Milbank, and S. Žižek. Durham, N.C., and London: Duke University Press, 2005.

———. "The Politics of Fear and the Gospel of Life." In *Veritas: Belief and Metaphysics*, edited by C. Cunningham and P. Candler Jr., pp. 426-51. Norwich: SCM, 2007.

Bell, R. *Illuminations for Legislator and for Sentimentalists*. London: Robert Bell, 1784.

Bellah, R., and H. Joas. *The Axial Age and Its Consequences*. Cambridge: Harvard University Press, Belknap Press, 2012.

Bellah, R., R. Madsen, W. Sullivan, A. Swidler, and S. Tipton. *Habits of the Heart: Individualism and Commitment in American Life*. Berkeley: University of California Press, 1985.

Bellows, H. "The Downward Tendency." *The City: An Illustrated Magazine* 1, no. 1 (1872).

Benjamin, W. "Theses on the Philosophy of History." In *Illuminations: Essays and Reflections*. New York: Schocken Books, 1968.

Benkler, Y. *The Penguin and the Leviathan: How Cooperation Triumphs over Self-Interest*. New York: Random House, Crown Business, 2011.

Benoit, P., T. Milik, and R. de Vaux. *Discoveries in the Judaean Desert*. Vol. 2, *Les Grottes de Murabba'at*. New York: Oxford University Press, 1961.

Benson, B., M. Berry, and P. Heltzel, eds. *Prophetic Evangelicals*. Grand Rapids: Eerdmans, 2012.

Berger, P. "On the Obsolescence of the Concept of Honor." *European Journal of Sociology* 11 (1970): 339-47.

Bergson, H. *The Two Sources of Morality and Religion*. Notre Dame: University of Notre Dame Press, 1932, 1977.

Berkhof, H. *Christian Faith*. Grand Rapids: Eerdmans, 1979, 1986.

Berkowitz, P. *Virtue and the Making of Modern Liberalism*. Princeton: Princeton University Press, 1999.

Berlin, I. *Four Essays on Liberty*. Oxford: Oxford University Press, 1969.

———. *Vico and Herder*. New York: Viking Press, 1976.

———. *The Crooked Timber of Humanity*. Princeton: Princeton University Press, 1998.

———. *Three Critics of Enlightenment*. Princeton: Princeton University Press, 2000.

———. *The Roots of Romanticism*. Princeton: Princeton University Press, 2001.

———. *Political Ideas in the Romantic Age: Their Rise and Influence on Modern Thought*. Princeton: Princeton University Press, 2006.

Berman, J. *Narrative Analogy in the Hebrew Bible: Battle Stories and Their Equivalent Non-Battle Narratives*. Leiden: Brill, 2004.

———. *Created Equal: How the Bible Broke with Ancient Political Thought*. New York: Oxford University Press, 2008.

Bernardin, J. Cardinal. *Consistent Ethic of Life*. Kansas City, Mo.: Sheed and Ward, 1988.

Betz, J. "Enlightenment Revisited: Hamann as the First and Best Critic of Kant's Philosophy." *Modern Theology* 20, no. 2 (April 2004): 292-301.

———. "Hamann's London Writings." *Pro Ecclesia* 14, no. 2 (Spring 2005): 191-234.

———. "Beyond the Sublime: The Aesthetics of the Analogy of Being (Part One)." *Modern Theology* 21, no. 3 (July 2005): 367-411.

———. "Beyond the Sublime: The Aesthetics of the Analogy of Being (Part Two)." *Modern Theology* 22, no. 1 (January 2006): 1-50.

———. "The Beauty of the Metaphysical Imagination." In *Veritas: Belief and Metaphysics*, edited by C. Cunningham and P. Candler Jr., pp. 41-65. Norwich: SCM, 2007.

———. "Hamann before Kierkegaard: A Systematic Theological Oversight." *Pro Ecclesia* 16, no. 3 (Summer 2007): 299-333.

———. *After Enlightenment: The Post-Secular Vision of J. G. Hamann*. Chichester: Wiley-Blackwell, 2009.

———. "Reading 'Sibylline Leaves': J. G. Hamann in the History of Ideas." *Journal of the History of Ideas* 70, no. 1 (2009): 93-118.

Bird, C. *The Myth of Liberal Individualism*. Cambridge: Cambridge University Press, 1999.

Bird, M. F. "When the Dust Finally Settles: Reaching a Post–New Perspective Perspective." *Criswell Theological Review* 2 (2005): 57-69.

———. "Justification as Forensic Declaration and Covenant Membership: A Via Media between Reformed and Revisionist Readings of Paul." *Tyndale Bulletin* 57, no. 1 (2006): 109-30.

———. "What Is There between Minneapolis and St. Andrews? A Third Way in the Piper-Wright Debate." *Journal of the Evangelical Theological Society* 54, no. 2 (2011): 299-310.

Blanchard, T. *How Relational Perspectives Can Transform Society.* New York: Fordham Law School, 2012.

Blank, R., and W. McGurn. *Is the Market Moral?* Washington, D.C.: Brookings Institution, 2004.

Bloch, E. *Principle of Hope.* Translated by N. Plaice, S. Plaice, and P. Knight. Cambridge: MIT Press, 1959.

Blondel, M. *Action: Essay on a Critique of Life and a Science of Practice.* Translated by O. Blanchette. Notre Dame: University of Notre Dame Press, 2004; original 1893.

Blumenfeld, B. *The Political Paul: Justice, Democracy, and Kingship in a Hellenistic Framework.* London: Continuum, 2001.

Blumhardt, C. *Action in Waiting.* Rifton, N.Y.: Plough Publishing, 2011.

Boethius. *Contra Eutychen.* In *Theological Tractates and the Consolation of Philosophy,* vol. 4, translated by H. Stewart, E. Rand, and S. Tester. Cambridge: Harvard University Press, 1978; original ca. 512.

Boff, L. *Passion of Christ, Passion of the World: The Facts, Their Interpretation, and Their Meaning Yesterday and Today.* Translated by R. Barr. Maryknoll, N.Y.: Orbis, 1988.

———. *Holy Trinity, Perfect Community.* Translated by P. Berryman. Maryknoll, N.Y.: Orbis, 2000.

Bonhoeffer, D. *Life Together.* Translated by J. W. Doberstein. New York: Harper, 1954.

———. *Sanctorum Communio.* Translated by R. G. Smith. London: Collins, 1963.

———. *Letters and Papers from Prison.* Edited by E. Bethge. New York: Simon and Schuster, 1971.

———. *Christ the Center.* Translated by E. H. Robertson. New York: Harper and Row, 1978.

———. *Letters and Papers from Prison.* Translated by R. Fuller et al. Enlarged ed. New York: Simon and Schuster, 1979.

———. *Discipleship.* Translated by B. Green and R. Krauss. Minneapolis: Fortress, 2001.

———. *Discipleship.* Dietrich Bonhoeffer Works, vol. 4. Minneapolis: Fortress, 2003.

———. *Ethics.* Translated by C. C. West, D. W. Stott, and R. Krauss. Dietrich Bonhoeffer Works, vol. 6. Minneapolis: Fortress, 2005.

———. *Letters and Papers from Prison.* Translated by I. Best, L. Dahill, R. Krauss, and N. Lukens. Dietrich Bonhoeffer Works, vol. 8. Minneapolis: Fortress, 2010.

Borgmann, A. *Technology and the Character of Contemporary Life.* Chicago: University of Chicago Press, 1984.

———. "Communities of Celebration: Technology and Public Life." In *Research in Phi-*

losophy and Technology: Technology and Religion, vol. 10, edited by F. Frerré. Greenwich, Conn., and London, U.K.: AI Press, 1990.

Borowitz, E. *A New Jewish Theology in the Making.* Philadelphia: Westminster, 1968.

———. "The Chosen People Concept as It Affects Life in the Diaspora." *Journal of Ecumenical Studies* 12, no. 4 (Fall 1975): 553-68.

———. "The Autonomous Self and the Commanding Community." *Theological Studies* 45 (1984): 34-56.

———. *Exploring Jewish Ethics: Papers on Covenant Responsibility.* Detroit: Wayne State University Press, 1990.

——— "The Dialectic of Living in Covenant." In *Renewing the Covenant: A Theology for the Postmodern Jew,* pp. 221-34. Philadelphia: Jewish Publication Society, 1991.

———. *Renewing the Covenant: A Theology for the Postmodern Jew.* Philadelphia: Jewish Publication Society, 1991.

———. "Covenant." In *Judaism after Modernity: Papers from a Decade of Fruition,* pp. 195-204. Lanham, Md.: University Press of America, 1999.

Boucher, J. *On Civil Liberty, Passive Obedience, and Non-Resistance.* In *A View of the Causes and Consequences of the American Revolution: In Thirteen Discourses, 1763-1775,* pp. 495-560. New York: Russell and Russell, 1967; original 1797.

Bowles, S., and H. Ginties. *A Cooperative Species: Human Reciprocity and Its Evolution.* Princeton: Princeton University Press, 2013.

Boyarin, D. *Carnal Israel: Reading Sex in Talmudic Culture.* Berkeley and Los Angeles: University of California Press, 1993.

———. *The Jewish Gospels: The Story of the Jewish Christ.* New York: New Press, 2012.

Boyd, G. *God at War: The Bible and Spiritual Conflict.* Downers Grove, Ill.: InterVarsity, 1997.

———. *Repenting of Religion: Turning from Judgment to the Love of God.* Grand Rapids: Baker, 2004.

———. *The Myth of a Christian Nation: How the Quest for Power Is Destroying the Church.* Grand Rapids: Zondervan, 2006.

———. "Don't Weep for the Demise of American Christianity." April 8, 2009. Retrieved from http://www.gregboyd.org/blog/dont-weep-for-the-demise-of-american-christianity/.

———. *The Myth of a Christian Religion: Losing Your Religion for the Beauty of a Revolution.* Grand Rapids: Zondervan, 2009.

Boyd, G., and P. Eddy. *Across the Spectrum: Understanding Issues in Evangelical Theology.* Grand Rapids: Baker Academic, 2009.

Boyle, R. *The Sceptical Chymist.* Mineola, N.Y.: Dover Publications, 2003; original 1661.

———. *The Christian Virtuoso, the First Part.* Whitefish, Mont.: Kessinger Publishing Co., 2007; original 1690.

Bradshaw, D. *Aristotle East and West: Metaphysics and the Division of Christendom.* Cambridge, U.K., and New York: Cambridge University Press, 2007.

Breen, T. "Persistent Localism: English Social Change and the Shaping of New England Institutions." *William and Mary Quarterly,* 3rd ser., 32, no. 19 (January 1975): 3-28.

Breslauer, S. D. "Toward a Theory of Covenant for Contemporary Jews." *Covenant* 1, no.

1 (November 2006). Retrieved from http://www.covenant.idc.ac.il/en/vol1/issue1/breslauer.html.

Bretherton, L. *Hospitality as Holiness: Christian Witness amid Moral Diversity.* Farnham, U.K., and Burlington, Vt.: Ashgate, 2006.

———. "A Postsecular Politics? Inter-faith Relations as a Civic Practice." *Journal of the American Academy of Religion* 79, no. 2 (2011): 346-77.

———. "Coming to Judgment: Methodological Reflections on the Relationship between Ecclesiology, Ethnography and Political Theory." *Modern Theology* 28, no. 2 (April 2012): 167-96.

Brewer, P. "Demographic Features of the Shaker Decline, 1787-1900." *Journal of Interdisciplinary History* 15, no. 1 (Summer 1984): 31-52.

Brooke, H. *Liberty and Common-sense to the People of Ireland, Greeting.* London: J. William, 1759/1760.

Brown, P. "Late Antiquity." In *A History of Private Life,* vol. 1, *From Pagan Rome to Byzantium,* edited by P. Aries and Georges Duby, translated by A. Goldhammer, pp. 235-311. Cambridge: Harvard University Press, Belknap Press, 1987.

———. *The Body and Society: Men, Women, and Sexual Renunciation in Early Christianity. Lectures on the History of Religion,* vol. 13. New York: Columbia University Press, 1988.

———. *Poverty and Leadership in the Later Roman Empire.* Hanover, N.H.: University Press of New England, 2002.

Bruce, F. F. *The Epistles to the Colossians, to Philemon, and to the Ephesians.* New International Commentary on the New Testament. Grand Rapids: Eerdmans, 1984.

Bruckstein, A. Sh. "On Jewish Hermeneutics: Maimonides and Bachya as Vectors in Cohen's Philosophy of Origin." In *Hermann Cohen's Philosophy of Religion: International Conference in Jerusalem 1996,* edited by S. Moses and H. Wiedebach. Hildesheim: Georg Olms Verlag, 1997.

Brueggemann, W. *A Social Reading of the Old Testament: Prophetic Approaches to Israel's Communal Life.* Minneapolis: Fortress, 1994.

———. *The Prophetic Imagination.* Minneapolis: Fortress, 2001.

———. *Journey to the Common Good.* Louisville: Westminster John Knox, 2010.

———. *Rich, Free, and Miserable: The Failure of "Success" in America.* Lanham, Md.: Rowman and Littlefield, 2010.

———. *Truth Speaks to Power: The Countercultural Nature of Scripture.* Louisville: Westminster John Knox, 2013.

———. *Reality, Grief, Hope.* Grand Rapids: Eerdmans, 2014.

Bruni, L. *The Wound and the Blessing: Economics, Relationships, and Happiness.* Translated by N. M. Brennen. Hyde Park, N.Y.: New City Press, 2012.

Bruni, L., and S. Zamagni. *Civil Economy: Efficiency, Equity, Public Happiness.* Bern: Peter Lang, 2007.

Brunner, E. *Man in Revolt: A Christian Anthropology.* Translated by O. Wyon. London: Lutterworth, 1939.

Bryce, J. *Modern Democracies.* Vols. 1-2. New York: Macmillan, 1921.

Buber, M. *I and Thou*. Prologue and notes translated by W. Kaufmann. New York: Charles Scribner's Sons, 1970.

———. *Between Man and Man*. New York: Routledge, 1993.

———. *I and Thou*. Eastford, Conn.: Martino Fine Books, 2010; original 1923.

Buber, S., ed. *Midrash Aggadah*. Agadischer Commentar zum Pentateuch nach einer Handschrift aus Aleppo. Vienna: AUT, 1894.

Bulgakov, S. *The Lamb of God*. Translated by B. Jakim. Grand Rapids: Eerdmans, 2008; original 1933.

Bullinger, H. *De Testamento seu foedere Dei unico et aeterno*. Tiguri, in aedibus C. Frosch, 1534.

———. "A Brief Exposition of the One and Eternal Testament or Covenant of God." In *Fountainhead of Federalism: Heinrich Bullinger and the Covenantal Tradition*, edited by C. McCoy and J. W. Baker. Louisville: Westminster John Knox, 1991; original 1534.

Bultmann, R. *Theology of the New Testament*. Translated by K. Grobel. Vols. 1-2. New York: Scribner, 1951, 1955.

Burke, E. "The Correspondence." In *The Works of the Right Honourable Edmund Burke*, vol. 3. London: John C. Nimmo, 1899.

———. "Letters on a Regicide Peace, Letter 1." In *The Works of the Right Honourable Edmund Burke*, vol. 5. London: John C. Nimmo, 1899.

———. "Letter to a Member of the French National Assembly." In *The Works of the Right Honourable Edmund Burke*, vol. 4. London: John C. Nimmo, 1899.

———. "Letter to a Noble Lord." In *The Works of the Right Honourable Edmund Burke*, vol. 5. London: John C. Nimmo, 1899.

———. "Letter to Sheriffs of Bristol." In *The Works of the Right Honourable Edmund Burke*, vol. 2. London: John C. Nimmo, 1899.

———. "New to the Old Whigs." In *The Works of the Right Honourable Edmund Burke*, vol. 4. London: John C. Nimmo, 1899.

———. "Revolution in France." In *The Works of the Right Honourable Edmund Burke*, vol. 3. London: John C. Nimmo, 1899.

———. *The Works of the Right Honourable Edmund Burke*. Vols. 2-5. London: John C. Nimmo, 1899.

———. *On the American Revolution: Selected Speeches and Letters*. Edited by E. Barkan. New York: Harper and Row, 1966.

———. "Reflections on the Revolution in France." In *The Works of the Right Honourable Edmund Burke*, vol. 3. London: John C. Nimmo, 1992.

Burke, P. *Reinterpreting Rahner: A Critical Study of His Major Themes*. New York: Fordham University Press, 2002.

Burrell, D. *Knowing the Unknowable God: Ibn-Sina, Maimonides, Aquinas*. Notre Dame: University of Notre Dame Press, 1986.

———. "The Christian Distinction Celebrated and Expanded." In *Faith and Freedom: An Interfaith Perspective*. Oxford: Blackwell, 2004.

———. *Towards a Jewish-Christian-Muslim Theology*. Chichester, UK, and Malden, Mass.: Wiley-Blackwell, 2011.

Burrow, R. *Personalism: A Critical Introduction*. St. Louis: Chalice, 1999.

Butler, J. *Analogy of Religion*. Los Angeles: Classworks, 1986; original 1726.

———. *Fifteen Sermons Preached at the Rolls Chapel and a Dissertation on the Nature of Virtue*. Los Angeles: Classworks, 1986.

Byrne, B. *Romans*. Edited by D. J. Harrington. Sacra Pagina, vol. 6. Collegeville, Minn.: Liturgical Press, 1996.

———. "Interpreting Romans Theologically in a Post-'New Perspective' Perspective." *Harvard Theological Review* 94 (2001): 227-41.

Caird, E. *Hegel*. New York: AMS Press, 1983; original 1883.

Calvin, J. *Institutes of the Christian Religion*. Edited by J. McNeill. Translated by F. Battles. Vols. 1-2. Philadelphia: Westminster, 1960; original 1536.

———. *The Epistles of Paul the Apostle to the Galatians, Ephesians, Philippians, and Colossians*. Edited by D. W. Torrance and T. F. Torrance. Translated by T. H. L. Parker. Edinburgh: Oliver and Boyd, 1965.

———. *Commentary on Genesis*. In *Calvin's Commentaries*, vol. 1. Translated by J. King. Grand Rapids: Baker, 1981.

———. *Commentary on the Gospel according to John*. Translated by W. Pringle. Grand Rapids: Baker, 1996; original 1847.

Campbell, C. "The Romantic Ethic and the Spirit of Modern Consumption." 1987. Retrieved from http://www.writersservices.com/wbs/books/Romantic_ethic.htm.

Campolo, T. *Red Letter Christians: A Citizen's Guide to Faith and Politics*. Ventura, Calif.: Regal, 2008.

Candler, P. M., Jr. "Liturgically Trained Memory: A Reading of *Summa Theologiae* III 83." *Modern Theology* 20, no. 3 (July 2004): 423-45.

Candler, P., and C. Cunningham, eds. *The Grandeur of Reason: Religion, Tradition, and Universalism*. London: SCM, 2010.

Capon, R. *The Supper of the Lamb: A Culinary Reflection*. New York: Harcourt, Brace, 1967.

Caputo, J. "What Do I Love When I Love My God? Deconstruction and Radical Orthodoxy." In *Questioning God*, edited by J. Caputo, M. Dooley, and M. Scanlon, pp. 291-317. Bloomington and Indianapolis: Indiana University Press, 2001.

Caputo, J., M. Dooley, and M. Scanlon, eds. *Questioning God*. Bloomington and Indianapolis: Indiana University Press, 2001.

Carson, D. A. "Summaries and Conclusions." In *Justification and Variegated Nomism: The Complexities of Second Temple Judaism*, vol. 1, edited by D. A. Carson, P. T. O'Brien, and M. A. Seifrid. Grand Rapids: Baker, 2001.

Carwardine, R. "Methodist Ministers and the Second Party System." In *Rethinking Methodist History: A Bicentennial Historical Consultation*, edited by R. Richey and K. Rowe. Nashville: Kingswood Books, 1985.

Casanova, J. *Public Religions in the Modern World*. Chicago: University of Chicago Press, 1994.

Castellio, S. *Concerning Heretics and Whether They Should Be Persecuted, and How They Should Be Treated*. Edited and translated by R. Bainton. New York: Octagon Books, 1965; original 1554.

Cavanaugh, W. *Being Consumed: Economics and Christian Desire*. Grand Rapids: Eerdmans, 2008.

Cheney, D. "Extent and Limits of Cooperation in Animals." *Proceedings of the National Academy of Sciences* 108, suppl. 2 (2011): 10902-909.

Chepurin, K. "Spirit and Utopia: (German) Idealism as Political Theology." *Crisis and Critique* 2, no. 1 (2015): 327-48.

Chesterton, G. K. "The Ethics of Elfland." In *Orthodoxy,* pp. 66-103. London: Bodley Head, 1957.

Chevalier, M. *Society, Manners, and Politics in the United States.* New York: Augustus M. Kelley, 1966; original 1839.

Christakis, N., and J. Fowler, *Connected: The Surprising Power of Our Social Networks and How They Shape Our Lives — How Your Friends' Friends' Friends Affect Everything You Feel, Think, and Do.* New York: Little, Brown, 2009.

Chronica and *Paradoxa ducenta octoginta.* In J. Lecler, *Toleration and the Reformation.* London: Longmans, Green; New York: Longmans, 1960; original 1534.

Churchland, R. *Braintrust: What Neuroscience Tells Us about Morality.* Princeton: Princeton University Press, 2012.

Claiborne, S. *Irresistible Revolution: Living as an Ordinary Radical.* Grand Rapids: Zondervan, 2006.

Claiborne, S., and T. Campolo. *Red Letter Revolution: What If Jesus Really Meant What He Said?* Nashville: Thomas Nelson/HarperCollins, 2012.

Clapp, R. "Why the Devil Takes VISA: A Christian Response to the Triumph of Consumerism." *Christianity Today,* October 7, 1996. Retrieved from http://www .christianitytoday.com/ct/1996/october7/6tb018.html?paging=off.

Clark, K. J. *Return to Reason: A Critique of Enlightenment Evidentialism and a Defense of Reason and Belief in God.* Grand Rapids: Eerdmans, 1990.

Clarke, W. *An Outline of Christian Theology.* Cambridge: John Wilson, 1894.

Clement of Alexandria. *Stromata (Miscellanies)* 6.12. In *The Ante-Nicene Fathers,* edited by A. Roberts, J. Donaldson, and A. C. Coxe. Peabody, Mass.: Hendrickson, 1994.

Clines, D. J. A. "The Image of God in Man." *Tyndale Bulletin* 19, no. 1 (1968): 53-103.

Cohen, H. *Ethik des reinen Willens. System der Philosophie.* Vol. 2. Berlin: Bruno Cassirer, 1904, 1907.

————. *Die Religion der Vernunft aus den Quellen des Judentums.* Leipzig: Fock, 1919. ET: *Religion of Reason: Out of the Sources of Judaism,* translated by S. Kaplan. New York: Frederick Unger, 1919.

Coleridge, S. T. *Aids to the Reflection in the Formation of a Manly Character.* London: Taylor & Hessey, 1825.

Collins, A., and J. Collins. *King and Messiah as Son of God: Divine, Human, and Angelic Messianic Figures in Biblical and Related Literatures.* Grand Rapids: Eerdmans, 2008.

Collins, J. J. *Apocalypticism in the Dead Sea Scrolls.* London and New York: Routledge, 1997.

Colpe, C. "Ho Huios Tou Anthropou." In *Theological Dictionary of the New Testament,* vol. 8. Grand Rapids: Eerdmans, 1972.

Condorcet, Marquis de. *Sketch for a Historical Picture of the Progress of the Human Mind.* London: Weidenfeld and Nicholson, 1980; original 1795.

Conklin, P. "Freedom: Past Meaning and Present Prospects." In *Freedom in America,* edited by N. Graebner, pp. 205-22. University Park: Pennsylvania State University Press, 1977.

Constant, B. "Liberty of the Ancients Compared with That of the Moderns." In *Political Writings*, edited and translated by B. Fontana, pp. 307-28. Cambridge: Cambridge University Press, 1988; original 1819.

Cooperative Extension Service. *Can Churches Respond to the Farm Crisis?* Columbia: University of Missouri, June 17, 1985.

Countryman, E. *American Revolution*. New York: Hill and Wang, 1985.

Crossan, J. *The Historical Jesus: The Life of a Mediterranean Jewish Peasant*. New York: Harper One, 1991, 1993.

————. *God and Empire: Jesus against Rome, Then and Now*. San Francisco: HarperSanFrancisco, 2007.

Cumings, H. *Massachusetts Election Sermon*. Boston: T. and J. Fleet, 1783.

Cunningham, C., and P. Candler, eds. *Veritas: Belief and Metaphysics*. Norwich: SCM, 2007.

Cunningham, L. A. "A Prescription to Retire the Rhetoric of 'Principles-Based Systems' in Corporate Law, Securities Regulation, and Accounting." *Vanderbilt Law Review* 60 (2007): 1409-94.

Cutler, W., and J. Cutler. *Life, Journals, and Correspondence of Rev. Manasseh Cutler*. Vols. 1-2. Cincinnati: Ohio University Press, 1888.

Danby, H. *The Mishnah*. Translated by S. Danby. London: Oxford University Press, 1933.

Darwin, C. *The Portable Darwin*. Edited by D. Porter and P. Graham. London and New York: Penguin Books, 1993; original 1859/1871.

————. *The Descent of Man*. New York: Penguin Classics, 2004; original 1871.

Davidson, I. "Theologizing the Human Jesus: An Ancient (and Modern) Approach to Christology Reassessed." *International Journal of Systematic Theology* 3, no. 2 (2001): 129-53.

Davidson, R. *The Emotional Life of Your Brain*. New York: Penguin Group, 2012.

Davies, S. *Religion and the Public Spirit: A Valedictory Address to the Senior Class*. New York: James Parker, 1761.

Davies, W. *Paul and Rabbinic Judaism: Some Rabbinic Elements in Pauline Theology*. 4th ed. London: SPCK; Philadelphia: Fortress, 1980; original 1948.

Davis, C., J. Milbank, and S. Žižek, eds. *Theology and the Political: The New Debate*. Durham, N.C., and London: Duke University Press, 2005.

Davis, C., and P. A. Riches. "The Theological Praxis of Revolution." In *Theology and the Political: The New Debate*, edited by C. Davis, J. Milbank, and S. Žižek. Durham, N.C., and London: Duke University Press, 2005.

Davis, E. F. *Getting Involved with God: Rediscovering the Old Testament*. Cambridge, Mass.: Cowley, 2001.

Dawkins, R. *The Selfish Gene*. Oxford and New York: Oxford University Press, 1976, 1990.

Day, D. *Selected Writings*. Maryknoll, N.Y.: Orbis, 1992.

Dearborn, T. "God, Grace and Salvation." In *Christ in Our Place: The Humanity of God in Christ for the Reconciliation of the World*, edited by T. Hart and D. Thimell, pp. 265-93. Eugene, Ore.: Wipf and Stock, 1989.

Dees, M., and J. Corcoran. *Gathering Storm*. New York: HarperCollins, 1996.

Dees, M., and M. Potok. "The Future of American Terrorism." *New York Times*, June 6, 2001, pp. 4, 15.

Derrida, J. "Shibboleth for Paul Celan." In *Word Traces: Readings of Paul Celan*, edited by A. Fioretos. Baltimore: Johns Hopkins University Press, 1994.

———. *On Grammatology*. Baltimore: Johns Hopkins University Press, 1998.

———. "Specters of Marx." In *Futures of Jacques Derrida*, edited by R. Rand. Stanford: Stanford University Press, 2001.

———. "A Testimony Given." In *Questioning Judaism: Interviews by Elisabeth Weber*, translated by R. Bowlby. Stanford. Stanford University Press, 2004.

Desmond, W. "Between Metaphysics and Politics." In *Theology and the Political: The New Debate*, edited by C. Davis, J. Milbank, and S. Žižek. Durham, N.C., and London: Duke University Press, 2005.

———. "The Confidence of Thought." In *Veritas: Belief and Metaphysics*, edited by C. Cunningham and P. Candler Jr. Norwich: SCM, 2007.

De Waal, F. *The Age of Empathy*. London: Souvenir Press, 2010.

Dewey, J. "The Public and Its Problems." In *John Dewey: The Later Works*, vol. 2, 1925-1927, edited by J. Boydston. Carbondale and Edwardsville: Southern Illinois University Press, 1984.

DeWolf, L. H. *A Theology of the Living Church*. New York: Harper, 1953.

Didache, The. In *Ancient Christian Writers*, edited by J. Quasten and J. Plumpe, translated by J. Kleist. New York: Newman Press, 1948.

Directory for the Publick Worship of God. An Act of the Parliament of the Kingdom of Scottland, approving and establishing the Directory for Publick Worship. February 1645. Retrieved from http://www.reformed.org/documents/wcf_standards/index .html?mainframe=/documents/wcf_standards/p369-direct_pub_worship.html.

Dobie, R. *Logos and Revelation: Ibn 'Arabi, Meister Eckhart, and Mystical Hermeneutics*. Washington, D.C.: Catholic University of America Press, 2010.

Documentary History of the Ratification of the Constitution. Edited by J. Kaminski and G. Saladino. Madison: Wisconsin Historical Society, 1996-2012.

Dodds, E. *Pagan and Christian in an Age of Anxiety: Some Aspects of Religious Experience from Marcus Aurelius to Constantine*. Cambridge: Cambridge University Press, 1965.

Donaldson, J., ed. *Constitutions of the Holy Apostles*. In *The Ante-Nicene Fathers*, edited by A. Roberts and J. Robertson. Grand Rapids: Eerdmans, 1985.

Doran, R. *Theology and the Dialectics of History*. Toronto: University of Toronto Press, 1990, 2001.

———. *What Is Systematic Theology?* Toronto: University of Toronto Press, 2005.

Dorff, E., and L. Newman. *Contemporary Jewish Theology: A Reader*. New York: Oxford University Press, 1999.

Drabinski, J. *Sensibility and Singularity: The Problem of Phenomenology in Levinas*. Albany: State University of New York Press, 2001.

Duck, S., and M. Collier. *The Thresher's Labor/Women's Labor: Two Eighteenth Century Poems*. London: Merlin Press, 1990; original 1736.

Dunn, J. D. G. "The Incident at Antioch (Galatians 2:11-18)." *Journal for the Study of the New Testament* 18 (1983): 3-57.

―――. "Works of the Law and the Curse of the Law (Galatians 3:10-14)." *New Testament Studies* 31, no. 4 (1985): 523-42.

―――. *Romans 1–8.* Dallas: Word, 1988.

―――. *Jesus, Paul, and the Law: Studies in Mark and Galatians.* London: SPCK, 1990.

―――. *Romans 9–16.* Dallas: Word, 1990.

―――. *The Partings of the Ways: Between Christianity and Judaism and Their Significance for the Character of Christianity.* London: SCM, 1991.

―――. "How New Was Paul's Gospel? The Problem of Continuity and Discontinuity." In *Gospel in Paul: Studies on Corinthians, Galatians, and Romans for Richard N. Longenecker,* edited by L. A. Jervis and P. Richardson. Sheffield: Sheffield Academic Press, 1994.

―――. *The Theology of Paul the Apostle.* Grand Rapids: Eerdmans, 1998.

Dunn, J. D. G., and A. M. Suggate. *The Justice of God: A Fresh Look at the Old Doctrine of Justification by Faith.* Grand Rapids: Eerdmans, 1994.

Dupuis, J. *Toward a Christian Theology of Religious Pluralism.* Maryknoll, N.Y.: Orbis, 1997.

―――. "Christianity and Religions: From Confrontation to Encounter." 2001. Retrieved from http://www.thetablet.co.uk/page/jacquesdupuislecture.

Durkheim, E. *Rules of Sociological Method.* Translated by W. Halls. London and New York: Free Press, 1982; original 1895.

―――. *Readings from Emile Durkheim.* Edited by K. Thompson. New York: Routledge, 1984.

―――. *Elementary Forms of the Religious Life.* Translated by K. Fields. London and New York: Free Press, 1995; original 1912.

―――. *The Division of Labor in Society.* Translated by W. Halls. London and New York: Free Press, 1997; original 1893.

―――. *Suicide: A Study in Sociology.* Translated by J. Spaulding and G. Simpson. London and New York: Free Press, 1997; original 1897.

Durkheim, E., and M. Mauss. *Primitive Classification.* Translated by R. Needham. Chicago: University of Chicago Press, 1967; original 1903.

Dyer, J. *Harvest of Rage: Why Oklahoma City Is Only the Beginning.* New York: Westview Press/HarperCollins, 1997.

Eckermann, J. *Conversations with Goethe.* Edited by J. Moorhead. Translated by J. Oxenford. New York: Dutton, 1970; original 1836, amended in 1848.

Edgar, O. "Seeing as Communion: Merleau-Ponty's Embodied Phenomenology of Vision and the Trinitarian Ontology of John Zizioulas." Paper presented at the Centre of Theology and Philosophy conference on the Soul, St. Anne's College, Oxford, June 28–July 1, 2013.

Edwards, J. "Religious Affections." In *The Works of Jonathan Edwards,* vol. 2, edited by J. E. Smith. New Haven: Yale University Press, 1959.

Eichhorn, A. *The Lord's Supper in the New Testament.* Translated by J. Cayzer. Atlanta: Society of Biblical Literature, 2007; original 1898.

Eisen, A. "Covenant." May 19, 2011. Retrieved from http://www.jtsa.edu/prebuilt/blog/covenant.html.

Eisenbaum, P. *Paul Was Not a Christian: The Original Message of a Misunderstood Apostle.* New York: HarperOne, 2009.

Eisenhower, D. *The Papers of Dwight David Eisenhower.* Vol. 15, *The Presidency: The Middle Way Part VI; Crises Abroad, Party Problems at Home; September 1954 to December 1954.* Retrieved from http://www.usmessageboard.com/threads/dwight -d-eisenhowers-1954-letter-to-his-brother-edgar.266267/.

Eisenstadt, S. *The Origins and Diversity of Axial Age Civilizations.* Albany: State University of New York Press, 1986.

Elliot, N. *The Arrogance of Nations: Reading Romans in the Shadow of Empire.* Minneapolis: Fortress, 2008.

Emerson, R. W. "Self-Reliance." In *Essays: First Series.* 1841. Retrieved from http://www .emersoncentral.com/selfreliance.htm.

———. "Nature, 4." In *Selected Prose and Poetry,* edited by R. L. Cook. New York: Holt Rinehart Winston, 1950.

———. "The Over-Soul." In *Selected Prose and Poetry,* edited by R. L. Cook. New York: Holt Rinehart Winston, 1950.

———. *Selected Prose and Poetry.* Edited by R. L. Cook. New York: Holt Rinehart Winston, 1950.

———. *Representative Men.* Edited by P. Schirmeister. New York: Marsilio, 1995; original 1850.

Engel, K. C. "Religion and Profit: Moravians in Early America." In *Early American Studies.* Philadelphia: University of Pennsylvania Press, 2011.

England, J., and S. Albrecht. "Boomtowns and Social Disruption." *Rural Sociology* 4 (Summer 1984): 230-46.

Epstein, J. "White Mischief." *New York Review of Books,* 1996, pp. 30-32.

Ezell, M., ed. *The Poems and Prose of Mary, Lady Chudleigh.* New York: Oxford University Press, 1993; original 1700-1710.

Federal Farmer. Letter VI. In *The Anti-Federalist,* edited by Herbert Storing. Chicago: University of Chicago Press, 1985; original 1787.

Feil, E. *The Theology of Dietrich Bonhoeffer.* Philadelphia: Fortress, 1985.

Felber, C. *Change Everything: Creating an Economy for the Common Good.* London: Zed Books, 2015.

Felsenthal, B. "The Law of Release, as Understood and Practiced in the Apostolic Age." *Old Testament Student* 3, no. 5 (1884): 145-49.

Ferguson, M. *First Feminists: British Women Writers, 1578-1799.* Bloomington: Indiana University Press, 1985.

Feuerbach, L. *Gesammelte Werke.* Edited by W. Schuffenhauer. Berlin: Akademie Verlag, 1981-1989.

———. *Principles of the Philosophy of the Future.* Translated by M. Vogel. Indianapolis: Hackett, 1986; also in *Gesammelte Werke,* vol. 9, pp. 264-341. Berlin: Akademie Verlag, 1981-1989.

Fichte, J. G. *The Vocation of Man.* Translated by W. Smith. LaSalle, Ill.: Open Court, 1965; original published as *Die Bestimmung des Menschen,* 1800.

Fichte, J. S. *The Science of Knowledge.* Edited and translated by P. Heath and J. Lachs. Cambridge: Cambridge University Press, 1980.

Finn, R. *Almsgiving in the Later Roman Empire: Christian Promotion and Practice, 313-450.* Oxford: Oxford University Press, 2006.

Fischer, D. *Albion's Seed: Four British Folkways in America.* Vol. 1. New York: Oxford University Press, 1989.

Fishman, C. "The Insourcing Boom." *Atlantic,* November 28, 2012. Retrieved from http://www.theatlantic.com/magazine/archive/2012/12/the-insourcing-boom/309166/?single_page=true.

Fleck, L. *Genesis and the Development of a Scientific Fact.* Chicago: University of Chicago Press, 1981; original 1935.

Florensky, P. *The Pillar and Ground of Truth.* Translated by B. Jakim. Princeton: Princeton University Press, 1997.

Foley, D. *Adam's Fallacy: A Guide to Economic Theology.* Cambridge: Harvard University Press, Belknap Press, 2006.

Forbes, G. "The Letter of the Galatians." In *All Things to All Cultures: Paul among Jews, Greeks, and Romans,* edited by J. Harding and A. Nobbs, pp. 243-68. Grand Rapids: Eerdmans, 2013.

Foucault, M. *Archeology of Knowledge and the Discourse on Language.* Translated by A. Sheridan. New York: Pantheon Books, 1982.

———. *Madness and Civilization: A History of Insanity in the Age of Reason.* New York: Vintage Books, 1988.

———. *The History of Sexuality: An Introduction.* New York: Vintage Books, 1990.

———. *The Use of Pleasure.* New York: Vintage Books, 1990.

———. *The Birth of the Clinic: An Archeology of Medical Perception.* Translated by A. Sheridan. New York: Vintage Books, 1994.

———. *The Order of Things: An Archeology of Human Sciences.* New York: Vintage Books, 1994.

———. *Discipline and Punish: The Birth of the Prison.* Translated by A. Sheridan. New York: Vintage Books, 1995.

———. *Ethics, Subjectivity, and Truth: Essential Works of Foucault.* Vol. 1, *1954-1984.* Edited by P. Rabinow. Translated by R. Hurley. New York: New Press, 1997.

———. *Aesthetics, Method, and Epistemology: Essential Works of Foucault.* Vol. 2, *1954-1984.* Edited by J. Faubion and P. Rabinow. Translated by R. Hurley. New York: New Press, 1998.

———. *Power: Essential Works of Foucault.* Vol. 3, *1954-1984.* Translated by R. Hurley. New York: New Press, 2000.

———. *The Birth of Biopolitics: Lectures at the College de France, 1978-1979.* Edited by M. Senellart. Translated by G. Burchell. New York: Palgrave Macmillan, 2004.

Fournier Beaulieu, J.-P., and H. Fournier Beaulieu. *Marie LeJars de Gournay.* New York: Rodopi Press, 1997.

Frame, J. *The Doctrine of the Knowledge of God.* Phillipsburg, N.J.: P&R Publishing, 1987.

Francis. *Evangelii gaudium*. Rome. November 24, 2013. Retrieved from http://www
.vatican.va/holy_father/francesco/apost_exhortations/documents/papa-francesco
_esortazione-ap_20131124_evangelii-gaudium_en.html.

Frank, R. *Luxury Fever: Money and Happiness in an Era of Excess.* Princeton: Princeton
University Press, 2000.

Franke, J. "Church." In *Prophetic Evangelicals,* edited by B. Benson, M. Berry, and P. Heltzel, pp. 134-42. Grand Rapids: Eerdmans, 2012.

Frankfort, H., and H. A. Frankfort. *Before Philosophy.* Harmondsworth, U.K.: Penguin,
1959.

Fretheim, T. *God and World in the Old Testament: A Relational Theology of Creation.*
Nashville: Abingdon, 2005.

Freud, S. *The Standard Edition of the Complete Psychological Works of Sigmund Freud.*
Edited by J. Strachey. London: Hogarth, 1958.

Fried, A., ed. *Socialism in America from the Shakers to the Third International.* New York:
Columbia University Press, 1993.

Frohnen, B. *Virtue and the Promise of Conservatism: The Legacy of Burke and Tocqueville.*
Lawrence: University Press of Kansas, 1993.

Fruehwald, E. S. "Reciprocal Altruism as the Basis for Contract." *University of Louisville
Law Review* 47, no. 3 (2009). Hofstra University Legal Studies Research Paper no.
08-09. Available at SSRN: http://ssrn.com/abstract=1270117.

Frum, D. "When Did the GOP Lose Touch with Reality?" *New York Magazine,* November 20, 2011. Retrieved from http://nymag.com/news/politics/conservatives-david
-frum-2011-11.

Fry, D. *Beyond War: The Human Potential for Peace.* Oxford: Oxford University Press,
2007.

Funkenstein, A. *Theology and the Scientific Imagination.* Princeton: Princeton University
Press, 1996.

Gadamer, H.-G. *Truth and Method.* Translated by J. Weinsheimer and D. Marshall. 2nd
rev. ed. New York: Continuum, 1999.

Galileo, G. *Dialogue concerning the Two Chief World Systems.* Translated by A. de Salvio.
New York: Prometheus Books, 1991; original 1632.

Gamoran, H. "The *Prozbul:* Accommodation to Reality." *Jewish Law Association Studies*
22 (2012).

Gardoski, K. "The *Imago Dei* Revisited." *Journal of Ministry and Theology* 11, no. 2 (2007):
5-37.

Garfinkle, G. *Stress, Depression, and Suicide: A Study of Adolescents in Minnesota, Responding to High Risk Youth.* Minneapolis: Minnesota Extension Service, State
Health Reports: Mental Health, Alcoholism, and Drug Abuse, 1986.

Garrison, R. *Redemptive Almsgiving in Early Christianity.* Sheffield: JSOT Press, 1993.

Gebara, I. *Longing for Running Water: Ecofeminism and Liberation.* Minneapolis: Fortress, 1999.

Geller, S. "The Sack of Shechem: The Use of Typology in Biblical Covenant Religion."
Prooftexts 10, no. 1 (1990): 1-15.

————. "Manna and Sabbath: A Literary-Theological Reading of Exodus 16." *Interpretation* 59, no. 1 (January 2005): 5-16.

Genesis Rabbah. In *The Midrash Rabbah.* New compact ed. London and Jerusalem, ISR; New York: Soncino Press/Oxford University Press, 1977.

Genovesi, A. *Lezioni di commercio o sia di economia civile.* Edited by M. L. Perna. Naples: Instituti italiano per gli studi filosofici, 2005; original 1765-1767.

Georgi, D. *Theocracy in Paul's Praxis and Theology.* Minneapolis: Fortress, 1991.

Gibbs, R. "Returning/Forgiving: Ethics and Theology." In *Questioning God,* edited by J. Caputo, M. Dooley, and M. Scanlon, pp. 73-91. Bloomington and Indianapolis: Indiana University Press, 2001.

Gilmore, R. *A Poor Harvest: The Clash of Politics and Interests in the Grain Trade.* New York: Longman, 1982.

Given, M., ed. *Paul Unbound: Other Perspectives on the Apostle.* Peabody, Mass.: Hendrickson, 2010.

Godbout, J., and A. Caillé. *The World of the Gift.* Translated by D. Winkler. Montreal: McGill-Queen's University Press, 1998.

Godwin, W. *The Anarchist Writings of William Godwin.* Edited by P. Marshall. London: Freedom Press, 1986.

————. *An Enquiry concerning the Principles of Political Justice and Its Influence on General Virtue and Happiness.* New York: Viking Press, 1993; original 1793.

Goethe, J. von. *Goethe on Art.* Edited and translated by J. Cage. Berkeley: University of California Press, 1980.

————. *Ecrits sur l'art.* Edited and translated by J.-M. Schaeffer and T. Todorov. Paris: Klincksieck, 1983.

Goffman, E. *The Presentation of Self in Everyday Life.* Garden City, N.Y.: Doubleday, 1959.

————. *Forms of Talk.* Philadelphia: University of Pennsylvania Press, 1981.

Goldberg, M. *Jews and Christians: Getting Our Stories Straight.* Eugene, Ore.: Wipf and Stock, 1985, 2001.

Goldin, J. "Hillel the Elder." *Journal of Religion* 26, no. 4 (1946): 263-77.

Goldingay, J. "Old Testament Sacrifice and the Death of Christ." In *Atonement Today,* edited by J. Goldingay. London: SPCK, 1995.

González, J. *Out of Every Tribe and Nation: Christian Theology at the Ethnic Roundtable.* Nashville: Abingdon, 1992.

Goodchild, P. "Capital and Kingdom." In *Theology and the Political: The New Debate,* edited by C. Davis, J. Milbank, and S. Žižek. Durham, N.C., and London: Duke University Press, 2005.

Goodman, L. *On Justice: An Essay in Jewish Philosophy.* New Haven: Yale University Press, 1991.

Goodman, M. "The First Jewish Revolt: Social Conflict and the Problem of Debt." *Journal of Jewish Studies* 33, nos. 1-2 (1982): 417-27.

Gordon, G. *Ultimate Conceptions of the Faith.* Boston: Houghton and Mifflin, 1903.

Goss, C. *Statistical History of the First Century of American Methodism.* New York: Carlton and Porter, 1866.

Gottstein, A. "The Body as Image of God in Rabbinic Literature." *Harvard Theological Review* 87 (1994): 171-95.

Graebner, N. *Freedom in America.* University Park: Pennsylvania State University Press, 1990.

Gray, A. "Redemptive Almsgiving and the Rabbis of Late Antiquity." *Jewish Studies Quarterly* 18 (2011): 144-84.

Gray, J. *Post-Liberalism: Studies in Political Thought.* New York and London: Routledge, 1993.

Green, D. *Sermon Delivered at Hanover, April, 22, 1778.* Chatham, N.J.: Sherpard Kollock, 1778.

Greenberg, I. "Easing the Divine Suffering." In *The Life of Meaning: Reflections on Faith, Doubt, and Repairing the World,* edited by B. Abernethy and W. Bole. New York: Seven Stories, 2002.

———. *For the Sake of Heaven and Earth: The New Encounter between Judaism and Christianity.* Philadelphia: Jewish Publication Society, 2004.

Greene, J. P. *Diary of Colonel Landon Carter of Sabine Hall, 1752-1758.* Virginia Historical Society Documents. 1987.

Greenhouse, S. "Take Up a New Career at 50? In Syracuse, Life after Layoffs." *New York Times,* June 20, 2005. Retrieved from http://www.nytimes.com/2005/06/20/nyregion/20workers.html?pagewanted=all&_r=0.

Gregory of Nyssa. *The Great Catechism.* In *The Nicene and Post-Nicene Fathers,* vol. 5, edited by P. Schaff and H. Wace. Peabody, Mass.: Hendrickson, 1903.

———. *Of the Making of Man (De hominis opificio).* In *The Nicene and Post-Nicene Fathers,* edited by P. Schaff and H. Wace, 8.5, 8.8. Peabody, Mass.: Hendrickson, 1903.

———. *Ad petrium.* In *Saint Basil: The Letters,* translated by R. J. Deferrari, vol. 2, *Epp.* 197-227. Loeb Classical Library. London: Heinemann, 1961.

Greider, W. *One World, Ready or Not: The Manic Logic of Global Capitalism.* New York: Simon and Schuster, Touchstone, 1997.

Grenz, S. *The Social God and the Relational Self.* Louisville: Westminster John Knox, 2001.

Grey, J. *Liberalism.* 2nd ed. Minneapolis: University of Minnesota Press, 1995.

Grisez, G. *Beyond the New Theism: A Philosophy of Religion.* Notre Dame: University of Notre Dame Press, 1975.

———. *The Way of the Lord Jesus: Living a Christian Life.* Vols. 1-3. Quincy, Ill.: Franciscan Press, 1993.

Grisez, G., J. Boyle, and J. Finnis. "Practical Principles, Moral Truth, and Ultimate Ends." *American Journal of Jurisprudence* 32 (1987): 99-151.

Grisez, G., J. Boyle, and O. Tollefsen. *Free Choice: A Self-Referential Argument.* Notre Dame: University of Notre Dame Press, 1976.

Gruchy, J. de. "Salvation as Healing and Humanization." In *Christ in Our Place: The Humanity of God in Christ for the Reconciliation of the World,* edited by T. Hart and D. Thimell, pp. 32-47. Eugene, Ore.: Wipf and Stock, 1989.

Gunton, C. *Enlightenment and Alienation: An Essay towards a Trinitarian Theology.* Grand Rapids: Eerdmans, 1985.

———. "The Church on Earth: The Roots of Community." In *On Being the Church:*

Essays on the Christian Community, edited by C. Gunton and D. Hardy. London: T. & T. Clark, 1993.

———. *One, the Three, and the Many.* Cambridge: Cambridge University Press, 1993.

Gunton, C., and D. Hardy, eds. *On Being the Church: Essays on the Christian Community.* London: T. & T. Clark, 1993.

Gupta, J. "Suffering Violence at Your Own Hands: Hegel on Ethical and Political Alienation." Paper presented at the 2015 Telos Conference on universal history, philosophical history, and the fate of humanity, February 13-15, 2015, New York University, New York.

Gushee, D. *Righteous Gentiles of the Holocaust: Genocide and Moral Obligation.* 2nd ed. St. Paul: Paragon House, 2003.

———. *The Future of Faith in American Politics: The Public Witness of the Evangelical Center.* Waco: Baylor University Press, 2008.

———. "Shalom." In *Prophetic Evangelicals,* edited by B. Benson, M. Berry, and P. Heltzel, pp. 59-75. Grand Rapids: Eerdmans, 2012.

———. *The Sacredness of Human Life: Why an Ancient Biblical Vision Is the Key to the World's Future.* Grand Rapids: Eerdmans, 2013.

———, ed. *A New Evangelical Manifesto: A Kingdom Vision for the Common Good.* St. Louis: Chalice, 2012.

Gutiérrez, G. *A Theology of Liberation.* Maryknoll, N.Y.: Orbis, 1973.

Haakonssen, K., ed. *The Cambridge Companion to Adam Smith.* Cambridge: Cambridge University Press, 2006.

Haakonssen, K., and D. Winch. "The Legacy of Adam Smith." In *The Cambridge Companion to Adam Smith,* edited by K. Haakonssen, pp. 366-94. Cambridge: Cambridge University Press, 2006.

Habgood, J. *Being a Person: Where Faith and Science Meet.* London: Hodder and Stoughton, 1998.

Haidt, J., and J. Graham. "When Morality Opposes Justice: Conservatives Have Moral Intuitions That Liberals May Not Recognize." *Social Justice Research* 20, no. 1 (2007): 98-116.

Halbertal, M. *On Sacrifice.* Princeton: Princeton University Press, 2012.

Hall, D. J. *Imaging God: Dominion as Stewardship.* Grand Rapids: Eerdmans, 1986.

Haller, W. *The Rise of Puritanism.* Philadelphia: University of Pennsylvania Press, 1972.

Haller, W., and G. Davies, eds. *The Leveller Tracts: 1647-1653.* New York: Columbia University Press, 1944.

Hallmann, J. *The Descent of God: Divine Suffering in History and Theology.* Minneapolis: Fortress, 1991.

Hamacher, W. "The Right Not to Use Rights." In *Political Theologies: Public Religions in a Post-Secular World,* edited by H. de Vries and L. E. Sullivan, pp. 671-90. New York: Fordham University Press, 2006.

Hamann, J. G. *Sämtliche Werke.* Edited by J. Nadler. Vienna: Herder Verlag, 1949-1957.

———. *Hamann's Socratic Memorabilia: A Translation and Commentary.* Translated by J. C. O'Flaherty. Baltimore: Johns Hopkins University Press, 1967.

―――. *Londoner Schriften, Historisch-kritische Neuedition.* Edited by O. Bayer and B. Weissenborn. Munich: C. H. Beck, 1993; original 1758.

―――. *Writings on Philosophy and Language.* Edited and translated by K. Haynes. Cambridge: Cambridge University Press, 2007.

Hamel, G. *Poverty and Charity in Roman Palestine: First Three Centuries c.e.* Berkeley: University of California Press, 1990.

Hammond, P., R. P. Stevens, and T. Svanoe. *The Marketplace Annotated Bibliography.* Downers Grove, Ill.: InterVarsity, 2002.

Handlin, O., and L. Handlin. *Liberty and Power: 1600-1760.* New York: Harper and Row, 1986.

Haque, U. *Betterness: Economics for Humans.* Cambridge: Harvard Business Review Press, 2011.

―――. "Is America Giving Up on the Future?" *Harvard Business Review,* September 28, 2011. Retrieved from http://blogs.hbr.org/2011/09/is-america-giving-up-on-the-fu/.

Harding, M., and A. Nobbs, eds. *All Things to All Cultures: Paul among Jews, Greeks, and Romans.* Grand Rapids: Eerdmans, 2013.

Harrison, J. *Paul and the Imperial Authorities at Thessalonica and Rome: A Study in the Conflict of Ideology.* Tübingen: Mohr Siebeck, 2011.

―――. "Paul among the Romans." In *All Things to All Cultures: Paul among Jews, Greeks, and Romans,* edited by J. Harding and A. Nobbs, pp. 143-76. Grand Rapids: Eerdmans, 2013.

Hart, D. B. "A Gift Exceeding Every Debt: An Eastern Orthodox Appreciation of Anselm's *Cur Deus Homo.*" *Pro Ecclesia* 7 (1993): 333-49.

―――. *Atheist Delusions: The Christian Revolution and Its Fashionable Enemies.* New Haven: Yale University Press, 2009.

―――. *In the Aftermath: Provocations and Laments.* Grand Rapids: Eerdmans, 2009.

―――. *The Experience of God: Being, Consciousness, Bliss.* New Haven: Yale University Press, 2013.

Hart, T., and D. Thimell, eds. *Christ in Our Place: The Humanity of God in Christ for the Reconciliation of the World.* Eugene, Ore.: Wipf and Stock, 1989.

Hartman, D. *A Living Covenant: The Innovative Spirit in Traditional Judaism.* New York: Free Press, 1985.

Hatch, N. *The Democratization of American Christianity.* New Haven: Yale University Press, 1989.

Hauerwas, S. *A Community of Character: Towards a Constructive Christian Social Ethic.* Notre Dame: University of Notre Dame Press, 1981.

―――. *The Peaceable Kingdom: A Primer in Christian Ethics.* Notre Dame: University of Notre Dame Press, 1983.

―――. *Sanctify Them in the Truth: Holiness Exemplified.* Nashville: Abingdon, 1989.

―――. *After Christendom.* Nashville: Abingdon, 1999.

―――. "Bonhoeffer: The Truthful Witness." *Homiletics online* (2004). Retrieved from http://www.homileticsonline.com/subscriber/interviews/hauerwas.asp.

―――. *Performing the Faith: Bonhoeffer and the Practice of Nonviolence.* Grand Rapids: Baker Academic and Brazos Press, 2004.

————. *The State of the University.* Oxford: Blackwell, 2007.

————. *Hannah's Child: A Theologian's Memoir.* London: SCM, 2010.

————. *War and the American Difference.* Grand Rapids: Baker Academic, 2011.

Hauerwas, S., and C. Pinches. *Christians among the Virtues: Theological Conversations with Ancient and Modern Ethics.* Notre Dame: University of Notre Dame Press, 1997.

Hauerwas, S., and W. Willimon. *Resident Aliens: A Provocative Christian Assessment of Culture and Ministry for People Who Know That Something Is Wrong.* Nashville: Abingdon, 1989.

Hauptman, J. *Rereading the Mishnah: A New Approach to Ancient Jewish Texts.* Tübingen: Mohr Siebeck, 2005.

Hausman, D., and M. McPherson. *Economic Analysis and Moral Philosophy.* Cambridge: Cambridge University Press, 1996.

Hayek, F. *The Road to Serfdom.* Chicago: University of Chicago Press, 1944.

————. *The Constitution of Liberty.* Chicago: Henry Regnery and University of Chicago Press, 1960, 2011.

Haynes, L. "Nature and Importance of True Republicanism." In *Black Preacher to White America: The Collected Writings of Lemuel Haynes, 1774-1833,* edited by R. Newman, pp. 77-88. Brooklyn, N.Y.: Carlson Publishing, 1990; original 1801.

Hazony, Y. *The Philosophy of Hebrew Scripture.* Cambridge: Cambridge University Press, 2012.

Hedges, C. *War Is a Force That Gives Us Meaning.* New York: Anchor Books, 2003.

Heffernan, W., and J. Heffernan. "Social Consequences of the Economic Crisis in Agriculture." In *Agricultural Change,* edited by J. Molnar. Boulder, Colo.: Westview Press, 1986.

Hege, A.-K. "On Earth as It Is in Heaven: Christian Covenantal Communities in the U.S. and Their Longing for a Better World, with a Close Examination of the New Monasticism Movement." Unpublished manuscript, 2014.

Hegel, G. W. F. *The Philosophy of Right.* Edited by A. Wood. Translated by T. Knox. Oxford: Oxford University Press, 1942; original 1821.

————. *Philosophy of History.* Translated by J. Sibree. New York: Dover, 1956; original 1837.

————. *The Phenomenology of Mind.* Translated by J. Baillie. New York: Harper and Row, 1967; original 1807.

————. *The Phenomenology of Spirit.* Translated by J. Findley. Oxford: Oxford University Press, 1979; original 1817.

————. *The Difference between Fichte's and Schelling's Systems of Philosophy.* Edited by W. Cerf and H. Harris. Albany: State University of New York Press, 1988; original 1801.

Heidegger, M. *Being and Time.* Translated by J. Macquarrie and E. Robinson. Oxford: Basil Blackwell, 1962; original 1927.

————. "What Is Metaphysics?" In *Martin Heidegger: Basic Writings,* translated by D. Krell. New York: Harper and Row, 1977; original 1929. Also available at http://wagner.wpengine.netdna-cdn.com/psychology/files/2013/01/Heidegger-What-Is-Metaphysics-Translation-GROTH.pdf.

————. *Schelling's Treatise of the Essence of Human Thought*. Athens: Ohio University Press, 1984.

Heim, M. *The Depths of the Riches: A Trinitarian Theology of Religious Ends*. Grand Rapids: Eerdmans, 2001.

Hendricks, O., Jr. *The Politics of Jesus*. New York: Doubleday, 2006.

Henry, M. *The Essence of Manifestation*. Translated by G. Etzkorn. The Hague: Martinus Nijhoff, 1973.

Henshke, H. "The Prozbol of Hillel — on the History of Its Talmudic Explanations." *Shenaton Ha-Mishpat Ha-Ivri* 71 (2001-2003).

Herder, J. "Ideas for the Philosophy of History of Humanity." In *F. G. Herder on Social and Political Culture*, edited and translated by F. Barnard. London: Cambridge University Press, 1969; original 1784-1791.

————. "Yet Another Philosophy of History concerning the Development of Mankind." In *F. G. Herder on Social and Political Culture*, edited and translated by F. Barnard. London: Cambridge University Press, 1969; original 1774.

Heschel, A. J. *Man's Quest for God: Studies in Prayer and Symbolism*. New York: Scribner, 1954.

————. "Religion and Race." In *The Insecurity of Freedom: Essays on Human Existence*. New York: Noonday Press, 1967.

————. *God in Search of Man*. New York: Farrar, Straus and Giroux, 1997.

————. *The Prophets*. New York: Harper Perennial Classics, 2001.

Hicks, D. *Inequality and Christian Ethics*. Cambridge: Cambridge University Press, 2000.

Hicks, D., and M. Valeri, eds. *Global Neighbors: Christian Faith and Moral Obligation in Today's Economy*. Grand Rapids: Eerdmans, 2008.

Himmelfarb, D. "Freedom, Virtue, and the Founding Fathers: A Review Essay." *Public Interest* 90 (Winter 1988): 15-120.

Hobbes, T. *Behemoth, or the Long Parliament*. Chicago: University of Chicago Press, 1990; original 1679.

————. *Leviathan*. Edited by E. Curly. Indianapolis: Hackett, 1994; original 1651.

————. *Leviathan*. Edited by R. Tuck. Cambridge: Cambridge University Press, 1996; original 1651.

————. *On the Citizen*. New York: Cambridge University Press, 1998; original 1642.

————. *On Liberty and Necessity*. Cambridge and New York: Cambridge University Press, 1999; original 1656.

Hodge, C. *Systematic Theology*. Vols. 1-3. New York: Scribner, Armstrong, and Co, 1872-1873.

Hoeflich, M. "Legal Ethics in the Nineteenth Century: The 'Other' Tradition." *University of Kansas Law Review* 47 (1999): 793-99.

Hoekema, A. *Created in God's Image*. Grand Rapids: Eerdmans, 1986.

Hoff, J. *The Analogical Turn: Rethinking Modernity with Nicholas of Cusa*. Grand Rapids: Eerdmans, 2013.

Hofstadter, R. *America at 1750: A Social Portrait*. New York: Vintage Books, 1971.

Hollenbach, D. *The Common Good and Christian Ethics*. New York: Cambridge University Press, 2002.

———. "The Common Good and Issues in U.S. Politics: A Critical Catholic Approach." *Journal of Religion and Society* 4 (2008): 33-46.

———. "Sustaining Catholic Social Engagement: A Key Role for Movements in the Church Today." *Journal of Catholic Social Thought* 10 (2013): 431-47. Special issue entitled "Social Movements in Context."

Hollingsworth, S. "Simone Weil and the Theo-Poetics of Compassion." *Modern Theology* 29, no. 3 (July 2013): 203-29.

Holloway, M. *Utopian Communities in America: 1680-1880.* Mineola, N.Y.: Dover Publications, 1966.

Holman, S. *The Hungry Are Dying: Beggars and Bishops in Roman Cappadocia.* New York: Oxford University Press, 2001.

Honner, J. "Unity-in-Difference: Karl Rahner and Niels Bohr." *Theological Studies* 46 (1985): 480-506.

Horkheimer, M., and T. Adorno. *Dialectic of Enlightenment.* London: Continuum, 1976; original 1947.

Horsley, R., ed. *Paul and Empire: Religion and Power in Roman Imperial Society.* Harrisburg, Pa.: Trinity, 1997.

Horton, M. *Covenant and Salvation: Union with Christ.* Louisville: Westminster, 2007.

Hoskyns, E., and N. Davey. *The Riddle of the New Testament.* London: Faber and Faber, 1947, 1957.

Houston, J. "Spirituality and the Doctrine of the Trinity." In *Christ in Our Place: The Humanity of God in Christ for the Reconciliation of the World,* edited by T. Hart and D. Thimell, pp. 48-69. Eugene, Ore.: Wipf and Stock, 1989.

Hrdy, S. *Mothers and Others.* Cambridge: Harvard University Press, Belknap Press, 2009.

Hudson, M. "Reconstructing the Origins of Interest-Bearing Debt and the Logic of Clean Slates." In *Debt and Economic Renewal in the Ancient Near East,* edited by M. Hudson and M. van de Mieroop. Bethesda, Md.: CDL Press, 2002. Retrieved from http://tinyurl.com/ckfv3rj.

Hughes, J. *The End of Work: Theological Critiques of Capitalism.* Malden, Mass., and Oxford: Blackwell, 2007.

Hume, D. *An Enquiry concerning Human Understanding.* Edited by L. A. Selby-Bigge and P. H. Nidditch. 3rd ed. Oxford: Oxford University Press, 1975.

Hunt, L., ed. and trans. *The French Revolution and Human Rights.* Boston and New York: Bedford Books, 1996.

Hunter, J. *Prayer, Politics, and Power: What Really Happens When Religion and Politics Mix.* Carol Stream, Ill.: Tyndale House, 1988.

———. *Right Wing, Wrong Bird: Why the Tactics of the Religious Right Won't Fly with Most Conservative Christians.* Longwood, Fla.: Church Press, 2006.

———. *A New Kind of Conservative.* Ventura, Calif.: Gospel Light, 2008.

Huntington, S. *American Politics: The Promise of Disharmony.* Cambridge: Harvard University Press, 1981.

Hurtado, A. M., and K. Hill. *Ache Life History: The Ecology and Demography of a Foraging People.* Livingston, N.J.: Aldine Transaction, 1996.

Hurtado, L. *Lord Jesus Christ: Devotion to Jesus in Earliest Christianity.* Grand Rapids: Eerdmans, 2003.

Husserl, E. *Cartesian Meditations: An Introduction to Phenomenology.* Translated by D. Cairns. The Hague: Martinus Nijhoff, 1977. See §42, p. 89.

Hyde, L. *The Gift: Imagination and the Erotic Life of Property.* New York: Vintage Books, 1983.

Hyneman, C., and D. Lutz. *American Political Writing during the Founding Era, 1760-1805.* Vols. 1-2. Indianapolis: Liberty Press, 1983.

Ibekwe, L. *The Universality of Salvation in Jesus Christ in the Thought of Karl Rahner.* Würzburg: Echter Verlag, 2006.

Illingworth, J. R. *The Doctrine of the Trinity.* London: Macmillan, 1907.

International Theological Commission. "Select Questions on Christology." In *International Theological Commission: Texts and Documents, 1969-1985,* edited by M. Sharkey, pp. 185-206. San Francisco: Ignatius, 1989.

Irenaeus. *Against Heresies (Adversus haereses).* Edited by A. Roberts and J. Donaldson. Grand Rapids: Eerdmans, 1989; original ca. 180.

———. *Against Heretics (Adversus haereses).* In *The Ante-Nicene Fathers,* edited by A. Roberts, J. Donaldson, and A. C. Coxe. Peabody, Mass.: Hendrickson, 1994; original ca. 180.

Jacobsen, T. "The Eridu Genesis." *Journal of Biblical Literature* 100 (1981): 513-29.

James, W. *The Works of William James.* Edited by F. Burkhardt, F. Bowers, and I. Skrupskelis. Cambridge: Harvard University Press, 1975-1988.

———. *Writings: 1902-1910: "The Varieties of Religious Experience"; "Pragmatism"; "Some Problems of Philosophy"; "A Pluralist Universe"; "The Meaning of Truth"; "Essays."* Edited by B. Kuklick. New York: Library of America, 1988.

Jaspers, K. *The Origin and Goal of History.* New York: Routlege, 2010.

Jay, M. "Faith-Based History." *History and Theory* 48 (February 2009): 76-84.

Jennings, W. J. *The Christian Imagination: Theology and the Origins of Race.* New Haven: Yale University Press, 2011.

Jensen, M., ed. "The Documentary History of the Ratification of the Constitution." In *Commentaries on the Constitution, Public and Private: 10 May to 13 September 1788,* vol. 18. Madison: Madison State Historical Society of Wisconsin, 1997.

Jenson, R. W. "Appeal to the Person of the Future." In *The Futurist Option,* edited by R. W. Jenson and C. E. Braaten. New York: Newman Press, 1970.

———. *Systematic Theology.* Vol. 1, *The Triune God.* New York: Oxford University Press, 1997.

———. *Systematic Theology.* Vol. 2, *The Works of God.* New York: Oxford University Press, 1999.

Jenson, R. W., and C. Gunton, eds. *Trinity, Time, and Church: A Response to the Theology of Robert W. Jenson.* Grand Rapids: Eerdmans, 2000.

Jewett, P. *Infant Baptism and the Covenant of Grace.* Grand Rapids: Eerdmans, 1978.

Jewett, R. *Romans: A Commentary.* Minneapolis: Fortress, 2007.

Joh, W. A. *The Heart of the Cross: A Postcolonial Christology.* Louisville: Westminster John Knox, 2006.

John of Damascus. *On the Divine Images.* Translated by D. Anderson. New York: St. Vladimir's Seminary Press, 1980.

John Paul II. *Redemptor hominis.* 1979. Retrieved from http://www.vatican.va/holy _father/john_paul_ii/encyclicals/documents/hf_jp-ii_enc_04031979_redemptor -hominis_en.html.

———. *Redemptoris missio.* 1990. Retrieved from http://www.vatican.va/holy_father/ john_paul_ii/encyclicals/documents/hf_jp-ii_enc_07121990_redemptoris-missio _en.html.

Johnson, K. "Reconsidering Barth's Rejection of Przywara's *Analogia Entis.*" *Modern Theology* 26, no. 4 (2010): 632-50.

Jones, L. G. *Embodying Forgiveness: A Theological Analysis.* Grand Rapids: Eerdmans, 1995.

Justin Martyr. *Apology (Apologia).* In *The Ante-Nicene Fathers,* edited by A. Roberts, J. Donaldson, and A. C. Coxe. Peabody, Mass.: Hendrickson, 1994; original 155-157.

Kamenev, M. "The World's Happiest Country." *Business Week,* October 11, 2006. Retrieved from http://images.businessweek.com/ss/06/10/happiest_countries/index_01.htm.

Kant, I. *Groundwork for the Metaphysics of Morals.* In *The Moral Law,* edited and translated by H. Paton. London: Hutchinson, 1948.

———. *Groundwork of the Metaphysics of Morals.* Translated by H. Paton. New York: Harper and Row, 1964.

———. *Grounding for the Metaphysics of Morals.* Translated by J. W. Ellington. 3rd ed. Indianapolis: Hackett, 1993; original 1785.

———. *Critique of Pure Reason.* Translated by N. Smith. New York: St. Martin's Press, 1965; original 1781.

———. *Kant's Political Writings.* Edited by H. Reiss. Cambridge: Cambridge University Press, 1970.

———. "Perpetual Peace." In *Kant's Political Writings,* edited by H. Reiss. Cambridge: Cambridge University Press, 1970.

———. *The Metaphysics of Morals.* Translated by M. Gregor. Cambridge: Cambridge University Press, 1991.

Käsemann, E. "The Beginnings of Christian Theology." In *New Testament Questions of Today,* edited by E. Käsemann, pp. 108-37. London: SCM, 1969.

———. "The Righteousness of God in Paul." In *New Testament Questions of Today,* edited by E. Käsemann, pp. 168-82. London: SCM, 1969.

———. "Justification and Salvation History in the Epistle to the Romans." In *Perspectives on Paul.* London: SCM, 1971.

———. *Commentary on Romans.* Translated by G. W. Bromiley. 4th ed. Grand Rapids: Eerdmans, 1980.

Kass, L. *The Beginning of Wisdom: Reading Genesis.* New York: Free Press, 2003.

Kaufman, W. *Hegel: A Reinterpretation.* Notre Dame: University of Notre Dame Press, 1997.

Kearney, R. "The God Who May Be." In *Questioning God,* edited by J. Caputo, M. Dooley, and M. Scanlon, pp. 153-85. Bloomington and Indianapolis: Indiana University Press, 2001.

———. "Philosophizing the Gift." In *The Hermeneutics of Charity: Interpretation, Selfhood, and Postmodern Faith; Studies in Honor of James H. Olthuis,* edited by J. K. Smith and H. I. Venema, pp. 52-72. Grand Rapids: Brazos, 2004.

———. "Sacramental Aesthetics." In *Transcendence and Phenomenology,* edited by P. Candler and C. Cunningham, pp. 334-69. London: SCM, 2007.

———. *Anatheism: Returning to God after God.* New York: Columbia University Press, 2009.

———. "Paul's Notion of Dunamis: Between the Possible and the Impossible." In *St. Paul among the Philosophers,* edited by J. Caputo and L. Alcoff, pp. 142-59. Bloomington and Indianapolis: Indiana University Press, 2009.

———. "Sacramental Imagination and Eschatology." In *Phenomenology and Eschatology: Not Yet in the Now,* edited by N. DeRoo and J. P. Manoussakis. Surrey, U.K.: Ashgate, 2013.

Keller, C. *From a Broken Web: Separation, Sexism, and Self.* Boston: Beacon Press, 1986.

———. "The Flesh of God: A Metaphor in the Wild." In *Theology That Matters: Ecology, Economy, and God,* edited by D. K. Ray. Minneapolis: Fortress, 2006.

———. "The Apophasis of Gender: A Fourfold Unsaying of Feminist Theology." *Journal of the American Academy of Religion* 76 (2008): 905-33.

———. *On the Mystery: Discerning Divinity in Process.* Minneapolis: Fortress, 2008.

———. "Theology's Multitude: Polydoxy Reviewed and Renewed." *Modern Theology* 30, no. 3 (2014): 127-39.

Keller, C., and L. Schneider, eds. *Polydoxy: Theology of Multiplicity and Relation.* New York: Routledge, 2010.

Kelly, A. "Gross National Happiness in Bhutan: The Big Idea from a Tiny State That Could Change the World." *Guardian,* December 1, 2012. Retrieved from http://www.theguardian.com/world/2012/dec/01/bhutan-wealth-happiness-counts.

Kelsey, D. "Wisdom, Theological Anthropology, and Modern Secular Interpretation of Humanity." In *God's Life in Trinity,* edited by M. Volf and M. Welker, pp. 44-60. Minneapolis: Augsburg Fortress, 2006.

Kepler, J. *The Epitome of Copernican Astronomy and Harmonies of the World.* Translated by C. Wallis. New York: Prometheus Books, 1995; original 1621.

Kesaris, P., and M. Hunter, eds. *Letters and Papers of Robert Boyle: From the Archives of the Royal Society.* Lanham, Md.: University Press of America, 1990.

Kierkegaard, S. *Works of Love: Some Christian Reflections in the Forms of Discourses.* Translated by H. Hong and E. Hong. New York: Harper and Row, 1962.

———. *The Concept of Anxiety.* In *Kierkegaard's Writings,* translated by R. Thomas. Princeton: Princeton University Press, 1980.

Kim, S. *Christ and Caesar: The Gospel and the Roman Empire in the Writings of Paul and Luke.* Grand Rapids: Eerdmans, 2008.

King, M. L., Jr. *Where Do We Go from Here: Chaos or Community?* Boston: Beacon Press, 1967, 2010.

———. "God (Amos)." In *The Papers of Martin Luther King, Jr.,* vol. 2, *Rediscovering Precious Values, July 1951-1955,* edited by C. Carson. Berkeley: University of California Press, 1992.

Klinck, D. *The French Counter-Revolutionary Theorist, Louis de Bonald.* New York: Peter Lang, 1996.

Knohl, I. *The Messiah before Jesus.* Berkeley and Los Angeles: University of California Press, 2000.

Kochen, M. "'It Was Not for Naught That They Called It *Hekdesh*': Divine Ownership and the Medieval Charitable Foundation." In *The Bar-Ilan Conference Volume,* edited by J. Fleishman, pp. 131-42. Jewish Law Association Studies, vol. 18. Liverpool: Jewish Law Association, 2008.

Kojève, A. "La métaphysique religieuse de Vladimir Soloviev." *Revue d'histoire et de philosophie religieuse* 14 (1934): 534-54; 15 (1935): 110-52.

———. *Introduction to the Reading of Hegel.* Edited by A. Bloom. Translated by J. Nichols. New York: Basic Books, 1969.

———. *Outline of a Phenomenology of Right.* Edited by B. Frost. Translated by B. Frost and R. Howe. Lanham, Md.: Rowman and Littlefield, 2000.

Korff, E. von. *Die Anfänge der Föderaltheologie und ihre erste Ausgestaltung in Zürich und Holland.* Bonn: Emil Eisele, 1908.

Korten, D. *When Corporations Rule the World.* West Hartford, Conn.: Kumarian Press; San Francisco: Berrett-Koehler Publishers, 1995.

Kotsko, A. *The Politics of Redemption.* London: T. & T. Clark, 2010.

Kovacs, K. *The Relational Theology of James E. Loder: Encounter and Conviction.* Frankfurt, New York, and Oxford: Peter Lang, 2011.

Kraemer, D. *The Mind of the Talmud: An Intellectual History of the Bavli.* New York: Oxford University Press, 1990.

Kramnick, I. *Republicanism and Bourgeois Radicalism: Political Ideology in Late Eighteenth Century England and America.* Ithaca, N.Y.: Cornell University Press, 1990.

Kraynak, R. *History and Modernity in Hobbes.* Ithaca, N.Y.: Cornell University Press, 1990.

Kress, G. "Design and Transformation: New Theories of Meaning." In *Multiliteracies: Literacy Learning and the Design of Social Futures,* edited by B. Cope and M. Kalantzis, pp. 151-63. London: Routledge, 2000.

Kuhn, T. *The Copernican Revolution.* Cambridge: Harvard University Press, 1957.

———. *The Essential Tension.* Chicago: University of Chicago Press, 1979.

———. *The Structure of Scientific Revolutions.* Chicago: University of Chicago Press, 1996.

Kutter, H. *They Must; or, God and the Social Democracy; A Frank Word to Christian Men and Women.* Miami: HardPress Publishing, 1979; original 1908.

Kuyper, A. *Calvinism: Six Stone Foundation Lectures.* Grand Rapids: Eerdmans, 1943.

Kymlicka, W. *Liberalism, Community, and Culture.* Oxford: Oxford University Press, 1989.

Labe, L. *Debate of Folly and Love: A New English Translation with the Original French Text.* Translated by A. Bourbon. New York: Peter Lang, 2000; original 1555.

Lachs, S. "On Matthew." *Novum Testamentum* 17, fasc. 1 (1975): 6-8. Retrieved from http://www.jstor.org/stable/1560193.

LaCocque, A., and P. Ricoeur. "From Interpretation to Translation." In *Thinking Biblically: Exegetical and Hermeneutical Studies,* translated by D. Pellauer. Chicago: University of Chicago Press, 1998.

LaCugna, C. *God for Us: The Trinity and Christian Life*. San Francisco: HarperSanFrancisco, 1992.

Lakoff, G. *Women, Fire, and Dangerous Things: What Categories Reveal about the Mind*. Chicago: University of Chicago Press, 1987.

———. *Whose Freedom? The Battle over America's Most Important Idea*. New York: Farrar, Straus and Giroux, 2006.

Lakoff, G., and M. Johnson. *Metaphors We Live By*. Chicago: University of Chicago Press, 1980, 2003.

———. *Philosophy in the Flesh: The Embodied Mind and Its Challenge to Western Thought*. New York: Basic Books, 1999.

Lamy, P. *Millennium Rage: Survivalists, White Supremacists, and the Doomsday Prophecy*. New York: Plenum Press, 1996.

Lang, U. M. "Anhypostatos — Enhypostatos: Church Fathers, Protestant Orthodoxy and Karl Barth." *Journal of Theological Studies* 49 (1998): 630-57.

Lantolf, J., ed. *Sociocultural Theory and Second Language Learning*. Oxford: Oxford University Press, 2000.

Lash, N. *Easter in Ordinary: Reflections on Human Experience and the Knowledge of God*. Notre Dame: University of Notre Dame Press, 1988.

———. *Believing Three Ways in One God: A Reading of the Apostles' Creed*. London: SCM, 1992.

Latour, B. *We Have Never Been Modern*. Translated by C. Porter. Cambridge: Harvard University Press, 1991, 1993.

Lebrun, R. *Joseph de Maistre: An Intellectual Militant*. Montreal: McGill-Queen's University Press, 1988.

———, ed. *Joseph de Maistre's Life, Thought, and Influence: Selected Studies*. Montreal: McGill-Queen's University Press, 2001.

Lejeune, R. *Christoph Blumhardt and His Message*. Rifton, N.Y.: Plough Publishing, 2011.

Levenson, J. "Poverty and the State in Biblical Thought." *Judaism* 25, no. 2 (1976): 230-41.

———. *Sinai and Zion: An Entry into the Jewish Bible*. Minneapolis: Winston Press, 1985.

———. *Creation and the Persistence of Evil: The Jewish Drama of Divine Omnipotence*. Princeton: Princeton University Press, 1988.

———. *The Hebrew Bible, the Old Testament, and Historical Criticism: Jews and Christians in Biblical Studies*. Louisville: Westminster John Knox, 1993.

Levinas, E. *Totality and Infinity*. Translated by A. Lingis. Pittsburgh: Duquesne University Press, 1969.

———. *Totality and Infinity: An Essay on Exteriority*. Dordrecht: Kluwer Academic Publishers, 1979.

———. *Ethics and Infinity: Conversations with Philippe Nemo*. Translated by R. Cohen. Pittsburgh: Duquesne University Press, 1985.

———. *Time and the Other*. Translated by R. Cohen. Pittsburgh: Duquesne University Press, 1987.

———. *Otherwise Than Being or Beyond Essence*. Translated by A. Lingis. Dordrecht: Kluwer Academic Publishers, 1991.

———. *Beyond the Verse: Talmudic Readings and Lectures*. New York: Bloomsbury, 1994.

————. *In the Time of the Nations.* Translated by M. Smith. London: Athlone, 1994.

————. "Revelation in the Jewish Tradition." In *Beyond the Verse: Talmudic Readings and Lectures,* translated by G. Mole, pp. 129-50. Bloomington: Indiana University Press, 1994.

————. *Basic Philosophical Writings.* Edited by A. Peperzak, S. Critchley, and R. Bernasconi. Translated by A. Lingis and R. A. Cohen. Bloomington: Indiana University Press, 1996.

————. *Proper Names.* Translated by M. Smith. Stanford: Stanford University Press, 1996.

————. *Existence and Existents.* Translated by A. Lingis. Pittsburgh: Duquesne University Press, 2001.

————. *Oeuvres 1: Carnets de captivité suivi de Écrits sur la captivité et Notes philosophiques diverses.* Edited by R. Calin. Preface and notes by R. Calin and C. Chalier. General preface by J.-L. Marion. Paris: Éditions Grasset & Fasquelle, 2009.

Levine, L. *The Ancient Synagogue: The First Thousand Years.* New Haven: Yale University Press, 2000.

Lévy-Bruhl, L. *How Natives Think.* Princeton: Princeton University Press, 1985.

Lewis, P. *Preventable Agricultural Deaths in Oklahoma, 1983-1988: Self-Inflicted or Suicides.* Edited by Agricultural Engineering Department. Stillwater: Oklahoma State University Press, 1989.

Lifshitz, J. I. "Secret of the Sabbath." *Azure* 10 (Winter 2001): 85-117.

Lind, M. *The Next American Nation: The New Nationalism and the Fourth American Revolution.* New York: Free Press, 1995.

Link, C. *Die Welt als Gleichnis: Studien zum Problem der natürlichen Theologie.* Munich: Kaiser, 1976.

Linklater, A. *Owning the Earth: The Transforming History of Land Ownership.* London: Bloomsbury, 2014.

Livingston, W. "Of the Use, Abuse, and Liberty of the Press." In *Independent Reflector; or, Weekly Essays on Sundry Important Subjects More Particularly Adapted to the Province of New York.* Cambridge: Harvard University Press, 1963; original 1753.

Locke, J. *An Essay concerning Human Understanding.* Edited by P. Nidditch. Oxford: Oxford University Press, 1975; original 1690.

————. *Two Treatises of Government.* Edited by P. Laslett. Cambridge: Cambridge University Press, 1988; original 1690.

————. *Letter concerning Toleration.* Edited by J. Horton and S. Mendus. New York: Routledge, 1991. Also available at http://www.let.rug.nl/usa/documents/1651-1700/john-locke-letter-concerning-toleration-1689.php.

————. *The Political Writings of John Locke.* Edited by D. Wootton. New York: Mentor, 1993.

————. *An Essay concerning Human Understanding.* In *Some Thoughts concerning Education: And, Of the Conduct of the Understanding,* edited by R. Grant and N. Tarcov. Indianapolis: Hackett, 1996.

————. *Some Thoughts concerning Education.* In *Some Thoughts concerning Education: And, Of the Conduct of the Understanding,* edited by R. Grant and N. Tarcov. Indianapolis: Hackett, 1996.

Lockwood, J. *The worth and excellence of civil freedom and liberty, illustrated, and a public spirit and the love of our country recommended.* New London, Conn.: Timothy Green, 1759.

Loder, J. *Transforming Moment.* 2nd ed. Colorado Springs: Helmers and Howard, 1989.

Loder, J., and W. J. Neidhardt. *The Knight's Move: The Relational Logic of the Spirit in Theology and Science.* Colorado Springs: Helmers and Howard, 1992.

Lofgren, M. "Goodbye to All That: Reflections of a GOP Operative Who Left the Cult." *Truthout.* 2011. Retrieved from http://www.truth-out.org/goodbye-all-reflections -gop-operative-who-left-cult/1314907779.

Lonergan, B. *De Deo trino, Pars systematica.* Translated by M. Shields. Rome: Gregorian University Press, 1964.

———. "Mission and the Spirit." In *A Third Collection: Papers by J. F. Lonergan,* edited by F. E. Crowe, pp. 23-34. Mahwah, N.J.: Paulist, 1985.

———. *Insight: A Study of Human Understanding.* Collected Works of Bernard Lonergan, vol. 3, edited by F. Crowe and R. Doran. Toronto: University of Toronto Press, 1992.

———. *The Lonergan Reader.* Edited by E. Morelli and M. Morelli. Toronto: University of Toronto Press, 1997.

———. *Method in Theology.* Toronto: University of Toronto Press, 2000.

———. *The Triune God: Systematics.* Collected Works of Bernard Lonergan, edited by R. Doran and D. Monsour, translated by M. Shields. Toronto: University of Toronto Press, 2009.

Long, D. S. *Divine Economy: Theology and the Market.* London and New York: Routledge, 2000.

Löning, K., and E. Zenger. *To Begin with, God Created . . . : Biblical Theologies of Creation.* Translated by O. Kaste. Collegeville, Minn.: Liturgical Press, 2000.

Lovin, R. "Covenantal Relationships and Political Legitimacy." *Journal of Religion* 60, no. 16 (1980): 1-16.

———. *Christian Ethics: An Essential Guide.* Nashville: Abingdon, 2000.

Luban, D. "Rediscovering Fuller's Legal Ethics." In *Rediscovering Fuller: Essays on Implicit Law and Institutional Design,* edited by W. J. Witteveen and W. van der Burg. Amsterdam: Amsterdam University Press, 1998.

———. *Legal Ethics and Human Dignity.* Cambridge and New York: Cambridge University Press, 2007.

Luther, M. *Lectures on Galatians (Galatervorlesung).* In *Luther's Works,* edited by J. Pelikan and H. Lehmann, translated by J. Pelikan. Vols. 1-55. St. Louis: Concordia, 1955-1986.

———. *Luther's Works.* Vol. 31. Edited by J. Pelikan and H. T. Lehmann. Philadelphia: Fortress, 1957.

———. *Lectures on Genesis (Genesisvorlesung).* In *Luther's Works,* translated by G. Schick. St. Louis: Concordia, 1958.

———. *The Freedom of a Christian (De libertate Christiana).* In *Martin Luther: Selections from His Writings,* edited by J. Dillenberger. Garden City, N.Y.: Anchor Books, 1961.

Macchia, F. *Spirituality and Social Liberation: The Message of the Blumhardts in the Light of Wuerttemberg Pietism.* Metuchen, N.J., and London: Scarecrow Press, 1993.

Mace, W. "Gibson's Strategy for Perceiving: Ask Not What's Inside Your Head but What

Your Head Is Inside Of." In *Perceiving, Acting, and Knowing,* edited by R. Shaw and J. Brandsford. Hillsdale, N.J.: Erlbaum, 1974.

MacIntyre, A. *After Virtue: A Study in Moral Theory.* London: Duckworth, 1981.

――――. "The Virtues, and Unity of a Human Life and the Concept of Tradition." In *Liberalism and Its Critics,* edited by M. Sandel. New York: New York University Press, 1984.

――――. "Community, Law and the Idiom and Rhetoric of Rights." *Listening: Journal of Religion and Culture* 5 (1991): 96-110.

――――. "Justice as Virtue: Changing Conceptions." In *Communitarianism and Individualism,* edited by S. Avineri and A. De-shalit, pp. 51-64. Oxford: Oxford University Press, 1992.

――――. "First Principles, Final Ends, and Contemporary Philosophical Issues." In *The MacIntyre Reader,* edited by K. Knight, pp. 171-201. London: Polity Press, 1998.

――――. "Politics, Philosophy, and the Common Good." In *The MacIntyre Reader,* edited by K. Knight, pp. 234-52. Notre Dame: University of Notre Dame Press, 1998.

――――. *Dependent Rational Animals: Why Human Beings Need the Virtues.* London: Duckworth, 1999.

――――. "Moral Philosophy and Contemporary Social Practice: What Holds Them Apart?" In A. MacIntyre, *The Tasks of Philosophy: Selected Essays,* vol. 1. Cambridge: Cambridge University Press, 2006.

Macmurray, J. *Persons in Relation.* Atlantic Highlands, N.J.: Humanities Press, 1991.

Madrick, J. *Why Economics Grow: The Forces That Shape Prosperity and How We Can Get Them Working Again.* New York: Basic Books, Century Foundation Book, 2002.

Maghen, Z. "Dancing in Chains: The Baffling Coexistence of Legalism and Exuberance in Judaic and Islamic Tradition." In *Judaic Sources and Western Thought,* edited by J. Jacobs, pp. 217-37. New York: Oxford University Press, 2011.

Mahmood, S. *Politics of Piety.* Princeton: Princeton University Press, 2005.

Maid in Manhattan (motion picture). Directed by W. Wang. Produced by R. Baratta and E. Goldsmith-Thomas. Los Angeles: Columbia Pictures/Sony Pictures Entertainment, 2002.

Maimonides, M. *Guide for the Perplexed.* Translated by A. H. Friedländer. New York: Dover, 1956.

Maistre, J. de. *Consideration on France.* Translated by R. Lebrun. Cambridge: Cambridge University Press, 1994; original 1796.

Maloney, R. "Usury in Greek, Roman and Rabbinic Thought." *Traditio* 27 (1971): 79-109. Retrieved from http://www.jstor.org/stable/27830917.

Mansfield, H., Jr. *Statesmanship and Party Government: A Study of Burke and Bolingbroke.* Chicago: University of Chicago Press, 1965.

Marcel, P. *The Biblical Doctrine of Infant Baptism.* London: James Clarke, 1953.

Marechal, J. *Le point de départ de la métaphysique.* Cahiers 1-5. Bruges: Charles Beyaert, 1922-1947. Retrieved from http://www.barnesandnoble.com/w/le-point-de-d-part -de-la-m-taphysique-joseph-mar-chal/1027340657.

Marion, J.-L. "Does the Cogito Affect Itself? Generosity and Phenomenology; Remarks on Michel Henry's Interpretation, and Does the Ego Alter the Other?" In *Cartesian Questions: Method and Metaphysics.* Chicago: University of Chicago Press, 1999.

———. "In the Name: How to Avoid Speaking of 'Negative Theology.'" In *God, the Gift, and Postmodernism,* edited by J. Caputo and M. Scanlon. Bloomington: Indiana University Press, 1999.

Maritain, J. *Person and the Common Good.* Notre Dame: University of Notre Dame Press, 1973.

———. *Man and the State.* Washington, D.C.: Catholic University of America Press, 1998.

———. *Christianity and Democracy, and the Rights of Man and Natural Law.* San Francisco: Ignatius, 2012.

Marks, E., and I. de Courtivron, eds. *New French Feminisms.* New York: Schocken Books, 1981.

Markschies, C. "God's Body: A Neglected Dimension of Ancient Christian Religion and Theology." Paper presented at a meeting of the North American Patristics Society, Chicago, 2014.

———. "Glaubten antike Christenmenschen an ihre Bilder für Himmel und Hölle?" In *The Metaphorical Use of Language in Deuterocanonical and Cognate Literature,* edited by M. Witte and S. Behnke, pp. 509-35. Deuterocanonical and Cognate Literature Yearbook, 2014-2015, edited by F. V. Reiterer, P. C. Beentjes, N. Calduch-Benages, and B. G. Wright. Berlin: De Gruyter, 2015.

Marsden, G. *Understanding Fundamentalism and Evangelicalism.* Grand Rapids: Eerdmans, 1991.

Marsh, C. *Reclaiming Dietrich Bonhoeffer: The Promise of His Theology.* New York and Oxford: Oxford University Press, 1994.

Marshall, C. *Crowned with Glory and Honor: Human Rights in the Biblical Tradition.* Studies in Peace and Scripture, vol. 6. Telford, Pa.: Cascadia Publishing House, 2002.

Martin, M. *The Submerged Reality: Sophiology and the Turn to a Poetic Metaphysics.* Tacoma, Wash.: Angelico Press, 2015.

Marx, K. *Grundrisse.* Edited by M. Niklaus. Harmondsworth, U.K.: Penguin, 1973; original 1858.

Marx, K., and F. Engels. *The German Ideology.* Edited by C. Arthur. London: Lawrence and Wishart, 1970; original 1846.

Marx, W. *The Philosophy of F. W. J. Schelling: History, System, and Freedom.* Bloomington: Indiana University Press, 1984.

Mauss, M. *The Gift: Form and Function of Exchange in Archaic Societies.* New York: Routledge, 1990.

———. *The Gift: The Form and Reason for Exchange in Archaic Society.* Translated by W. D. Halls. London: Routledge, 1990; original 1925, *Essai sur le don: Sociologie et anthropologie.*

May, H. *The Enlightenment in America.* New York: Oxford University Press, 1976.

Mayflower Compact. 1620. Retrieved from http://www.let.rug.nl/usa/documents/1600 -1650/mayflower-compact-1620.php.

Mayhew, J. "Memorandum on 25 August, 1765 Sermon: Appended to Bailyn, B. *Reli-*

gion and Revolution: Three Biographical Studies." *Perspectives in American History* 4 (1970): 140-43; original 1765.

McBride, J. *The Church for the World: A Theology of Public Witness.* New York: Oxford University Press, 2010.

McBrien, R. *Catholicism.* London: HarperCollins, 1994, 2000.

McCoy, C., and J. W. Baker. *Fountainhead of Federalism: Heinrich Bullinger and the Covenantal Tradition.* Louisville: Westminster John Knox, 1991.

McDonald, F. *Novus Ordo Seclorum: The Intellectual Origins of the Constitution.* Lawrence: University Press of Kansas, 1985.

McFague, S. *Literature and the Christian Life.* New Haven: Yale University Press, 1966.

———. *The Body of God: An Ecological Theology.* Minneapolis: Fortress, 1993.

McFadyen, A. *The Call to Personhood: A Christian Theory of the Individual in Social Relationships.* Cambridge: Cambridge University Press, 1990.

McGinn, B. "Seeing and Not Seeing: Nicholas of Cusa's *De visione Dei* in the History of Western Mysticism." In *Cusanus: The Legacy of Learned Ignorance,* edited by P. J. Casarella. Washington, D.C.: University of America Press, 2006.

McMahon, R. *The Two Poets of Paradise Lost.* Baton Rouge and London: Louisiana State University Press, 1998.

Meacham, J. *American Gospel: God, the Founding Fathers, and the Making of a Nation.* New York: Random House, 2006.

Meek, E. *Loving to Know: Covenant Epistemology.* Eugene, Ore.: Wipf and Stock, Cascade Books, 2011.

Meeks, M. D. "The Social Trinity and Property." In *God's Life in Trinity,* edited by M. Volf and M. Welker, pp. 13-24. Minneapolis: Augsburg Fortress, 2006.

Meir, E. *Interreligious Theology: Its Value and Mooring in Modern Jewish Philosophy.* Berlin: De Gruyter, 2015.

Mekiltha on Exodus. Tractate Kaspa (Ex. 22.24-29) 3.147. Translated by J. Z. Lauterbach. Jewish Publication Society, 1933.

Meltzoff, A. *Words, Thoughts, and Theories.* Cambridge: MIT Press, 1997.

———. *The Scientist in the Crib: What Early Learning Tells Us about the Mind.* New York: Morrow, 2000.

Merleau-Ponty, M. "The Primacy of Perception and Its Philosophical Consequences." Translated by J. Edie. In *The Primacy of Perception and Other Essays.* Evanston, Ill.: Northwestern University Press, 1964.

———. *Signs.* Translated by R. McCleary. Evanston, Ill.: Northwestern University Press, 1964.

———. "Working Notes." In *The Visible and the Invisible,* edited by C. Lefort. Evanston, Ill.: Northwestern University Press, 1973.

———. *The Phenomenology of Perception.* Translated by C. Smith. London: Routledge, 2002.

Michea, J.-C. *The Realm of Lesser Evil: An Essay on Liberal Civilization.* Translated by D. Fernbach. Malden, Mass.: Polity Press, 2009.

Migliore. D. "The Trinity and the Theology of Religions." In *God's Life in Trinity,* edited by M. Volf and M. Welker, pp. 101-17. Minneapolis: Augsburg Fortress, 2006.

Milbank, J. *Theology and Social Theory: Beyond Secular Reason.* Oxford: Basil Blackwell, 1990.

———. "The Name of Jesus: Incarnation, Atonement, Ecclesiology." *Modern Theology* 7, no. 4 (1991): 311-33.

———. "Can the Gift Be Given? Prolegomena to Any Future Trinitarian Metaphysic." *Modern Theology* 11, no. 1 (1995): 119-61.

———. "Postmodern Critical Augustinianism: A Short Summa in Forty-Two Responses to Unasked Questions." In *The Postmodern God: A Theological Reader,* edited by G. Ward, pp. 265-78. Oxford: Blackwell, 1997.

———, *The World Made Strange: Theology, Language, Culture.* Oxford: Blackwell, 1997.

———. "The Theological Critique of Philosophy in Hamann and Jacobi." In *Radical Orthodoxy: A New Theology,* edited by J. Milbank, C. Pickstock, and G. Ward, pp. 21-37. London: Routledge, 1999.

———. "The Soul of Reciprocity. Part One: Reciprocity Refused." *Modern Theology* 17, no. 3 (2001): 335-91.

———. "The Soul of Reciprocity. Part Two: Reciprocity Granted." *Modern Theology* 17, no. 4 (2001): 485-507.

———. *Being Reconciled: Ontology and Pardon.* Radical Orthodoxy. New York: Routledge, 2003.

———. "Sublimity: The Modern Transcendent." In *Transcendence: Philosophy, Literature, and Theology Approach the Beyond,* edited by R. Schwartz, pp. 211-34. London and New York: Routledge, 2004.

———. "Materialism and Transcendence." In *Theology and the Political: The New Debate,* edited by C. Davis, J. Milbank, and S. Žižek, pp. 393-426. Durham, N.C., and London: Duke University Press, 2005.

———. *The Suspended Middle: Henri de Lubac and the Debate concerning the Supernatural.* Grand Rapids: Eerdmans, 2005.

———. "Liberality vs. Liberalism." *Telos* 134 (2006): 6-21.

———. "Only Theology Saves Metaphysics." In *Veritas: Belief and Metaphysics,* edited by C. Cunningham and P. Candler Jr., pp. 452-500. Norwich: SCM, 2007.

———. "Paul against Biopolitics." *Theory, Culture, and Society* 25 (2008): 125-72.

———. "Can a Gift Be Given?" Unpublished manuscript, 2010.

———. "Materialism and Transcendence." In *Theology and the Soul of the Liberal State,* edited by L. Kaplan and C. Cohen, pp. 221-54. Lanham, Md.: Rowman and Littlefield, Lexington Books, 2010.

———. "Paul against Biopolitics." In *Paul's New Moment: Continental Philosophy and the Future of Christian Theology,* edited by J. Milbank, S. Žižek, and C. Davis, pp. 21-73. Grand Rapids: Brazos, 2010.

———. "Hume against Kant: Community, Faith, Reason and Feeling." *Modern Theology* 27 (March 2011): 276-97. Retrieved from http://onlinelibrary.wiley.com/doi/10.1111/j .1468-0025.2011.01676.x/abstract.

———. "The Real Third Way: For a New Metanarrative of Capital and the Associationist Alternative." In *The Crisis of Global Capitalism: Pope Benedict XVI's Social Encyclical and the Future of Political Economy,* edited by A. Pabst, pp. 27-70. Eugene, Ore.: Wipf and Stock, 2011.

―――. "Stanton Lecture 7: The Objectivity of Feeling." 2011. Retrieved from http:// theologyphilosophycentre.co.uk/papers/Milbank_StantonLecture7.pdf.

―――. "On 'Thomistic Kabbalah.'" *Modern Theology* 27, no. 1 (2011): 147-85.

―――. "Christianity and Platonism in East and West." In *Divine Essence and Divine Energies: Ecumenical Reflections on the Presence of God in Eastern Orthodoxy,* edited by C. Athanasopoulos and C. Schneider, pp. 158-209. Cambridge: James Clarke, 2013.

―――. "Dignity Rather Than Right." In *Understanding Human Dignity,* edited by C. Mc-Crudden. Oxford: Oxford University Press, 2013.

―――. *Beyond Secular Order: The Representation of Being and the Representation of the People.* Chichester: Wiley Blackwell, 2014.

―――. "Ethical Economy beyond 'Shared Value.'" In *Ethical Economy — a ResPublica Report,* edited by Phillip Blond and Adrian Pabst. London: ResPublica, 2014.

―――. "*Mathesis* and *Methexis:* The Post-Nominalist Realism of Nicholas of Cusa." Forthcoming.

Milbank, J., and A. Pabst. *The Politics of Virtue: Britain and the Post-Liberal Future.* Lanham, Md.: Rowman and Littlefield, 2016.

Milbank, J., and C. Pickstock. *Truth in Aquinas.* London and New York: Routledge, 2001.

Mill, J. S. "Theism." In *Essays on Ethics, Religion, and Society: Collected Works of John Stuart Mill,* edited by J. Robson. Toronto: University of Toronto Press, 1969.

―――. "Utilitarianism." In *Essays on Ethics, Religion, and Society: Collected Works of John Stuart Mill,* edited by J. Robson. Toronto: University of Toronto Press, 1969.

―――. "The Utility of Religion." In *Essays on Ethics, Religion, and Society: Collected Works of John Stuart Mill,* edited by J. Robson. Toronto: University of Toronto Press, 1969.

―――. "Considerations on Representative Government." In *Essays on Politics and Society: Collected Works of John Stuart Mill,* edited by J. Robson. Toronto: University of Toronto Press, 1977.

―――. "On Liberty." In *Essays on Politics and Society: Collected Works of John Stuart Mill,* edited by J. Robson. Toronto: University of Toronto Press, 1977.

―――. "The Subjection of Women." In *Essays on Equality, Law, and Education: Collected Works of John Stuart Mill,* edited by J. Robson. Toronto: University of Toronto Press, 1984.

Miller, D. "Responsible Relationship: *Imago Dei* and the Moral Distinction between Humans and Other Animals." *International Journal of Systematic Theology* 13, no. 3 (2011): 323-39.

Miller, N. *The Religious Roots of the First Amendment: Dissenting Protestants and the Separation of Church and State.* New York: Oxford University Press, 2012.

Milton, J. *Complete Poems and Major Prose: Milton.* Edited by M. Hughes. New York: Prentice-Hall, 1957.

―――. *Political Writings.* Edited by M. Dzelzainis. Translated by C. Gruzelier. Cambridge: Cambridge University Press, 1991.

―――. *Areopagitica and Other Political Writings of John Milton.* Edited by J. Alvis. Indianapolis: Liberty Fund, 1999. *Areopagitica* published 1644.

Mir, A. "A Panentheist Reading of John Milbank." *Modern Theology* 28, no. 3 (2012): 526-60.

Missouri Rural Crisis Center. *Hog Wars: The Corporate Grab for Control of the Hog Industry and How Citizens Are Fighting Back.* Columbia: Missouri Rural Crisis Center, 1996.

Mitchell, M. *The Politics of Gratitude: Scale, Place, and Community in a Global Age.* Dulles, Va.: Potomac Books, 2012.

―――. "What Exactly Do I Have a Right To?" *Front Porch Republic.* 2013. Retrieved from http://www.frontporchrepublic.com/2013/03/i-have-a-right-to-be-unlimited/.

Moltmann, J. *The Crucified God.* Translated by R. Wilson and John Bowden. New York: Harper and Row, 1973.

―――. *Trinity and the Kingdom.* Translated by M. Kohl. San Francisco: Harper and Row, 1981, 1991.

―――. *God in Creation: A New Theology of Creation and the Spirit of God.* Translated by M. Kohl. San Francisco: Harper and Row, 1985.

―――. *The Way of Jesus Christ: Christology in Messianic Dimensions.* Translated by M. Kohl. Minneapolis: Fortress, 1989, 1993.

―――. *The Coming God: Christian Eschatology.* Translated by M. Kohl. Minneapolis: Fortress, 1996.

―――. *Experiences in Theology: Ways and Forms of Christian Theology.* Translated by M. Kohl. London: SCM, 2000.

―――. *Ethics of Hope.* Translated by M. Kohl. Minneapolis: Fortress, 2012.

Moltmann-Wendel, E. *I Am My Body: A Theology of Embodiment.* New York: Continuum, 1995.

Montefiore, C. "Rabbinic Judaism and the Epistles of St. Paul." *Jewish Quarterly Review* 13 (1900-1901): 161-217.

―――. *Judaism and St. Paul: Two Essays.* London: Max Goschen, 1914.

Montesquieu, Baron de. *The Spirit of the Laws.* Translated by T. Nugent. London: G. Bell & Sons, 1914; original 1748.

―――. *Persian Letters.* Translated by J. Betts. New York: Penguin, 1977; original 1721.

Montgomery, B., T. Oord, and K. Winslow. *Relational Theology: A Contemporary Introduction.* Eugene, Ore.: Wipf and Stock, 2012.

Moore, G. *History of Religions: Judaism.* International Theological Library, vol. 2. Edinburgh: T. & T. Clark, 1914.

―――. "Christian Writers on Judaism." *Harvard Theological Review* 14 (1921): 197-254.

―――. *Judaism in the First Centuries of the Christian Era: The Age of the Tannaim.* Vols. 1-3. Cambridge: Harvard University Press, 1927-1930.

Moorhead, J. "Prophecy, Millennialism, and Biblical Interpretation in Nineteenth-Century America." In *Biblical Hermeneutics in Historical Perspective: Studies in Honor of Karlfried Froehlich on His Sixtieth Birthday,* edited by M. Burrows and P. Rorem. Grand Rapids: Eerdmans, 1991.

Moran, J., and A. Gode. *On the Origin of Language*. Chicago: University of Chicago Press, 1986.

Morgan, E. *Inventing the People: The Rise of Popular Sovereignty in England and America*. New York: Norton, 1988.

Morgenstern, M. *Conceiving a Nation: The Development of Political Discourse in the Hebrew Bible*. University Park: Penn State University Press, 2009.

Mudge, L. *We Can Make the World Economy a Sustainable Global Home*. Grand Rapids: Eerdmans, 2014.

Mühling, M. *Resonances: Neurobiology, Evolution, and Theology: Evolutionary Niche Construction, the Ecological Brain, and Relational-Narrative Theology*. Göttingen: Vandenhoeck & Ruprecht, 2014.

Mure, G. *The Philosophy of Hegel*. Westport, Conn.: Greenwood Publishing, 1965.

Nagel, T. "Rawls on Justice." In *Reading Rawls: Critical Studies of "A Theory of Justice,"* edited by N. Daniels. New York: Oxford University Press, 1975.

Nancy, J.-L. *The Inoperative Community*. Edited by P. Conor. Translated by P. Conor, L. Garbus, M. Holland, and S. Sawhney. Minneapolis: University of Minnesota Press, 1991.

———. "On Communism." In *Critical Legal Thoughts*. 2009. Retrieved from http://www .egs.edu/faculty/jean-luc-nancy/quotes/.

Nasar, S. *Grand Pursuit: The Story of Economic Genius*. New York: Simon and Schuster, 2011.

National Mental Health Association. *Report of the National Action Committee on the Mental Health of Rural Americans*. Alexandria, Va., 1988.

Navarre, M. de. *Heptameron*. Translated by P. Chilton. London: Penguin, 1984; original 1559.

Nelson, W. *Americanization of the Common Law: The Impact of Legal Change on Massachusetts Society, 1760-1830*. Cambridge: Harvard University Press, 1975.

Nelson, W., and R. Palmer. *Liberty and Community: Constitution and Rights in the Early American Republic*. New York: Oceana, 1987.

Neusner, J., and B. Chilton. *Jewish and Christian Doctrines*. New York: Routledge, 2000.

New London Group. "A Pedagogy of Multiliteracies: Designing Social Futures." *Harvard Educational Review* 66 (1996): 60-92.

Newman, L. "Covenant and Contract: A Framework for the Analysis of Jewish Ethics." *Journal of Law and Religion* 9, no. 1 (1991): 89-112. Retrieved from http://www.jstor .org/stable/1051109.

Nicholas of Cusa. *De quaerendo Deum*. 1444/1445.

———. *Reformatio generalis*. 1459.

———. *De visione Dei*. 1453.

———. *De ludo globi*. 1463.

———. *De aspice theoriae*. 1464.

———. *Nicholas of Cusa: Selected Spiritual Writings*. Translated by H. L. Bond. Mahwah, N.J.: Paulist, 1997.

———. *The Vision of God*. Translated by E. G. Salter. Introduction by E. Underhill. New York: Cosimo Classics, 2007.

Niebuhr, H. R. "Radical Monotheism and Western Culture." 1960. Retrieved from http://media.sabda.org/alkitab-2/Religion-Online.org%20Books/Niebuhr,%20H.%20Richard%20%20Radical%20Monotheism%20and%20Western%20Culture.pdf.

Niesel, W. *The Theology of Calvin.* Translated by H. Knight. Philadelphia: Westminster, 1956.

Niles, N. "[First of] Two Discourses of Liberty." In *American Political Writing during the Founding Era, 1760-1805,* edited by C. Hyneman and D. Lutz, pp. 257-76. 2 vols. Indianapolis: Liberty Press, 1774.

Nisbet, R. *Slavery not forbidden by Scripture; or a defence of the West India planters.* Philadelphia, Pa., 1773.

Noble, T. A. "Paradox in Gregory Nazianzen's Doctrine of the Trinity." In *Studia Patristica,* edited by E. A. Livingstone, pp. 94-99. Leuven: Peeters, 1993.

Noll, M. *America's God: From Jonathan Edwards to Abraham Lincoln.* New York: Oxford University Press, 2002.

Nordhoff, C. *The Communistic Societies of the United States: Harmony, Oneida, the Shakers, and Others.* St. Petersburg, Fla.: Red and Black Publishers, 1875.

Nordlander, A. "The Wonder of Immanence: Merleau-Ponty and the Problem of Creation." *Modern Theology* 29, no. 2 (April 2013): 104-23.

Novalis. *Philosophical Writings.* Translated and edited by M. M. Stoljar. Albany: State University of New York Press, 1997.

———. "Fichte Studies." In *Cambridge Texts in the History of Philosophy,* edited by J. Kneller. New York: Cambridge University Press, 2003; original 1795-1796.

———. *Notes for a Romantic Encyclopedia.* Translated and edited by D. Wood. Albany: State University of New York Press, 2007.

———. *Glauben und Liebe.* Contumax GmbH & Co. KG, 2010; original 1798.

Noyes, J. H. *Essay on Scientific Propagation.* Oneida, N.Y., 1875.

Nozick, R. *Anarchy, State, and Utopia.* New York: Basic Books, 1974.

NPR Staff. "Not Just Patriotic, U.S. Manufacturing May Be Smart." *NCPR.* December 8, 2012. Retrieved from http://www.northcountrypublicradio.org/news/npr/166801322/not-just-patriotic-u-s-manufacturing-may-be-smart.

Nussbaum, M. *Women and Human Development: The Capabilities Approach.* Cambridge: Cambridge University Press, 2000.

Oakes, K. "The Question of Nature and Grace in Karl Barth: Humanity as Creature and as Covenant-Partner." *Modern Theology* 23, no. 4 (November 2007): 595-616.

Oakeshott, M. "Introduction to Leviathan." In *Rationalism in Politics and Other Essays,* edited by T. Fuller. Indianapolis: Liberty Press, 1991.

Oakman, D. E. "The Ancient Economy in the Bible: BTB Readers Guide." *Biblical Theology Bulletin* 21 (1991): 34-39.

O'Connell, T. *Principles for a Catholic Morality.* New York: Seabury Press, 1978.

O'Donovan, O. "Moral Disagreement as an Ecumenical Issue." *Studies in Christian Ethics* 1, no. 1 (1988): 5-19.

———. *The Desire of the Nations: Rediscovering the Roots of Political Theory.* Cambridge: Cambridge University Press, 1996.

Olthuis, J. "Face-to-Face: Ethical Asymmetry of the Symmetry of Mutuality?" In *The*

Hermeneutics of Charity: Interpretation, Selfhood, and Postmodern Faith; Studies in Honor of James H. Olthuis, edited by J. K. Smith and H. I. Venema, pp. 135-56. Grand Rapids: Brazos, 1996, 2004.

———. "Face-to-Face: Ethical Asymmetry of the Symmetry of Mutuality?" In *Knowing Other-Wise: Philosophy at the Threshold of Spirituality,* edited by J. Olthius, pp. 131-58. New York: Fordham University Press, 1997.

———. *The Beautiful Risk.* Grand Rapids: Zondervan, 2001.

O'Neill, J., ed. *Hegel's Dialectic of Desire and Recognition: Texts and Commentary.* Albany: State University of New York Press, 1996.

Origen. *De oratione.* Retrieved from http://www.documentacatholicaomnia.eu/03d/0185 -0254,_Origenes,_Prayer,_EN.pdf.

Osterkamp, E. *Lucifer: Stationen eines Motivs.* Komparatistische Studien, vol. 9. Berlin and New York: De Gruyter, 1979.

Overton, R. "An Appeal to the Free People." In *Leveller Manifestoes of the Puritan Revolution,* edited by D. Wolfe. New York: T. Nelson and Sons, 1944; original 1647.

Pabst, A. "Modern Sovereignty in Question: Theology, Democracy and Capitalism." *Modern Theology* 26, no. 4 (2010): 570-602.

———. *Metaphysics: The Creation of Hierarchy.* Grand Rapids: Eerdmans, 2012.

———. "Prosperity and Justice for All: Why Solidarity and Fraternity Are Key to an Efficient, Ethical Economy." Paper presented at the Conference of the Fondazione Centesimus Annus Pro Pontifice, "The Good Society and the Future of Jobs: Can Solidarity and Fraternity Be Part of Business Decisions?" Vatican City, May 8-10, 2014.

Padilla-DeBorst, R. "Mary." In *Prophetic Evangelicals,* edited by B. Benson, M. Berry, and P. Heltzel, pp. 115-25. Grand Rapids: Eerdmans, 2012.

Palley, T. *Plenty of Nothing: The Downsizing of the American Dream and the Case for Structural Keynesianism.* Princeton: Princeton University Press, 1998.

Pally, M. *The New Evangelicals: Expanding the Vision of the Common Good.* Grand Rapids: Eerdmans, 2011.

———. "The Hebrew Bible Is a Problem Set." In *Die Gewalt des einen Gottes: Die Monotheismus Debatte,* edited by R. Schieder. Berlin: Berlin University Press, 2014.

Palmer, P. *To Know as We Are Known: Education as a Spiritual Journey.* San Francisco: HarperSanFrancisco, 1996.

Palmer, R. "Liberties as Constitutional Provisions: 1776-1791." In *Liberty and Community: Constitution and Rights in the Early American Republic,* edited by W. Nelson and R. Palmer, pp. 55-148. New York: Oceana, 1987.

Pambrun, J. "The Relationship between Theology and Philosophy: Augustine, Ricoeur, and Hermeneutics." *Theoform* 36, no. 3 (2005): 292-319.

Pan, D. "Language and Metaphysics in Johann Georg Hamann's Aesthetica in Nuce and Philologische Einfälle und Zweifel." *Monatshefte* 106, no. 3 (Fall 2014): 351-75.

Pannenberg, W. *Theology and the Kingdom of God.* Edited by R. J. Neuhaus. Philadelphia: Westminster, 1969.

———. *Basic Questions in Theology.* Edited by G. H. Kelm. Vols. 1-2. Philadelphia: Fortress, 1971.

————. *Jesus — God and Man*. Translated by L. Wilkins and D. Priebe. 2nd ed. Philadelphia: Westminster, 1977.

————. *Systematic Theology*. Translated by G. Bromiley. Vols. 1-3. Grand Rapids: Eerdmans, 1991-1998.

Parrington, V. *Main Currents in American Thought*. Vol. 2. New York: Harcourt Brace, 1927.

Parsons, T. *Social Structure and Personality*. New York: Free Press, 1964.

————. *Theories of Society: Foundations of Modern Sociological Theory*. Edited by K. Naegele. New York: Free Press, 1965.

————. *The System of Modern Societies*. New York: Prentice-Hall, 1971

————. *Economics and Society: A Study in the Integration of Economic and Social Theory*. New York: Routledge, 1999.

Patton, G. S., Jr. *Quotes*. Retrieved from http://www.goodreads.com/author/quotes/370054 .George_S_Patton_Jr_.

Paul VI. Encyclical Letter *Populorum Progressio*. March 26, 1967. Retreived from http://www.vatican.va/holy_father/paul_vi/encyclicals/documents/hf_p-vi_enc_26031967 _populorum_en.html.

Pavlenko, A., and J. Lantolf. "Second Language Learning as Participation and the (Re)construction of Selves." In *Sociocultural Theory and Second Language Learning*, edited by J. Lantolf, pp. 155-77. Oxford: Oxford University Press, 2000.

Pearce, R. "Rediscovering the Republican Origins of the Legal Ethics Codes." *Georgetown Journal of Legal Ethics* 6 (1992): 241-82.

————. "The Professionalism Paradigm Shift." *New York University Law Review* 70 (1995): 1229-78.

————. "The Legal Profession as a Blue State: Reflections on Public Philosophy, Jurisprudence, and Legal Ethics." *Fordham Law Review* 75, no. 3 (2006): 1338-68.

Pearce, R., and E. Wald. "Rethinking Lawyer Regulation: How a Relational Approach Would Improve Professional Rules and Roles." *Michigan State Law Review* (2012): 513-36.

Penn, William. Pennsylvania charter of privileges. October 18, 1701. Retrieved from http://www.constitution.org/bcp/penncharpriv.htm.

Penuel, W., and J. Wertsch. "Vygotsky and Identity Formation: A Sociocultural Approach." *Educational Psychologist* 30 (1995): 83-92.

Peperzak, T. *Beyond: The Philosophy of Emmanuel Levinas*. Evanston, Ill.: Northwestern University Press, 1997.

Perceptor, The. "Social Duties of the Political Kind." In *American Political Writing during the Founding Era, 1760-1805*, edited by C. Hyneman and D. Lutz. Vols. 1-2. Indianapolis: Liberty Press, 1983; original 1772.

Perkins, W. *A Golden Chain: The Description of Theology Containing the Order of the Causes of Salvation & Damnation, according to God's Word*. Puritan Reprints, 2010; original 1590.

Peters, T. *God as Trinity: Relationality and Temporality in the Divine*. Louisville: Westminster John Knox, 1993.

Pfaff, D. *The Altruistic Brain: How We Are Naturally Good.* New York: Oxford University Press, 2014.

Pfleiderer, O. *Das Urchristentum.* Berlin: G. Reimer, 1887.

Philo. *De specialibus legibus.* In *Philo, Complete Works.* Loeb Classical Library. Cambridge: Harvard University Press, 1929.

———. *De virtutibus.* In *Philo, Complete Works.* Loeb Classical Library. Cambridge: Harvard University Press, 1929.

———. *The Giants (De gigantibus).* In *Philo of Alexandria: The Contemplative Life, The Giants, and Selections,* edited and translated by D. Winston, pp. 59-72. Classics of Western Spirituality. New York: Paulist, 1981.

Pickstock, C. *After Writing: On the Liturgical Consummation of Philosophy.* Oxford: Blackwell, 1989.

———. "Music: Soul, City and Cosmos after Augustine." In *Radical Orthodoxy: A New Theology,* edited by J. Milbank, C. Pickstock, and G. Ward, pp. 243-77. London: Routledge, 1999.

———. "Justice and Prudence: Principles of Order in the Platonic City." *Telos* 119 (2001): 3-17.

———. "Modernity and Scholasticism: A Critique of Recent Innovations of Univocity." *Antonianum* 78 (2003): 3-46.

———. "Duns Scotus: His Historical and Contemporary Significance." *Modern Theology* 21 (2005): 543-74.

Piketty, T. *Le capital au XXIᵉ siècle.* Paris: Ed. Seuil, 2013.

———. *Capital in the Twenty-First Century.* Translated by A. Goldhammer. Cambridge: Harvard University Press, 2014.

Pinckaers, S., O.P. *The Sources of Christian Ethics.* Washington, D.C.: Catholic University of America Press, 1995.

Pinker, S. *The Language Instinct.* New York: Morrow, 1994.

———. *How the Mind Works.* New York: Norton, 1997.

———. *The Blank Slate: The Modern Denial of Human Nature.* New York: Viking Press, 2002.

———. *The Stuff of Thought: Language as a Window into Human Nature.* New York: Viking Press, 2007.

Pinker, S., and G. Lakoff. "Does Language Frame Politics?" *Public Policy Research* 14, no. 1 (2007): 59-71.

Pitzer D., ed. *America's Communal Utopias.* Chapel Hill: University of North Carolina Press, 1997.

Plantinga, C., Jr. *Not the Way It's Supposed to Be: A Breviary of Sin.* Grand Rapids: Eerdmans, 1995.

Platt, D. *Radical: Taking Back Your Faith from the American Dream.* Colorado Springs: Multnomah, 2010.

———. *Radical Together: Unleashing the People of God for the Purpose of God.* Colorado Springs: Multnomah, 2011.

Polanyi, K. *Primitive, Archaic, and Modern Economies: Essays of Karl Polanyi.* Edited by G. Dalton. New York: Anchor Books, 1968.

―――. *The Livelihood of Man.* New York: Academic Press, 1977.

―――. *The Great Transformation: The Political and Economic Origins of Our Time.* Boston: Beacon Press, 2001; original 1944.

Polanyi, M. *Personal Knowledge: Towards a Post-Critical Philosophy.* Chicago: University of Chicago Press, 1962.

―――. "Science and Reality." *British Journal for the Philosophy of Science* 18 (1967): 177-96.

―――. *Knowing and Being: Essays by Michael Polanyi.* Edited by M. Greene. Chicago: University of Chicago Press, 1969.

―――. *The Tacit Dimension.* Chicago: University of Chicago Press, 2009.

Polkinghorne, J., ed. *The Work of Love: Creation as Kenosis.* Grand Rapids: Eerdmans, 2001.

―――. *The Trinity and an Entangled World: Relationality in Physical Science and Theology.* Grand Rapids: Eerdmans, 2010.

Polzin, R. *Moses and the Deuteronomist: Deuteronomy, Joshua, Judges.* Literary Study of the Deuteronomic History. New York: Seabury Press, 1980.

Popper, K. *The Open Society and Its Enemies.* Princeton: Princeton University Press, 1950.

―――. *The Poverty of Historicism.* London: Routledge and Kegan Paul, 1961.

Prestige, G. *God in Patristic Thought.* London: SPCK, 1950.

Przywara, E. *Religionsphilosophie Katholischer Theologie.* Munich: R. Oldenbourg, 1927.

―――. *In und Gegen: Stellungnahmen zur Zeit.* Nürnberg: Glock und Lutz, 1955.

―――. *Analogia Entis: Metaphysics; Original Structure and Universal Rhythm.* Grand Rapids: Eerdmans, 2014; original 1932.

Rah, S.-C. *The Next Evangelicalism: Freeing the Church from Western Cultural Captivity.* Nottingham: IVP, 2009.

Rahner, K. *The Christian Commitment: Essays in Pastoral Theology.* New York: Sheed and Ward, 1963.

―――. *Theological Investigations.* Translated by K.-H. Kruger. Baltimore: Helicon Press, 1966.

―――. "The Theology of Power." In *Theological Investigations,* vol. 4. London: Darton, Longman and Todd, 1966.

―――. *Spirit in the World.* London: Sheed and Ward, 1968.

―――. *The Trinity.* Translated by J. Donceel. New York: Seabury Press, 1970, 1997.

―――. "Experience of the Spirit and Existential Commitment." In *Theological Investigations,* vol. 11. London: Darton, Longman and Todd, 1974.

―――. "Ideas for a Theology of Death." In *Theological Investigations,* vol. 13. London: Darton, Longman and Todd, 1975.

―――. *Foundations of Christian Faith: An Introduction to the Idea of Christianity.* Translated by W. V. Dych. New York: Seabury Press, 1978.

―――. *Grundkurs des Glaubens: Einfuehrung in den Begriff des Christentums.* 6th ed. Freiburg, Germany; Basel, Switzerland; Vienna: Herder, 1978.

―――. *Concern for the Church.* New York: Crossroad, 1981.

―――. "Reflections on the Unity of the Love of Neighbour and the Love of God." In *Theological Investigations,* vol. 6, *Concerning Vatican Council II,* translated by K.-H.

Kruger and B. Kruger. New York: Crossroad, 1982; original published as *Schriften zur Theologie*, vol. 6. Einsiedeln, Switzerland: Verlagsanstalt Benziger & Co. AG, 1969.

Ramsey, P. *Basic Christian Ethics.* New York: Charles Scribner, 1950.

Rasmussen, L. *Moral Fragments and Moral Community: A Proposal for Church in Society.* Minneapolis: Augsburg Fortress, 1993.

Rasmusson, A. "Science as Salvation: George Lakoff and Steven Pinker as Secular Political Theologians." *Modern Theology* 28, no. 2 (2012): 197-228.

Ratzinger, J. *Dogma and Preaching.* Translated by M. J. O'Connell. Chicago: Franciscan Herald, 1985.

Rauschenbusch, W. *Christianity and the Social Crisis.* Edited by D. Ottati. Louisville: Westminster John Knox, 1992; original 1907.

———. *Christianity and the Social Crisis in the 21st Century: The Classic That Woke Up the Church.* New York: HarperOne, 2007; original 1907.

Rawls, J. *A Theory of Justice.* Cambridge: Harvard University Press, 1971.

———. "The Basic Liberties and Their Priority." Tanner Lectures on Human Values, April 10, 1981. Ann Arbor: University of Michigan, 1981. Retrieved from http://tannerlectures.utah.edu/lectures/documents/rawls82.pdf.

———. "Justice as Fairness: Political Not Metaphysical." In *Communitarianism and Individualism,* edited by S. Avineri and A. De-shalit. New York: Oxford University Press, 1992.

Reese, T. *Essay on the Influence of Religion in Civil Society.* Charleston, S.C.: Markland and M'Iver, 1788.

Reinhard, K. "Toward a Political Theology of the Neighbor." In *The Neighbor: Three Inquiries in Political Theology,* edited by S. Žižek, E. Santner, and K. Reinhard. Chicago: University of Chicago Press, 2005.

Renan, E. "What Is a Nation?" In *Becoming National: A Reader,* edited by G. Eley and R. Suny, pp. 41-55. New York: Oxford University Press, 1996; original 1882.

Reynolds, S. *Fiefs and Vassals: The Medieval Evidence Reinterpreted.* Oxford: Oxford University Press, 1994.

Riches, A. "After Chalcedon: The Oneness of Christ and the Dyothelite Mediation of His Theandric Unity." *Modern Theology* 24, no. 2 (April 2008): 199-224.

———. "Christology and the *Duplex Hominis Beatitudo:* Re-sketching the Supernatural Again." *International Journal of Systematic Theology* 14, no. 1 (January 2012): 44-69.

———. "Hannah's Child: A Life Given and Therefore Lived." *Modern Theology* 28, no. 2 (April 2012): 327-38.

———. "Christology and Anti-Humanism." *Modern Theology* 29, no. 3 (July 2013): 311-37.

Richmond, W. *Essay on Personality as a Philosophical Principle.* London: Edward Arnold, 1900.

Ricoeur, P. *Oneself as Another.* Translated by K. Blamey. Chicago: University of Chicago Press, 1995.

———. "Reflections on a New Ethos for Europe." In *Paul Ricoeur: The Hermeneutics of Action,* edited by R. Kearney. London: Sage, 1996.

———. *On Translation.* Translated by E. Brennan. London: Routledge, 2006.

Roca, C., and D. Helbing. "Emergence of Social Cohesion in a Model Society of Greedy,

Mobile Individuals." *Proceedings of the National Academy of Sciences*. 2011. Retrieved from http://www.pnas.org/content/108/28/11370.full.

Rodgers, D. *Contested Truths: Keywords in American Politics Since Independence*. New York: Basic Books, 1987.

Rolnick, P. *Person, Grace, and God*. Grand Rapids: Eerdmans, 2007.

Rorty, R. *The Linguistic Turn: Essays in Philosophical Method*. Chicago: University of Chicago Press, 1992.

Rosato, P. "Spirit-Christology as Access to Trinitarian Theology." In *God's Life in Trinity*, edited by M. Volf and M. Welker, pp. 166-76. Minneapolis: Augsburg Fortress, 2006.

Rose, G. *Hegel contra Sociology*. London: Athlone, 1981.

_____. *Dialectic of Nihilism: Post-Structuralism and Law*. Oxford: Blackwell, 1984.

———. *The Broken Middle: Out of Our Ancient Society*. Oxford: Blackwell, 1992.

———. *Judaism and Modernity: Philosophical Essays*. Oxford: Blackwell, 1993.

Rosenzweig, F. *The Star of Redemption*. Translated by W. W. Hallo. New York: Holt, Rinehart and Winston, 1971; original 1921.

———. *Ninety-Two Poems and Hymns of Yehuda Halevi*. Edited by R. Cohen. Translated by T. Kovach, E. Jospe, and G. Schmidt. Albany: State University of New York Press, 2000.

———. *Star of Redemption*. Translated by B. Galli. Madison: University of Wisconsin Press, 2005; original 1921.

Roskies, D. "Terumah, the Art of Being a Jew." Lecture conducted from Ansche Chesed, New York, February 2014.

Ross, E. *Social Control: A Survey of the Foundations of Order*. Cleveland: Case Western Reserve University, 1969.

Rothschild, E. *Economic Sentiments: Adam Smith, Condorcet, and the Enlightenment*. Cambridge: Harvard University Press, 2001.

Rousseau, J.-J. *The Social Contract and Discourses*. Translated by G. Cole. New York: Dutton, 1950; original 1762.

———. *On the Social Contract*. Translated by J. Masters. New York: St. Martin's Press, 1978; original 1762.

Rubenstein, M.-J. "Introducing Polydoxy." *Modern Theology* 30, no. 3 (2014): 1-6.

Rudolph, D. "Paul's 'Rule in All Churches' (1 Cor 7:17-24) and Torah-Defined Ecclesiological Variegation." *Studies in Christian-Jewish Relations* 5 (2010): 1-23.

Rush, B. *Letters of Benjamin Rush*. Edited by L. H. Butterfield. Vols. 1-2. Princeton: Princeton University Press, 1951. Letter of November 12, 1791.

Ruskin, J. *"Unto This Last" and "Munera Pulveris."* London: George Allen and Sons, 1911.

Russell, B. *Unpopular Essays*. New York: Simon and Schuster, 1951.

Russell, J. *Mephistopheles: The Devil in the Modern World*. Ithaca, N.Y.: Cornell University Press, 1986.

Sacks, J. *The Dignity of Difference: How to Avoid the Clash of Civilizations*. London: Continuum, 2007.

Salguero, G. "The Cross." In *Prophetic Evangelicals*, edited by B. Benson, M. Berry, and P. Heltzel, pp. 126-33. Grand Rapids: Eerdmans, 2012.

Samuelson, P. "The Keynes Centenary: Sympathy from the Other Cambridge." *Economist* 287 (1983): 19-21.

Sandel, M. "Justice and the Good." In *Liberalism and Its Critics.* New York: New York University Press, 1984.

―――. *Public Philosophy: Essays on Morality in Politics.* Cambridge: Harvard University Press, 2005.

Sanders, E. P. "Patterns of Religion in Paul and Rabbinic Judaism: A Holistic Method of Comparison." *Harvard Theological Review* 66 (1973): 455-78.

―――. "The Covenant as a Soteriological Category and the Nature of Salvation in Palestinian and Hellenistic Judaism." In *Jews, Greeks, and Christians,* edited by R. Hamerton-Kelly and R. Scroggs, pp. 11-44. Leiden: Brill, 1976.

―――. *Paul and Palestinian Judaism: A Comparison of Patterns of Religion.* Philadelphia: Fortress, 1977.

―――. "On the Question of Fulfilling the Law in Paul and Rabbinic Judaism." In *Donum Gentilicum,* edited by E. Bammel, pp. 103-26. Oxford: Oxford University Press, 1978.

―――. *Paul, the Law, and the Jewish People.* Philadelphia: Fortress, 1983.

Santner, E. *On the Psychotheology of Everyday Life: Reflections on Freud and Rosenzweig.* Chicago: University of Chicago Press, 2001.

Sarna, N. *Genesis.* Jewish Publication Society Torah Commentary. Philadelphia: Jewish Publication Society, 1989.

Sartori G. "Liberty and Law." In *The Politicization of Society,* edited by K. Templeton Jr., pp. 249-312. Indianapolis: Liberty Press, 1979.

Saussure, F. *Course in General Linguistics.* London: Duckworth, 1983; original 1916.

Sauter, G. *What Dare We Hope? Reconsidering Eschatology.* Harrisburg, Pa.: Trinity, 1999.

Schaff, P., ed. *A Select Library of the Nicene and Post-Nicene Fathers.* Vols. 1-14. Grand Rapids: Eerdmans, 1981.

Scheler, M. "The Sense of Unity with the Cosmos." In *The Nature of Sympathy.* London: Routledge and Kegan Paul, 1954.

Schelling, F. W. J. von. *Schellings Sämmliche Werke.* Edited by K. F. A. Schelling. Stuttgart: Cotta, 1856-1861.

―――. *Werke: Historisch-kritische Ausgabe.* Edited by H. M. Baumgartner, W. G. Jacobs, and H. Krings. Stuttgart-Bad Cannstatt: Frommann-Holzboog, 1976-.

Scherer, M. "Saint John." In *Political Theologies: Public Religions in a Post-Secular World,* edited by H. de Vries and L. E. Sullivan, pp. 341-62. New York: Fordham University Press, 2006.

Schindler, D. "The Embodied Person as Gift and the Cultural Task on America: *Status Quaestionis.*" *Communio: International Catholic Review* 35 (2008): 397-443.

Schipper, B. "From Milton to Modern Satanism: The History of the Devil and the Dynamics between Religion and Literature." *Journal of Religion in Europe* 3 (2010): 103-24.

Schleiermacher, Friedrich. *The Christian Faith,* edited by H. R. Mackintosh and J. S. Stewart. 2nd ed. Edinburgh: T. & T. Clark, 1999; original 1830/1831.

Schmitt, C. *Political Theology: Four Chapters on the Concept of Sovereignty.* Translated by G. Schwab. Cambridge: MIT Press, 1985.

Schnarch, D. *Passionate Marriage: Keeping Love and Intimacy Alive in Committed Relationships*. New York: Henry Holt, 1997.

Scholem, G. "Zum Verstaendnis der messianischen Idee." *Judaica* (1963): 7-74.

Schwartz, D. *Aquinas on Friendship*. New York: Oxford University Press, 2007.

Schwartz, S. *Imperialism and Jewish Society, 200 B.C.E. to 640 C.E.* Princeton and Oxford: Princeton University Press, 2001.

Schwarzschild, S. "On Jewish Eschatology." In *The Pursuit of the Ideal: Jewish Writings of Steven Schwarzschild*, edited by M. Kellner, pp. 209-29. Albany: State University of New York Press, 1990.

Schweitzer, A. *Die Mystik des Apostels Paulus*. Tübingen: Mohr Siebeck, 1930.

———. *The Mysticism of Paul the Apostle*. Translated by W. Montgomery. Baltimore: Johns Hopkins University Press, 1998; original 1931.

———. *The Quest of the Historical Jesus*. Translated by W. Montgomery. Mineola, N.Y.: Dover Publications, 2005; original 1906.

Scitovsky, T. *The Joyless Economy: The Psychology of Human Satisfaction*. New York and Oxford: Oxford University Press, 1976, 1992.

Searle, A. *Americans against Liberty; or, An Essay on the Nature and Principles of True Freedom*. 2nd ed. London: J. Mathews, 1776. Retrieved from http://archive.org/stream/cihm_20487#page/n7/mode/2up.

Seebeck, D., and T. Stoner. *My Business, My Mission: Fighting Global Poverty through Partnerships*. Grand Rapids: Faith Alive Christian Resources, 2009.

Selznick, P. *The Moral Commonwealth: Social Theory and the Promise of Community*. Berkeley: University of California Press, 1992.

Sen, A. "What Do We Want from a Theory of Justice?" *Journal of Philosophy* 3 (2006): 215-38.

Seyfarth, R., and D. Cheney. "The Evolutionary Origins of Friendship." *Annual Review of Psychology* 63 (2012): 179-99.

Seyhan, A. *Representation and Its Discontents: The Critical Legacy of German Romanticism*. Berkeley and Los Angeles: University of California Press, 1992.

Sfard, A. "On Two Metaphors for Learning and the Dangers of Choosing Just One." *Educational Researcher* 27, no. 2 (1998): 6.

Shain, B. *The Myth of American Individualism: The Protestant Origins of American Political Thought*. Princeton: Princeton University Press, 1994.

Shambaugh, B. *Amana: The Community of True Inspiration*. Iowa City: State Historical Society of Iowa, 1908.

Shanahan, W. O. *German Protestants Face the Social Question*. Notre Dame: University of Notre Dame Press, 1954.

Shanks, A. *Against Innocence: Gillian Rose's Reception of Gift of Faith*. London: SCM, 2008.

Sharswood, G. "An Essay on Professional Ethics." *32 Annual Report of the American Bar Association* (1907).

Shelley, P. *Prometheus Unbound: A Lyrical Drama in Four Acts*. In *Shelley's Poetry and Prose: Authoritative Texts, Criticism*, edited by D. Reiman and S. Powers. New York: Norton, 1977. See act 4, scene 4.1, verse 321.

————. *Shelley's Poetry and Prose: Authoritative Texts, Criticism.* Edited by D. Reiman and S. Powers. New York: Norton, 1977.

Sider, R. *Fixing the Moral Deficit: A Balanced Way to Balance the Budget.* Downers Grove, Ill.: InterVarsity, 2012.

Sigurdson, O. "Beyond Secularism? Towards a Post-Secular Political Theology." *Modern Theology* 26, no. 2 (April 2010): 177-96.

Silk, J., and B. House. "Evolutionary Foundations of Human Prosocial Sentiments." *Proceedings of the National Academy of Sciences* 108, suppl. 2 (2011): 10910-17.

Sittler, J. *Gravity and Grace: Reflections and Provocations.* Minneapolis: Augsburg, 1986.

Skidelsky, R., and E. Skidelsky. *How Much Is Enough? Money and the Good Life.* New York: Other Press, 2012.

Skinner, A. *A System of Social Science: Papers Relating to Adam Smith.* Oxford: Oxford University Press, 1996.

Skinner, Q. "Thomas Hobbes and His Disciples in France and England." *Comparative Studies in Society and History* 8, no. 2 (January 1966).

Smigel, E. O. *The Wall Street Lawyer: Professional Organization Man?* New York: Free Press of Glencoe, Collier-Macmillan, 1964.

Smith, A. *The Theory of Moral Sentiments.* Edited by D. Raphael and A. Macfie. Oxford: Clarendon, 1976; original 1759/1790.

————. *A Theory of Moral Sentiments.* New York: Prometheus Books, 2000; original 1759/1790.

————. *A Wealth of Nations.* Edited by E. Cannan. New York: Random House, Modern Library, 2000; original 1776.

Smith, C. *Moral, Believing Animals: Human Personhood and Culture.* New York: Oxford University Press, 2003.

Smith, G. "Why I Am Leaving Goldman Sachs." *New York Times,* March 14, 2012. Retrieved from http://www.nytimes.com/2012/03/14/opinion/why-i-am-leaving-goldman-sachs.html?pagewanted=all.

Smith, I. K. "The Later Pauline Letters." In *All Things to All Cultures: Paul among Jews, Greeks, and Romans,* edited by J. Harding and A. Nobbs, pp. 302-27. Grand Rapids: Eerdmans, 2013.

Smith, J. K. A. *The Fall of Interpretation: Philosophical Foundations for a Creational Hermeneutic.* Downers Grove, Ill.: InterVarsity, 2000.

————. "Formation, Grace, and Pneumatology: Or, Where's the Spirit in Gregory's Augustine?" *Journal of Religious Ethics* 38, no. 3 (September 2011): 556-69.

————. *How (Not) to Be Secular: Reading Charles Taylor.* Grand Rapids: Eerdmans, 2014.

Smith, J. K. A., and H. I. Venema. *The Hermeneutics of Charity: Interpretation, Selfhood, and Postmodern Faith; Studies in Honor of James H. Olthuis.* Grand Rapids: Brazos, 2004.

Smith, M. "The Thessalonian Correspondence." In *All Things to All Cultures: Paul among Jews, Greeks, and Romans,* edited by J. Harding and A. Nobbs, pp. 269-301. Grand Rapids: Eerdmans, 2013.

Smith, S. "What Is 'Right' in Hegel's Philosophy of Right?" *American Political Science Review* 83, no. 1 (1989): 3-18.

Smith, T. *Revivalism and Social Reform: American Protestantism on the Eve of the Civil War.* New York: Abingdon, 1957.

Soelle, D. *Christ the Representative: An Essay in Theology after the "Death of God."* Translated by D. Lewis. Philadelphia: Fortress, 1967.

Söhngen, G. "Analogia Fidei." *Catholica* 3 (1934): 176-208.

Sokolowski, R. *The God of Faith and Reason: Foundations of Christian Theology.* Washington, D.C.: Catholic University of America Press, 1995.

Soloveitchick, J. *The Halakhic Mind.* New York: Free Press, 1986.

Solovyov, V. *The Crisis of Western Philosophy: Against the Positivists.* Translated and edited by B. Jakim. Hudson, N.Y.: Lindisfarne Press, 1996; original 1873.

Sparling, R. "Transfiguring the Enlightenment: J. G. Hamann and the Problem of Public Reason." *Monatshefte* 98, no. 1 (Spring 2006): 12-29.

———. *Johann Georg Hamann and the Enlightenment Project.* Toronto: University of Toronto Press, 2011.

Spencer, H. *Political Writings.* Edited by J. Offer. Cambridge: Cambridge University Press, 1994.

Spengler, O. *Man and Technics: Contribution to a Philosophy of Life.* Honolulu: University Press of the Pacific, 2002.

Spidlik, T. *The Spirituality of the Christian East: A Systematic Handbook.* Translated by A. Gythiel. Cistercian Study Series, vol. 79. Kalamazoo, Mich.: Cistercian Publications, 1986.

Stafford, M. "Christian Resistance to the Cult of the Self." *Religion and Ethics,* March 21, 2013. Retrieved from http://www.abc.net.au/religion/articles/2013/03/21/3720786.htm.

Stanley, T. "Barth after Kant?" *Modern Theology* 28, no. 3 (July 2012): 423-45.

Stassen, G. *Living the Sermon on the Mount: A Practical Hope for Grace and Deliverance.* Hoboken, N.J.: Jossey-Bass/Wiley, 2006.

———. *A Thicker Jesus: Incarnational Discipleship in a Secular Age.* Louisville: Westminster John Knox, 2012.

"Statement of Berkshire County Representatives." In *The Populist Sources of Political Authority: Documents on the Massachusetts Constitution of 1780,* edited by O. Handlin and M. Handlin. Cambridge: Harvard University Press, 1996; original 1778.

Stein, E. *Endliches und Ewiges Sein.* Leuven: Nauwelaerts; Freiburg: Herder, 1950.

———. *On the Problem of Empathy.* Washington, D.C.: ICS Publications, 1989.

Stein, S. "Shaker Gift and Shaker Order: A Study of Religious Tension in Nineteenth-Century America." *Communal Societies* 10 (1990): 102-13.

Steinbock, A. *Home and Beyond: Generative Phenomenology after Husserl.* Evanston, Ill.: Northwestern University Press, 1995.

Stendahl, K. "The Apostle Paul and the Introspective Conscience of the West." *Harvard Theological Review* 56 (1963).

———. *Paul among Jews and Gentiles.* London: SCM, 1976.

Stern, D. *The Interpersonal World of the Infant: A View from Psychoanalysis and Developmental Psychology.* New York: Basic Books, 2000.

Stern, K. *A Force upon the Plain: The American Militia Movement and the Politics of Hate.* New York: Simon and Schuster, 1996.

Stern, M. *Greek and Latin Authors on Jews and Judaism: From Tacitus to Simplicius.* Jerusalem: Israel Academy of Sciences and Humanities, 1980.

Sternberg, M. *The Poetics of Biblical Narrative.* Bloomington: Indiana University Press, 1985.

Stevenson, K. *The Lord's Prayer: A Text in Tradition.* Minneapolis: Fortress, 2004.

Stiglitz, J. "Information and Change in the Paradigm in Economics." *American Economics Review* 92, no. 3 (2002): 460-501.

―――. *The Price of Inequality: How Today's Divided Society Endangers Our Future.* New York: Norton, 2013.

Storing, H., ed. *The Anti-Federalist.* Chicago: University of Chicago Press, 1985.

Story, I. *The Love of Our Country Recommended and Enforced.* Boston: John Boyle, 1775.

Strand, M. *I/You: Paradoxical Constructions of Self and Other in Early German Romanticism.* New York: Peter Lang, 1998.

Strauss, L. *Natural Right and History.* Chicago: University of Chicago Press, 1953.

―――. *Spinoza's Critique of Religion.* New York: Schocken Books, 1965.

Stump, E. *Wandering in Darkness: Narrative and the Problem of Suffering.* New York: Oxford University Press, 2012.

Suchocki, M. *The Fall to Violence: Original Sin in Relational Theology.* New York: Continuum, 1994.

Swart, K. "'Individualism' in the Mid–Nineteenth Century (1826-1860)." *Journal of the History of Ideas* 23 (1962): 77-90.

Talbot, M., R. Lints, and M. Horton. *Personal Identity in Theological Perspective.* Grand Rapids: Eerdmans, 2006.

Taylor, A. *Visions of Harmony: A Study in Nineteenth-Century Millenarianism.* Oxford: Oxford University Press, 1987.

Taylor, C. *Hegel.* Cambridge: Cambridge University Press, 1975.

―――. "Atomism." In *Philosophy and the Human Sciences: Philosophical Papers,* vol. 2, pp. 187-210. Cambridge: Cambridge University Press, 1985.

―――. "Language and Human Nature." In C. Taylor, *Human Agency and Language: Philosophical Papers,* vol. 1, pp. 215-47. Cambridge: Cambridge University Press, 1985.

―――. "Atomism." In *Communitarianism and Individualism,* edited by S. Avineri and A. De-shalit, pp. 29-50. Oxford: Oxford University Press, 1992.

―――. *The Ethics of Authenticity.* Cambridge: Harvard University Press, 1992.

―――. *Sources of the Self: The Making of the Modern Identity.* Cambridge: Harvard University Press, 1992.

―――. *Modern Social Imaginaries.* Durham, N.C.: Duke University Press, 2003.

―――. *A Secular Age.* Cambridge: Harvard University Press, 2007.

―――. "Buffered and Porous Selves." *The Immanent Frame,* September 2, 2008. Retrieved from http://blogs.ssrc.org/tif/2008/09/02/buffered-and-porous-selves/.

Taylor, M. L. *The Executed God: The Way of the Cross in Lockdown America.* Minneapolis: Fortress, 2001.

Taylor, R. *Metaphysics.* Englewood Cliffs, N.J.: Prentice-Hall, 1992.

Templeton, K., Jr., ed. *The Politicization of Society.* Indianapolis: Liberty Press, 1979.

Teresa of Avila. *The Collected Works.* Vol. 3. Translated by K. Kavanagh and O. Rodriguez. Washington, D.C.: ICS Publications, 1980.

Tertullian. *On Prayer (De oratione).* Retrieved from http://www.tertullian.org/articles/evans_orat/evans_orat_04english.htm. Ch 7.

Theunissen, M. *The Other: Studies in the Social Ontology of Husserl, Heidegger, Sartre, and Buber.* Translated by C. Macann. Cambridge: MIT Press, 1984.

Thiemann, R. "Beyond Exclusivism and Absolutism." In *God's Life in Trinity,* edited by M. Volf and M. Welker, pp. 118-29. Minneapolis: Augsburg Fortress, 2006.

Thomas, K. *Religion and the Decline of Magic.* New York: Charles Scribner's Sons, 1971.

Thompson, D. *Studies in the Theory of Ideology.* Berkeley: University of California Press, 1984.

Thompson, J. "Christology and Reconciliation in the Theology of Karl Barth." In *Christ in Our Place: The Humanity of God in Christ for the Reconciliation of the World,* edited by T. Hart and D. Thimell, pp. 207-23. Eugene, Ore.: Wipf and Stock, 1989.

Thurow, L. *The Future of Capitalism: How Today's Economic Forces Shape Tomorrow's World.* New York: Morrow, 1996.

Ticciati, S. "The Castration of Signs: Conversing with Augustine on Creation." *Modern Theology* 23, no. 2 (April 2007): 161-79.

Tillich, P. *The Courage to Be.* New Haven: Yale University Press, 1951, 2008.

―――. *Systematic Theology.* Vols. 1-3. Chicago: University of Chicago Press, 1951.

Tocqueville, A. de. *The Old Regime and the French Revolution.* Translated by S. Gilbert. Garden City, N.Y.: Doubleday, 1955.

―――. *Recollections on the French Revolution of 1848.* Edited by J. P. Mayer. Translated by A. Teixeira de Mattos. Cleveland: World Publishing, 1959.

―――. *Democracy in America.* Edited by J. P. Mayer. Translated by G. Lawrence. Vol. 1. Garden City, N.Y.: Doubleday, 1966, 1969; original 1835; also available at http://www2.hn.psu.edu/faculty/jmanis/toqueville/dem-in-america1.pdf.

Toft, M. D., D. Philpott, and T. Shah. *God's Century: Resurgent Religion and Global Politics.* New York: Norton, 2011.

Tomasello, M. *Why We Cooperate.* Cambridge: MIT Press, 2009.

Torrance, J. "The Doctrine of the Trinity in Our Contemporary Situation." In *The Forgotten Trinity,* edited by A. Heron. Vol. 3. London: BC/CCBI Inter-Church House, 1989.

Torrance, T. "Karl Barth." *Union Seminary Quarterly Review* 12, no. 1 (1956): 21-31.

―――. *Theology in Reconciliation: Essays towards Evangelical and Catholic Unity in East and West.* London: Geoffrey Chapman, 1975.

―――. "The Goodness and Dignity of Man in the Christian Tradition." *Modern Theology* 4, no. 4 (July 1988): 309-22; also in *Christ in Our Place: The Humanity of God in Christ for the Reconciliation of the World,* edited by T. Hart and D. Thimell, pp. 369-87. Eugene, Ore.: Wipf and Stock, 1989.

―――. "The Doctrine of the Holy Trinity according to St. Athanasius." *Anglican Theological Review* 71, no. 4 (Fall 1989): 398-405.

―――. "Calvin's Doctrine of the Trinity." *Calvin Theological Journal* 25, no. 2 (1990): 165-93.

————. *Trinitarian Perspectives: Toward Doctrinal Agreement.* Edinburgh: T. & T. Clark, 1994.

Tracy, D. *Plurality and Ambiguity: Hermeneutics, Religion, Hope.* Chicago: University of Chicago Press, 1904.

Trinterud, L. *The Forming of an American Tradition: A Re-examination of Colonial Presbyterianism.* Philadelphia: Westminster, 1949.

Trivers, R. "The Evolution of Reciprocal Altruism." *Quarterly Review of Biology* 46, no. 1 (1971): 35-57.

Trocmé, A. *Jesus and the Nonviolent Revolution.* Maryknoll, N.Y.: Orbis, 2004; original 1961.

Troeltsch, E. *The Social Teaching of the Christian Churches.* Louisville: Westminster John Knox, 1992; original 1912.

Tuck, R. *Hobbes.* Oxford: Oxford University Press, 1989.

Tucker, D., and M. Stafford. "A Phoenix Rising: Common-Good Conservatism." *Truthout,* April 27, 2012. Retrieved from http://truth-out.org/opinion/item/8643-a-phoenix-rising-common-good-conservatism.

Tyson, J. R. *The Way of the Wesleys.* Kindle ed. Grand Rapids: Eerdmans, 2014.

Tyson, P. "Plato against Ontotheology." In *Veritas: Belief and Metaphysics,* edited by C. Cunningham and P. Candler Jr., pp. 393-412. Norwich: SCM, 2007.

United States Conference of Catholic Bishops. "Pastoral Letter: Forming Conscience for Faithful Citizenship." November 2007. Retreived from http://www.usccb.org/issues-and-action/faithful-citizenship/upload/forming-consciences-for-faithful-citizenship.pdf.

Urbach, E. "Kol Ha'Meqayyem Nefesh Ahat . . ." (Development of the version, vicissitudes of censorship, and business manipulations of printers; in Hebrew with English summary). *Tarbiz* 40 (1971): 268-84.

Velde, R. de. "Metaphysics and the Question of Creation." In *Veritas: Belief and Metaphysics,* edited by C. Cunningham and P. Candler Jr., pp. 73-99. Norwich: SCM, 2007.

Venard, O.-T. *Thomas d'Aquin, poète théologien.* Vol. 1, *Littérature et théologie: Une saison en enfer;* Vol. 2, *Le langue de l'ineffable: Essai sur le fondement théologique de la métaphysique;* Vol. 3, *Pagina Sacra: Le passage de l'écriture sainte à l'écriture théologique.* Paris: Cerf; Geneva: Ad Solem, 2002, 2009, 2010.

Vermes, G. *Jesus the Jew.* Minneapolis: Fortress, 1981.

Vico, G. *The New Science of Giambattista Vico.* Translated by T. Bergin and M. Fisch. Ithaca, N.Y.: Cornell University Press, 1994; original 1725.

Virginia Declaration of Rights. 1776. Retrieved from http://www.let.rug.nl/usa/documents/1776-1785/the-virginia-declaration-of-rights-1776.php.

Volf, M. *Exclusion and Embrace: A Theological Exploration of Identity, Otherness, and Reconciliation.* Nashville: Abingdon, 1996.

————. "Being as God Is." In *God's Life in Trinity,* edited by M. Volf and M. Welker, pp. 3-12. Minneapolis: Augsburg Fortress, 2006.

————. *A Public Faith: How Followers of Christ Should Serve the Common Good.* Grand Rapids: Brazos, 2011.

Volf, M., and M. Welker, eds. *God's Life in Trinity.* Minneapolis: Augsburg Fortress, 2006.

Voltaire, F.-M. *The History of Charles XII, King of Sweden.* New York: Dutton, 1925.

———. *The Complete Works of Voltaire.* Edited by T. Besterman et al. Toronto: University of Toronto Press, 1968.

———. *The Philosophical Dictionary.* Edited by T. Besterman. New York: Viking Press, 1984; original 1769.

———. *Candide and Other Stories.* Translated by R. Pearson. New York: Knopf, 1992; original 1759.

———. *Voltaire: Political Writing.* Edited by D. Williams. Cambridge: Cambridge University Press, 1994.

———. *Letters on England* or *The Philosophical Letters.* Translated by L. Tancock. New York: Penguin, 1995; original 1734.

———. *Treatise on Tolerance and Other Writings.* Edited by S. Harvey. Translated by B. Masters. Cambridge: Cambridge University Press, 2000; original 1763.

Vries, H. de, and L. E. Sullivan, eds. *Political Theologies: Public Religions in a Post-Secular World.* New York: Fordham University Press, 2006.

Wald, E., and R. Pearce. "The Obligation of Lawyers to Heal Civic Culture: Confronting the Ideal of Incivility in the Practice of Law." University of Denver Sturm College of Law, legal research paper series, working paper 11-27. *University of Arkansas Law Review* 34 (2011): 1-52. Retrieved from http://ssrn.com/abstract=1969961.

Waldron, J. *Liberal Rights: Collected Papers, 1981-1991.* Cambridge: Cambridge University Press, 1993.

———. *God, Locke, and Equality: Christian Foundations in Locke's Political Thought.* Cambridge: Cambridge University Press, 2002.

Wallace, M. *Fragments of the Spirit: Nature, Violence, and the Renewal of Creation.* London and New York: Continuum, 1996.

Wallis, J. *The Great Awakening: Reviving Faith and Politics in a Post–Religious Right America.* New York: HarperOne, 2008.

Walls, R. "The Church: A Communion of Persons." In *Christ in Our Place: The Humanity of God in Christ for the Reconciliation of the World,* edited by T. Hart and D. Thimell, pp. 102-9. Eugene, Ore.: Wipf and Stock, 1989.

Walzer, M. *The Revolution of the Saints: A Study in the Origins of Radical Politics.* Cambridge: Harvard University Press, 1965.

———. *Spheres of Justice.* New York: Basic Books, 1983.

Ward, G. "Receiving the Gift." *Modern Theology* 30, no. 3 (2014): 74-88.

Ward, W. R. *Theology, Sociology, and Politics: The German Protestant Social Conscience, 1890-1933.* Bern, Frankfurt am Main, and Las Vegas: Peter Lang, 1979.

Warfield, B. B. "The Polemics of Infant Baptism." 1899. Retrieved from http://www.the-highway.com/InfantBaptism_Warfield.html.

Weber, M. *The Protestant Ethic and the Spirit of Capitalism.* Translated by T. Parson. New York: Charles Scribner's Sons, 1958. Also available at Digireads.com.

Webster, J. "God's Perfect Life." In *God's Life in Trinity,* edited by M. Volf and M. Welker, pp. 143-52. Minneapolis: Augsburg Fortress, 2006.

Weil, S. *La pesanteur et la grace.* Paris: Plon, 1947.

———. *Waiting for God.* New York: HarperCollins, 1951, 2001.

———. *Gravity and Grace.* Translated by E. Craufurd. London: Routledge and Kegan Paul, 1952.

———. "La connaissance surnaturelle." Translated by R. Rees. In *The First and Last Notebooks.* London: Oxford University Press, 1970; original 1950.

———. *Gateway to God.* Edited by D. Raper. London: Collins, Fontana Books, 1974.

———. *Judaism and Modernity: Philosophical Essays.* Oxford: Blackwell, 1993.

———. *The Need for Roots: Prelude to a Declaration of Duties towards Mankind.* New York: Routledge, 2011; French 1949; English 1952.

Weir, D. *Early New England: A Covenantal Society.* Grand Rapids: Eerdmans, 2005.

Wenham, G. *Genesis 1–15.* Edited by D. Hubbard, G. Barker, and J. D. W. Watts. Word Biblical Commentary, vol. 1. Waco: Word, 1987.

———. *Story as Torah: Reading Old Testament Narrative Ethically.* Grand Rapids: Baker Academic, 2004.

Wesley, C., J. Wesley, and G. Osborn. *The Poetical Works of John and Charles Wesley.* Andesite Press, 2015.

Wesley, J. "Thoughts upon Methodism." August 4, 1786. London. Retrieved from http://www.imarc.cc/one_meth/vol-02-no-02.html.

———. "Further Appeal to Men of Reason and Religion (Part I, 3)." In *The Works of John Wesley,* edited by A. C. Outler. Nashville: Abingdon, 1986; original 1745.

———. "Sermon 91: On Charity, III:12." In *The Works of John Wesley,* edited by A. C. Outler. Nashville: Abingdon, 1986.

———. "On Working Out Our Own Salvation." Retrieved from http://wesley.nnu.edu/john-wesley/the-sermons-of-john-wesley-1872-edition/sermon-85-on-working-out-our-own-salvation/.

West, C. *Prophesy Deliverance! An Afro-American Revolutionary Christianity.* Louisville: Westminster John Knox, 1982, 2002.

———. *Keeping Faith: Philosophy and Race in America.* New York: Routledge, 1994.

West, C., with C. Buschendorf. *Black Prophetic Fire.* Boston: Beacon Press, 2014.

Westbrook, R. "Lex Talionis and Exodus 21, 22-25." *Revue biblique* 93, no. 1 (1986): 52-69.

Westermann, C. *Creation.* Translated by J. Scullion. Philadelphia: SPCK and Fortress, 1974.

Whitaker, N. *Antidote against Toryism.* Newburyport, Mass.: John Mycall, 1777.

Whitehead, A. N. *Science and Modern World.* New York: Macmillan/Free Press, 1967.

Whitman, W. *Complete Prose Works.* 2008. Retrieved from Google e-books: MobileReference.

Wilde, Marc de. "Violence in the State of Exception." In *Political Theologies: Public Religions in a Post-Secular World,* edited by H. de Vries and L. E. Sullivan, pp. 188-200. New York: Fordham University Press, 2006.

Williams, D. *Sisters in the Wilderness: The Challenge of Womanist God-Talk.* Maryknoll, N.Y.: Orbis, 1993.

———. "Black Women's Surrogacy Experience and the Christian Notion of Redemption." In *Cross Examinations: Readings on the Meaning of the Cross Today,* edited by M. Trelstad. Minneapolis: Augsburg Fortress, 2006.

Williams, M. *Far as the Curse Is Found: The Biblical Drama of Redemption.* Phillipsburg, N.J.: P&R Publishing, 2005.

———, ed. *Child Labor and Sweatshops.* San Diego: Greenhaven Press, 1999.

Williams, Robert. *Hegel's Ethics of Recognition.* Berkeley: University of California Press, 2000.

Williams, Roger. *The bloudy tenent of persecution for cause of conscience.* In *The Complete Writings of Roger Williams.* New York: Russell and Russell, 1963; original 1644.

Williams, Rowen. "Language, Reality and Desire in Augustine's *De Doctrina.*" *Journal of Literature and Theology* 3, no. 2 (July 1989): 138-50.

———. *Being Christian: Baptism, Bible, Eucharist, Prayer.* Grand Rapids: Eerdmans, 2014.

Williamson, R. *Jews in the Hellenistic World: Philo.* Cambridge Commentaries on Writings of the Jewish and Christian World, 200 B.C. to A.D. 200. Cambridge: Cambridge University Press, 1989.

Wilson, E. O. *The Social Conquest of Earth.* New York: Norton, Liveright, 2013.

Wilson, J., and D. Drakeman, eds. *Church and State in American History: Key Documents, Decisions, and Commentary from the Past Three Centuries.* 3rd ed. Boulder, Colo.: Westview Press, 2003.

Wilson, K. *Women Writers of the Seventeenth Century.* Edited by F. Warnke. Athens: University of Georgia Press, 1989.

Wilson-Hartgrove, J. *New Monasticism: What It Has to Say to Today's Church.* Grand Rapids: Brazos, 2008.

Winn, C. *Jesus Is Victor! The Significance of the Blumhardts for the Theology of Karl Barth.* Eugene, Ore.: Pickwick, 2008.

———. "Kingdom." In *Prophetic Evangelicals,* edited by B. Benson, M. Berry, and P. Heltzel, pp. 82-94. Grand Rapids: Eerdmans, 2012.

Winthrop, J. *A modell of Christian charity.* Collections of the Massachusetts Historical Society. 3rd ser., 7:31-48. Boston, 1630, 1838. Retrieved from http://history.hanover .edu/texts/winthmod.html.

Witherspoon J. *Dominion of Providence over the Passions of Men.* Philadelphia: R. Aitken, 1776.

Wittgenstein, L. *Philosophical Investigations.* Oxford: Blackwell, 1958.

———. *On Certainty.* Oxford: Blackwell, 1969.

Wolfson, Elliot R. *Giving beyond the Gift: Apophasis and Overcoming Theomania.* Kindle ed. New York: Fordham University Press, 2014.

Wollstonecraft, M. *On the Vindication of the Rights of Women.* New York: Cosimo Inc., 2010.

Wolters, A. *Creation Regained.* Grand Rapids: Eerdmans, 1985.

Wolterstorff, N. *Justice, Rights and Wrongs.* Princeton: Princeton University Press, 2008.

Wood, G. *Rising Glory of America: 1760-1820.* New York: George Braziller, 1971.

———. "American Religion: The Great Retreat." *New York Review of Books* 53, no. 10 (June 8, 2006): 60-63.

Worthington, W. *The evidence of Christianity deduced from facts: and the testimony of sense, throughout all ages of the church, to the present time. In a series of discourses preached for the lecture founded by the honourable Robert Boyle in the parish church of St. James, Westminster, in the years MDCCLXVI, MDCCLXVII, MDCCLXVII.* London: W. Bowyer and J. Nichols, 1769.

Wright, N. T. "Justification: The Biblical Basis and Its Relevance for Contemporary Evangelicalism." In *The Great Acquittal: Justification by Faith and Current Christian Thought,* edited by G. Reid, pp. 13-119. London: Collins, 1980.

————. *The Epistles of Paul to the Colossians and to Philemon: An Introduction and Commentary.* Leicester: IVP, 1986.

————. *The Climax of the Covenant: Christ and the Law in Pauline Theology.* Edinburgh: T. & T. Clark, 1991; Minneapolis: Fortress, 1992.

————. "Romans and the Theology of Paul." In *Pauline Theology,* vol. 3, edited by D. M. Hay and E. E. Johnson, pp. 30-67. Minneapolis: Fortress, 1995.

————. *Jesus and the Victory of God: Christian Origins and the Question of God.* London: SPCK, 1996.

————. "Paul's Gospel and Caesar's Empire." In *Paul and Politics: Ekklesia, Israel, Imperium, Interpretation; Essays in Honor of Krister Stendahl,* edited by R. A. Horsley, pp. 160-83. Harrisburg, Pa.: Trinity, 2000.

————. "Romans." In *New Interpreter's Bible,* edited by L. Keck. Nashville: Abingdon, 2002.

————. *Paul: In Fresh Perspective.* Minneapolis: Fortress, 2005.

————. "New Perspectives on Paul." In *Justification in Perspective: Historical Developments and Contemporary Challenges,* edited by B. L. McCormack. Grand Rapids: Baker, 2006.

————. *Justification: God's Plan and Paul's Vision.* Downers Grove, Ill.: IVP Academic, 2009.

————. "Justification: Yesterday, Today, and Forever." *Journal of the Evangelical Theological Society* 54, no. 1 (2011): 49-64.

————. "Israel's Scriptures in Paul's Narrative Theology." *Theology* 115, no. 5 (2012): 323-29.

————. "Paul and the Patriarch: The Role of Abraham in Romans 4." *Journal for the Study of the New Testament* 35 (2013): 207-41.

Wuthnow, R. *Caring for Others and Helping Ourselves.* Princeton: Princeton University Press, 1991.

Wyschogrod, E. *Saints and Postmodernism: Revisioning Moral Philosophy.* Chicago: University of Chicago Press, 1990.

————. "Trends in Postmodern Jewish Philosophy: Contexts of a Conversation." In *Reasoning after Revelation: Dialogues in Postmodern Jewish Philosophy,* edited by P. Ochs, R. Gibbs, and S. Kepnes. Boulder, Colo.: Westview Press, 1998.

————. *Emmanuel Levinas: The Problem of Ethical Metaphysics.* New York: Fordham University Press, 2000.

————. *Crossover Queries: Dwelling with Negatives, Embodying Philosophy's Others.* New York: Fordham University Press, 2006.

Yale Law School. Charter of Rhode Island and Providence Plantations — July 15, 1663. In the Avalon project. Documents in law, history and diplomacy. Lillian Goldman Law Library (2008). Retrieved from http://avalon.law.yale.edu/17th_century/ri04.asp.

————. The Fundamental Constitutions of Carolina: March 1, 1669. In the Avalon project. Documents in law, history and diplomacy. Lillian Goldman Law Library (2008). Retrieved from http://avalon.law.yale.edu/17th_century/nc05.asp.

Yoder, J. *The Politics of Jesus*. Grand Rapids and Cambridge: Eerdmans, 1972, 1994.

———. "The Power Equation, Jesus and the Politics of King." In *For the Nations: Essays Evangelical and Public*. Grand Rapids: Eerdmans, 1997.

Zamagni, S. "Catholic Social Teaching, Civil Economy, and the Spirit of Capitalism." In *The True Wealth of Nations: Catholic Social Thought and Economic Life*, edited by Daniel K. Finn. Oxford: Oxford University Press, 2010.

Zetterholm, M. *Approaches to Paul: A Student's Guide to Recent Scholarship*. Minneapolis: Fortress, 2009.

Žižek, S., E. Santner, and K. Reinhard. *The Neighbor: Three Inquiries in Political Theology*. Chicago: University of Chicago Press, 2005.

Zizioulas, J. "Human Capacity and Incapacity: A Theological Exploration of Personhood." *Scottish Journal of Theology* 28 (1975): 401-48.

———. *Being in Communion: Studies in Personhood and the Church*. Contemporary Greek Theologians, vol. 4. Crestwood, N.Y.: St. Vladimir's Seminary Press, 1985.

Index of Names and Subjects